THE RANGER IDEAL VOLUME 1

Texas Rangers in the Hall of Fame, 1823–1861

by
Darren L. Ivey

University of North Texas Press
Denton, Texas

Printed in the United States of America.

10 9 8 7 6 5 4 3 2 1

Permissions:
University of North Texas Press
1155 Union Circle #311336
Denton, TX 76203-5017

The paper used in this book meets the minimum requirements of the American National Standard for Permanence of Paper for Printed Library Materials, z39.48.1984. Binding materials have been chosen for durability.

Library of Congress Cataloging-in-Publication Data

Ivey, Darren L., 1970- author.
The Ranger ideal / Darren L. Ivey.
pages cm
Includes bibliographical references and index.
ISBN-13 978-1-57441-690-9 (cloth : alk. paper)
ISBN-13 978-1-57441-701-2 (ebook)
1. Texas Rangers in the Hall of Fame, 1823–1861 2. Texas Rangers—Biography. 3. Texas—History, Military.

F385 .I94 2017
363.209764–dc23

2017027901

Front cover images: Pistol and gun belt, courtesy of *Texas Ranger Hall of Fame and Museum, Waco, Texas; John Coffee Hays and Samuel Hamilton Walker, Library of Congress, Washington, D.C.;* and *William A. A. Wallace, author's collection.*

The electronic edition of this book was made possible by the support of the Vick Family Foundation. Typeset by vPrompt eServices.

As always, for Dusti
My best girl

And this time for my parents,
Glenn and Jeanne ne

THE RANGER'S SONG

Mount! mount! and away o'er the green prairie wide—
The sword is our sceptre, the fleet steed our pride;
Up! up! with our flag—let its bright star gleam out—
Mount! mount! and away on the wild border-scout!
We care not for danger, we heed not the foe—
Where our brave steeds can bear us, right onward we go,
And never, as cowards, can we fly from the fight,
While our belts bear a blade, our star sheds its light.
Then mount and away! give the fleet steed the rein—
The Ranger's at home on the prairies again;
Spur! spur in the chase, dash on to the fight,
Cry Vengeance for Texas! and God speed the right.
The might of the foe gathers thick on our way—
They hear our wild shout as we rush to the fray; What to us is the
fear of the death-stricken plain—
We have "braved it before, and will brave it again."
The death-dealing bullets around us may fall—
They may strike, they may kill, but they cannot appal;
Through the red field of carnage right onward we'll wade,
While our guns carry ball, and our hands wield the blade.
Hurrah, my brave boys! ye may fare as ye please,
No Mexican banner now floats in the breeze! 'Tis the flag
of Columbia that waves o'er each height,
While on its proud folds our star sheds its light.
Then mount and away! give the fleet steed the rein—
The Ranger's at home on the prairies again;
Spur! spur in the chase, dash on to the fight,
Cry Vengeance for Texas! and God speed the right.

—Captain James T. Lytle, c. 1848.

Contents

Preface and Acknowledgments

The Texas Rangers: legendary men of story and song. Professor Walter Prescott Webb, the renowned Texas historian, opined that "no man could lead or control these Indian and Mexican fighters simply because some political authority had given him an appointment to do so. The leaders had to *emerge* from the group, and all that the state could do was to confirm and legalize a fact." The professor went on to affirm the obligatory qualities of a successful Ranger captain: physical courage, intelligence, boldness coupled with judgment, strength, and endurance.

Byron A. Johnson, executive director of the Texas Ranger Hall of Fame and Museum in Waco, has observed other traits beneficial to the Texas Rangers' continuing mission. These qualities include a respect for and pursuit of moral courage, a commitment to selflessness, and a conviction that an honorable individual can triumph over tremendous adversity. In formulating his perspective, Johnson has coined the phrase: "The Ranger Ideal." The expression can be appreciated in two ways. First, the men featured in this series were honored by their brethren, those both serving and retired, and represent the ideal Rangers to the other members of the service. Secondly, the attributes of the men in the Hall of Fame inspire contemporary and future Rangers to perform their duties with "honor, self-sacrifice, perseverance, dedication, valor, duty and humility," and further the ideal that Johnson perceived.

The seven men featured in these pages were leaders in the molds Webb and Johnson have espoused. Stephen Austin was not a member of the Texas Rangers per se, but the contributions he made to the service remain significant. His visionary leadership in the shaping of Texas is, of course, obvious. The other six individuals presented in this book—Jack Hays, Ben McCulloch, Bigfoot Wallace, Sam Walker, Rip Ford, and Sul Ross—did lead rangers into the fray, all before the beginning of the

Civil War. They waged war against hostile Indians or Mexicans, or both, in the untamed borderlands; they preserved the lives of settlers and forged a nation; and they served their state and country in a variety of civil offices. Five of them were soldiers in the war with Mexico; two of those five plus one more fought for Texas and the Confederate States of America in the next great conflict. All of them, although born outside the borders of Texas, lived lives of service and sacrifice for their adopted home. Interestingly, only three ever married and fathered children. Two died facing the enemy in combat. Six of them were among the first the Ranger service chose to honor for their commitment to Texas.

Despite their induction into the Texas Ranger Hall of Fame, some Rangers have since been underserved by history. They may rate a mention in a book dealing with a larger issue, but they are usually overlooked in favor of other men on the list. Not included in this observation are Austin, McCulloch, and Ford, who have been the subjects of relatively recent biographies. Since the book concerning Ross was written more than thirty years ago, his story would benefit from research more in-depth than can be done in these pages. Similarly, the lives of Hays and Wallace are in severe need of updated interpretations. Incredibly, Walker has gone without a full-length biographical work. The lives of Texas Rangers in the latter half of the nineteenth century, which will be covered in Volume 2, have been more fully documented. When the twentieth-century Rangers are considered in Volume 3, one will again notice an absence of books on worthy men, including, but not limited to, Will Wright, Bob Crowder, and Bobby Paul Doherty. Having noted the absence of up-to-date biographies on a significant number of these men, I have decided to help fill the void. This series of three books, of which you hold the first in your hands, seeks to introduce men unfamiliar to all but the more knowledgeable students of Ranger history, while honoring those who are already known.

In these pages, and in the volumes yet to come, will be presented the Texas Rangers as they slowly developed from makeshift bands of Indian fighters to professional law enforcement officers. In the forty years between Stephen Austin's founding of his colony and the Civil War, the service was not a formal organization, permanent or otherwise. Rather, they were an evolving institution answering to the demands of the perilous borderlands. The tradition of the Texas Rangers furnishing their own weapons, ammunition, horses, and equipment has its genesis in this time. Furthermore, these individuals were not the stalwart lawmen that the most casual observer associates with the popular tradition. Instead, they were citizen-soldiers who formed in response to an emergency and, once the threat was resolved, returned home to resume their normal lives. As the years passed, and the opportunities for border service increased, these men would do much to transform the service from a collection of local ad hoc parties to a more seasoned, semi-professional arm of government. They confronted the Comanches, Kiowas, and other Indians who raided settlements from the Red River to the Rio Grande. They challenged Mexican bandits who preyed upon the merchant caravans conducting trade along the border. They were among the vanguard of the United States Army that crossed the Rio Grande into Mexico. While they did these things, they dealt with another common theme that runs through the story of the Texas Rangers in both the republican and antebellum eras: the lack of money to properly equip and maintain companies in the field. Most men served only an enlistment or two since a rangering career was financially unsustainable, and the turnover rate was high. A few, including some of the men featured in this book, would return time and again out of a love for the life, or out of a sense of duty. Despite the meager funding, the shared dangers and hardships the rangers of the 1840s and 1850s experienced went far in developing an *espirit de corps* that would impact the establishment of the first, permanent body of Texas Rangers in the 1870s.

In recent years, Walter Webb's landmark book has been rightfully criticized for being biased in favor of the Texas Rangers and turning a blind eye to their repeated and documented acts of brutality. Once the pendulum of historical interpretation swings in the opposite direction, the contrasting extreme view usually emerges. The recent trend in revisionist histories has been to portray the Texas Ranger as no longer Webb's hard-riding defender of law and order, but instead a cruel, trigger-happy racist engaged in, as one historian declared, "ethnic cleansing." Not to put too fine a point on the matter, but the attempt to compare the entire Texas Ranger service with those guilty of the systematic murder of thousands or millions of innocent people is both historically inaccurate and decidedly unfair. As Byron Johnson has commented elsewhere, the mistake of the revisionist is to judge individuals and societies by current standards rather than to assess them according to the time in which they lived. The obvious caveat would be those horrific instances that exceed all cultural norms in their malevolence. This book seeks to find a reasonable middle-ground that can acknowledge the Texas Rangers as ordinary flesh-and-blood mortals, not dime novel champions or rogues, who lived in a harsh land ruled by equally unforgiving laws of survival. From 1821 to 1861, and beyond, the borderlands of Texas were locked in a seemingly endless cycle of violence where acts were committed by Indians, Mexicans, and Texans alike that the modern observer might find appalling, sometimes with good reason. Wars great and small were fought in these lands, normally without the benefit of uniforms and flags, and the basic mission of Texan rangers was to defend their people from what were perceived as external threats. In truth, good and bad, heroes and villains, can be found in any of these ethnic and national groups. In a just application of moral standards, none had a monopoly on righteousness or wickedness. Each culture has their own heroes and those "others" they view as villains. The Comanches have their Buffalo Hump and Quanah Parker; the Mexicans have their Juan Cortina, Gregorio Cortez, and Catarino Garza; and Anglo Texans have their Texas Rangers. In developing this personal interpretation after nearly thirty years of amateur study, I find I am in agreement with Robert Utley and, to a lesser extent, Mike Cox, which is good company indeed. The seven men in this book may be judged as ruthless sinners or selfless saints according to one's own perspective. The objective historian may realize they are neither the mythical heroes of Webb's thesis nor are they the racist brutes of the revisionist. They were simply men who lived for a time by the gun on the ragged edge of the frontier.

The issue of change can also involve language. This book and the succeeding volumes encompass nearly two hundred years of Texas, American, and Mexican history. In that time, descriptive nomenclature for inhabitants has come and gone. Texas grew to be a land populated by people who hailed from a wide variety of countries, and the term "Anglo" has come to refer to any white-skinned person of European ancestry. The word "Texian" generally denoted an Anglo-American who immigrated to Texas either in its colonial or republican days. While the expression continued into the 1860s, its use began to diminish after the annexation of Texas in favor of "Texan." "*Tejano*" described a Texas citizen of Spanish or Mexican descent, while "Mexican" (or *mexicano*) was used broadly in the nineteenth century to describe equally a Mexican-born citizen of the United States or a Mexican national. A review of Texas newspapers shows the term "Hispanic" came into use in the early 1890s and seems to have replaced *tejano* in the popular lexicon of the day. While citizens of the United States and Mexico reside in North America, the expression "American" will be applied here for the sake of clarity to refer to those individuals from north of the Rio Grande. Readers will doubtless notice other words, such as Río Grande and Béxar, that use Spanish accented characters. These were in vogue in Texas before the 1842 Woll Invasion, only to be phased out in favor of their Anglicized forms, and to disappear altogether after statehood. Likewise, I have chosen to call the present Mexican cities of Monterrey and Veracruz by their older spellings, Monterey and Vera Cruz, that were common until shortly after the U.S.-Mexican War. These language choices were made deliberatively in order to give the reader a flavor of the times in which the men and women of this book lived.

As I noted in my first work, the process of historical writing is a collaborative affair. A great many people are owed thanks for their assistance in either helping this book to be possible, or in making me an improved author and, more importantly, a better historian. These generous contributors to whom I am obliged include: Christina Stopka, Christina Smith Clariday, Amanda Crowley, and Shelly Crittendon, Texas Ranger Hall of Fame and Museum, Waco, Texas; Jean Eckstein, Former Texas Rangers Association, Fredericksburg, Texas; Sergio Velasco, Texas State Library & Archives Commission, Austin, Texas; Arthur House, National Archives and Records Administration, Washington, D.C.; David S. Turk, U.S. Marshals Service, Washington, D.C.; Kevin Klaus, Daniel Alonzo, and Mary White, Texas General Land Office, Austin; Anita Tufts, Historical Research Center, Texas Heritage Museum, Hill College, Hillsboro, Texas; the reference staffs at the Manhattan Public Library, Manhattan, Kansas, the Kansas State University Libraries, the Midwest Genealogy Center, Independence,

Missouri, the Kansas Historical Society, Topeka, the Louis Round Wilson Special Collections Library, University of North Carolina at Chapel Hill, Austin History Center, Austin, Texas, and the Briscoe Center for American History, University of Texas at Austin; J. P. "Pat" McDaniel and Cathy Smith, Haley Memorial Library and History Center, Midland, Texas; Benna Vaughan, Texas Collection, Baylor University; Jacquelyn Slater Reese, Western History Collections, University of Oklahoma Libraries; Beverly Carver, Special Collections, University of Texas at Austin Libraries; Cathy Spitzenberger, Special Collections, University of Texas at Arlington Libraries; Nicole Grady, Special Collections, University of the Pacific Library; Tai Kreidler, West Texas Historical Association, Texas Tech University; Nicci Hester, Southwest Collections Library/Special Collections, Texas Tech University; Pilar Baskett, Cushing Memorial Library & Archives, Texas A&M University; Alan Zoellner, College of William and Mary Libraries; Teresa Gray, Special Collections and University Archives, Vanderbilt University Library; Nancy Armstrong, Mount Juliet-Wilson County Public Library, Mt. Juliet, Tennessee; Judy Glick, Rockbridge Regional Library, Lexington, Virginia; Sean Sutcliffe, Waco-McClennan County Public Library, Waco, Texas; Steve Lapp, Medina County Museum, Hondo, Texas; Mary Ellen Lindstrom, Medina Community Library, Medina, Texas; Chuck Bradner, Jones Memorial Library, Lynchburg, Virginia; Noel Kalenian, Western History and Genealogy Department, Denver Public Library, Denver, Colorado; Stephanie Arage Bennett, Genealogy Division, Dallas Public Library, Dallas, Texas; Mandy Roane, Marfa Public Library, Marfa, Texas; Martha Bergmann and Kathleen Leles DiGiovanni, Oakland Public Library, Oakland, California; Carol Borchardt and Karen Miles, Prince George's County Genealogical Society, Bowie, Maryland; Holly Hasenfratz, Dickinson Research Center, National Cowboy & Western Heritage Museum, Oklahoma City, Oklahoma; Lizette Pelletier, Mel Smith, and Christine Pittsley, Connecticut State Library, Hartford, Connecticut; Sara Azam, Beinecke Rare Book and Manuscript Library, Yale University; Connie Langum and Alan Chilton, Wilson's Creek National Battlefield, Republic, Missouri; Larry J. Walker, The Magazine House, La Pine, Oregon; Donaly E. Brice, Lockhart, Texas; Stephen L. Moore, Lantana,

Texas; Kristina Harville, University of Texas at San Antonio; Michelle Herbelin, Baylor University; Professors M. J. Morgan and David Defries, History Department, Kansas State University; Annalee Allen and Dennis Evanosky, Oakland, California; Donna G. Ferrell, Mt. Juliet, Tennessee; Carolyn Bausinger, Willow Street, Pennsylvania; the late Louis L'Amour; William Adams, Dallas, Texas; Tracy Stivers, Leesburg, Virginia; Dina Thomas, Carthage, Missouri; Holly Taylor, Bridgeman Images, New York City; Erin Meskill, The Greenwich Workshop, Seymour, Connecticut; and Don Troiani, Southbury, Connecticut. There were likely some names I overlooked; if that is the case, my deepest apologies.

Special thanks are tendered to the staff of the University of North Texas Press: Ron Chrisman, director, Karen J. DeVinney, managing editor, and Elizabeth "Bess" Whitby, marketing manager, for their expert guidance and assistance in getting this work published and into the hands of readers. My heartfelt appreciation goes to Dr. Richard B. McCaslin, professor of history at the University of North Texas, and Dr. Harold J. Weiss, Jr., emeritus professor of history, Leander, Texas, for reviewing the manuscript and for their invaluable recommendations. A special thanks to Byron Johnson for his support and for allowing me to borrow "The Ranger Ideal" phrase that became the title of this series.

My most profound gratitude is reserved for Dusti, my beautiful bride of a quarter-century, who remains my muse. Her love, patience, understanding, and heroic efforts copy-editing a subject for which she has little personal interest had a greater impact on my efforts than she possibly knows.

Introduction

The Homer Garrison Texas Ranger Museum, located at historic Fort Fisher on the banks of the Brazos River, officially opened to the public on October 25, 1968. The fulfillment of a desire to honor Texas Rangers, past and present, took years, and its guiding force was Senior Captain, and later U.S. Marshal, Clint Peoples. While the project was his brainchild, Peoples had the assistance of the Fort Fisher Committee, the Fort Fisher Ranger Museum Committee, the Texas Ranger Commemorative Commission, the Texas Ranger Commemorative Foundation, and scores of other dedicated and civic-minded individuals. As part of the agreements the project required, the museum's management was turned over to the City of Waco. At the same time, the facility was certified by the Texas Department of Public Safety as the Official Museum of the Texas Rangers. Presently, the museum showcases exhibits related to the Rangers and pioneer history of Texas, and has grown to include, but is not limited to, firearms, badges, clothing, saddles, equipment, and an extensive art collection. Starting in 1978 and continuing through the 1980s, several additions were built to expand the museum space.

The Texas Ranger Commemorative Commission, established by the legislature in June 1971, was appointed to oversee the celebration of the famed service's sesquicentennial anniversary in 1973. A subsidiary organization, the Texas Ranger Commemorative Foundation, chaired by Captain Peoples, became responsible for building and financing a Texas Ranger Hall of Fame. During a banquet that followed the groundbreaking ceremony at Fort Fisher on August 4, 1973, a film, entitled *The Texas Rangers: A Certain Kind of Man*, was shown to the audience. The program portrayed several historical events involving the Texas Ranger service, including the shootings of outlaws Sam Bass and Bonnie and Clyde. Country western singer Johnny Rodriguez, a good friend of the late Ranger Joaquin Jackson, sang "They Took It Up," which had been composed specifically for the occasion by Tom T. Hall and Allan Pace. In addition, the future facility was named the Official Hall of Fame of the Texas Rangers by the Texas Ranger Commemorative Commission. After months of construction that cost the taxpayers not one cent, the Hall of Fame was dedicated at high noon on February 7, 1976. An integral component of the Hall of Fame and Museum, the Moody Texas Ranger Memorial Library was established to house an ever-growing collection of service records, case files, correspondence, photographs, microfilm, periodicals, and books.

Twenty Texas Rangers were initially inducted, including Hays, McCulloch, Wallace, Walker, Ford, and Ross. Stephen Austin would be nominated for induction by Texas Ranger Lieutenant George Turner and installed into the Hall of Fame in June 2004. The inclusion of some men has later stirred debate, but as Byron Johnson commented to me in an email, "The serving Rangers who make induction decisions for the Texas Ranger Hall of Fame have a unique perspective on the service—*at their point in the continuum* … We have urged them to consider candidates based on criteria: who made major contributions to the development of the service, displayed exceptional valor—outside that normally expected of their contemporaries, or gave their lives in the line of duty under extraordinary circumstances. We think these adapt well to changing times, mores and mindsets."

On May 29, 1997, the Seventy-fifth Legislature passed House Concurrent Resolution No. 55 which designated the Texas Ranger Hall of Fame and Museum as the official state repository, library, and archives for the service. As well, the Moody Library was renamed the Texas Ranger Research Center. Governor George W. Bush, later to become the nation's forty-third president, signed the measure into law. With the archival collection growing too immense for the available space by the mid-2000s, the family of the late Tobin and Anne Armstrong, descendants of Texas Ranger John B. Armstrong, headed a fundraising campaign for the renovation and expansion of the Research Center. The facility was dedicated on June 7, 2012, as the Tobin and Anne Armstrong Texas Ranger Research Center.

Timeline of Texas Ranger History (1821–1861)

1821	Stephen Austin takes up his father's last request and establishes an Anglo colony in *Tejas*.
1823	Moses Morrison recruits volunteers for what is viewed by many as the first Texas Ranger company. Austin pens a document that proposes employing ten "rangers" to defend the colony.
1824	Austin disseminates twenty-six Criminal Regulations in Texas's first official codification of law. Later in the year, Austin supervises the colony's first Indian campaign.
1827	Abner Kuykendall raises a company to "range" the northern boundaries of the colony.
1835	Robert M. Coleman recruits a company, the members of whom are later recognized by some as the first official Texas Rangers. The Permanent Council authorizes a regional ranging system. The Corps of Rangers is established by virtue of the military ordinance act.
1836	The skirmish at Walnut Creek initiates forty years of war between rangers and Comanches. Ben McCulloch arrives in Texas. The victory at San Jacinto allows the formation of the Republic of Texas. John S. Ford reaches Texas.
1837	William A. A. "Bigfoot" Wallace travels to Texas to avenge his murdered relatives.
1838	John C. Hays emigrates to Texas.

1840	Battle of Plum Creek: McCulloch has a leading role in the fight, while Hays and Wallace are in the ranks of the ad hoc companies.
1841–1846	Hays commands ranger companies that establish the standard for others to follow. McCulloch and Wallace perform heroic service as rangers.
1844	Battle of Walker's Creek: Hays and Walker both participate in this momentous engagement.
1845	Texas is annexed by the United States.
1846	Battle of Monterey: Hays, McCulloch, Wallace, and Walker all serve in the campaign and fight throughout the three-day struggle.
1847	Battle of Buena Vista: Prior to the engagement, McCulloch undertakes a reconnaissance mission that adds to his legend. Battle of Huamantla: Walker dies while leading his men into battle.
1848	Hays and Ford fight guerrillas in Central Mexico.
1849–1851	Ford and Wallace command federalized ranger companies in South Texas.
1858	Battle of Antelope Hills: Ford leads a major force of rangers and Indian auxiliaries into the Comanche heartland, and wins a decisive victory.
1860–1861	Cortina War: Ford leads Texan forces in pursuing the bandit-revolutionary Juan Cortina. "Battle" of Pease River: Sul Ross commands the ranger contingent at this controversial fight and recovers Cynthia Ann Parker.
1861	Southern forces fire on Fort Sumter, which begins armed hostilities between the North and the South. McCulloch, Ford, and Ross enter Confederate service. Wallace remains on the frontier.
1862	Battle of Pea Ridge (or Elkhorn Tavern): McCulloch is killed while reconnoitering Union positions.

Stephen F. Austin. Portrait attributed to George Catlin, but the provenance has been disputed. #1/102–24. *Courtesy Prints and Photographs Collection, Texas State Library and Archives Commission, Austin, Texas.*

Chapter 1

Stephen F. Austin: "Introduced the Concept of Rangers into the Texas Lexicon"

Stephen Fuller Austin is rightfully considered the "Father of Texas." As Mike Cox observed, "The land clearly spoke to Austin. The grassy prairies and timbered river bottoms influenced him every bit as strongly as his father's dying wish that he continue with his colonization plans." He did indeed succeed his father in establishing an Anglo colony in the Mexican province of *Tejas*, and spent the next fifteen years guiding the region into becoming a sovereign nation. While the Republic of Texas, and the later American state, would owe its existence to Austin's labors, he also introduced the concept of rangers into the Texas lexicon. The results of his inspiration, the subsequent spies, mounted gunmen, mounted volunteers, and ranging companies of Texas, would form and disband countless times until they became in effect a permanent force in 1874. Similar to the state that it protects, the present Texas Ranger Division is beholden to Austin for founding the antecedents of that renowned law enforcement agency.

He was born in Austinville, Wythe County, Virginia, on November 3, 1793, the eldest son of Moses and Mary "Maria" (Brown) Austin. Stephen's father had been born a British subject in Durham, Connecticut, on October 4, 1761, while Maria was a native of Morris County, New Jersey. Their citizenship would change once the thirteen colonies declared and secured their independence as the United States of America. Entering the world of commerce, Moses was a partner in a mercantile business in Philadelphia and Richmond. In the former city, Moses met Maria, and they married on September 28, 1785. He first leased, and then purchased, Colonel John Chiswell's old lead mines in Wythe County, and engaged in the extraction and manufacturing of lead. Two of Stephen's sisters, Anna Maria Austin and Eliza Fuller Austin, did not survive infancy, but another sister, Emily Margaret Austin, born June 22, 1795, and one brother, James Elijah Brown Austin, born October 3, 1803, reached adulthood. Pursuing new opportunities, the extended Austin family traveled to Ste. Genevieve, Missouri, then part of Spanish Upper Louisiana, in the summer of 1798, and became Spanish subjects. Moses engaged in lead mining at Mine á Breton while the ownership of Louisiana transferred to France and then to the United States. His operations turned a quick profit and Moses amassed an impressively large personal fortune of $200,000. In time, Moses constructed Durham Hall, a stately mansion on Breton Creek, for his family, and also opened a dry goods store.[1]

In 1804, Stephen was sent to Bacon Academy in Colchester, Connecticut, where he studied for three years. He left the East in January 1808, and attended Transylvania University in Lexington, Kentucky, later the same year. In April 1810, due to some losses in the lead market, and the subsequent cash shortage, Austin was forced to leave school before obtaining his degree. He returned home and managed his father's commercial affairs while Moses took a trip to New York City to obtain investors. Even after the elder Austin's return, Stephen continued to take on more responsibility for the family's mercantile and mining ventures.[2]

Three years later, while American forces were fighting the British to the east, the Illinois and Missouri frontier was the scene of several Indian attacks. The governors of the two territories received authorization from Congress to raise militia troops to answer the threat. Governor Benjamin Howard of Missouri mustered in companies for the purpose of clearing hostile Indians from the country along the Illinois and Mississippi Rivers. Desiring to join the campaign, Stephen enlisted as a private in the First Regiment of Mounted Militia under the command of Colonel Alexander McNair. He soon earned promotion to regimental quartermaster sergeant. Dividing his forces on September 10, 1813, Howard, in his new rank of brigadier-general, sent an element of regulars up the Illinois River on gunboats, and marched the Illinois regiment under Colonel Benjamin Stephenson along the east side of the Mississippi and the Missourians on the west. They then swept through the area for seven weeks, burning deserted villages and fighting small skirmishes, but failing to engage any Indians in decisive combat. The volunteers were disbanded at Fort Russell on October 21. Two years later, Stephen was promoted to the position of adjutant of the Sixth Militia Regiment. A few months after, he was elected to the lower house of the territorial legislature. On December 4, 1815, he took his seat and represented Washington County in the Second and Third Legislatures, and in a special session that convened from October 26 to December 23, 1818.[3]

Beginning in 1817, Stephen made unspecified improvements to public lands along the Red River in Arkansas, particularly at a tract dubbed Long Prairie. Even without ever seeing the ground, he had established a foundation for a preemption claim when the government opened the area for settlement. He further amassed goods to sell to the immigrants he was positive would rush into the territory. With two partners, he located five New Madrid claims at two locations: the Ouachita River near the mouth of the Caddo River and the sandstone formation known as the Little Rock on the south bank of the Arkansas River. Austin arrived at Long Prairie in June 1819, and spent the summer and fall performing the preliminary work to establish Mount Prairie, his anticipated plantation. For reasons known only to himself, he sold his interest in the Little Rock claim to his brother-in-law, and acted as the latter's agent in promoting the new town of Fulton. He also lobbied to have the seat of the territorial government moved from Arkansas Post to the more advantageous Little Rock location. In May 1820, he decided to divest himself of his interest in Mount Prairie, but the real estate market was glutted with others also looking to sell. By the summer, Austin was forced to admit his Arkansas ventures had proven to be embarrassing failures.[4]

Stephen was not alone in his commercial disappointments. The War of 1812 had disrupted trade along the Mississippi River and adversely affected Moses Austin's already overextended finances. Adding to his troubles, the Panic of 1819, which began in the East earlier in the year, spread to Missouri by the fall.

Moses Austin. The authenticity of this portrait has been questioned, but it is the only known presumed likeness. *Courtesy Photograph Collection, The State Historical Society of Missouri, Columbia, Missouri.*

The general contraction of the territory's economy was fueled by excessive land speculation and debt, waning migration, the depreciation of bank notes, and a steep decline in the value of land. Creditors, who were themselves ensnared in the financial crisis, began to sue Moses for outstanding debts, and win their civil judgements in court. When the Bank of St. Louis went bankrupt on July 12, Moses, a founder and major stockholder, was personally ruined. Stephen had assumed his father's place as a director on December 14, 1818, and this failure would have a profound effect on the younger man. In his private life, Moses was an arrogant and domineering man who goaded his eldest son to achieve "greatness in life." Conversely, Stephen was anxious to escape his father's stifling ambitions and pursue his own aspirations. Even while respecting and revering the elder Austin, Stephen would blame Moses for destroying the family's assets and reputation. These dynamics would drive Stephen to realize his own dreams while still creating a legacy to his father's memory.[5]

On July 10, 1820, Stephen was appointed judge of the First Circuit Court at Little Rock, a town named for the stone outcropping where he had once held a land title. Hoping to use the position to mitigate his financial woes, he was frustrated in his plans when the legislature, on October 25, abolished the circuit courts in favor of another system. Desperate to start anew, and find steady employment, Austin traveled down the Red and Mississippi Rivers to New Orleans, arriving in November.[6]

Meanwhile, seeking to recover his own personal fortunes, Moses looked to the opportunities accorded by Spanish *Tejas*. The state of affairs there looked promising as James Long's second filibustering expedition had purportedly failed, the Spanish government was supposedly in control of the province, and the constitution of 1812 had been reinstated. Spain and the United States had signed the Adams-Onís Treaty in February 1819, which, among other things, ceded the latter's claims to *Tejas*. The accord prompted Spanish administrators to relax immigration restrictions and issue land grants to colonists of all nationalities.[7]

Moses Austin arrived in San Antonio de Béxar on December 23, 1820, and secured an audience with Governor Antonio María Martínez. In the meeting, Austin requested permission to settle Anglo settlers in the province. Unfortunately, the speculator had made his appeal at an inopportune time as the Spanish

Crown was preparing to suppress James Long's renewed filibustering expedition into *Tejas*. Pointing to Austin's U.S. citizenship, Martínez ordered him to quit the province immediately. After leaving the governor's palace, the disappointed Austin encountered Felipe Enrique Neri, the self-styled Baron de Bastrop, in the Military Plaza. The baron, an old associate from New Orleans, was living in San Antonio and possessed some influence with the provincial authorities. Austin and Bastrop returned to the palace where the baron appealed to Martínez, employing several arguments. The settlements were increasingly coming under Comanche attack, *rancheros* and farmers were being ruthlessly plundered of livestock, and traders refused to travel because of the danger. Even after a century of occupation, emigration to *Tejas* continued to be minimal and the land remained virtually empty. As historian Pekka Hämäläinen later noted, "The province, for all practical purposes, had ceased to function as a Spanish colony." Bastrop promised Americans, with an established record of fighting Indians, would prove to be a benefit. He also pointed to the successful influx of Americans into Spanish Louisiana, which included one Moses Austin. Seeing the advantages in colonists loyal to Spain developing the untamed *frontera*, providing a market for Spanish goods and a source of tax revenue, offering a channel for trade with the United States, and creating a buffer zone to counter Comanche incursions, the superior government of the Eastern Interior Provinces approved the petition on January 17, 1821. However, the Spanish viceroyalty in Mexico City was soon overthrown and a new Mexican regime emerged.[8]

Even as three hundred years of colonial rule came to an end, Moses Austin had returned to the United States to settle his affairs and begin to organize the colony project. However, he developed a severe cold that, due to age and exhaustion, deteriorated into pneumonia. Moses died on June 10, 1821, in Herculaneum, Missouri, but his deathbed wish was for Stephen to continue in his father's stead:

> I now can go forward with confidence and I hope and pray you will discharge your doubts as to the enterprise and, if any means can be commanded, use your utmost to have every thing brought into motion … raise your Spirits, times are changing. A new chance presents itself. Nothing is wanting but Concert and firmness.

By this time, the younger Austin was reading law in the office of the highly regarded New Orleans attorney, Joseph H. Hawkins, and working for the *Louisiana Advertiser*. However, to Stephen's thinking, *Tejas* represented a better opportunity to recoup the family's lost fortunes, settle his own debts, achieve personal success, and fulfill his obligations to his late father.[9]

He left New Orleans on June 18, and met with Juan José María Erasmo de Jesús Seguín in Natchitoches, Louisiana. There Austin received formal confirmation of his grant. Departing Natchitoches on July 13, he crossed the Sabine and entered *Tejas* on the sixteenth. Upon seeing the rich country on which he would stake his future, and that of potential colonists, Austin's dutiful filial obligations quickly grew into excitement. Meeting with Governor Martínez in Béxar, the new *empresario* submitted his plan for allocating the lands to new settlers: each family would receive 320 acres of farm land along a river and another 640 acres for grazing. The head of each household would likewise be granted two hundred acres for his wife, one hundred for each child, and fifty for each slave. The governor gave his provisional approval, and the first of three hundred carefully chosen families readied themselves to immigrate to the new colony site between the Colorado and Brazos Rivers.[10]

To finance the project, Austin, still struggling to manage his massive debts in Missouri and Arkansas, entered into a partnership with Hawkins and other Louisiana investors. As *empresario*, he planned to "exact from each settler a sufficient per cent on the land grant[d] to compensate him for his trouble and expense in attending to the business." He decided twelve and one-half cents per acre would be a fair recompense. To convey immigrants to their new homes, he acquired the *Lively*, a thirty-ton schooner, and hired a crew. The first settlers set out for Texas by both land and sea. One group departed New Orleans aboard the *Lively* on November 27 for the mouth of the Colorado, while the other had left Pecan Point, Arkansas, in July en route to the La Bahia crossing of the same river. The *Lively* failed to arrive on schedule when her captain mistook the mouth of the Brazos for the Colorado and landed his passengers there. Even while Austin waited impatiently for the missing colonists and the much-needed supplies, other settlers were trickling into the colony by January and February of 1822.[11]

Austin was not the image of the hardy soldier or ranger found elsewhere in the pages of this book. Moses Austin Bryan, his sister's son, would describe him as "slender, sinewy, of graceful figure and easy, elastic movements, with small hands and feet, dark hair inclined to curl when damp, with large, hazel eyes, fair skin when not sun-burned, about five feet eight or nine inches in height." Historian and author H. W. Brands remarked: "Where the Texas project came naturally to Moses, Stephen, left to himself, would never have dreamed of anything so bold. If not for his father's deathbed request, he likely would have become a lawyer, perhaps a state judge, and spent his life pondering the perplexities of human nature, his own included." Stephen's tale is not notable for his skills on the battlefield or in tracking dangerous desperadoes, but rather for an indomitable will that would surmount any obstacle in order to realize his newfound vision. Never physically robust, and suffering from reoccurring bouts of malaria, Austin would ultimately work himself to death, driven onward by often-conflicting motivations: personal ambition, and a sense of duty and obligation to his fellow colonists.[12]

Because final permission for colonization had not been given by the new government, Austin had to travel to Mexico City to press for recognition of his *empresario* contract. He was to spend most of 1822 and the early part of 1823 resolving the validity of his Spanish grant in light of Mexico's independence. En route to the capital, he traveled by way of Laredo and Monterey. He and his two companions were near the Nueces when they were taken by Comanches, who appropriated all their possessions. This particular tribe had not yet treated with Anglo Texians, but they remained intermittently hostile to Mexicans and *tejanos*, depending on the ability of the latter two groups to bestow gifts (i.e. tribute payments). Although their attitude toward all white men would change in the years to come, the Comanches were initially friendly. The Indians released Austin and his companions and returned their property, except for four blankets, a bridle, and a Spanish grammar book.[13]

Austin and his party reached Mexico City on April 29 and found the capital's state of affairs in turmoil. The *empresario* met with the colonization committee of the Mexican Congress and cultivated relationships with key officials. Due in part to his innate skill at diplomacy, and having the time to learn Spanish and the customs of Mexico, he was allowed to assist in drafting the first colonization act. Austin was on hand to witness Agustín de Iturbide crowned as Emperor Agustín I on May 19. On the verge of success, his efforts were temporarily stymied when the Emperor dissolved the Congress *sine die*. After a brief interlude in limbo, the Imperial Colonization Law was finished by the Emperor's *junta nacional instituyente* on January 4, 1823. Among the terms of the agreement was that each family would receive one *sitio* (league, or 4,428 acres) of land for stock raising, or one *labor* (177 acres) for farming. Further, all colonists were required to convert to Catholicism. For his services Austin would receive twenty-two leagues of land, a sixty-dollar fee from each colonist family, and one *medio*, or twelve and one-half cents, for each league granted to settlers. The monarch decreed on February 18 the law would only grant concessions to Austin's colony and no other.[14]

Before Austin could depart the city, he was again thwarted when the autocratic Agustín was overthrown on February 21. Once the restored National Congress met in March, they nullified every action taken by the Emperor and his *junta instituyente*. Austin was forced to petition this new body and the ruling triumvirate for another concession. Approval was finally granted on April 14. Austin left Mexico City with 307 separate grants scattered throughout the Colorado and Brazos River country. After his leave-taking, the Congress voted for a new constitutional convention to create a federal system of government with limited executive powers, an autonomous legislative body, and sovereign states.[15]

Meanwhile, in the wake of Mexican independence, most of the military garrisons were withdrawn, and Austin's colonists were forced to provide for their own defense. For a time, they remained beyond the reach of the Comanches who raided *ranchos* and villages between the Nueces River and Coahuila. Instead, the Anglos frequently clashed with the Huacos (Wacos), Tonkawas, Tahuacanos, and the cannibalistic Karankawas. José Felix Trespalacios, the governor of *Tejas*, directed in June 1822 the colony be divided into two districts situated along the Colorado and the Brazos Rivers. Each one was authorized to elect an *alcalde* to govern the civil administration, and a captain and lieutenant to command the militia. On November 20, John Jackson Tumlinson, Sr. was chosen as *alcalde* of the Colorado district, Robert Hardin (or Hampton) Kuykendall as captain, and Moses Morrison as lieutenant. In the Brazos district, Josiah Hughes Bell was elected *alcalde*, Samuel Gates captain, and Gibson Kuykendall (Robert's nephew) lieutenant. Male citizens of the colony aged eighteen to fifty-five were required to participate in the militia, which gave the Colorado district a fighting force of seventy-four men.[16]

On January 7, 1823, Tumlinson sent a letter to Governor Trespalacios requesting authorization to raise a fifteen-man company for protection against Indians, and nominated Lieutenant Morrison to command the detachment. The *alcalde* also detailed his plan to erect a chain of blockhouses beginning near the mouth of the Colorado and use the waterway to mount combined land and riverine operations. The governor responded on January 31 by granting permission for the company's establishment and requesting an estimation of the cost to build the blockhouses. Morrison and another nine volunteers were mustered into the new company by May 5. The modern Texas Rangers trace the lineage of their service to this outfit, which began a long-standing tradition of supplying their own arms, horses, clothing, and equipment. On the other hand, some historians, such as Allen G. Hatley, adamantly contest this notion in favor of later companies. The proposed blockhouses were never constructed as Morrison's men spent most of their time trying to stay alive in the harsh wilderness. The company's supply of gunpowder—used more for hunting than for combat—and other necessities was dwindling by the time of the second monthly inspection on July 5.[17]

The colony was dealt a severe blow on July 6 when John Tumlinson was killed by Karankawa and Huaco Indians while en route to San Antonio. His body was never recovered. As no Indians had been found near the mouth of the river, Captain Kuykendall requested permission to withdraw Morrison's company and place them in a position where they could do more good. The interim governor, Don Luciano García, did not reply.[18]

On August 4, Austin returned to his colony after a sixteen-month absence. The grants he carried instructed him to confer with the governor to allocate the land among the colonists. The Baron de Bastrop had been appointed by Governor García to issue land titles and joined Austin in the colony. The baron was also ordered to locate the colonial capital which was to be named San Felipe de Austin. Austin was invested with the authority to rule the colony

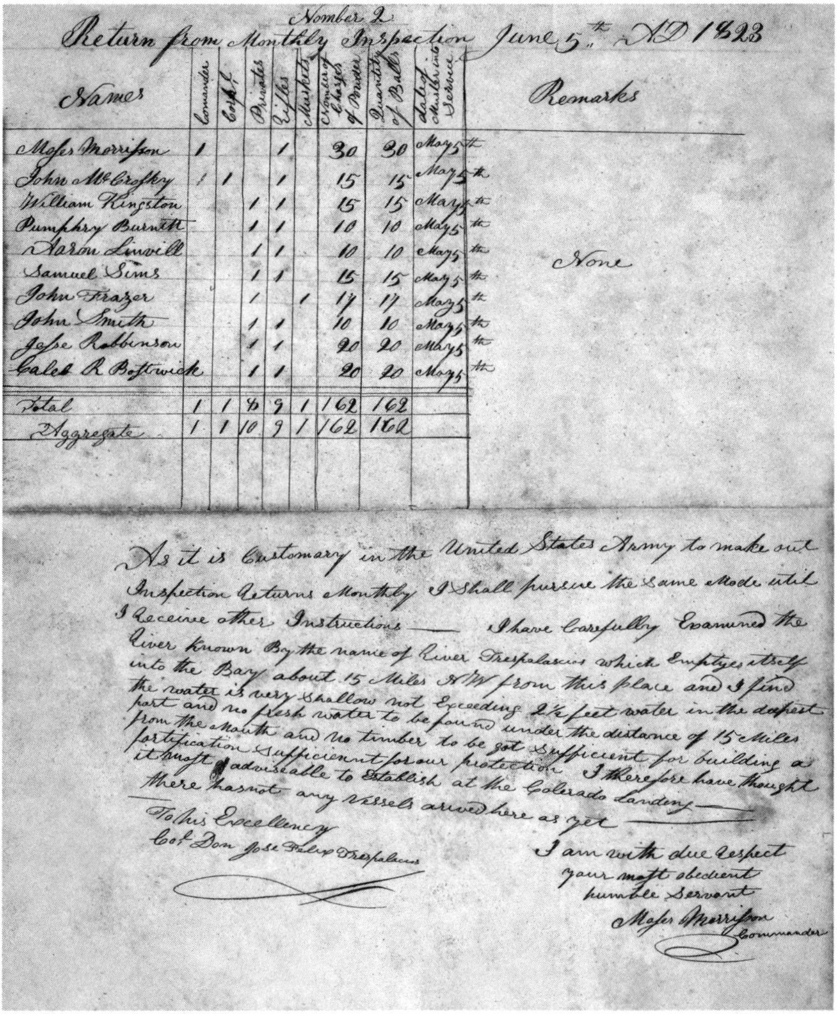

Nomber 2

Return from Monthly Inspection June 5th AD 1823

Names	Comander	Corpl	Privates	Rifles	Muskets	Number of Charges of Powder	Quantity of Balls	Date of Mustering into Service	Remarks
Moses Morrison	1			1		30	30	May 5th	
John McCroskey		1		1		15	15	May 5th	
William Kingston			1	1		15	15	May 5th	
Pumphry Burnett			1	1		10	10	May 5th	
Aaron Linvill			1	1		10	10	May 5th	None
Samuel Sims			1	1		15	15	May 5th	
John Frazer			1		1	17	17	May 5th	
John Smith			1	1		10	10	May 5th	
Jesse Robbinson			1	1		20	20	May 5th	
Caleb R Bostwick			1	1		20	20	May 5th	
Total	1	1	8	9	1	162	162		
Aggregate	1	1	10	9	1	162	162		

As it is Customary in the United States Army to make out Inspection Returns Monthly I Shall pursue the Same Mode util I Receive other Instructions — I have Carefully Examined the River known By the name of River Trespalacios which Emptyes itself into the Bay about 15 Miles N W from this place and I find the water is very Shallow not Exceeding 2½ feet water in the deepest part and no fresh water to be found under the distance of 15 Miles from the Mouth and no timber to be got Sufficient for building a fortification Sufficient for our protection I therefore have thought it most advisable to Establish at the Colorado Landing — there has not any vessels arrived here as yet —

To his Excellency
Col Don Jose Felipe Trespalacios

I am with due respect
your most obedient
humble Servant
Moses Morrison
Commander

Morrison's Muster Roll. Bexar Archives, di_10849. *Courtesy The Dolph Briscoe Center for American History, The University of Texas at Austin.*

until the state government extended its laws to the area. He was further named commander-in-chief of the militia with the rank of lieutenant-colonel, and also chief official for the administration of justice.[19]

One of the items he intended to handle upon his arrival was the need to ensure protection for the colonists. On the back of a proclamation signed by the Baron de Bastrop, dated August 4, 1823, he wrote:

> … I have determined to augment at my own private expense the company of men which was raised by order of the late Govr [*sic*] Trespalacios for the defense of the Colony against hostile Indians. I therefore by these presents give public notice that I will employ ten men in addition to those employed by the Govervnt to act as rangers for the common defence of the Colony. The said ten men will form a part of Lieut. Moses Morrisons [*sic*] Company and the whole will be subject to my orders. The wages I will give the said ten men is fifteen Dollars a month payable in property …[20]

There is no evidence the additional ten men ever took the field, but this document marks the first time the term "ranger" was used in print in Texas. Instead, "Austin's Address to Colonists," as historian Eugene C. Barker called it, may have been merely a notion he explored and later abandoned. In its place, Austin ordered Morrison to remain at the mouth of the Colorado and protect the northern frontier. However, the promised wages for Morison's men never materialized and the company was disbanded by the fall.[21]

The initial period of relative peace the settlers experienced began fading in the autumn of 1823. Indian raiding parties commenced to infiltrate the settlements, including two Tonkawa forays along the Brazos in September that stole horses and intimidated colonists. On October 2, Austin and thirty militiamen rode into the Indian camp, and forced the chief to, first, identify the guilty parties and, second, administer a lashing to them. Austin then ordered the Indians to cease their looting and depart the country between the Brazos and the Colorado. If they failed to heed his warning, the militia chief promised they would be killed. After a period of comparative inactivity, the Tonkawas would return to the war path.[22]

On January 22, 1824, in addition to a civil code, Austin promulgated his Criminal Regulations—a body of laws that provided for a system of justice, and structured the militia. The first five of the twenty-six articles he approved sanctioned "all and every person" to apprehend suspicious, aggressive, or insolent Indians and remand them to the custody of the *alcalde* or militia captain of their district. The *empresario* further cautioned his people to avoid the use of violence unless necessary. If the number of Indians was too many for individuals in the vicinity to handle, militia commanders were authorized to call upon as many citizens as needed. Detained Indians were to be brought before the *alcaldes* or captains who would hear testimony pertaining to their conduct. If the Indians were found guilty of violating the regulations, they were either banished from the colony, returned under guard to their home villages, or subjected to not more than twenty-five lashes. Lastly, he instructed his colonists to treat innocent Indians justly until they ceased to deserve it.[23]

The sixth article authorized "the nearest militia officer or *alcalde*" to form posses and pursue criminals. If offenders submitted to arrest, they were delivered before the *alcalde* for trial. Defendants accused of serious crimes were required to perform hard labor in public works projects until they were brought before Mexican judges in Monterey or Saltillo. If fugitives resisted, the militiamen were permitted to use deadly force.[24]

At first, Texian responses to coastal Indian raiding were light infantry affairs, but, as settlements expanded onto the prairies, mounted combat would become the norm. The successors of Moses Morrison's outfit would over time combine aspects of Spanish *compañías volantes* (flying companies), who had guarded the *frontera* of New Spain in the eighteenth and early nineteenth centuries, with those of eastern American colonial irregulars. The *tejano* troopers were characterized by innate horsemanship, endurance, rapid response, and effective offensive patrolling. These informal militia companies, manned by tough *rancheros* and *vaqueros*, understood their swift-moving Comanche foes could not be countered with a defensive attitude. Captain John Smith, commanding "ranging" parties in New England in the 1620s, and Major Robert Rogers, who led Rangers in the French and Indian War, were among the earliest examples of the rough-hewn frontier tradition on the Atlantic coast. These men pioneered light infantry tactics for waging *petite guerre* ("little war," or partisan warfare) that emphasized marksmanship, scouting, ambushing, and fieldcraft. Concepts synthesized from these far-flung yet similar groups of nonprofessional soldiers would facilitate the development of the Texan rangers. While the colonial volunteers were not Rangers as traditionally defined, they were also not, strictly-speaking, militiamen. As shown, the *empresario* used them as much for law enforcement as he did for frontier defense. His captains were given wide latitude to conduct their own operations in the field and lead their men through personal example. These traits of tactical independence and dynamic leadership would become added cornerstones of the Texas Ranger tradition. Beginning in December 1823, Austin oversaw the reorganization of the militia. Robert Kuykendall resigned his position in the Colorado District militia and Austin appointed John Ross to the captaincy. Josiah Bell was named the lieutenant of a company in the new Lower Brazos District. In total, five companies under Captains Andrew Robinson, Horatio Chriesman, Randall Jones, Jesse Burnam, and Amos Rawls would be formed into a battalion by June 22, 1824.[25]

Depredations, usually involving Karankawas between 1821 and 1824, became so onerous that, in June 1824, Austin organized the first campaign in Texas's Indian wars. Amos Rawls was ordered to lead his company in pursuit of a raiding party that had been stealing cattle. The militiamen located the Karankawas and killed one warrior in the subsequent skirmish; one of the Texians was struck by an arrow through the elbow. The Indians escaped into the canebrakes, and Rawls called for reinforcements. Volunteers marched on the main camp on the coast and killed five Karankawas near the mouth of the Colorado River. In the same month, Rawls and Jesse Burnam set out with twenty-four men to rescue two sailors who were being held for ransom at the mouth of the Colorado. Reaching the site of the proposed exchange, the militiamen lay in ambush until nine Karankawas arrived in canoes. The settlers' first volley killed seven Indians, and the two survivors dove into the water to escape; one paused to look back and was fatally shot.[26]

Austin set out on August 30 at the head of an expedition of approximately one hundred men, including thirty slaves. Their prey was the Karankawas.

The Settlement of Austin's Colony, or The Log Cabin. Oil on canvas painting by Henry Arthur McArdle. *Courtesy Prints and Photographs Collection, Texas State Library and Archives Commission, Austin, Texas.*

Deployed into three companies, Austin marched his force down both banks of the Brazos. Ahead of the column were men Austin referred to as "spies" who scouted for sign of Indians. The expedition's supplies were nearly exhausted by September 7, and Austin ordered his force to retire to San Felipe to resupply and assemble reinforcements. At the same time, Randall Jones and twenty-three militiamen moved down the Brazos to chastise a band of Karankawas suspected of murdering several families in the area. Attacking the camp near what came to be called Jones Creek, the captain's force lost three men killed, but approximately fifteen Indians were slain. On the march once more in mid-September, Austin's expedition drove the Karankawas west without bloodshed until the two sides concluded a treaty at La Bahía del Espíritu Santo. The Karankawas consented to remain west of the San Antonio River and cease raiding the colony; however, the peace did not last long.[27]

By late 1824, the three hundred families stipulated in the original application had arrived in the colony. The "Old Three Hundred" would assume prominent roles in the political and social circles of the growing community. On August 18, the Mexican Congress passed a national colonization law that directed future land grants would be the responsibility of the state governments. Furthermore, land codes had to adhere to the constitution, no person could possess more than eleven leagues of land, and all immigrants must become Mexican citizens.[28]

Early in 1826, the Tawakonis began infiltrating the settlements for the purpose of killing their Tonkawa enemies and stealing horses. On April 4, Captain James Jeffres Ross and thirty-one militiamen engaged sixteen of the raiders on the Colorado, killing eight and wounding five. Austin recommended a campaign using Cherokees, Shawnees, and Delawares as auxiliaries. Vetoing the idea of such an alliance, Colonel Mateo Ahumada, the Mexican commandant in Béxar, suspended a response until reinforcements could be obtained from the interior. Rather than simply wait, Austin ordered Aylett "Strap" Buckner, the senior militia captain and overall field commander, to proceed without the assistance of allied Indians. Four companies under Captains Rawson Alley, William Hall, Horatio Chriesman, and Bartlett Sims rode north amid heavy spring rains, which flooded the

Brazos River and its tributaries. After an especially arduous ride, Buckner and his 185 men arrived at the Indian villages near present Waco and found them deserted. Extremely frustrated, the militiamen turned around and rode back to the colony.[29]

By June 14, the five companies were commanded by Sims, Chriesman, Hall, James Ross, and Buckner. Another two platoons, or *tercios*, were led by Lieutenants Samuel C. Hirams and Samuel Millar. In total, the colonial militia consisted of 519 privates, twenty-two noncommissioned officers, and twenty-four officers. Finally boasting ample numbers, Austin offered a comprehensive proposal on August 28 to restructure the organization. He wrote the *jefe político* in San Antonio and suggested the force be reorganized into twelve divisions, "one section to be sent to the frontier every month, to do duty as spies, or frontier guards. The object of the plan is to keep twenty or thirty mounted men continually on the frontier as spies; as well for the preventing of incursions of small parties of Indians, as to give timely notice should they come in force to make a formal attack." As with the ten-man ranger company he had proposed three years earlier, there exists no evidence the plan was ever acted upon.[30]

However, the militia had proven successful in securing a measure of security for the colony as the Karankawas were decimated by battle and disease. In one such engagement, Captain Buckner led a party of men in an attack on these Indians along the coast, and killed an estimated thirty warriors. Once the Texians spread beyond the coastal plains, the Tawakonis, Wacos, and other tribes would pose a threat, especially the ferocious Comanches who would in time become the Texians' most implacable foes.[31]

For the moment, though, Mexico was to be the next great challenge. The men who headed the Old Three Hundred families were often veterans of the War of 1812 and General Andrew Jackson's Indian campaigns. They were among the first and second generations to be born after the American War of Independence and, so, fiercely defended the God-given guarantee of personal liberty and property rights that was their forefathers' legacy. Many of them were well-educated, professional men, including lawyers, doctors, and surveyors. Even after they immigrated to Mexico, they found difficulty in accepting they were foreigners in a land with different customs and traditions, and where they no longer enjoyed the rights and privileges of U.S. citizenship. They typically remained Protestants, albeit unofficially, as the law requiring the conversion to Catholicism was never strictly enforced. They made their home in a land that reluctantly tolerated or outright opposed slavery, while bringing their slaves with them. They also carried their prejudices regarding darker-skinned people who were seemingly idle and unsophisticated. The proud Mexicans, in return, grew to mistrust *Yanqui* intentions toward Texas and shared their lack of respect and their ethnic hostility. The constitution of 1824, which established Mexico as a federal republic, also created the state of *Coahuila y Tejas* on May 7. Rather than a provincial governor in Béxar, Texians and *tejanos*, both resenting the loss of their autonomy, now answered to a chief magistrate in distant Saltillo. Further, Texas was allowed only one delegate in the state legislature, which assured her citizens had no representation at all. In time, they would be allowed a lieutenant governor in San Antonio and one more seat in the legislature, but they came to believe officials in Mexico City and Saltillo cared little about the people north of the Río Bravo. The distances between Austin's colony, as well as the others that were later authorized, and the Mexican administrative centers prevented the Anglos from assimilating into Mexican society and helped to foster an emerging discontent.[32]

Austin would write of his colonists:

> The settlers have done their duty, and have been much clearer from internal dissensions, than could be expected, under all the circumstances. They have uniformly been unshaken in their fidelity, and ready and willing to discharge their obligations as Mexican citizens; they have borne, with the most inflexible fortitude, all the privations to which their situation exposed them, and have contributed largely in laying a foundation for the future prosperity of Texas, by commencing the settlement of its wilderness.[33]

Another factor was that the national government was continually distracted as the liberal *federalistas* and the conservative *centralistas* struggled for dominance. The former implemented the 1824 constitution, which envisioned a federal republic with a limited central government restraining the power of the great landowners and the Church. They also favored foreign trade and supported the influx of Anglos into the country. Texians, by nature, were usually sympathetic to the federalist cause, as it shared similarities with the principles found in the United States Constitution. Unfortunately, centuries of oppressive rule by the Spanish had left Mexico unprepared for democracy. The conservatives, composed of the wealthy *hacendados*, monarchists, and the clergy, pursued a policy of protectionist isolationism and desired a strong, autocratic government that would protect their age-old privileges. The country descended into political chaos and *caudillaje* as a succession of generals won the presidency only to be overthrown in almost continual military revolts.[34]

Even before the promulgation of the general colonization law, Martín de León had received permission to settle forty-one Mexican families on the lower Guadalupe River; sixteen Anglo and Irish families would also join him there. On March 24, 1825, the legislature at Saltillo passed an act to standardize the *empresario* system and promote generous offers of land to new settlers. On April 15, the state authorized grants to other *empresarios*, including Green DeWitt, with four hundred families between the Guadalupe and the Lavaca Rivers; Robert Leftwich and four hundred families north of the San Antonio road and between the Brazos and the Colorado; and Haden Edwards and Frost Thorn, each with four hundred families in the vicinity of Nacogdoches. Ultimately, twenty-five *empresarios* would be granted commissions, although only Austin's and DeWitt's colonies would enjoy real success. On the twenty-seventh, Austin was awarded another concession which authorized him to locate an additional three hundred families within the boundaries of his existing grant. Austin would receive two more grants: one between the Brazos and San Jacinto, and the second from the mouth of the Lavaca to the mouth of the San Jacinto. The two administrative districts originally established in 1823 had expanded to seven, including those of San Felipe, San Jacinto, Mina, and Victoria.[35]

Mexican officialdom hardened their attitudes toward *Tejas* after *empresario* Haden Edwards confronted the central government over land and electoral disputes. The quarrel turned into full-scale revolution on December 16, 1826, when Edwards's supporters proclaimed themselves the Republic of Fredonia. On January 22, 1827, one battalion of Mexican regulars marched on the insurgents' capital at Nacogdoches; Austin followed with more than four hundred of his colonists. His intention was to assist the Mexican soldiers in suppressing what became known as the "Fredonian Rebellion" and prove the loyalty of his colony. The disorganized movement's leaders escaped across the Sabine, and the uprising collapsed on the twentieth-eighth before Austin's militiamen could even reach the scene.[36] At the same time, with so much of the militia gone, Austin had commissioned Abner Kuykendall in February 1827, to recruit eight men and "range the country between the Colorado and Brazos along the San Antonio road, in order to detect any inroad of the Wacoes or other northern tribes." In the debate as to who were the first Texas Rangers, some historians assert this company represents the first official body in the service. Kuykendall disbanded his men at the end of the Fredonian disturbance.[37]

While relations between the colonists and Mexico City slowly declined, the frequency of Indian depredations in 1828 and 1829 increased. Following a fight on the Colorado in July 1829, between ten Texians and an Indian war party that resulted in four dead warriors, Austin organized two companies of fifty volunteers each. Abner Kuykendall was appointed to command the expedition while Captains Oliver Jones and Bartlett Sims led the companies. A third, under Captain Henry Stevenson Brown, was raised in Gonzales to answer the growing number of raids into Green DeWitt's colony. The three groups marched up the Colorado in search of hostile Indians. Scouts reported locating a camp of Wacos and Tawakonis near the junction of the Colorado and the San Saba Rivers. The colonists were discovered by the Indians, who fled the Texian charge, leaving behind one dead warrior and their camp equipage. Captain Sims gathered fifteen men and pursued the retreating Indians for several miles before capturing most of their pony herd. Believing the loss of their stock and equipment would deter the Indians from further raiding, the Texians arrived home after an absence of thirty-two days.[38]

Even though the Fredonian revolt had been quickly put down, the damage was done as the Mexican government began to view *norteamericano* colonists as invaders rather than invited guests. Approximately eleven thousand Anglos and three thousand slaves lived in Texas by 1830 and comprised nearly 75 percent of the population; alongside them were five thousand *tejanos*. Settlers who came after the Old Three Hundred usually did so under the sponsorship of an *empresario*, but some others simply squatted along the Red River and around San Augustine. The émigrés were seeking inexpensive farmland, escaping creditors and financial failures, or fleeing the law in the United States. Most of the inhabitants remained more or less loyal to Mexico, but a few firebrands desired independence. Acting on the findings of General Manuel de Mier y Terán's inspection tour of Texas, *Presidente* Anastacio Bustamente and Congress enacted the Law of April 6, 1830, which prohibited further emigration from the United States, banned the importation of additional slaves, imposed tariffs on necessary goods imported into the province, and garrisoned Nacogdoches, Anahuac, Velasco, and Goliad with federal convict-soldiers. Anglos and *tejanos* alike protested the decree. The two representatives in the legislature objected to the administration's course of action and were scorned and criticized; one delegate was even ejected from the assembly. Austin was able to gain exemptions from the immigration ban and the tariff, but all of these undertakings increasingly alienated the Texians in the years to come.[39]

Simultaneously, Austin was steadily losing the authority he had exercised over his own colony. He had turned over control of the colonial government to the *ayuntamiento* of San Felipe de Austin in February 1828. The settlers then elected officials of their own choosing, the land fees he had once collected had been invalidated by the Mexican government, some malcontents had accused him of seeking to benefit at their expense and favoring his friends with larger grants of land, and he had sold off a great deal of his assets to pay his outstanding debts. The success of the colonization project was evident, even if he did not personally profit in the end. Indeed, his home at San Felipe was a two-room log cabin: one for his living quarters, and the other his office. Instead of governance, the colonists now looked to him for counsel, and Austin readily gave them the benefit of his wisdom and experience.[40]

As his role in the colony changed, Austin began to dream of a life he could have once Texas was secure in her fortunes. The first inkling of these aspirations might have commenced when his widowed cousin, Mary Austin Holley, came to visit her brother near Brazoria. H. W. Brands described the affection Austin felt for her:

> He had had a crush on her as a youth, and the fond memories of that time returned when he heard she was coming for a visit. To Austin, Mary Holley represented grace and beauty and refinement—qualities often absent on the frontier. Austin was no elitist, and he never spoke ill of the plain folks who formed the majority of his colony, but he was a college man who knew something of literature and the arts, and he hoped to attract at least a few kindred spirits to his corner of the wilderness.[41]

Meeting her for the first time in twenty-five years, Austin was captivated by the vivacious Mary, who was also an aspiring writer. "She is a very superior woman, and the most agreeable company I have met with for many years," he wrote his sister. They spent ten days together in Brazoria before Mary returned east to complete her book and consider relocating to the colony. Whatever chances for romance were lost while Austin fulfilled his obligations to Texas must remain conjecture. Although they corresponded regularly, she never would move west, and Austin would briefly see her only once more before his death.[42]

He was elected to the state legislature to fill the vacant seat, and traveled to Saltillo in December 1830 to take his place among the lawmakers. Events in the summer of 1832 would prove the need for the absent Austin's steadying hand. Outbreaks of violence between *americano* settlers and Mexican authorities at Anahuac, Velasco, and Nacogdoches encouraged agitation for the creation of Texas as a separate state within the Mexican federation. The revolt of the seemingly liberal general Antonio López de Santa Anna against the Bustamente regime was seen as a welcome sign by this activist movement. [43]

In August 1832, the *ayuntamiento* of San Felipe called for a convention to discuss the issues confronting Texas. Fifty-eight delegates from sixteen municipalities met on October 1, but Béxar and Victoria, with their largely

Don Antonio Lopez de Santa Anna in the Year 1829. Lithograph of Carlos Paris painting by the Widow of Murguia and Sons' studio, Mexico City. *Courtesy Special Collections, The University of Texas at Arlington Libraries, Arlington, Texas.*

tejano populations, opted not to send anyone and indicated such a gathering was unlawful. Sensing he was losing control of events, Austin supported the actions of the colonists with the hope of influencing the outcome. Indeed, he was elected president of the convention. The delegates adopted resolutions requesting a three-year exemption to the tariff established by the act of 1830, a repeal to the immigration ban, improvements to the process of issuing land titles, the funding of bilingual schools for Anglo and *tejano* children through the sale of public lands, and independence from Coahuila and statehood for Texas. They bade permission to organize a militia regiment comprised of two battalions of six companies each. They also recommended raising a forty-man company to range the frontiers of Austin's and DeWitt's colonies. No record has been found that indicates this latter company was ever formed. Similarly, the motions reached by the convention, which adjourned on October 6, were, for undetermined reasons, never presented to the Mexican government.[44]

Unbeknownst to the colonists, their assembly, while embracing long-standing Anglo-Saxon political traditions, was viewed by Mexican authorities to be seditious and treasonous, and furthered a suspicion that they secretly desired full independence from Mexico. A second meeting was held at San Felipe between April 1 and April 13, 1833, during which time the delegates drafted a proposed state constitution, reintroduced a call for the repeal of the Law of April 6, and approved new resolutions requesting improved frontier defense, better delivery of the mails, and another exemption to the tariffs. Lastly, they ratified once more an application for separate statehood. Austin was still not convinced of the wisdom of the summit's actions. As Professor Barker commented, "He sincerely believed until the beginning of 1836 that the best interest of Texas lay in its loyalty to Mexico, that the colonists and the government had, therefore, a common interest in its development, and he was the efficient apostle of that faith." Despite his misgivings, Austin traveled to Mexico City to submit the most recent convention's resolutions and petition. Reaching the capital on July 18, he was able to present the memorial to the Mexican Congress. Through his efforts, the emigration ban of the decree of 1830 was revoked, but Austin perceived a decided mistrust of Texians in official circles. To make matters worse, he wrote an "exceedingly rash" letter to the San Antonio *ayuntamiento* on October 2 urging statehood for *Tejas*. The correspondence was intercepted, and Austin was cast into prison without trial for eleven months and placed under house arrest for another six.[45]

Relations between the central government and the Texian colonists had seemed on the verge of improving when Santa Anna forced Bustamente into exile. Instead, the *centralistas* gained political ascendency when the former assumed the presidency on April 1. Although he had publicly assumed the role of the federalist who reluctantly seized power in order to save the country, once in office, Santa Anna adopted the policies of the very same conservatives and clergy he had once opposed. He dissolved the national congress on June 12, 1834, and the state legislatures on October 3, 1835. He strengthened the power and privileges of the Church. He formed a new, meticulously selected *Congreso Nacional* that rubber-stamped his actions and abrogated the 1824 constitution. Opposition to Santa Anna's increasingly despotic rule arose in the states of Puebla and Zacatecas. In the latter, the *presidente* allowed his troops to sack the capital city. The federalist governor of *Coahuila y Tejas* and his staff were arrested before they could mount their own rebellion.[46]

As the calls for revolution began to grow louder, on the frontier, Robert Morris Coleman of Mina raised a company of twenty-five mounted riflemen on June 12, and led them in a campaign against the Tawakonis. Leaving Mina on July 2, and crossing the Brazos at Washington on the fourth, Coleman was nearing the village at Tehuacana Springs one week later when the volunteers were discovered. Both sides fought fiercely, but the Indians' superior numbers forced Coleman to retire with one man killed and four wounded. The Tawakonis lost "a considerable number."[47]

Coleman withdrew to John and Daniel Parker's fort near the headwaters of the Navasota River from which he sent a message calling for assistance. Answering the summons, four companies of volunteers, under Captains Robert McAlpin Williamson, Michael R. Goheen, Philip Haddox Coe, and George Washington Barnett, arrived at the fort on August 5. Coleman's company would be discharged on August 28, but his men seem to have been dispersed among the other commands for the immediate campaign. John Henry Moore was elected major of the ad hoc battalion and James Clinton Neill was named adjutant. The rangers returned to the springs, but the Tawakonis had already fled. For sixty days, the Texians scouted the Trinity River country as far as the forks, then rode down the Brazos. They encountered five or six Indians in total and, in one skirmish, dispatched one warrior and took several women and children prisoner. One of the females killed her child after being captured, and was immediately shot. The captives were returned to the settlements and sold as slaves—the only occurrence of this decision in all of Texas's Indian wars.[48]

After requesting aid, Coleman had written a letter to Henry Rueg, political chief for the Department of Nacogdoches, and proposed the raising of four garrisons of rangers at government expense, the sites where they would be posted, and their system of command and control. His views would be incorporated into *An Act Defining the pay of Mounted Riflemen, now and hereafter in the ranging service on the Frontier*, dated December 10, 1836. The legislation was made retroactive to July 1, 1835. Based on his suggestions, and the fact he was the first captain in the field that month, Coleman has been credited by some as being the organizer of the earliest Texas Ranger company.[49]

Far from the northern borderlands, Austin was freed in a general amnesty authorized by the Mexican Congress on May 6, 1835. While he was preparing to leave the capital, Mexican troops assigned to customs collection in Anahuac clashed with colonists on June 29. The episode polarized the various factions in the province into a "War Party" and a "Peace Party." Reaching the mouth of the Brazos on August 30, the "sadder and wiser" Austin had by this time accepted the need for an independent Texas. "We must rely on ourselves and prepare for the worst," he wrote Mary. He found that most communities had established committees of safety and correspondence in his absence, and he assumed control of the body at San Felipe on September 12. Further, the separatist movement had gained popular support among both *norteamericanos* and *tejanos* by this time, and Austin came to direct the revolutionary effort.[50]

Learning that Santa Anna had dispatched reinforcements to the garrison at Béxar, Austin issued a call for an election of delegates to a general consultation in order to decide the correct course of action. Before any representatives could be chosen, colonists at Gonzales defied Mexican troops who had orders to retrieve an artillery piece from that town. The two sides clashed in a short skirmish on October 2 that repulsed the *soldados*, leaving one or two dead on the ground. With blood spilled, Texian political leaders echoed Austin's call on October 5, and the convention was scheduled to meet on the fifteenth. For the former *empresario*, the choice had become clear: "There must now be no half measures—War in full—The sword is drawn and the scabbard must be put on one side until the military are all driven out of Texas."[51]

Austin felt the local committees lacked the authority to prosecute a war and the revolution needed a unifying structure. In the interlude before the Consultation met, Austin called for delegates from each *ayuntamiento* to form a temporary governing body with the power to make decisions. The assembly Austin proposed gathered on October 11 in San Felipe with the intent to form a provisional government. Richard Royster Royall was elected president and Charles Stewart secretary. During its brief existence, the ironically named Permanent Council directed supplies and volunteers to the army organizing in the field, commissioned privateers to operate in the Gulf of Mexico, established a postal system, and authorized agents to go to the United States and appeal for men, funding, and supplies. The Consultation met at San Felipe on October 15, but lacked a quorum due to many of the delegates being with the army. Those who were present voted to adjourn until November 1.[52]

While a government was being shaped, Austin was unanimously elected on October 11 commander-in-chief of the "Texas Army of the People," initially comprising some three hundred volunteers. Austin and his men began the march for San Antonio the following day. Although many were equipped with Kentucky rifles or shotguns, a significant number of the rebels carried no firearms at all. They were short of gunpowder and lead as well. Initially, the army suffered from a lack of mounted troops to counter the *centralista* cavalry they were sure to meet. As Austin advanced toward his objective, though, he was joined by bands of capable federalist *rancheros*, including Juan Nepomuceno Seguín and his thirty-seven horsemen. While on the road, an election for regimental officers saw John H. Moore chosen as colonel, Edward Burleson as lieutenant-colonel, and Alexander Somervell as major.[53]

Marching at a rate of ten miles per day, the army reached the left bank of Cíbolo Creek on October 16. Convening a council of war, Austin and his officers decided the former should open negotiations with *santanista* general Martín Perfecto de Cós. In a note, written on the seventeenth, the *americano* commander specified the reasons the Texians had revolted and offered the terms that would see them peacefully return home. Cós unequivocally refused to treat with the insurrectionists until they disarmed, dispersed, and submitted petitions through the regular channels. Resuming the advance on the twentieth, the rebels made camp the following morning, five miles from Béxar on Salado Creek. Seguín, having been appointed a captain, and other *tejanos* rode the countryside, searching for corn, beef, beans, salt, and other supplies. Dispatching Benjamin Rush Milam to scout the best approaches to the city, the Mexican positions, and the intentions of Cós, Austin determined to wait for reinforcements before moving on the town.[54]

By October 21, the Texas army was comprised of eleven companies totaling approximately 453 men. The captains serving under Austin's command were James Walker Fannin, Michael R. Goheen, Robert M. Coleman, I. Hall, Jacob Eberly, Randall Jones, Albert Martin, Thomas Alley, John Bird, J. Robinson, and James C. Neill. In the meantime, the entrenched Mexican force at Béxar had been reinforced to at least 650 *soldados* and twenty cannons. Austin rejected carrying the works by direct assault and decided instead to lay siege to the town in the hopes of starving out the garrison. On the twentieth-seventh, James Bowie and Fannin led an advance element of ninety-two men to find a suitable location for a base from which to invest the city. Locating a defensible camp at Mission Purísima Concepción de Acuna, they engaged one hundred Mexican infantrymen and three hundred dragoons early the next morning, and held the position until Austin arrived later in the day. Sheltered behind the steep banks of the San Antonio River, Bowie's men were able to kill or wound approximately seventy-six *soldados*, while only losing one of their own.[55]

While Austin's army was marching on Béxar, delegate Daniel Parker of Nacogdoches rose during the October 17 meeting of the Permanent Council and proposed his brother Silas Mercer Parker, Garrison Greenwood, and Daniel Boone Friar be authorized to form ranger districts and "superintend" companies in the field. Parker's twenty-five men would range the country between the Brazos and Trinity Rivers; the same number supervised by Friar between the Brazos and the Colorado; and Greenwood would oversee ten between the Trinity and the Neches. From Parker's Fort, also known as Fort Sterling, Silas recruited a company under Eli Hillhouse and sent them on October 23 to follow a fresh Indian trail. Hillhouse's irregulars returned to their post by November 2 without having engaged any hostile parties. A second company of ten men was authorized on the ninth, and would be mustered into service under the command of James W. Parker on January 1.[56]

On November 1, Friar raised a company of sixteen men at Viesca, and was elected the captain in addition to his position as superintendent. To outfit his rangers, he paid for provisions and ammunition from his personal funds. Friar led his men to the Waco village on the Brazos and swept the country to the Colorado and back. On the twenty-third, he added six more volunteers to his company rolls. Between November 19 and December 31, a detachment of Friar's company engaged hostile Indians near the San Gabriel with only two horses being lost.[57]

Another twenty-five men were authorized to be added to Greenwood's command, headquartered at the town of Houston in Anderson County, on the twenty-sixth. A fourth ranging company under George Washington Davis was approved on November 9 to patrol between the Colorado and the Cíbolo.[58]

On the political front, delegates to the Consultation began to gather at San Felipe on November 1, but did not achieve an actual quorum and commence business until the third. On that day, Doctor Branch Tanner Archer was elected president. Deliberations got underway on the fifth, and two days later they adopted a declaration of causes, which proclaimed their belief that Mexico's representative democracy had been supplanted by dictatorship, affirmed Texas's prerogative to defend her citizens' "natural rights" by armed force, and asserted their privilege to quit the republic if these grievances were not addressed. In order to ensure the security of any loans made to the cause of Texas, Austin and other patriotic citizens began at this time to donate their personal property to the Consultation as collateral.[59]

The Consultation approved an interim charter known as the Organic Law on November 13, which authorized the formation of a provisional

Volunteers ready themselves to pursue Indian raiders. Walter Prescott Webb Papers. *Courtesy Archives and Manuscript Division, Texas State Library and Archives Commission, Austin, Texas.*

government that would be headed by a governor and a lieutenant governor. The governor was to have full executive powers, and be named the commander-in-chief of the army and the navy. The Consultation would also elect a General Council to advise and assist the executive. Each district was to choose a delegate to the council, which was presided over by the lieutenant governor. The council was responsible for the well-being and administration of the armed forces, the defense of the state, contracting for loans, and imposing taxes and duties. Austin and Henry Smith had been nominated for the office of governor. Smith won the election on November 12 by a vote of thirty-one to twenty-two, and James W. Robinson was chosen as lieutenant governor. The Consultation adjourned on the fourteenth, and the General Council convened the same day.[60]

The military ordinance act was approved on November 24, which created a regular army of 1,120 men. This force was to be divided into one regiment of infantry and one of artillery. Sam Houston was named major-general of the regular military, which at this time only existed on paper. One important caveat was that Houston held no command authority over Austin's volunteers. Further, all able-bodied men between the ages of sixteen and fifty were enrolled in a militia, and the law required them to assemble the following month to muster into companies.[61] The regional ranging system established the previous month had barely begun to take effect when the General Council created another organization. The discussion over the identity of the first Texas Rangers is further muddled with this development. Whether one believes Morrison, Kuykendall, or Coleman was the original Ranger captain, the role of Texas rangers was formalized for the first time in Article IX of the ordinance, which stated:

> There shall be a corps of rangers under the command of a major, to consist of one hundred and fifty men, to be divided into three or more detachments, and which shall compose a battalion under the Commander-in-Chief, when in the field.[62]

The four ranging districts were not immediately replaced by the new ranger corps, but any further recruiting was halted. Garrison Greenwood had already organized a ten-man company commanded by Captain William Turner Sadler, which was mustered into service on January 1, 1836. As George Davis had not yet raised any companies for his district, his command was allowed to lapse. Henry Smith asserted the rangers needed a "bold, energetic and enterprising commander at their head," and Robert McAlpin Williamson was elected the battalion's major on the twenty-eighth. To command three companies of fifty-six men each, Isaac Watts Burton, John Jackson Tumlinson, Jr., and William Willis Arrington were appointed the same day. On December 1, Williamson was ordered to raise a force of thirty to seventy men and proceed to the source of Mill Creek in order to overtake and punish a party of hostile Indians. Eighteen days later, he was instructed to establish his headquarters at Mina and begin to recruit additional men for the battalion.[63]

Meanwhile, Austin and his ragtag army sat in front of Béxar, while the general struggled to organize, train, and supply his men. Cós performed the same vexing task inside San Antonio, and active operations ground to a halt. The strength of the Army of the People fluctuated between six hundred and eight hundred as Texian militiamen returned to their farms and volunteers began arriving from the southern United States. The enforced idleness caused restless men to become insubordinate, which led to drinking and desertions. Edward Burleson replaced John Moore on November 7 in a general reorganization of the armed forces. In a candid November 8 letter to the government, Austin discussed his physical limitations as an army commander and recognized the need for an experienced soldier to take charge.[64]

However, Austin's future lay in a direction different from that of military affairs. He took on another role when he, William Harris Wharton, and Branch Archer were appointed commissioners to the United States, and directed to proceed to Washington, D.C. at once to secure financial assistance. The general was notified of the Consultation's intentions and formally relieved of command on November 18, but he decided to press on with the assault on San Antonio before his departure. When his chief lieutenants reported the troops were opposed to the offensive scheduled to begin on the twenty-second, Austin disgustedly cancelled the attack. Informing the men of his appointment, they elected Burleson as their new commander on November 24.[65]

Believing the Consultation's declaration of causes to be ineffectual, Austin addressed the Council on December 2. He called for a new convention to either organize a state government under the constitution of 1824, or declare full independence. He would not support any vacillating options, and vowed to refuse the commissioner's position if they did not act resolutely. Two days later, the General Council concurred with Austin's viewpoint and scheduled the convention for March 1 of the following year. Before he departed San Felipe, the delegates, on behalf of the people of Texas, presented to Austin the thanks and compliments of the Council on December 11.[66]

The three commissioners took passage for New Orleans on December 26. Austin had scant confidence in the provisional government he was leaving behind. He and his fellow envoys had been instructed to negotiate a million-dollar loan, solicit donations, purchase supplies and munitions for the army, acquire warships for the navy, and recruit volunteers. They were further ordered to assess the position of the United States government regarding the annexation of Texas. Any subsequent negotiations would have to wait for Governor Smith's approval.[67]

On December 4, after Burleson announced he was cancelling the siege, Ben Milam roused three hundred Texian and *tejano* volunteers to follow him in storming Béxar. The attack was launched on the fifth, and the fighting was bitter and bloody as the defenders stubbornly contested "every inch of ground." Once the assault party lost contact with its logistical base, numerous *bexareños* exposed themselves to enemy fire to bring ammunition, food, and water to the rebels fighting in the streets. San Antonio was in Texian hands by the dawn of December 9, but tragically at the cost of Milam who had been killed by a sharpshooter on the seventh. Three other insurgents died and fourteen were severely wounded, while the Mexicans lost 150 killed or wounded.[68]

As Texas readied itself for war, the two forces of rangers on the frontier were facing hardships of their own. By December 17, Silas Parker had employed thirty rangers for his district. The men had experienced great difficulty in procuring horses and provisions. The superintendent placed the blame on the indifference of the people to the cause, and paid for the supplies he could acquire from his own pocket. Captain Hillhouse died on December 24 and was replaced by Eli Seale. Beginning on November 28 and December 19 respectively, Tumlinson and Burton were busily raising their companies. By the middle of January, Tumlinson assembled his men at Hornsby's Station, then marched them to the headwaters of Brushy Creek. The third captain, Arrington, seems to have never organized his company.[69]

For years, *tejanos* in the western half of Texas, and the lower Río Grande, had suffered from the steady onslaught of Comanche raids. By 1834 or 1835, Anglo Texians began to feel their wrath. On January 19, 1836, Tumlinson and his men were surprised by the appearance of a ragged white woman who reported most of her family had been wiped out by thirteen Comanches on Rocky Creek in present Lavaca County. After her husband's and her brother's deaths, and the murder of her infant son, the woman, Sarah Hibbins, and her eldest son were taken prisoner. Forced to leave her child behind, she escaped and walked for an entire day before she chanced upon Tumlinson's camp. The next morning, the captain's scouts found a fresh trail that indicated the Comanches were heedless of any pursuit. At nine o'clock, the rangers unexpectedly found the Indians in the midst of departing their encampment on Walnut Creek, located in the present city of Austin. In the subsequent fight, four Comanches were killed and two Texians were wounded. The surviving Indians escaped into the cedar thicket. The captive boy was recovered, and all of the enemy's horses and equipment were seized. This skirmish was the first known violent encounter between Comanche Indians and Texas Rangers, and set the stage for forty years of bitter warfare.[70]

By January 25, Eli Seale's company, under Silas Parker's superintendence, completed its three months' service and was discharged at Fort Sterling. James A. Head raised another company in Parker's district on the twentieth-seventh and served for three months. James Parker's outfit continued in service for several more months, then disbanded. Daniel Friar's company similarly completed their enlistment on February 1. William Sadler mustered his men out on March 16.[71] Three of the four ranger districts had been able to raise men and patrol their areas of operation over the winter of 1835 and 1836. Despite Tumlinson's initial success in battle, by February 4, Williamson's ranger corps was being called a failure as a sufficient number of men could not be induced to enlist at the authorized rate of pay. Prospective rangers also objected to not being allowed to elect their own officers. Regardless of negative opinion, the major continued to complete the organization of his battalion and "fortify strategic points so as to more surely protect the frontier from Indian attacks." In late February, Tumlinson would move his company to Mina to act as a picket line watching for Mexican troop movements.[72]

Based on the attitudes of New Orleans capitalists, Austin realized financial assistance for Texas would be more forthcoming if the struggle became one for independence. The commissioners solicited the promise of loans totaling over $200,000 and bearing an annual interest of 8 percent. They further attempted to raise money by offering 500,000 acres of Texas public land to speculators. Austin and his colleagues continued to speak at public meetings in Nashville, Louisville, Cincinnati, and Maysville before reaching Washington. Their efforts to secure financial assistance and official recognition from the federal government became dependent upon a Texian declaration of independence from Mexico.[73]

At home, the Texian provisional government was coming apart at the seams. Due to the unrealistic expectations of the Organic Law concerning shared powers, and following a dispute over an expedition to Matamoros, the intractable Governor Smith formally suspended the General Council on January 9. He then assumed absolute authority over the affairs of state. The councilors immediately deposed the executive, and appointed Lieutenant Governor Robinson in his place. Smith stubbornly refused to vacate his office or surrender the public documents in his possession, but bowed to the inevitable on January 10. Unable to maintain a quorum, the Council adjourned on January 17, which hamstrung Robinson in adopting the role of executive.[74]

Divided by petty ambition and rank egotism, the political leadership nevertheless gathered at Washington-on-the-Brazos on March 1. Forty-five delegates representing twenty-one municipalities chose Richard Ellis president of the convention, and quickly got down to the business of fashioning a permanent government. The following day, they adopted a declaration of independence, which the members began to sign on the third. Sam Houston was appointed commander-in-chief of all regular, volunteer, and militia land forces, and ordered to take charge immediately. The lawmakers proceeded to draft a constitution, but the approach of the Mexican army would prevent ratification and cause the Convention to hastily adjourn on March 17. Before they departed, though, the delegates elected *ad interim* officials, including David Gouverneur Burnet as president, until the commencement of a constitutional government.[75]

In the U.S. capital, Austin and his fellow commissioners waited impatiently for word that Texas had formally severed ties to Mexico. The newspapers reported such an event had occurred, but, without official notification, the Texan emissaries lacked authorization to negotiate either recognition or annexation. After a week of forced idleness, Archer traveled to Richmond, and Austin to Baltimore, Philadelphia, and New York, while Wharton remained in Washington.[76]

Even as the commissioners implored for assistance in the East, the Texian cause experienced several reverses, then one critical moment of triumph. At the outset of the thirteen-day siege of the Alamo, Santa Anna had directed the raising of a blood-red flag and the playing of the *degüello*, both to signify no quarter was to be given to the insurgents. The mission-turned-fortress fell on March 6 and the entire garrison was slain either during the fighting or immediately afterward. Further south, Fannin's command, despite some initial success, was defeated piecemeal at Refugio and at Coleto Creek. The survivors were taken to Goliad as prisoners where, on Palm Sunday, approximately 342 were executed according to the Supreme Government's standing orders. The manner in which these Texians met their deaths galvanized the people of Texas, and provoked sympathy and outrage in the United States. When Houston and the rebel army met Santa Anna and his Mexican *soldados* at the San Jacinto River on April 21, Texian soldiers continually shouted "Remember the Alamo!" and "Remember Goliad!" as they routed the opposing troops.[77]

Not knowing military victory had been achieved, the commissioners went about their business discouraged by the lack of results. Failing to secure a half-million-dollar loan from the Bank of the United States, Austin reached New York and met with the city's most prominent financiers and politicians.

Fall of the Alamo. Oil on canvas painting by Theodore Gentilz. #1/075. *Courtesy Prints and Photographs Collection, Texas State Library & Archives Commission, Austin, Texas.*

He addressed a public meeting at the Masonic Hall on April 26. The Texians' time thus far had produced only a 10 percent installment on the promised loan of $200,000, and that money had been expended before they reached Washington. Austin spoke at another meeting in Philadelphia before returning to New York.[78] Once there, Austin penned a letter to Senator Lewis Fields Linn of Missouri which explained the origins and goals for Texas declaring her independence. He characterized the struggle as "a war of barbarism and of despotic principles" waged against civilization and liberty and encouraged his readers to,

> take up the history of Mexican misrule in Texas, and all over Mexico; let them inquire into the present state of things in that important nation; let them ascertain whether the present consolidated despotism which exists there, has or has not been established by revolutionary means, by force, fraud, and violence; whether the federal social compact of Mexico, to which the People of Texas bound their allegiance, is not illegally dissolved; whether the People of Texas did or did not oppose this illegal dissolution of their Government, as they were bound by their oaths to do, and whether they did not grimly adhere to THEIR duty and obligations as Mexican citizens, under the Constitution, so long as it existed … In short, let them understand the question, before they attempt to approve or condemn, and I am confident they can form but ONE OPINION, which is, that the Texians are RIGHT, and that under similar circumstances all freemen ought to, and would have done as they have.[79]

The correspondence was published in many of the country's newspapers, which allowed Austin to reach a far wider audience.[80] Despite the extent of their solicitations, though, the efforts of the commissioners resulted in a paltry $75,000 in loans from private donors. The news of the Texian battlefield triumph made further petitioning unnecessary and the commissioners discontinued their activities. The issue of official recognition by the United States proved even less successful as Texas still lacked an accredited government. On May 13, Austin entrained for Washington, and for Baltimore eleven days later, before traveling overland to Wheeling. From there he took a steamboat down the Ohio River toward the Mississippi. He landed in New Orleans on June 10.[81]

Reaching Velasco on June 27, Austin accurately predicted the treaties made between Santa Anna and the *ad interim* government would not be honored by Mexico City. He resumed a central role in Texas affairs and acted unofficially as the primary diplomatic strategist. Endeavoring to secure a more permanent peace, and official recognition of Texan independence, he met with Santa Anna and convinced the *generalissimo* to write Andrew Jackson asking for the American president's mediation. The courteous letter reached the White House after Jackson had been notified the Mexican government had deposed Santa Anna *in absentia*. Instead, the president offered to negotiate a peaceful settlement between Texas and the current regime in Mexico City through regular channels.[82]

The unpopular Burnet called for the election of a permanent government, and Austin announced his candidacy for the presidency on August 4. The contest quickly turned ugly as opponents charged Austin with involvement in fraudulent land speculations at Monclova, with opposing independence, and being a lackey of the disgraced Burnet administration. Henry Smith and Sam Houston, the latter fresh from his victory at San Jacinto, also entered the race.[83]

Although he would not win the highest political office, Austin was to see his life's work become the Republic of Texas on September 5, 1836. On that day, his fellow Texians voted to approve the constitution and elect Sam Houston and Mirabeau Buonaparte Lamar president and vice president respectively. Twenty-two counties sent representatives to the bicameral First Congress in Columbia, which convened on October 3. The seat of government would reside there until April 1, 1837, when the new city of Houston became the capital. Meanwhile, General Houston and Lamar were inaugurated on the twenty-second.[84]

Despite losing the presidency to Houston, Austin, both privately and publicly, praised the republic's new chief executive. In turn, Houston graciously nominated Austin for the post of secretary of state. The president wrote Austin on October 30 announcing the confirmation of his appointment.

Austin accepted the offer the next day. Upon assuming office, Austin set to creating the diplomatic machinery of the new republic. The primary goals of the government included securing international recognition of Texian independence and the country's annexation to the United States. Shortly before his death, he wrote about Texas: "I feel a more lively interest for its welfare than can be expressed—one that is greatly superior to all pecuniary or personal views of any kind. The prosperity of Texas has been the object of my labors, the idol of my existence—it has assumed the character of a *religion* for the guidance of my thoughts and actions for fifteen years."[85]

The traditions of the Texas Rangers Austin had inaugurated in 1823 continued under the auspices of the Republic of Texas. In the wake of the Revolution, every ranger district but Silas Parker's had ceased to exist, Major Williamson had left the service, and Tumlinson's and Burton's companies had transferred to a ranger battalion commanded by Lieutenant-Colonel Griffin Bayne. Companies under Eleazar Louis Ripley Wheelock and William C. Wilson were similarly assigned to Bayne's command. Throughout the remainder of the year, Edward Burleson, Robert Coleman, and James Smith would each command ranger battalions on the frontier.[86]

In one example of early ranger activities, Burton was ordered on May 29 to range the coastal plain from the Guadalupe River to Mission Bay. Two days later, the company was near Refugio when they learned a questionable vessel had been spotted in Copano Bay. The rangers rode to the inlet where, on June 3, they concealed themselves in the brush atop the bluff overlooking the water. They observed a two-masted schooner flying no flag, but bearing the name *Watchman*. By eight a.m., the suspicious Burton instructed two of his men to signal the ship while feigning distress. The vessel raised the American flag, but when the rangers did not respond the crew raised the Mexican banner in its place. The Texians then beckoned the ship's captain to send a boat ashore. The rangers quietly seized the captain and four of his crew and, leaving the five sailors under guard, took the boat back out to the *Watchman* which they captured without bloodshed. While Burton waited for favorable winds in order to set sail for Velasco, two more schooners, subsequently identified as the *Comanche* and the *Fanny Butler*, were sighted and the rangers were able to board these vessels as well. All three ships were found to be American vessels chartered by the Mexican government to haul supplies to the latter's army. The cargoes were later forfeited to the Republic of Texas, but the schooners were returned to their rightful owners.[87]

While the service he had helped to create protected the borderlands, Austin continued to set an exhausting pace in his Columbia office. In his role as the republic's chief diplomat, he "worked almost day and night, by the dim light of the tallow candle, in a room without fire, thus contracting a severe cold." His condition worsening, he died of pneumonia on December 27, 1836, and his body lay in state for two days. Secretary of War William S. Fisher directed that every officer was required to wear crêpe on his right arm for thirty days. All officers commanding posts, garrisons, or detachments were to order twenty-three guns to be fired in salute—one for each county in Texas. Furthermore, garrison and regimental colors were to be hung black during the period of mourning. Secretary of the Navy Samuel Rhoads Fisher issued similar orders to the commanders of every squadron, naval depot and station, and individual vessel. Austin's remains were then brought aboard the steamer *Yellowstone*, and conveyed down the Brazos to his sister's home at Peach Point for interment. On October 19, 1910, he was exhumed in order that he be reburied at the State Cemetery the following day with full honors. Among the local and state officials escorting the "Father of Texas" to his permanent resting place were Captain John Harris Rogers and a detachment of Texas Rangers.[88]

Even though he never commanded Texas Rangers in the field, Austin was nevertheless the catalyst for the creation of that vaunted corps. In his roles of *empresario*, militia commander, administrator, and diplomat, he proved himself a man of action, commitment, and will. Regardless of whether the ten men mentioned in his "Address to the Colonists" ever actually served, the notion of rangers in Texas began with Stephen Austin.

John Coffee Hays. Salted paper photographic print attributed to Mathew Brady, Washington, D.C. *Courtesy Prints and Photographs Division, Library of Congress, Washington, D.C.*

Chapter 2

John C. Hays: "Ideal Texas Ranger"

John Coffee "Jack" Hays is the standard for the ideal Texas Ranger. He was a soft-spoken, unassuming gentleman who looked far too youthful to be the dreaded *El Diablo* of the Río Grande country. Untrained in the military arts, his natural genius for combat leadership made him a savior to a people beset with Indian and bandit raids. His ability to inspire greatness in others was evidenced by his four subordinates also enshrined in the Texas Ranger Hall of Fame. Thanks to his foresight and tactical proficiency, the rangers Hays commanded in 1844 would utilize Samuel Colt's innovative revolving pistol and establish a singular combination of mobility and firepower. A captain by the age of twenty-four, and a colonel by twenty-nine, he would become, in a few short years, arguably the greatest ranger chief in the history of the Lone Star State. The ranger and author known to posterity as "Brazos" commented: "He was all that has been said of him, and more … his coolness inspired the faltering, and his presence was worth a regiment … So much faith did all of us have in the military abilities of this extraordinary man that any half dozen veterans would have followed him in a charge against the whole Mexican army."

The eldest child of Harmon A. and Elizabeth (Cage) Hays, he was born on January 28, 1817, on the family plantation near Little Cedar Lick Creek in

Wilson County, Tennessee. Harmon was born in 1787 in neighboring Sumner County. He had been appointed a cornet in the Regiment of Light Dragoons in March 1812 and, under the command of Major-General Andrew Jackson, fought the British and the Creek Indians. Hays resigned his commission of second lieutenant in the Second Light Dragoons in July 1814. John himself was named for his father's commanding officer, Brigadier-General John Coffee, who had been Jackson's most trusted subordinate.[1] In addition to Jack, Harmon and Elizabeth's offspring included William Cage Hays, born later in 1817; Mary Anne Hays, born on December 14, 1818; Harry Thompson Hays, born on April 14, 1820; Sarah Elizabeth "Sallie" Hays, born in 1822; Rachel Jane Hays, born on July 23, 1827; and Robert B. Hays, born in 1830.[2]

By 1820, the family was living in Wilkinson County, Mississippi, where some of Elizabeth's relatives also dwelt. Ten years later, they were once more residing in Wilson County, where Harmon obtained at least three pieces of land on the Cumberland River near Cairo.[3]

Following the deaths of his father on October 21, 1833, and his mother on November 21, Jack and his siblings moved to their uncle's plantation in Yazoo County, Mississippi. While there, Robert Hall Cage, their mother's brother, urged Jack to prepare himself for a career in business, but Hays wanted to earn an appointment to the military academy at West Point. The two were unable to come to an agreement so Jack left the plantation to seek his fortune. Needing a marketable skill, the fifteen-year-old Hays began to learn the trade of surveying. He started as a chain carrier, and by the end of two years he was heading his own crew. Isaac Dunbar Affleck and James Kimmins Greer, two of Hays's biographers, asserted he enrolled in Davidson Academy in Nashville using the money he had saved from his surveying work. Due to diligent studying and strenuous recreation, he supposedly became sick during a bad winter and had to leave school. Whether the episode as conveyed is accurate, that institution, founded in 1785, changed its name to Cumberland College in 1806, then to the University of Nashville in 1826.[4]

Joined by his brother William, Hays left Tennessee and Mississippi and drifted westward until the two reached Texas in early 1838. Hays's emigration to the Republic has been the subject of some debate. John Caperton, Affleck, and Greer each state Hays reached Texas shortly after the battle of

San Jacinto in 1836. He purportedly joined Captain Erastus "Deaf" Smith's ranger company and fought in a skirmish with Mexican troops at Laredo. The 1838 date, however, is supported by a letter of introduction from Harry Cage, an uncle of the Hays brothers living in Wilkinson County, Mississippi, to President Sam Houston, which is found among the records of the Texas State Archives. The chief executive had been a lieutenant in the Seventh and Thirty-ninth U.S. Infantry Regiments, and had known Harmon Hays during the Creek War. Bearing the date of November 29, 1837, the note describes Cage's nephews as "having nothing to rely upon but their personal exertions" and that "they visit your Republic believing they will there find a fairer field for the Pursuit of their energies, industry and objects." The phrasing of Cage's missive suggests the brothers arrived in Texas sometime after the letter was written rather than in the previous year. Furthermore, the records of the General Land Office include a transcript of second- and third-class land grants prepared by the clerk for the Board of Land Commissioners in Béxar County. This November 20, 1839, document certified Hays's claim to 320 acres and noted his arrival in Texas as occurring in the first part of 1838. By law, second-class headrights of 640 acres were presented to single men who settled in Texas after March 2, 1836, and before October 1, 1837. Third-class grants of 320 acres went to single men who immigrated after October 1, 1837, and before January 1, 1840. The version advanced by Caperton, Affleck, and Greer is almost certainly false based on this evidence. In addition, Deaf Smith provided the names of his men in his after-action report, and Hays's name was not among them.[5]

Making San Antonio his home, Hays commenced to busily survey the land grants given to veterans of the Revolution and to new settlers. He soon received an appointment of deputy surveyor of the Béxar District, which at that time encompassed all of western Texas. As white settlement began to encroach on the *Comanchería*, the Edwards Plateau uplands west of the Balcones Escarpment, raiding parties attacked farms, killed homesteaders, and stole livestock and captives. While in the field with his transit and chain, Hays survived several brushes with the Comanches.[6]

Colonel Henry Wax Karnes was in charge of the defense of the southwestern borderlands in 1838. In the summer of that year, he led an expedition of twenty-one volunteers, including Hays, out of San Antonio. They rode west of the Medina River and halted at the Arroyo Seco on August 10. While allowing their horses to rest, they were suddenly confronted by two hundred charging Comanches. The colonel quickly ordered his men to safeguard the horses and prepare to meet the attack. They were sheltered in a slight ravine amidst chaparral, and fired in alternate platoons so that one-third of the company always held loaded rifles ready for close-quarters battle. Hays shot the Comanche chief, possibly Essomanny, from his horse, which caused the Indians to withdraw beyond rifle range and regroup. Behind a volley of arrows, the Comanches charged again. The marksmanship of the Texians was deadly, and numerous warriors fell to the ground dead or wounded. Outnumbering Karnes's volunteers by ten to one, the warriors were not easily persuaded to retire. Loosing another shower of arrows, they charged for a third time. They retrieved their casualties on this last, failed attempt before dashing away, having lost twenty dead and as many wounded. Several times during the engagement, the fearless Karnes had exposed himself to the enemy's fire. He received an arrow wound in the hip while standing on the ravine's edge to get a better view of the battlefield. The rest of the men were uninjured, but most of the horses were wounded or killed by the Indians' arrows.[7]

Hays returned to San Antonio, then left again on September 21 for a month-long survey in the Leon River country. This time he had no encounters with hostile Indians. In total, he located seventy-six headrights in 1838, although he only worked part of the year.[8]

Hays continued to combine surveying with service as a frontier scout or ranger during 1839.[9] He signed up once more with Henry Karnes on June 6, when the colonel was organizing another campaign against the Comanches. His party was comprised of two mounted companies commanded by Captains Louis B. Franks and Juan Nepomuceno Seguín; Hays became a member of Franks's volunteers. The expedition numbered one hundred men, with forty-five of those being Anglos. Karnes led his troops out of San Antonio on June 10, and rode along winding trails in Pasa del Bandera. Hays commanded the scouting party, and they were constantly in advance of the column choosing the best route. Indian sign was plentiful, but indications were that they were falling back before the Texians.[10]

The expedition ranged above the forks of the Medina River and on to the Río Frio where Hays's scouts had reported seeing Indians. On June 19, they discovered recently abandoned campsites as they approached the Cañon de Uvalde, including one where the men found a bound human corpse roasted over a fire. As the column continued the march, Karnes realized the Indians were driving their herds beyond the reach of the Texians. He reasoned his men were under observation, and the Indians were not inclined to offer him battle. Karnes decided to call a halt to the excursion and return to San Antonio, but some of the volunteers were loath to end the hunt. Consequently, the colonel divided his men into three squads; the first would backtrack and gather up supplies left at an earlier camp, and the other two would follow circuitous routes home while looking for Indians. Hays led one of the detachments and scouted the country surrounding Cañon de Uvalde. His squad destroyed several abandoned Indian *rancherías*, and later reported having killed a small number of Indians in brief skirmishes. The last of the expedition reached San Antonio on June 23, and the two companies were discharged. The men were not paid at this time as the bulk of the Texas military and its paymasters were fighting the Cherokees in East Texas.[11]

Hays served under Karnes for a third time later in the fall. The colonel was raising a force of 105 men assembled into two mounted companies under Captains William F. Wilson and José María Gonzales. Hays enrolled in the latter unit on September 8. Along with twenty-eight *tejanos*, and eighteen other Anglo surveyors and ex-rangers, he was called into service two days later. On October 20, the colonel led his command on another expedition out of San Antonio, this time bound for the San Saba hill country. The column rode for two days through a pair of picturesque valleys before reaching a steep, rocky ravine strewn with wild pine and junipers. The volunteers dismounted and led their horses in a slide downhill. On the bottom of the gorge, one of Gonzales's men was seriously wounded when a comrade's rifle accidentally discharged. One more volunteer, this time from Wilson's company, was mortally wounded on October 26 in another unintentional shooting. He died approximately one-and-a-half hours after the accident and was buried the following day. The first man to be wounded died on the twenty-eighth and was laid to rest next to his fellow ranger.[12]

The march continued through the country between the Guadalupe and San Saba Rivers and on to the Pedernales. On November 1, near present-day Fredericksburg, a scout reported the presence of Indians. Karnes ordered his men to fall back to a position eight miles away where they made camp. Hays was leading a small spy detachment drawn from Gonzales's company, and he reported the *tejano* scouts refused to leave the camp for fear of an Indian attack. He instead took three other spies and left to locate the enemy. Karnes's continual choice of Hays for reconnaissance into hostile country indicates the younger man's growing expertise in the field. The scouts pinpointed the Indian encampment after dark, and Hays was able to infiltrate to within eighty yards of the fire and count thirty sleeping forms. He later reported the warriors were led by the notorious Comanche chieftain Isomania.[13]

The Texians returned to their own camp where they reported their discoveries to Karnes. The colonel took Hays's detachment and half of Wilson's company that very night and marched on the Indians' position. The balance of the expedition was left behind to guard the camp. Hays and his spies guided their comrades to the Comanche camp, arriving about an hour before daybreak. As the rangers approached, one of the Indians' horses became spooked and alerted the sleeping warriors. The stunned Comanches seized their weapons, and both sides began to fire. The Indians fled, leaving behind ten or twelve dead. The Texians suffered no casualties. Karnes and his rangers arrived back at their camp about noon the following day. They were accompanied by forty captured horses and mules, as well as equipment, bridles, robes, and other spoils.[14]

The next day, the expedition resumed, and they were encamped in the Llano River valley by November 5. Karnes, who had not fully recuperated from the arrow wound taken at Arroyo Seco, had fallen ill and the volunteers were forced to wait for his recovery. The idleness, dwindling provisions, and cold weather caused many of them to consider returning home. On November 10, Hays and his fellow surveyors elected to leave the expedition and travel to Austin. Others, either singly or in groups, did the same, and the remaining body was back in San Antonio by November 21 for disbandment.[15]

On February 15, 1840, Hays was appointed by President Mirabeau Buonaparte Lamar to plot the northwestern boundary line of Travis County.

His services as a surveyor were in high demand as he located eighty-nine land certificates throughout the year. Twenty-three projects were as far as the Pedernales River, sixty miles from San Antonio. He was working a tract of land below Béxar on the San Antonio River in March, and so missed the Council House Fight.[16]

Twelve Comanche chiefs, eighteen warriors, three women, and two children had been killed in the failed peace conference in San Antonio. In early August, more than six hundred vengeful Penatʉkas launched an offensive that became known as the Great Comanche Raid. They cut a swath of death and destruction between the Lavaca area and Gonzales that resulted in twenty people killed, three women and three children taken, and over two thousand horses and mules stolen. The raiding party was finally cornered at Plum Creek where Texian volunteers under Felix Huston, Edward Burleson, and Mathew "Old Paint" Caldwell defeated them. While not a key participant in the battle, Hays's conduct at Plum Creek, as well as in the earlier campaigns with Henry Karnes, earned him "an enviable reputation for bravery, daring, endurance, and skill in commanding men."[17]

The Texas Congress enacted a joint resolution on December 26, 1840, "Authorizing the President to employ three Spy Companies for the Western Frontier." The legislation approved the appointment and commissioning of three men to raise and command companies of fifteen men, each for four months' service. On January 10, 1841, Hays formally became a captain of rangers when he was selected to lead one of two companies based in Béxar. The other was commanded by Antonio Pérez, while John T. Price's outfit was stationed at Victoria.[18]

Hays never looked the part of a "bold and dashing Indian fighter." Standing five foot eight inches, with a slim build, a clear, high voice, wavy brown hair, and a "lean but bold Roman face," he was described by a contemporary as a "delicate-looking young man." Mary Ann Adams Maverick, wife of Samuel Augustus Maverick, a leading citizen of San Antonio, wrote: "Hays displayed such rare military skill and daring, that very soon by consent of all, he was looked upon as the leader and his orders were obeyed and he himself loved by all. In a fight he was utterly fearless and invincible."[19]

In his biography of Hays, Caperton described the type of men who would have enlisted in Hays's ranger company:

> Each man was armed with a rifle, a pistol, and a knife, and with a Mexican blanket tied behind his saddle, and a small wallet in which he carried salt and ammunition, and perhaps a little panola or parched corn, spiced and sweetened, a great allayer of thirst, and tobacco, he was equipped for months; and the little body of men, unencumbered by baggage wagons or pack trains, moved as lightly over the prairie as the Indians did, and lived as they did, without tents, with a saddle for a pillow at night, blankets over them, and their feet to the fire … The men were splendid riders, and used the Mexican saddle, improved somewhat by the Americans, and carried the Mexican *riata*, made of rawhide, the *cabrista* also, a hair rope and the lariat, used to rope horses with.[20]

Hays began his storied career as a ranger captain by conducting a scout from the mouth of the Frio along the Nueces toward the Río Grande. Entering Laredo, he seized a number of horses, frightened the *soldados* who were on hand, and withdrew to his camp outside of town. The following day, Hays returned the horses to their rightful owners and informed the Mexicans he had not stolen them. Instead, he wanted to impress upon the residents of the border country the folly of raiding into Texas, as any depredations would be returned in kind.[21]

Known as the *Llanos Mesteñas* (Wild Horse Prairie) or *El Desierto Muerto* (the Dead Desert), the area between the Nueces and the Río Grande had seen the development of a lucrative smuggling trade between San Antonio, Goliad, Victoria, Matagorda, Corpus Christi, and Houston, and smaller communities in Tamaulipas, Nuevo León, and Coahuila. The Texians trafficked in cloth, hardware, and tobacco with the Mexicans who, in turn, ran beans, sugar, flour, and leather goods. At the same time the region developed commercially, it also became a battleground between roving bands of Texas "cowboys" and Mexican *bandidos*. The Mexican marauders, who plundered Texian settlements and merchant caravans from San Antonio, Goliad, and Refugio, were usually *rancheros*, common brigands, or partisans of the *federalista* or *centralista* factions fighting in northern Mexico. The *desperadoes* of bandit chieftains Agatón Quinoñes, Manuel Leal, and Calixto Bravo were the most notorious of these gangs. Captain Ignacio García, Mexican garrison commander at Laredo, offered them military protection in exchange for a portion of their loot. According to some Texas newspapers, higher-ranking Mexican frontier commanders issued roving commissions to the leaders of these robbers, who styled themselves as "customs guards" to project an air of legitimacy.[22]

Two Anglo traders rode into San Antonio in early March 1841, and reported their pack train had been robbed by Quinoñes and thirty raiders near Laredo. Local merchants dispatched a representative to Austin to implore the government to raise a ranger company. President Lamar instructed the chief justice of Béxar County to notify Hays, who was in the field, of his orders to take command of the military response. Captain Pérez, "a daring Indian fighter and reliable citizen," and his company of twelve *bexareño* spies agreed to place themselves under Hays's leadership.[23]

Hays's thirteen rangers and Pérez's *tejanos* left San Antonio on March 15. They rode toward Laredo until they confronted Captain García's dismounted cavalry company on April 7, ten miles east of town. The fifteen Mexican troopers, supported by twenty-five suspected bandits, charged and opened up on the Texians with their *escopetas*, which did little damage. Hays ordered his men to dismount and return fire. Their Kentucky long rifles had a maximum range of two hundred yards, and an effective range of one hundred yards. The first volley killed one Mexican and wounded another. The enemy then withdrew a short distance and attempted to surround the Texians.[24]

Remounting, Hays and his rangers jumped their horses over a deep ravine on their left and rode to a copse of *chapotes* (black persimmons) two hundred yards from the enemy. The captain ordered his two companies to alight, left the horses in the care of five men, and led his remaining twenty toward the Mexicans. The rangers advanced through the brush to within sixty yards of García's position on a rise before they delivered a devastating fire. They killed two Mexicans and wounded several others. Returning to their saddles, loading as they moved forward, the Rangers pursued the demoralized enemy force for several hundred yards. The Mexicans almost regrouped, then wavered, and finally broke under another dismounted Texian charge. Hays's men secured all but three of García's horses, which the captain and two of his men used to flee. In total, three Mexicans were killed and three severely wounded. Several more were wounded early in the action and managed to escape before the end; twenty-five were taken prisoner, along with their arms and ammunition; and twenty-eight horses, complete with saddles and bridles, were captured.[25]

García returned to Laredo with tales of horrific slaughter at the hands of the Texians. The *alcalde* and several deputies rode to Hays's camp under a flag of truce. The terrified town officials begged Hays to spare Laredo, and the captain assured them all he wished was the apprehension of Agatón Quinoñes and Manuel Leal. He also wanted traders traveling to and from San Antonio to be accorded safe passage. The *alcalde* promised Hays his requirements would be met. The captain took his men back to San Antonio, leaving some prisoners with the *alcalde* and taking others with him. The two spy companies arrived in Béxar on or about April 14.[26]

Despite his victory, Hays still faced dangerous enemies. He received word in early May of Calixto Bravo heading a large Mexican force at the point where the Presidio del Río Grande road crossed the Nueces River, some sixty miles from San Antonio. Bravo had reportedly merged his band with that of Quinoñes, as well as several others. These *bandidos*, and their Texian "cowboy" counterparts, were interrupting the border trade and stealing any valuable commodity they could attain. Since the source of the information was identified as a spy working for the Mexicans, Hays suspected a trap designed to wipe out his command. Nevertheless, he still decided to seek out the enemy force. The spy picked up on a rumor spread by a *mexicano* friendly to the captain that Hays was gathering one hundred men to launch an attack. On May 9, the spy rode hard to inform his leaders that Hays was coming. He was followed by the ranger captain and forty men.[27] The Texians encountered Bravo's three hundred regular soldiers and *bandidos* and, despite his inferior numbers and exhausted horses, Hays ordered his men to charge as if they were a larger force. The ruse was successful and the Mexicans fled. Hays and his rangers pursued the Mexicans all the way to the Río Grande. The captain returned to San Antonio on May 10, and, their enlistment completed, disbanded his company.[28]

Hays was not inactive for long. On February 4, 1841, the Congress had passed "An Act to encourage frontier protection," which authorized the citizens of each of twenty counties, including Béxar, to raise companies of twenty to fifty-six minutemen and hold themselves in readiness for future Indian depredations. The chief justices of the counties were directed to approve and forward muster rolls and expense vouchers to the secretary of war. On the fifth, $75,000 was appropriated for the maintenance of the frontier service. Under this law, Hays raised a new company on June 1, although he was the only member until he recruited five men on the twelfth, and another nine on June 23.[29]

During the same month, President and Mrs. Lamar visited San Antonio in order to organize an expedition to Santa Fé. A grand ball was thrown in their honor at the home of Mrs. Maria Josefa Yturri Castillo. Colonel Juan Seguín, the recently elected mayor of San Antonio, and his wife were also in attendance. Mrs. Maverick, a guest at the party, noticed some of the rangers were present. She later wrote in her memoirs that John Howard, Hays, and Michael H. Chevallie "had but one coat between them, and they agreed to use the coat and dance in turn." The two men not on the dance floor would wait at the door to the long reception room, watching the one who was enjoying the dancing. They were also quick to remind him when it was time to give up the coat. Mrs. Maverick continued, "Great fun it was watching them and listening to their wit and mischief as they made faces and shook their fists at the dancing one."[30]

All was not parties and frivolity, though, as Hays readied his company of Béxar County minutemen to take the field. Losing one man who quit after only ten days' service, Hays led his remaining thirteen out on June 27 in pursuit of Indian cattle thieves who recently struck the settlements around San Antonio. The company was joined on the trail by Captain Salvador Flores and twenty *tejanos*. The Indians' tracks led to Cañon de Uvalde (presently the Frio Canyon in Real and Uvalde Counties) approximately fifty miles west of Béxar at the headwaters of the Río Frio. Hays discovered the presence of a large Comanche camp near the canyon. The twenty-four men under his command were too few to successfully attack the encampment so Hays concealed the company and took a *mexicano* with him to reconnoiter. The captain and his companion approached to within two miles of the mouth of the canyon. They spied a party of approximately ten Comanches leaving the vicinity of the camp and apparently headed for San Antonio. Hays assembled his company and immediately attacked the potential raiders.[31]

The rangers charged and the Indians fell back into a dogwood thicket, fighting at every backward step. The brush was too dense to continue the advance so Hays took two men with him into the thicket, while the rest of the company surrounded it. The three rangers were soon joined by a fourth and they resumed the fighting amid the grove. The Comanches were encircled by horsemen ready to kill them if they tried to escape, and confronted by well-armed attackers in their midst. They only possessed one firearm, and were unable to use their bows and arrows because of the dense thicket. Instead, they could only fight and die well.[32]

In his July 1 after-action report for Uvalde Canyon, Hays listed eight of the ten Comanches were killed, and the other two were taken prisoner. The Texians also captured all of the Indians' horses and equipment. Recounting the battle three years later, he claimed the actual tally had been ten of twelve Indians were killed.[33]

Hays wanted to move against the main camp, but decided the distance was too great for his worn-out horses. He was also concerned about the disparity in numbers between his force and the Indians. He reluctantly led his men back to San Antonio, arriving on July 1, where his only casualty, who had received a minor wound, was treated. Hays then began recruiting in order to return to Uvalde Canyon and finish the task. By the middle of the month, he had succeeded in enrolling an additional twenty-seven rangers, including "some ten or fifteen from Gonzales." He secured the services of Flacco, son of old Chief Flacco, and twenty-five Lipan Apaches and Tonkawas to act as scouts. Flacco the younger, a seasoned veteran of ranger expeditions, would comment on Hays: "Me and Blue Wing not afraid to go to hell together. Captain Jack great brave, not afraid to go to hell by himself." The cadre of the expanded company included all of the men who had fought at Cañon de Uvalde some two weeks earlier.[34]

Lipan Warrior. Lithograph by Sarony & Co., New York City. *Courtesy Prints and Photographs Division, Library of Congress, Washington, D.C.*

Hays led the expedition out of San Antonio on July 12. He was accompanied by forty-three rangers, the Lipans and Tonkawas, and eight *tejanos*. Acting on intelligence that the enemy was still in the area, the Texians returned to the site of Hays's earlier fight with the Comanches on the Frio River, "where [the captain] had been informed they were still encamped in a considerable body." Instead, the rangers found that the Indians, alarmed by the fate of their fellow tribesmen, had murdered some prisoners in their camp and then bolted. Hays and his men relentlessly pursued the fleeing Comanches through the mountains surrounding the headwaters of the western fork of the Río Frio and the Llano River. The hunt, exhausting for both man and horse, took them into contemporary Real and Edwards Counties, approximately twenty miles west of present-day Kerrville. Hays's Lipan and Tonkawa scouts grew concerned as the sign left by the Comanches indicated a growing number of tribesmen. On July 24, fearing they would be overwhelmed, the Indian auxiliaries diverted to an alternate trail some eight miles lower in elevation. The next day, the expedition was discovered by a Comanche hunting party who sped away to raise the alarm. Hays picked the two dozen rangers mounted on the best horses and immediately gave chase. They engaged nearly fifty warriors who were covering the withdrawal of the noncombatants about a mile from the Comanche camp. The captain recounted, "A running fight ensued between these and a few of our best horses; which lasted some two hours, over six miles of rugged Country." Professor Webb later labeled this engagement "the Battle of the Llano."[35]

An account found in Mirabeau Lamar's papers described the action:

> In the fight, the Indians would retreat, halt, form a line, and prepare for battle. On one occasion, Capt. Hays charged alone within a short distance of the enemy intending to discharge his piece, and retreat; but his horse, seizing the bit in his teeth, dashed off and ran entirely thro [*sic*] the Indian ranks; Flacco, perceiving this, followed his leader in rapid pursuit and broke thro [*sic*] the Indian ranks & came off safely with his Captain — Their escape was a miracle. After the fight, Flacco remarked that he would never be left behind by anyone; but that his Capt. was "*Bravo too much*."[36]

Hays reported the enemy numbers to be two hundred men, women, and children with a herd of six hundred horses. The warriors fell back slowly as the main party made its escape. By the end of the year, the entire Penatuka band had roamed to the northwest and fashioned *rancherías* on the upper Colorado, Brazos, and Red Rivers. Meanwhile, the lengthy fight left the rangers completely spent. Hays reckoned eight to ten Comanches were killed or wounded. The Texians suffered two wounded and one killed. Beginning the return trip to San Antonio, the Lipans left the expedition on August 2, while the remainder reached home two days later. The rangers mustered out on August 31.[37]

At the same time, Hays was elected surveyor of Béxar County. He had never been active in politics, but he was still prepared to give his opinion on current affairs. Due to the pressing demands on his time as a ranger captain, he employed deputy surveyors and, indeed, only personally located five land titles in the remainder of that year.[38]

Hays took the field on September 1 with a company of nineteen men; all of whom had been with him since the Cañon de Uvalde action. They returned to San Antonio on October 1, at which time the company was disbanded. The rangers Hays had commanded in 1841 proved most efficient and had "almost completely broken-up the old haunts of the Comanches in the vicinity of Bexar." Apparently, though, more work was needed. On October 2, President Lamar authorized the captain to raise a new force of one hundred men under the terms and conditions of May 27, 1841. Hays was ordered to have "the entire Western country cleared of the enemy" until Congress could devise a better means of protecting the borderlands. No verifiable evidence has been found to suggest he resumed ranging operations in the waning days of 1841. Instead, for the remainder of the year, Hays attended to his county surveying duties while working to collect the wages owed his men.[39]

The documented exploits of "Devil Jack" Hays were guaranteed to give rise to a larger-than-life legend. In the first of several examples of this trend, he purportedly made his fabled stand atop Enchanted Rock "in the year 1841, or '42." No after-action report or contemporary newspaper article exists to give any details of the engagement. The first mention of Enchanted Rock was published in 1847 in *The Scouting Expeditions of McCulloch's Texas*

Rangers by Samuel Chester Reid, Jr. Reid had learned of Hays's feats while collecting material for his book around ranger campfires during the later war with Mexico. John Caperton, John Wesley Wilbarger, James DeShields, A. J. Sowell, and Ben C. Stuart also wrote of the fight in their own works which featured new details, as well as some borrowed from Reid's description. Professor Webb chose not to mention the fight in his seminal 1935 book, *The Texas Rangers*. In recounting his past exploits, Hays talked of the fight and, given his characteristic modesty, one has to consider the incident at least possible. Stephen L. Moore presents a persuasive argument that places the Enchanted Rock battle between September 1841 and the beginning of 1842, if indeed it occurred.[40]

Sam Houston returned to the presidency on December 13, 1841. His approach to governance contrasted sharply with that of his predecessor. Lamar's Indian wars had cost Texas approximately $2.5 million. Overall, government expenditures totaling $4.85 million had exceeded revenue of $1.08 million. The price of land had fallen and trade had virtually ceased as the country suffered the recession that followed the Panic of 1837. Since the republic was bankrupt, Houston moved to suspend payment of the public debt, which stood at seven million dollars, and replace the depreciated paper currency with one backed by gold and silver.[41] He characterized Lamar's frontier policies as costly, inefficient failures. He further believed the threat from Mexico to have ended, and that the Indian menace could be mitigated. To that end, Houston eliminated the minutemen and the regular army, and requested congressional approval to raise small ranging companies under the auspices of the War Department. The president believed these economized, semi-professional formations would deter brigandage on the border and protect the chain of trading posts he sought to construct. On January 29, 1842, the Sixth Congress authorized him to "employ one company of mounted men, to act as rangers, on the southern frontier, on such terms as he may deem most beneficial to the public interest." The one man Houston had in mind to lead the new company was Jack Hays.[42]

All seemed quiet during the winter, but indications of invasion began to surface in late January and early February. Nine-tenths of San Antonio's two thousand inhabitants were *mexicanos*, and some of them secretly left town with Antonio Pérez to enlist with the enemy forces gathering south of the border. Amid rumors of an attack, the leading men of San Antonio unanimously named Hays chief of the town's protective efforts, and authorized him to declare martial law. Similarly, Congress appropriated twenty thousand dollars and placed the funds at the president's discretion for the purpose of frontier defense.[43]

In March 1842, the Mexican Supreme Government dispatched *General de brigade* Ráfael Vásquez and his Reserve Brigade to raid Texas. Composed of four hundred regular cavalry troopers, two hundred *defensores* (militia), seventy infantrymen, and thirty Caddo Indians, the purpose of the incursion was to retaliate for Texas's disastrous Santa Fé Expedition, probe the republic's defenses, disrupt any further campaigns, and demonstrate Mexico's military supremacy. Volunteers from Lavaca, Cuero, and Seguín answered Hays's call to arms and made their way to Béxar. The Mexicans easily occupied San Antonio on March 5, when Hays and his one hundred men elected to fall back to the Guadalupe. The rangers made camp on the bank of Cíbolo Creek the evening of March 6. After sending a courier to Austin, Hays relocated to the Guadalupe opposite Seguín the following night. The Mexicans held the town for two days, then departed for home with their plunder. Hays's men, accompanied by Juan Seguín and numerous *tejanos*, pursued the raiding party beyond the Nueces, but they lacked sufficient strength to attack the invaders. The Texians withdrew to the Nueces, and scouts soon reported Vásquez and his *soldados* had crossed the Río Grande back into Mexico.[44]

Hays and his men returned to San Antonio and found that Vice President Edward Burleson had assumed command of the ill-equipped and inadequately armed volunteers drifting into town. Hays promptly placed himself and his company under the general's orders. Acting aggressively to preempt critics, while still realizing Texas could not prosecute an all-out offensive war, President Houston authorized spies and scouts to probe the border country and gather intelligence on the enemy's intentions. With the opportunity for active operations dwindling, Burleson disbanded his motley force on April 2.[45]

During the spring, the Comanches were active to the west of San Antonio. Hays and his company, augmented by new recruits and by fifty-two Lipans under the younger Flacco, went into camp near the old Mission Concepción on the San Antonio River. The rangers were only there a few days when they were informed that Yellow Wolf and a band of eighty Comanches had raided near town the previous day. They carried off horses, murdered several Mexicans and a black sheepherder, and kidnapped an Irish shepherd.[46]

Hays and sixteen rangers set out after the marauders and overtook them on the Guadalupe at what was known as the Pinta Trail Crossing. The location of the subsequent engagement is in present Kendall County, northeast of Bandera, and would be mistakenly remembered as the "Battle of Bandera Pass." In their own works, Stephen Moore, Clifford R. Caldwell, and Mike Cox have discussed the actual date and location in which the skirmish took place. In the most reliable eyewitness account, Jim Nichols wrote the engagement occurred two years after Plum Creek, while his editor gives the year as 1841. Three additional Texians—Benjamin Franklin Highsmith, Thomas Galbreath, and Creed Taylor—recounted their memories of serving with Hays to A. J. Sowell, including this fight. Highsmith and Taylor remembered the skirmish as taking place in 1841, and Galbreath in 1843. Neither Highsmith nor Galbreath appear in muster rolls for 1841 or 1843 to 1845, so there is a reasonable probability they were in Hays's company in 1842. Taylor did serve in Hays's company during 1842. Another narrative written by Taylor, "Jack Hays Fight on the Guadalupe," was more precise in details, although he did place the battle in the autumn of 1840.[47]

The assigning of the battle to the actual landmark of Bandera Pass rests solely on the sketches presented by Sowell. No post-action report, newspaper article, or other primary source material has been found to substantiate his assertion. In their remembrances, Nichols and Taylor separately pointed to a site in Kendall County, along or near the Guadalupe, where the present town of Waring is located. Equally troublesome in Sowell's writings is the fact he seems to have blended that story with the later engagement at Walker's Creek. He wrote that Peter "Fore" (properly spelled Fohr) was killed and Sam Walker was wounded by a lance thrust. As will be seen, both casualties were confirmed to have occurred at Walker's Creek two years later.

However, the uncertainty that would muddle the story of the fight was not of any concern to Hays's men that day. Once the rangers approached the river, they opened fire on the Comanches as the Indians retreated up the opposite bank. Several Indians were killed in the volley, and numerous others were wounded. The raiders continued to run over the adjacent hill and disappeared from view. Hays and his men pursued to the top of the rise and halted. Below them the Comanches had formed a line of battle. Appreciating that his company had ridden into a trap, the captain coolly instructed his men, "Steady there, boys! Dismount and tie those horses; we can whip them; no doubt about that." Hays continued to exhort the rangers as they readied themselves for combat, "Come on boys, and when you shoot, shoot to hit."[48]

The Texians delivered another volley into the Indian ranks that forced them to scatter. The rangers then fell back down the hill to reload. Before they could finish, the top of the hill was swarming with Indians. The Comanches gave a war whoop and raced down at the rangers. Observing the Texians were standing fast, the Indians only rode halfway, discharged their *escopetas* and arrows, and wheeled about for the summit. Another volley of Texian bullets followed them. After reloading, the rangers dashed up the slope and over the crest of the hill. They continued halfway down the other side to within sixty yards of the enemy's line. After firing, they fell back as they had before. The Comanches responded again by charging, firing, and withdrawing. Hays then directed half of the company to charge and draw the enemy out. When the Indians emptied their firearms, the rangers held in reserve rushed forward and killed several Comanches; Yellow Wolf was severely wounded and carried off by his fellow tribesmen. Once their chief had been shot from his horse, the Indians quit the field. A prisoner, who later escaped from the Comanches, reported the raiders had suffered twenty-three killed and thirty wounded, thirteen of which would prove mortal.[49]

Toward the end of June, Hays was left as the only man commanding an established military force in the South Texas borderlands. Congress was aware of the republic's vulnerability and, through a joint resolution on July 23, authorized President Houston to raise two companies to alleviate the threat. Two thousand dollars was appropriated for their maintenance. Houston appointed Hays to the rank of major that same month, and made him the military chief of the southwestern line. In addition to his own company already in service, Hays was ordered to supervise Captain José Antonio Menchaca's outfit, which was intended to range between the San Antonio River and the Río Grande.[50]

Morgan Calvin Hamilton, the acting Secretary of War and Marine, would later remark in his annual report about the obstacles confronting the ranging service:

> Few men could be found at once able to mount and equip themselves and willing to enter a service which promised little else than fatigue and danger. Those who were willing to enlist were for the most part utterly destitute of means to fit themselves for the field; the government was equally so—it could neither furnish the means to equip and mount a force, nor sustain them for any length of time when in the field.[51]

Since Captain Menchaca could not enlist enough men, Hays was instructed by Secretary Hamilton to increase his company to 150 rangers to defend the entire Río Grande frontier. Unfortunately, the major also had difficulty acquiring men to fill his ranks. By September 7, he had nearly fifty recruits, or one-third of his authorized strength.[52]

In the early days of September 1842, rumors were rife concerning a second foray from Mexico. Hays was instructed by the president to preserve the peace on the Río Grande and to keep the border open to trade. In addition to economic benefits, the soldier turned chief executive believed such a policy would offer the best chance for the gathering of intelligence on enemy troop movements. On September 10, Hays learned that *General de brigade* Adrián Woll and the Second Division of the Mexican Army Corps of the North was marching on San Antonio. The leading citizens of the town elected Hays colonel, and organized themselves into a one hundred-man company of *bexareños* under Salvador Flores, and another of seventy-five Texians under Chauncey Johnson. Five prominent residents dispatched a messenger to Gonzales relating the latest reports, and declared "if fifty or a hundred of the brave men of Gonzales can put foot in stirrup immediately it will be for the best."[53]

Accompanied by five volunteers that night, Hays scouted the Laredo road for the enemy *soldados*, but the Mexicans had circled through the hills in a dense fog to approach San Antonio from the north. For once, Hays had been outmaneuvered, and he returned to town the following morning to find it occupied. For an entire day, he observed the Mexican force, which consisted of four companies of infantry, or approximately four hundred men; four cavalry squadrons of four companies each, or two hundred soldiers; two 4-pound cannons, and approximately thirty gunners; five presidial companies of 221 militiamen; two companies of *defensores*, or 187 irregulars; and forty Cherokee Indian auxiliaries under Vicente Córdova (a leader of the 1838 Indian rebellion that bore his name). One of the irregular companies, the *Defensore de Bejar*, was led by Juan Seguín, who had been forced by slanderous rumors and threats to his personal safety earlier in the year to decamp to Mexico.[54]

Hays sent couriers to raise the alarm that San Antonio had fallen and fifty-two citizens had been captured. On September 13, he and fourteen rangers united with Mathew Caldwell's forces assembling at Seguín. Hays and ten volunteers returned to the vicinity of San Antonio and chose a position on Salado Creek, eight miles east of town, from which to reconnoiter enemy movements. Henry McCulloch brought thirteen men and badly needed provisions to the camp. The two groups combined, with Hays remaining as commander and McCulloch being named first lieutenant. Four days later, 225 Texians, including Hays's rangers, rendezvoused on the Cíbolo. Caldwell was elected commander with the rank of major, Canah C. Colley was named as adjutant, Doctor Caleb S. Brown as surgeon, and Reverend Zachariah (or Zenos) Nehemiah Morrell as chaplain. Caldwell organized his force into four line companies, with enough of the best mounted men detached to Hays to bring his total number to forty.[55]

That evening, the Texians were situated on Salado Creek, two miles closer to San Antonio than the previous camp. Wanting to face the Mexicans in a decisive battle, but knowing his numbers were too few, Caldwell planned to lure Woll into attacking the Texians' prepared defenses. To that end, the major took particular care in arranging his battlefield. The Salado, some forty feet wide and eight to twelve deep, flowed more or less southeast, but the defenders were placed on the north side of the creek bed at a portion that ran from west to east before again flowing south. The Texians were able to take cover behind the bank, and shelter their horses amidst forty yards of elm and pecan trees on the creek bottom. The right flank was secured by a deep ravine that opened into the Salado for some 150 yards. The ground in front of the position was open prairie interspaced with sparse clumps of mesquite and live oak.[56]

At ten o'clock the next morning, Caldwell detailed Hays to lead the decoy mission with thirty-eight men mounted on the freshest horses. They rode to the outskirts of San Antonio and enticed the Mexicans to come out and fight. Led by former ranger turned renegade Antonio Pérez, the invaders did so in numbers approximated at 150 cavalrymen. Hays and his rangers raced back toward Caldwell's position with the Mexicans close behind. The Texians reached the Salado barely escaping disaster. Throughout the remainder of the morning, the Mexican army arrived on the field, including four hundred infantrymen, 160 cavalry troopers, Vicente Córdova's forty Cherokees, one hundred *tejano* volunteers from San Antonio, and two cannons. Hays and his spy company were assigned to hold the left flank, while James Nichols's detachment secured the ravine on the right. The Texian battle line was spread thin to cover the space in the center. The thick stand of pecan trees in front of Hays's location would thwart any cavalry charge. Rather than offering a prayer, Baptist preacher Morrell exhorted his countrymen to shoot low and kill "every man that has an officer's hat or sword."[57]

As the day progressed, Caldwell repeatedly sent squads of fifteen to twenty skirmishers to harass the enemy before withdrawing to the safety of the creek. By late in the afternoon, General Woll shifted into the attack with his two artillery pieces belching canister and grapeshot, but the cannonade spent itself in the trees over the Texians' heads. Woll then advanced his right and left wings leaving the center open for the guns. The fortified Texians repulsed the assault in about fifteen minutes, shooting Mexicans down in the open within thirty paces of the creek bed. One column of *soldados* stormed the Texian left in an attempt to enfilade the line. Hays countered this move by deploying ten men armed with double-barreled shotguns to cover the exposed flank. The detachment waited until the attack was thirty feet away, then delivered a smashing blast that felled every Mexican in front of the position.[58]

Ignoring any attempt to send his cavalry on wide flanking maneuvers to attack the Texian rear, Woll continued to order his forces forward in sporadic frontal assaults that were steadily foiled. During the long intervals between each advance, the Mexicans would collect their dead and wounded. Late in the afternoon, Vicente Córdova led his Cherokees and some Mexicans into the ravine on the right flank. Men from Ewen Cameron's company met them and killed fourteen in hand-to-hand combat. Córdova himself was shot through the heart by a rifleman standing ninety yards away. As the sun set, the firing ceased and Woll withdrew from the field. Taking many of his casualties with him back to San Antonio, he abandoned sixty of his *soldados*; many of those not already dead expired throughout the night. The Texians had one man killed and a dozen lightly wounded.[59]

The day after the battle, heavy rains fell, and Caldwell held off any subsequent operations against Woll's force. Hays, the McCulloch brothers, and other rangers scouted the Mexican lines in San Antonio at various times. From them, Caldwell realized on the morning of the twentieth that Woll was withdrawing to the Río Grande.[60]

Gathering reinforcements as they advanced, Caldwell's command moved off in pursuit; Hays's horsemen were in the lead. The Mexican retreat was slowed by the train of carts and wagons bearing approximately two hundred wounded *soldados* and assorted loot. On September 22, the fifty rangers caught up with the Mexican rear at Arroyo Hondo where they attacked a deployed cannon. The Texians killed the gun's crew, but were driven back by one hundred Mexican infantrymen, fifty cavalry troopers, and a second artillery piece. Woll reported Agatón Quinoñes commanded the Mexican rearguard and claimed the Texian van of "100 haughty men" was bloodily repulsed. Further pursuit became impossible as night fell and some of the Texian commanders began to quarrel amongst themselves.[61]

Their passions roused to a fever pitch, Texians everywhere demanded a response to this most recent invasion. Unable to deny the citizenry their vengeance, President Houston reluctantly sanctioned a retaliatory mission into Mexico. He knew full well the republic could not field the required force of well-equipped and disciplined troops, but he had to placate the outraged electorate. Therefore, on October 3, the cagy president assigned Brigadier-General Alexander Somervell to the task. Already the commander of the First Brigade of the Texas militia, Somervell was a weak, indecisive man unsuited to lead the rowdy volunteers assembling in San Antonio. Houston shifted the operational decisions for the expedition squarely onto Somervell's shoulders, thus freeing himself from any responsibility.[62]

One favor the President did extend to Somervell was to recommend Hays and his rangers:

> You may rely upon the gallant Hays and his companions; and I desire that you should obtain his services and co-operation, and assure him and all the brave and subordinate men in the field, that the hopes of the country and the confidence of the Executive point to them as objects of constant solicitude. Insubordination and a disregard of command, will bring ruin and disgrace upon our arms.[63]

As military commander of the southwestern frontier, Major Hays possessed an independent status with extensive powers, including the authority to declare martial law in Béxar County. Neither Houston nor Somervell made any attempt to define his place in the expedition's chain of command. Never carried on the Southwestern Army of Operations's muster rolls, Hays cooperated with its commander without actually being under his orders. By the time Somervell reached San Antonio on November 4, the assembled army numbered some twelve hundred mounted volunteers and militiamen. Somervell made little effort to impose any sense of discipline in his unruly troops; instead he dithered over administrative and logistical details that could have been accomplished quickly by a more competent commander.[64]

When the Somervell Expedition began in earnest on November 25, the Southwestern Army was composed of 750 men. Many of the more reliable had returned home, while those remaining were often hard-drinking troublemakers. Hays's eighteen (increased later to sixty) rangers and a number of Lipan Apache scouts under young Flacco accompanied the command. Henry McCulloch served as the company's first lieutenant, Ephraim Walton McLean as second lieutenant, and James Wilson "Smokey" Henderson as first sergeant. Even the rangers added to the contentious atmosphere as they quarreled with Samuel Bogart's sixty Washington County spies over whose company was to constitute the vanguard. The expedition marched cross-country through heavy, unseasonably cold rains. After a setback in the

"Atascosa Bogs," the rivalry between Hays's rangers and Bogart's spies reached a critical moment. While Hays was away on a scout, Bogart ordered the rangers to bivouac with his own company. Some of Hays's men refused in an insulting manner. Once Hays returned, Bogart discussed the matter with him in the presence of Somervell and a number of rangers. A few of the more vocal began haranguing Bogart and he left the meeting. Bogart later preferred charges against the two most insubordinate rangers, and Somervell promised to convene a court-martial when circumstances allowed. The general never dealt with this breach of discipline, and the already miniscule amount of respect he enjoyed dwindled still further.[65]

Instead, on November 30, Somervell declared that Hays's rangers would be the expedition's spy company, while Bogart's men would become a line company with the lead position in the column, normally a place of honor. When the march resumed the next morning, Bogart's men refused to follow the rangers. Instead they cantered beside them step for step for several miles before an enraged Somervell rode up and put an end to the farce. He ordered Bogart's company to take the second place in the column, and most of the Washington County men declared they were leaving for home. After some deliberation, and not wanting to be blamed for jeopardizing the success of the expedition, Bogart's men agreed to stay.[66]

With the rangers riding a day ahead, the column reached Laredo in the early morning of December 8, only to find the Mexican garrison had fled. Sometime around noon, various-sized groups of disgruntled soldiers went into town without orders, and proceeded to ransack homes and businesses. Somervell responded by moving the camp to a site three miles away. The following morning, two hundred men swept into Laredo and continued their plundering. In the early afternoon, Somervell dispatched his officers to round up the looters and return them to camp. He further ordered all stolen items be returned to their rightful owners. Some of the men obeyed, but not all.[67]

Somervell led his troops down the east bank of the Río Grande before abruptly turning east into the chaparral. The expedition commander was at a loss. He knew he led an army comprised of an insubordinate and fractious rabble, exhausted horses, and dwindling provisions. He had no idea of the location and numbers of the enemy possibly gathering in order to destroy the

Texian invaders. He also had received communications from the president obliquely encouraging the general to abandon the entire enterprise.[68]

On the morning of December 10, he consulted his company commanders on the next course of action. Eleven of the fourteen captains favored marching across the river and bringing the Mexican army to battle. Not hearing the answer he desired, Somervell called for a vote of all ranks. Any who wanted to end the expedition and return home were free to go. One hundred elected to fall out and were joined by another eighty-seven the next day. Somervell's reduced command rode on toward Guerrero with Hays's rangers reconnoitering the line of march. On December 14, they reached the Río Grande, and Hays and Bogart begun crossing their respective companies, sharing two dugout canoes found nearby. As the troops crossed twelve at a time, the remaining men waited by the river and were subjected to rain and sleet. The freezing soldiers insisted they be allowed to return to Guerrero six miles distant and loot the town. Remembering the Laredo fiasco, Somervell refused and ordered the troops already in Mexico to return to Texas on the seventeenth.[69]

On December 19, having at last decided the expedition was unlikely to end in success, Somervell ordered the troops to commence countermarching for home. The rank and file were livid the army had made the difficult journey to Mexico and was now turning back without the promised fight or plunder. Somervell was obeyed by only a small portion of his army; instead five captains and more than three hundred troops mutinied and resolved to press on. Those who refused to return to San Antonio elected William S. Fisher their colonel and continued the march. Somervell led his smaller force north. Hays obeyed the general's order, but when he was one hundred miles from the border he discovered his prized horse had gotten loose. The captain returned to the Río Grande and retrieved his steed from a *ranchero* without being detected. He reached San Antonio approximately one week after Somervell's January 6 arrival. Flacco also headed for home, but he was brutally slain on the Medina by an unknown party, possibly some of Somervell's returning men.[70]

On January 16, 1843, Congress empowered Houston to declare martial law between the Río Frio and Nueces River to the Río Grande for the duration of hostilities. The same day, the lawmakers passed "An Act to Authorize the President to Accept the Services of One Company of Mounted Men, to Act as Spies on the Southwestern Frontier" and appropriated five hundred dollars for its maintenance. Due to "his indomitable energy and generous perseverance, skill and daring," Hays was appointed to lead the company on the twentieth. For the remainder of the year, Hays was to be the only formal military commander, and his company the only armed force sanctioned by Texas law.[71]

Hays began recruiting in February, but the recent turmoil in South Texas made the task difficult. At the end of the first nine days, he had only managed to enlist two privates. By March 1, when the company was mustered in, he had fifteen men on the rolls.[72]

In late April, Hays led fifteen rangers out of San Antonio to hunt down and destroy Agatón Quinoñes's band of one hundred to three hundred marauders. The *bandidos* had been attacking traders on the Laredo and San Antonio road, as well as near Corpus Christi. The rangers rode to the Río Grande opposite Matamoros where they caught two Frenchmen illegally entering Texas. Hays learned from the prisoners that four hundred Mexican *soldados* were at Matamoros. In the meantime, Quinoñes's spies in San Antonio reported to him that Hays was on the move. The bandit chieftain, accompanied by seventy of his followers, rode to intercept the rangers. They found Hays and his men camped on the Nueces with a *caballada* of horses and mules confiscated from Mexicans on the border. The bandits hesitated to attack and instead hid in the river bottoms. After nightfall, they stampeded the Texians' captured stock, but the wily Hays had hidden his men's horses in another location. Saddling up, the rangers were on the trail to San Antonio the following morning.[73]

President Houston was committed to crushing the banditry in the disputed *brasada*, the South Texas brush country of live oak thickets and chaparral, and he gave Hays special legal powers to perform that mission. First, the president reaffirmed martial law and ordered all armed groups in the region to disperse, save those commanded by Major Hays. Second, he authorized Hays "to execute without delay all whom he can arrest, and who are guilty of these infamous offences [*sic*]." In early July, the major moved his camp west to Leon Creek to escape the prying eyes of Mexican agents. The same month,

Hays captured three Mexicans suspected of spying for Quinoñes. The leader confessed under interrogation to numerous thefts and murders, and Hays ordered the prisoners to be executed by firing squad.[74]

Hays's recruiting efforts were more successful in the summer. Several of the new men were frontier veterans, including Ben McCulloch. The captain was able to field twenty-five privates by August and September. In the latter month, Hays was in town when he was informed that a band of spies under Manuel Perez, a lieutenant of Quinoñes, was on the Medina River. Perez supposedly had one hundred men and planned to conduct raids in the Béxar area. Hays and fifteen rangers left San Antonio on September 17 and scouted the bandit camp located on a small stream west of the river. They came under fire from Perez's men who had spotted them. The two sides exchanged shots and the *bandidos* moved downstream. Brave but not foolhardy, the outnumbered Hays cautiously trailed them, waging a running fight as Perez's band rode onto an open prairie. The outlaws fired the grass and the resulting smoke forced the Texians to stop. Anticipating the Mexicans would attack under cover of the blaze, Hays ordered his men into a defensive position. Once the smoke cleared, the rangers discovered Perez and his followers had fled. Hays and his company returned home in late September. For the next several months, they were almost constantly patrolling the *brasada*. On September 26, Houston authorized the acting treasurer to advance $520 for the use of Hays's command.[75]

On their last scout taken that year, the rangers surprised four or five Mexicans on the Río Frio, wounding one through the shoulder and capturing another. The prisoner was sent to Béxar, and the company returned on November 1. While in the field, Hays had learned from traders and Mexican prisoners that Agatón Quinoñes had been killed and the raiding companies sanctioned by the Mexican government had been disbanded. Rather than ushering in a new era of peace, the ranger imagined the lawless men who had made up those bands, and who lacked any means to make an honest living, would continue their depredations. On November 12, he was forced to furlough the twenty-odd men remaining in the company as he was without the funds to provide for their expenses. Even after the government appropriations were exhausted, he had kept them in the field by using four hundred dollars of his own money. Recognizing Hays to be a man of honor, patriotic merchants and tradesmen in San Antonio had provided goods and services for the company with the understanding they would have to wait for recompense at a later date.[76]

Hays took advantage of the interlude to call on the Calvert family in Seguin over the holidays. Chief among his reasons for the visit was the attractive Susan Sophia Calvert, whom he had met earlier in San Antonio. Her father was Judge Jeremiah Strother Calvert, who had recently moved his family to Texas from Alabama, where Susan had been born on February 2, 1827. His stay with the judge's family began a courtship with the dark-haired and brown-eyed Susan that lasted for several years.[77]

While Hays was away, Manuel Leal interrupted commerce on the Río Grande and even boldly rode into Béxar on several occasions. His raiders stole horses, needlessly killed thirty or forty milch cows, and robbed the only trader to leave the city of five thousand dollars in property. The captain returned to duty when the Congress enacted a law on January 23, 1844, "Authorizing John C. Hays to raise a Company of Mounted Gun-men, to act as Rangers, on the Western and South-Western Frontier." He was empowered to enlist forty privates and directed to range from Béxar County to Refugio County and westward as needed. The rangers were to serve for four months, but the president could prolong their enlistments if necessary. Their monthly wages were set at seventy-five dollars for Hays, fifty-five dollars for Lieutenant Ben McCulloch, and thirty for each private.[78]

On January 31, Congress legitimized Hays's earlier actions when they passed "An Act For the protection of the South-Western Frontier." The measure instructed all persons known to have borne arms against the republic to leave Texas within twenty days. Section one of the legislation further authorized Hays, as commander of the borderlands, to court-martial any who failed to comply with the order. Citizens captured while not under arms, but still suspected of treason, were to be delivered to the civil authorities. Non-citizens suspected of hostile acts were to be subjected to any penalty the court-martial deemed proper. Section two directed Hays and county chief justices to regulate legal trade with Mexico, including the issuing of passports for crossing the Río Grande and the suppression of smuggling.[79]

The January 23 legislation instructed Hays to organize his company by February 1, or as soon as possible thereafter. Unfortunately, he was not able to muster his rangers in on that date, but he had twenty-five privates by February 25. Around the twentieth, before the company was organized, Hays, Colonel William Gordon Cooke, Major George Thomas Howard, and Frank Paschal went on a scout to the country between Gonzales and La Grange. They confronted three or four *bandidos* along Peach Creek and captured a horse, but lost the Mexicans in the creek bottom.[80]

Hays mustered his company into service by March 15, but he still lacked his full complement. He left San Antonio again in mid-March to pursue a gang of white outlaws who had raided ranches in the area and were riding for the Colorado River with almost two thousand head of stolen cattle. The newspaper accounts do not mention if Hays caught up to the rustlers and recovered the stock, but they do reveal that his rangers in 1844 were performing at the very least a quasi-law enforcement role. Returning to San Antonio, Hays continued to recruit and managed to achieve his authorized strength in April and May. During the former month, Hays and a portion of his command captured nine of Leal's *bandidos* who had been lying in wait for traders from Béxar. The Mexicans were tried by court-martial and found guilty of treasonable conduct. Absent license to punish the raiders, Hays turned them over to civil authorities for the next term of district court.[81]

The captain made a quick trip to Washington-on-the-Brazos to confer with President Houston, who had come to hold a high regard for Hays: "The frontier of our country would be defenceless [*sic*] but for his gallantry and vigilance united With fine capacity … If Hays had a battalion of spies, or a regiment, in my opinion, no man on earth could be equally efficient on the frontier, and particularly that of the Rio Grande." John Washington Lockhart, later a prominent physician in Chappell Hill, was in the lobby of the hotel, possibly Nathaniel Norwood's establishment, when he noticed a stranger signing his name in the register book. Lockhart was later surprised to learn the "small, boyish looking youngster, [with] not a particle of beard on his face" was the redoubtable "Captain Jack" who was "considered one of the best Indian trailers on the border." Hays stayed in town for one night and half a day completing his business, then hurried back to camp.[82]

Colt-Paterson Holster Model No. 5. *Courtesy Dickinson Research Center, National Cowboy & Western Heritage Museum, Oklahoma City, Oklahoma.*

The company he led in that year was the finest he had ever commanded. The ranks were filled with experienced, well-mounted veterans who only needed one more tool to truly become a force with which to be reckoned. The battle at Walker's Creek on June 8, 1844, proved to be a moment of singular importance in the Indian wars of Texas, as well as in the history of the Texas Rangers. In their engagement with Yellow Wolf's Comanche raiders on a small stream in the Hill Country north of San Antonio, Hays's rangers utilized the revolutionary new Colt Paterson No. 5 Holster pistol and forever changed the nature of Indian fighting.[83]

Five years previously, 180 Colt .36-caliber revolvers had been purchased for the Texas navy from the Patent Arms Manufacturing Company of Paterson, New Jersey. In a letter to General Waddy Thompson, chairman of the U.S. House of Representatives' Military Affairs Committee, Colonel Charles Downing, delegate from Florida, praised the Texas military for adopting Samuel Colt's invention: "Texas … surrounded by enemies on all sides, with but a few soldiers to call to her defense, has sought to judiciously multiply her means, by placing in the hands of the soldiery the most efficient weapons so as to equalize her army to her enemy—not by men … but by the arms they carry."[84]

After the navy was disbanded in 1843, Hays, quick to see the revolver's advantages in mounted combat, acquired a fair number of them. Prior to Walker's Creek, when Texians were able to bring Comanches to battle, they would dismount to fight. Remaining on horseback, the Indians would use their bows and arrows as effective close-range, rapid-firing weapons. To counter Indian fire superiority, the rangers would discharge their slower-loading muskets in alternating volleys so a portion of the men would always remain loaded. In addition to a rifle, Hays's men carried two Patersons and extra five-shot cylinders. With the pistols in hand, one mounted ranger could deliver ten aimed shots in forty seconds.[85]

On June 1, 1844, Hays rode north out of his camp on the Medina with fifteen men. They scouted the country between the Pedernales and Llano Rivers and found abundant signs of Indians before beginning the return trip home. By June 8, they had reached Walker's Creek, a tributary of the Guadalupe River, approximately fifty miles north of Seguin in present Kendall County. Dismounting their horses, the men unsaddled or loosened the cinches. Hays designated four men to act as pickets while Christopher Black "Kit" Acklin and Alexander Coleman procured honey from a bee hive in a large cypress tree. The pickets soon came in to report ten Indians on the rangers' trail.[86]

After saddling up, the Texians observed the aforementioned Indians leisurely retreating toward a stand of timber. Determining that they were attempting to draw the rangers out, Hays rode slowly toward the woods. Realizing their subterfuge was unsuccessful, other Comanches, some sixty or seventy in number, rushed out of the timber. Hays deployed his outnumbered men in a line and continued to advance. With the rangers following, the Indians withdrew across a shallow ravine and up a rocky slope spotted with scrub oak and underbrush. Once on top of the ridge, they dismounted in a line and taunted the rangers to attack. Hays was too experienced an Indian fighter to do something so foolish. Instead, once he reached the ravine and was temporarily hidden from the Comanches' view, the captain led his men down the gap and around the hill. Galloping up the ridge, the rangers took the Comanches in the flank. As the surprised Indians reacted in confusion, the rangers fired their rifles into the teeming Indians, emptying quite a few saddles.[87]

The running *mêlée* surged down the slope and onto the level ground. The Comanches overcame their initial surprise and counterattacked from two directions in numbers sufficient to overwhelm the Texians. As the Indians bore down on them, Hays ordered his men to drop their rifles and pull out their Patersons. The experienced veterans received the Comanches' charge and delivered a deadly, rolling fire with their five-shooters. The surviving warriors fell back, but the advancing Texans kept up the pressure for two miles. More than once, the Indians would turn to face the rangers, but always the Paterson pistols forced them to once again flee. Finally, Yellow Wolf rallied his twenty remaining men to confront the rangers. By this time, the battle had stretched out over three miles. Hays's men had nearly exhausted their ammunition. Every ranger had been at least grazed in the close-quarters fighting. The captain asked for anyone possessing a loaded rifle and Robert Addison "Ad" Gillespie, despite his wounds, walked his horse forward. Hays then ordered Gillespie to dismount and "shoot that damned chief!" The ranger private did so at a range of approximately thirty paces and Yellow Wolf fell to the ground dead. Once their leader was downed, the remaining Comanches broke and fled from the scene.[88]

The results of the battle were twenty-three Indians slain and another thirty wounded. Hays had lost only one man, German-born Peter Fohr. The exhausted rangers remained on the field nursing their injuries. Within fifteen minutes, Hays had secured a place in history for not only the Texas Rangers, but also himself. With his personal example of adroit daring and cool courage, Hays deployed his men in a manner that made the best use of their skills, the terrain, and his new weaponry. On June 11, four Comanches appeared on the scene likely for the purpose of recovering their dead. Hays promptly ordered an attack and six of his men killed three of them after a one-mile chase. The rangers were back in San Antonio around the fifteenth. They remained in town until sometime after June 27, when they filled out new muster rolls.[89]

In the fall, Hays divided the company into detachments to more effectively cover the vast territory for which he was responsible. He completed a new muster roll on October 29 listing himself, Lieutenant McCulloch, and thirty-five privates, but the ever-present obstacle of funding soon forced him to furlough a number of the men. He discharged two rangers on November 14, five men five days later, two on November 24, eight more on November 29, and another five in the month of December. On the first day of 1845, Hays was in command of nine rangers.[90]

On February 1, 1845, Congress authorized Hays to "organize and command" two ten-man detachments in Robertson and Milam Counties, a fifteen-man squad in Travis County, and fifteen men in Refugio and Goliad Counties. Hays personally led one company of a lieutenant and thirty men in Bexar County, while the others were each directed by a first lieutenant. As the overall commander, Hays received seventy-five dollars per month, while the lieutenants were paid thirty dollars per month and the privates twenty dollars. Sam Houston's policies in his second administration had stabilized the republic's economy through a combination of retrenchment, customs revenues, property tax collection, and public land sales. By the time Anson Jones succeeded Houston as president, Texas was enjoying a small budget surplus, despite the ongoing public debt. Therefore, an appropriation of thirty thousand dollars was provided to suitably maintain the new battalion. Hays and First Lieutenant Robert Gillespie had their company ready for duty by February 12, while the others—Peter Hansborough Bell, Corpus Christi; Thomas Ingles Smith, Robertson County; Alexander Coleman, Travis County; and Richard S. Teal, Milam County—were in service by March. Hays's command was active in patrolling, engaged a large party of Comanches near Agua Dulce, and suppressed banditry before disbanding on September 28.[91]

Even while Hays had led his company, Mexico had not relinquished claims to its former colony, nor had it accepted the decision of Texas to be annexed by the United States. On May 28, Brevet Brigadier-General Zachary Taylor, commanding Fort Jesup, Louisiana, was ordered to prepare his garrison and attached troops for a march to Texas. His instructions were to provide protection "from foreign invasions and Indian incursions" as soon as the Texas Congress ratified the terms of the agreement. When Texas consented to annexation, Taylor was directed on June 15 to move his "Army of Observation" to a tactically advantageous position on or near the Rio Grande. On July 23, the general and his troops began their journey to the Nueces.[92]

As the United States and Mexico moved closer toward open hostilities, Hays was commissioned a major of Texas Mounted Rangers in United States service on September 28, 1845. Taylor acknowledged "The commander of the rangers at San Antonio, Major Hays, has reputation as a partisan," but issued him "strict injunctions … to molest no Mexican establishments on this side of the river." In command of four companies under Captains Robert Gillespie at San Antonio, Peter Bell at Corpus Christi, John T. Price at Victoria, and David C. Cady at Austin, Hays was charged with "procuring intelligence of the movements of the Mexicans and protecting the Frontier against Indian Depredations." While the rangers carried out the general's orders, the three brigades under Taylor organized and conducted camp and field instruction at Corpus Christi. The Texan served two enlistments as chief of the San Antonio Ranging Corps, then mustered out on May 16, 1846.[93]

During this time, Hays was said to have been involved in yet another fight with an uncertain basis in fact. Similar to the battles Hays allegedly fought at Bandera Pass and Enchanted Rock, the engagement at Paint Rock is a mixture of fact, supposition, and myth. Like Enchanted Rock, Paint Rock received no mention in contemporary newspapers, nor have any after-action reports or firsthand accounts surfaced. The first published mention of the battle was written by Isaac Affleck in the *El Paso Times*, possibly in 1910.[94]

Early Texan writers, such as Andrew Sowell, John Henry Brown, and John Wilbarger, were silent concerning the battle. Walter Webb, Robert Utley, and Charles Robinson have been reluctant to give credence to the tale. Mike Cox and Stephen Moore each addressed the doubts concerning the battle's authenticity, while holding out the possibility for the uncovering of conclusive evidence. As the former states, "Absence of evidence is not evidence of absence."[95]

Despite possibly apocryphal accounts, the service Hays and his early rangers had provided Texas was remarkable. When the First Legislature had met on March 14, Senator Edward Burleson had risen before his colleagues of the Texas Senate and recognized the gallant and daring deeds of Hays, Ben McCulloch, and Ad Gillespie. In his speech, he asserted his belief they were "entitled to the gratitude of the people of Texas and the admiration of the world." His resolution was unanimously adopted.[96]

The lengthy process by which Texas was annexed by the United States is outside the scope of this work. Suffice to say, President James Knox Polk signed the Texas Admission Act on December 29, 1845, and Texas became the twenty-eighth state of the Union. Regrettably, Mexico was determined to defend its national honor by force of arms if necessary.[97]

On April 24, in response to a report of Mexicans crossing the Rio Grande in force, Captain Seth Barton Thornton, commanding a squadron of the Second Dragoons, was ordered to reconnoiter above Fort Texas. The following day, Thornton's sixty-three horsemen were trapped in a field near La Rosia by *General de brigade* Anastosio Torrejón and a force of five hundred Mexican cavalrymen. The regulars lost nine men killed, two wounded, and forty-nine captured, including Captain Thornton. On May 11, President Polk requested a declaration of war from Congress, affirming Mexico had "shed American blood upon the American soil." The president's appeal was granted and, on May 13, the United States formally declared war on her southern neighbor. The same congressional act also authorized Polk to accept the services of volunteers for twelve-month terms.[98]

Answering the call to arms, Hays enrolled in Kit Acklin's company on May 19 in San Antonio. The volunteers trekked south to Corpus Christi, then on to General Taylor's depot at Point Isabel. Acklin's company, designated as Company B, was mustered into federal service on June 6. Hays was on the rolls as a private, but he was eligible for a more senior rank. When six ranger companies were present and organized, an election for regimental officers was held on June 24. Hays was chosen as colonel, Samuel H. Walker as lieutenant-colonel, and Mike Chevallie as major. The company commanders were Acklin, Thomas Green, Samuel Leonard Smith Ballowe, Claibourn C. Herbert, Frank S. Early, and James Gillaspie. The First Texas Mounted Rifles was formally mustered in the same day, less four companies. The eighth company, commanded by Jerome B. McCown, would join the regiment on July 13. Eli Chandler's men would be present five days later. The last two, under Ben McCulloch and Robert Gillespie, were detached to Taylor's headquarters for the time being. Once the regiment was organized, the rangers were ordered to march to Matamoros and report to the commanding general.[99]

Although a part of Taylor's army, Hays and his men operated independently at first, ranging south out of Matamoros on August 10, and west toward the town of China (pronounced *Cheena*). Their mission was to clear the area of the enemy and prevent a surprise attack on the American southern flank. The regiment entered San Fernando on the thirteenth and met little resistance.

As the Texans arrived, a Mexican soldier attempted to flee before he was shot and killed. After resting for three days, the mounted riflemen made ready to depart and discovered twelve of their horses had been stolen. The thief was caught within three hours, but several horses were not recovered. The prisoner was duly tried by court-martial, found guilty, and, rather than being shot or hung, was sentenced to one hundred lashes. After the punishment was carried out and the Mexican released, the regiment took to the trail.[100]

Arriving in China on August 23, Hays was ordered to remain in town or a nearby, convenient location and send his companies to Camargo to have their horses shod. The army's quartermaster and subsistence departments also were to provide funds for the purchase of the regiment's supplies. Another three horses were stolen and, as before, the culprit was apprehended, tried, and convicted. This time, though, the offender was shot.[101]

The month of September brought a turnover of personnel in the regiment. As the enlistments of those who enrolled for three months expired, some men in the regimental staff and the various companies declined to sign on again, while others changed to a different rank. Since the companies had mustered in on different dates and for varying lengths of time, the discharges were likewise spread over a period of weeks.[102]

Hays's regiment was ordered to patrol the China and Cadereita road parallel to the main army's axis of advance, and rendezvous with Taylor at Marin. They arrived on September 18 and marched to Monterey the following morning. Upon reaching the city, military engineers, escorted by Gillespie's rangers, began to reconnoiter the enemy's dispositions. They determined the hills known as Loma de Federación and Loma de Independencia were the most vulnerable and offered the best chance of carrying the fortified town by assault. Gaining control of the nearby Saltillo road would also sever the Mexican line of supply and retreat. General Taylor assigned this crucial task to Brigadier-General William Jenkins Worth, commanding the Second Division. Worth's command consisted of two brigades of regular infantry and two batteries of horse artillery. Hays and 250 rangers were attached to the division on September 20. The column advanced the same day, and Acklin and Ballowe fought a brief skirmish with the enemy before going into camp.[103]

William Jenkins Worth. Steel engraving by John Sartain, Philadelphia, Pennsylvania. *Courtesy Prints and Photographs Division, Library of Congress, Washington, D.C..*

On September 21, Taylor, and the First and Third Divisions, struck the northeast environs of Monterey. After having spent an uncomfortably wet night, Worth and his forces moved at six a.m. to assault the enemy positions atop the less intimidating Federación. Captain Charles Ferguson Smith led one attacking party of three hundred dismounted rangers and regular artillerymen acting as infantry up the rocky slope to the redoubt on the western summit. Determined to carry the bastion, the general ordered Colonel Persifor Frazer Smith to support the charge with six companies of Major Martin Scott's Fifth Infantry, and with Albert Gallatin Blanchard's company of Louisiana volunteers. Hays, Walker, and the ranger companies of Early, Gillaspie, and Acklin joined the latter Smith's detachment. After linking up with the other assault parties, Colonel Smith assumed command of the entire attack. Deciding the original force was sufficient to take the heights, he led the remaining Americans along the southern side of the hill and launched a frontal assault on the Soldado fort. Reaching the crest, Captain Smith's command seized the first gun, a nine-pounder, and turned it to capture the second before moving on to take the Soldado fort from the rear. The Americans encountered determined resistance, but the Mexicans could not withstand the concentrated effort of the attackers. Striving through a shower of rifle balls and grapeshot, the rangers and regulars competed with each other to be the first to reach the heights. The Mexican defenses were breached and the surviving garrison members fled to the Obispado, an abandoned bishop's palace across the Santa Catarina. One of the soldiers of the Fifth Infantry called to several of the Texans, "Well, boys, we almost beat you!" as he wrote "Texas Rangers and Fifth Infantry" on a captured cannon with a piece of chalk. Leaving a detachment of regulars to hold Federación, Worth ordered the remainder of his men back to Walnut Springs to rest. They spent another miserable night with little to eat.[104]

On September 22, the force assaulting Independencia consisted of Companies A, B, C, D, E, G, and I of Hays's regiment, three companies of dismounted artillery, and three of the Eighth Infantry. The mission proved to be grueling, but not impossible. In order to reach the ramparts, the attackers had to climb a height of 350 to four hundred yards, the last twenty nearly vertical. In addition, the defenders of the stronghold were protected by a breastwork of sandbags. Worth, though, was determined to take the summit at all costs. The Texans were able to deliver the general a victory, but at the loss of Robert Gillespie. With his captain dead, William A. A. "Bigfoot" Wallace took over command of the company.[105]

The seizure of the hill, renamed Gillespie's Height by the Texans, enabled Worth to launch his noontime attack on the Obispado. The regulars and rangers rested in the outer works under cover from the brisk fire

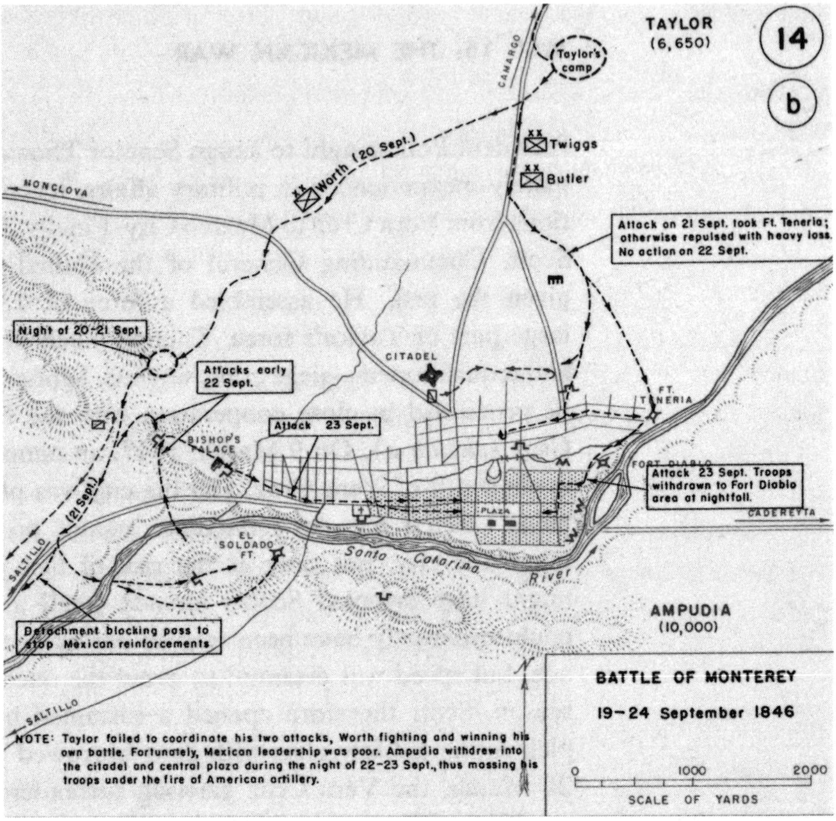

Map of Monterey. From *West Point Atlas of American Wars. Courtesy Geography and Maps Division, Library of Congress, Washington, D.C.*

the Mexicans in the palace were delivering. American skirmishers in an advanced position kept the enemy in check. A twelve-pound howitzer was brought up the hill and fired at the palace, while the Mexicans were receiving reinforcements from the city and preparing a counterattack. The position was carried when defenders were lured into pursuing retreating Louisiana volunteers and regular army troops and rangers attacked the Mexican front and flanks in a double envelopment at point-blank range. The garrison fled, some back into the palace and the others into the city. The Americans breached the palace's gates and the remaining Mexicans were routed, leaving behind four artillery pieces, a large quantity of ammunition, and thirty *soldados* who were taken prisoner. The Obispado was firmly in American hands by four o'clock that afternoon.[106]

On the afternoon of September 23, General Worth ordered his men into the city down parallel streets, advancing in two columns led by Hays and Walker. The colonel and Major Chevallie commanded the right flank of the assault down the *Calle de Monterey*, which extended to the right before finally reaching the plaza. Accompanying Hays were five ranger companies, including those of McCulloch and Wallace, four companies of the Seventh Infantry, and First Lieutenant William Whann Mackall's twelve-pound howitzer. According to Samuel Reid, the men in Hays's detachment,

> steadily advanced inch by inch—our artillery was heard rumbling over the paved streets, galloping here and there, as the emergency required, and pouring forth a blazing fire of grape and ball—volley after volley of musketry, and the continued peals of artillery became almost deafening—the artillery of both sides raked the streets, the balls striking the houses with a terrible crash, while amid the roar of battle were heard the battering instruments used by the Texians. Doors were forced open, walls were battered down—entrances made through the longitudinal walls, and the enemy driven from room to room, and from house to house, followed by the shrieks of women, and the sharp crack of the Texian rifles. Cheer after cheer was heard in proud and exulting defiance, as the Texians or regulars gained the house-tops by means of ladders, while they poured in a rain of bullets upon the enemy on the opposite houses. It was indeed a most strange and novel scene of warfare.

By nightfall the onslaught was within one block of the enemy works in the central plaza, and the Americans readied themselves for the final push on the cathedral the following morning. Upon daybreak of the twenty-fourth, though, Worth received an order from Taylor to suspend any further advance in order to coordinate plans.[107]

In the interim, Mexican envoys under a flag of truce called for a cease-fire. In the subsequent noontime meeting, the Mexicans offered to evacuate the city, and Taylor reciprocated by allowing them to leave with full honors and declaring an eight weeks' truce. The rangers' prominent role in storming the city had been purchased at the cost of five killed and seventeen wounded. They and Texans at home were left "very much dissatisfied" their sacrifices and their victory had been cheapened. Believing the general had violated his orders, President Polk wrote of the armistice, "It will only enable the Mexican army to reorganize and make another stand." The men of the First Texas Mounted Rifles, except for McCulloch's and Wallace's companies, which had been discharged earlier, were mustered out on October 2, and returned to Texas in disgust. General Taylor commented of the Texans, "With their departure we may look for a restoration of quiet and order in Monterey, for I regret to report that some shameful atrocities have been perpetrated by them since the capitulation of the town." Such cases sometimes involved other volunteer regiments, but Taylor seems to have given special emphasis to instances involving Texans. Conversely, General Worth thanked Hays, Walker, and McCulloch by name in his after-action report for their conspicuous conduct and courage.[108]

Delayed by the need to complete his official reports, Hays returned to San Antonio and endured an enthusiastic welcome from his fellow citizens. Lauded in scores of newspapers, Hays modestly accepted the accolades, and shunned any public office his fame could have gained him, choosing instead to return to private life. Even though he had but recently come home, the colonel was authorized by Governor James Pinckney Henderson on November 7 to recruit men for another regiment. He first undertook a business trip to Mississippi and returned in December. After conferring with the governor on January 1, 1847, Hays was occupied with raising the regiment from January 4 to May 9. The War Department insisted on enlistments lasting until the cessation of open hostilities, but few men wished to sign up for the duration. Instead, Hays and his prospective recruits were only willing to enlist for twelve months in accordance with the Act of May 13, 1846. Given the notable service Texans had already rendered, Hays believed the president and the War Department should permit any realistic request the volunteers might submit.[109]

The colonel announced his desire to travel to Washington and discuss the matter personally with President Polk. The governor agreed and Hays, as Henderson's personal representative, carried a letter to the chief executive.

Hays's conversation with Polk resulted in the War Department issuing an order on March 20 authorizing him to raise the proposed regiment, which would serve for twelve months. The Texan was instructed to employ as many companies as he deemed necessary to protect the frontier, and to utilize the remainder to end the pillaging of *guerrilleros* on the Rio Grande. Indicative of the respect Hays enjoyed, the president offered him an appointment as major of infantry in the Regular Army, but the ranger politely declined. He departed Washington for Texas on March 21 by way of the river route.[110]

Arriving home, the military hero turned his attentions from war to matrimony. He married his sweetheart Susan on April 29, 1847, at the Magnolia Hotel in Seguin. While he was away on his honeymoon, Colonel Samuel Ryan Curtis, ranking officer at Camargo, issued a call on March 2 for two thousand mounted Texans under the terms set forth in the law. One week later, Captain Marshall Saxe Howe of the Second Dragoons, commanding in San Antonio, indicated he would begin receiving volunteers for the terms of six months, notwithstanding the earlier War Department directive. On March 11, Adjutant General William Cooke ordered the rendezvous to be located at San Antonio. The governor approved the call on the twenty-third.[111]

By May 11, eight hundred recruits had enrolled into ten companies, which were to be organized into a regiment. Hays, recently back in San Antonio, was unanimously chosen by the men to be colonel. In appreciation for his service to the nation, he was gifted with a sorrel charger by a Mr. Prescot of New Orleans. The steed had been shipped to Galveston aboard the steamer *Yatch*, then brought overland to San Antonio. The First Texas Mounted Volunteers departed San Antonio on May 14, bound for Laredo where Hays planned to cross the border. Shortly after the regiment marched, Taylor declared his intention to only accept enlistments for twelve months, or the duration of the war, and ordered the discharge of all six-month volunteers. The message reached Colonel Hays and his command on the Nueces River, whereupon he returned the men to San Antonio. They disbanded on June 5.[112]

Once Hays was home, he assumed responsibility for the frontier from Captain Howe on July 6. Two days later, he received authorization to form another regiment, also to be called the First Texas Mounted Volunteers, with the enlistments set once more at twelve months. In the election for officers,

Hays was chosen as colonel and Peter Bell as lieutenant-colonel; the regiment was mustered into federal service on July 10.[113]

Hays was actively readying his men for field service when he received additional instructions from the War Department. He was to take all or part of the regiment and join General Taylor in Monterey. The general sent Hays a directive to detail "such force as the governor of Texas may deem necessary for the protection of the frontier," then proceed with the remainder of his command to Mier to await further orders. Two of the regiment's seven companies were left on the frontier under Lieutenant-Colonel Bell, while Hays departed San Antonio on August 12 with the other five. The captains who accompanied the colonel to Mexico were Alfred Marion Truit (or Truitt), Company E; Jacob Roberts, Company F; Gabriel M. Armstrong, Company G; Isaac Ferguson, Company I; and Stephen Kinsey, Company K. The oversized battalion rode to Laredo, forded the Rio Grande, and followed the river to their destination. Arriving on the twenty-eighth, they rested and enjoyed the hospitality, or hostility, of Mier's citizens.[114]

Their brief respite ended when Hays received fresh orders from the War Department directing the regiment to report to General Winfield Scott in Vera Cruz.[115] The reason for the change was the National Road, a well-trod dirt lane which ran for 260 miles between Vera Cruz and Mexico City, and served as Scott's main communications and supply line. With commands "to attack and destroy the invaders, in every manner imaginable," guerrilla bands had risen in the rear of Scott's army as it advanced into the interior, posing a strategic threat to the movement of reinforcements, munitions, and monies. "War without pity, unto death" was the rallying call of these partisans. Wagon trains were commonly two miles in length and, with the guards typically posted at the front and rear, the center was the most vulnerable to the fast-riding Mexican irregulars. With their speed and thorough knowledge of the terrain, *guerrilleros* were a menace to the slower American infantry and artillery, and President Polk was concerned Scott could lose control of the road. He had suggested on July 16, "that the mounted Regiment from Texas under the command of Col. John C. Hays, who has a high character as an officer, be ordered to proceed without delay to Vera Cruz to co-operate with other troops in dispersing the bands of guerrillas who infest the roads from Vera Cruz in Gen'l Scott's rear." Secretary of War William Learned Marcy concurred and declared guerrilla tactics were "hardly recognized as a legitimate mode of warfare, and should be met with the utmost allowable severity." Hays's assignment was to keep the road free of prowling *lanceros* and *guerrilleros*.[116]

The Texans rode to Camargo, Matamoros, Point Isabel, and finally Brazos Santiago, where they set sail for Vera Cruz. The companies of Captains Truit and Ferguson preceded the rest of the regiment to Vera Cruz and established

Hays' Regiment of Texas Mounted Volunteers in 1847, 2008 (w/c & gouache on paper), Troiani, Don (b. 1949) / Private Collection / Bridgeman Images.

a camp three miles inland at Vergara. The last of the 417 rangers disembarked on October 17 and, in the four months prior to the signing of the Treaty of Guadalupe Hidalgo, they would once more display a proclivity for hard fighting and troublemaking.[117]

On October 19, and again on the twenty-sixth, Hays drew a total of 394 Walker Colts from the Vera Cruz supply depot to supplement the Patersons his men already possessed. Many of those who had not served in the colonel's previous commands were ignorant of how the revolving pistols functioned. Several accidental explosions of the cylinders occurred before the men became proficient in their use.[118]

The rangers were ordered to sweep the road of *guerrilleros* while en route to Mexico City, and Hays decided to march with Major-General Robert Patterson's volunteer division. On November 2, the regiment struck their tents and departed Vera Cruz. The Americans reached Jalapa on November 4. Leaving the remainder of his men to rest and then catch up, Hays took the companies of Armstrong and Roberts and continued on to Puebla. There Hays met Brigadier-General Joseph Lane, a politician who commanded a brigade of Indiana and Ohio volunteers. The general had brought eighteen hundred men from Vera Cruz to Puebla to relieve the beleaguered city. Among the actions they fought along the way was a battle at Huamantla that had claimed the life of Sam Walker. Lane had resumed his march to Puebla where, after two hours of shooting, he lifted the siege on October 12. Alike in personality in several ways, Hays and Lane established a fast friendship. The rangers would often be nominally attached to Lane's command once the general became Scott's *de facto* chief of counter-guerrilla operations.[119]

The same month, Lane received word that enemy forces were concentrating at Izúcar de Matamoros for the purpose of launching attacks on American supply trains. Large numbers of artillery, munitions, and other stolen public property were reported to be held in a military depot at that location. Several American soldiers were also being held as prisoners there. On November 22, at seven p.m., the general and Hays departed Puebla with Roberts's ranger company and Captain Lorenzo Lewis's company of Louisiana cavalry, 135 mounted men in total. Accompanying them was Brevet Captain Horace B. Field of the Third Artillery, twenty-five cannoneers, and one gun. The soldiers

Joseph Lane. Wet process collodion glass plate negative attributed to Mathew Brady, New York City. *Courtesy Prints and Photographs Division, Library of Congress, Washington, D.C.*

marched fifty-four miles through a persistent rain and arrived at Izúcar de Matamoros twelve hours later on November 23.[120]

The mounted Americans charged the enemy's advance guard and drove it into the main element of the Mexican force, which caused the whole body to flee through the streets and into a nearby forest. The strength of the charge, the swiftness with which the Mexican opposition collapsed, and the multiple avenues they took to escape made calculating their numbers difficult, although estimates ranged from four to six hundred. Mexican casualties numbered between sixty and eighty killed or wounded without a single friendly loss. Colonel José de las Piedras, the Mexican commander at Nacogdoches in the early 1830s, was among the enemy dead. Twenty-one prisoners were liberated, and were given arms and horses taken from the enemy. Lane's rescue party also captured three field pieces, five hundred muskets and an equal number of sabers, one hundred horses, and a large store of cannon and musket ammunition. They took only what could be transported and destroyed the rest.[121]

Returning to Puebla the following morning, most of Captain Roberts's company was in the van, followed by the artillery, the balance of the rangers, and finally the Louisiana dragoons acting as the rearguard. The column became extended as it moved along the rough ground of Galaxa Pass, some five miles from Izúcar de Matamoros. The captured cannons and four wagons of confiscated equipment fell to the rear due to obstructions in the trail and Lane went back to personally supervise their progress. He received word the enemy was present in front, and he ordered Hays to go forward and take command. After two hundred Mexican *lanceros* had pushed back the pickets, Hays and Roberts counter-charged and drove the enemy over the summit into flight. On the other side, the rangers found another five hundred lancers drawn up under General Joaquín Rea. Their rifles and pistols empty, the Texans fell back in good order, reloading as they rode. Hays personally covered the withdrawal in the face of superior enemy numbers and "deliberately shot two of them dead." Once the rangers reached the main column, the entire command rode forward and drove the lancers off. The American losses were two killed and two slightly wounded. Mexican casualties were estimated to have been at least fifty killed and wounded.[122]

On December 6, General Patterson's train at last entered Mexico City. Professor Irving W. Levinson noted: "To the dismay of the US Army, [Mexican] partisans promptly displayed their ability to wage unconventional warfare in urban as well as rural environments." He continued, "In Mexico City, partisans took cover in houses and commercial buildings just as they had concealed themselves behind hills and in forests. Back streets and alleyways offered the same opportunity for rapid withdrawal as did foot paths in the countryside." Roaming the city's avenues, packs of *leperos* (semi-criminal, professional beggars) targeted lone soldiers or unarmed groups of Americans. In this contentious atmosphere, the citizens of the capital, similar to those in Monterey, experienced the swift vengeance of the Texas Rangers. Hays's men were to answer insult, theft, thrown stone, and assault with the business end of a Walker Colt.[123] Endeavoring to maintain control over a hostile populace, General Scott was not amused by the Texans' conduct. He summoned Hays to report to him. Hays promptly stood before his commanding general and, saluting, stated, "I, sir, am Colonel Hays, commander of the Texas Rangers and report myself to you in accordance with an order just received."

Scott icily declared, "I have been informed, sir, since the arrival of your command in this city, two Mexicans have been killed. I hold you, sir, responsible for the acts of your men. I will not be disgraced, nor shall the army of my country be, by such outrages. I require you, sir, to say whether my information is correct, and if so, you will render me a satisfactory explanation."

Hays answered, "Your information is correct. General, the Texas Rangers are not accustomed to being insulted without resenting it. They did kill two Mexicans as I entered the city, and I, sir, am willing to be held responsible for it."

The colonel's respectful manner and forthright bearing persuaded Scott that Hays believed his men to have been justified. The general invited the ranger to sit and give a full account of the matter. Hays went on to briefly inform Scott of the numerous reasons Texans felt such amity for Mexico and Mexicans alike. Once the interview was completed, Hays was courteously dismissed and the episode was not discussed further. Throughout their stay in the Halls of the Montezumas, the rangers would well earn their sobriquet of *los diablos tejanos*, "the Texas Devils."[124]

Hays refused to be distracted by such events and undertook to combat the *guerrilleros* infesting the region. His principal nemesis was the infamous *Presbyterio* Celedonio Dómeco de Jarauta, a Spanish-born priest who carried a government *patente* for "light corps operations" in the Noreste de México region. The padre had earlier raided around Vera Cruz before shifting his endeavors to the Valley of Mexico.[125] Hays learned late in December that Jarauta was at Hacienda Tlalnepantla, approximately fifteen miles from Mexico City. On January 1, 1848, Lieutenants Ephraim Merrill Daggett and Hardy Jones, with thirty-eight rangers, and Colonel Francis Murray Wynkoop, commanding a small force of regulars, departed the capital to capture the *guerrillero* chieftain. When the Americans reached the *hacienda*, they rushed inside to discover Jarauta had left for Villa Toluca several hours before. The Texans interrogated some of the residents, and learned General Gabriel Valencia and his staff were at a *rancho* about eighteen miles away. The expedition mounted their horses and set out for a hard night's ride. They surrounded the *hacienda* and Wynkoop demanded entrance. The Americans were at first refused entry, but the door opened after he insisted on admittance a second time. Colonel Silea, a wounded and paroled officer, informed Wynkoop that General Valencia and his officers had traveled to Toluca that day. Wynkoop ordered his men to search the house and confirm Silea's story. The search was inconclusive, but the American colonel remained unconvinced. He told Silea that he and his men would not leave until Valencia was produced. The general suddenly appeared and identified himself. After Valencia dressed for the trip, he and a colonel of his staff were escorted back to Mexico City.[126]

On the evening of January 11, Hays led his men from their camp at San Àngel for an undisclosed location. The general consensus of the rangers was that they were hunting Jarauta, and the speculation was proven correct the next morning when the command entered Otumba, approximately thirty miles northwest of Mexico City. The bandit chieftain had been reported to be lurking in the area. When the Texans arrived in the village, Hays discovered Jarauta was instead in San Juan Teotihuacán, closer to the capital and ten miles from the Mexico City-Otumba road. Hays drove his regiment hard for their new destination, but their quarry had already departed.[127]

Hays quartered his men in a large stone building that encompassed almost an entire side of the central plaza. The horses were stabled in an enclosed space adjacent to the main structure. The fatigued rangers prepared their beds on benches and on the floor in the *cuartel* (barracks) and were quickly fast asleep. The sound of spooked horses awakened Lieutenant Daggett. He went out into the enclosure and looked over the high wall. Beyond terrified citizens who were scattering, the ranger observed Jarauta and seventy-five *lanceros* charging across the plaza at a full gallop. Yelling the alarm, Daggett leapt into the barracks to seize his pistols. Before he could buckle on his gun belt, partisans were crowding into the doorway and the ranger lieutenant opened fire. Although he was temporarily blinded by powder from a pistol fired close to his face, Daggett wounded Jarauta in the wrist and in the "beefsteak," and Jarauta's lieutenant in the shoulder. The determined Daggett, believing he was about to die, resolved to give the bandits a "coon fight."[128]

The roar of gunfire and shouts of men locked in mortal combat roused the sleeping rangers. Springing to their feet, weapons in hand, Hays and his men rushed to the door to assist Daggett. As the rangers forced the lancers away from the entrance, Jarauta formed his men for another charge. The Texans rushed into the plaza outside the *cuartel* and prepared to meet the *guerrilleros*. Ignoring the fire from the Mexicans' *escopetas*, the Texan skirmish line broke the enemy advance. As the Mexicans began to fall back, sharpshooters Hays had positioned on the roof went into action. Jarauta was preparing his *guerrilleros* for a third charge when a rifle bullet fired at long-range knocked him from his horse. Forsaking the engagement, the lancers carried their wounded chieftain from the scene. The enemy casualties were estimated at eight dead, while the powder-burned Daggett was the only ranger to suffer a wound. Later in the early afternoon, the regiment took up the march for Mexico City. The command reached its destination about ten o'clock that night.[129]

In the early morning hours of January 18, General Lane assembled Hays and four companies of his regiment to patrol the countryside and suppress brigandage. They were accompanied by the president's younger brother, Major William Hawkins Polk, commanding detachments from Companies A, B, H, and I, Third Dragoons, and Company I of the Mounted

Riflemen. Assigning two ranger companies to escort a military supply train, Lane led the rest of his command in a southeasterly search for hostile forces. During the night of January 22, forty miles from the town of Tehuacán, the horsemen encountered a coach escorted by eight to twelve armed men. The Americans disarmed the bodyguards and were about to take the entire party prisoner when a person stepped down from the carriage and produced a safe-conduct pass signed by General Persifor F. Smith. Having no alternative, Lane returned the escort's weapons, and ordered the release of the guards and the coach.[130]

Lane and his command continued the march for Tehuacán, eighty miles southeast of Puebla. Spies had reported the presence of *Generalissimo* Antonio López de Santa Anna in the town, protected by one hundred regular cavalrymen and an undetermined number of *guerrilleros*. At four a.m., the column arrived at the outskirts of Tehuacán where signals were immediately lit, and a shot was fired at the Americans. Hays, Lane, and two Texas companies charged into the center of the plaza, while Polk's troopers surrounded the town. They found traces of the recent residence of soldiery, but any combatants had since disappeared. The house where Santa Anna had been quartered was located and his furniture, uniforms, and valuables were captured, as was the wardrobe of his wife. Without disturbing any of Doña Santa Anna's clothing, Hays chivalrously arranged for all of the articles to be returned to the *señora*. Lane learned from the *alcalde* that a courier had arrived two hours earlier, and warned the dictator of the approaching American cavalry. The messenger was determined to have been one of the escorts encountered the previous evening. Moreover, Santa Anna's retainers had taken all the available horses away with them, and Lane's exhausted mounts were unable to pursue.[131]

Lane and his command continued to patrol the region, accepting the surrenders of Orizaba and Córdova, before returning to Puebla on February 3. He took the same force out again on the fifth in the direction of Tlaxcala and the rugged country to the north. On February 8, the Americans approached San Juan Teotihuacán (the scene of the fight with Jarauta the previous month) and Lane was informed that the enemy under Colonel Manuel Falcón was present in the field. The general ordered Polk's horsemen to pursue the

Mexicans, while Hays's Texans were to seize the town. Polk's detachment killed seventeen of Falcón's partisans, captured three, and chased the remainder into the mountains for seven miles before their wearied horses caused them to return to town. Meanwhile, Hays captured 250 muskets, a number of *escopetas*, and a large quantity of ammunition, all of which was destroyed since they had no wagons to transport the matériel. He also presented Falcón's papers to Lane. The following morning, the brigadier's command returned to Mexico City.[132]

Although the Treaty of Guadalupe Hidalgo was signed on February 2, 1848, the United States and Mexico would not ratify the document until March 10 and May 30, respectively. In the interim, *gringos* were being murdered nightly in the streets of Mexico City. On the afternoon of February 13, Private Adam Alsans of Roberts's company was hacked nearly to death by a mob in a squalid area of the city the Texans knew as "Cutthroat." He perished after eight agonizing hours and was buried with full military honors. The eerily quiet mood in the Texan camp following the funeral foretold ominous events ahead. On the night of the fourteenth, Alsans's unforgiving comrades went into the quarter to exact "a terrible revenge." At ten o'clock, Hays was in his headquarters conversing with Captain Parry W. Humphreys and Adjutant John S. Ford when they heard a steady roll of gunshots. Hays immediately contended the firing was due to U.S. Marines drilling outside the city walls. According to Ford, all three men knew the true nature of the shooting, but maintained the polite fiction. Around midnight, Humphreys looked outside and abruptly asked, "I wonder what the commanding general's orderly is coming for?" Desiring to remain officially unaware of what was occurring that night, Hays quickly absented himself from the room and disappeared until daybreak. Obviously, the captain had not seen the orderly, but merely wanted to test the colonel's stated opinion. Once Hays had vanished, the two remaining officers listened to the gunfire until after one o'clock. The next morning eighty corpses were counted in the city's morgue, which did not include those bodies already retrieved by relatives. General Scott had questioned Hays and his Texans concerning other clashes with the local populace, but he apparently decided to let this particular episode alone. He did, however, order the regiment to take the field.[133]

On February 17, General Lane, Hays's 250 rangers, Polk's 130 dragoons and mounted riflemen, and Colonel Manuel Domínguez's spy company of *contra-guerrilleros* rode to search the mountainous country north of the Río Frio. After following the National Road as far as San Felipe, then riding to Tulancingo on February 22, the general learned a now-recovered Padre Jarauta was at Zacualtipán, seventy-five miles to the north. Sending the sick personnel back to Mexico City under Domínguez's care, the balance of the American column undertook a forced march to confront their tenacious foe. Arriving at daybreak on February 25, Lane and the rangers led the charge into town. The van came under fire from a *cuartel* on the right flank, which was returned with unerring marksmanship. Leaving Major Truit, Adjutant Ford, and fifteen to eighteen rangers to hold the fifty or sixty Mexicans in check, the others continued to the main plaza, taking fire from both sides.[134]

Hays perceived a strong detachment of lancers and infantry issuing forth from a barracks on a street to the left. He divided his command and took the majority of them to engage the enemy. Lane led the remaining fifteen or sixteen rangers into the plaza. After Hays's detachment received fire from the Mexicans in front of the barracks and behind its walls, a running fight ensued that covered a half-mile of the street until the enemy was able to escape, leaving behind thirty dead. Three hundred yards beyond Lane's position in the plaza, more Mexicans were situated in front of a *cuartel* and lancers were poised behind the structure. Hays sent Captain Daggett's company to assist the brigadier and, as the enemy fire redoubled, the general ordered the rangers to dismount and attack in desperate street fighting reminiscent of Monterey. The Texans advanced to within thirty feet of the Mexican positions, and a determined charge pushed the enemy back into the *cuartel*. Fighting at point-blank range, the Mexicans bitterly contested the Texans as the latter cleared each room. Thirty Mexicans were killed and several were captured, while the remainder escaped through the rear of the building.[135]

Major Polk and his men fought in another street to the left of the plaza, then battled fugitives in the western quarter who were fleeing from Hays and Lane's fronts. He returned to the plaza in time to disperse the *lanceros* behind the *cuartel* where Lane's detachment was hotly engaged. The Americans learned from a prisoner that Jarauta was quartered in the cathedral facing the plaza. Unfortunately, the elusive priest managed to escape from the church only moments before Polk's regulars fought their way to the structure, killing a large number of the enemy. Despite the hard nature of the fighting, Lane's command suffered one man mortally wounded, three severely injured, and two slightly hurt. Out of four hundred lancers and fifty infantrymen, at least 150 Mexicans were killed, while a considerable number were wounded and fifty-six were captured (including three American deserters).[136]

The American troops departed the town on February 26, and reached Mexico City on March 1. Once he returned to his headquarters, Hays signed his after-action report, not as commander of the First Texas Mounted Volunteers, but as "Colonel Texas Rangers." Zacualtipán ended the guerrilla effort in Central Mexico, and Jarauta ceased to trouble the *Yanquis*. Indeed, the battle was the last significant engagement of the war.[137]

Once the conflict was at an end, the rangers leisurely departed Mexico City on March 18, bound for Vera Cruz. As they traveled by easy marches along the National Road, the rangers occasionally skirmished with outlawed *guerrilleros* who had repudiated the armistice and refused to disarm. By the end of the month, the rangers were bivouacked near Jalapa, some fifty miles from the port. Santa Anna, on his way to exile in Jamaica, was billeted four miles away at San Miguel and dining with American army officers. On March 28, Hays learned of the *generalissimo's* presence and rode into the village to meet him. The ranger colonel entered the dining room where the deposed president was sitting at a table eating fruit. Hays was formally presented to *El Napoleón del Oeste* ("the Napoleon of the West") as he rose to greet the newcomer. When he heard the name of his country's mortal enemy, the former dictator's face turned scarlet and he began to splutter; his young wife went pale. Swiftly regaining his composure, Santa Anna resumed his place at the table. Hays courteously bowed, paid his respects, and strode from the room. On April 30, 1848, except for Hays and Ford, the men of the First Texas Mounted Volunteers were discharged from federal service at Vera Cruz. They took ship on May 5 and sailed for home.[138]

After Hays returned to Texas, the citizens of San Antonio organized a celebration for the rangers on May 20 to thank them for their war service.

The party was attended by more than three hundred people and the dancing lasted well into the early hours. Furthermore, the First Legislature had created Hays County on March 1 in honor of the legendary ranger. The colonel then traveled to Austin and Washington to wrap up the administrative details of his regiment. He completed his business and was discharged on July 10.[139]

Later in the summer, Hays was approached by San Antonio merchants eager to open new markets in Mexico. His thirst for adventure unquenched, the colonel agreed to lead an expedition for the purpose of blazing a trade road between San Antonio and Chihuahua by way of Paso del Norte. Interest also grew in establishing an all-season overland route from the latter location to San Diego and San Francisco. Setting forth on August 27, Hays and his party, escorted by Captain Samuel Highsmith's thirty-five rangers, rode to Enchanted Rock, then crossed the Devil's and Pecos Rivers, and trekked through the rough expanse of the Big Bend, where they were without food for twelve days. They reached the village of San Carlos and went on to Presidio del Norte after a grueling journey of over fifty days. After resting at Ben Leaton's private fort for ten days, Hays led his battered expedition back to San Antonio, arriving on December 12. Hays recommended a wagon route to Presidio del Norte by way of the San Saba and Pecos Rivers, and believed a road could be constructed from there to Paso del Norte.[140]

On April 11, 1849, Commissioner of Indian Affairs William Medill wrote a letter to Hays enclosing his commission as Indian sub-agent to the Lipan Apaches along the Gila River in New Mexico. The notification also included details on his salary, authorization to employ an interpreter, and reports from various officials in the territory. Since so little was known of the Gila country, the department could not supply the colonel with any specific instructions regarding the Indians there. Nevertheless, Hays accepted the appointment and submitted a bond of two thousand dollars to the Office of Indian Affairs on June 8. The surety was received and approved by the Secretary of the Interior.[141]

On June 6, Hays, Major John Caperton, and a small party departed San Antonio on the lower road bound for El Paso. For most of the overland trek, they banded together for mutual protection with the Frémont Association, a wagon train of thirty-nine New York emigrants. In turn, the colonel and his increased number of companions were allowed to accompany Brevet Lieutenant-Colonel Joseph Eggleston Johnston and a contingent of topographical engineers, one company of the First Infantry, and six companies of the Third Infantry under Major Jefferson Van Horne, all of whom were tasked with testing the practicality of the route. The government expedition was a serious endeavor, as the caravan included 275 supply wagons and 2,500 head of livestock. The road took the civilian and military travelers across the Leon, Medina, Seco, Sabinal, Leona, and Nueces Rivers, Las Moras Creek, the Devil's and Pecos Rivers, and on to the Rio Grande Valley. The emigrant party parted with the soldiers twenty-five miles above El Paso, and the former reached the town on September 10 after a journey of 693 miles. Once they resumed the journey west, the Forty-niners reorganized, and Hays was elected captain of the one hundred men driving the mule train.[142]

Hiring renegade Peter Worthington "Jack" Gordon as an intermediary, Hays attempted to parley with the Lipans at Ben Moore Mountain on October 16, but his entreaties were rebuffed. The days of the easy friendships Texans had enjoyed with the band had deteriorated in the wake of Flacco's murder. Hays described his new charges as "hostile with feelings aroused against the whites," and indeed twenty-five German emigrants were attacked shortly thereafter. In the end, Hays came to believe the only means to bring about a lasting peace was war. He continued with the Frémont Association along the cut-off between the Burro Mountains and Tucson, across the Sonoran Desert, and over the Colorado River into California. They reached the New River on the twenty-second of December. On January 3, 1850, Hays submitted his resignation letter from San Diego stating, "The only Indians in my department are the Apaches, and to effect any thing with them requires much time, a number of troops, and a large expenditure of money. My inability to be of any service whatever, with the means furnished, compels me to abandon the undertaking."[143]

Rather than return to Texas, Hays decided to join the gold rush to northern California. From San Diego, he took the SS *Colonel Frémont*, a side-wheel steamship under the command of Captain J. D. Nason, to San Francisco. For four days of the fifteen-day voyage, the brig was battered by a violent storm, but sailed safely though the Golden Gate strait on January 25. As wharves would not be constructed for several more months, the *Frémont* dropped anchor off North Point, and the passengers, drenched by a cold rain, were forced to take a dingy to the shore to disembark. They then trudged through the mud over Telegraph Hill into town. Word of Hays's impending arrival had spread throughout the Bay area, and all of San Francisco was talking about the famous Texas Ranger.[144]

Despite the warm welcome he received, the colonel's financial resources remained meager. He desired to bring Susan to California and wanted to ensure they could live in comfort. Although he was determined to be engaged in a suitable occupation, Hays was almost immediately sought for public office. In the first county elections set for April 1, 1850, the Whigs and the Democrats had their own candidates, but a group of independents approached Hays and begged him to run for county sheriff. The *Alta California* published a flattering article on the national war hero's career and character. The same issue announced "At the solicitation of numerous friends Colonel Jack Hays has consented to place himself before the public as a candidate for the Sheriffalty when the election for that office shall take place."[145]

The Democrat challenger was "Colonel" J. J. Bryant, an ambitious and successful gambler whose real-estate holdings included the opulent Bryant House hotel. The establishment was a meeting place for the area's political elite, and Bryant provided prospective voters a band that played music daily on the balcony, free lunches served in the saloon, and even an open bar on the day of his nomination. Interestingly, Hays was leading the Whig candidates in the days before the March 22 primary. He accepted the party's nomination, but withdrew his response the next day, reiterating his status as an independent. Instead Colonel John Townes became the nominee, but he soon dropped out and the real contest lay between Hays and Bryant.[146]

Two days prior to the election, Hays's supporters staged a rally in Portsmouth Square, which culminated in a parade with a brass band. That same evening, the Democrats also held a meeting complete with a parade, a concert, and a torchlight procession. By noon of Election Day, the popularity of Colonel Hays caused the Bryant camp some distress. They presented another elaborate rally with a procession of horsemen and a carriage-drawn band complete with banners. The spectacle was winning over the crowd when Hays, mounted on a spirited black horse, dashed into the gathering and put on a display of horsemanship that awed the roaring spectators.[147] Hays handily won the election, receiving 789 votes to Bryant's 283 and Townes's seventy-four. The new sheriff swore his oath and assumed his duties on April 9. His office was located on the second floor of the town hall. Neighboring rooms housed the common council, the courtrooms for the district and superior courts, the police station, and a space for two fire engines. The members of Hays's staff included Undersheriff John Caperton, and deputies John Anderson Freaner, Thomas Hayes, and Captain B. F. Harley. John L. Powers served as a guard.[148]

Upon assuming office, Sheriff Hays inherited as his county jail the brig *Euphemia* floating near the Central Wharf. The *Euphemia* had been acquired for that purpose in October 1849, along with fifty sets of ball and chains for shackling prisoners. Because of the high costs of construction and rents in the city, the use of berthed ships as buildings was widespread, and included hotels, offices,warehouses, and a church. By February 1850, the ship had begun its life as a lockup, as well as an insane asylum. Conditions onboard worsened as the number of prisoners increased. After he accepted responsibility for the *Euphemia*, Hays led an unsuccessful effort to solicit private donations for the completion of the new, permanent county jail on Broadway between Kearney and Dupont Streets. In the end, he had to spend fourteen to fifteen hundred dollars of his own money to finish the project. Large sums of public funds had already been expended, but the effort was hampered by charges of official misconduct against members of the Court of Sessions. By an act of the California Assembly on April 25, 1851, Mariano G. Vallejo and James M. Estell were awarded a contract for the safekeeping, guarding, and maintenance of all state convict labor. The governor then gave notice that all prisoners were to be delivered to the custody of Hays and Undersheriff Caperton, who had sub-contracted for the privilege.[149]

Hays lived in the Marine Hospital for several months as a lodger, while Susan stayed at her father's residence in Guadalupe County, Texas. On December 7, 1850, the sheriff was on hand at the wharves to welcome his bride to their new home. She had sailed down the Gulf of Mexico, crossed over the Isthmus of Panama, and cruised up the California coastline to San Francisco. Before her arrival, Hays, Caperton, and James Galbraith had each purchased from sawmill operator Charles Brown a one-third interest in two thousand acres of the Mountain Home Ranch, a spread thirty miles south of town in present San Mateo County. The property was once part of the old Rancho Cañada de Raymundo. The remaining 880 acres were leased as "Frank Turk's old ranch." Moreover, Hays and his associates individually owned a one-ninth interest in the ranch's steam-powered sawmill, while the firm of Howe & Howe possessed the remaining two-thirds. Apparently the managing partner of the venture, Hays used Brown's old adobe as a boardinghouse for the lumbermen, and built a two-story frame house on the property for Susan. However, the long ride to and from town proved too time consuming, and the couple moved to a house on Powell Street the following year.[150]

San Francisco was a rough, boisterous, intimidating town of tents, shacks, and shanties. Merchants, land speculators, traders, gamblers, saloon-keepers, and prostitutes had all come west to profit from the riches of the goldfields, while alongside them was a significant criminal element responsible for extensive lawlessness and frequent arsons. The "Hounds," a gang of New York veterans discharged in California, and the "Sydney Ducks," Australians from the penal colony at Botany Bay, were particularly notorious for preying on immigrants. Additionally, whether they were honest or crooked, the Americans, *Californios*, Mexicans, Chileans, Peruvians, Chinese, and every other national and ethnic demographic were divided by animosities and prejudices. Outside the city limits, the Bay area was infested with a gang of military deserters and former convicts who were raiding remote *ranchos* and missions. The efficient administration of governmental affairs was hampered by the high turnover in local offices, the widespread corruption and incompetence of these bureaucrats, and the lack of qualified jurists and prosecutors due to low salaries. However, defense attorneys were able to earn a substantial living. Fortunately, in Sheriff Hays, law-abiding citizens had a strong, equally dangerous individual who had been tempered by years of war and handling tough men. Months into his tenure, Hays began to have dealings with a volunteer night patrol formed to assist the inadequate city police force. This auxiliary organization would become notorious as the "Committee of Vigilance." William A. Howard, a member of the group, wrote to that body's president: "The Sheriff & his officers are with us *Heart* and *Soul.*" Declaring their confidence in Hays's integrity as a public official, the committee raised one thousand dollars in funds to improve the county jail and reimburse him for his earlier outlay. In spite of the vigilantes' generosity, there is no indication the sheriff or his deputies actively endorsed the extralegal actions of the committee.[151]

The vigilantes' first victim was John Jenkins, a member of the Sydney Ducks, who, during the evening of June 10, 1851, had stolen a safe from a store on the Long Wharf. Before morning, he had been captured, tried by a panel of sixty to eighty townsmen, and strung up on Portsmouth Square in front of a crowd of one thousand. Nearly two hundred citizens confessed to the act in the newspaper, but public approval barred any prosecution of the lynching.[152]

Soon after that incident, Hays locked horns with Captain Edgar "Ned" Wakeman, the vigilantes' "Captain of the Water Police." The sheriff had placed an attachment on the steamship *New Orleans* commanded by Wakeman. Since $65,000 was involved, Hays ensured the steamer was watched. One day he received word the ship was being readied to depart from the Long Wharf and hurried to the scene. Observing a sailor handling the moorings, Hays ordered him to cease. Wakeman approached and the sheriff informed him the line was to be left alone. "Suppose I choose to cast it off, what then?" the captain asked. "I will kill you," Hays coolly replied with a deadly look in his eyes, Wakeman chose not to challenge the law officer any further.[153]

The sheriff's once-cordial relations with the Committee of Vigilance became strained through the summer of 1851. On July 1, the vigilantes extracted a confession from career criminal James Stuart, another Duck, that implicated Samuel Whittaker and Robert McKenzie, two ex-convicts from Sydney. City Attorney Frank Morrison Pixley had secured a writ of *habeas corpus* for Stuart and requested Hays take the lawbreaker into custody. The sheriff went to the committee's headquarters on Battery Street, but Stuart had already been hidden elsewhere and the members averred they did not have him in their possession. Despite their false claims, Stuart was lynched from the gallows constructed on the Market Street wharf on July 11. Whittaker and McKenzie were captured by the vigilantes in late

July and early August, and scheduled to be hung from a ship's yardarm on August 20. The night before the slated execution, Hays and Caperton, serving another writ at the behest of Governor John McDougal, went to the committee's headquarters and rescued the condemned men without having to resort to violence. The vigilantes were not disconcerted, but instead laid plans to recapture the two culprits. On the twenty-fourth, Hays was lured to the bullfight occurring at the Mission Dolores, while a force of vigilantes gained entry to the town hall and seized the deputies inside. A messenger alerted Hays, but Whittaker and McKenzie were dragged from the basement cells and hung before he could get to the jail. They were the last to be executed by the committee, although a subsequent association would rise several years later. Hays would oppose them as a captain of the Law and Order Party.[154]

Despite the lynchings, Hays was handily reelected on September 3. Even before his second term was half-complete, he had begun to look to the town of Oakland as his future home. Shortly after arriving in California, he had become acquainted with the Peralta family who owned the Encinal de Temescal and Encinal de San Antonio land grants. On March 13, 1852, Hays and a consortium of investors purchased from Don Vicente Peralta all the dry land north of the estuary and south of Lake Merritt. The don, whose family had been awarded the grant in 1820, sold the tract for ten thousand dollars. Since the end of the Mexican War, and subsequent gold rush, the Peraltas and other *Californios* had been forced to deal with squatters taking up residence on their properties. In the case of Don Vicente, Edson Adams, Horace Walpole Carpentier, and Andrew Moon had each filed claims on 160 acres of the Encinal de Temescal in 1850, alleging the land was on the public domain. They then arranged for the surveying of city lots and streets, and persuaded the legislature to incorporate the town of Contra Costa, later renamed Oakland, on May 4, 1852. Other squatters followed the trio's example and began seizing more Peralta acreage. Don Vicente had reasoned relinquishing his estate to Hays's group for a profit was better than seeing the land stripped away bit by bit in hopeless lawsuits. As the property included Oakland and its environs, and the claims of Carpentier, Adams, and Moon, the transaction led to court cases between the opposing syndicates that lasted for more than fifteen years. In the interim, Hays and his associates improved upon the land and

The Hanging of Samuel Whittaker and Robert McKenzie. Lithograph by Justh, Quirot & Co., San Francisco, California. *Courtesy Yale Collection of Western Americana, Beinecke Rare Book and Manuscript Library, Yale University, New Haven, Connecticut.*

divided it into city lots. When their titles were finally upheld in 1869, they sold their investment for a handsome return.[155] Even as the sheriff laid the groundwork for his imminent financial success, his first son, John Caperton Hays, was born on August 25, 1852. His second, Richard, would follow on April 29, 1855, as would his eldest daughter, Kitty, on May 4, 1856.[156]

Although Hays had won the sheriff's office as an independent, he was active in Democratic party politics. When Franklin Pierce was elected president, Hays took a four-month leave of absence and sailed to Washington to petition for the recently established post of United States surveyor-general for California. His past experience as a surveyor in Mississippi and Texas was considered valuable, and the president nominated him on March 16, 1853. The Senate proceeded to consider and then confirm the appointment the same day. Hays returned to California aboard the steamer *Pacific*, arriving in San Francisco on June 15. He resigned as sheriff two days later and entered the surveyor-general's office on July 15.[157]

Hays assumed his new duties at a time when the future of Spanish and Mexican land grants was being determined. The U.S. government had declared all valid titles were to be honored, but land-hungry emigrants protested the ownership of enormous tracts by a small group of individuals. Once the Golden State was admitted to the Union, the California Land Act of 1851 established a federal board of three land commissioners for the purpose of dividing privately held properties, mainly old *ranchos*, missions, and pueblos, from the public domain. *Californios* and Anglos possessing Spanish and Mexican grants were required to appear before the board and prove with documentation and testimony their ownership; the burden of proof was upon the claimant. Decisions by the land board could be appealed to the federal district courts and to the U.S. Supreme Court. Resolution of the average case took seventeen years from the original filing of the claim before the commissioners to the final court ruling. Even though Don Vicente would sell to Hays, the Peralta family was still compelled to submit their claims regarding their two grants to the commissioners in January 1852. The validity of their titles would be upheld by the supreme court in 1856, after they had sold almost all of their properties. For the cases that were decided quickly, once ownership was confirmed, Hays was responsible for surveying the lands and determining the exact boundaries. He began immediately to press for surveys that would give clear title to residents for the lands they occupied and increase the tax base for the state. Land, as well as mining, would present the most lucrative business opportunities in California, so Hays gave priority to properties that would benefit the real estate and agricultural markets. In September and October 1854, accompanied by celebrated traveler and writer J. Ross Browne, he made a personal tour of the state's public lands in the San Joaquin Valley. Hays experienced his own issues with property rights in 1855, when he accused the firm of Baker & Burham, owners of a sawmill on the other side of Bear Gulch from the Mountain Home Ranch, of poaching his timber. Hays was able to obtain a writ of injunction against the offending lumber company that inadvertently aided in hastening their commercial demise.[158]

Once James Buchanan was inaugurated president, members of the California congressional delegation, as well as other officials, began to urge for Hays's reappointment. However, on July 13, 1857, the president selected Hays for the open position of federal surveyor-general for Utah Territory on a temporary basis. The reasons stated were that Buchanan believed in the principle of rotation in office. The *Alta California* took a different view and reported, "Hays had in contracts for survey exceeded the legal appropriations by near $175,000. One of the first acts of the new administration was to have no 'deficiency' to ask for … it was decided in cabinet council to shuffle Colonel Jack out of California, and to send him into honorable exile among the Mormons."[159]

Hays's commission as surveyor-general for California expired on September 8, 1857. His deputies, and a number of personal friends, presented him a testimonial consisting of six sizable pieces of silver plate. The Buchanan administration affirmed they "retained the highest opinion of his integrity, services, and great executive abilities as a public officer." Indeed, his term in office had been successful, the surpassing of his funding indicated the volume of work he had performed, and the offer of a less-significant post was considered as almost an insult. As the territory was troubled by the threat of violence between the federal government and the Mormon population, the Utah assignment would have entailed physical risks for his family, not to mention financial loss. While he was confirmed for the permanent Utah appointment, the colonel declined on February 19, 1859. Becoming a private citizen once again, Hays continued to acquire and develop real estate properties in Oakland, Berkeley, and Alameda.[160]

Meanwhile, the Hays family was experiencing its own personal trial when Kitty died on May 14, 1858. She was buried in the old Oakland Cemetery and later reinterred at Mountain View Cemetery. On a brighter note, another daughter, Mary Susan, known as "Susie," was born later in the year.[161] On February 17, 1858, Hays, Caperton, and Galbraith sold their interests in the Mountain Home Ranch to Colonel Ralph W. Norris. In the late autumn of 1859, the Hays family moved to Fernwood, an eight hundred-acre ranch along Temescal Creek in the Oakland Hills. The main house was characterized as

> one of the most beautiful in the State. It is located at the base of the verdure-clad hills of the Coast Range, in a quiet nook, secluded from the bustle and turmoil of that busy world in which this hero so long maintained a gallant and successful career. Lordly oaks surround a handsome building, and exquisite art has been made an assistant in adorning the natural beauties of the scene.[162]

The colonel's nephew, mining engineer and diplomat John Hays Hammond, would recall:

> During my boyhood, every country place was called a ranch, but my uncle's was really a ranch de luxe. Although in extent not comparable with some of the enormous ranches of the day, it held cattle and, of course, many horses. With its alternating hills and wild ravines, it was an ideal place for a boy with an adventurous spirit.[163]

Even as he enjoyed the benefits of success after a lifetime of conflict, Hays was called upon to fight one last time. On May 8, 1860, Paiute Indians in Nevada, once friendly to white settlers, killed five men at Williams Station on the Carson River, and set the trading post on fire. Lost in the subsequent furor over the "massacre" was the fact one or all of the men slain at Williams

Station had earlier kidnapped and raped two young Paiute girls. Ignorant of the reasons for the killings, the grim news alarmed residents of Virginia City, Silver City, Carson City, and Genoa, and a force of 105 miners was organized to punish the Paiutes. Led by Major William Matthew Ormsby, the volunteers were poorly equipped, ill-disciplined, and badly mounted. The few seasoned veterans in their ranks were not enough to compensate for the command's shortcomings. The Indians were found on a plateau above the Truckee River, near Pyramid Lake, on May 12. Lured into an ambush, the surrounded Nevadans engaged some two to three hundred warriors who delivered murderous volleys of bullets and arrows. The volunteers tried to make a stand, but the fury of the Paiutes forced them into a terrified retreat. The warriors followed for twenty to thirty miles, overtaking and slaying stragglers. Of the men who began the expedition, seventy-six were killed at the Truckee or after taking flight, including Ormsby, while all of the survivors were wounded.[164]

News of the slaughter sent the Comstock range into a panic, and rumors spread of vast hordes of Indians rushing to attack the settlements in a welter of blood and fire. Many people fled west over the Sierra Nevada to escape. The army was caught unprepared as troops elsewhere in the territory were few in number. At the same time, Colonel Hays happened to be in the Carson Valley on personal business. Alerted to his presence, citizens unanimously pressed him to command the "Washoe Regiment" and he accepted on May 24.[165]

Three days later, Hays led eight companies of infantry and six of cavalry down the Carson River. He was assisted by Lieutenant-Colonel E. J. Saunders and Major Daniel Elihu Hungerford. All of the 550 volunteers had been equipped with Sharps rifles and Minié balls supplied by the California militia. The colonel was supported by 144 detached regulars from the First Dragoons, Sixth Infantry, and Third Artillery—the latter fielding two 12-pound mountain howitzers—under the overall command of Captain Joseph "Jasper" Stewart. The expedition reached Williams Station on the twenty-eighth. The following morning, forty-five men of Hays's spy company, who were two miles away at Big Meadows, were attacked by 150 well-armed and well-mounted Indians. The scouts were pursued by the Paiutes until the volunteers neared the main camp and elected to make a stand. Hays and thirty horsemen rode to their comrades' assistance and skirmished with the Paiutes for forty-five minutes before the warriors withdrew, leaving six or seven of their number dead on the field.[166]

At three p.m. on June 2, eight hundred to one thousand Paiutes were located on the Truckee near Pyramid Lake, a short distance from the earlier battlefield. Beyond the river a half-mile was a range of mountains from which extended toward the regiment a plateau of pedregal that broke off into deep ravines and sandy ridges. Approximately one hundred regulars marched in open order as skirmishers, followed a half-mile behind by Hays and Saunders with two hundred mounted volunteers. The volunteer infantry was left in reserve under Major Hungerford to secure a possible line of retreat. Hays hoped to draw out the Indians with a display of supposedly inferior numbers and bring on a decisive battle. The Secretary of War would later report to President Buchanan, "The Indians were very powerful in numbers and strong in position … But the practiced eye of the cool and daring leader enabled him to lead the assault with such skill that the vastly superior number of the Indians availed them nothing."[167]

Gaining the plateau, Hays dismounted his cavalry and, together with some of the regulars, deployed them in skirmish order. A large gathering of Indians formed to his left and, predicting they would attempt to turn his flank, Hays led a portion of his command to engage them. The troops filtered into the ravines and split into two or three separate groups. At the same time, Saunders and Captain Stewart advanced with the remainder upon the enemy who were situated in a ravine to the front. The Indians were driven across a succession of crests, which enabled Hays's left flank and center to link up and make a concentrated assault. Other Paiutes were positioned atop the chain of mountains from which they directed an enfilade fire on the right flank of Hays's troops. A detachment of regulars and another of volunteers scaled the heights in the face of a murderous barrage and drove the Indians from the summit. The two howitzers were brought onto the plateau, but were never able to range the enemy.[168]

The battle covered a distance of some three miles and ended three hours after it began with the general dispersion of the Indians. Twenty to fifty warriors were killed and a great number were wounded. Hays suffered only seven volunteers and four regulars killed or wounded. Following the fight, the mutilated and putrefying remains of Ormsby's doomed men were gathered for a proper burial. Hays disbanded the volunteer regiment at Virginia City on June 12, ordered the return of arms and public property, and departed for Fernwood.[169]

His fighting days at last behind him, Hays was named to be one of Alameda County's delegates to the state Democratic convention, and supported the candidacy of John Cabell Breckenridge. As a Jacksonian Democrat who had shed blood to bring Texas into the republic, he believed in preserving that Union, but he also refused to fight against friends and family in Texas or Tennessee. His considerable military capabilities led both sides of the coming conflict to seek his services; instead, Hays pursued a neutral course. He did, however, accept an appointment from Governor John Gately Downey to the state militia as inspector of the First Brigade, Second Division.[170]

Hays became one of the major developers of Oakland, and held financial interests in waterfront property and city lots, the Union National and Union Savings banks, and the Oakland Gas Light Company. The 1860 federal census valued his real estate holdings at $160,000, while his personal estate was assessed at six thousand dollars. Hays had been an advocate for making Oakland the seat of state government and contributed Franklin and Washington Squares to the county. The two locations became the sites for the Hall of Records and the Hall of Justice. He also donated tracts to various churches. His civic involvements included membership on the University of California Board of Regents and a directorship of the Deaf, Dumb, and Blind Asylum. By 1870, the federal census valued his real property at $200,000, and his personal estate at ten thousand dollars. In 1876, Hays represented the Second Congressional District as a delegate to the Democratic national convention in St. Louis, and nominated Samuel Jones Tilden for president.[171]

Even as the colonel prospered in business, his family experienced both joy and sorrow. His son, Henry Thompson, nicknamed "Harry," was born in 1861, but he died on August 27, 1877; Richard and Susie died in 1862 and 1863 respectively; and Elizabeth Brenham, also known as "Betty," was born on December 28, 1869. Richard and Susie were buried in Old

Oakland Cemetery and later removed to Mountain View Cemetery, where Harry was laid to rest.[172]

For years, Hays had suffered from the effects of rheumatism and exposure due to his years of active field service, including the Washoe campaign of 1860. Ever the planner, he transferred the assets of his extensive portfolio to his wife, his eldest son, and other family members, retaining land worth ten thousand dollars in his own name. Surrounded by family members and a few friends, he died on April 21, 1883, of a pulmonary hemorrhage. Following a funeral service at St. John's Church attended by members of the Veterans of the Mexican War organization, and the Society of California Pioneers, he was interred in the family plot at Mountain View Cemetery.[173]

Following Hays's death, Susan sold Fernwood to water magnate William Jackson Dingee and purchased the latter's home in Oakland. For the last twenty years of her life, she resided with Betty's family in Denver and Oakland. She died on May 18, 1913, of old age, and was buried eleven days later at Mountain View.[174]

John Caperton Hays attended Washington and Lee University in Lexington, Virginia. Returning to California, he married Anna McMullen on November 3, 1880, and fathered two sons. He was engaged in reclamation work on the Sacramento River and farming in Alameda County, and worked as a cashier for the Mount Whitney Power and Electric Company in Visalia. He died on June 13, 1911, at Adler's sanatorium of Bright's disease, and was buried in Mountain View Cemetery.[175]

Betty married Princeton University graduate John McMullen, Jr. on January 4, 1888, and they lived in Denver, Colorado, for a time. Along with business ventures in mining and agriculture, he served as president of the Fresno National Bank with headquarters in San Francisco. Betty bore him two sons and a daughter. John died on January 8, 1903, while in Tucson, Arizona, seeking relief for his consumption. Betty then married insurance agent Joseph Hewes Norris in a private ceremony on October 1, 1908, but they divorced sometime prior to 1920. She was active in the Red Cross, and was a member of the Town and Country Club of San Francisco. Betty died of influenza on January 31, 1944, at Peralta Hospital in Oakland, and was buried in Mountain View.[176]

Given his stamp on the ranger service, one may be forgiven for failing to recall Jack Hays spent only eleven years in Texas. His campaigns against Comanche raiders and Mexican bandits, and the battles fought by his two regiments in Mexico, made him the archetype of the Texas Ranger. Even though ranger companies, battalions, and regiments had taken the field in previous years, Hays was the man who set the traditions of personal courage and gallant leadership that would be expected of future Texas Ranger captains.

Ben McCulloch. Engraving from Civil War Photograph Collection. *Courtesy Prints and Photographs Division, Library of Congress, Washington, D.C.*

Chapter 3

Ben McCulloch: "A Man Who Personified Courage and Daring"

Ben McCulloch was a man of many qualities. A scion of the eastern planter aristocracy, he was nevertheless at home on the borderlands. He was the chivalrous Southern gentleman who was on familiar terms with presidents and senators, as well as the backwoods brawler. Although without much formal education, he was an avid student of military history, and was considered to be one of the nation's foremost experts on firearms and military affairs. These combined traits served him well in a long, adventurous career, and enabled him to be a man who personified courage and daring. William H. Tunnard pronounced McCulloch "a bold, graceful rider, a desperate fighter, a reckless charger, a border man, and an Indian fighter of the highest type." His greatest ambition was to be a professional soldier and a leader of fighting men, but when opportunities to achieve that goal were not available, he sought position and fortune in various business endeavors and public offices. Chief among the abilities he possessed were the essential skills of the partisan scout. From battlefields in Mexico to Arkansas, his special talents involved penetrating the enemy's lines, acquiring intelligence on strength and dispositions, and escaping with not only the information, but also his life. This long-standing practice of personally observing his foe's designs would eventually lead to his demise.

He was born November 11, 1811, on the family plantation along Stone's River in Rutherford County, Tennessee. His parents were Major Alexander and Frances Fisher (Le Noir) McCulloch. Born on April 16, 1777, in Lunenburg County, Virginia, reared mainly in North Carolina, and educated at Yale College, Alexander had served as volunteer aide-de-camp to Generals Andrew Jackson and John Coffee during the Creek War. Frances had been born in Virginia on April 11, 1780. Besides Ben, the children of Alexander and Frances included Alexander McCulloch III; John Stokes McCulloch; Sarah Montfort Stokes McCulloch; Samuel McCulloch; Mary Ann McCulloch; Andrew Jackson McCulloch; Frances Olivia McCulloch; Harriet Maria McCulloch; Henry Eustace McCulloch, born December 6, 1816; James Coffee McCulloch; Elizabeth Julia McCulloch; and Adelaide Delia McCulloch. The family had once been prominent in colonial North Carolina, but much of their affluence had been lost in the course of the Revolutionary War, or squandered by Alexander. In fact, he so misused his birthright he was financially unable to formally school his younger sons. In 1820, the family transplanted to Florence, Alabama, but moved back to Tennessee ten years later, settling in Dyer County.[1]

Ben McCulloch spent his formative years hunting meat for the family table, clearing the forest for farmland, and piloting cypress log rafts of merchandise down the Mississippi River to Natchez and New Orleans. The hard work toughened his body and gave him the abilities of marksman, woodsman, and boatman—worthwhile skills for later wars in Texas, Mexico, and Arkansas.[2]

In 1835, Ben and his younger brother, Henry, determined they would seek their fortunes in Texas. Their friend and neighbor, Colonel David Crockett, was in the midst of a heated political campaign to retain his congressional seat. If he should lose the race, the legendary frontiersman planned to accompany the McCullochs to Texas. Once Crockett was defeated in the election, he was anxious to begin the journey and left without the brothers. Delayed by family business, Ben and Henry departed home in the fall, crossed the Mississippi River at Memphis, and entered Texas at Gaines' Ferry in January 1836. Once they reached Nacogdoches, Ben convinced his younger brother to return home and care for their aging parents. The older sibling followed the Crockett party across the Trinity River to Nashville. Here he was stricken with measles and had to be nursed back to health. Meanwhile, Crockett kept his rendezvous with destiny in San Antonio and entered into the pantheon of Texas heroes.[3]

After the fall of the Alamo, Major-General Sam Houston, Alexander McCulloch's old Creek War comrade, assumed command at the Texas army's Gonzales camp on March 11. The general found a disorganized and ill-trained rabble of "three hundred and seventy-four effective men, without two days' provisions, many without arms, and others without ammunition." Two days later, Houston ordered the destruction of the stores that could not be moved and sank his two brass 24-pounders in the Guadalupe River. With those disagreeable chores completed, he led a retreat eastward to seek more favorable ground. The army reached Burnham's Crossing on the Colorado on the sixteenth, remained two days, then continued their retrograde movement. Panicked Texian and *tejano* civilians fled ahead of the advancing Mexican columns in a mad flight that became known as the "Runaway Scrape." Once Houston's men were encamped at Jared Ellison Groce's plantation on the Brazos River on March 31, he struggled to organize his ever-changing number of troops into a proper fighting force of two regular infantry companies, two volunteer regiments (including two cavalry companies), and one artillery battery.[4]

Having recovered from his illness, Ben arrived at Groce's Crossing and enlisted in Captain William Hester Patton's Columbia Company on April 8. He then transferred to Lieutenant-Colonel James Clinton Neill's artillery corps on the thirteenth. Two days prior, Captain Isaac Newton Moreland's battery had taken possession of the "Twin Sisters," two 6-pound iron field-pieces donated to the Texian cause by the citizens of Cincinnati, Ohio. The Twin Sisters were to be the only cannons in the army's inventory. Private McCulloch was assigned to take charge of gun No. 1.[5]

With the massacre of James Fannin's men at Goliad, Houston's army was the last hope for the nascent Republic of Texas. His prudent refusal to advance upon the numerically and logistically superior enemy nevertheless caused the men to grumble, and President David Burnet to lose confidence in his general. Undeterred, Houston withdrew to Harrisburg, arriving on the eighteenth. *Generalissimo* Antonio López de Santa Anna had grown complacent and dismissed Houston's force as a threat. At the same time, Captain Henry Wax Karnes's scouts discovered that the Texans were now fortuitously on the road behind the Mexican Army of Operations. Leaving his baggage train and his sick in camp under guard, Houston ferried his men across Buffalo Bayou and marched along its east bank toward the San Jacinto River. Reaching Lynch's Ferry on April 20, his scouts found the Mexicans also arriving. The Texians withdrew a half-mile to a position in a live-oak grove with Buffalo Bayou to their backs, and an open prairie to their front extending two miles from Vince's Bayou on the right to the San Jacinto on the left.[6]

By eleven-thirty a.m., Mexican cavalrymen were approaching the thicket where Houston's army was arrayed. The rebels' volunteer infantry was deployed in the woods on the flanks; the Twin Sisters were in the center supported by the two regular infantry companies. The Texian artillery spoke before the enemy horse could draw closer. Not yet having fired their weapon in the campaign, even in practice, the gun crew overshot their first round, but the Mexicans panicked and galloped back to the main body. Santa Anna ordered his single cannon, thought to be a twelve-pounder, to deploy forward and engage the Texians. The Mexican piece, dubbed the Golden Standard, opened fire, but the cannonball crashed through the treetops and smacked harmlessly into Buffalo Bayou. The Twin Sisters advanced ten paces to meet the enemy, and their barrage resulted in two Mexican pack mules killed and a caisson and ammunition box destroyed. Colonel Neill was wounded in the exchange. The opposing artillery and infantry skirmished for a time, but the commanders kept their respective forces from a general engagement. At three o'clock, the *santanistas* withdrew to the other end of the clearing, and fortified their position behind breastworks of timber and pack saddles. Later in the day, the Texian cavalry made an attempt to seize the enemy cannon until their Mexican counterparts forced them to retreat after a sharp fight.[7]

The next day, Houston dispatched Erastus "Deaf" Smith and six volunteers to destroy Vince's Bridge and cut Santa Anna off from reinforcements. Meanwhile, 930 tired and angry Texians were deployed on the high ground. At four-thirty in the afternoon, General Houston gave the order for which his men had been yearning when he instructed the troops to advance on the Mexican camp. Colonel Mirabeau Buonaparte Lamar, and the cavalry, was posted on the right flank; the artillery, under acting commander Colonel George Washington Hockley, in the center; Lieutenant-Colonel Henry Millard's regulars next; then the two volunteer regiments of Colonels Edward "Ned" Burleson and Sidney Sherman on the left. Captain Juan Nepomuceno Seguín and his company of *bexareños* marched shoulder to shoulder with the Anglos of Sherman's regiment. Commanding one of the Twin Sisters, McCulloch and his nine-man crew moved forward with the infantry line until the enemy was approximately two hundred yards distant. They commenced a steady fire and advanced after each discharge, keeping to the fore of the line of infantry. As Colonel John Milton Swisher later recalled, "I have never heard two pieces of cannon fired as rapidly as those two pieces were on that day." The Mexican twelve-pounder managed three shots before a Texian cannonball smashed the field-piece's water bucket and frightened the gunners into fleeing. McCulloch stopped less than one hundred yards from the enemy breastworks, prepared the gun to fire again, but paused when General Houston rode across the front of the Texian line. "The Raven" then advanced upon the Mexican army, approximately one-third of the distance between the opposing forces. Mexican soldiers chose this moment to charge the Texian artillery, but Burleson's screaming infantrymen rushed the enemy barricades first. With the other rebel forces also storming the camp, the Mexicans were overrun and fled in panic. The vengeful Texians and *tejanos*, remembering the massacres at Goliad and the Alamo, pursued and mercilessly slew fugitives floundering in Peggy's Lake and the surrounding marsh. Scores of other *soldados* attempted to escape along the road to Vince's Bridge and the lane became littered with their corpses. As one unapologetic participant recounted, "We just killed 'em till we got tired." In eighteen minutes of actual battle, and a slaughter that lasted until nightfall, Houston and his army scored a surprising and historically significant victory. At a loss of seven dead and thirty-four wounded, four of them mortally, the Texians and *tejanos* killed 630 Mexicans and captured more than seven hundred; the most important of the prisoners proved to be Santa Anna himself.[8]

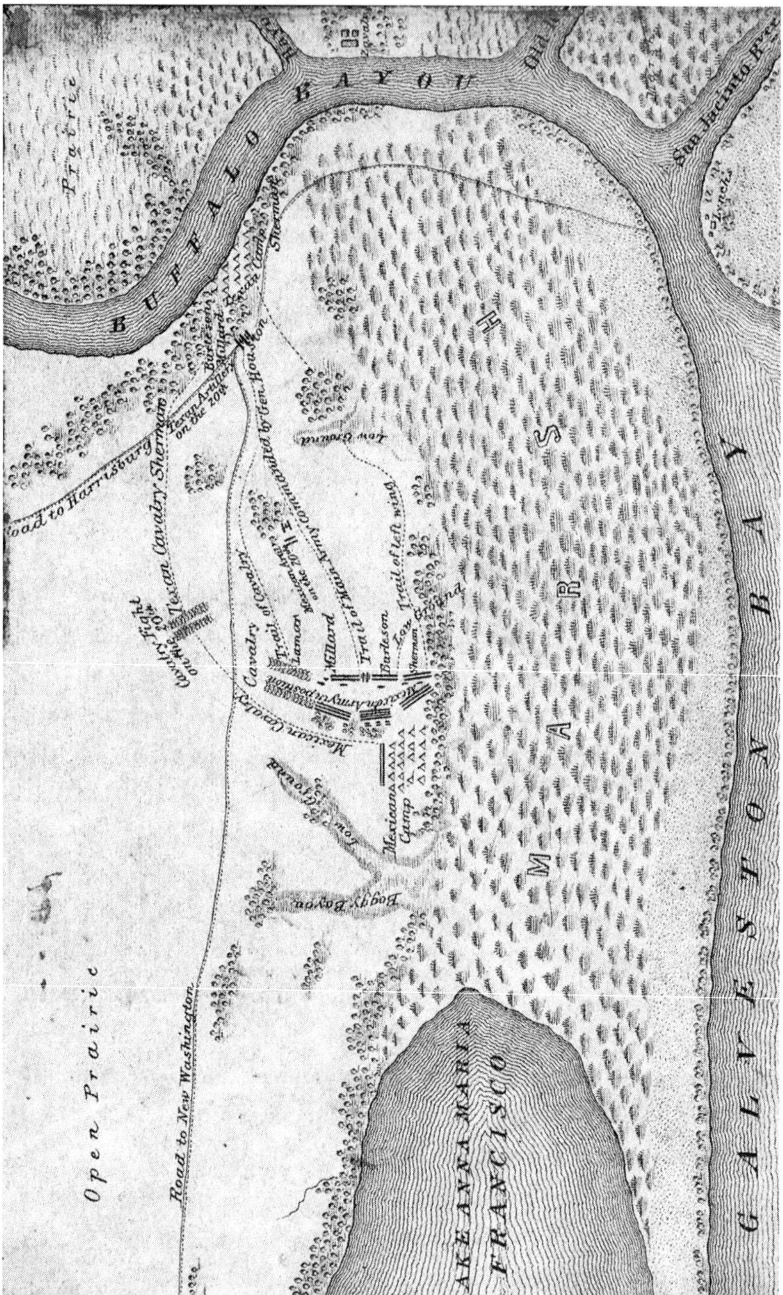

Map of San Jacinto. From Henderson King Yoakum's *History of Texas.*

McCulloch's courage and ability in the battle won him praise, and he was elected first lieutenant on May 6. Later a poem, entitled "Ben McCulloch at San Jacinto," was written about his exploits.[9] Victor Rose, his first biographer, would declare of the fledgling soldier with, perhaps, a touch of hyperbole:

> There was an air about the thoughtful, cool and courageous young man which arrested the attention. Scrupulously neat in his dress, which was the plain "homespun" of the backwoods, and courteous in his manners, he seemed in the surging mass of wild, rough humanity which celebrated the victory with boisterous hurrahs, a being *sui generis*; for though his bright, intelligent blue eyes would kindle on such occasions with unwonted animation, the emotions swelling within his bosom were held in abeyance by an inflexible force of the will but rarely witnessed.[10]

In the aftermath of the Texian victory, the Mexican Supreme Government was unwilling or unable to prosecute the war further, at least for the time being. Vicente Filisola, the second-in-command of the Army of Operations, was under orders to not risk Santa Anna's life and consequently led his four thousand men through mud and rain toward the Río Grande. By June 18, when the last fatigued and dispirited Mexican soldier crossed the river, Texas had achieved *de facto* independence. For ten years, though, Mexico would refuse to recognize Texian sovereignty or relinquish its claims to the lost province, despite being incapable of regaining the territory.[11]

Desiring more active service, McCulloch resigned his commission to enlist as a private in Captain Thomas Robbins's cavalry company on June 5. Still not finding the action he craved, McCulloch resigned on July 19, and left to explore the Lavaca and Guadalupe River valleys. He then operated a sawmill in Houston before returning to Tennessee to study surveying under his father. In February 1838, he departed his home state and settled in Gonzales, working as a surveyor on the expanding frontier. Later in the year, he plotted the proposed location for the town of Seguín. Henry finally traveled to Texas in July of the same year, and the two McCullochs shared a cabin until the younger brother's marriage in 1840.[12]

Comanches struck the Guadalupe River settlements in October 1838, and carried away thirteen-year-old Matilda Lockhart and four other children from the Mitchell Putnam home. Hearing of the raid in Gonzales, the McCulloch brothers joined with Captain Mathew "Old Paint" Caldwell, a veteran ranger and Indian fighter, in raising volunteers to pursue the Indians and liberate the children. The settlers pursued the Indians up the Comal River to its mouth, but lost the trail when it entered the Hill Country. Andrew Lockhart urged his neighbors to continue, but they persuaded him to return to the settlements, collect more men, and resume the search. Their efforts would prove futile.[13]

In early 1839, McCulloch organized a private expedition intended to capitalize on Colonel John Henry Moore's February 15 fight at Spring Creek. He also continued to hope he could recover Matilda Lockhart and the Putnam children. To this end McCulloch gained the assistance of the nearby Tonkawa Indians. In mid-February, a two-week period of brutally cold sleet and snow caused him to postpone the expedition. Once the temperatures warmed, he experienced some difficulty finding volunteers willing to risk a renewal of the unusually harsh winter weather. Finally, on March 1, he led four Texians, including Henry, and thirty-five Tonkawas in a search for the Comanches' winter camp. The friendly Indians were headed by "Captain Jim Kerr," a chief who had adopted the name of a Gonzales settler he admired as his own. On the second day of the march, McCulloch's party was near the headwaters of Peach Creek when they discovered the fresh footprints of Indians headed for Gonzales. The find caused the men to change their plans, and McCulloch determined they would follow the trail and, if necessary, attack the suspected raiders.[14]

The volunteers tracked the Indians for three or four hours before they sighted thirteen Wacos and Comanches, who responded by entering a dense thicket. The enemy warriors held the tactical advantage from their concealed position, and any move by the Texians or Tonkawas to approach exposed them to their hidden foes' fire. The two sides exchanged a number of shots for several hours. One Tonkawa was killed while situated behind the only tree available to the attackers. Declaring the hazards to be too great and his tribesmen too few to risk losing, Captain Jim had opposed entering the thicket since the beginning of the fight. At last, McCulloch obtained a promise from the chief to position his warriors at the lower end of the thicket and kill any raider who tried to flee. Meanwhile, McCulloch would take his men and crawl into the heavy brush from the upper end; one of the Texians chose to stay behind.[15]

McCulloch and his three volunteers cautiously crept through the scrub and each killed an Indian in succession. They also wounded two or three others. The Indians responded with an ineffective fire of musket balls and arrows. Finally, nine of the original nineteen broke and fled toward the lower end of the brush. Captain Jim and his Tonkawas allowed them to escape into the next large thicket and disappear.[16]

The cannibalistic Tonkawas scalped the four dead Indians, removed portions of the slain men's thighs and breasts, and hacked off their limbs. Afterwards they started for home to celebrate the victory. Along the way they stopped to perform a mystic war dance bewailing the loss of their fellow tribesman, and exalting in the deaths of their enemies. Once the ceremony was completed, they hurried onward to repeat the gruesome spectacle at their village. McCulloch and his men followed at a more sedate pace and returned to Gonzales for a hero's welcome.[17]

Following his successful fight with the Indians, McCulloch stood for election to the House of Representatives in the spring of 1839. His opponent was Alonzo B. Sweitzer, a doctor hailing from Ohio. McCulloch won the seat by a significant margin, and Sweitzer responded by calling the new congressman a "moral coward" for having refused to debate him. The argument might have turned violent then and there but for the reemergence of Vicente Córdova.[18]

After the defeat of his uprising the previous August, the rebel leader had continued to agitate the Texas Indians in opposition to the Republic. Once Córdova's location was confirmed, Colonel Edward Burleson, commander of the Texas army, hurriedly raised eighty volunteers and defeated three hundred revolutionaries at Mill Creek on March 29. Córdova was wounded in the arm before he fled. Following the Mill Creek fight, Córdova's insurgents headed to the Guadalupe River, but discovered it too perilous to cross. Instead, they marched through the night and struck the river six miles above Seguín.[19]

In response to the emergency, Mathew Caldwell had raised the Gonzales County ranger company and mustered it into service on March 16. McCulloch refused the position of first lieutenant, but promised his assistance in recruiting men. A portion of the company was stationed at Seguín under First Lieutenant James Campbell, while the remainder under Caldwell was camped on the Guadalupe, positioned midway between Gonzales and Seguín. Caldwell was in Gonzales in the early hours of March 30, when he learned of the previous day's battle. He called for volunteers to supplement his company, and informed them he would pull out at daybreak.[20]

Along with approximately fifty other men, McCulloch and Sweitzer both agreed to serve with Caldwell. The feud flared again when each man believed he was responsible for locating Córdova's trail. Sweitzer formally challenged McCulloch to a duel, but the latter demurred as the existing rebel menace took precedence over their personal quarrel. The chase led past the Guadalupe, through the country north of San Antonio, west-northwest to the Old Presidio de Río Grande Road, where it crossed the Río Frio, and down the road to the Nueces. Córdova maintained a steady lead of thirty to forty miles on his pursuers.[21]

Shortly thereafter, the trail was lost again, and McCulloch approached Caldwell on the Blanco River to ask him if the hunt had ended. Caldwell replied that, indeed, the chase was over for now. Carrying his rifle, McCulloch confronted Sweitzer, who was sitting nearby, with the offer to resume their dispute. The doctor arose but, not liking the look in McCulloch's eyes, kept his hands empty and stated he was not ready to fight. McCulloch observed that Sweitzer's weapons were at hand and promised him every opportunity to use them. The cowed doctor still refused. Even though Sweitzer had "been publicly disgraced without resenting it," McCulloch decided he also could not be shot down "like a dog." Instead, McCulloch contented himself with ridiculing his enemy as "a black-hearted, cowardly villain, in every respect beneath the notice of a gentleman."[22]

The company lingered in San Antonio to acquire supplies. A severely wounded chestnut horse, abandoned by one of Córdova's men on the trail, had caught McCulloch's eye. Obtaining Caldwell's permission to leave, McCulloch and a companion found the horse, later known as "Old Pike," and soon nursed the animal back to health. Caldwell returned to Seguín where he disbanded his company on June 16.[23]

In the summer, McCulloch and Henry were engaged in surveying a new wagon road from Gonzales to the seat of government being formed at Austin. Returning to Gonzales, McCulloch received another challenge from Sweitzer, this time delivered by Colonel Reuben Ross, Sweitzer's second. According to the *code duello*, since Sweitzer had proven he was not a gentleman, McCulloch was obliged to refuse the invitation. However, protocol also required Ross, an honorable man and McCulloch's social equal, to take up the matter. The two men, who had no actual personal quarrel, were now set at odds by deeply ingrained traditions of principle and pride. Acclaimed historian Bertram Wyatt-Brown, who primarily studied the South, reflected that "almost all [dueling] arose because one antagonist cast doubt on the manliness and bearing of the other, usually through the recitation of ritual words—liar, poltroon, coward. The stigma had to be dealt with or the labels would haunt the bearer forever." He went on to observe that:

> dueling was a means to demonstrate status and manliness among those calling themselves gentlemen … the duel set the boundaries of the upper circle of honor. They excluded the allegedly unworthy and therefore made ordinary brawling appear ungentlemanly, vulgar, and immoral. In a hierarchal society, all these factors were socially significant. They made violence a part of the social order even in the upper ranks, but at least duels helped to restrict the bloodletting, which otherwise would have been much more chaotic and endlessly vindictive.[24]

The principal and the second faced each other on October 6, 1839, in a field two miles north of town. Standing forty paces apart, McCulloch and Ross leveled their rifles at each other and fired when the word was given. Ross, an experienced duelist, was slightly quicker and shot McCulloch in the right arm. The ranger's own aim was spoiled and his bullet missed its intended target. With honor satisfied, they left the field as friends. Ross went so far as to arrange for his personal surgeon to treat McCulloch's wound.[25]

With his injured arm unusable and resting in a sling, McCulloch took his seat in the Fourth Congress on November 15. The legislature had convened its first session four days previously. In time, he was named to the committees on Finance and Enrolled Bills, and to a select committee deliberating on a petition for the financial relief of a citizen. McCulloch's votes were mostly routine, including those on the election of judges, the construction of a bridge across the Guadalupe River, the creation of the Houston Chamber of Commerce, the regulation of elections, and the incorporation of Rutersville College in Fayette County. He did take to the floor to offer a joint resolution authorizing the Gonzales County surveyor to maintain his office in his private home.[26]

Although McCulloch and Ross had considered their dispute ended, the former was indicted by a grand jury in November for "contriving and intending to break the peace of this Republic, setting at naught the quiet and good morals of this community." He was arrested on March 13, 1840, and brought to trial on April 6. The district attorney refused to prosecute.[27]

After the recovery of the cruelly tortured Matilda Lockhart, and the affair at the Council House in San Antonio in March 1840, the Penatʉka Comanches began organizing a raid on the Texian settlements in late July. The Indians deliberately ceased their normal pursuits, and instead busily procured firearms and ammunition. They parlayed with their ancient foes, the Cheyennes and Arapahos, to acquire a large herd of horses in exchange for guns, blankets, and kettles.[28]

On August 4, five to six hundred warriors, women, and children led by Potsanaquahip (Buffalo Hump) descended out of the Hill Country west of Austin, and dashed for the coast. The next day, a mail carrier riding from Austin to Gonzales discovered the trail of a large number of Indians in the vicinity of Plum Creek heading southeast. The postman hurried to Gonzales and raised the alarm. McCulloch assembled twenty-four volunteers and rode to examine the tracks. He also issued a call for settlers along the Guadalupe and Lavaca Rivers to come aid in stopping the marauders.[29]

McCulloch's party left Gonzales at four a.m. on August 6 bound for the Big Hill settlement, some sixteen miles from town in the direction of the Lavaca River. Making camp on the six-hundred-foot-high ridge that evening, the volunteers found the trail made by the Comanches early the following morning. They were joined at that point by Captain Adam Zumwalt and thirty-six men. The Gonzales and Lavaca volunteers followed the tracks of the Indians toward Victoria, deploying scouts to the front and on both flanks. At approximately noon, the outriders spotted a party of horsemen moving toward the trail, and the two groups warily approached each other. The newcomers were revealed to be sixty-five men from the Cuero and Victoria settlements, led by Captain John Jackson Tumlinson, Jr.[30]

Tumlinson brought word that Victoria had been attacked the previous afternoon. The Comanches had entered the outskirts of town at four o'clock and ultimately killed ten residents, kidnapped a black girl, and stole fifteen hundred horses and mules. Despite being caught unawares the determined townsmen were able to keep the raiders from reaching the populated neighborhoods. The three companies combined forces and, by mutual agreement, Captain Tumlinson was given command of the 125 volunteers. Unbeknownst to the Texians, the Indians returned to Victoria on August 7 and killed two more men, one of them long-time army quartermaster Pinckney Coatsworth Caldwell. The Comanches burned one house and robbed several others before the heavily armed townsmen drove them off. Riding south, the raiders captured Nancy Crosby and her infant near Nine Mile Point. They later murdered Mrs. Crosby's baby when the child grew hungry and could not be quieted. The war party then rode to the east across the prairie, ultimately for Linnville in Calhoun County. As they moved toward the unsuspecting town, they killed another man.[31]

On the early morning of August 8, the Comanches rode in and slew four residents, kidnapped two women and a child, stole a number of goods, and fired the buildings. The survivors could only watch from the boats anchored in the bay to which they had fled. By the late afternoon, the jubilant Comanches, their thirst for vengeance quenched, began their return trip to the Hill Country along the west bank of Garcitas Creek, fifteen miles east of Victoria.[32]

Tumlinson's combined force arrived in Victoria about sundown, when he and his fellow captains received the news of Linnville's sacking. The three companies took a short rest and gathered supplies before moving out. They made camp at Casa Blanca Creek, a small branch of the Garcitas, at midnight. Tumlinson dispatched a courier to recruit additional men from Texana and La Grange.[33]

On the morning of August 9, scouts reported the considerable party of Comanches making their way back from Linnville laden with booty. Tumlinson moved his men to intercept the Indians on a flat, treeless prairie near the Garcitas. The Gonzales and Lavaca companies under McCulloch and Zumwalt were deployed on the right, closest to the enemy, and the Cuero and Victoria volunteers under Tumlinson twenty paces to the left. Tumlinson dismounted his men as they moved to attack. A portion of the Comanches encircled the Texians, while the balance kept riding on with the loot. Tumlinson's force and the Indians exchanged fire for approximately twenty minutes, which resulted in one volunteer killed and three horses wounded. At least three, and possibly four, dead Indians bore witness to the Texians' marksmanship.[34]

McCulloch strongly advised a charge to scatter the Comanches, but Tumlinson feared the less battle-hardened of his men would fall behind and risk annihilation in detail. The option was lost as the last of the Indians slipped away along the same route they had ridden to the coast. The horses of Tumlinson's battalion were spent, and the captain decided to pursue at a slow, steady pace. He wanted to keep the enemy concentrated, rather than forcing them to disperse. He also hoped to find a wooded area where he could engage the Comanches again, using the timber to his advantage. They rode for some twenty miles and made camp at Chicolete Creek that night.[35]

McCulloch was furious Tumlinson had not seized the earlier opportunity to smash the Comanches. He turned command of his company over to his lieutenant and took three trusted subordinates to Gonzales to raise more men. He also sent messages to Colonel Burleson and Captain Caldwell to rendezvous with him, and any other armed volunteers, at Isham Good's crossing on Plum Creek in present Caldwell County. Tumlinson's force continued to pursue the fleeing Comanches throughout the next day in the hopes of bringing them to battle. He was ultimately unsuccessful, but he did drive them toward the Texians gathering at Plum Creek.[36]

Helping to raise volunteers in Gonzales, McCulloch, his three men, and Henry joined a thirty-man company under Captain James Bird. While the citizens were assembling, Henry scouted ahead for signs of the Comanches. He rode east fourteen miles to Big Hill and spied the raiding party with Tumlinson's three companies still trailing. Henry returned to town and reported his sighting to his brother and Bird. The latter assembled his company, and they made for Plum Creek. Shortly after Bird's departure, fifty-nine Gonzales men under Captain Caldwell and twenty-two Lavaca volunteers under Captain Lafayette Ward arrived in Gonzales. They joined forces and left town one hour later. The various volunteer companies reached the rendezvous throughout the morning, afternoon, and evening of August 11. The last to arrive that day was militia commander Major-General Felix Huston and his aide.[37]

At six a.m., on August 12, a scout from Bird's company reported the Comanches were three miles away and approaching the crossing. Caldwell spoke briefly to the assembled one hundred volunteers. He acknowledged the numerical superiority of the enemy, but stated his belief in the necessity of attacking. The emboldened men were mounted and lined up for battle within twenty minutes. "Old Paint" rode again to the front of the formation and courteously called on General Huston to take command. The general was an experienced soldier, but he had never before fought Indians. Demonstrating respect for Huston's rank, none of the men protested, although most would have preferred Caldwell lead them.[38]

Huston ordered his men forward three miles from the crossing and across several ravines. They entered a small clearing separated from the larger prairie by a thicket of trees and brush along a creek bed. Having received word Burleson was rushing to the scene, Huston formulated his battle plan, which called for a "hollow square" to be employed. The front side would be left open while he would deploy Burleson's troops to form the right face of the square and Caldwell's men the left. The rear side, acting as the reserve, would be Bird's and Ward's companies under the command of Major Thomas Monroe Hardeman.[39]

As the volunteers watched from their places of concealment, the gaudy column of Comanches, which extended for nearly a quarter-mile, rode onto the prairie. At the same moment, Burleson and his men reached the scene and Huston informed the newly arrived colonel of his arrangements. Burleson, undoubtedly the most experienced Indian fighter on the field, wasted no time in debating who should command. Instead, he cordially accepted Huston's leadership. Once assembled, the Texian force advanced on the Comanches at a trot. By this time, the retreating Comanches were a mile and a half away. As Huston's troops drew within striking range, their pace increased to a gallop. The Indians spotted the Texians and several bands broke away from the main body to confront the white men.[40]

The rearguard skirmished with the pursuing Texians, while the rest of the Comanche cavalcade drove the stolen livestock and plunder toward safety. Huston's riders steadily closed the distance until the Indians turned at bay at some oak trees near a place later known as Kelley Springs. To the Comanches' rear was the Clear Fork of Plum Creek, while to their left was a boggy stream that blocked their line of retreat. The Texians were able to avoid the swampy portion, which only stretched a short distance. Once within two hundred yards of the Comanches, Huston ordered his troops to halt and dismount on the open prairie. He then directed them to form the hollow square he had earlier devised. A number of the old hands at Indian fighting were reluctant to abandon the advantages offered by their horses. As they secured their mounts, a small band of Indians began to ride in circles around them, while darting in and firing from behind their shields. When the range closed to within eighty yards, the Comanches would wheel their horses away before moving in again. The distance kept the combatants from doing any real damage.[41]

In this early phase of the battle, Henry was credited with saving the life of Alonzo Sweitzer, his brother's old enemy. Sweitzer had gone forward to shoot at an Indian, only to be charged by eight to ten Comanches. He was seriously wounded by an arrow that pinned his arm to his body. Henry and another volunteer advanced to hold back the Comanches and allow the injured man to escape. Sweitzer later returned the favor when he shot an Indian closing on Henry, while the latter was reloading his weapon. Although the two Texians had saved each other's lives, neither expressed any gratitude.[42]

The main element of the Comanches continued to herd their *caballado* of stolen horses and mules northwest, while the rearguard delayed the Texians. After a notable chief was either killed or gravely wounded, the Indians let out a loud, sorrowful howl. Burleson, Caldwell, and Ben McCulloch all urged

Battle of Plum Creek. Oil on canvas painting by Lee Herring. *Courtesy William Adams and Collections Division, Texas Ranger Hall of Fame and Museum, Waco, Texas.*

Huston to drive into the Indian formation and check their escape. Caldwell exclaimed, "Now, General, is your time to charge them! They are whipped." McCulloch galloped up to his commander and, with flashing eyes, shouted, "General Huston, this is no way to fight Indians; they are fooling with us. They are running off with their captives and plunder—order a charge, and we can kill hundreds and rescue the women and children."[43]

Huston heeded his more experienced subordinates and ordered his troops to break through the Comanche lines. The Indians quickly dispersed into smaller bands and fled, but they continued to fight as they ran. Once the boggy branch of the creek was passed, Huston's control over his men ceased as they likewise scattered and pursued individual targets for up to fifteen miles. The Comanches abandoned horses and booty-laden pack mules in their flight, and some took refuge in the thickets. McCulloch led thirty mounted men to a marshy creek where they ambushed fleeing Indians slowed by the mud. Henry slew one, but the rest made it across. McCulloch and his detachment raced after them. One by one, the Texians overtook and killed at least five of the enemy; Ben accounted for one warrior. The chase stopped when the Comanches reached the timber on Morrison's Creek, a tributary of the San Marcos River. The McCulloch brothers and two other men scouted up the San Marcos and across to the Clear Fork of Plum Creek. They were not able to find more combatants, but they did discover an abandoned Indian woman and a child. With the prisoners in hand, McCulloch and his comrades returned to camp, arriving about dusk.[44]

Huston's volunteers suffered one killed and seven wounded. Two of the female captives had been murdered by the Comanches. Another had been seriously wounded, but she would recover. Huston estimated the enemy's casualties to have been forty killed. The tally was increased to eighty on August 14, and to 186 on September 28. The Texians recovered two hundred horses and mules, many of them laden with plunder. They also took a total of thirty prisoners, most of them women and children. Huston wanted to send men in pursuit of the Comanches, but the horses were too exhausted to resume the chase.[45]

The following month, Huston was authorized by President Lamar to exploit his victory and lead a major expedition into Indian country.

The general planned to recruit sixteen hundred men, using volunteers from the general public and members of the militia brigades. His efforts to raise the manpower were "coolly" received and ultimately futile.[46]

Even while Huston was unable to mount his campaign, Colonel John H. Moore received eager approval from the president for his own foray. In addition to Fayette County, the call for volunteers was also circulated in Gonzales. McCulloch wrote a letter on September 9 encouraging the citizens of Victoria and Texana to join up. Despite gathering slightly over a hundred volunteers, Moore set out for the upper waters of the Colorado River and won a smashing victory at the Red Fork on October 24.[47]

Meanwhile, the regular army's Frontier Regiment decided to conduct their own expedition. Major George Thomas Howard was appointed to command, and his orders were to sweep through the Cañon de Uvalde and on to the headwaters of the Colorado. Howard issued a call for volunteers, and the always reliable Paint Caldwell answered. He raised a Gonzales ranger company on September 25 that boasted several veterans of the recent Plum Creek battle, including Ben McCulloch. McCulloch had been intent on going with any of the recent expeditions. On September 9, he had co-signed another letter to the citizens of Victoria and Texana petitioning for a suspension of the district court's fall term so volunteers could go into the field.[48]

The Gonzales volunteers rode to San Antonio and joined Howard's two regular infantry companies, a company of Anglo Béxar citizens, and another of fourteen *tejanos*. The entire force was estimated to be 180 men. Howard led his column out of San Antonio on September 29. They marched north and west for the first two weeks, encountering the headwaters of the Nueces, Frio, Pedernales, Llano, and San Saba Rivers. Howard had received intelligence that the latest small raids in the Béxar area were initiated by Indians encamped to the west of San Antonio. Once the expedition had reached the Nueces, Howard's scouts reported fresh tracks indicating a large concentration of Indians. They continued on past tributaries of the Nueces and the Río Grande and found more sign of a recent Indian presence. On the afternoon of October 12, the major ordered the heavy supplies to be left with a small detail, while the remainder of the expedition would make a forced march in pursuit of the hostiles. He hoped to reach the enemy camp before dawn the following morning. The Texians trudged on until midnight when the spies lost the trail.[49] Howard later reported:

> The men were halted, ready to move on at any moment. The guides, however, could not discover the trail during the night. At daybreak, it was found on our right, and I dispatched Capt. Caldwell, Mr. McCulloch, and a Mexican to examine it. They soon returned and reported to have seen Indians, and that we were discovered.[50]

Howard swiftly ordered his men into their saddles, and they rode hard the ten miles toward the Comanche *ranchería* located at the head of Las Moras Springs. Previously alerted to the Texians' presence, the Indians had already fled. The soldiers and rangers found few inhabitants left in the camp. The Texians with the best mounts were able to kill three Comanches. Howard's men also quickly captured a young Indian woman, who was later killed, and a stolen Mexican child. The chase continued for approximately five miles, during which four Comanches were overtaken and dispatched. With this minor victory, Howard called a halt as the horses were exhausted. The Texians rode back to the *ranchería* in the late afternoon. There they found a large store of provisions and sturdy winter quarters. Howard ordered the food and tents destroyed. On October 14, the expedition left the camp with several captured Comanche rifles and 125 horses and mules. They marched to the heads of the Frio, Guadalupe, and Llano Rivers. After sending a detachment of scouts to the San Saba, the rest of the column moved downriver to the Pedernales. The scouts returned on November 6 and reported no fresh signs of Indians in that region. Hopeful that Moore was faring better, Howard decided to call an end to his own campaign the following day. He left the Pedernales country and reached San Antonio on November 11. The Gonzales rangers arrived home five days later, at which time they disbanded.[51]

McCulloch was involved in his community as more than just an Indian fighter. The home schooling he had received from his Yale-educated father had left him with an unquenchable thirst for learning. As a result, he helped to found Guadalupe College on January 30, 1841, and served on its board of trustees. In this capacity, he was also responsible for developing the school's curriculum.[52]

In late April or early May 1841, a war party of twenty-two Indians made a nighttime raid into the Gonzales area. They stole a sizeable number of horses and were headed back to their mountain stronghold before daybreak. McCulloch gathered together Henry, James Hughes Callahan, and thirteen other companions to pursue the marauders. Instead of immediately rushing after them, he decided to remain in town for a few days, and lull the Indians into a false sense of security. Once he felt the Indians had come to believe the Texians were refusing to follow, McCulloch and his party set out after them. They found the trail, which crossed the San Marcos River at the mouth of Mule Creek. They followed the tracks north and west to the head of York's Creek, through the hill country to the Guadalupe, and then up the river to the main northern mountain tributary of the Guadalupe, presently known as Johnson's Fork, in Kerr County. The volunteers followed the trail along this fork to its source, then northwest to the head of Johnson's Fork of the Llano in Kimble County and down to its junction with the Llano.[53]

Before striking the river, the captain halted his company in an isolated area. He was certain they were near the Indian encampment. Alone, he made a personal reconnaissance of the enemy position. McCulloch was able to approach close to the Indian camp, make an accurate survey, and afterwards lead his men into their own bivouac. At dawn, the volunteers attacked, taking the Indians completely by surprise. They killed five warriors and wounded all but eight. The Indians fled, leaving behind horses, saddles, camp equipage, blankets, robes, and moccasins. By the actions of McCulloch and his men, the raiders had learned they could be hunted down and punished, even in that distant and wild location.[54]

McCulloch decided to not seek a second term in Congress, even though Henry asserted he "could have beaten any man in the county" regardless of the type of election. Instead, he devoted himself to surveying and Indian fighting. On the Texas borderlands, the two were often one and the same. Surveyor and author Wilson Forrest Daniell observed:

> The surveyor with compass became a main enemy of the Indian. With rifles at their sides, the surveyors read the compass, cut brush along the boundary lines, and chained distances. The surveying parties, in drawing

> the fire of hostile Indians, were the first line of defense of the weak colonists. Usually working beyond the frontier, the surveyors frequently were first to encounter Indians bent on depredations and the first to spread the alarm among the settlements.[55]

When the opportunity arose, McCulloch volunteered for a more official role. James Callahan raised a company of Gonzales County minutemen on July 7, 1841, and McCulloch joined on the eleventh. He re-enlisted on October 24, and continued to serve until December 18.[56]

On January 9, 1842, *General de división* Mariano Arista declared that Mexico would never recognize Texas as a sovereign nation and would, instead, seek to recover her lost colony. At the request of John C. "Jack" Hays, McCulloch traveled to San Antonio in early March and enlisted in the former's ranging company. On March 2, he and Alsey Silvanus Miller reconnoitered toward the Medina River. The two rangers were near Hondo Creek on the fourth, scouting the road leading from San Antonio to the Río Grande. Situated in a concealed position in the chaparral, they observed *General de brigade* Ráfael Vásquez leading a column of seven hundred *soldados*, militia, and Caddo Indians. Vásquez occupied San Antonio without difficulty and ordered the town plundered. McCulloch and Miller rode some eighty miles to the Nueces to scout the enemy there, then rejoined Hays on March 6 as the ranger company withdrew to the Flores *rancho* near the Guadalupe River. The captain knew reinforcements would be on the march as soon as news of the invasion spread. Before additional support arrived, though, Vásquez pulled his troops out of San Antonio and moved them to the border.[57]

The Texan Congress responded by passing a bill that granted President Sam Houston near-dictatorial powers and declared war on Mexico. Reasoning the measure was impractical and unconstitutional, and understanding the republic's limitations, the president vetoed the pronouncement on July 22. Given the foul mood on both sides of the border, conflict was certain.[58]

Still believing in taking some proactive measures, President Houston authorized McCulloch, on June 18, to raise a spy company of between fifty-six and sixty-six men. The executive instructed McCulloch to only take men who could provide "a first rate horse and the arms and equipment requisite and appropriate for the service contemplated." Available records do not indicate whether McCulloch successfully organized the company. He went on to make additional, albeit unproductive, efforts for the republic after July 21. On that date, he received orders from Secretary of War and Marine George Washington Hockley to report to Colonel Moore on the Medina River by August 15. Moore had been authorized to raise a regiment "for the purpose of securing the country upon this side of the Rio Grande, and, if necessary, operating upon the enemy's country." The planned expedition was canceled when word reached Texas that the Mexican government, in a gesture of goodwill, was releasing prisoners taken in the failed Santa Fé Expedition. On August 21, Colonel Hugh McLeod and 182 captives were delivered to Galveston by a Mexican warship.[59]

In September 1842, *General de brigade* Adrián Woll, a French-born soldier of fortune, and fifteen hundred Mexican troops crossed the Río Grande and marched on San Antonio. President Houston responded by issuing orders to the fighting men of Matagorda, Brazoria, Victoria, Colorado, Fort Bend, Fayette, Gonzales, Austin, Washington, and Bastrop Counties to assemble for the emergency. McCulloch was visiting friends living on the upper Colorado River when the invasion began. He arrived at the Texian camp just hours after the battle at Salado Creek ended on September 18. Mathew Caldwell and 225 volunteers had soundly defeated a numerically superior Mexican force at relatively little cost to themselves. Later that evening, McCulloch reconnoitered the Mexican positions around San Antonio and penetrated the lines to the walls of the Alamo. He reported to Caldwell and advised an attack the next morning. Hard rains on the nineteenth impeded any further progress, and another scout conducted about midnight revealed Woll had evacuated the city under the cover of darkness.[60]

At ten a.m., on September 20, Caldwell learned of the Mexican retreat and immediately set forth in pursuit. The Texians reached the Medina, two miles above the Presidio Road crossing, around midnight. While Caldwell's troops rested, McCulloch and Hays went forward to scout the Mexican camp near the Cañon Ford of the same river. The two rangers returned with one captive. Later in the morning, members of Hays's company again reconnoitered and succeeded in taking another four prisoners. While these enemy troops were being captured, the entire Texian force was at odds on whether to assail Woll's retreating column. By four o'clock that afternoon, more reinforcements had arrived to swell the pursuers' ranks to between 489 and five hundred men, and the decision was made to attack. Before moving upriver, Caldwell's fortified command divided into two battalions under John Moore as lieutenant-colonel and James Shannon Mayfield as major. Caldwell remained in charge and was elevated to the rank of colonel. The volunteers advanced to within four miles of Woll, but Hays reported at midnight that the invaders had broken camp and were retreating toward Mexico. Caldwell's troops followed straightaway, although they were delayed by having to cross the flooded Medina.[61]

The rangers raced ahead and overtook the Mexican rearguard about three p.m. on September 22. Concealed in a creek bed, the *soldados* opened fire on the approaching Texians. The rangers hurriedly dismounted and formed to engage the ambushers. Caldwell's forces were a mile and a half to the rear, and the outnumbered Texians waited thirty minutes for the anticipated attack. Hays learned Woll was moving toward the Arroyo Hondo, some fifty miles from San Antonio, with the intention of crossing the river. The Mexican general reached the Hondo slightly below the mouth of Quihi Creek and prepared a defensive position on the east side. On a bluff, he placed one cannon with a twenty-man gun crew and infantry support to cover the troops crossing the river to the west side.[62]

Colonel Caldwell marched his volunteers faster to reach Hays. An additional 150 horsemen were dispatched to reinforce the ranger captain. His numbers thus enlarged, Hays gave the order to charge the cannon on the hill. Fifty Texians pounded up the slope while the Mexican artillerymen failed to account for the inclining ground, and overshot the racing horsemen. The rangers and volunteers gave a great shout, which unnerved the enemy infantrymen and prompted them to fire at the rapidly advancing charge. Several Texians were wounded, but the rush continued unabated. The gun crew had time for one more missed shot before the horsemen were among them, shotguns and pistols blazing. The Mexican infantry was dispersed, and the artillerymen were all killed or wounded in the *mêlée*. Woll would report he lost five killed and an undetermined number wounded. Four Texians were injured.[63]

Although they had successfully seized the artillery piece, the Texians were only to keep possession for ten minutes. A large number of Mexican infantrymen advanced on the bluff, and Hays was forced to withdraw just as Caldwell's troops were beginning to arrive. The two sides traded a few random shots as night fell. Woll made camp a short distance away, and the large fires he ordered built lulled the Texians into believing his force would remain. Instead the Mexicans slipped away in the night. Ranger scouts later discovered the ruse.[64]

Caldwell convened a council of war on the morning of September 23. Hays and his rangers favored a resumption of the pursuit, but other voices thought the fights on Salado Creek and in the Arroyo Hondo were sufficient and wanted to return home. McCulloch stepped forward and urged those who were willing to join him in attacking. Dissent among the leaders surfaced, and the majority chose Colonel Moore to replace Caldwell. The latter's followers refused to support the former. In the end, the volunteers returned to San Antonio.[65]

The McCulloch brothers remained in town to await the forthcoming offensive campaign. Brigadier-General Alexander Somervell was appointed to be the expedition's commander, and was ordered to satisfy the popular demand for action:

> You will proceed to the most eligible point on the South Western frontier of Texas, and concentrate with the force now under your command, all troops who may submit to your orders, and if you can advance with a prospect of success into the enemy's territory, you will do so forthwith.[66]

Somervell subsequently received instructions on October 13 to make his headquarters on the Cíbolo, east of San Antonio. The general was tardy in arriving, and found his Army of Southwestern Operations already assembling in town. On October 17, Ben enlisted in Hays's ranger company as a private, while Henry retained his rank of first lieutenant. On November 7, the recruits concentrated at the Mission of San José in order to organize the army's two regiments. Five days later, the brigade moved to Camp León on León Creek, seven miles west of San Antonio.[67]

Most of the expedition departed San Antonio on November 12, and marched to the Medina River; Hays's rangers followed three days later. Once there, Somervell waited nearly two weeks for the arrival of a cannon and the gun's commander. Both appeared on November 23, and the general at the last moment elected to leave the artillery piece behind. Meanwhile, the brigade was decimated by desertions and forced to reorganize into a single regiment and several unattached companies. Major Hays's rangers retained their independent status. Setting out for the Río Grande, the column missed the dirt road to Laredo, due to the driving rain, and instead marched across the wet prairie. They literally stumbled into a vast bog and fought through the thick mire for nearly three days before reaching firm ground. Numerous horses were lost in the struggle to escape, and most of the rest were "damaged."[68]

When the army finally reached the Río Grande on December 6, they found the river to be at flood stage. The men refused to cross without the aid of rafts or boats. Hays detailed McCulloch, Samuel H. Walker, and others to steal all the Mexican boats available and hold them for the army's use. On December 8, at about four a.m., the companies of Hays and Bogart were sent on foot into Laredo to seize the town. McCulloch captured a young boy who had come to the river to water his mule. From the youth, the Texians learned the Mexican garrison and many of the citizens had fled, abandoning women, children, and a few old men. The townspeople left behind professed joy at seeing the rangers and, indeed, the *alcalde* surrendered to the Texians. When General Somervell marched into town with the remainder of the army, he found the Texas flag flying over the town square.[69]

After a number of the men elected to return home, Somervell led his army, now numbering fewer than 550, in a meandering tramp through difficult terrain along the east bank of the Río Grande. On December 15, several small boats were found, and the expedition went downriver toward the Mexican town of Guerrero, sixty miles below Laredo. McCulloch and ten rangers reconnoitered the road to the town.[70]

Finally realizing the futility of continuing the campaign, Somervell issued Order No. 64 on December 19, which instructed the army to march to the junction of the Frio and the Nueces Rivers, and thereafter to Gonzales for disbandment. The expedition splintered with only 189 officers and men obeying the directive. The rest decided to carry on, and elected William S. Fisher as their new commander. McCulloch was persuaded to accompany the insubordinate group for a few days. On the twenty-second, while Fisher's command moved down the east side of the Río Grande, McCulloch led twelve rangers in scouting the west bank to the town of Mier. Finding a large number of Mexicans in the area, he returned to Texas and delivered the sobering news to Fisher. Undaunted, the colonel decided to invade Mexico and capture Mier. McCulloch persuaded him to hold off until a more thorough search could be made. The following day, McCulloch and twenty-five men rode back to Mier and accepted the *alcalde's* surrender. While there, the private learned that a Mexican force of fifteen hundred *soldados* and assorted militia was marching on the town. McCulloch reported to Fisher and strongly advocated returning to the interior. The colonel refused, confidant in the prowess of his Texians, and the men were intent on looting the town. On December 24, Ben and Henry, Thomas Green, Robert Addison "Ad" Gillespie, and some others decided they had had enough. They left Fisher's ragtag army on the banks of the Río Grande and returned to San Antonio. McCulloch was officially discharged on January 17, 1843.[71]

Having missed the ensuing battle at Mier, and avoided months spent in Mexican prisons, McCulloch returned to the ranger service. He volunteered for Hays's company on September 10, and served until the end of the month. He signed up again on February 25, 1844, and was elected first lieutenant. McCulloch was not present for the historic fight at Walker's Creek, although he did provide details in a letter to Thomas J. Green. He mustered out on June 26 and reenlisted the following day, serving until October 28. His next enlistment began on October 29, and ended on December 29. In late August, and again in December, McCulloch supplemented his income by carrying dispatches from San Antonio to Washington-on-the-Brazos. The Texas government had moved from Austin to that location after the Woll invasion of the previous year. Employing Hays's company was deemed the only secure method of transmitting official messages to and from the temporary capital.[72]

Texas would not remain a sovereign nation for long, and her annexation, and the deployment of United States troops to Corpus Christi and the

Río Grande, would come to dominate the lives of men like McCulloch. In early September 1845, he assisted Jack Hays in recruiting men for new ranger companies in federal service, and designated Gonzales as the place of rendezvous. He himself enlisted in Captain Robert Gillespie's company of Texas Mounted Rangers on the twenty-eighth. In addition to being carried on the rolls of Gillespie's command, McCulloch was elected to the House of Representatives of the First Legislature in December and, on February 16, 1846, he was appointed one of the body's three tellers. Four days later, he was named to the committee on the militia. He mustered out of Gillespie's company on March 29. On April 21, the state militia reorganized into five districts, each one commanded by a major-general. McCulloch was elected the commanding general of the Fifth District, which encompassed lands west of the Colorado River.[73]

Once the United States and Mexico were at war, Brevet Brigadier-General Zachary Taylor exercised the authority given him by President James Knox Polk to call up the Texas militia. The general requested Governor James Pinckney Henderson to raise four regiments of volunteers, two mounted and two infantry, "to serve for the longest period authorized by law, unless sooner discharged."[74] After hearing of Taylor's appeal for troops, McCulloch raised a company on his own initiative rather than wait for a gubernatorial directive. Thirty-six hours after he had begun, he had collected sixty-two men from the Guadalupe settlements, and the company was enrolled at Gonzales on May 11. McCulloch was elected captain, John McMullen first lieutenant, and James S. Allen second lieutenant. Immediately heading south, the men passed through San Patricio and Corpus Christi, down Padre Island, and reached Matamoros on May 23.[75]

After spending two or three horrid weeks at "Camp Maggot," opposite Matamoros, the officers and forty-one privates were mustered into federal service on June 13 as McCulloch's Company of Texas Militia; their enlistment was fixed at three months. Although they had originally intended to form Company A of Hays's First Texas Mounted Rifles, the change in their status was due to General Taylor's detaching the company from Hays's command and assigning the rangers to his headquarters as an independent spy company.[76] At this time, McCulloch was thirty-five years old and possessed a

Zachary Taylor. Engraving by Alexander Hay Ritchie, New York City.
Courtesy Prints and Photographs Division, Library of Congress, Washington, D.C.

decade of experience fighting Mexicans and Indians. One of his men would later describe the "celebrated partisan scout" as

> a man of rather delicate frame, about five feet ten inches in height, with light hair and complexion. His features are regular and pleasing, though, from long exposure on the frontier, they have a weather beaten cast. His quick and bright blue eye, with a mouth of thin, compressed lips, indicate the cool, calculating, as well as the brave and daring energy of the man.[77]

Unlike their regular army counterparts, the Texas ranger companies traveled light, needing little in the way of logistical stores, and were comfortable with living off the land. For instance, on June 15, Taylor's assistant adjutant general issued instructions that a lieutenant of McCulloch's company, to be designated by the captain, was to draw funds from the senior assistant quartermaster in order to procure supplies along their route. However, by then, the company was already gone on a scout. McCulloch had been detailed by General Taylor to reconnoiter between Fort Brown and Monterey, capital of the state of Nuevo León, "to gain information touching the number and position of the enemy, and the resources of the country." On June 12, even before the company was officially enrolled, he and forty men rode from Matamoros toward Linares in the wake of General Arista's army withdrawing from their defeat at Resaca de la Palma.[78]

Three days later, they engaged a mounted party under Blas Falcón, a notorious *guerrillero*. McCulloch and several rangers had risen in the early morning and were saddling up when they heard the sound of approaching horsemen. Immediately mounting, McCulloch and an ever-growing number of rangers rode to where a party of *rancheros* had been halted by the posted sentinels. The Texans and Mexicans were dressed alike, and in the predawn darkness the guerrilla leader could not see whom he faced. The Mexican asked, "*Quien vive*?" Fluent in Spanish, McCulloch answered, "*Amigos*." Evidently his accent alerted the partisan who shouted, "*Los malditos americanos*!" The *rancheros* turned and galloped away, which gave them a good lead on the rangers filing onto the road. All of the horsemen dashed into the chaparral, the raiders dividing right and left over the rocky ground. Several

Texan horses stepped into holes and fell; one threw its rider. Finally, the rangers reined in as the *guerrilleros* jumped from their horses, dropped their weapons, and vanished into the brush. Disgusted at being denied a fight, the Texans returned to camp, retrieving the Mexicans' abandoned horses, guns, and gear along the way. McCulloch and his men pushed on, often finding evidence of the retreating Mexican army's passing. Within sixty miles of their goal by June 20, the rangers decided the road was impracticable as a route of invasion, being without sources of water and subsistence. McCulloch also learned Arista and his battered forces had arrived at Monterey. The company rode on to Reynosa arriving two days later. They had been gone for ten days and had traveled 250 miles through enemy territory.[79]

McCulloch's company rested in Reynosa for three weeks. Several members of the company were veterans of the Mier Expedition, and had spent an unpleasant time in the village. A number of the local Mexicans also foolishly boasted of killing and pillaging north of the Rio Grande. These braggarts were often later found shot or hanging from tree limbs. No one ever officially connected the Texans with the deaths, and one wit opined the men were so remorseful over their raids they committed suicide.[80]

One evening, while McCulloch was in Matamoros on business, Lieutenant McMullen was informed that *ranchero* chieftain Antonio Canales Rosillo (the "Chaparral Fox") was attending a *fandango* at a ranch six miles from Reynosa. Formally a colonel of militia, Canales was believed to be responsible for the murder of Colonel Truman Cross, Taylor's quartermaster. Assembling the company, McMullen rode for the ranch.[81] They observed lights emanating from their intended target at a distance of a mile. As they stealthily approached, they saw that

> the dance was held in the open air; and the bright fires kindled at different points, the candles and torches moving to and fro, the animated groups of revelers clustered on every side, the white robes of the girls prettily contrasting in the fire-light with the dusky apparel of their partners; while gay forms, replete with life and motion, bounded in the lively dance, or floated in the graceful waltz, in sweet accord with the spirit-stirring strains of music which the night-breeze wafted to our ears.

"Halt!" McMullen ordered. "Dismount! Creep up cautiously, men, and surround the house—and when I call you, come up quickly and firmly at the charge."[82]

The lieutenant then loosened his pistols in their holsters and sauntered into the midst of the crowd. The Mexicans were surprised and, before they could react, they were encircled by the rangers. The women exclaimed, and the men attempted to break through the ring of Texans before leveled rifles forced them back. McMullen directed a search of the house but no trace of Canales could be found. The lieutenant was inclined to avoid a confrontation with the crowd and apologized for disturbing the festivities. He explained the rangers had heard the noise of the dance and stopped to investigate. As the celebrators calmed, they invited the rangers to join them, and the two or three best dancers in the company chose partners from among the girls. The rangers spent an enjoyable evening before they departed for camp. Their only disappointment was in not finding Canales.[83]

Samuel Chester Reid, Jr., an attorney who became adjutant of the Sixth Louisiana Volunteers, had heard of the exploits of the Texas Rangers. Through the efforts of newspaper correspondent George Wilkins Kendall, Reid was introduced to Captain McCulloch in Matamoros, and informed the ranger that he wanted to join the troop. After examining the applicant's horse, McCulloch agreed to take him on. Reid was mustered into the company on June 24.[84] In the book he would subsequently write of his experiences, the lawyer-turned-ranger described seeing his new comrades for the first time:

> Men in groups with long beards and moustaches, dressed in every variety of garment, with one exception, the slouched hat, the unmistakable uniform of a Texas Ranger, and a belt of pistols around their waists, were occupied drying their blankets, cleaning and fixing their guns, and some employed cooking at different fires, while others were grooming their horses. A rougher looking set we never saw. They were without tents, and a miserable shed afforded them the only shelter … Notwithstanding their ferocious and outlaw look, there were among them doctors and lawyers, and many a college graduate.[85]

McCulloch returned to Reynosa on July 7 before moving with his men to join the advance guard at Camargo. On the sixteenth, General Taylor appointed McCulloch to his staff as quartermaster with the rank of major, although his primary role was that of chief of scouts. On the twentieth, and again on the twenty-third, McCulloch requested permission for his company to proceed in the direction of Monterey. Approval for the task was eventually given. Seeking the best route by which to take the city, McCulloch and fifty rangers conducted a reconnaissance on August 3 up the San Juan valley to the town of China. After a forced march of some sixty miles along the western road, they arrived at one o'clock on the morning of the fifth. McCulloch learned Juan Seguín, who had been obliged to defect to Mexico in 1842, was leading a band of 115 *rancheros* in the area. He made preparations to attack the former *tejano* patriot, but Seguín fled when he learned of the ranger company's approach. McCulloch rode back to Camargo on August 6. When Taylor's headquarters reached the town on the eighth, the major reported the China road, while possessing nearby water sources, was unsuitable for heavy wheeled transports.[86]

The general then ordered detachments of McCulloch's and Gillespie's companies on August 12, to reconnoiter the Mier route. The rangers were accompanied by artillery officer Captain James Duncan and topographical engineer Brevet Second Lieutenant Thomas John Wood. Once in Mier, which still bore evidence of the desperate battle fought four years previously, McCulloch took to his sickbed and remained behind while Captain Duncan assumed command. The reconnaissance also became an offensive as Duncan forced the surrender of Cerralvo on August 14. The town would be used as a supply depot. Duncan returned to Camargo on August 17 to report the Mier route to be the best option. The rangers, in the meantime, detoured to Mier to retrieve their captain, who had nearly recovered.[87]

The company's enlistment expired on August 18, and all but twenty men were reorganized on the thirtieth into Company A, First Texas Mounted Rifles. McCulloch and James Allen retained their ranks, and William H. Kelley was elected first lieutenant; Fielding Alston was commissioned as an additional second lieutenant. McCulloch's men would not join their regiment just yet, as General Taylor still had work for them. On the same day, Taylor reorganized his army into two divisions. The first was comprised of the Second Dragoons, the First, Second, Third, and Fourth Regiments of infantry, and Braxton Bragg's and Randolph Ridgely's batteries; while the second included the Artillery Battalion, the Fifth, Seventh, and Eighth Infantry Regiments, Duncan's battery, and a company of Louisiana volunteers.[88]

Taylor began the campaign on August 21 by marching his troops south along the San Juan River. On September 1, McCulloch and Gillespie were ordered to report to Brigadier-General William Jenkins Worth, commanding the Second Division at Cerralvo. The Texans were on the road almost immediately, scouting the country in front of the American army. They arrived at Cerralvo on September 5. Seven days later, a party of pioneers and topographical engineers, escorted by McCulloch and twenty-five rangers, as well as a squadron of dragoons, marched ahead of the van to prepare the road to Monterey for the artillery and supply trains. Continuously screening the pioneer party by riding at least a mile in advance, McCulloch and thirty-five men encountered two hundred Mexican cavalry troopers near Ramos on September 14. The two sides exchanged a few shots that wounded two Mexicans and a Texan horse. The enemy formed to charge, but then inexplicably retreated. McCulloch's detachment entered nearly deserted Marin on September 15, and was joined by Taylor and the First Division that evening.[89]

Taylor waited at Marin for three days while the army concentrated. Hays's outfit was among them, and McCulloch's company finally joined its parent regiment. In the early morning hours of September 19, the American divisions broke camp and continued the march to Monterey. Later in the day, the commanding general, his staff, and McCulloch and twenty rangers rode ahead of the column to within one-and-a-half miles of Monterey. As Taylor extended his telescope to survey the city's defenses, a battery at the citadel, or the "Black Fort," about one thousand yards north of Monterey, began firing twelve-pound cannonballs at the reconnaissance party. When one of the projectiles landed twenty feet away, Taylor called for the group to move back to the approaching army and established an encampment at Walnut Springs.[90]

Worth's troops, with McCulloch's and Gillespie's companies in the van, then moved to their designated position to the west on the afternoon of September 20. Early the following morning, the division advanced with the Texans first in line, marching in close order, followed by Captain Charles Ferguson Smith's light companies of the First Brigade deployed as skirmishers, Captain Duncan's and Lieutenant William Whann Mackall's six-pounders, and finally three regular infantry regiments. Two or three hundred yards from the Saltillo road, at the *hacienda* of San Jeronimo, some two hundred Jalisco and Guanajuato *lanceros* commanded by Lieutenant-Colonels Juan N. Najéra and Mariano Moret were seen preparing to charge. Behind the horsemen were infantry, which combined with the cavalry totaled approximately fifteen hundred *soldados*.[91]

Under fire from Mexican artillery, five ranger companies dismounted and took cover behind a roadside hedge fence. Hays kept McCulloch's company in the saddle to protect his exposed right flank. The enemy cavalry formed into columns of six, fired a volley at the mounted Texans, and slammed spurs to their horses. McCulloch's riders met the charge with accurate fire, which failed to check the advance, and then crashed into the Mexicans. Professor Justin H. Smith remarked: "The shock was terrible; and like a lion and a tiger grappling the two bodies writhed and fought. The weight of the American horses proved a great advantage, but numbers were on the other side." The combatants fired their pistols, hacked and slashed with their sabers and knives, and battered their foes with clubbed rifles and shotguns. Only a few feet away, Hays shouted to his dismounted companies, "Here they come, boys, here they come, Give them hell."[92]

Captain Smith's battalion, still advancing in open order on the road, fired a volley. The Texans behind the fence delivered another that sent the *lanceros* reeling, but they gathered themselves for a second charge. Worth's infantry rushed forward and kept the supporting Mexican infantry from advancing, while the batteries of Duncan and Mackall dropped an effective fire upon the enemy foot. In fifteen minutes, the exertions of rangers and regulars forced the enemy into flight. Having charged into the center of the Mexican squadrons, McCulloch and several of his men were carried along with the retreat. They cut their way back to their regiment with seven bearing lance wounds, but over one hundred dead and wounded *lanceros* were strewn along the road, including the gallant Najéra. Despite the ferocity of the clash, only one Texan was killed.[93]

With the Saltillo road secured, Worth moved to take the western approaches to Monterey. Both Federación and Independencia were captured after fierce fighting. Once the garrison in the Obispado was decimated in an ambush, the Americans launched their attack on the city itself on September 23. The Texans led the way in clearing each house and street toward the central plaza. In the three days of fighting, McCulloch's company lost one man killed and seven wounded, four of the latter severely.[94] In analyzing the battle more than a century later, one professional soldier wrote the rangers introduced

> a new mode of fighting; one that greatly reduced friendly casualties while wreaking havoc on the Mexican defenders. These tactics stood in bold contrast to the massed infantry attacks across open ground that had been employed only two days prior at such dreadful cost. Despite the advantages of being on the defensive and enjoying interior lines, the Mexicans were unable to withstand the multi-pronged, three-dimensional attack of the Texas Rangers and continually gave ground.[95]

Before Worth could give the order to resume operations on the twenty-fourth, he received word that *General de división* Pedro de Ampudia had sent an emissary under a flag of truce to request a brief suspension of fighting; Taylor had granted the appeal. The two army commanders met in person later in the afternoon, and agreed to form a commission to negotiate terms for the city's surrender. The commissioners assembled the same day. They drew up nine articles of agreement that stipulated, among other items, the evacuation of Monterey by the Mexican army, that Mexican officers be permitted to retain their personal sidearms and enlisted soldiers their arms and accoutrements, that the Mexican army withdraw into the interior, and that Taylor's forces not advance beyond a predetermined line for a period of eight weeks.[96]

With the fighting ended for a time, the Texans were mustered out of the service on September 30, and the First Texas Mounted Rifles was disbanded. In his report to the War Department, General Worth extoled the martial qualities of the rangers, observing "every individual in the command unites with him in admiration of the distinguished gallantry and conduct of Col.

Hays and his noble band … We can desire no better guarantee of success than by their association." After touring the city and visiting friends, McCulloch left the army around October 8 with the understanding he would return if hostilities resumed. Accompanied by sixteen of his men, McCulloch headed for San Antonio. After crossing the Nueces, the Texans would have lost their horses to a pair of audacious Comanches, but for the quick actions of McCulloch and Captain James Cheshire, who drove off the Indians.[97]

The terms of Monterey's capitulation did not meet with overwhelming approval in the White House. President Polk, rejecting Taylor's cease-fire, ordered the general to end the truce and continue the war. Honoring the provisions of the agreement, Taylor notified *Presidente* Santa Anna at San Luis Potosí he would cross the line of demarcation on November 13. The American army occupied Saltillo three days after the armistice expired.[98]

In the months after the fall of Monterey, General-in-Chief Winfield Scott made plans to personally command an invasion into Central Mexico. He sent orders to Taylor instructing him to cease any further offensive operations, possibly to forestall the latter's political ambitions. Scott took nine thousand of Taylor's best troops and left him with a skeleton force. A fuming Taylor ordered Brigadier-General John Ellis Wool, who was campaigning in Chihuahua, to march to Nuevo León and join him there. When the reorganization was complete, the Army of Occupation had been reduced to five hundred experienced regulars, mostly artillery. The balance of the 4,759 troops were volunteers, most of whom had not seen action. Taylor's forces were arrayed in a defensive line stretching from Saltillo and Monterey to Camargo to the mouth of the Rio Grande.[99]

The Texas mounted companies that operated in northern Mexico throughout the war were a mixed blessing for the general, and, while he frequently complained of their conduct, he never discharged them until his purpose had been served. Despite his contradictory feelings for Texans, Taylor knew he required a troop of first-class scouts for his upcoming campaign. As Robert Utley observed, "Never did Zachary Taylor succeed in resolving his ambivalence about Texas Rangers." Having developed a warm personal relationship with McCulloch, Taylor recalled the veteran captain. McCulloch had been reelected major-general of the Fifth Texas Militia Division, but he answered the summons nevertheless. With some difficulty, he raised a company of twenty-seven men, mostly in Gonzales and Fayette Counties, and returned to Mexico, arriving in Monterey on January 31, 1847. He went on to Saltillo where Taylor had established his headquarters, and reported for duty on February 4. The rangers refused to enlist for the war's duration or even for twelve months. Since Taylor was in such desperate need for their services, the general ignored army regulations and agreed to their terms: "I determined to accept them for the period of six [months]; trusting that the peculiar necessity for their services would justify this departure from the prescriptions of the law." The outfit was mustered in as McCulloch's Company, Texas Mounted Volunteers (Spies) retroactive to January 31. Although enrolled as a captain, McCulloch resumed his old post of staff quartermaster and his rank of major.[100]

On the eve of commencing his overland campaign, General Scott ordered Taylor to abandon Saltillo and fall back to Monterey, but "Old Rough and Ready" declined to obey. Unwilling to cede the advantageous terrain around Saltillo to the enemy, he instead advanced his forces to a site eighteen miles southwest of Agua Nuéva on February 5. At the same time, having returned from exile in Cuba and reclaimed the presidency, Santa Anna intercepted a message from Scott to Taylor detailing the state of American forces in Northern Mexico. The dictator incorporated this information into his plans to attack and crush the *gringos*. His ill-trained and poorly equipped main element left San Luis Potosí on January 28, and began arriving at Rancho La Encarnación on February 17. He was situated only thirty-five miles from Taylor's lines.[101]

McCulloch was detailed to scout the enemy's position and left with sixteen men. Slipping into the dense chaparral and cactus, they reached the vicinity of Encarnación late on February 16, where they chanced upon the Mexican vanguard. The major shouted, "Charge 'em boys!" as the enemy began shooting. He was followed by only six men as the remaining horses were terrified by the gunfire. The Texans forced the Mexican pickets to retreat toward their camp. Once he heard a bugle call urging cavalrymen to stand to horse, McCulloch decided discretion was the better part of valor and turned his men around. They returned to Agua Nuéva early the next morning without having gathered the needed intelligence on the Mexican army.[102]

Undaunted, McCulloch and six rangers returned to the same area at four p.m. on February 20. The Texans successfully infiltrated the Mexican picket line that night, and gathered exceedingly accurate information on the size of Santa Anna's force. McCulloch sent Lieutenant Fielding Alston and four men back to Taylor to report their findings, while he and Sergeant William J. Phillips stayed behind to observe the camp in the daylight. After reveille sounded, and they slipped through three separate Mexican picket lines, McCulloch and his companion returned to Taylor's headquarters at two p.m. and reported the enemy force was divided into three grand divisions totaling twenty thousand *soldados*.[103]

Since the Agua Nuéva position was vulnerable to attack, Taylor redeployed his 4,800 soldiers fifteen miles to more defensible ground behind the defile of La Angostura ("The Narrows"), one and a quarter-mile south of the *Hacienda de Buena Vista*. The inaccessible arroyos to the west of the American position limited Santa Anna to three avenues of approach: the main road, the rising plateaus to the east, and a long, narrow ridge beyond.[104]

On the morning of February 22, McCulloch dispatched Lieutenant William Kelley and fifteen men to scout the Mexican lines near Agua Nuéva. The rangers had only gone two miles before they encountered the enemy. Lulled into a false sense of security by the captured letter and Taylor's retrograde movement, the "Napoleon of the West" was marching in great haste, and fifteen thousand Mexicans began arriving on the field at eleven a.m. General Wool, second-in-command of Taylor's army, made the initial placement of the American forces and was assigned to oversee the defense. McCulloch's company and Captain Enoch Steen's two troops of the First Dragoons were placed in reserve on the eastern heights to support the Arkansas and Kentucky mounted volunteers on the left flank. They took up a position in a ravine behind and to the right of Lieutenant George Henry Thomas's artillery section. As they settled in to await the enemy, the Texans, past masters at fighting Mexicans, were far more relaxed than the novice volunteers around them.[105]

Beginning at three in the afternoon, the Mexicans endeavored to force the American left, but the *Yanquis* held against the superior numbers. The more serious attack on that position occurred the following morning. Santa Anna's men repeatedly struggled to break Taylor's line, but each attempt failed. Steen's dragoons were ordered to fall back to a ravine closer to the American infantry, while the rangers relocated themselves to the head of a gorge in front of army headquarters. As these movements were being made, a renewed Mexican assault on the left drove the Arkansas and Kentucky volunteers back in confusion, followed by the Second Indiana regiment, and the Mexican horse plunged through the gap in the line. Colonel Jefferson Davis and the First Mississippi Rifles were ordered to plug the hole, while Captain Charles Augustus May instructed his dragoons and McCulloch's rangers to pursue the enemy cavalry. As the Mexicans reached the American wagon park at Buena Vista, they were met with a galling fire from the waggoneers and supporting infantry. May's horsemen arrived in time to finish the rout. After the Mexican charge was repelled, McCulloch convinced May to order an assault on the enemy's right wing with the dragoons' two cannons. McCulloch rode forward to reconnoiter the ground, and discovered an unhorsed *lancero* officer attempting to regain the Mexican lines. The ranger seized him and took him back to Taylor's paymaster. McCulloch's subsequent attempts to capture more prisoners were unsuccessful as the remaining lancers retreated under covering fire from the enemy infantry. Santa Anna sent an attacking force along the ridge on Taylor's extreme left, but excellent leadership provided by the general's staff, the gallantry of Davis's Mississippians, and deadly execution by the American artillery all contributed to the Mexicans being bloodily repulsed. The entire Mexican army finally withdrew toward Agua Nuéva during the night.[106]

Taylor wrote in his official report, "The services rendered by Major McCulloch and his men, particularly in reconnoitering the enemy's camp at Encarnación, and advising us certainly of his presences there, were of the highest importance." The Americans suffered 272 killed and 387 wounded, while Mexican casualties were 591 killed, 1,048 wounded, and 1,894 missing. With these losses, the enemy was rendered ineffective in Northern Mexico.[107]

After the Mexicans had withdrawn, McCulloch and his men were dispatched to trail the retreating army. On the night of the twenty-sixth, the rangers discovered Santa Anna's cavalry had formed a rearguard at

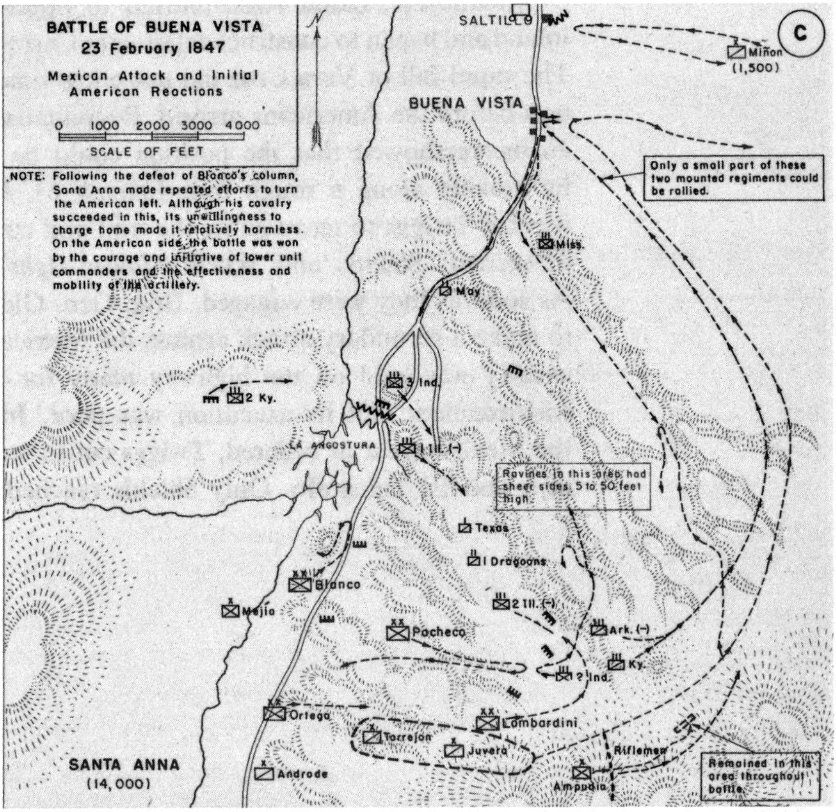

Map of Buena Vista. From *West Point Atlas of American Wars. Courtesy Geography and Maps Division, Library of Congress, Washington, D.C.*

Agua Nuéva, behind which the infantry and artillery had retired toward San Luis Potosí. Once the enemy horsemen abandoned their position on February 27, the American army reoccupied Agua Nuéva, and Taylor sent a strong command, including McCulloch's company, to retake Encarnación on March 1. They found there sixty unhurt Mexican soldiers and over two hundred wounded who had been abandoned by Santa Anna. Taylor later reported, "The dead and dying were strewed upon the road and crowded the buildings of the hacienda."[108]

Following the successful end of the campaign, McCulloch was detached from his troop and took up his duties as a staff quartermaster. The major was granted leave to return to Texas on March 5. Departing two days later, he proceeded to purchase 150 horses for the dragoons and the mounted Texas volunteers. While in La Grange, McCulloch also enrolled forty-two more men for his company on May 1. On the thirty-first, he and the new recruits herded the remounts from the Guadalupe to the Rio Grande where he passed them on to the appropriate officers. They then escorted a wagon train from Camargo to Monterey. Arriving at Taylor's headquarters on July 31, McCulloch discovered his company had been discharged in his absence on June 14. Taylor decided since the new volunteers had enlisted in good faith and had already supported the war effort, they were entitled to wages and allowances for the time they had served. Thus the recruits were mustered into and then out of federal service on the same day.[109]

During the time McCulloch was absent from the army, Texans had been causing problems for the commanding general. Even though he had benefitted from their endeavors, Taylor wrote, "The mounted men from Texas have scarcely made one expedition without unwarrantedly killing a Mexican … The constant recurrence of such atrocities, which I have been reluctant to report to the department, is my motive for requesting that no more troops may be sent to this column from the State of Texas." While rangers did wage war on Mexicans not in uniform, the general, regular and volunteer officers, correspondents, and later historians, until relatively recently, have each contributed to a shared, one-sided mindset. This outlook has led these individuals to blame all Texans in Mexico rather than individuals, sometimes without firsthand knowledge or primary evidence, wholeheartedly accept the testimony of enemy authorities, publish hyperbolic accounts in newspapers, and ignore or tolerate the misdeeds of other volunteers. While not excusing unrestrained behavior, Professor Jimmy L. Bryan, Jr. has noted how pacifists and anti-expansionists used "the Texas Ranger as an emblem of the degenerative influences of war and conquest" in order to denounce the conflict. Detractors have also rarely taken into account that Comanche warriors usually slew and mutilated captives, while Mexican soldiers and irregulars on numerous occasions declared *degüello* (no quarter), or used cease-fires and capitulation as a means to escape defeat. Such conduct on the part of their enemies would tend to make

Texans view the prosecution of war far differently than would soldiers from the older states.[110]

Resigning his staff commission on September 6, McCulloch returned to Texas and resumed the business of surveying. He also lobbied U.S. Senator Thomas Jefferson Rusk for assistance in obtaining a military command on the frontier. If securing a commission was not to be possible, he further petitioned Congress for an appointment as superintendent of Indian affairs in Texas when the law creating that position was enacted. McCulloch made a trip to Washington in the beginning of 1848, but was unsuccessful in gaining either office. Once Congress finally passed an Indian appropriations bill on September 30, 1850, the Taylor administration appointed three agents for Texas. None of the men named were Ben McCulloch.[111]

McCulloch was not on hand to express any disappointment. Like his friend Jack Hays, he had decided to seek his fortune in far-off California. He departed Austin on September 9, 1849, and planned to add several more men to his party in San Antonio. Following a long but "agreeable" journey of 934 miles, which included a ride through the rough country of the Sierra Madre, the argonauts arrived in Mazatlán on November 9. After waiting fifteen days in the midst of a cholera outbreak, the greater part of the company took the side-wheel steamer SS *Oregon* to San Francisco, arriving on December 1.[112]

Before he could begin to acquire any riches, McCulloch was appointed by Governor Peter Hardeman Burnett to be "collector of foreign mining licenses" for Mariposa County. As the title implies, his duties were to collect a fee of twenty dollars from each foreign miner in the county for the privilege to work their claims. Finding the position to be disagreeable and unprofitable, McCulloch remained in office for only two months before he returned to San Francisco on June 2. He went to the American River, but his mining claim there would not prove viable. Soon controversy in the new state would lead him to again enter public service. A legal contest between John Augustus Sutter and squatters questioning his Spanish land titles had turned ugly the previous November when he forcibly removed trespassers from his land. The latter individuals seized vacant private property around Sacramento as their own and built shanties. After one interloper was evicted from the lot he had appropriated and jailed, thirty to forty other armed squatters moved to release their compatriot and reclaim the land on August 14, 1850. Opposing them was Mayor Hardin Bigelow, Sheriff Joseph McKinney, and a party of vigilantes. In the street fighting that followed, the sheriff, the city assessor, and three squatters were killed; Bigelow was severely wounded.[113]

The death of McKinney created a void that demanded a special election on September 2. Within four days, as many as ten contenders advertised their candidacies. His reputation having preceded him, McCulloch was persuaded by his friends to enter the race. Even though he announced his intentions on the very day of the vote, he was elected sheriff of Sacramento County, and sworn into office on September 8. The job proved to be disappointing, and paid only slightly better than his previous position of tax collector. Regardless, the sheriff was regarded well enough to be appointed delegate for the city's Second District to the county Democratic convention. After Chauchila, Potoyanti, and Tomquit Indians attacked a trading post on the Fresno River, a ferry on the San Joaquin, and other mining camps and towns in the region, a militia force, dubbed the "Mariposa Battalion," was raised in January 1851 to punish the raiders. McCulloch was offered the command of the two hundred volunteers, but he refused on the grounds "it would bring him neither honor nor pecuniary advantage." Trader James D. Savage took the leadership role, and the battalion conducted three campaigns that convinced hostile tribes to surrender and accept reservation life.[114]

Once news of a new strike was announced, McCulloch made one last trip to the central valley's goldfields in the spring of 1851 and inspected several quartz mines; he purchased an interest in fourteen claims. His term as sheriff was to expire on April 1, 1852, and he chose not to run for reelection. Instead, he left his deputy in charge of the office and made plans to return to Texas. He sold his claim on the American River for one hundred dollars, but kept his holdings in the quartz mines. He left Sacramento on October 11, 1851, spent four days settling his affairs in the south, then departed California aboard the steamer *New Orleans*.[115]

After returning to Texas, he twice traveled to Washington, D.C. to press his petition for a regimental command. On the evening of March 5, 1853,

McCulloch was dining at the Brown Hotel when he was insulted by Elias Putnam West, the U.S. attorney for New Mexico Territory, who threw the contents of a water glass in his face. The Texan responded by striking West with a tumbler, then breaking plates over his head. He finished the brawl by severely beating the federal attorney with a chair. Although he was disenchanted with the nation's capital, and despite the affray with West, McCulloch was appointed U.S. Marshal for the District of Texas on March 29 by President Franklin Pierce.[116]

McCulloch arrived in Galveston on April 16, accompanied by Jack Hays, who was returning to California to assume his duties as federal surveyor-general. McCulloch went on to Tyler about May 15 to take his oath of office. The judge of McCulloch's district was John Charles Watrous, a virulent political enemy of Sam Houston, and one of the most notorious jurists ever to sit on the federal bench. On June 20, Watrous convened court in Tyler with U.S. Attorney Samuel D. Hay, Marshal McCulloch, and Deputy George Rosenbaum in attendance. Once the term at Tyler closed, the judge, the federal prosecutor, and the marshal headed for Brownsville. There they would handle a dilemma that had been brewing for months. In January 1852, Watrous had responded to a direct request from President Millard Fillmore and impaneled a grand jury to investigate José María Carvajal. The revolutionary had been using South Texas as a base from which to mount armed incursions into Mexico, and the embarrassed administration was anxious to resolve the diplomatic crisis. The jurors quickly returned a true bill on Carvajal and eleven Americans for violating the Neutrality Act of 1818. To allow Hay time to gather evidence and witnesses, the case was continued until the next term in Brownsville, which would not be held until the first two weeks of July 1853. Once court was in session, and the Carvajal case was heard, Watrous granted eight of the defendants a change of venue to the upcoming term in Galveston. The judge adjourned on July 18, and the next session was set to convene in Austin on November 28. McCulloch went to the state capital in October, and appointed Joseph Harrel as a deputy marshal. The term at Galveston convened on January 2, 1854, and Carvajal's case was swiftly thrown out by Watrous on a technicality. In addition, the trials of three of Carvajal's associates ended in acquittals. Hindered by a lack of support from local residents and the Pierce administration, Hay admitted defeat and entered a *nolle prosequi* (dismissal of charges) for the remaining accomplices awaiting trial. All was not lost as McCulloch learned of a new filibuster plot being organized near Brownsville in October, and took decisive action to quash the conspirators' designs.[117]

Despite the momentary excitement offered by quelling freelance military schemes, the life of a U.S. marshal in the 1850s was fairly routine. Rather than personally pursuing outlaws, McCulloch's general duties included the housing and care of federal prisoners, the leasing of county courthouses in which to hold district court, and the auctioning of seized assets, although his principal task was accounting for the court's monies. He was responsible for preparing estimates of the court's costs prior to each term, and allocating congressional appropriations to the judge, U.S. attorney, clerks, deputy marshals, and grand jurors. By law, federal marshals were the sole officials authorized to manage the court's expenditures, much to the chagrin of judges and prosecutors. In 1849, the newly created Department of the Interior had assumed oversight responsibilities for the marshals' accounts. As McCulloch attended court in Tyler, Galveston, and Austin for the next several years, his tenure was marked by incessant demands from the Interior Department for detailed reports, receipts and vouchers, and other administrative documentation. In return, the department was often tardy in providing the increasingly exasperated marshal the financial means to manage his office.[118]

Even as McCulloch struggled with the federal bureaucracy, momentous events were occurring on the national stage. From 1845 to 1848, the size of the United States expanded by more than a million square miles, and the Kansas-Nebraska Act of May 30, 1854, added even more territory to the nation. The resulting westward migration into the Great Plains and onward to Utah, Oregon, and California forced Congress to consider increasing the size of the peacetime army. Once the volunteer force that had marched into Mexico was demobilized, the regular military establishment stood at a mere ten thousand officers and men. The wagon trains traveling westward, and the pioneers settling on new lands, all required military protection, and the army was hard-pressed to satisfy their demands. Secretary of War Jefferson Davis advocated a larger force, especially in the mounted arm. Due to his efforts, on March 3, 1855, Congress passed an army appropriations bill authorizing two additional regiments of cavalry and another two of infantry. President Pierce signed the measure into law the following day.[119]

The command of a cavalry regiment had been McCulloch's dream for years. Since his time in the Texas revolutionary army, he had carefully examined the military campaigns of the Great Captains, including Alexander, Pyrrhus of Epirus, Hannibal, Julius Caesar, Charlemagne, Turenne, Vauban, Frederick the Great, and Napoleon. The libraries of Washington had offered him this opportunity the previous year between court sessions. As the *Encyclopedia of the New West* noted, "The popular impression was that he was a splendid scout and dashing cavalry officer; but only those familiar with his laborious studies and intercourse with our most eminent military men after the Mexican war, were aware of his profound knowledge of war as a science." Sam Houston, Congressman Peter Hansborough Bell, and other influential friends recommended the marshal for a colonelcy in one of the new regiments, and President Pierce personally promised him the appointment. Senator Rusk, although well-disposed toward McCulloch, promoted the case of Albert Sidney Johnston. Unfortunately, the endorsements for the ranger did not carry sufficient weight as Secretary Davis favored West Point graduates, in particular Johnston, his old academy classmate. Instead, the president called McCulloch to the White House on March 3, and tendered him a lieutenant-colonel's commission in the élite Second Cavalry. McCulloch replied he could not accept without first consulting with Rusk and Bell. The Texans spent the day discussing the offer, and McCulloch then informed Pierce at eight p.m. he would let Rusk, Bell, and the president decide whether he should accept. He did add that naming Henry as his replacement in the marshal's office would encourage him to agree.[120]

McCulloch went to his rooms at the Brown Hotel and received Secretary Davis the following morning. Davis informed him that the previous proposal was no longer on the table as Robert Edward Lee would be offered the rank of lieutenant-colonel. McCulloch would now receive a junior major's commission in the First Cavalry. Referring to the customary practice of selecting at least some officers from civil life, McCulloch argued that "the country had some claim upon these appointments, and that they ought not to fill them all from the army." After further consultations with Houston and Rusk, he wrote the president declining the rather insulting offer. Although his martial aspirations would go unrealized for the time being, the renowned ranger may have been pleased when, on August 27, 1856, the Sixth Legislature created McCulloch County in his honor.[121]

On November 4, 1856, James Buchanan was elected to the presidency. Still smarting from his failure to gain a colonelcy, and despite the unending frustrations, McCulloch decided to seek continued employment as a U.S. marshal. The original federal judicial district for Texas was reorganized into an eastern district and a western district on February 21, 1857. McCulloch was selected marshal of the Eastern District, with a recess appointment on April 9, earning him a monthly salary of two hundred dollars plus associated fees. The court sessions in Galveston opened on the first Mondays of May and December, and those in Brownsville on the first Monday of March and October.[122]

In May 1857, President Buchanan was faced with the possibility of armed insurrection in distant Utah Territory. Among other grievances, Brigham Young and his Mormon followers were objecting to the influx of Gentile settlers along the Overland Trail, fearing a resumption of the persecution that had driven them from Illinois and Missouri years earlier. For their safety, all federal officials had left Utah, and Young seized control of the territorial government. Effective July 15, Brigadier-General William Selby Harney assumed command of the expedition being raised to suppress the uprising. Seven days earlier, McCulloch, once more in the nation's capital, had been requested by Secretary of War John Buchanan Floyd to travel to Fort Leavenworth, confer with Harney, and use his frontier and military expertise to ascertain whether the troops were prepared for the task at hand. McCulloch traveled to Kansas Territory, examined the Utah Expedition's readiness, and returned to Washington on the twenty-first to write his report. In his commentary, he made recommendations on the number of soldiers to leave in "Bleeding Kansas" for emergencies, advised the recall to Fort Laramie of Colonel Edwin Vose Sumner's Cheyenne Expedition, and counselled the War Department to place Forts Kearney and Laramie under Harney's command.

He also suggested the procurement of supplies for the men on the march. When Harney was ordered to remain at Leavenworth due to possible Free State and pro-slavery strife, Brevet Brigadier-General Albert Sidney Johnston was placed in charge of the "Army of Utah."[123]

McCulloch had earlier indicated an interest in the governorship of troubled Utah if he should be considered. When the offer was formally tendered, though, he declined after a month of careful deliberation. His name was also mentioned as a possible successor to Sam Houston when the latter's Senate term ended in March 1859. Despite his experiences two years earlier, McCulloch still desired a military command, and was inclined to refuse any political office. The senatorial matter was decided with John Hemphill's nomination to the seat on November 9, 1857.[124] One San Antonio editor opined of McCulloch's suitability for political office:

> As to statesmanship he makes no pretensions, and has neither experience nor aspirations. He has too much common sense to place himself in a false position, as an aspirant for the Senate. Were it proposed to place him at the head of a troop or regiment of mounted men, for which he has nerve, talent and experience, we should second the move heartily. *That* is in his line—statesmanship is not.[125]

Early the following year, the Senate was considering a bill to increase the size of the Regular Army once more. On February 1, 1858, Houston rose in opposition and decried the stationing of infantry upon the Texas borderlands. He also criticized the competence of the professional military in general, and the costs of maintaining the frontier army in garrison and in the field. He informed his colleagues "Texas desires to have a more efficient force" and called for the formation of a federalized ranger regiment of one thousand men. Doctor Stephen L. Hardin observed: "The inherited animosity against professionals remained at the core of the ranger ethic. Volunteers defending hearth and home thought themselves on higher moral ground than brass-buttoned hirelings." The matter was still being debated on March 17, when an amendment to a similar House bill was introduced authorizing the president to receive into service one regiment of Texas mounted volunteers.

Jefferson Davis, by this time a senator from Mississippi, resented Houston's slurs upon the military establishment he had shaped while secretary of war. Facing the Texan on the floor of the Senate, Davis hotly defended the performance of the Regular Army in the Mexican war, and alluded to General Taylor's misgivings concerning the Texas mounted troops. In response to an earlier statement by Houston, Davis rendered McCulloch "high qualities as a partisan officer, and credit for valuable services wherever employed." He then extolled Captain Charles May's reconnaissance to Hediona on February 20, 1847, as being more vital to the subsequent victory at Buena Vista than the scout to Encarnación. Having no direct role in the argument, McCulloch had hoped to be nominated for the command of the prospective ranger regiment, but that honor would ultimately go to John S. "Rip" Ford. Any disappointment he felt from being passed over might have been mollified by the fact the outfit was never created.[126]

Even if he would not lead rangers on the frontier, McCulloch was still deemed ideal for a special mission. In a last effort to "spare the effusion of blood" in Utah, he and Senator-elect Lazarus Whitehead Powell of Kentucky were appointed as peace commissioners on April 12, 1858, and charged with delivering the president's offer of reconciliation to Mormon leaders. If Young and his followers would "obey the law, keep the peace, and respect the just rights of others," they were to receive a pardon from any charges of treason or sedition. The commissioners and their thirteen-man escort departed Fort Leavenworth on April 25. Traveling by way of Fort Kearney and Fort Laramie, they covered some eleven hundred miles before reaching Camp Scott in Utah on the twenty-ninth of May. Upon their arrival, McCulloch and Powell met with General Johnston and territorial governor Alfred Cumming to discuss their task.[127]

McCulloch and Powell left camp on June 2 and reached Salt Lake City five days later. On the tenth, they met with Mormon leaders for two days of private and public conferences. The commissioners secured a pledge that Young's followers would "yield obedience to the Constitution and laws of the United States" and "make no resistance to the army of the United States in its march to the valley of Salt Lake or elsewhere." On June 12, McCulloch and Powell reported their success to Secretary Floyd and General Johnston,

Sam Houston. Half plate daguerreotype by Matthew Brady, Washington, D.C. *Courtesy Prints and Photographs Division, Library of Congress, Washington, D.C.*

then explained the agreement to crowds in Provo and Lehi. Before having received word of the peace commission's accomplishment, Johnston marched the Army of Utah into the Salt Lake Valley on the thirteenth, and took up a position on Bear River. With an uncertain reconciliation achieved, McCulloch assisted Johnston in locating the site for a new military post beginning on the twenty-eighth. The soldiers marched through the Mormon capital on June 29, discreetly underscored the federal government's primacy, and camped on the Jordan River for three days. The colonel moved his forces to Cedar Valley on July 3, and erected the cantonment, which had been named Camp Floyd.[128]

While McCulloch was occupied in Utah, he had been retained as United States marshal on June 3, 1858. Returning home, his reappointment was confirmed by the Senate on September 14. He had little time to devote to his office, since he was subsequently dispatched to Sonora as a confidential agent for President Buchanan. The administration was keenly aware of its obligation to protect American citizens south of the border from civil strife and government corruption. The federal government was also duty-bound to suppress brutal raids from Mexico into the United States. Traveling to El Paso, McCulloch was instructed to "visit Mexico and report to [the president] the actual conditions and prospects of the contending parties." Buchanan favored military intervention to establish a protectorate over the northern portions of Sonora and Chihuahua, but he would ultimately fail to convince Congress to approve his plans. The president's schemes notwithstanding, once McCulloch completed his assignment, he traveled to Washington by way of Arizona, and submitted his resignation on March 7, 1859, effective April 1. He gave no reason for his decision, but he did succeed in ensuring Henry replaced his brother as federal marshal.[129]

Free from the demands of public office, McCulloch pursued several commercial ventures that invariably proved disappointing. He purchased an interest in George Woodward Morse's patent for a breech-loading modification to the United States Model 1816 musket and the Model 1841 rifle. For several months, McCulloch worked as a sales agent, and promoted the gun maker's design to the War Department and to state governments throughout the South. Any revenue derived from his investment in the rifle was to be interrupted by the imminent war. He next offered bids on contracts for carrying the U.S. mails in Washington and Oregon territories, but his submissions were not accepted. His name also appeared in newspaper articles announcing he and Benjamin Franklin Ficklin had been awarded the contract for carrying the mail between Fort Leavenworth and Coraville in the Pike's Peak mining district. This opportunity likewise fell through as the post office in the latter town only operated from March 22 to June 25, 1859. With his business endeavors failing to produce fruit, McCulloch returned to the occupation he knew best.[130]

On April 20, 1858, Senator Houston, supportive of Buchanan's designs for Mexico, had risen to address his colleagues, and called for a resolution establishing a protectorate over the northern part of that country in order to bring peace to the region. In his speech, he called the senators' attention to the length of the border, to the depredations committed by Comanches and other tribes, to the depopulation of the border country, and to the dubious prospect of Mexico improving her anarchic condition. Even though Congress would not act on his or any of Buchanan's calls for military action, the senator remained undeterred. While the Cortina War raged on the southern border, McCulloch served as Houston's liaison in the halls of power of the nation's capital. Writing to another ally in the budding scheme, the crafty former general described McCulloch as a "very 'big Captain' as my Red brothers say." On February 13, 1860, Houston, who had assumed the governorship of Texas, sent McCulloch a letter proclaiming "there will be stirring times on the Rio Grande ere long. What are you doing? See the President and Secretary of War. Reply at once." McCulloch quickly responded, "I am at all times ready to serve Texas." Answering a summons from Houston, the old ranger returned home confident he would soon be at the head of a regiment of Texas volunteers on the Rio Grande. Despite McCulloch's willingness to invade Mexico, which was reflected in widespread popular support in Texas, the Cortina War was decisively ended by Major Samuel Peter Heintzelman, Rip Ford, and Lieutenant-Colonel Lee, and the filibustering plot ultimately came to naught.[131]

Once the Secession Convention voted to remove Texas from the Union, they appointed commissioners to meet with Brevet Major-General David Emanuel Twiggs at the Post of San Antonio. The convention also instituted a Committee of Public Safety to raise an Army of Texas and ready the state for war. On February 5, 1861, the Committee engaged McCulloch as a colonel of cavalry and commander of the Middle District. Ordered on the ninth to seize United States government property in and around San Antonio, McCulloch assembled eleven hundred men on the Salado on February 15. Early the next morning, with four hundred of this force, he peacefully compelled the evacuation of Union troops from the Alamo and accepted the surrender of General Twiggs. Unknown to McCulloch, Twiggs had been removed from command effective January 28, and received the order on the fifteenth of February, presumably before he capitulated to McCulloch. The general stepped down four days later. Regardless of the surrender's uncertain legality, the deed was done and the two federal companies in San Antonio were allowed to take their arms, clothing, camp and garrison equipment, light artillery, and other necessities on the march to the coast. Remaining in the arsenal were four thousand muskets and rifles, which McCulloch seized for the Southern cause.[132]

On March 4, Confederate Secretary of War Leroy Pope Walker requested McCulloch raise a regiment of mounted riflemen to protect the frontier. Desiring a field command in the coming fight, he declined in favor of Henry. He did assist in recruiting for his brother's new regiment, though. While in Richmond in April and May, McCulloch's living legend status—and the fame of the Texas Rangers—initiated a wave of panic in Washington. Rumors raced through the Yankee capital that McCulloch and five hundred rangers, "a desperate set of fellows," were in northern Virginia ready to sweep across the Potomac, kidnap or kill President Abraham Lincoln, and seize control of the city.[133]

Anxious to obtain a leading role in fighting the Union, the veteran soldier was equally keen for Texas to take her "place in the picture, near the flashing of the guns." To that end, McCulloch resigned his commission from the Committee, and accepted a new assignment to procure one thousand Morse breech-loading rifles, or a like number of Colt revolvers, for the cavalry. He was able to obtain the pistols, which were issued to the regiment authorized by the Secession Convention. The rifles were never delivered. He terminated his services on March 20 in order to apply for a regimental command in the Provisional Army of the Confederate States.[134]

By this time, Jefferson Davis had been elected president of the Confederacy. The relationship McCulloch had with the former secretary of war and senator had been epitomized by a "qualified coolness" ever since Davis had thwarted the Texan's several attempts at frontier commands. However, the chief executive remembered the famed ranger's service in Mexico, particularly at Monterey and Buena Vista. With those past exploits in mind, Davis finally gave McCulloch the opportunity he had desired for years and commissioned him a brigadier-general on May 11, 1861, to take effect from the first. The same day, McCulloch was ordered to Fort Smith, Arkansas to assume command of the Indian Territory.[135]

Arriving in Fort Smith on May 30, and establishing his headquarters at Camp Walker, McCulloch and his staff began the monumental task of building an army from scratch. They were faced with a myriad of logistical complications, including a deficiency in provisions, ammunition, and serviceable firearms. In an effort to rectify the situation, twenty thousand dollars was placed at the general's disposal to purchase essential supplies. In addition, McCulloch, with the assistance of Confederate commissioner Albert Pike, was able to establish vital alliances with the Cherokees, Choctaws, Creeks, and other tribes of the territory.[136] Proclaiming a call for volunteers, the limited forces he soon had at his personal command included Colonel Thomas James Churchill's First Arkansas Mounted Rifles, Colonel James McQueen McIntosh's Second Arkansas Mounted Rifles, Captain Dandridge McRae's Arkansas Battalion, and Colonel Louis Hébert's Third Louisiana Infantry. Independent of McCulloch, but working under his supervision, Brigadier-General Nicholas Bartlett Pearce commanded Colonel John Rene Gratiot's Third Arkansas Infantry, Colonel Jonathan David Walker's Fourth Arkansas Infantry, Colonel Thomas Pleasant Dockery's Fifth Arkansas Infantry, Colonel DeRosey Carroll's First Arkansas Cavalry, Captain James G. Reid's Fort Smith Battery, and Captain William Edward Woodruff, Jr.'s Pulaski Light Battery.[137]

One Louisiana soldier assigned to McCulloch's command observed:

> He was a thoroughly practical general. He gave much attention to the nature of the country in which he was going to operate. He made himself acquainted with every road or passage through which an army with trains could pass or operate in. He examined every river, creek, ford, or bridge where an enemy could be checked or met to advantage. He took care to know where forage and supplies were to be procured readiest, and noted where a pass could be guarded, defended, or stopped up, or where a bridge could be burned or blown up. He was an excellent

> horseman and a most able leader of rangers or irregular cavalry, and could take them through and over almost impassable barriers of rivers, swamps, hills, rocks, woods, or copses. He was not so particular about clock-work movements in drill or in having the ranks dressed straight as an arrow, but he was particular in brigade movements, that proper distances were kept, and that corps passed regularly in order without any doubling up or confusion, and, above all, that the men knew well to handle their arms and were good shots.[138]

McCulloch's primary mission was to protect Arkansas and the Indian Territory from invasion by Federal forces headquartered in St. Louis, but the Confederate War Department ordered him on June 26 to also assist secessionist forces in Missouri. The status of Missouri as "a Southern State still in the Union" required the general to act with a great deal of judiciousness. On July 4, McCulloch led Churchill's regiment and twelve hundred of Pearce's Arkansawyers into the Show-Me State, where they united at Cassville with seventeen hundred militiamen of Major-General Sterling "Old Pap" Price's Missouri State Guard. In the meantime, Brigadier-General Nathaniel Lyon had assumed command of the Union Army of the West and organized his five thousand troops into four brigades. Brigadier-General Franz Sigel, commanding the Second Brigade, clashed with Governor Claiborne Fox Jackson's troops on July 5 at Carthage, then withdrew to join Lyon at Springfield. The Confederate forces marched rapidly to attack Sigel at Neosho, but the Union troops fell back leaving one detachment behind. These 137 Yankees surrendered unconditionally when two columns of Rebel cavalry approached the town. McCulloch's army concentrated at Neosho and, after a rest of an hour or two, resumed the march to meet with Governor Jackson. Following a conference, McCulloch, Pearce, and Price agreed to forego pursuing the enemy due to a scarcity of water and supplies, but instead relocated to camps in Arkansas on Little Sugar Creek near Bentonville, on Cowskin Prairie, and near Maysville. On July 20, the Southern commanders decided to advance once more into Missouri and offer battle to the Federals. McCulloch only reluctantly assented, as Missouri had not yet seceded, and President Davis was wary of militarily entering her territory without an official request for assistance. McCulloch, with 3,200 men, Pearce, with 2,500, and Price, with ten thousand, each moved toward Springfield on July 28 and rendezvoused at Cassville the following day.[139]

Beginning on July 31, McCulloch's "Forces in Missouri" marched along the Telegraph (or Wire) Road to Dug Spring, where James Spencer Rains's

Sterling Price. Wet process collodion glass plate negative made from an original watercolor portrait held by DeGolyer Library, Southern Methodist University. *Courtesy Prints and Photographs Division, Library of Congress, Washington, D.C.*

Second Division of the Missouri State Guard fought a brief skirmish with Lyon's vanguard on August 2. Rains's men were forced to retreat across Cane Creek, but the Federals declined to press their advantage, and instead withdrew to Springfield. While at Cane Creek, Price continued to advocate for an advance farther north. A man of soaring ego, the Missourian imperiously spoke to McCulloch as if the Texan were an inferior:

> Now, sir, I am an older man than you … and I am not only your senior in rank now, but I was a brig-gen [*sic*] in the Mexican War, with an independent command, when you were only a captain; I have fought and won more battles than you have ever witnessed; my force is twice as great as yours; and some of my officers rank, and have seen more service than you; we are upon the soil of our own state; but, Gen. McCulloch, if you will consent to help us whip Lyon and to repossess Missouri, I will put myself and all my forces under your command, and we will obey you as faithfully as the humblest of your own men. We can whip Lyon, and we will whip him and drive the enemy out of Missouri, and all the honor and all the glory shall be yours … If you refuse to accept this offer, I will move with the Missourians alone, against Lyon …[140]

Regardless of whether Price's state rank could properly be considered senior or junior to McCulloch's Confederate commission, the former issued Special Order No. 16 on August 4, which directed that the Missouri State Guard was subject to the orders of McCulloch in his role as the commanding general of the new "Western Army." The troops were now assembled into three elements: McCulloch's Confederate Army brigade comprised of his Arkansas regiments, Hébert's Louisiana infantry, and Colonel Elkanah Bracklin Greer's Third Texas Cavalry; Pearce's brigade of Arkansas militia troops; and Price's six Missouri State Guard divisions, all totaling 5,300 infantry, six thousand cavalry, and fifteen field guns. In spite of the Missouri general's show of support, McCulloch had a complete difference of opinion with Price over strategic objectives. McCulloch also mistrusted him, Rains, and the mettle of all the ragged Missouri troops; the latter carried a haphazard assortment of shotguns, hunting rifles, and antique muskets, except for the two or three thousand without weapons of any kind.[141]

McCulloch and his men continued the march and reached Wilson Creek, twelve miles southwest of Springfield, on the sixth. While Price impulsively called for an immediate advance, McCulloch dispatched scouts to seek the location and strength of Lyon's Army of the West. Once he had attained the necessary information, the Texan ordered the Western Army would resume at nine p.m. on August 9, but rainfall delayed the anticipated movement until the next morning. Meanwhile, lacking support from his superiors, Lyon was nevertheless determined to seize the initiative. To that end, he approved Franz Sigel's plan which called for a concentric assault on McCulloch's position. While Lyon himself led the main attack from the north along the Mount Vernon road, Sigel was to march south and west on the Fayetteville road and fall on the Confederate right flank and rear. The two Union forces camped for the night on August 9, a short distance from the unsuspecting Confederates.[142]

About five a.m., the first of two pincers attacked the Confederate camp. McCulloch and Colonel McIntosh were breakfasting at Price's headquarters tent while Lyon's main element of Kansas and Unionist Missouri volunteers moved along the west side of Wilson Creek. On the opposite bank, Captain Joseph Bennett Plummer, commanding a mixed battalion of regular infantry and mounted Missouri Home Guards, marched toward John Ray's cornfield in support of Lyon's left flank. Receiving the first blow, nine hundred poorly armed cavalrymen of General Rains' division were driven off the crest of Oak Hill (later remembered as "Bloody Hill") by Lyon's men after an hour of fighting. Woodruff's battery, positioned across the creek near the Guinn farm, responded by enfilading the Yankees, while four divisions of Price's infantry rushed up through the dense underbrush and scrub oak covering the slopes to regain the lost positions. The secessionist Missouri volunteers attacked the Union line twice, but failed to break through.[143]

Meanwhile, Plummer's force bore down on the Pulaski Battery's flank at the same time Gratiot's Third Arkansas moved to support Woodruff's guns. As the foot soldiers maneuvered around them, the rebel artillery dueled with their Union counterparts throughout the battle. Crossing Wilson Creek

The Battle of Bloody Hill. Painting by Greg Harlin. *Courtesy Wilson's Creek National Battlefield, Republic, Missouri.*

and assuming command of the eastern sector of the battle, McCulloch ordered McIntosh to take the brigade's infantry and attack Plummer. The Third Louisiana and the dismounted Second Arkansas deployed along the fence surrounding the cornfield, opened a galling fire, and drove the Federals back upon the enemy's center. Union artillery atop Bloody Hill saw the plight of Plummer's withdrawing battalion and opened fire with canister, grape, and shot. The Confederates were themselves forced to retreat.[144]

At around five-thirty a.m., four cannons of Sigel's pincer were positioned on a ridge east of Wilson and Terrell Creeks, where they proceeded to shell the camp of Colonels Churchill and Greer. Caught under the bombardment, the Southern horsemen were thrown into confusion and forced to shelter in the nearby woods. Sigel and his nine hundred men crossed Terrell Creek and advanced along the southern edge of Joseph Sharp's cornfield, pausing once to disperse Rebel cavalry massing near the Sharp house. Reaching the Telegraph Road, the Union general's six guns commenced a harassing fire on the Southerners opposing Lyon on Oak Hill. With the fighting concluded east of Wilson Creek, McCulloch rallied a battalion of the Third Louisiana, a detachment of seventy Missouri infantrymen, Colonel Thomas Henry Rosser's First Infantry Regiment, and Colonel Benjamin Johnson Brown's cavalry regiment, both of the Missouri State Guard, and McRae's Arkansas infantry. Leading the combined force of one thousand men, he skillfully deployed them across the road at Skegg's Branch. While the Confederate foot soldiers and dismounted horsemen struck Sigel's front and left flank, Reid's battery raked the Federals' right from the high ground east of the creek. By ten o'clock, Sigel had been routed with a loss of four cannons, and he took no further part in the action.[145]

Once the threat of Sigel's brigade had been neutralized, McCulloch dispatched his troops to reinforce Price's right flank. Lyon had been killed during the fighting for Bloody Hill, and Major Samuel David Sturgis assumed command. Following Price's third and final attack, which ended at eleven a.m., Sturgis recognized his ammunition was becoming depleted and his exhausted men could simply not continue the engagement, so they withdrew to Springfield in good order. The Confederates were too disorganized and ill-equipped to follow, and McCulloch soon retired to Arkansas.

The Rebel casualties numbered 265 men killed, eight hundred wounded, and thirty missing. The Union army lost 258 killed and 873 wounded.[146]

Despite the near parity of casualty figures, the battle was judged a Southern victory. The Rebels held the field in the end and consequently control of southwestern Missouri. On August 21, the following resolution would be offered on the floor of the Confederate Congress:

> That the Thanks of Congress are cordially tendered to Brigadier-General Ben McCulloch and the officers and soldiers of his brave command for their gallant conduct in defeating, after a battle of six and a half hours, a force of the enemy equal in numbers and greatly superior in all their appointments; thus proving that a right cause nerves the hearts and strengthens the arms of the Southern people, fighting, as they are, for their liberty, their homes, and firesides, against an unholy despotism.
>
> *Resolved*, That in the opinion of Congress General McCulloch and his gallant troops are entitled to, and will receive, the grateful thanks of our people.[147]

Although they had saved their army from certain defeat, and trounced the enemy in the bargain, relations between McCulloch and Price continued to sour and made any meaningful future cooperation moot. Desperate to see the Yankees leave his state, Price beseeched McCulloch to march north for a new campaign to retake Missouri, but the Texan refused. An infuriated Price countermanded his earlier directive with Special Order No. 18 on August 14, and reclaimed the sole command of the Missouri forces. The three elements parted company, each general to pursue his own strategy. McCulloch pulled back to Fayetteville to ready his weary men for further action, Pearce returned to Little Rock and disbanded his troops, and Price recklessly marched his militia north for the Missouri River.[148]

The Missouri general seized Lexington on September 20, but he lacked the means to keep his prize, let alone to conquer the entire state. Price then appealed to McCulloch for assistance, but the latter only conducted a reconnaissance-in-force along the Springfield road before falling back to the

Boston Mountains. McCulloch had expected to muster Pearce's Arkansas regiments into the Confederate Army, but he found them unwilling to reenlist. Hampered by their lack of resolve, McCulloch's division included Colonel Evander McNair's Fourth Arkansas Infantry, Colonel William Christmas Mitchell's Fourteenth Arkansas Infantry, Colonel Barton Warren Stone's Sixth Texas Cavalry, Major John W. Whitfield's Fourth Texas Cavalry Battalion, McRae's battalion reorganized as the Twenty-first Arkansas Infantry, and the regiments of Hébert, McIntosh, Churchill, and Greer. His artillery was composed of Captain William Hart's Dallas (Arkansas) Battery, Captain David Provence's Fort Smith Battery, and Captain John Jay Good's First Texas Battery. With such limited resources, the Texan determined his best option was to go on the defensive, recruit additional troops, procure badly needed supplies, and allow the enemy to assume the risks of offensive operations. His course of action was militarily sound, but he also missed opportunities to destroy scattered Yankee forces piecemeal. The strategy did not sit well with the Confederate high command, and McCulloch was required to travel to Richmond and explain himself. On October 31, the Missouri government-in-exile seceded from the Union, and all the secessionist forces, arms, and matériel were tendered to President Davis.[149]

McCulloch and Price's ongoing failure to come to a consensus caused the president, on January 10, 1862, to appoint Major-General Earl Van Dorn to the command of the Trans-Mississippi District; as such he was the direct superior of both McCulloch and Price. The new district commander traveled to Bowling Green, Kentucky, and reported to General Albert Sidney Johnston, who led all Confederate forces west of the Appalachians. During the conference, Van Dorn learned his role in the overall strategy was to invade Missouri and alleviate Union pressure in Kentucky and Tennessee. Moving on to Little Rock, he formally assumed command of his district on January 29, and selected Pocahontas to be his headquarters. McCulloch and his ten thousand men were ordered to proceed from Little Rock and join Van Dorn there.[150]

Even while Van Dorn prepared his movement into Missouri, Union Brigadier-General Samuel Ryan Curtis and his Army of the Southwest forced Price to abandon Springfield on February 12. The Missourian conducted a fighting withdrawal into Arkansas to join McCulloch in the White River Valley near the Boston Mountains. Curtis followed until he reached a point two miles south of Bentonville. Price continued to press for retaking his native state, while McCulloch still saw his duty as protecting Arkansas and the Indian Territory.[151] Analyzing the Texas general's appreciation for the military situation in the Trans-Mississippi, one historian contended:

> "Here … lay McCulloch's greatest weakness as a Confederate commander. He could not come to realize that the Indian Territory … was really of secondary importance in comparison with other fields of operation. The general either did not see, or chose to ignore, the fact that his area of operations was but a part of the operations of the entire western theatre … But, on the other hand, there was good reason for believing that Price's designs in Missouri could not be carried out even with McCulloch's aid."[152]

Van Dorn left Jacksonport on February 24, and arrived at Price's headquarters at Cove Creek on March 2. He visited with McCulloch at Strickler's Station the following morning. The district commander planned to move west of the dispersed Union forces in order to outflank them, cut their supply line, and fall on them from the rear. The expedition was one McCulloch indignantly opposed, but to no avail. The same day, Van Dorn ordered his two senior commanders to begin the march toward Fayetteville on March 4. He also instructed Brigadier-General Albert Pike to rendezvous with him at Elm Springs, ten miles north of Fayetteville.[153]

The assembled forces assumed the name "Army of the West." McCulloch's division consisted of Colonel Hébert's infantry brigade, Brigadier-General McIntosh's cavalry brigade, and Captain James J. Gaines's John D. Adams Battery, as well as those of Hart, Provence, and Good. The division's fifteen guns were organized into an artillery battalion attached to Hébert's brigade and commanded by Captain William R. Bradfute. Price's division was comprised of three infantry brigades and forty-seven field-pieces. The Missouri State Guard of six, severely reduced divisions was also placed under Price. General Pike commanded two cavalry regiments of Cherokees and a mounted squadron of Texans. In all, Van Dorn possessed a strength of approximately sixteen thousand.[154]

Van Dorn moved swiftly in the early hours of the fourth. The snowy weather allowed the Army of the West to steal a march on Curtis. The Union commander was not informed of the Rebel advance until March 5, after they had passed through Fayetteville and were in Elm Springs. Curtis ordered his four divisions to fall back and concentrate south of Pea Ridge. Van Dorn pushed his troops through Bentonville in pursuit of Curtis's retreating column, but was unable to overtake the Federals before they reached entrenched positions at Little Sugar Creek on March 6. Once Curtis had his army assembled, the force under his command numbered some 10,500 soldiers and forty-nine artillery pieces. Van Dorn halted his marching troops at nightfall of the same day astride the Bentonville Road. Price's division bivouacked two miles southwest of the Federal position. The men were cold, hungry, and exhausted by marching fifty miles in three days through snow drifts and across the rugged terrain. Unfortunately, they would not get their much-needed rest.[155]

Desiring to avoid a frontal assault on the Union line, Van Dorn consulted with McCulloch and McIntosh and learned of the Bentonville Detour, which allowed access to the left flank and rear of Curtis's position. Seizing the opportunity, Van Dorn moved his army behind Pea Ridge and, screened by the mountains, advanced southward by the Telegraph Road and Elkhorn Tavern. In the night, Van Dorn and his staff accompanied Price's division on the march, followed by McCulloch's troops and Pike's horsemen. Missouri militiamen remained in camp to guard the baggage train and hold the position in case of attack. The trek was slow and demanding due to the difficult crossing of an icy Sugar Creek, inevitable delays, and removing felled trees from the road. By ten a.m., only Price was in a position to attack the Union pickets around Elkhorn Tavern. McCulloch and Pike were still on the detour four or five miles to the rear. Van Dorn sent orders for them to countermarch and take a shortcut that approached Elkhorn Tavern from the west. The two wings were now separated by the ridge and woods, and would fight two distinct actions, unable to support one another.[156]

Curtis learned of the Confederate movement sometime after daybreak on March 7. Originally expecting an attack from the south, he ordered a change

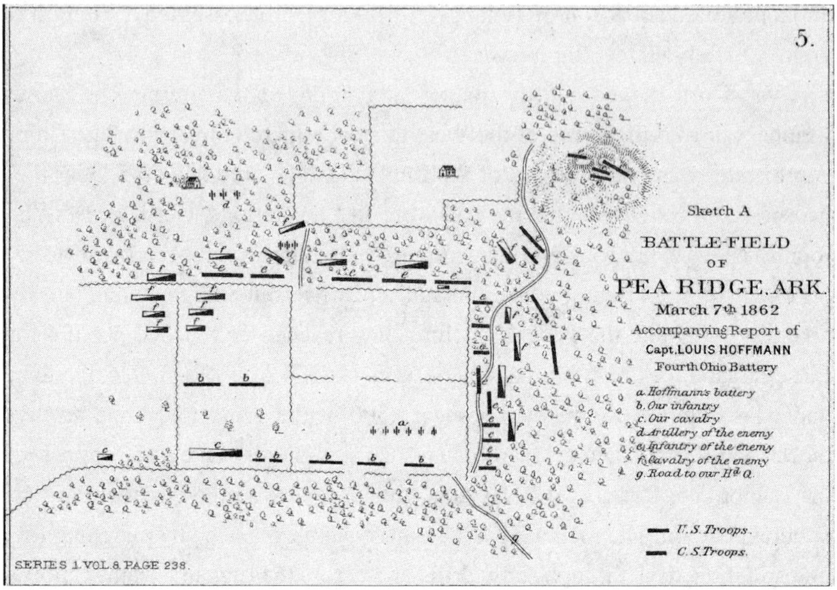

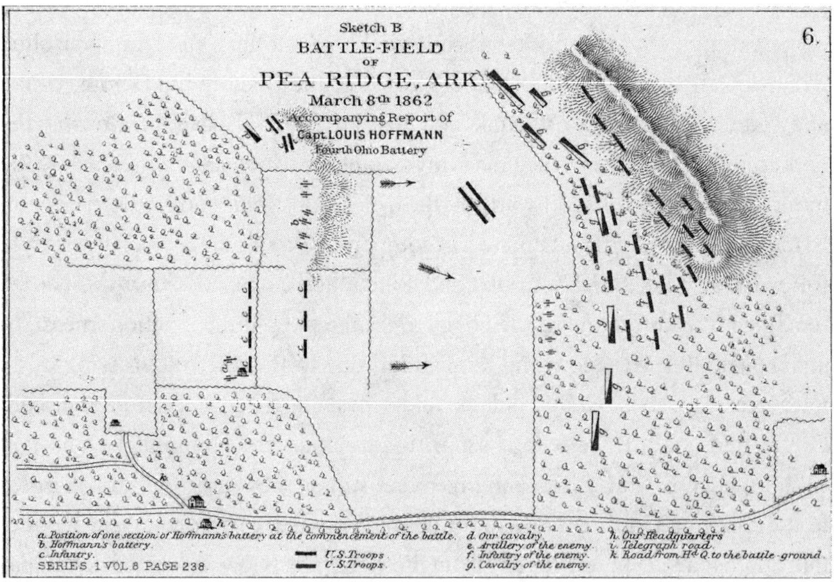

Map of Pea Ridge. From *Atlas to Accompany the Official Records of the Union and Confederate Armies.*

of front to meet the new tactical situation with his left flank anchored on Sugar Creek. Price assaulted the Federal right later in the morning. Union infantry rushed to reinforce, but the Confederates possessed superior numbers and firepower. Successive infantry and artillery onslaughts pushed the Yankees back to Benjamin Ruddick's field. Late in the afternoon, Curtis readied his forces for a counterattack, but he later recalled the order.[157]

On the other front, McCulloch was marching his division east on Ford Road, when, just before noon, they encountered the Union left flank in the open fields north of Leetown. McCulloch deployed Hébert's infantry to the left of the road and McIntosh's cavalry to the right. Pike's Indian horsemen formed to the rear of McIntosh in support. Federal artillery opened fire, and Union infantry made ready to attack the Confederate left flank, but the Rebel foot soldiers ran forward at the double-quick and reached the shelter of the thick oak scrub nearby. Before the enemy could advance, a mounted charge of Texans broke through the Federals' front lines and threw them into confusion. The Southern infantry reformed in the woods, then steadily closed upon the Yankees, braving a shower of musketry, grape, and canister. McCulloch ruled the battlefield for almost two hours, but his advance stalled by one-thirty p.m. in the face of a robust Federal counterattack. McCulloch brought up five of Hébert's regiments and battalions to meet the enemy who were positioned in Samuel Oberson's field. Deciding to personally reconnoiter the Union lines, the Texas general slung his Morse rifle over his shoulder, mounted his tall sorrel, and rode forward. While leading skirmishers of the Sixteenth Arkansas through a brushy thicket, McCulloch, conspicuous in a narrow-brimmed hat and black velvet coat, was fatally shot through the heart. As his body had tumbled into the brush, the nearby Confederate troops were ignorant of their commander's death for a few minutes. Once the news became known, General McIntosh rallied the division and charged the Union infantry in the dense woods. He also fell before the enemy and perished; fifteen minutes later, Colonel Hébert, the third-ranking officer, was captured. The leaderless remnants of McCulloch's division soon fell into disorder. Once Union reserves arrived on the field in the midafternoon, the demoralized Rebels were forced to withdraw and link up with Van Dorn at Elkhorn Tavern.[158]

Two Generals Die. Oil on canvas painting by Andy Thomas. *Courtesy of the artist.*

John Henry Brown, a member of McCulloch's staff, suggested in his diary the general's body was buried on the field, then disinterred that night. He probably took possession of the remains at Bentonville sometime the same evening. Twenty-four hours later, he and the two men accompanying McCulloch home were six miles below Fayetteville. On March 10, they were in Fort Smith where the general's wound was examined. Seven days later, the escort departed and reached the Red River on the twenty-fourth. The cavalcade arrived in Austin late on April 9, and McCulloch was given a state funeral in the capitol building the following day. The body was laid to rest in the State Cemetery.[159]

On April 21, the Confederate Congress passed a joint resolution of thanks to "Major-Generals Van Dorn and Price, and the officers and soldiers under their command, for their valor, skill, and good conduct in the battle of Elkhorn, in the State of Arkansas, and of respect for the memory of Generals McCulloch and McIntosh." President Davis signed the act the same day.[160]

McCulloch died a much-loved hero of Texas. On the national stage, he had proven himself to be a bold and resourceful ranger and soldier. Throughout his twenty-six-year career as a fighting man, he displayed an exceptional military talent, a natural gift for leadership and organization, and an absolute genius for reconnaissance. While not commanding large bodies of men at Plum Creek, he was nevertheless instrumental in defeating the Comanche raiding party. By virtue of his scouting, he influenced the success of two campaigns in Mexico. His shrewd and dynamic actions saved the Confederate army at Wilson Creek. Had he survived the battle at Pea Ridge, he may well have advanced to higher rank and responsibility in the Confederate service. With his death, the Southern cause lost Missouri and northern Arkansas, and was deprived of a desperately needed general. If he had outlived the war, the further contributions he could have made to Texas in a peacetime setting might have been equally substantial.

William A. A. "Bigfoot" Wallace. Albumen photograph by Michael Miley's Stonewall Art Gallery, Lexington, Virginia. *Author's Collection.*

Chapter 4

William A. A. Wallace: "True Texas Folk Hero"

William Alexander Anderson "Bigfoot" Wallace was a true Texas folk hero. Like Davy Crockett or "Deaf" Smith, his exploits were the stuff of legend, and, even before his death, he became a larger-than-life figure in the popular culture. Wallace was the epitome of the bold, colorful individualist who could not abide the confines of civilization and kept following the frontier line west. Regrettably, his life story is not easily verifiable, and some of this unhappy circumstance is the responsibility of Wallace himself. J. Frank Dobie called him an "authentic liar," an engaging storyteller who "knows what he is lying about, knows that his listeners—unless they are tenderfeet, greenhorns—know also, and hence makes no pretense of fooling either himself or them." Regardless of how much Wallace "stretched the blanket," the separating of fact from fiction has not diminished the valuable services he rendered to the people of Texas.

He was born on April 3, 1817, in Lexington, Rockbridge County, Virginia, to Andrew and Rachel Jane (Blair) Wallace. According to family tradition, he was purportedly a descendant of the Scottish Highlanders William Wallace on his paternal side and Robert the Bruce on his maternal. He did definitely come from fighting stock, as his grandfather and four great-uncles had served in the Continental Army during the American Revolution. His father was born on

August 8, 1784, in Rockbridge County, and his mother was born in Staunton County on June 22, 1790. They married on March 10, 1812. In addition to William, their children were Sarah Lapsley Wallace, born in 1812; Grover Wallace, born on February 5, 1813; Samuel P. Wallace, born on February 5, 1815; Rebecca Jane Wallace, born on April 7, 1819; Andrew Wallace, Jr., born on August 11, 1821; Elizabeth Wallace, born on November 4, 1823; James Eli Wallace, born in 1825; Joseph Blair Wallace, born on March 4, 1826; Martha Ruff Wallace, born on July 31, 1828; and Alexander Anderson Wallace, born on July 13, 1831. After Rachel died on May 5, 1832, Andrew married Mary C. (Blair) Poage the following year. The elder Wallace owned and operated a tobacco farm, and the 1820 federal census noted nine free white persons and five slaves were living on the property.[1]

Having heard of the revolution being fought in Texas, Samuel went there as third sergeant in Captain William A. O. Wadsworth's company of Columbus, Georgia, volunteers. He and his comrades were part of James Walker Fannin's command at Goliad. Taken prisoner by José Urrea's forces, they were massacred on March 27, 1836. Two cousins, William Wallace and Major Benjamin Wallace, also perished.[2]

Wallace resolved to travel to Texas and avenge his kin's deaths. Andrew tried to dissuade him from such a course, but the younger Wallace vowed he would spend the rest of his life killing Mexicans. In the end, his father relented provided William's uncle, Joseph Blair, and cousin, James Paxton, accompany him. News arrived of the Texian victory at San Jacinto, but Wallace was still determined to go. The trio journeyed to New Orleans in order to take passage to Galveston. Sailing aboard the schooner *Diadem* through a storm-tossed Gulf, they arrived on October 5, 1837, more than seventeen months after the Mexican defeat. From the port, the party rode to Bastrop. Once they arrived on the Colorado River, Joseph and James decided such wild country was not for them; the former returned to Virginia and the latter resided in Houston. For Wallace, the frontier was now home. He settled near the hamlet of La Grange, and built himself a cabin.[3]

In the same month, Wallace accompanied a surveying party into present-day Palo Pinto County. He became separated from his companions and was discovered by an Indian war party. He killed one warrior before managing to elude the others. An injury to his ankle compelled him to hide in a cave from October 28 to November 20, living on pecans and wild game. When he emerged the last time, he was captured by hostile Indians. Wallace was taken to their village where his captors decided to burn him at the stake. Once the wood had been heaped around him, an old woman and her son came to Wallace's aid and convinced the other Indians to spare his life. After being held in the village for a time, he escaped and returned safely to La Grange.[4]

Men who had served in the Texian army during the recent revolution were entitled to a land grant. As his brother had fought and died in the conflict, Wallace claimed the land bounty to which Samuel, or his heirs, was entitled. He traveled to Houston and received the warrant for 960 acres on December 28.[5]

The following year, Wallace and seven other Texians were camped overnight on the Lavaca River when Indians stole their horses. The eight men packed their gear on foot several miles to the village of Zumwalt. There they procured new horses and recruited five volunteers to pursue the thieves. On the trail, the thirteen Texians were joined by Jefferson Turner, an "Indian hater" whose family had been massacred a decade earlier and who now lived only for vengeance. Tuner expertly tracked the Indian horse thieves to their camp by late afternoon. Wallace and the other Texians dismounted and crept to within fifty yards of the position before they were spotted. They opened fire and the two sides engaged in a brisk fight for fifteen minutes. Wallace took aim at an Indian at close range, but an arrow grazed his head and caused him to miss the easy shot. The Indians broke and ran, leaving four dead to be scalped by Turner. Only one Texian was wounded.[6]

Some months later, fifteen Lipan Apaches raided near La Grange, swept up the livestock in the neighborhood, and slaughtered the family of a man named Black. Volunteering to accompany the grieving survivor in pursuit of the warriors, Wallace and four to six other volunteers rode down the valley of the Colorado. When the raiders spotted the hunters, they "scattered like quail" and tried to draw the white men off in different directions. Wallace and his companions galloped after their quarry for several miles. Dodging three arrows, Wallace closed to within fifty yards of one warrior and killed him with one rifle shot. One more Lipan was killed and one wounded before the others escaped. The Texians ended the fight with no casualties. Hearing that a black servant from a nearby immigrant wagon train had shot an Indian wearing a bearskin, Wallace, Black, and the others took out after the wounded warrior. The next day, they found the man and Black, murderous after the killing of his family, shot the Indian a second time. He then whipped out his knife and scalped the dying Lipan. After he finished, Black cut strips of flesh from the warrior's back to use as razor strops. These acts shocked Wallace, who had not yet become hardened to the grim realities of border warfare. While he would kill many Indians and Mexicans in his lifetime, Wallace never once scalped or otherwise mutilated a foe in any of the multiple battles he fought.[7]

On February 24, 1839, Wallace heard that Caddo, Waco, and Kichai Indians, allied with another war party of Comanches, had killed Elizabeth Coleman, the widow of Colonel Robert Morris Coleman, and her young son Albert. Wallace and approximately twenty men immediately set out to assist in running down the Indians. They stopped at the Coleman farm on Wells' Prairie near the Colorado and found the bodies of Mrs. Coleman and her boy. After burying the two, Wallace and his companions learned the Comanches had turned north toward Brushy Creek, and Captains Jacob Burleson and James Rogers were leading a force in pursuit. They were anxious to reach the anticipated fight, but arrived too late to participate. Reaching Josiah Wilbarger's fort, Wallace and the others beheld the survivors of the battle as they rode in.[8]

Wallace moved to the growing town of Austin later in the year, and spent his time digging wells. One saloonkeeper paid him twelve dollars per foot for just such a job. Proficient with a broadax, he also cut timber to be used as building material for two hundred dollars per month and board. After two months, he worked with a man named William Leggett and floated cedar logs from upstream to Austin. The number of Indians in the area where they were working grew too large for comfort, and the two men returned to town. They were fortunate to leave when they did, as another party of loggers working the same stream as Wallace were wiped out to a man.[9]

Tiring of life in town, Wallace became filled with a wanderlust that had him roving the Colorado valley and the surrounding hills above the capital.

He lived off the land and slept wherever he found a likely spot. The growing population of Austin demanded large quantities of fresh meat, and Wallace returned to town to partner with William Fox, a jovial Irishman, in opening a smokehouse. The two entrepreneurs made a prosperous living selling the deer, wild turkeys, and bears Wallace killed. They also hauled building stone from the hills to town.[10]

Once in his prime, Wallace was, like all his male kin, a physically powerful man. He stood six foot two inches in his moccasins, and weighed 240 pounds. He had long arms and enormous hands, and his thick black hair tended to curl. Despite the sobriquet he would be given, his feet were, in fact, normal sized.[11]

Residing in the area was a notorious Waco chief named Bigfoot, who made a regular practice of stealing horses and killing white men. The enormous Indian's footprint was said to measure twelve to fourteen inches, and was notable for the big toe that extended from his moccasin. One night, Chief Bigfoot crept into the kitchen of a man named Gravis and stole food. He then left tracks leading to the door of the house Wallace and Fox shared. Gravis accused Wallace, also a towering man, of theft. Wallace resented the accusation and proceeded to make his displeasure known with his fists. Wallace then went to one of the footprints the Waco chief had left and put his own moccasin inside the larger track. Gravis apologized for his false allegation. Fox came outside to see about the ruckus and, after being informed of the situation, laughingly took to calling Wallace "Bigfoot." The nickname stuck.[12]

With the new moniker, the legend of Bigfoot Wallace began to grow. In the fall of 1839, he was traversing a trail across Mount Bonnell, eleven miles above Austin. While hunting, he suddenly encountered a Waco on the same path. Reacting first, Wallace snapped a rifle shot from the hip, and the Indian plunged into the Colorado River below. Returning to the spot the next day with seven other men, Wallace found signs that a passing band of Wacos had pulled the dead Indian from the water and carried him off.[13]

The big frontiersman continued his free and untamed existence, and the next time he battled Indians would be perhaps the most significant for Texas. Following the Comanche attacks on Victoria and Linnville, Reverend Zachariah (or Zenos) Nehemiah Morrell rushed to Austin to recruit volunteers for Colonel Edward Burleson. Wallace, residing in town at the time, and confirmed to have been present at the forthcoming fight, was likely among the men who stepped forward. Colonel Burleson assembled eighty-seven horsemen and thirteen of Chief Plácido's Tonkawa scouts, and led them to the rendezvous at Plum Creek. Major-General Felix Huston had assumed command of the volunteer force and was tracking the Comanche raiders. When the colonel and his party arrived, they took their assigned place on the right wing. After skirmishing for a half-hour, Burleson's men and their Tonkawa allies charged around the woods, while Caldwell on the left went into the trees. Together they drove the Comanches into retreat. While their collective nose had been bloodied, Comanche war bands increased the size of their raiding expeditions into northern and central Mexico for livestock and Mexican and Apache slaves. They would not mount another large-scale attack into the Texas settlements until the Elm Creek Raid of 1864.[14]

After the decisive victory at Plum Creek, Wallace left Austin and decided to settle on the Medina, ten miles below the present town of Castroville. There he built his cabin on the west side of the river. According to F. E. Harris, who knew Wallace in the 1880s, the frontiersman "never acquired title to any of the ranch land he ranged. At that time, vacant land was everywhere about him. He never made costly or permanent improvements, and when his range deteriorated he moved his stock to new range." Harris was more or less correct as the Medina County tax rolls do not show land with either Samuel Wallace, as the original grantee, or William Wallace as the owner until 1866.[15]

Following Ráfael Vásquez's sortie into Texas, Wallace enlisted in Major John C. "Jack" Hays's ranging company on March 10, 1842. That same day, at least seven hundred volunteers answered President Houston's general call to arms and streamed into San Antonio. Hays's company also rendezvoused with those assembling. Vice President Edward Burleson, arriving on the fifteenth, assumed command of the irregular force, but President Sam Houston ordered Brigadier-General Alexander Somervell to take charge. Once the general arrived on March 18, he found the volunteers unwilling to submit to his orders, preferring instead Burleson. As Houston had realized the Vásquez raid was not a prelude to a major invasion, he ordered the discharge of those men needed on their farms. Burleson would wait nearly a month before he released the remainder of his force.[16]

Although the disappointed volunteers were sent home, Hays and his rangers remained active throughout the remainder of the year. Volunteering for the company in the summer of 1842, Private John Forester described his fellow rangers:

> The men were, in physical make-up, as fine a body of men as I ever saw, but the uniform was altogether new, unique and picturesque. Most of them were dressed in skins, some wearing parts of buffalo robes, deer skins and bear skins, and some entirely naked to the waist, but having leggings and necessary breechclouts. All were well armed and well mounted.[17]

In late August or early September, Wallace informed Hays that at least a dozen Mexicans, who were not known residents, were suspiciously loitering around San Antonio. At the same time, only ten to fifteen Anglos were residing in town and business was completely suspended. Wallace knew a fight was coming and, when his enlistment expired on September 1, he immediately reentered the service. Several days later, Hays sent Wallace and Nathaniel Mallon to the arsenal in Austin to procure gunpowder, percussion caps, and lead. After stopping along the trail to help bury two men who had been killed by Indians, the two rangers were only able to acquire a small amount of caps and lead and one barrel of powder. Wallace wrapped the barrel in a blanket and Mallon did likewise with the munitions. Each bundle was strapped to the pommels of their saddles. The pair rode back toward Seguín, some seventy miles, where they halted at José Antonio Navarro's *rancho* on San Geronimo Creek to obtain corn for their horses. They found there James Rice and Jack Johnson, two of Hays's rangers, sitting on the ground while two Mexican women removed prickly pear spines from their feet. Reining in and seeing their plight, Wallace laughingly said, "Hello, boys. What are you doing here?" From their comrades, Wallace and Mallon learned that General Adrián Woll had taken Béxar. The pair hurried with their badly needed supplies to join Hays's company in Seguín. While he welcomed a chance to fight Mexicans,

Wallace mourned the probable loss of the new Sunday-go-to-meeting pants he had purchased before leaving for Austin.[18]

Texian volunteers had organized into a combined force on September 17 at Salado Creek. The company commanders were Daniel Boone Friar of Cuero, with thirty-five men; James Bird and James Henry Callahan, with sixty men from Gonzales and Seguín; Adam Zumwalt, assisted by John Henry Brown, with twenty-five men from the Lavaca; and Ewen Cameron of Victoria with forty "cowboys." Forty of the best-mounted men, including Wallace, were assembled into a spy company under Hays. In an election for commanding officer, Mathew "Old Paint" Caldwell was chosen and he assumed the rank of major.[19]

Caldwell's men took a strong position on the east side of the creek. The major's plan was to entice the Mexicans out of San Antonio and deceive them into accepting battle on ground of his choosing. Acting on Caldwell's orders on September 18, Hays led a party of horsemen, including Wallace, Henry McCulloch, Robert Addison "Ad" Gillespie, Christopher Black "Kit" Acklin, Tom Galbreath, George Neill, Andrew Sowell, Creed Taylor, and Michael H. Chevallie, to within a half-mile of the Alamo. Taking the bait, four companies of Mexican cavalry wheeled into line and prepared to charge. Wallace was riding a sturdy mule, and Hays ordered him to start for camp even before the Mexicans advanced. Wallace thought his mule could beat them, but he obeyed his commander and kept up with his comrades when they raced for the creek and safety.[20]

Behind the Mexican cavalry came their infantry and artillery. The enemy opened their attack at eleven o'clock with a desultory cannonade. Following the barrage, Woll ordered his infantry to advance. As the battle was joined, Wallace was fired on at close range by a Mexican infantryman with an *escopeta*. The ranger's nose was grazed by a ball. Henry Whaling, one of Ewen Cameron's mounted gunmen, standing nearby commented, "Damn such shooting as that!" He then demonstrated superior marksmanship with his rifle and saw the Mexican collapse against a mesquite tree. While repulsing the next charge, a man of Hays's company pointed out a Mexican assisting a wounded *soldado* off the field. "Bigfoot, yonder is a Mexican who has on a pair of pants large enough to fit you," his fellow ranger said. Wallace's spare pair of trousers was still in enemy-occupied San Antonio. He fired at the tall Mexican and the ranger's bullet struck true. Wallace then ran out to strip the fallen man of his leggings. He would wear the trousers, made of a fine material, for the subsequent Somervell and Mier Expeditions.[21]

Thomas Jefferson Green, who wrote of the Woll invasion, estimated the Mexican general departed San Antonio with over two hundred casualties, most of whom died on the journey south. The Texians, their numbers increased to about five hundred, followed in their wake. The swift-riding rangers of Jack Hays caught up with the Mexican rearguard at the Arroyo Hondo. Hays formed his men to charge and capture the artillery that had unlimbered at the crossing. The rangers raced toward the cannon, killing six gunners, but they were forced to withdraw before the advancing Mexican infantry. Astride his mule, Wallace tried to turn back, but the stubborn animal instead headed straight for the enemy foot soldiers. Using all his strength, Wallace struggled to reverse his course while the braying mule kept on through a storm of lead. A short distance from the Mexican bayonets, the mule suddenly whirled around, shook her head as if bee-stung, nearly unseated Wallace, and raced for the Texian line. Wallace lay low in the saddle to avoid the balls whistling by his head. Once he reached the safety of Caldwell's force, he halted the mule and discovered her nose had been burned by a bullet.[22]

Occurring between the withdrawal of Woll's invasion force and the subsequent retaliation by the Texian government, numerous Comanche raids in the fall of 1842 prompted a punitive campaign of forty men; Wallace was one of them. Setting out, the volunteers quickly found an Indian trail and by the third day were at the headwaters of the Llano River. Spotting signal fires in the distance, Wallace persuaded the party's leader to allow him to go on a solitary scout. He left camp on foot a few hours before daybreak, and was soon clambering up a narrow canyon. Rounding a bend, he was suddenly face to face with a powerfully built Indian warrior. The two men instantly seized each other, but the task was made more difficult by the bear grease that coated the nearly naked Indian's body. Wallace outweighed his foe, but the Indian was quicker and hard to grasp. The Texian did manage to throw his enemy to the ground, whereupon the Comanche hit his head on a rock. Wallace snatched out his knife and drove the blade into the stunned Indian's heart. The mortally wounded warrior threw Wallace to the ground and leaped to his feet. He then whipped out his own knife and straddled the Texian, clutching him by the throat. Blinded by blood, the Indian struck, but his blade sank into the ground beside Wallace. The Comanche, at that point, dropped to the ground dead. Wallace disassembled the Indian's rifle and laid it beside the body. He then respectfully covered the fallen warrior with rocks.[23]

Wallace returned to San Antonio ready to fulfill the oath he had taken six years previously. He had come to Texas to avenge the deaths of his brother and other family members, and that task had not been sufficiently achieved. An invasion of Mexico offered him his chance. His participation in the Somervell Expedition as a member of Hays's ranger company was recorded as beginning on October 17.[24]

Wallace described his new comrades-in-arms as:

> A motley, mixed-up crowd … broken-down politicians from the "old States," that somehow had got on the wrong side of fence, and been left out in the cold; renegades and refugees from justice, that had "left their country for their country's good," and adventurers of all sorts, ready for anything or any enterprise that afforded a reasonable prospect of excitement and plunder. Dare-devils they were all …[25]

The expedition departed San Antonio on November 18, and reached the flooded Nueces River on December 2. After wandering through the Río Grande country, while the army deteriorated into a fractious mob, Brigadier-General Alexander Somervell at last decided, on the nineteenth, to end the campaign. He ordered the men to return to the interior of Texas. Most were furious; the expedition had formed to invade Mexico and plant the flag of Texas in enemy soil, and they had yet to complete that mission. Captains William S. Fisher, Ewen Cameron, William Mosby Eastland, William Ryon, John George Washington Pierson, Charles Keller Reese, and Claudius Buster refused to comply. A sizeable portion of the rank and file also chose to disobey Somervell's command and voted to continue on. Hays would return with Somervell, and Ben McCulloch followed a few days later. His original pledge unchanged, Wallace left Hays's outfit and enrolled in Reese's

Company E. The mutineers elected Fisher as their new commander and continued the march down the Río Grande. The expedition arrived opposite Mier on December 22. The next day, Wallace and several others advanced to the edge of the town where they encountered Agatón Quiñones and a sizeable force of enemy cavalry. The outnumbered Texians fled back to camp on the west side of the river.[26]

At dusk on December 25, Fisher led his 261 impetuous men in an attack on the estimated two thousand regular foot soldiers and one thousand cavalry troopers at Mier. Brushing aside the picket guard, the invaders halted briefly on the east side of the Río Alcantro atop a high bluff overlooking the town. Captain Reese and Joseph Berry were dispatched to the extreme left flank to distract the Mexican picket stationed there. General Green and Captain John Reagan Baker's twenty-five spies attacked the enemy cavalry picket on the lower ford, while the main body of Texians descended the steep clay hillside and crossed the Alcantro through a steady drizzle. Driving in another Mexican picket, they marched steadily west in column toward the block east of the Plaza de Armas.[27]

As darkness fell, Fisher's right wing turned north behind the cover of the houses bordering the square. The Mexicans had positioned artillery on the northeast and southeast corners of the plaza, which commanded the two lanes leading eastward to the Texian line. Once Fisher's men turned the corner, the gunners opened up with a barrage of grape and canister. Bordering each side of a street leading to the plaza was a row of stone houses separated only by partition walls. The Texians smashed in the doors of the corner house on the north side and began to break through the walls separating each successive house in an effort to reach the square. As they advanced, they made loopholes in the front walls to engage the enemy outside.[28]

In the forefront of the attack, Wallace manned some of the openings as the Texians smashed their way through the houses. He found an abandoned baby in one room, and dashed out the back door to place the infant on the other side of the wall surrounding the yard. He then ran back inside to take his place at the loopholes. As the evening fell, Wallace found himself in an officer's quarters with a banquet-laden table. He and his hungry comrades feasted and toasted their anticipated victory amid the gunfire and sounds of demolition.[29]

The Texians reached the fourth house and discovered the adjacent lot was vacant. The distance to the artillery was too great and without any cover. Nearly one hundred men led by Major Thomas W. Murray dashed across the street to seize a house on the opposite side. Once they reached their goal, some forty of the Texians "amused themselves by picking their chance to fire upon the enemy's artillery, which was planted within one hundred yards of the position of the Texan army." The Mexicans attempted three times to man the guns the following morning, and on each instance Fisher's men cut them down. Denied the use of their artillery, the Mexicans posted marksmen on the rooftops, while ropes were used to drag the cannons behind the houses on the plaza. The best of the Texian riflemen picked off sharpshooters while the others reloaded the discharged weapons.[30]

After midday, the battle experienced a respite as the opposing infantry quit the roofs and began massing for a charge. Fisher led forty or fifty men into the street and formed a line to receive the attack. The Mexican foot rushed forward, heedless of the Texians' deadly marksmanship. Wallace was moved by the infantry's bravery even as he killed one after another. He later reported he fired fifteen bullets in the fight and had a bead on a Mexican each time he squeezed the trigger. The enemy fell back to reform their ranks, then advanced twice more. The third charge almost reached the Texian line before they fell.[31]

Outnumbered ten to one, the Texians suffered sixteen killed and seventeen wounded, but they reportedly dispatched hundreds of the enemy. They continued to fight hard until they were induced to surrender that afternoon. Wallace opposed any capitulation and joined Captain Cameron, who was determined to fight to the bitter end. When the last of the other companies had yielded to the Mexicans in the plaza, Cameron was left with forty men to oppose 2,500 of the enemy. Suffocated by rage and shame, Cameron admitted the best chance for survival was to submit. Fisher was assured he and his men would be treated "with all the honor and consideration of prisoners of war." Wallace and his fellow prisoners were marched to Camargo, then to Matamoros, arriving at the latter place on January 9, 1843. When he laid down his arms, Wallace remarked, "Never shall I forget the humiliation of my feelings."[32]

General de división Pedro de Ampudia ordered Colonel Antonio Canales Rosillo and five hundred *rancheros* to take the Texians south. The colonel, who was known as an ignoble enemy of Texas, forced his half-starved and exhausted charges to walk at a rate of twelve to fifteen miles per day, arriving at Monterey on January 29, and at Saltillo on February 5. In addition, the guards proved to be brutal and tyrannical in their treatment of the prisoners. Colonel Manuel Barragán, a more humane officer, took custody of the Texians at Saltillo, and marched them toward San Luis Potosí and Agua Nuéva.[33]

On February 11, while at Hacienda del Salado, Wallace seized a bayonet from the muzzle of a Mexican musket and joined his fellow captives in overpowering their guards. The prisoners fled into the arid, rugged Sierra de la Paila near Saltillo. Over the next several days, they abandoned their makeshift weapons to lighten their load, ate snakes, grasshoppers, and their own horses, and clawed the ground in the hopes of finding moist dirt to quench their searing thirst. Their tongues became so swollen they could not close their mouths, and finally some resorted to drinking their own urine. The results of this desperate act were appalling. Mexican cavalry hunted the scattered fugitives, and when Wallace and three equally exhausted and starving companions stumbled across one patrol on February 19, they once more surrendered. Most of the escapees were recaptured within two weeks; seven died of starvation and thirst, five were successful in reaching Texas, and three completely disappeared.[34]

Wallace had begun the expedition dressed in top-quality trousers, a felt hat, and a buckskin jacket. By the time of his second capture, he was a tattered figure in a ragged coat, shredded pants, one shoe with numerous holes, and one rawhide sandal. His hat was gone and he had covered his head with a red bandanna.[35]

Presidente Antonio López de Santa Anna was incensed over the five Mexicans killed in the escape attempt, and he ordered the execution of every tenth man among the escapees. Returning to Salado in chains on March 24, the gaunt and filthy Texians paraded the following day and drew beans from a pot to choose whether they lived or died. Carefully observing the event, Wallace noticed the black beans, signifying death, were larger than the white ones. When his turn came, the tall ranger reached deep into the jar,

The Mier Expedition: The Drawing of the Black Bean (Prisoners Drawing their Beans) 1869 (oil on canvas), Remington, Frederic (1861-1909) / Museum of Fine Arts, Houston, Texas, USA / The Hogg Brothers Collection, Gift of Miss Ima Hogg / Bridgeman Images.

sifted several through his fingers, and pulled out a small bean of an indistinct grayish hue. Fortunately for Wallace, the Mexican officer in charge of the lottery declared it to be white.[36]

Following the execution of those who had drawn the black beans, the surviving 159 Texians were marched to the prison of Santiago. Within the week, Wallace and his fellow prisoners were taken to an old powder mill, where they were forced to work on the six hundred-yard public road connecting the Archbishop's Palace with nearby Tacubaya. The captives were forced to wear heavy fetters, and their rations consisted of "one pint of thin gruel, with a small cake of brown bread for breakfast, about two ounces of poor beef for dinner, with the water it is boiled in, and another cake of brown bread for supper." The quality and quantity of the food was insufficient to keep the men from slowly starving or becoming sick. While some carried heavy stones or other building materials, Wallace was hitched to a cart and forced to haul dirt.

He was so disgusted with this treatment that, while pulling the cart along the edge of the embankment, he pretended to take fright and ran down the road like a runaway steed. When he reached the next turn, he sent the cart whirling into the bottom of the embankment where it smashed into the rocks. Wallace ran on for another hundred yards, stopped, turned, and whinnied like a horse. The Mexican guards appreciated the joke and instead of punishing Wallace gave him a shovel. He never had to pull another cart.[37]

On September 12, the Texians were removed to the Castle of San Carlos de Perote, some 160 miles east of Mexico City on the Vera Cruz road. Arriving on the twenty-first, they were thrown into the dank, vile dungeon where they suffered for want of clothing and blankets. Observing Wallace's arrival, Edward Manton, a fellow prisoner, remarked that the Mexicans had "worked him thin." Chained together in pairs, the prisoners endured near-starvation, dreadful monotony, and an outbreak of typhus. Except for three Texians, the entire prison population fell victim to the epidemic, including Wallace. He became wild in his delirium and attempted to attack the guards and hospital staff. Until his fever broke, he had to be so securely restrained to his bed that the ropes left livid marks.[38]

As the year 1844 progressed, prisoners would sporadically gain their freedom. On March 23, Santa Anna ordered the release of the Béxar-Dawson prisoners taken during Woll's incursion. Wallace, William Ryon, William F. Wilson, Thomas S. Tatum, and James C. Armstrong were ordered to be liberated on August 24 due to a petition "from many members of the United States Congress."[39] At four p.m. the following day, Wallace and his four companions walked to Vera Cruz only to find the city wracked by a yellow fever epidemic. Consequently, no ships were available to sail to New Orleans. The five Texians waited for eleven days before they were finally able to board the French bark *Anax*. The passengers and most of the crew contracted the fever, but with the assistance of the ship's captain they all recovered and reached New Orleans on September 30. From there, Wallace, Armstrong, Ryon, and Wilson took passage aboard the steamship *Republic*, and arrived at Galveston on October 20. Wallace would receive pay for his services through October 16, 1844.[40]

While Wallace and the others were making their way back to Texas, the remaining 104 Texians had their manacles struck off on September 15.

The following day, before they were formally released, the prisoners were compelled to swear an oath and sign a document to never take up arms against Mexico. None of them took the pledge seriously, but they did all privately vow to avenge the deaths of their countrymen and the treatment they had received from their captors.[41]

Wallace returned to his homestead on the Medina River to "do a little farming." There he enjoyed the peace and solitude he so badly needed after his recent harrowing experiences. His convalescence ended after about two months when he enlisted in Hays's company on December 30. The ranger camp was near Wallace's cabin so he was able to serve and still work his farm. As the hunting was plentiful, his cultivation efforts proved haphazard and unenthusiastic. He realized only one good crop of corn. Wallace served a total of four enlistments with the rangers and was discharged on September 28, 1845.[42]

When Hays was appointed to command a battalion of rangers, Wallace enrolled in Captain Robert A. Gillespie's company of Texas Mounted Rangers on September 28 and was appointed first sergeant. The battalion operated under the auspices of Brigadier-General Zachary Taylor, commanding the American army at Corpus Christi. In November, the rangers guided First Lieutenant Jacob Edmund Blake's survey expedition westward to the Presidio crossing of the Rio Grande. Once the reconnaissance had been completed, Gillespie's men, the largest and most seasoned of the four companies in federal service, were situated on the probable avenue of approach for a Mexican invasion column from Laredo, as well as being expected to watch the hills north and west of San Antonio for Indian trouble. On January 13, a band of Wacos and Kichais managed to steal thirty-five horses in the Bexar area before Gillespie's company took up the chase. After a hard ride of seventy miles, the rangers overtook the Indians at the edge of a cedar brake. The raiders fled into the thick brush at the Texians' approach, leaving further pursuit impossible. Gillespie and his men gathered the horses together and drove them back to San Antonio, arriving on the sixteenth. The remainder of the rangers' tour of duty passed without incident, and Wallace mustered out on March 29, 1846.[43]

With the outbreak of the war with Mexico, Gillespie raised another company on June 29 in San Antonio. Wallace was elected first lieutenant, and Gouverneur Howard Nelson second lieutenant. Intent on seeing action with Taylor's army, the Texans rode from San Antonio to the Rio Grande, passing through Laredo and Mier, before being mustered into service in Camargo on August 30. Gillespie's men were nominally Company I of Hays's First Texas Mounted Rifles, but they would perform the role of an independent spy company for the time being. For the Texans, the war proved to be merely a continuation of the blood feud they had been waging with the Mexicans for over a decade. Throughout their service south of the border, all the rangers would acquire a fierce and well-deserved reputation. As Lieutenant Rankin Dilworth, First U.S. Infantry, observed, "The Mexicans dread the Texians more than they do the devil, and they have good reason for it." The Mier and Perote men were particularly notorious for having "fearfully punished their old oppressors." Two Mexicans who had allegedly insulted the prisoners on their way from Mier to Matamoros were attacked in the latter city; one was killed and the other severely wounded. Another who had "shamefully ill-treated" the captives at Perote was dangerously injured at a faro table. A third Mexican was shot in a billiard room because he had "been instrumental in adding to the distress of the Mier prisoners some years ago." Troubled by the Texans' insistence on retaliating against Mexicans they deemed guilty, General Taylor would lament, "I have not the power to remedy it or apply the corrective, I fear they are a lawless set."[44]

Nevertheless, the rangers were vital to the prosecution of the campaign. The companies of Gillespie and Ben McCulloch were ordered to report to Brigadier-General William Jenkins Worth at Cerralvo. Before departing that town, Taylor directed the company be divided with Gillespie and half the men being assigned to Major-General William Orlando Butler's Third Division, and Wallace and the other half to Worth's Second Division. Both detachments were employed as outriders and vedettes, and dispatch riders between Taylor's headquarters and the columns. On September 12, an advance party of ninety pioneers set out to prepare the roads for the supply trains. The next day, the First Division marched for Monterey, followed by the Second Division on the fourteenth, and the Third on the fifteenth.[45]

Making camp at Marin on September 17, General Taylor issued instructions that the Texas mounted volunteers would form the advance the following day and commence the march at five-thirty a.m. Four men were left with each of Worth's and Butler's divisions, while the remainder became part of the vanguard. Rejoining its parent regiment, Gillespie's company was the advance element of the column when the army broke camp at daylight on September 19. Wallace and his comrades were followed by the rest of the First Texas Mounted Rifles, the Second Texas Regiment, and the infantry divisions in numerical order.[46]

When the Army of Occupation arrived at Monterey, Company I was attached to Brevet Major Joseph Fenno King Mansfield's reconnaissance party. Mansfield, Taylor's chief engineer, was assigned to survey the southwestern side of the city and determine whether the road that led from Saltillo could be secured. At four p.m., Mansfield and Gillespie's detachment slipped out of Walnut Springs. They rode to within five hundred yards of Monterey and continually came under fire from the Black Fort's artillery. In an act of bravado intended to show contempt for the enemy's accuracy, the bold Texans competed to see how close they could get to the batteries near the city walls, while the Mexican artillerists attempted to hit them. "Now a cheer would ring from the citadel as a well-aimed shot produce some confusion among the Texans," a Maryland volunteer later wrote. As the mounted riflemen regained control of their horses, they would shower the defenders with a stream of expletives.[47]

Mansfield and the others returned to headquarters at ten o'clock and reported that if the Saltillo road were cut, the enemy supply line to Monterey would be choked off and the city's defenses could be taken. Taylor convened a council of war and announced his plans for a double envelopment. Worth's Second Division, Hays's regiment, and a company of Louisiana volunteers would capture the Saltillo road. If he deemed it practical, Worth would then assault the Federación and Independencia, which were two vital links in the city's chain of defenses. At the same time, Taylor and the balance of the army would strike the eastern sector.[48]

On September 20, Worth's command advanced from its camp at El Bosque de Santo at two p.m. Hays's 250 mounted rifles led the division in columns of five. One hour before sunset, while the general and some thirty rangers were observing the enemy dispositions near Independencia, they skirmished with a body of dismounted Mexican cavalry, which was quickly repulsed. Worth halted for the night at six o'clock beyond the range of the Mexican artillery atop Independencia. The Americans made camp and waited through the cold downpour without benefit of food, fires, blankets, or shelters. Despite their discomfort, the rangers were eager to even the score for the Alamo, Goliad, Mier, and countless other wrongs done to Texas in the last ten years. For his part, Taylor sought a crushing victory that would end the war in one stroke. The army he marshaled in front of Monterey was comprised of more than six thousand troops, nearly evenly split between regulars and volunteers. Standing ready to keep both the Texans and the American general from their respective goals were Pedro de Ampudia's seven thousand regulars and three thousand irregulars.[49]

By a quarter past eight the next morning, Worth and his men had reached the road. A fierce cannonade from the heights of Federación and Independencia began falling on the Americans, obliging them to move a half-mile down the road. Convinced he would have to take the guns on the peaks before he could assault the city, the general formed and discarded numerous plans to deal with the enemy artillery. At around noon, he ordered four artillery companies and Gillespie's company, along with those of Ben McCulloch, Thomas Green, Samuel Leonard Smith Ballowe, Jerome B. McCown, and Eli Chandler, to storm Federación. Major Mike Chevallie volunteered to lead his fellow Texans, but Worth refused on the grounds that Chevallie outranked Captain Charles Ferguson Smith, the general's choice for commanding the operation. The major waived his higher grade and told Worth, "There shall be no difficulty about that … I'll go under Capt. Smith."[50]

The assault party—three hundred strong—forded the "swift, running current" of the Santa Catarina River under a heavy artillery fire. Once they were on dry land, they hurried through the chaparral toward the hill. As they reached the base of their objective, they discovered reinforcements waiting for them. The foot soldiers of the Seventh Infantry under Captain Dixon Stansbury Miles had found a ford across the river closer to the hill and had actually arrived sooner. Smith reconnoitered the ground ahead, and observed the rocky hill rising some four hundred feet and covered in thick chaparral. Once he had seen enough, he ordered the attackers forward. The five hundred enemy troops on the summit spotted the advance and attempted to shell the attackers, but the gun crews could not depress their barrels enough to engage the Americans. With their artillery ineffectual, skirmishers descended the slope to engage the *Yanquis*. The U.S. regulars advanced by the heads of companies, while, on either flank, the Texans scrambled up the slope in loose order, shouting encouragement to one another, and exacting retribution with every rifle ball. The Mexican center faltered under the onslaught, then collapsed in disarray. The Americans reached the entrenchments and, seizing a nine-pounder, turned the gun upon the retreating enemy. The soldiers at the base of Federación gave a great shout when they saw the Stars and Stripes raised over the bastion.[51]

The victorious Texans retired to the Saltillo road where they slept until three a.m. on the twenty-second. Another assault party, this time under the command of Lieutenant-Colonel Thomas Childs and Colonel Hays, stormed up the western slope of Independencia. Making the daring ascent were three companies of the Eighth Infantry, three companies of the Third and Fourth Artillery Regiments, and two hundred dismounted rangers. In the lead, Gillespie's men charged through the fog and their captain was first over the enemy parapets. Lieutenant Wallace was close behind his friend and commanding officer. As the mist thinned, Wallace saw a Mexican sergeant standing atop the wall surrounding the bishop's palace and shot him. At the same time, Gillespie's foot slipped on a rock and he fell against the fortification. His staggering attracted the attention of another sentinel on the rampart. The Mexican fired at Gillespie, and the ball hit the captain's pistol whereupon it split and one fragment lodged in his bowels. The enemy soldier then fell to Lieutenant Nelson's rifle. As he lay on the ground, the gutshot Gillespie exhorted his men to carry on and "rush to the fore." Hays was nearby readying his rangers for a counterattack. The colonel instructed the men, "dont [*sic*] one of you fire until they get within 15 feet—short fifteen—let them come jam up." Gillespie heard the orders, rose up on an elbow, and told his subordinates, "Boys place me behind that ledge and rock … and give me my revolver, I will do some execution on them yet before I die." The defenders behind the breastworks were quickly driven from the position, leaving one of the six-pounders behind. The American forces breached the defenses of the Obispado and compelled the Mexicans to flee. In great pain for twenty-two hours, Gillespie would expire the next day. In the meantime, Wallace succeeded to command of Company I.[52]

On September 23, Hays's men led the assault into the city. During the advance down the *Calle de Monterey* to the plaza, Wallace and some other Texans fought their way to the Hidalgo Hotel, where they took a respite. After the terrified cooks found in the restaurant protested they had no food left, several of the famished rangers went out to search for provisions and soon returned with thirteen butchered sheep. The cooks began making a meal, but the mounted riflemen realized there was no bread to accompany the mutton. A vagrant sitting nearby offered to find bread if the Texans would pay him a dollar. Wallace agreed to the bargain and handed over the money. The little Mexican left and shortly came back with an impressive amount of fresh bread tied up in a blanket. Before they could tear into the loaves, one of the rangers uttered his concern the bread might be poisoned. Wallace assured his fellow Texans he would confirm whether the loaves were tainted. He called the Mexican vagrant over and ordered him to eat some of the bread. The man balked at first, but Wallace's cocked revolver convinced him otherwise. He struggled to finish four of the loaves, but he finally succeeded with the aid of copious amounts of water. Once the bread was eaten, Wallace told the man to sit and wait for any potential poison to kill him. After two minutes with no ill-effects, the smell of the cooked mutton convinced the Texans the bread was safe. They then began eating their improvised meal with gusto.[53]

Thus far, the company had only suffered one man killed and another slightly wounded. As an American victory seemed certain, General Ampudia sent a party under a flag of truce to request a parley. When he observed the Mexican officer holding the white flag, a suddenly enraged Wallace raised his rifle and prepared to shoot him. His fellow Texans intervened, reminding the lieutenant of the inviolability of a truce. Wallace revealed his motivations: the man in question had held the jar during the lottery at Salado and had cruelly mocked the condemned men. The Mexican denied he had been there, but Wallace loudly cursed him as a coward and "a coyote." Wallace was disgusted the man would escape justice amid the general armistice granted by General Taylor.[54]

Third Day of the Siege of Monterey. Lithograph by Sarony & Major, New York City. *Courtesy Prints and Photographs Division, Library of Congress, Washington, D.C.*

Despite these disappointments, not all was lost. Wallace had first come west to avenge the deaths of his kinsmen. When marching into Mexico, he passed through Mier and other places where he had suffered at the hands of Mexicans. By all accounts, he killed enough of his foes to consider these old scores well on the way to being settled. The last of Ampudia's army marched out of the city on September 28. With Monterey securely in American hands, and the Texas Rangers' place in history assured, Wallace and the rest of Company I was discharged the next day.[55] Luther Giddings, an Ohio volunteer officer, described a sentiment common among other soldiers of the army:

> The departure of the Rangers would have caused more regret than was generally felt, had it not been for the lawless and vindictive spirit some of them had displayed in the week that elapsed between the capitulation of the city and their discharge … Gifted with the

> intelligence and courage of back-woods hunters, well-mounted and skilled in arms, they were excellent light troops. Had they remained and given their whole attention to the guerrillas, they might have been exceedingly useful. The commanding general took occasion to thank them for the efficient service they had rendered, and we saw them turn their faces toward the blood-bought State they represented, with many good wishes and the hope that all honest Mexicans were at a safe distance from their path.[56]

After almost a year spent at his homestead, Wallace traveled to San Antonio and enlisted in Captain William G. Crump's ranger company on September 28, 1847. The company was mustered into Colonel Peter Hansborough Bell's Regiment of Texas Mounted Volunteers two days later. As the colonel deployed his companies along the frontier line, Crump's command was posted within the settlements on the Medina and assigned to protect San Antonio and Goliad. Later, Wallace and his comrades would be shifted to the Arroyo Seco with a detachment thirty miles away on the Leona. He mustered out on September 30, 1848, as a private.[57]

Becoming a civilian once more, Wallace found himself the owner of a substantial amount of land. By virtue of Third-Class Certificate No. 14, issued by the Travis County Board of Land Commissioners, he was entitled to a headright of 320 acres. On November 24, 1846, Survey No. 152 had been conducted on the northeast side of what came to be called Wallace Creek in present Bandera County, about fifty-eight miles northwest of San Antonio. The warrant would be patented on June 21, 1856. The surveys for the 960 acres Wallace had received as Samuel's heir in 1837 were completed and patented by May 2, 1848. This tract was situated on the north bank of the Guadalupe River in present Kerr County, about fifty-five miles northwest of San Antonio. By August 1849, Wallace was running three horses and two head of cattle on his headright and paying taxes on the land in Kerr County. The following year, the acreage in Bandera was no longer in his possession and no livestock was assessed on the bounty land. By October 1852, Wallace had evidently sold the property, as his name no longer appears on the tax rolls.[58]

Presumably after Wallace's discharge from Bell's regiment, Chiquito and Chipota, two chiefs leading a war party of Lipan Apaches, were raiding the Medina country and stole 190 horses and mules, including two of Wallace's own stock. He advised his neighbors to wait before striking back as the Indians would be expecting a response. The following month, Wallace and Edward Dixon Westfall led a party of thirty volunteers in pursuit and located the raiders' camp on the head of the Frio River. Wallace and Westfall scouted the site on foot and discovered the Indians busy gorging themselves on buffalo meat. They returned to the men and led them in a mounted charge on the raiders. The surprised warriors took flight and the Texians galloped after them. After Wallace's mare stumbled on a rock and fell, the ranger toppled to within a few feet of an enemy warrior. He scrambled to shoot the Indian, but his rifle's flint broke. Westfall and the settlers charged again and the Indians were overrun. Wallace then aimed at another warrior and his gun discharged upon this attempt. The rifle ball severed the Indian's spine, killing him instantly. The engagement concluded with ten Indians slain. Nearly all the stolen animals were recovered, but Wallace's horse and mule were not among them.[59]

In the summer of 1849, Governor George Tyler Wood received appeals from residents of Corpus Christi and the Rio Grande country regarding the large bands of hostile Indians raiding in their area. Major-General George Mercer Brooke, commanding the Eighth Military Department, requested the governor raise three ranger companies for federal service. Later in the year, Wood sought to convey to Secretary of War George Walker Crawford the vast amount of territory in need of protection, and implored more troops be sent to the area. On March 6, 1850, Brooke asked Peter Bell, by then serving as the state's third governor, to authorize an additional company for six months. The company was to be composed of one captain, one first lieutenant, one second lieutenant, four sergeants, four corporals, two musicians, two farriers, two blacksmiths, and sixty-four privates. Petitions on behalf of Bigfoot Wallace were sent to the governor imploring he be given the commission. Bell acquiesced and designated Wallace, "an energetic and enterprising old ranger," to raise the company.[60]

Company elections were held on March 23, 1850, in Austin. Wallace was chosen captain; Peter Rainsford Brady, first lieutenant; Absalom King

Vansickle, second lieutenant; and Elisha Briggs, first sergeant. Wallace's men were mustered into federal service the same day, and the company was ordered to San Antonio to receive supplies following its organization. Once their stores had been issued, the rangers departed on April 9 for their station on Chacon Creek, approximately twenty miles from Eagle Pass.[61]

Wallace was later posted to Fort Inge where he received orders to make immediate preparations for two months of field duty, or until the Nueces Strip was cleared of Lipan Apaches. Utilizing all available dragoons and mounted infantry, as well as the rangers, Brevet Lieutenant-Colonel William Joseph Hardee was to command the campaign. Brevet Captain James Oakes, commanding Company G, Second Dragoons, and Captain Wallace took their companies toward Fort Merrill. On June 23, Wallace moved down the right bank of the Nueces, while Oakes rode down the left bank of the Frio. Hardee marched with the dragoons of Company C between the two rivers, crossing the Nueces about twenty-five miles above Fort Merrill. Oakes arrived at the post on July 3, Wallace and Hardee two days later. In skirmishes with two war parties, they had killed nine Lipans and wounded another nine. On July 8, news came of Indian depredations near Corpus Christi. Wallace was ordered to head to the scene and "follow the Indians wherever they might go." The captain returned to Fort Merrill without having found any victims or indication of Indian raiders. Ten days later, Wallace, with nineteen rangers, was directed to scout up the Nueces to Espantosa Lake. In an area known as the Black Hills, sixteen miles from the present town of Cotulla, the company rode through the blistering heat and found one dried-up water hole after another. Stopping at Todos Santos Creek, they came across a band of eighty Comanches. The Indians charged four times and were repeatedly repulsed. Wallace's men killed seven of the attacking warriors and wounded nine, while suffering three wounded themselves. The warriors retreated to their camp at another water hole farther up the creek and, after slaking their own thirst, Wallace's men followed. Comanche reinforcements came up unexpectedly and pushed the rangers back. The Texans returned to the place where they had left their wounded. Later, Wallace reconnoitered the Indian camp and found they had departed. The rangers stayed at the water hole several days resting their horses. In August, Captain Jerome B. McCown's rangers found twenty-five to thirty Comanches encamped on the Nueces. The captain would later determine they were of the same party Wallace had fought the previous month. Leaving eleven behind in reserve, McCown and ten men charged the Indians, killing two and capturing forty-five horses, two mules, two firearms, assorted clothing articles, and all the camp equipage. One of the rangers was killed.[62]

Wallace's company remustered for another six-month term on September 23, 1850, at Fort Inge. Vansickle chose not to reenlist, and William F. Powell became the new second lieutenant. John F. Spratt replaced Elisha Briggs as first sergeant. An enumerator for the 1850 federal census found the members of Wallace's company encamped on the west side of the Leona River on October 14. Vansickle was listed as the third lieutenant. In addition to four officers, the record tallied eight noncommissioned officers, seventy-three privates, two musicians, and one farrier. Displaying the cosmopolitan nature of the American borderlands, ten of the rangers were born in Germany, three in Ireland, one in Canada, and one in Scotland. Of the native-born recruits, eleven hailed from Tennessee while fifty-one were from other Southern states; only four had been born in Texas.[63]

By September, the Nueces Valley was deemed free of Indian troubles. General Brooke approved of the results derived from Hardee's operations, and he ordered more reconnoiters of the Frio and Nueces valleys and nearby passes where warriors might be prowling. Prior to one such scout, Wallace and his rangers were encamped on Turkey Creek. During the month of November, Wallace, two corporals, and eighteen privates were positioned at Tortuga Lake, while Brady, Powell, Spratt, and fifty-six rangers were assigned to detached duty at Fort Inge. Private Benjamin F. Wilson died in camp on December 26, but the cause was not recorded.[64]

By February 1851, the company was back on the Leona while potentially hostile Indians were increasing their numbers along the border. General Brooke was concerned the ranger stations be kept occupied and the settlements protected during the coming muster of the ranger companies. In a February 20 skirmish with Indians on the Nueces, Private William Fiega was killed. The incident occurred when a detachment of the company was scouting and camped for the night. Fiega and another ranger had ridden out to

Comanche War Trail. ©Frank C. McCarthy, licensed by The Greenwich Workshop, Inc. wwwgreenwichworkshop.com.

hunt turtles and encountered a party of Indians in the darkness. The sudden appearance of the warriors spooked the Texans' horses, and Fiega was thrown to the ground while his companion fled. The next morning, the rangers found their slain comrade scalped with his chest cavity cut open and a fire built within. The following month, Wallace was absent on recruiting duty, and the company was remustered on the twenty-third at Fort Inge. George Witting became first sergeant in the reorganization. Peter Brady resigned on July 16, and Wallace's old friend, Edward Westfall, became the company's first lieutenant ten days later.[65]

On July 1, scouts reported to the captain that a party of Indians was moving down between Mina Creek and the Nueces. The next day, Wallace and thirty-seven rangers rode out in pursuit. On the fifth, they found evidence the war party was on the Nueces in a dense thicket twenty-five miles below the old Presidio road. Wallace and three men dismounted and crept through the chaparral to the edge of a lagoon where they saw seven Comanches on the opposite bank. Because of the brush, and the muddy soil, the captain left a small horse-guard behind and advanced toward the Indian camp on foot. In the ensuing fight, the warriors briefly stood their ground, then fled with the rangers in pursuit. Despite his superior numbers, Wallace could not get sufficiently close to the raiders due to the terrain. Some forty shots were fired and only one Comanche was killed, but the rangers were able to capture all of the enemy's rifles, lances, shields, saddles, horses, and camp equipage.[66]

The company was discharged on September 23, 1851, at Fort Inge, and Wallace returned to "his ranch on the Medina, where he raised cattle and horses." He found little time to work his spread as he was kept occupied with hunting, fighting Indians, and tracking runaway slaves with his dogs. With the dream of freedom beckoning from across the Rio Grande, the human chattel belonging to planters along the Brazos and Colorado Rivers would sometimes escape and flee for Mexico. Indeed, southern Texas had become a major route for slaves attempting to cross the border throughout the 1840s and 1850s. The common dilemma for Southern slaveholders in recapturing their property from free states and territories had prompted the passage of the second Fugitive Slave Act as part of the greater Compromise of 1850. Legally empowered to demand up to fifty dollars per head in bounties, Wallace's reputation as a successful slave catcher became widespread, and he earned a substantial, albeit shameful, sum in reward money.[67]

While Wallace had commanded his rangers, the Postmaster General solicited bids to carry the U.S. mails from San Antonio to Doña Ana, New Mexico Territory, via Eagle Pass, Presidio del Norte, and San Elizario on a bi-monthly basis. Wallace and Richard A. "Dick" Howard had offered to fulfill the contract for $25,000 annually. The Postmaster General rejected their bid on April 14, 1851, as "extravagant and not according to advertisement." Instead, Captain Henry Skillman, an experienced frontiersman, was awarded the mail service contract on September 20.[68]

Two months later, Wallace hired on with Captain Skillman to direct a mail train between San Antonio and San Elizario. The caravan usually consisted of a stagecoach for passengers, two heavy wagons for supplies and baggage, and six heavily armed guards. Four mules were harnessed to each vehicle with one spare mule per team. Running some six hundred miles through Comanche and Apache lands, the road lay west out of San Antonio to Fort Clark and on to the Devil's River. From there, it turned northwest to Fort Lancaster, then west to Camp Stockton and Fort Davis. Skirting the Davis Mountains, the route continued on to Van Horn Wells before bearing toward the Rio Grande and San Elizario. Indian trouble was only one of the trials facing the stage lines as the arid terrain, rugged mountains, and wild animals proved daunting as well.[69]

For more than five years, Wallace drove the stage road while the government contract changed hands several times. Skillman lost out to Daniel Wasson, who sub-contracted to George Henry Giddings on March 13, 1855. The franchise then went to James E. Birch on June 22, 1857. Appointing Giddings and Robert Emmett Doyle as his agents, and Isaiah Churchill Woods as general superintendent, Birch started operations on July 9, but he died in a shipwreck off the California coast three months later. Shortly thereafter, Wallace would leave the stage line's employment.[70]

While he embarked on a new career with the stage line, Wallace continued to acquire land. On April 27, 1838, the Harrisburg County Board of

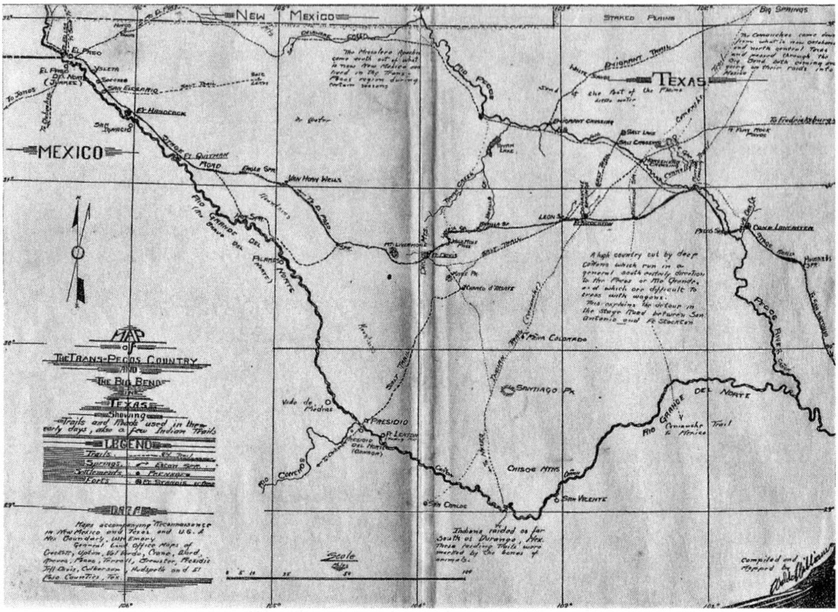

Map of Stagecoach Route. Compiled and mapped by Waldo Williams. *Courtesy Marfa Public Library, Marfa, Texas.*

Land Commissioners had issued Wallace, as administrator of his brother's estate, First-Class Certificate No. 506, which entitled him to a headright of one-third of a league of land, or 1,476 acres. Surveys of two tracts composed of one-sixth of a league each were conducted on the north bank of the Guadalupe River, which were alongside the two parcels he already owned in Kerr County. The warrant was patented on December 19, 1851.[71]

Wallace would find little time to enjoy his new property as the demands and dangers of driving the San Antonio–El Paso road consumed his attentions. On September 9, 1852, during a trip between Leona Station and Fort Fillmore, New Mexico, five men, all but one a seasoned Indian fighter, were escorting the stagecoach Wallace was driving. The coach stopped for the afternoon meal at Big Bluff, five miles below the California Springs and seven miles above the Painted Caves, near the Devil's River. The Texans were just preparing to resume their journey when Wallace heard the sound of horses dashing across the rocky ground and alerted his men. In scant moments, thirty-two Comanches charged toward the coach and loosed a shower of arrows. Only one of the Texans returned fire, seemingly without effect. The warriors gained the top of Big Bluff and the two sides skirmished until nightfall. One mule was killed and Adolph Fry was grazed by a bullet fragment. Three of the attackers were killed and a fourth was badly wounded. As the sun set, the Comanches were reinforced by seven or eight more warriors. Wallace moved his stagecoach and two wagons into a triangle, and the Texans settled down to wait. At daybreak, with no further attacks, Wallace and a companion climbed to the top of Big Bluff and discovered the Indians had vanished during the night.[72]

While his men were harnessing the mule teams, Wallace observed a party of forty Indians approaching. He shouted defiance in Spanish and challenged the warriors to fight him on the trail to California Springs. The Comanches rode to the proposed meeting place, but Wallace took an alternate route to Fort Clark. There, and at Fort Inge, he failed to obtain a military escort, and was forced to return to San Antonio and hire one on his own. He then continued to El Paso with three arrows jutting from the side of the coach.[73]

During another mail run, on April 28, 1853, Wallace was headed for San Antonio while three of his men drove eight spare mules ahead of the main caravan. The trio were attacked by a party of fifteen Mescalero Apaches twelve miles east of Van Horn's Wells. One of the stage company employees took an arrow in his right side, and the Indians stampeded the mules; all but four were recovered. The wounded man and his companions rode back to the safety of Van Horn's Wells. Soon after, Wallace was camped for the night on the Pecos. Noticing one of his mules was acting uneasy, Wallace alerted his men and readied his rifle and a brace of long-barreled dueling pistols for action. Despite the preparations, though, nothing happened for hours and the guards began to relax. Without warning, nine warriors slipped toward the coach around nine p.m., and Wallace shouted for his men to "nip them quick." Both sides opened fire; one Indian discharged an old blunderbuss that peppered the side of the coach with shot. Wallace pursued the raiders for a short time in the darkness, and he narrowly escaped becoming a casualty. The skirmish ended quickly with none hurt on either side.

Wallace, plagued by a severe fever, arrived in San Antonio slightly less than fourteen days after he had begun the trip.[74]

Wallace took the mail to Santa Fé in January 1854. On his return trip, he was in El Paso County where his involvement in local matters led him to become a fugitive from justice. The issue began when El Paso merchant James Wiley Magoffin asserted ownership of the salt lakes at Los Chinos in New Mexico. He claimed people from the village of Doña Ana were taking salt from the deposits without compensating him. As was the case in El Paso County, which would explode into violence some twenty years later, the salt lakes had been considered a public resource for decades. Magoffin swore out a complaint and an arrest warrant was issued. An El Paso deputy sheriff and a posse of thirty well-armed men rode to the deposits to arrest the *salineros* gathering the salt. Wallace, ever ready to make war upon Mexicans, accompanied the party. One hundred New Mexicans in twenty-six carts arrived at Los Chinos at one a.m. and were confronted by the possemen. A shot rang out and the gunfire continued for another ten minutes. The *salineros* quit the scene and the Texans confiscated several mules. The posse returned to Magoffinsville confident they had served notice on the New Mexicans that the salt deposits were off-limits. Instead, bad blood was created, and the territorial governor issued arrest warrants for the posse members in March 1854. Wallace was one of those on the list, but since he never returned to New Mexico the warrant went unserved.[75]

Wallace failed to deliver the mail on schedule only twice. The first time was while he was en route to El Paso and had stopped at the stage station at *Ojo del Muerto* in present Jeff Davis County. The mules were taken to graze under the watch of one guard while Wallace sat mending some harness. Hearing a slight noise behind him, he turned and saw an Indian on a large rock ten feet away bringing his gun to bear. Wallace whipped out his pistol and the Indian dodged behind cover. At the same time, the guards had wandered away and a band of Indians were taking advantage of the lapse to drive off the mules. Wallace called for his inattentive companions to save the stock, but the raiders were too swift and were quickly out of sight with the stolen *mulada* (drove of mules). Wallace's only choice to complete his run was to walk the eighty miles to El Paso, acquire another team, and return for the stage.[76]

More Indian raids engulfed the Medina and Atascosa countries in the late summer of 1855. On September 3, they attacked the Briggs ranch on Elm Creek and stole twenty-five horses. Wallace, at home between trips to El Paso, raised a company of fifteen volunteers on the fifth and took to the trail. The *San Antonio Ledger* noted that settlers, badly mounted and often ill-armed, had lately followed the "Parthian-like marauders" with only trifling success. Unfortunately, the results of Wallace's foray in early September went unrecorded. Another war party struck ranches nine miles below Castroville on the twenty-sixth, stealing thee ponies, killing three others and four head of cattle, and wounding another horse. Wallace gathered thirteen of his neighbors together the next day and set out in pursuit of the raiders. By noon, after a chase of twenty-five miles, they caught up to their quarry, four in number, cooking one of the stolen cows. The settlers attacked, and one of the Indians was killed and another was wounded in the brief engagement. Wallace's party suffered only one casualty, an arrow wound in the shoulder. The surviving Indians fled into the brush, leaving their horses behind.[77]

While at home the following April, Wallace, alerted by his dogs, captured a young Indian hiding in a gulley near his cabin. He brought his prisoner into Castroville where he allowed inquisitive townspeople to satisfy their curiosity. A self-important county officer informed Wallace he would take custody of the Indian, but Wallace told him, "This is my Indian; I caught him. If you want an Indian, go catch you an Indian." Wallace then took his captive to San Antonio and turned him over to Indian agent Robert Simpson Neighbors.[78]

Stage line superintendent Isaiah Woods dispatched Wallace to Forts Clark and Lancaster on July 19, 1857, with an extra train of stores and twenty-seven mules to stock relay stations. On the twenty-fifth, Wallace's stage was eighteen miles north of Camp Hudson near the upper crossing of the Devil's River. Suddenly, Comanches sprang from the chaparral and fired on the six mules pulling the coach. The terrified animals dashed into the mesquite, turned suddenly, and snapped the pole. Wallace, who was driving, dove from the box and called on his passenger, a young man named William Clifford, to assist him. Clifford ran ahead to help the five men driving the *mulada* and was severely wounded; he and another of the escort soon died in hand-to-hand fights with the Indians. Although wounded, Wallace succeeded in turning the herd into the brush in an attempt to escape his pursuers, but they were too close. Calling on the outriders to flee for their lives, he barely managed to escape on a saddled mule leaving the livestock, coach, and baggage to the Comanches.[79]

Wallace reached Camp Hudson a few hours later where, by coincidence, Captain Charles Jarvis Whiting and a patrol of Company K, Second Cavalry from Fort Clark had halted. Whiting immediately set out after the raiders. The troopers overtook the Indians and recovered most of the stage company's property, including all of the stolen stock. Returning to the scene of the ambush, a detachment from Company G, Eighth Infantry salvaged the smashed coach and gave Clifford a proper burial. Meanwhile, presumably having retrieved the mail, Wallace and his men returned to San Antonio to wait for further instructions.[80]

In late 1857, grasshoppers plagued much of South Texas, including the Medina range, and Wallace decided to quit the stage company. He packed his rifle and gear, gathered his stock and dogs, and set out for the untamed country to the southwest. He found a wild and lonely spot on Chacon Creek east of the Hondo River in which to locate his new homestead. In keeping with his casual attitudes regarding land ownership, Wallace neglected to legally file on his claim, a decision that would cost him in the years ahead.[81]

His choice of ranchlands also exposed him to new dangers. Settlers along the Hondo, Sabinal, and Seco were being plagued by depredations, and they looked to Wallace as one man "better acquainted with the Indian character and their intrigues of warfare" than any other. The ex-ranger was guiding a band of settlers in pursuit of marauding Indians when the raiders decided to set an ambush in a brushy area. Intent on following the trail, Wallace looked up in time to see a warrior stand and take aim with his rifle. The ranger threw himself off the back of his horse, narrowly avoiding the ball. Wallace fired from a prone position and dealt the Indian a mortal wound. Several other warriors also stood, and J. M. Smith wounded one of them. The demoralized raiders vanished. Smith later said Wallace dodging the Indian's bullet "was the quickest work he ever saw done."[82]

In 1859, Wallace elected to take a trip to Virginia and visit his kinfolk. He first stopped in his birthplace of Rockbridge County, then made a short side trip to Canada in order to see Niagara Falls. Wallace was still in Virginia in time for the 1860 federal census. While staying at the home of his sister Rebecca and her husband Marion Sehorn in Wytheville, he reported his occupation to the enumerator as "Capt. U.S.A. Texas Mounted Volunteers."[83]

Wallace returned to the Medina country before the onset of the Civil War. The old ranger believed the secession of Texas from the Union in February 1861 to have been a mistake. He would later recount, "I wanted nothing to do with that foolish war. I did not want to see the Union dissolved, and I could not fight against old Virginia, and I would have fought a regiment before I would have shouldered a musket on either side." As male settlers began to join the Confederate Army and leave the frontier exposed, Wallace resolved to stay and protect the women and children remaining behind. While the conflict raged in New Mexico, and north and east of the Red River, Wallace fought Indians and bandits, tracked down escaped slaves, and hunted wolves. In October 1861, after a war party of twenty-five Indians swept through the Hondo settlements, he raised a band of thirty volunteers and followed the raiders' trail between the D'Hanis and Rancho Creeks. Riding approximately thirty miles up Seco Creek, the settlers began to ascend a steep hill when they were ambushed by twelve to fifteen Indians; William Davenport was severely wounded. Wallace led his men to the foot of the hill where they sought cover in a grove of trees. Five Indians were slain by the sharpshooting Texans and three more were wounded. The Indians fled, leaving behind two double-barreled shotguns, one rifle, and one horse. Wallace took Davenport to the military camp on the Sabinal, seven miles distant, then resumed the pursuit. He and his party outpaced the Indians and set their own ambush, killing three and forcing the others to flee. One hundred and fifty head of stolen horses were recovered.[84]

Once the war ended, Wallace settled down to ranching as a full-time occupation. As mentioned previously, the Medina County tax rolls for 1866 have the first positive mention of him owning property in that locale. He also owned a herd of forty horses valued at twelve hundred dollars. In 1867, Wallace and three cowboys—Jeff Bonds, Bill Dukes (or Decker), and Tom Jones—were working on the old ranger's ranch when they noticed the smell of roasting meat. Assuming Indians were nearby, the four men readied their rifles and pistols and searched on foot for the campfire. They advanced through the brush and discovered five Tonkawas cooking one of Wallace's unbranded cows. Wallace leveled his rifle at the Indian he believed to be the leader and directed his hands to fire on the other Tonkawas. At the order, all four rifles cracked simultaneously. The leader fell head first into the fire even as he was raising a chunk of beef to his lips; another Indian also died, one was wounded, and the three surviving warriors vanished into the brush.[85]

Even as Wallace was engaging hostile Indians for possibly the last time, he was building his ranching interests, including his 2,436 acres in Kerr County and 496 acres in Bandera. His horse herd would number between seventy-two and 104. By 1870, his real estate was valued at two thousand dollars. Over the next few years, though, Wallace's business acumen would not match his expertise as a hunter and scout, and, through an unmanageable accumulation of debt, his holdings would slowly become forfeit. On May 8, 1871, Wallace agreed to transfer title for 1,956 acres in Kerr County to William Speer in order to satisfy a liability of $3,200. On December 7, he entered into a similar arrangement with Joshua D. Brown when he decided to hand over his remaining 480 acres in Kerr to fulfill an obligation of seven hundred dollars. The following year, Wallace conveyed title for 320 acres in Bandera County to James W. Chamberlain in recompense for a debt of $640. On May 15, Wallace and Speer agreed to withdraw 738 acres from their title bond so Wallace could sell the tract to Roland Christal for the sum of $691. By 1872, his ranch in Medina County encompassed 960 acres and his livestock numbered eighty-seven horses. In 1875, he acquired two tracts covering one hundred and 320 acres respectively, but he sold them two years later.[86]

On July 27, 1874, Wallace applied for a pension citing his service in the Mier Expedition. The claim was approved on August 8, and Wallace received $250. He would sorely need the money as his attempts at ranching proved unsuccessful. According to John Wesley Wilbarger, Wallace was "unable to hold his own against the manipulations of the shrewd land shark … some one discovered a flaw in Wallace's land title and succeeded in ejecting him from his little ranch, which he had occupied for some fifteen or twenty years without any one ever disputing the right of his occupancy." In 1879, his forty horses, twenty-two head of cattle, and twelve hogs were seized by the sheriff in a civil suit, and his ranch was listed on the county tax rolls as unrendered acreage. The following year, his name did not appear in the rolls, and he was residing in the home of laborer Antonio Baldares in Frio County. The *Statesman* noted he was living in "reduced circumstances." Moreover, old age, deprivations experienced in Mexican prisons, and a hard life out-of-doors had taken a physical toll on the once powerful ranger. Suffering from palsy, Wallace could no longer care for himself and had to depend on the hospitality of friends.[87]

Moving to the tiny hamlet of Big Foot, he lived with Judge John Smart Thomas and, later, the jurist's brother-in-law MacHenry Bramlette. Wallace continued to hunt and kept the Bramlette household in fresh meat. He worked in the garden and enthralled the children with colorful stories of the frontier. He would continue to run cattle and horses on his neighbors' ranches until the spring of 1892 when he sold the last of his herds.[88]

Wallace traveled to Austin in early February 1889. In the state capitol, he met with Governor Lawrence S. "Sul" Ross and several members of the Twenty-first Legislature to ask for redress regarding the land certificate error that had cost him his ranch. By virtue of "An Act for the relief of William A. A. Wallace," approved March 30, 1889, he was issued a certificate for 1,280 acres of land on July 6. Wallace offered John W. Maddox, a co-owner in Maddox Bros. & Anderson of Austin, a nine-tenths interest in return for one thousand dollars and named him, on April 22, to serve as the agent in regards to the property. Several surveys were made on the tract, which was located on the east end of Galveston Island. Wallace also received 252 acres in several tracts on Tally Island, approximately four miles south of Rockport in Aransas County, and on Blackberry Island in the shallow bay near Aransas Harbor. Wallace grew to mistrust Maddox and lamented, "I'll never live to get anything out of this deal." Through the intercession of friends, Wallace was able to realize some profit when he sold his acreage in Aransas, and his claim on the east end of Blackberry Island, to Kerr County businessman William H. Bonnell for the sum of five hundred dollars.[89]

Remaining in the town that bore his nickname, Wallace spent his twilight years in the home of William West "Doc" Cochran, Bramlette's son-in-law. The physical weakness and involuntary tremors that plagued him made eating a simple meal impossible without assistance. Despite his impairments, he was able to attend the State Fair and Dallas Exposition in October 1898; author and former ranger A. J. Sowell was present as a chaperon. Wallace died of pneumonia on January 7, 1899, and was laid to rest in the Devine Cemetery in Medina County. On February 20, the Twenty-sixth Legislature passed a bill authorizing his disinterment and reburial in the State Cemetery in Austin.[90]

The life of Bigfoot Wallace was an exciting, rough-and-tumble adventure, and his colorful exploits as hunter, Indian fighter, ranger, and stagecoach driver were told and retold until they became all but tall tales. Nonetheless, his deeds in the service of Texas, however fanciful the exaggeration, merit the respect shown him by a grateful state. He deserves no less than the modest epitaph that marks his gravestone:

BIG FOOT WALLACE
Here Lies He Who Spent His
Manhood Defending the Homes
of Texas
Brave Honest and Faithful
Born April 3, 1817
Died Jan. 7, 1899

Samuel H. Walker. Half plate daguerreotype by Mathew Brady, New York City. *Courtesy Prints and Photographs Division, Library of Congress, Washington, D.C.*

Chapter 5

Samuel H. Walker: "Fighting Man par Excellence"

Samuel Hamilton Walker was a fighting man *par excellence*. J. J. Oswandel said of him, "War is his element, the bivouac his delight, and the battlefield his playground." His actions as a ranger captain in the early stages of the Mexican war thrust the once local renown of the Texas Rangers into nationwide prominence. In just four years, this formidable soldier of fortune would grow from an unknown Marylander into a Texas hero and a national celebrity. This fame would moreover allow him to make significant contributions to one of the most legendary firearms in American history. While Hays may have set the benchmark for future Texas Rangers, Walker cemented the service's reputation and made them a household name.

He was born on February 24, 1817, at Toaping Castle, the family plantation in Prince George's County, Maryland. Beginning as a log cabin in the late 1750s, the subsequent white oak manor house was located at the headwaters of Bear Garden Branch, nine miles from Washington, D.C. Samuel's father, Nathan, had been born on the estate in 1756, and served in the Revolutionary War as a private in Captain Thomas Beall's Company of the Upper Battalion of Militia. He was a carpenter by trade, and began farming full-time in 1820. Nathan had married Nancy Ann (Baggerly) Beck of Montgomery County on July 21, 1798, but she died in 1804. Samuel had two half-siblings from his father's first marriage: Henry B. Walker, born August 31, 1799, and Elizabeth Ann "Betsy" Walker. On October 3, 1810, Nathan married Elizabeth Thomas, who had been born in Charles County in 1783. Samuel's six brothers and sisters from the second marriage were Jonathan Thomas Walker, born August 4, 1811; Nathan Walker, born December 8, 1812; Catherine Walker, born April 30, 1814; Jane Walker, born July 20, 1815; Charles Edward Walker, born December 18, 1818; and Mary Thomas Walker, born November 28, 1820. As a boy, Samuel attended the common country school, and afterward learned carpentry from his father.[1]

Census records indicate ten members of the family were living on the plantation in 1820: four boys and two girls under the age of ten, two males between sixteen and twenty-six, one female between twenty-six and forty-five, and one over the age of forty-five. Additionally, Nathan owned one male and two female slaves between the ages of fourteen and twenty-six, and one female between twenty-six and forty-five. Six members of the household were engaged in agriculture and two in manufactures. The 1830 census for Prince George's County no longer exists, but the 1828 county tax list shows Toaping Castle encompassed 169 acres that was valued at $388.70, and Nathan owned another 148 acres worth $406 and ten slaves with a total value of $474. The 1840 census reveals much of the family had left the estate with only one male between the ages of eighty and ninety, presumably Nathan, and two females, one fifteen to twenty and the other fifty to sixty, likely Mary and Elizabeth in that order. Nathan continued to hold slaves: two boys and one girl under the age of ten, one male and one female between ten and twenty-three, and one male twenty-four to thirty-four.[2]

Sam reminisced as a boy he had read of "the chivalry and noble deeds of our forefathers in the wars with Great Britain; and being naturally fond of military glory, I determined to try my fortune on the field of battle on the first opportunity that presented itself." He would soon receive his baptism of fire in the wilderness of the Southeast. Since the United States took possession of Florida in 1821, Washington had been negotiating for the removal of the Seminole people to lands west of the Mississippi River. The Indians were opposed to the proposed migration, and balked at being relocated alongside their traditional enemies, the Creeks. Slowly starving due to poor hunting, and claiming they had been tricked into signing away their homes, the Seminoles renounced the treaties. Frustration on both sides led to violence and, on December 28, 1835, Major Francis Langhorne Dade and more than one hundred soldiers were ambushed and killed near present-day Bushnell in Sumter County. At about the same time, similar events were unfolding in neighboring Alabama. Following the battle at Horseshoe Bend in 1814, the Creeks had, for years, steadily ceded their holdings in Georgia and Alabama to the federal government. Once the final treaty completely relinquished the tribe's rights to the land, white squatters rushed into the state and either swindled or outright stole the property of individual Creek families. Despite efforts by the Andrew Jackson administration to halt the land rush, Creek dissatisfaction, rampant fraud and speculation, and malicious rumors of an Indian uprising gave rise to bloodshed. During the bitterly frigid winter of 1835, Creek war parties burned homes and farms, killed entire families, disrupted the U.S. mails, and sacked the town of Roanoke, Georgia. With two Indian outbreaks in such close proximity, panicked settlers in the theaters of conflict clamored for protection from these "most horrid barbarities." In response, the War Department dispatched Brevet Major-General Winfield Scott to Florida in January 1836, and Brevet Major-General Thomas Sidney Jesup to Alabama five months later. Both generals were fully authorized to call into the field all U.S. soldiers, sailors, and marines that could be spared, as well as to make requests to the governors of Florida, South Carolina, Georgia, Alabama, and Tennessee for volunteers to supplement the regular troops. With these events, the federal government commenced waging its longest and costliest Indian war in the nation's history.[3]

During the first two years of hostilities, 23,530 Americans volunteered to serve in Alabama and Florida. The majority were raised in the southeastern states, except for one company from the District of Columbia. On May 23, 1836, citizens of the district met at City Hall to organize a volunteer corps for the purpose of suppressing the Creek uprising. On June 1, Walker enlisted in the Washington City Volunteers, whose services were tendered directly to the president for twelve months. Benjamin Lloyd Beall was to be the militiamen's commanding officer, but he had instead accepted a captaincy in the Second U.S. Dragoons on June 8. First Lieutenant Edward Branch Robinson, Second Lieutenant William A. T. Maddox, and Third Lieutenant George F. Howard all received their commissions the next day, and Robinson took command of the company on June 13.[4]

The following day, the seventy-nine members of the company left the city aboard the steamship *Columbia* bound for Norfolk. Once there, they embarked on the steam packet *Columbus* and sailed to Charleston on the sixteenth. Reaching the latter city, they left for Augusta, Georgia, and arrived on June 23. Their march then took them to Talbotton on July 8, and Columbus on the tenth.[5]

The Washington volunteers arrived at Fort Mitchell, Alabama, on July 11, and were placed under the command of Lieutenant-Colonel Archibald Henderson, Commandant of the Marine Corps. According to Walker, Captain Robinson revealed himself to be "entirely destitute of moral principles and behavior" while in Alabama. The captain unjustly charged Walker with insolence and disobedience and, while the accusation was proven to be without merit, the young private was still ordered by Henderson to beg Robinson's pardon. Walker's father Nathan had instilled in his children to be "always a true friend to the cause of freedom and justice between man and man." Trained since boyhood in the "true principles of freedom and fair dealing," Walker repeatedly refused to obey the Marine colonel's order, and was tied to a tree for two hours as punishment. He felt ill-treated by Henderson's callous attitude and further lamented the lack of any real action against the Creeks. His father wrote Adjutant General Roger ap Catesby Jones asking for Samuel's discharge. The request was denied, and Walker was subsequently pleased when the company saw more active service. His troubles with his captain would continue for the time being. On the first of August, the company was sent to Creek Stand on the Federal Road in Macon County. The post was commanded by Brevet Major Greenleaf Dearborn of the Second Infantry. There an intoxicated Robinson fought with an equally drunken subordinate and, when other company members sought to disarm him, the captain informed Major Dearborn the Washington volunteers were in a state of mutiny. The major immediately ordered seven or eight companies of regulars to remain under arms until the crisis was resolved. Walker and his comrades left Creek Stand at the end of August, and were assigned to a camp on Hatchechubbee Creek on September 3. Under the able command of Brevet Major John Munroe, Fourth Artillery, they were ordered to intercept any Indians attempting to escape through the swamp into Florida. On the twenty-eighth, the company was itself directed to proceed to the seat of war in Florida. By this time, the rank and file had grown exasperated with their captain's leadership, and Lieutenant Maddox preferred charges against Robinson in a letter to General Jesup. Robinson was consequently relieved and placed under arrest, while the respected Maddox assumed command. The company left Fort Mitchell aboard the steamship *Minerva* on October 2, and reached Apalachicola six days later. There they were subject to the orders of Brevet Major William L. McClintock of the Third Artillery until the arrival of the steamers *Anna Calhoun* and *Hyperion* from upriver. On the thirteenth, the Washington volunteers departed Apalachicola and escorted Jesup, who had been made the new commander of the Army of the South, to Fort Brooke at Tampa Bay. The company helped to garrison the post from the seventeenth to the twenty-sixth.[6]

The following month, Maddox's men, along with three companies of the Third Artillery, were assigned to the First Battalion commanded by Major McClintock. Not desiring a court-martial, Robinson resigned his commission in the meantime, and Lieutenant Charles Irwin won the subsequent election for the captaincy on November 20. McClintock's battalion was attached to the Fourth Infantry under Lieutenant-Colonel William Stanhope Foster, which marched into the interior of the territory on November 30. They reached the site of old Fort Alabama the next day, and were employed in the construction of new works on the Hillsborough River, including Fort Foster and a bridge connecting the post with two blockhouses. On December 22, Colonel Foster moved to the Withlacoochee in order to establish Fort Dade, leaving McClintock in command on the Hillsborough.[7]

On December 26, the company was instructed to return to Fort Brooke and report to Jesup's headquarters for further orders. Once arrived, the Washington volunteers were offered the choice of entering the quartermaster's office as teamsters and artificers at a wage of two dollars per day, or remaining at the fort as line soldiers for a daily rate of one dollar. Every member of the company chose the first option, and Walker was employed as a carpenter. The volunteers accompanied the general to Fort Armstrong in mid-February 1837, and were assigned to Fort Dade the following month. At the same time, the American victory at Hatcheelustee on January 27 had convinced the Seminoles to agree to a cease-fire and attend a peace conference at Dade on February 18. Irwin's men were assigned to guard the post during the event. The principal chiefs did not appear for the scheduled council, but Walker would witness the Seminoles' capitulation at another gathering on March 5. The peace did not last, though, and the conflict would drag on for another seven years.[8]

Even in the wilds of Florida, Walker was beginning to see a future for himself in the emerging Republic of Texas. In a letter to his brother Jonathan, dated March 5, 1837, Samuel wrote:

> I have found by experience that new settled countries are the places for young men and I have come to the determination to purchase a small tract of land in Texas … fifty dollars bounty, horse and saddle to ride, and twenty-four dollars per month is offered to volunteers. The Mexicans are daily expected.[9]

The Washington City Volunteers were discharged on May 31 at Fort Brooke, and General Jesup expressed his thanks to "Captain Irwin and his company for the correctness, faithfulness, and efficiency with which they have performed their duty, during the whole period of their arduous service, as well in Alabama as in Florida." Their tour of duty completed, Captain Irwin, Lieutenant William C. Irwin, six non-commissioned officers, and thirty-nine privates departed Tampa Bay aboard the brig *Maryland* and sailed for Baltimore, arriving on June 19.[10]

Walker ended his enlistment as a corporal, but he did not return with the company to Maryland, or strike out for Texas. Instead, he traveled to New Orleans to meet his brother Nathan, and arrived on June 13. On July 14, he and Nathan took passage for Florida, where Samuel had accepted a Quartermaster's Department contract to work as a carpenter at Fort Brooke for a wage of $2.75 per day plus rations. The following spring, they went into business together in the frontier village of Iola in Calhoun County. There the brothers operated a hotel and a construction company, and managed a steam-powered sawmill. The demands of their diversified ventures kept the partners fully occupied, but, in the first of several reverses, the sawmill, some of their best tools, and four to five thousand feet of juniper lumber were destroyed in a fire in February 1839. Further imperiling their commercial efforts, the Panic of 1837, the subsequent depression, and the ongoing war with the Seminoles began having severe consequences on the economy of northern Florida. Although the middle years of the decade had brought prosperity to the territory, paper currency became worth forty cents on the dollar, cotton prices fell, banks, including the one in neighboring St. Joseph, suspended operations, and the new thirty-mile rail line from St. Joseph to Iola almost immediately began failing. While the railroad's impending closure was due more to an inability to entice the cotton trade from the port of Apalachicola, Walker placed the blame for local financial hardships on the "villainy and faithlessness" of the St. Joseph Canal and Rail Road Company in selling out to the Apalachicola Land Company. In the unstable economy, he had no ready capital to complete the homes he still had under construction. Needing to raise some funds, Walker and his employee, Manuel Nevarro, went to St. Joseph in November 1839 to build a steamship cabin. They soon quit when their employer could not afford to pay wages. More misfortune struck the family when Nathan died in the same month, leaving his pregnant wife Ann.[11]

On January 21, 1840, Walker left Iola and traveled by way of Tallahassee and Charleston to Maryland for a visit. Once in Washington, on July 1, he wrote, and subsequently published, a pamphlet critical of the army and marine officer corps in Florida; he also publicly excoriated Captain Robinson for his "disgraceful conduct." While he was away, his business partner, John C. Taylor, wrote and suggested Walker stay in Maryland and allow his property to be attached in order to pay his debts. Resolved to settle his obligations in a more honorable fashion, Walker returned to Iola on October 2. After his arrival, he and seventy-four volunteers made two short excursions against the Seminoles on Pig Island. The expeditions were fruitless, as the citizens could not bear enough provisions for a campaign longer than ten days. Foreshadowing his later exploits in Texas, Walker attempted to raise an independent volunteer company to fight the Indians, but any men interested in joining were also too poor to properly equip themselves. On January 18, 1841, Walker moved to Tallahassee where he was employed as a construction supervisor for the Tallahassee Railroad Company at a wage of sixty dollars per month. Seeking the best use of his leisure time, he studied geometry and civil engineering. Despite the trusted position he held at the railroad, Walker debated whether to remain in Florida or return to Maryland. He indicated in a letter to Johnathan his intention to liquidate his holdings in Iola at a loss rather than try to save them on credit. Walker left the Tallahassee company in June on account of his wages being paid in depreciated paper currency rather than specie. Two months later, he accepted the railroad board's invitation to return with an increase in salary, disbursed this time in coin.[12]

The railroad job was not enough to keep Walker in Florida. In late January 1842, he wrote Nathan's widow, Ann, in Iola and revealed, "that unextinguishable love of chivalric immortal fame still clings to my heart … The love of fame still urges me on." In the same letter, he hinted at his decision to finally take that long-deferred trip to Texas. In many ways still the same young Marylander who had gone to seek glory in war, Walker's business difficulties may have prompted him to consider his real destiny, and a chance for fame and fortune, was to be found in the profession of arms. Writing on the search for renown in the age of American expansion, Doctor Jimmy L. Bryan remarked: "The Republic of Texas was a nation that suffered an interminable state of war—fertile fields for the martial adventurer." Landing in Galveston in mid-February, he found the country in turmoil. Since Mexico had never recognized the republic's independence, and hostile Indians were especially active, the southwestern borderlands continued to be a frequent battleground. The following month, Walker described in a letter to Ann the conditions in Texas and buoyantly predicted a Mexican invasion was imminent. Falling back on old skills, he declared to his sister-in-law his intention to meet the enemy on the frontier. Later in September, following *General de brigade* Adrián Woll's seizure of San Antonio, the young veteran enlisted in Captain Jesse Billingsley's mounted volunteer company for three weeks' service.[13]

The newly arrived adventurer was described as sandy-haired with a reddish beard, penetrating blue eyes, and a slender frame, weighing approximately 150 pounds. He was remembered as a "genial companion, open, frank, generous, always ready to do more than his share of the drudgery of camplife, truthful and proverbially unselfish … [he was] of sanguine temperament … with a lithe, active form, capable of great endurance, an unassuming manner, quiet yet alert, quick of perception, fertile in resources, prompt, and, as his whole life evinced, fearless in action."[14]

During the evening of September 18, Billingsley was leading his seventy-five men toward Mathew "Old Paint" Caldwell's position on Salado Creek. The volunteers reached the high ground overlooking the valley by five o'clock, where they observed the smoke produced by the Mexican artillery. The captain was unsure of Caldwell's exact location in the growing darkness, and he sent Walker and Cicero Rufus Perry ahead to search for the Texian camp. Rather than finding Caldwell's victorious men, the two scouts discovered a scene of horror. Captain Nicholas Dawson and his fifty-three La Grange volunteers had encountered two Mexican cavalry squadrons and one cannon near a mesquite thicket northeast of Salado Creek. After refusing to yield, Dawson's men positioned themselves in the thicket. There they were hammered by artillery fire, and many of the survivors were then cut down by dismounted cavalry, despite repeated efforts to capitulate. Thirty-six Texians were killed and fifteen were allowed to surrender, while the remainder were able to escape. Walker went back the three miles to inform his captain, then returned to the site of the massacre with four more men. Once at the thicket, he helped perform the grisly task of burying the mutilated bodies.[15]

The assembled Texians gathered at San Antonio on September 24. The next day, the volunteers were summoned to the Alamo, where Vice President Edward Burleson recommended all troops rendezvous at Béxar on October 25. Among the captains responding to the call were John C. "Jack" Hays and Ewen Cameron, the latter a "bold and chivalrous leader." The Scottish-born Cameron, known as the "Bruce of the West," had been a thorn in the collective side of Mexican border commanders for years. Before they could commence the march for the Río Grande,

Texas Rangers during the period of the Texas Republic (1836–45) 1842 (engraving), American School, (19th century) / Private Collection / Peter Newark American Pictures / Bridgeman Images.

though, President Houston formally appointed Brigadier-General Alexander Somervell to command a campaign into Mexico, which prevented Burleson from employing any more recruits.[16]

Signing on with Hays's rangers, Walker volunteered for Somervell's Army of Southwestern Operations, and took part in the actions around Laredo and Guerrero. Casting his lot with those who resolved to carry on without Somervell, Walker enlisted in Ewen Cameron's Company A. On December 25, the expedition, now under the command of Colonel William S. Fisher, learned Mexican troops under *General de división* Don Pedro de Ampudia, commander of the First Division of the Army Corps of the North, and Colonel Antonio Canales Rosillo, commanding a *ranchero* contingent, were encamped below them on the Río Grande at Mier. Convening a council of war, Fisher decided to cross the river with his men and offer battle to the assembled *soldados*. Walker was selected to be part of the fifteen-man spy detachment that Captain John Reagan Baker had taken over once Ben McCulloch left the expedition.[17]

The main body of Texians began to cross the river in boats at two p.m., and by four o'clock all were on the west side. Baker's spies were sent out to scout the surrounding area. Walker, Patrick Henry Lusk, John McMullen, and one other man encountered several of Ampudia's scouts and rode in pursuit. Walker soon found himself within rifle range of fifty well-armed Mexican horsemen. The four Texians beat a hasty retreat, closely chased by the enemy cavalry who continuously fired their *escopetas*. Lusk was captured when his horse's girth broke. Riding in the lead, McMullen took a wrong trail that led to a bullrush fence that was too high for the horses to jump. Walker's two companions dismounted and escaped over the barrier, while he paused to fire one last shot at the Mexicans now thirty feet away. Too late, he discovered both percussion caps on his shotgun were missing and, before he could ready his weapon, he was seized by six Mexicans. Taken before Ampudia, Walker answered the general's questions with evasive replies, except for when he brazenly declared the Texians were spoiling for a fight.[18]

Walker and several other men taken captive were held in a small cell next to the *alcalde's* office. There, they were tightly bound, and passed the night listening to the sounds of musketry and artillery as Fisher's command fought the Mexican troops in the plaza. The next afternoon, the prisoners learned Fisher had surrendered to Ampudia.[19]

The Texians, minus twenty-one wounded left in Mier, and their captors started for Matamoros on December 31. The next day, they crossed the San Juan River and entered Camargo as trophies in a parade honoring Ampudia and Canales for their victory. The same spectacle occurred in Reynosa on the fourth, and Matamoros on the ninth. The captives left the latter city on January 14, bound for Monterey and Saltillo.[20]

While on the way to San Luis Potosí, Walker participated in a mass bid for escape at Hacienda del Salado on February 11. Together with Ewen Cameron, he wrestled two guards to the ground while other captives seized weapons. Within five minutes, the prisoners had possession of the yard in which they had been held and the one adjacent. Five Texians and five Mexican guards were mortally wounded in the breakout. Seizing seventy horses and mules, saddles, 180 stands of arms, ammunition, rations, and approximately fourteen hundred dollars, the fugitives fled along the Monclova road before detouring into the barren mountains to the west, where a lack of food and water plagued them. On February 18, after a journey of 150 miles, the Texans dispersed into small groups to look for water. Walker was taken the next day after he and nine companions, having failed in their search, approached a Mexican camp and surrendered.[21]

An enraged Antonio López de Santa Anna ordered the execution of all those who had escaped and been recaptured. He subsequently relented when General Francisco Mexía, governor of Coahuila, objected to the illegal order. As the prisoners had not been paroled, they had every right to attempt escape under the recognized rules of warfare. Rather than perpetrate a massacre, the dictator instead ordered their decimation. Those seventeen who drew a black bean from an earthen jar were to be shot, while those who produced a white were to be spared. The deadly lottery was held at Hacienda Salado, the scene of the earlier escape attempt, on March 25. Walker extracted a white bean and was spared. Ewen Cameron, his accomplice in the escape, was not so fortunate. While stopping for the night at Huehuetoca on April 24, Cameron was ordered to be executed for his leadership in the prison break, and for his past activities against the Republic of Mexico. Some believed the order came, not from Santa Anna, but from Colonel Canales, who nursed a profound loathing for the Scottish-born "cowboy." Regardless of who made the decision, the next morning, Cameron bravely faced his firing squad without a blindfold and bared his own chest for the volley. He was killed instantly, pierced by eight musket balls. Walker wrote in his journal, "the blood of these men may yet cost [the Mexicans] the blood of thousands as circumstances will make it more lasting than the massacre of Fannin." Indeed, the executions would prove to be one of the most infamous atrocities of Santa Anna's violent career.[22]

Walker and his fellow prisoners reached Mexico City on April 26, and were incarcerated at Santiago Prison, north of the Vera Cruz road. On May 8, they were moved to Molino del Rey (King's Mill), where they were forced to build a road from Santa Anna's country residence to

Tacubaya, a suburb six miles outside the capital. On May 13, Walker was struck with a whip by an overseer, and the Texian responded by hitting him over the head with a shovel; the Texian then attacked his tormenter with his bare hands. Shortly thereafter, Walker was brutally beaten by the same overseer and a drunken guard. After a two-month stay in the hospital, he was regularly forced to carry three times the amount of sand as usual.[23]

By June 3, 189 prisoners remained of the 248 men who had fallen into captivity on December 26. Besides those who had died, eight had escaped at Mier, seventeen were at Perote Castle, five more in Matamoros, and 159 at Tacubaya. By the end of July 1843, nine more Texians had died at Tacubaya.[24]

Together with James Charles Wilson and D. H. Gattis, Walker successfully scaled the prison wall and escaped on July 30, 1843. Avoiding recapture four times, they made their way to Tampico where the Texians boarded the schooner *Richard St. John* bound for New Orleans. The trio arrived in the Crescent City on September 11, and left for San Antonio in January 1844. Walker's Old Testament philosophy of an eye for an eye, coupled with his experiences in Mexico, would leave him with an "anxiety & ambition to fight the mexicans [*sic*]."[25]

While the members of the Mier Expedition languished in prison, Sam Houston had written to the British *chargé d'affaires* that they had gone "without orders" and had "placed themselves out of the protection of the rules of war." Thus, according to the president, the government of Texas was not responsible for the expedition. A New Orleans newspaper opined of Houston's act: "It is equivalent to volunteering the information to the Mexican government that [Houston's] unfortunate countrymen in chains were a banditti, and unfit objects of humane and Christian treatment." Shortly after his return, Walker attempted to gain a copy of the message. Failing that, while in the city that bore the president's name, he confronted Houston who denied making any such declaration and asked the name of Walker's source. Once the chief executive was told Waddy Thompson, the American minister plenipotentiary to Mexico, had made the contention, Houston asked Walker to put the charges in writing. The president chose not to reply to Walker's subsequent letter. When the two later met on a staircase in Galveston, Houston thrust out his hand, but Walker ignored the cordial greeting and strode on. The president said to the former prisoner's back, "I am very sorry to see you indisposed Mr. Walker."[26]

Seeking another opportunity for action, Walker volunteered for Hays's ranger company in February 1844. When Indian raiders struck the area, Hays and a detachment of his company rode out to scout the country, and determine the identity of the marauders. As they were riding through the Pedernales country, they encountered a party of Yaparʉka Comanches above the San Antonio Road and near the "Pinta trail," about sixty miles from Béxar. The rangers, using new Colt Paterson revolvers and rapid mounted charges, successfully defeated about eighty Comanches. During the *mêlée*, Walker killed an enemy who was attempting to stab him. While his head was turned, another Comanche rode in and drove a lance into his back. As the warrior pulled his weapon from Walker's body, John Carlin shot the Indian through the head, then assisted Walker to a nearby thicket. The life-threatening nature of Walker's wound obliged Hays to forgo pursuing the defeated Comanches.[27]

After being returned to San Antonio, Walker was tended over the course of several months by Mrs. Catherine Louise Jaques, a boardinghouse owner, a selfless nurse to the suffering, and the wife of prominent merchant William Budd Jaques. Mr. Jaques wrote Walker a letter on July 15, 1846, inquiring as to his health, as well as that of Jack Hays and John McMullen. He admitted his wife and daughter Laura prayed nightly for Walker and the other rangers, but feared they would never see him again.[28]

Walker, once recovered, reenlisted in Hays's ranger company and served from February 12 to September 28, 1845. In mid-March, a band of Comanches, rumored to comprise two thousand warriors, women, and children, was reportedly encamped between Corpus Christi and the Río Grande. Several war parties were said to be committing raids on Mexican border villages and carrying off captives and plunder. One such, numbering four hundred under Penatʉka chief Santa Anna, was situated within fifteen or twenty miles west of Henry Lawrence Kinney's ranch. The companies of Hays and Peter Hansborough Bell readied themselves to ride out and offer the Indians battle. On April 25, the vanguard of seven rangers, which included Walker, was following an elusive Indian trail beyond the Agua Dulce when they spotted three Comanches one mile in the distance. The main body of Texians was ordered to press on, while the scouts continued to reconnoiter and soon encountered fifteen Indians in a small thicket of timber. The warriors were hailed, but they refused to answer. After a rifle inadvertently discharged, the Comanches began to retreat behind a relentless shower of arrows. The rangers pursued for five miles and, in the exchange of fire, six Indians were killed, eight were wounded, and most of the horses and camp equipage were seized. The remainder of the rangers arrived too late to participate in the skirmish. Walker and Captain Bell were the only Texians to receive wounds.[29]

While the rangers were battling Comanches, events involving Mexico were taking shape that would affect the remainder of Walker's life, and hasten his impending death. Texas was negotiating annexation with the United States, and tensions with Mexico were running high. Brevet Brigadier-General Zachary Taylor, colonel of the Sixth Infantry and commander of Fort Jesup, Louisiana, had two thousand troops positioned between the Red and Sabine Rivers. Assembled at Fort Jesup were the Third and Fourth Infantry Regiments, and seven companies of the Second Dragoons. Taylor received orders to hold that force in readiness to move at short notice and prevent hostile incursions by Mexico into Texas.[30]

Receiving his marching orders on June 29, 1845, Taylor's column, renamed the "Army of Occupation," began arriving in Corpus Christi on July 28. There they were met by Captain Bell's Texas Mounted Volunteers. Seven companies of the Seventh Infantry and two batteries of volunteer artillery reached the camp, which was soon dubbed Fort Marcy, by the end of the month. Additional reinforcements would follow in the coming weeks.[31]

On August 16, Taylor wrote Anson Jones, the last president of Texas, and recommended that any ranger companies presently active be continued in employment. Taylor offered to send an officer to enroll these companies into the service of the United States at the same pay rates provided by the Texas government. Jones replied to the general and indicated that three hundred rangers should be mustered in for the protection of the frontier.[32]

Walker was determined to "remain in the service until the final settlement of all our difficulties with Mexico." As historian Michael L. Collins observed,

"The horrors of war are never truly offset by the heroism of battle. And yet history is filled with accounts of uncommon courage and selfless sacrifice, reminding us that while warfare brings out the worst in some men, it summons forth the best in others." Sam Walker was one such who would discover his true self in the crucible of combat. Years later, James C. Wilson, Walker's fellow prisoner in Mexico, would eulogize his old comrade: "Walker in ordinary service seemed quite an ordinary man: retiring, silent, mild, apathetic, and rather melancholy, performing his duties merely from a sense of duty, and not that he delighted in them; yet never failing to perform them well." He went on to describe the transformation in Walker's personality when battle was at hand: "Walker was rapid, untiring, terrible. Like [Ewen] Cameron, he seemed to change his whole character and appearance, and arise a new being, entirely superior to himself … Walker had no sense of fear … Walker seemed to seek danger; to love it for itself."[33]

The border country was the perfect place for a born warrior, and Walker enrolled in Captain Robert Addison "Ad" Gillespie's Texas Mounted Rangers in San Antonio. As the *Texas Democrat* would declare the following year: "There is probably no set of men on earth readier for a fight, a chase, a fandango, or anything else which may come up, than the Texas Rangers." The company was mustered into federal service on September 28. Gillespie retained many of the men from Hays's old company, including First Lieutenant Michael H. Chevallie. These seventy-three men were assigned to defend the frontier. Walker spent part of October on recruiting duty, and received thirty dollars to cover his traveling expenses.[34]

Following the formal admittance of Texas into the Union on December 29, 1845, relations between the United States and Mexico further deteriorated. Orders were sent to General Taylor on January 13, 1846, to redeploy his troops to the Rio Grande. Receiving the directive on February 3, the dragoons, the artillery batteries, and the three infantry brigades by then amassed began their advance on March 8. In the largest assemblage of the U.S. army since the War of 1812, the field-grade officers of Taylor's forces had spent lengthy years in borderlands service, and, while not as seasoned, the company officers were capable and professionally educated West Point graduates. The rank and file were often from the lower classes of society, and seemingly prone to drinking and desertion, but they were rigorously trained and rigidly disciplined fighting men. Once the American military crossed the Nueces, they were in territory claimed by Mexico, who considered their presence to be an invasion, and therefore an act of war. After arriving at the Rio Grande on March 28, Taylor established his headquarters and supply depot at Point Isabel, and ordered his troops to begin constructing defensive works twenty-seven miles away opposite Matamoros; the earthen stronghold came to be called Fort Texas. On April 6, four 18-pound guns were placed in battery within easy range of Matamoros's central plaza.[35]

Opposing Taylor across the river were four to five thousand Mexican *soldados* under General Ampudia. Taylor received a note from his counterpart on April 12 advising him that unless the American army began withdrawing to beyond the Nueces within twenty-four hours, a state of war would exist between the two countries. In Taylor's reply to Ampudia, he rejected the demand and affirmed his intention to follow his orders from the War Department.[36]

On the very day Taylor reached the Rio Grande, the enlistments of the ranger companies in United States service expired. Walker and other Texans spoiling for a fight followed the army south. He conferred with the general on April 16 and, realizing the need for capable scouts, Taylor authorized Walker to raise a company of Texas Mounted Rangers for a three-month enlistment. The new captain initially recruited twenty-six men, and they were sworn into federal service on April 21. Walker was elected captain and Joseph P. Wells as first lieutenant.[37]

Walker established his base of operations at a camp between Point Isabel and Taylor's main force at Fort Texas. The day before the company was formally enrolled, he had requisitioned thirty-two Colt Paterson pistols, eight U. S. Model 1819 "Hall" rifles, and six U.S. Model 1833 "North" carbines from the Galveston depot. In addition, some of the rank and file Texans carried their personal rifles and shotguns. Sufficiently armed, his men ranged the army's line of supply against the *guerrilleros* of Antonio Canales, as well as regular Mexican troops.[38]

On April 28, Walker was doubly embarrassed while engaging the enemy. The captain and twenty-four men were on a scout and had ridden some fifteen to eighteen miles when they were attacked by approximately fifteen hundred Mexicans. Several of his men had never been in combat and, unnerved by the superior numbers, broke ranks and raced back toward camp. Walker and twelve rangers gallantly held the line and battled the enemy for fifteen minutes before they withdrew. Six rangers were killed while the Mexicans lost an estimated thirty men. Meanwhile, Walker had left First Sergeant Edward S. Radcliffe and fifteen raw recruits at his campsite. The Texans failed to post guards on their perimeter, and a band of *rancheros* took advantage of the lapse and attacked. Six rangers were killed, including Radcliffe, and four were listed as captured. Twelve Colt pistols, three North carbines, and four rifles were also lost in the raid.[39]

The enemy demonstrations on the American side of the river caused the commander of Point Isabel to believe an attack on his depot was imminent. On April 29, Walker and six rangers were sent to Taylor's headquarters at Fort Texas with a dispatch for the general. According to Nelson Lee, who claimed to have been a member of Walker's company, the Texans were within eight miles of the Rio Grande when they chanced upon a party of Mexican troops in their path. The rangers quickly discussed the best method to bypass the *soldados* until Walker "coolly announced he was going *through* them." The rangers walked their horses toward the Mexican line. Because their clothing resembled the garb worn by *rancheros*, the Texans were able to approach the Mexicans unsuspected. Once they were within fifty yards, Walker ordered a charge. "Instantly the spurs were buried deep in the sides of our good horses, which bounded forward like the wind, and greeting them with a terrific yell, we dashed right through," Lee wrote. The Mexicans were thrown into confusion, and the rangers were 150 yards past before the *soldados* were able to react. The rangers galloped toward Taylor's encampment, waving a white handkerchief to signal the dragoons rushing to meet them.[40]

On May 1, acting on the dispatch Walker had brought, Taylor left Major Jacob Brown in command of Fort Texas and its garrison: the Seventh Infantry, and elements of the Second, Third, and Fourth Artillery Regiments; some six hundred men in total. By three-thirty that afternoon, the general marched the bulk of the army to reinforce Point Isabel. The relief force of two brigades bivouacked for the night ten miles from their destination and entered the depot the following day. Along the way, the Americans saw no sign of the enemy.[41]

The anticipated attack turned out to be a false rumor, but Mexican forces crossed the border behind Taylor as the general and his troops marched downriver. On the night of May 2, Walker and a party of rangers reconnoitered the Mexican camp and briefly engaged their picket line. The captain was able to report the enemy was massing in strength and waiting for Taylor's column. Several of Walker's men had fled in the flurry of shots, and a New Orleans newspaper later reported that he had been deserted by seventeen Irishmen in his hour of peril. On July 21, Walker would take pen in hand and correct the record by stating that the deserters included one Englishman, two Americans, and three Germans. Furthermore, one of the Americans ran because he claimed his horse was lame.[42]

At five o'clock on the morning of May 3, Fort Texas was heard to be under Mexican artillery bombardment from Matamoros. Desiring to know of the situation, Taylor requested Walker return to the post. Together with an escort of dragoons commanded by Captain Charles Augustus May, Walker and ten rangers set out in the afternoon. Running numerous risks, Walker and six of his men left their party at the edge of the chaparral and slipped into the embattled stronghold at about three a.m. on May 4. There they made contact with Major Brown. Walker left the fort at about four and came back shortly after reveille. The rangers then returned to Point Isabel the following morning with a dispatch for Taylor from the major.[43]

While the army made preparations to move on Fort Texas, Walker was directed to conduct a reconnaissance of the Mexican positions. The captain located a significant number of the enemy about six miles from Point Isabel. A scout on the morning of May 7 revealed the Mexicans had retired. Leaving a sufficient force to hold Point Isabel, Taylor and the remainder of his troops departed at three o'clock the same afternoon. His company the only volunteers present, Walker and his men were attached to the Fifth Infantry, which, with the Third Artillery, constituted the advance element.[44]

At noon on May 8, Taylor's 2,300 soldiers encountered a Mexican force under *General de división* Mariano Arista (who had replaced Ampudia on April 24) at the edge of the chaparral adjacent to Palo Alto prairie.

As Walker, who was at the head of the column, rode close, he came under fire from a concealed Mexican cannon. The captain wheeled his horse and galloped back to Lieutenant-Colonel James Simmons McIntosh, commanding the Fifth Infantry, to report the presence of the enemy. He then identified the Mexican position to the Third Artillery's commander, who ordered counterbattery fire to commence. The two sides shelled one another for nearly three-quarters of an hour before general fighting began. The enemy consisted of six thousand foot soldiers on the right flank, eight hundred cavalrymen on the left, and seven artillery pieces in the center. The opposing battle lines, separated by three-quarters of a mile, readied themselves and both began their advance at three o'clock. Walker's company supported the Fifth Infantry and Brevet Major Samuel Ringgold's Battery C, Third Artillery on Taylor's extreme right flank, where the Mexican horse was particularly vigorous. McIntosh's infantry was ordered to turn the left flank of the enemy and advanced approximately a half-mile to the right. *General de brigade* Anastosio Torrejón and his *lanceros*, supported by two artillery pieces, extended their line to outflank them, and the American regulars maneuvered into a hollow square; Walker's rangers helped to reinforce the formation's right face. The Mexican horsemen fired as they rode to within eighty yards, wounding three or four Americans. The veteran infantrymen held their fire until the lancers were within fifty yards, then loosed a concentrated shower of lead killing several men and horses. The rangers fired a second volley, which was followed by a barrage of grape and canister. The Mexican charge dissolved and the lancers withdrew. Notwithstanding the hard-fought valor of the foot soldiers and the rangers, the enemy was mainly broken at Palo Alto by the skillfully deployed six- and eighteen-pound guns of the artillery. Enemy losses were approximately two hundred killed and four hundred wounded. Taylor's army suffered nine killed, forty-four wounded, and two missing.[45]

In evaluating Walker's performance at Palo Alto, Walter P. Webb wrote:

> Captain Walker, in the first engagement of the war, had set an example of heroic service for all Texas Rangers to emulate, and had gained a reputation for the organization which every member felt constrained

> to uphold. This act of Walker's is significant of the character of the services rendered by the Texas Rangers in the Mexican War. Their acts often had a strategic value that was inestimable, upon which the fate of an army, a battle, or even a campaign depended.[46]

The next morning, Walker and his men were sent to reconnoiter the Mexican lines and found the enemy army to be withdrawing down the Matamoros road. After being informed of the retreat, Taylor placed his troops under arms at the edge of the thick chaparral and made ready to march. He then directed an advance detachment of infantry and dragoons to pursue the Mexican army with Walker's Texans in front as scouts. The company rode along the road for approximately three miles until they met a small detachment of Mexican skirmishers. The rangers killed one of them and took another prisoner. The advance party resumed their march, and upon reaching Resaca de la Palma, received canister fire from a masked battery. Three dragoons were sent back to Taylor to inform him that the enemy was massing to his front along the Resaca de Guerrero. Receiving the news at three p.m., Taylor promptly ordered his troops to march to the sound of the guns and the American army reached the battlefield within the hour. Walker was directed to guide Lieutenant Randolph Ridgely, commanding the slain Ringgold's "flying artillery," forward a half-mile into position. As they neared the Mexican lines, they came under fire from the seven enemy cannons. Unlimbering three hundred yards from the Mexicans, Battery C's two guns went into action and continued to advance up the road. The four American infantry regiments deployed to either side of the lane and pressed forward to the edge of the resaca.[47]

During the engagement, Walker's horse was shot from under him. He struggled to free himself from his fallen mount even as a Mexican *lancero* charged him. When the enemy horseman was almost atop the captain, Walker coolly shot him out of the saddle, seized the steed's reins, and swung up ready to resume the fight. The clash became confused in the dense undergrowth, with neither side able to gain an advantage. The impasse ended when Captain May's squadron, sabers in hand, boldly charged the four enemy guns in the center and drove the artillerists from their pieces. Galloping

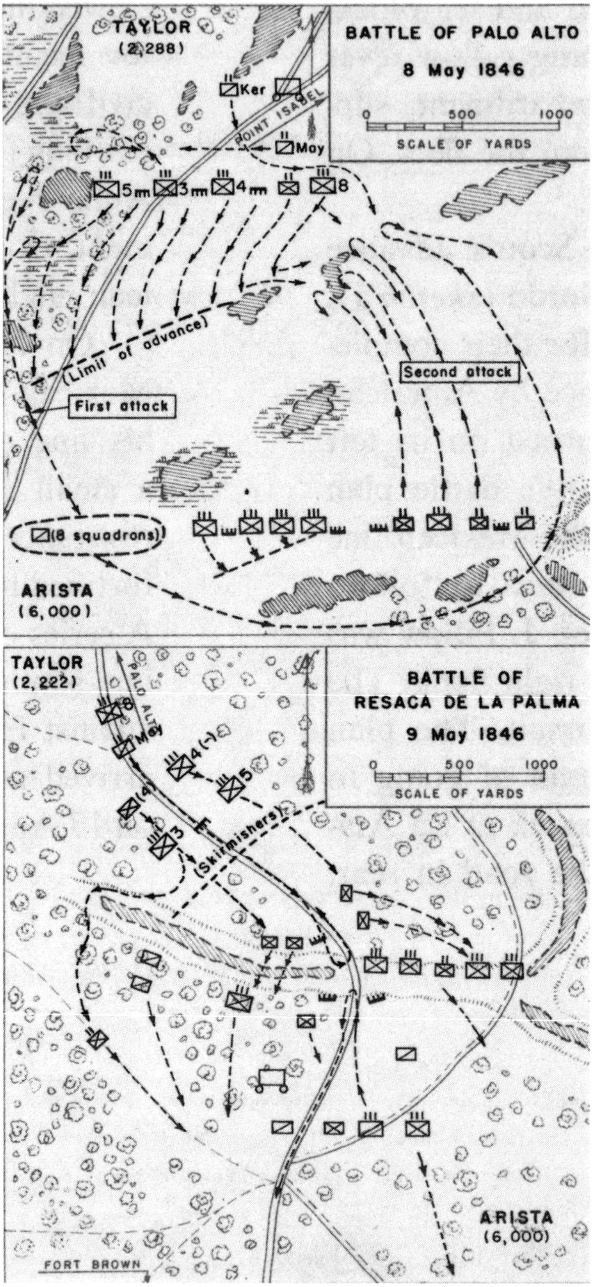

Maps of Palo Alto and Resaca de la Palma. From *West Point Atlas of American Wars. Courtesy Geography and Maps Division, Library of Congress, Washington, D.C.*

under heavy fire, the American dragoons lost eight men and eighteen horses killed, and ten soldiers and ten horses wounded. The cavalry charge was followed with an assault by elements of the Fifth and Eighth Infantry Regiments. The Third and Fourth Infantry Regiments advanced in support and the Mexican line broke.[48]

The *soldados* retreated toward the Rio Grande approximately three or four miles to the rear with Taylor's troops close behind. As the fleeing Mexicans came within range of Fort Brown, they were shelled by the garrison there, and the rout became complete. The Texans were in the forefront of the trailing American army shouting, "Drawing [*sic*] your sword boys and stay close together and remember the Black Bean!" Like their captain, many of Walker's men were seeking vengeance for past Mexican transgressions, including the callous treatment received after Mier. Any Mexican overtaken was killed. When the retreating soldiers attempted to escape across the Rio Grande, they were easy prey for the rifles of the American rangers and regulars. Many of those who survived the fusillade drowned. Captain May's dragoons and Walker's rangers continued pursuing the broken enemy a "considerable distance" beyond Matamoros and took thirty of them captive. Taylor's army did not possess a pontoon train, so the infantry was unable to immediately pursue the Mexican survivors across the Rio Grande. Thus the general missed his chance to capitalize on his victory and destroy Arista's force in detail. Taylor's reported casualties were thirty-nine killed and seventy-one wounded. The Mexican losses were estimated at 262 killed, 355 wounded, and 185 missing.[49]

Walker's élan, and the manner in which he lost one horse and gained another, was widely applauded in American newspapers from New Orleans to New York City. Several gentlemen in the former town raised enough donations to purchase him a magnificent steed named Tornado. An elegant but serviceable sword with an "appropriate inscription" was also presented to the ranger captain. In St. Louis, artist Charles Deas exhibited to rave reviews *The Last Shot*, a "wild and picturesque" portrayal of Walker slaying the dastardly "ranchero" who killed his horse. Interestingly, details of the painting exist only in written descriptions as it disappeared sometime after 1847. Securing Walker's reputation in the army, Taylor reported, "I would mention the services of Captain Walker, of the Texas Rangers, who was in both affairs with his company, and who has performed very meritorious services as a spy and partisan."[50]

Prior to the occupation of Matamoros by Taylor's troops, Walker's company and a contingent of regulars slipped into town to ascertain the particulars of the Mexican forces still in the city. Arista was discovered to have abandoned the town on the evening of May 17 with all his soldiers, except for three hundred sick and wounded men who were left behind. The American army commenced crossing the Rio Grande early the next day. While his troops planted the American flag on the Fort Paredes redoubt, the general accepted the surrender of Matamoros from the city's prefect.[51]

Jack Hays's First Texas Mounted Rifles arrived at the American camp, and Walker accepted the lieutenant-colonelcy of the regiment on June 24; he resigned his commission as captain of volunteers on the thirtieth. Because of his recent exploits, Walker was also appointed captain of Company C, Regiment of U.S. Mounted Rifles on July 17, to rank from May 27. During the recent campaign, Walker had come to admire General Taylor for his "determination and bravery," which had won the ranger captain's "esteem and confidence." The Texan requested he be allowed to remain in Hays's regiment where he could continue to serve with the general close to the action. The decision for when Walker should join his regulars was delegated to Taylor, who seems to have opted to leave the ranger with Hays for the time being.[52]

Simultaneously, the general was amassing the transportation and supplies needed for the next phase of the campaign. He also required intelligence on the enemy forces in his path. In late July, Lieutenant-Colonel Walker led a reconnaissance party to the outskirts of Monterey in order to observe the enemy's defensive works. He would subsequently conduct other patrols closer to Camargo. On one of them, Walker, commanding a party of eleven rangers disguised as *vaqueros*, approached twenty-five Mexican soldiers bivouacked at a *hacienda* on the San Juan River. Eight men stood on the riverbank watching bathers frolicking in the water, while two inattentive guards stood nearby. The Texans' costumes allowed them to come within one hundred feet of the Mexicans before the enemy captain became suspicious. The officer demanded to know the identities of the newcomers. Walker promptly shot him and the two guards quickly joined the captain in death. The bathers and those on the bank panicked and attempted to flee to the other side of the river. Few managed to escape being cut down by the sharpshooting rangers. The screams and the gunfire attracted the attention of the *hacienda's* residents. Somebody among those coming to investigate the clamor fired some shots at Walker's men, and the Texans burned down two *jacales* in retaliation. The slain *soldados'* weapons and uniforms were destroyed.[53]

On September 19, the army began to arrive at Monterey and encamped at Walnut Springs. The following day, Hays's regiment was assigned to Brigadier-General William Jenkins Worth's division. The audacious plan of attack was for the division to locate and block the Saltillo road and, if feasible, take the two fortified hills guarding the gateway to the city. Worth would be separated from the main army by eight miles, be hampered by severed communications, be equipped with four days' provisions, and be opposed by a numerically superior force. Taylor and the other two divisions would keep the Mexicans' attention fixed to the north and east and potentially gain entry into the city.[54]

Worth's column began advancing on the Saltillo road by two p.m. Hays's Texans led, followed by Lieutenant-Colonel Thomas Staniford's First Brigade and Colonel Persifor Frazer Smith's Second Brigade. They were six miles from Taylor's column and nearly in sight of their first objective by six. Twelve hours later, on September 21, following a rain shower that had lasted all night, the rangers, regular infantry, and the supporting horse artillery met an enemy charge at San Jeronimo. In fifteen minutes, more than a hundred Mexicans were killed or wounded, with the remainder fleeing in disorder up the Saltillo road. Walker was in the thick of the fighting, and his horse bore numerous wounds from lance thrusts. The Americans continued their progress and came into effective range of the Mexican artillery on the Loma de Federación and Loma de Independencia.[55]

Around noon, Worth determined the enemy batteries would need to be taken before the march could continue. He ordered his men to storm the redoubt on Federación, which commanded the Soldado fort lower to the east and the Obispado, or the Bishop's Palace, on Independencia six hundred yards across the valley. The first of two waves, commanded by Captain Charles Ferguson Smith, was composed of four regular companies of red-leg infantry (artillerymen acting as foot soldiers) and Companies A, C, D, H, I, and K of the Texas mounted riflemen. Two 9-pound cannons guarded the slopes of Federación, and Mexican light troops deployed to meet the Americans. More Mexican soldiers were observed to be forming on the summit, so Worth detached the Second Brigade—the Fifth and Seventh Infantry Regiments and Albert Gallatin Blanchard's "Phoenix Company"—and the remaining rangers led by Hays and Walker to support the first assault party. Soon after, despite determined resistance, the Americans took the hill.[56]

Any further operations were halted by a violent storm and the weary rangers and regulars, without food for over thirty-six hours, caught what sleep they could while exposed to the pelting rain. At three a.m., on September 22, Hays and Walker; the companies of McCulloch, Acklin, Green, Ballowe, Herbert, Gillaspie, and Gillespie; Captain John Rogers Vinton's three companies of artillery; and Captain Richard Bedon Screven's three companies of infantry were awakened to begin the assault on Independencia. Brevet Lieutenant-Colonel Thomas Childs was placed in charge of the sortie. The 450 men began their mist-shrouded ascent in two columns under a moonless sky. Walker and three ranger companies supported Vinton's one company of the Third Artillery and one company of the Eighth Infantry up the northern slope, while Hays and Childs led the remainder on the southern. The enemy had not posted pickets on the hillside, nor had they set guards on the summit. Climbing steadily over the jagged rocks and rain-soaked brush, the Americans were only one hundred yards from the top by dawn. With the morning light, the Mexicans became aware of the advance, and skirmishers were thrown forward to bar the climbers. War correspondent Thomas Bangs Thorpe later wrote of the attack:

> Regulars and rangers quickened their steps, the latter opening with their rifles; presently the regulars gave one united shout, and charged with their bayonets. The skirmishers of the Mexicans faltered, and fell back to their breastworks. The assailing party went on, seizing hold of

> the chapparel [*sic*] that grew from the perpendicular rocks. In spite of the encumbrance of heavy muskets, the natural obstacles of the ground, and the rolling fire of the enemy, the members of it made their way to the base of the fort, over which they rushed, the Texians clubbing their rifles, and the regulars using their bayonets. It was in vain that the enemy endeavored to check the charge.

The attackers were soon before the outworks of the vaunted Obispado, but any further progress without artillery would have been suicidal.[57]

One 12-pound howitzer was summoned and, after two hours of back-breaking labor in bringing it seven to eight hundred feet uphill, the gun was in position. The howitzer then opened fire on the palace and its outworks four hundred yards distant, producing "a visible sensation." While the bombardment was occurring, the Fifth Infantry regulars and Blanchard's Louisiana volunteers ascended Independencia to join the assault force. After some skirmishing, the Mexicans sallied forth from the palace with a strong force of cavalry and infantry to regain possession of the summit. The Americans were ready for them with a pincer movement: Childs had deployed forward of his main line a contingent of the Louisianans, which he then flanked with Hays and a detachment of Texans on the left, and Walker and another body of rangers on the right. The enemy bravely charged but was smashed by a single, massive volley. The Mexicans retreated in confusion, followed closely by Childs's and Hays's men into the palace itself. The pistols and double-barreled shotguns of the pursuing Texans cut down numerous Mexicans as they fled. In scant moments, the Americans replaced the Mexican flag with their own and the fort's capture was complete. The three enemy cannons, along with the two American horse artillery batteries, were turned upon the Mexicans retreating into the city's *Plaza la Capilla*. The plaza was in range of artillery fire from both hills, but the main assault force concentrated around the palace for the anticipated attack. In the meantime, the rangers and regulars saw to the care of the dead and wounded of both sides of the conflict.[58]

At ten a.m. on September 23, Worth heard a heavy fire from the east where Taylor's forces were located. Assuming orders to support the commanding general's attack had failed to reach the Obispado, Worth ordered his troops to commence their own assault into Monterey. Two columns were formed and directed to deploy skirmishers and march down the two parallel streets that led to the *Plaza la Capilla*. Once they had secured the square, the Americans were then to clear the buildings of the enemy. Light artillery would follow the advance at appropriate intervals and offer direct fire support. Just as Worth was to order his troops forward, Taylor inexplicably withdrew his own column from the city, and the Mexicans were able to reposition men and cannon to meet the western attack. Hays took five companies and worked down the right side, while Walker, with the commands of Green, Herbert, and Acklin, and two others, proceeded along the *Calle de Itúrbide* on the left. Following the lieutenant-colonel were four companies of the Eighth Infantry and four companies of Childs's Artillery Battalion, plus Brevet Lieutenant-Colonel James Duncan's two 6-pounders. The Americans moved steadily and fought their way over barricades that had been placed at strategic street corners, among buildings room by room, using pickaxes and crowbars to break through the common walls, and atop the roofs where they could choose sites to fire down on the enemy. By dark, they were within one block of the plaza and had gained possession of a building that offered a commanding view of the Mexican defenses.[59]

Worth's troops fell back a short distance to allow the American artillery to bombard the plaza. Walker and the five ranger companies with him had fought their way to the post office, but the message to retire never reached him. Thus he and his men spent the night in General Ampudia's living quarters, which they had seized earlier in the day. The Texan officer claimed Ampudia's bed for his own use, posted sentries on the roof, and suggested the remainder of the rangers get some sleep. His slumber was likely interrupted when the guards on top of the residence traded shots with Mexicans entrenched in adjacent houses. At some point in the darkness, two or three rangers slipped across the street and began hammering a hole in a house with a pickaxe. Once the masonry wall collapsed, a company of *soldados* located inside bolted out the front door, straight into the rifles of rangers positioned in the post office; nearly half of the enemy was killed. Throughout the night, two howitzers and a six-pound gun were hauled to the rooftop, and the attack was ready to resume at dawn.[60]

Even before daybreak on September 24, the Texans at the post office were battling furiously. Walker still believed the ranger detachment under Hays was in the area, and his men were careful to identify every combatant before shooting them. Due to low visibility in the early morning, the Texans would challenge the shadowy figure if he was an American. More than a few of the individuals in question answered "yes" in fluent English. Once they were persuaded the man was friendly, the mounted riflemen came out from behind their cover and exposed themselves to the fire of Mexicans hidden nearby. In each instance, the rangers responded with a murderous salvo, forcing the enemy to take shelter. Once this event had occurred several times, Walker came to realize he and his men were the only Americans in the immediate vicinity. Unconcerned with being surrounded, the formidable lieutenant-colonel continued to direct his nearly two hundred men in fighting off the numerically superior enemy. Using a *ruse de guerre* to confuse the Mexicans as to the exact number of Texans in the post office, he ordered his rangers to periodically shout at the top of their lungs. This also had the added benefit of maintaining high morale.[61]

Later in the morning, Major John Munroe of the Fourth Artillery, the same officer Walker had known in Alabama, placed a twelve-pound mortar atop an adjacent two-story building and shelled the enemy positions. Shortly thereafter, a Mexican officer and a trumpeter came forth under a flag of truce. The rangers disregarded the white flag and opened fire, killing the bugler and wounding the officer as he fled to safety behind a house. Once he learned of the incident, Walker instructed his men to refrain from shooting any more individuals requesting a parley. Another officer and trumpeter stepped into the street shortly thereafter, fully expecting to meet the same fate as their comrades. The rangers, obeying the orders of their commander, this time held their fire. Walker met with the Mexican officer, who informed him that General Ampudia wished to meet with the officer commanding the assault on Monterey. Walker and Captain Tom Green went to Ampudia's headquarters. When they arrived, they were informed the general would only talk to General Taylor, not junior officers. Walker replied by emphasizing how Taylor would never agree to meet with the enemy alone in his own fortifications. The Mexicans then requested permission to send an emissary through Walker's lines and deliver a message to Taylor. Walker gave his consent.[62]

Ampudia stated in his note that he had fulfilled all his obligations to duty and honor in defending Monterey. He conceded that "a continuation of the defence would only bring upon the population distresses to which they have already been sufficiently subjected." He proposed "to evacuate the citadel and city, taking with me the personnel and materiel of war which is left," provided "no prosecution ... be undertaken against the citizens who have taken part in the defence." In his reply, Taylor rejected Ampudia's offer and demanded "a complete surrender of the town and garrison, the latter as prisoners of war." He did suggest such a capitulation would be upon liberal terms. After laying down their arms, the garrison would be allowed to retire to the interior, provided they not serve again in the war, or until properly exchanged. He seemed to think it superfluous to declare "that the rights of non-combatants will be respected." Furthermore, Taylor required the Mexican general to reply by noon. The American conditions were accepted, and the troops of the defeated garrison began to depart for Saltillo on the twenty-fifth, a process that lasted three days.[63]

The terms of the surrender were not welcomed in Texas. Many in the Lone Star State regretted "Gen. Taylor received the capitulation of the Mexicans upon any other terms than as unconditional prisoners of war." If Taylor had been a Texan, "he would have thought of this; but the blood of Goliad and the Alamo has not printed the deep reflections of its color upon his heart, as it has upon the heart of every true Texan of '35 and 6."[64]

On October 1, Walker was directed to repair to Washington, D.C. for further orders. The next day, he mustered out of the volunteer service and took on his regular commission in the Mounted Rifles. Together with Hays, he journeyed to New Orleans, Galveston, and San Antonio, receiving a fervent welcome in each town. On October 17, Walker attended a meeting of citizens gathered at the Bexar County courthouse to honor Ad Gillespie. The assembly convened by calling Walker to the chair, and he appointed five persons to draft resolutions expressing sincere respect for the fallen ranger's memory, profound grief for his death, and sympathy for the captain's survivors. Two additional proclamations declared the intention to send a copy of the proceedings, and a biographical sketch, to Gillespie's nearest relatives and to the state's newspapers. His duty to his friend fulfilled, Walker proceeded to Washington by way of Austin to begin recruiting for his company. As he stopped in various towns on his trip eastward, citizens continued to honor him for his service.[65]

After Walker arrived in the nation's capital on November 22, he called on President James Knox Polk and on army officials, visited with relatives, attended a reception in his honor at the Odd Fellows' Hall, then journeyed to New York City. Samuel Colt had asked him for an endorsement of the Paterson pistol. The gun maker was hoping to win a contract from the Army's stubbornly traditional chief of ordnance, who distrusted the new technology. The ranger-turned-mounted rifleman was enthusiastic in his praise of the five-shooter, describing the 1844 victory at Walker's Creek. Walker first met with Colt on December 2, and their continuing discussions led to various improvements in terms of endurance and stopping power. Using his hard-won reputation, and enlisting the aid of the president and Secretary of War William Learned Marcy, Walker assisted Colt in side-stepping the Ordnance Department's opposition. Colt was so grateful he named the one thousand pistols purchased by the government on January 4, 1847 the "Walker Colt." The captain's description of Walker's Creek was immortalized in an engraving by artist Waterman Lilly Ormsby, which appeared on the cylinder of the weapon.[66]

Even while Walker worked with Colt on the revolver, the captain was recruiting for his company in Washington and at Fort McHenry, Maryland. Widely publicized in the national press, his battlefield fame rendered his efforts simpler, and he was able to enroll more than one hundred soldiers before he left for Newport Barracks, Kentucky, on March 1. Arriving five days later, a hard-pressed Walker dealt with the army's bureaucracy to obtain horses, arms, and equipment before he received orders on the twenty-fourth to proceed to the seat of war. Unfortunately for the regulars, Jack Hays was promised almost all of the one thousand Colt handguns for the regiment he was recruiting in the spring of 1847. Walker's own company of

Samuel Colt. Photographic print from PG 640, Colt's Patent Fire Arms Manufacturing Company Collection. *Courtesy State Archives, Connecticut State Library, Hartford, Connecticut.*

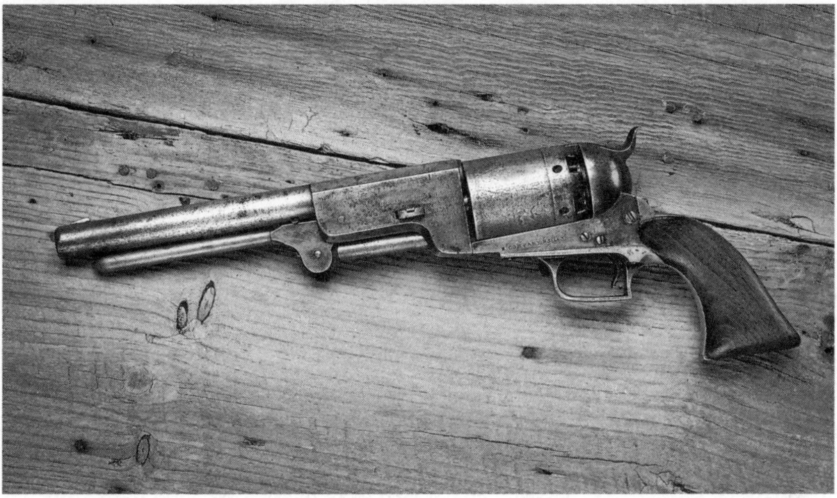

Colt Walker Pistol, or U.S. Model 1847. Catalog #2088. *Courtesy Collections Division, Texas Ranger Hall of Fame and Museum, Waco, Texas.*

mounted riflemen would not benefit from their captain's efforts, as a resentful Ordnance Department ensured they would be armed with U.S. Model 1841 "Mississippi" .54-caliber percussion rifles, Model 1840 heavy cavalry sabers, and flintlock pistols. Walker himself received, on October 5, a matched brace of revolvers sent to him personally by Sam Colt.[67]

After arriving at Vera Cruz on May 10 with 182 recruits, Walker was disgusted to learn he would only be able to keep seventy-eight soldiers to join the eighteen currently serving in Company C. As they had hoped to fight under the celebrated ranger, the remaining men were equally dismayed at having to go to other companies. Regardless of the soldiers' wishes, military requirements took precedence. Brigadier-General David Emanuel Twiggs's division had begun the march for Puebla and Mexico City on the ninth. They were followed by a train of two hundred wagons escorted by a squadron of the Second Dragoons and Company C. Walker's horsemen clashed twice with the enemy, the second time at the village of Santa Fé on the morning of the twelfth. The force of two hundred Mexicans was routed, losing ten killed and numerous wounded in the process. The dragoons had still been asleep when the *lanceros* attacked and the Americans suffered six killed and eleven wounded. Walker led his men in pursuit and captured a number of prisoners. The Mexicans were turned over to the dragoons and almost immediately executed. The caravan arrived at Jalapa on the twentieth and departed the next morning.[68]

Malicious rumormongers in Jalapa later spread the falsehood that Walker had hung the *alcalde* at Santa Fé and shot seventeen prisoners. His honor impugned, Walker intended to demand a court of inquiry into the matter once the regiment assembled. Regrettably, he would never have the opportunity to clear his name.[69]

A soldier writing in his journal described the arrival of the captain and his men at Castle San Carlos de Perote on May 25:

> This morning … Gen. Twiggs' division … arrived in Perote city. Among them I noticed Col. Harney and his regiment of dragoons, and Capt. Samuel Walker, the Texas Ranger, with two companies of mounted riflemen, mounted on fine spirited horses. They are all fine, strong, healthy and good looking men, nearly every one measured over six feet; they took up their quarters in the Castle Perote … I learn they are to remain with us to keep the National Road open between this castle and the city of Jalapa. So guerrillas, *robadors* (robbers), take warning … for the renowned Capt. Samuel H. Walker takes no prisoners.[70]

The diarist went on to describe Walker's movements the following day:

> In the afternoon, Capt. Samuel H. Walker, the celebrated Texas Ranger, with his two companies of mounted riflemen, and Col. William S. Harney's dragoons, left the Castle Perote for the town of Perote, placed there as a garrison to keep an eye on the guerrillas, robbers and blanket greasers—a class of people who watch in the daytime who they can kill, and what they can steal at night.[71]

Colonel Harney and his regiment would continue with General Scott on the campaign to Mexico City, while Walker and his men remained to fight guerrillas. The captain had only intended to stay long enough to further train his horses before pushing on, but his talents were needed there. Colonel

Francis Murray Wynkoop, leading the First Pennsylvania Volunteers, was appointed to command the Department of Perote, and he never issued specific orders allowing the mounted riflemen to proceed to the main army. Instead he kept Walker on frequent scouting expeditions.[72]

On June 16, Wynkoop received intelligence that a Mexican force of fifteen hundred was lurking at the pass of La Hoya with the intention of attacking a supply train under the command of Brigadier-General George Cadwalader of the Third Division. After confirming the information, Wynkoop dispatched a courier to Cadwalader telling the general they would rendezvous at the pass behind the enemy in the early morning of Sunday, June 20. At ten p.m. on June 19, Walker and his mounted riflemen accompanied five companies of Wynkoop's regiment down the National Road—some 250 soldiers in total. Encountering forty of the enemy's pickets at three in the morning, approximately one mile beyond the small village of Las Vegas, the Americans drove them in, killing one. While later routing some Mexicans on a curving road, Walker chanced upon an unseen fence, which caused two sets of fours to be thrown to the ground, some quite severely, and the eight horses—including the captain's—to bolt and likely fall into enemy hands.[73]

The column moved on and Walker received permission to ride ahead and locate water and forage for his horses. Between seven and nine o'clock, he observed a party of Mexican cavalry in the hills to the right. The captain dismounted half of his company to act as skirmishers and deployed them on the right and the left. Five stragglers were killed but the remainder of the enemy fled before they could be engaged. Wynkoop caught up to Walker's company and, having marched twenty-five miles, the American troops halted for a brief rest. The colonel was concerned the *guerrilleros* would cut off his line of retreat and ordered Walker to return to Perote. Walker refused to comply, and instead reconnoitered the village of La Hoya. At eleven o'clock, protected by a stone fence, the captain's three officers and forty-seven mounted riflemen became embroiled in a hot fight with a force of five hundred Mexicans under Padre Celedonio Dómeco de Jarauta. Although many of his company had never seen action, Walker's confidence in their bravery inspired them to continue holding the position. He ordered his men to ready their sabers for close-quarters battle, but the cool courage and deadly marksmanship of Company C held off the swarming enemy. After some forty minutes, Wynkoop hurried forward with his infantry and the Mexicans retreated. Walker and Wynkoop pursued the enemy in a running fight for several miles, killing a number of them. Brevet Colonel Thomas Childs, commanding the Second Brigade of General Cadwalader's division, was also pursuing the fleeing Mexicans, and the two converging American forces were able to drive their foes from hill to hill for more than two miles. Jarauta's losses were estimated to be at least forty and possibly exceeded one hundred killed and wounded. In his official report on the battle, Colonel Wynkoop stated, "Captain Walker and his company deserve the greatest share in the honor of the fight. Before the arrival of the infantry he held his position with 30 rifles against 500 of the enemy, and had killed a number of them."[74]

Relations between Walker and Wynkoop soured after the engagement at La Hoya. The former ranger considered Wynkoop's desire to retreat an act of cowardice, while the colonel resented Walker's refusal to obey his order. Their mutual aversion remained discreet until summer's end when they openly clashed over several instances of looting authorized by Wynkoop. On August 26, the colonel allowed the men to ransack homes in the town of Coatepec while searching for weapons; one individual even pillaged the church. Angered by such dishonorable conduct, the captain contemplated preferring charges against Wynkoop. The same behavior occurred at an unnamed village the following day where, in searching the church for arms and powder, Walker discovered Wynkoop's interpreter stealing a silver cross. The captain declared the soldiers of his company "had disgraced themselves" and acted contrary to the orders of the commanding general. On September 4, Walker and his mounted riflemen accompanied the colonel on a march north to Jalacingo and Altotonga. Three miles from the first village, while on a mountain road, Wynkoop instructed Walker to charge the town. The Texan declined to obey the tactically senseless order and moved his company forward leisurely. The colonel repeated the command, then galloped for Jalacingo, reaching the town a half-hour before Walker. The state of Wynkoop's horses after a three-mile dash over rough ground is unknown, but, in all likelihood, they entered the village exhausted and in no shape to fight. Upon his arrival, the captain was placed under arrest, but, accusing Wynkoop of planning to order more plundering, he refused to submit until the patrol had returned to Perote. The colonel furiously responded by calling Walker a "damned scoundrel," and the mounted rifleman returned the insult by angrily reminding everyone present of Wynkoop's timidity at La Hoya. The argument might have turned violent, but the two men were separated and Walker retained his command until the column was back at the castle. He then turned the company over to Lieutenant Thomas Claiborne and was confined to quarters.[75]

On August 7, before beginning his final push toward Mexico City, General Scott had appointed Colonel Childs military governor and commander in Puebla to protect the sick and wounded left there. Approximately four thousand brigands and *guerrilleros* under *General de brigade* Joaquín Rea besieged the Puebla garrison on September 13, and demanded Childs's surrender three days later. The colonel refused to yield. Nine days later, General Santa Anna and his army arrived after having evacuated Mexico City. Intent on regaining his lost power, the former dictator needed to take Puebla in order to cut Scott's line of communications and supply. His regular troops and Rea's irregulars totaled six thousand men and six cannons. Believing he held all the advantages, Santa Anna called for the garrison's capitulation, but Childs had received word Mexico City had fallen to Scott eight days previously and once more declined the ultimatum. For most of the siege, the Mexican commander settled for using near-constant sniping and harassment fire. On three occasions, he ordered direct assaults, all of which failed amid heavy casualties.[76]

Meanwhile, Brigadier-General Joseph Lane and his Fourth Indiana and Fourth Ohio Infantry Regiments arrived in Vera Cruz. The general would figure prominently in the story of the Texas Rangers and their war in Mexico. On September 19, he marched seventeen hundred men to lift the siege of Puebla. Organizational difficulties and *guerrilleros* hampered his progress, but he was able to depart Jalapa by October 1. The trek was punctuated by heavy rains, muddy roads, and scant provisions. The brigade reached Perote on October 2, integrated soldiers of that post into the relief force, which now totaled 3,300 men and seven guns, and resumed the march three days later. Despite Wynkoop's protests, Lane ordered Walker released from arrest, restored the captain to his command, and instructed him to join the column. The general also assigned to the Texan officer Captain John Loyall's Company of Georgia Mounted Volunteers, and Captain Lorenzo A. Besancon's Company A and Captain Lorenzo Lewis's Company E, both of the Mounted Battalion of Louisiana Volunteers. Due to the constraints of time, the general refused to grant Walker's request for a court of inquiry.[77]

In the early morning hours of October 9, at the *hacienda* of San Antonio Tamaris, Lane learned from a spy that Santa Anna was possibly at Huamantla. Placing his supply train under a strong guard, the general marched eighteen hundred infantrymen and five guns toward the town; Walker and his two hundred horsemen led the advance. Three miles from their objective, at one p.m., Walker spotted two thousand Mexican *lanceros* in a draw near Huamantla, and increased the pace of his detachment to a trot. On the outskirts of town, the American troopers closed up into columns of four, drew their sabers, and thundered into the plaza. Their swords carved a bloody path though the five hundred enemy artillerymen and lancers before their adversaries fled. In the fighting, Walker decapitated a Mexican officer with his blade. The Americans quickly captured three cannons before, thinking their task complete, they broke ranks to carouse, loot, or scrounge for other artillery and ammunition. Santa Anna, who had actually been near El Pinal some two miles distant, had observed the charge from a church tower and moved to attack with one to two thousand lancers; some five hundred rode to meet Walker's scattered force in the plaza. The opposing horsemen charged toward each other and, upon crashing together, engaged in close, desperate fighting. The determined Americans were able to drive the Mexicans back, when Walker, the pistols that bore his name in hand, was shot from his saddle at the head of his men. Before he breathed his last, he was heard to say, "Don't surrender boys; the infantry will soon be here." The American foot was indeed soon in action with well-directed fire and, even though their own reinforcements checked the withdrawal for a time, the Mexicans were finally forced to retire. Lane's force lost thirteen killed and eleven wounded, while the enemy losses were estimated to be between 150 and two hundred. In the

The Death of Capt. Walker, at Huamantla in Mexico. Lithograph by R. Magee and Thomas W. Strong, New York City. *Courtesy Special Collections, The University of Texas at Arlington Libraries, Arlington, Texas.*

aftermath of the battle, Walker's death enraged the American soldiers, and they sacked the town in a maddened rampage of looting, arson, rape, and murder. Lane regained control of his men that night and marched them to Puebla on October 12 where they raised the siege. As the Mexican defeat at Huamantla had finally ended Santa Anna's military career, the American general avoided punishment for the outrages that occurred there.[78]

General Lane would later eulogize his fallen subordinate in his after-action report:

> This victory is saddened by the loss of one of the most chivalric, noble-hearted men that graced the profession of arms—Captain Samuel H. Walker, of the mounted riflemen. Foremost in the advance, he had routed the enemy when he fell mortally wounded. In his death, the service has met with a loss which cannot be easily repaired.[79]

Following the conclusion of the Puebla siege, the captain's body was escorted back to Perote on November 5 in a carriage believed to have belonged to Santa Anna. He was buried at San Antonio Tamaris, and his old foe Colonel Wynkoop, who regretted the lost opportunity to make amends, conducted the funeral service. An honor guard of Ohio volunteers fired three volleys over his grave. His remains were exhumed later in the month and transported home to San Antonio by way of Vera Cruz, New Orleans, and Galveston. As the procession bearing Walker's remains passed through Austin, the cannon on President Hill prematurely fired the salute and struck an unnamed bystander. The unfortunate man was hurled several yards down the hill and badly injured, but he later recovered. Walker was interred in San Antonio's Old City Cemetery on January 8, 1848. On April 21, 1856, at the commemoration of the battle of San Jacinto, he was reburied in the Odd Fellows' Cemetery in San Antonio. His ashes had been mixed with those of Ad Gillespie, and the remains of the two friends were placed in the same grave.[80]

The ranger's service to Texas would continue to be recognized. In 1846, Walker County had originally been named for Robert John Walker, a senator from Mississippi who had supported the annexation of Texas. On December 16, 1863, after Walker declared himself for the Union cause, the Tenth Legislature publicly renamed the county in honor of the fallen ranger.[81]

Walker died doing what is expected of all Ranger commanders—leading from the front. From the battlefields of Palo Alto to Huamantla, he was always found where the action was hottest, and at the head of his men. Reports of his death were carried in newspapers from Matamoros to Louisville to Baltimore and New York City. His deeds, especially those of twice crossing enemy lines, made him a celebrated hero and helped to spread the fame of the Texas Rangers nationwide.

John S. Ford. *Courtesy Prints and Photographs Collection, Texas State Library and Archives Commission, Austin, Texas.*

Chapter 6

John S. Ford: “Combination of the Renaissance Man and the Frontier Warrior”

John Salmon Ford epitomized the dichotomy of the antebellum Texas Ranger. A combination of the Renaissance man and the frontier warrior, not only did he fight hostile Indians from the Red River to the Rio Grande, and Mexican bandits along the southern border, he was also a physician, lawyer, newspaperman, legislator, and educator. After Hays, McCulloch, and Wallace had left the service to engage in other pursuits, and Walker had died in Mexico, Ford was the one man primarily responsible for maintaining the Texas Ranger tradition through the 1850s. He was instrumental in bringing Texas into the United States, and in seceding fifteen years later to enter the Confederacy. After the Civil War, he was active in the endeavor to regain for Texas her status in the Union. “Equally at home with the most polished, literate, and well-mannered of Austin society as with the most savage and desperate characters infesting the borders of the Lone Star State,” Professor Michael L. Collins commented, “he arguably stood closer than any person then living to being the Texas everyman.”

He was born to William and Harriet (Salmon) Ford on the family plantation in the Greenville District of South Carolina on May 26, 1815. William had been born on March 25, 1785, and Harriet on December 27, 1791. They married on August 27, 1809. John had at least two older sisters, but only he and Elizabeth survived into adulthood. In 1817, the Ford family joined the westward migration and acquired land on the middle, west, and east forks of Mulberry Creek, a tributary of the Elk River in Lincoln County, Tennessee. Three years later, the federal census recorded William as being engaged in agriculture and owning one female slave under the age of fourteen. By 1829, William possessed 189 acres of deeded land and eighty-two acres of school land, and a year later had increased the number of his slaves to four. Meanwhile, Ford flourished on his father's plantation. In his youth, he learned to ride and shoot, fought and created mischief with other boys, and discovered girls. As a student, he was an avid reader and eager to learn. To this end, in 1834, he went to Shelbyville in Bedford County to study medicine under Doctor James Garden Barksdale.[1]

Heretofore, the details of Ford's first wife and their marriage have been scant. According to the accepted narrative, they had twin children: a son whose name is still unknown, and a daughter, Frances ("Fannie"). Their union was thought to have ended in the early summer of 1836, presumably through divorce. Following a brief mention in his memoirs, Ford never again commented on this failed marriage, or his firstborn son, in writing. The assertion concerning the date of the divorce is mainly drawn from Ford's reminiscences, and from several of his grandsons, but new interpretations of old evidence point to a fresh narrative. While Ford was engaged in his medical studies, he met Mary Thomas Davis, born on March 28, 1821, the daughter of prosperous local merchant Thomas Davis. According to the family Bible, they married on November 24, 1835. Additionally, Ford was supposed to have been awarded custody of Fannie before he moved to Texas in 1836, but her gravestone in Austin's Oakwood Cemetery bears the birth date of September 17, 1840.Therefore, Mary definitely made the trek to Texas as well, and the divorce almost certainly occurred sometime after 1840 and before Ford's second marriage in 1845. Mary and Fannie subsequently returned to Tennessee, and the 1850 federal census shows them living in the home of Doctor Augustus H. White in Rutherford County. The unidentified son is not recorded as being a member of the household, which likely indicates he had died earlier. His death might have been a painful reason for the Fords' divorce, but that notion is mere speculation.

Mary thereafter disappears from the historical record, and she possibly died while Fannie was young. William was still residing in Lincoln County in 1850, and he may have escorted Fannie to her father in Texas when he made the trip himself.[2]

Whether Mary accompanied him west or followed later, John Ford became infected with "Texas fever," and he soon embarked on the trail to the burgeoning republic. Arriving in San Augustine, Texas, in June, Ford settled into the practice of medicine and earned a reputation as a "skillful physician." Among his patients were refugees who had fled to the San Augustine area months prior in the "Runaway Scrape." In February 1838, the republic's government established a general land office to dispose of public lands, verify Spanish and Mexican land titles, and handle the claims of land grant and headright certificate holders. Richard Hooper, the Shelby County surveyor, appointed Ford to be his deputy. Leading a small party, Ford was active in surveying the lands attached to Shelby County, which now comprise present Harrison County.[3]

Later that summer, Mexican agents infiltrated Texas and sat in council with Caddo, Cherokee, Chickasaw, Choctaw, Kichai, Kickapoo, Tawakoni, and Waco tribal chiefs. The Indians were promised the return of their ancestral lands if they joined with Mexican forces in overthrowing the Texians. A number of *tejano* revolutionaries, bearing grudges against the republic, also joined the insurgency. The most prominent figure of the uprising would be Vicente Córdova, a former judge and *alcalde* of Nacogdoches during Mexican rule. The "Córdova Rebellion," as the series of bloody raids became known, spread alarm through the settlements. On August 8, President Sam Houston ordered the one hundred Mexicans assembling under Córdova on the Angelina River to disperse or face the consequences. The rebels refused on the tenth, demanded the government recognize their property rights, and swore to continue to the bitter end. At the same time, the president opened negotiations with Chief Duwali (also known as Bowles) in an attempt to keep the Cherokees out of the war.[4]

Major-General Thomas Jefferson Rusk, commanding the Texas militia, had meanwhile issued the call for volunteers to form an expedition against the rebels. Ford enlisted as assistant surgeon in a mounted volunteer company commanded by Captain Henry William Augustine; the unit was mustered into the First Regiment, Third Militia Brigade on August 8 in Nacogdoches. The insurgents camped on the Angelina were observed being joined by approximately three hundred Indians on August 10. After they sent their impudent letter to President Houston, the rebel force began to move out. Captain Augustine's company was ordered to track Córdova's movements, as the rebels were thought to be proceeding to Duwali's lands. The militiamen followed the Mexicans and Indians upriver while Rusk marched his main body of six hundred men along the Old San Antonio Road. The general wrote Duwali on August 13, and informed the chief of the depredations the insurgents had committed. He stressed he meant the Cherokees no harm but he believed Duwali was wrong to shelter enemies of Texas.[5]

After spending two days at Lacy's Fort, a well-protected farmhouse in present Cherokee County, Augustine's scouts started out in pursuit of Córdova. Rusk's force, now organized into the Third Militia Brigade under the immediate command of Brigadier-General Kelsey Harris Douglass, encountered Augustine's riders that morning past the fort. Ford and his comrades located Córdova's rebels approximately two miles from the Cherokee village. By August 14, indications were that they were well-armed and spoiling for a fight. Rusk moved the brigade from Lacy's Fort to Fort Houston, then marched to a camp near Duwali's village. The general met with the Cherokee chief on August 15 to discuss peace. Duwali promised his tribesmen would take no part in any fighting. Córdova's Mexican rebels broke camp and fled west for the headwaters of the Trinity River, while the Indians planned to slip back to their respective villages. While the bulk of the brigade remained camped on the Neches Saline, several scouts, Ford among them, followed Córdova's trail, which he noted "grew smaller as we advanced." Córdova would return the following year to trouble Texas again. With the rebellion scattered for a time, Houston ordered Rusk to disband his expedition, and Augustine's company was discharged on August 22.[6]

Although Texas signed a peace treaty with the Kichai, Tawakoni, Towash (Pawnee), and Waco Indians on September 2, 1838, relations between the republic and the Cherokees were deteriorating by 1839. The suspicion of their tribe's dealings with Mexican provocateurs, and the depredations for which they were blamed, were causing settlers to view them with increasing hostility. President Mirabeau Buonaparte Lamar, inaugurated on December 10, proclaimed in his first address to the Third Congress that Indians had no legal claim to land in Texas and he intended to bring about "their total extinction or total expulsion." Lamar wrote Duwali on May 26, 1839, and suggested his people leave Texas in return for fair compensation for the improvements they had made to their lands east of the Neches Saline. The chief replied that he wished for peace, but his younger men were ready to fight for their homes.[7]

Even while Texian troops were concentrating at Fort Kickapoo on the west bank of the Neches River, Secretary of War Albert Sidney Johnston, General Rusk, Vice President David Gouverneur Burnet, and two private citizens were dispatched on June 27 to negotiate Lamar's compensation proposal. Duwali, accompanied by twenty-one Cherokees, and representatives from the Shawnees and the Delawares, met with the commissioners near Saline Creek on July 10. The Cherokee chief appeared to be stalling for time in order to gather his forces, and the talks broke down within five days. General Douglass was placed in charge of the one thousand regulars and volunteers assembled into twenty-five companies at newly established Camp Johnston. Around noon on July 15, the Cherokees moved to the west of the Neches, and the Texian army quickly broke camp to pursue.[8]

In response to this latest crisis, Ford had enlisted under Captain William Kimbro, whose company was mustered into the Third Regiment of Douglass's brigade. While the negotiations were failing on the fifteenth, Kimbro's eighty volunteers were sent to disarm the Shawnees. The Texians surrounded the village at Big Spring the following day and seized the gunlocks from the Indians' rifles. While the Shawnee chief Jim Linney complied with the militiamen, Ford was of the opinion they merely surrendered the locks from useless weapons and hid the remainder in the brush. Nevertheless, the Indians offered no resistance and refrained from aiding the Cherokees. Kimbro's company marched on to Duwali's camp on the Neches River in present Van Zandt County. Ford and his comrades arrived at the village on July 16, one day too late to participate in the battle that killed Duwali and an estimated one hundred warriors. Ford viewed with admiration the body of the Cherokee chief, who had fallen fighting a courageous rearguard action while his people escaped. His esteem for Duwali remained intact, even after a Bible was found in an Indian hut. The book was marked with the names of the massacred white family from whom it had been stolen. This evidence confirmed for Ford the part the Cherokees had played in the raiding of the previous year.[9]

After Kimbro's company was disbanded on August 10, the ambitious Ford turned from war to politics. Twice he stood for election to the House of Representatives, and twice he lost by reasonable margins. Although he returned to his doctor's office on Main Street in San Augustine, he did read law, possibly to prepare himself for a future political career. Upon successful examination and the recommendations of attorneys Thomas Johnson, David Spangler Kaufman, and William C. Duffield, Ford was granted a law license. Despite his newly won certification, he does not seem to have followed the legal profession. Instead, he devoted his efforts to his medical practice for the next three years. He became successful enough to take on Doctor Thomas H. Lister as a partner and move to better offices in the business district. The partnership dissolved in June 1843, and Ford moved his practice to Columbia Street opposite the *Red-Lander* newspaper office.[10]

On September 21, 1844, Ford announced his candidacy for the Texas House and championed the issue of the annexation of Texas to the United States. In the election, he was able to secure one of the three seats available by polling 238 votes, thirty-two more than his next closest rival. The new representative took his seat when the Ninth Congress opened its session on December 2 at Washington-on-the-Brazos. Ford was appointed to committees focusing on Indian affairs, education, and finance, and to a special committee analyzing the report of the commissioner of the General Land Office. He was also named chairman of the Committee on Retrenchment. While on the Indian Affairs Committee, he encountered, for the first time, the concerns of the frontier counties, an issue he held dear for the remainder of his public career.[11]

Even after the House recessed on February 3, 1845, Ford remained in the capital where he learned President John Tyler had approved a joint resolution of the U.S. Congress on March 1 that provided for the annexation of Texas. Anson Jones, president of the Republic of Texas, convened the Ninth Congress into special session on June 16 to debate the issue. Ford was present when the House was called to order, and the following day he was given the honor of introducing a joint resolution that Texas consent to the proposition. One notable feature of the treaty was that Texas would retain ownership of its public lands, which could be applied toward the long-standing public debt. The Congress unanimously approved the motion on June 23, and also supported President Jones's request for a general convention to finalize the process and write a state constitution. Having performed its last official duties, the Congress of the Republic of Texas adjourned on June 28 for the final time.[12]

The convention approved the offer of annexation, absent one dissenting vote, on July 4. The new state constitution was adopted on August 27. After the delegates adjourned the following day, Ford returned to Washington to marry Louisa Swisher Lewis on September 26. His bride was described as possessing "the kind of grace and inner beauty that John Salmon wanted most in a woman." His memoirs are strangely silent on his second marriage (and indeed his first), but this union, however brief, seems to have brought him happiness.[13]

The new couple made ready to move to Austin, which, as a state capital, Ford saw was ripe for expansion and perfect for his new business endeavor. Ford had partnered with Michael Cronican, a former publisher from Galveston, to purchase the *Texas National Register* and transfer its operations from Washington to Austin. The name of the paper was changed to the *Texas Democrat* on January 3, 1846, as Ford intended to promote the Democratic Party platform in his editorial page. Becoming a fixture in town life, Ford published articles on local items, Indian depredations, and the undertakings of the new state legislature. This latter source of news was so plentiful that, beginning on March 7, the newspaper changed to a semi-weekly publication during legislative sessions. Furthermore, the relationships Ford created with the political leadership insured his continued prosperity. On April 13, the First Legislature narrowly elected Ford and Cronican the official state printers by a vote of forty-one to forty. The government contract for printing assured the solvency of the *Democrat* for the next two years. Two weeks later, on April 27, a number of legislators met to organize the Democratic Party in Texas and selected Ford for the state central committee.[14]

Ford was seemingly at the pinnacle of personal and professional achievement. He delighted in his new bride, he possessed the respect and friendship of his neighbors, he enjoyed financial success in his business, and he experienced the admiration of the state's political elite. Regrettably, his destiny lay elsewhere. In the first weeks of June, Louisa became ill with "pulmonary consumption," otherwise known as tuberculosis. Ford and other physicians in Austin were helpless to cure her. He shifted management of the paper to Cronican and faithfully tended to his wife through the humid summer. His efforts ultimately failed as Louisa died on August 21, and was buried in Oakwood Cemetery in Austin.[15]

Ford was left despondent but determined to find diversions from his grief. Current events were to present him with such an opportunity. On May 12, the United States had entered into a state of war with Mexico, and Texans were seeing action below the border. Major-General Zachary Taylor had found Colonel John C. "Jack" Hays's regiment of mounted riflemen, which was discharged in the fall of 1846, prone to troublemaking and difficult to discipline. However, his supply and communications lines came under *guerrillero* attack once the rangers had departed. Responding to appeals from the army, Hays raised another regiment in early 1847 to deal with the problem. Ford's opportunity to forget his heartache was at hand. He rode to San Antonio to be mustered into Captain Samuel Highsmith's Texas Mounted Volunteers on June 23, 1847. On July 7, Ford was promoted to the rank of first lieutenant and appointed regimental adjutant. Three days later, after the last enlistment was accepted, the regiment was mustered into federal service for twelve months.[16]

The need to sustain an adequate defense of the borderlands forced Hays to detail two companies of the First Texas to remain behind; one of them was Highsmith's outfit. The other five and the regimental headquarters, which included Ford, left San Antonio on August 12. Fully expecting to protect Taylor's line of operations from *guerrillero* raids, the rangers were instead directed on July 16 to provide that same service for

Major-General Winfield Scott from Vera Cruz to Mexico City. The new set of orders reached Hays at Mier.[17]

Captain Gabriel M. Armstrong's rangers reached Matamoros on September 7, where they encamped two miles below the city to await transport to Vera Cruz. The rest of the regiment arrived on the tenth. Approximately two weeks later, Ford and the companies of Isaac Ferguson and Alfred Marion Truit boarded a ship at Brazos Santiago in order to secure a regimental campsite in Vera Cruz. The advance party made landfall, and Major-General Robert Patterson, the garrison commander, assigned them a bivouac at Vergara, three miles north of the city on the Jalapa road. The camp location was relatively healthy, but humid and exposed to the wind. Irregular bands of Mexicans were constantly raiding the area, particularly one operating under Colonel Mariano Zenobia from the Hacienda de San Juan, approximately thirty miles from Vera Cruz. General Patterson believed the rangers would be able to campaign effectively in the dense jungle growth. Undaunted, the Texans requested they be allowed to conduct a reconnaissance. Patterson gave his permission and offered them a guide. Before dawn on October 13, Captain Truit, commanding the ranger party, was ready to depart but the guide was not present. Following verbal instructions he had received the night before, the captain led out 119 officers and men drawn from Companies E, I, and K.[18]

The rangers rode for about twenty-five miles along shadowy trails choked with thick vines and undergrowth. At the head of the column, Ford suddenly spotted three *guerrilleros* ahead. Without a word of warning to his comrades, the adjutant impetuously spurred his horse toward the enemy. Behind him, another ranger also spied the Mexicans and fired his rifle at them just as Ford's horse stepped in a mud hole, tumbled over in a somersault, and deposited the lieutenant in the same muck. The other members of the reconnaissance party believed Ford had been struck by friendly fire and berated the unfortunate rifleman. The adjutant rose dripping from the mire and remounted to continue the chase.[19]

As the rangers pursued the partisans across a small clearing where stood a crude hut, one Mexican was shot from his saddle. Ford thundered after another raider, but soaked percussion caps rendered his pistol useless.

The lieutenant instead drew his saber and rushed at the *guerrillero*. The fleeing irregular tumbled off his horse and leaped into the hut. Ford dismounted and followed, but he only found a woman standing in the middle of the room. The ranger exited the shanty and circled it a few times, but the Mexican had escaped. Fortunately, the third Mexican was captured and disarmed. The prisoner revealed Zenobia was located at the Rancho of San Juan with a gang of one hundred bandits.[20]

Ford and the other rangers rode the twelve miles to Zenobia's headquarters. Upon reaching their objective, Truit deployed his left wing under Captain Ferguson and his right under Lieutenant Preston Witt, while retaining the center under his personal command. Ford, continuing to lead the advance guard, rode forward and encountered three armed Mexicans who fled the Texans' approach. The rangers pursued and dispatched one Mexican, wounded another in a sharp firefight, and captured the third. Zenobia escaped. The Texans searched the large, marble-floored residence and found among its palatial furnishings blood-stained clothing, U.S. Army-issue firearms, powder and lead, five or six hundred bushels of corn, forage sacks, and other items taken from American troops. The rangers ordered the family residing at the *hacienda* outside and set fire to the structure, thereby depriving the *guerrilleros* of a rendezvous site. The Texans chose a different route in their return to Vergara and skirmished with the enemy along the way. After a march totaling sixty miles, they reported to General Patterson as the sun was setting.[21]

Once Colonel Hays and the balance of the regiment arrived in Vera Cruz, General Patterson continually sent them into the countryside to pursue raiders. Since Hays was the regiment's only field-grade officer, he ordered an election to be held to choose a major as the second-in-command. Alfred Truit was selected on October 26, and Chaucer Ashton succeeded him as captain of Company E. As the regimental staff was completing its organization, Ford's duties as adjutant frequently forced him to remain at the headquarters tent while others battled *guerrilleros*. When the entire regiment took to the field, only then could he fight. However, when a spy company was formed at Vergara using the best fifty men in the regiment, Ford was elected its captain and John Joel Glanton its lieutenant. The detachment was tasked with operations independent of the regiment; rather than chasing marauders after they attacked, Ford and his men hunted them amongst the nearby villages and hillsides. On the occasions the regiment moved in force, the spy company served as scouts. His selection as the commander of a picked body of rangers was a testament to Ford's capabilities and leadership.[22]

The men of the scout company were kept in a constant state of alert, so they were exempted from routine camp chores. Only Captain Armstrong, commander of Company G, objected to the arrangement. In order to maintain harmony within the regiment, Hays disbanded the scout detachment and returned the rangers to their respective companies. In his memoirs, Ford indicated he did not have much respect for Armstrong.[23]

The most enduring account of how Ford earned the nickname "Rip" was expressed by his great-grandson, Brownsville attorney Louis Rafael Cowen. According to him, one of Ford's chief duties as regimental adjutant was to prepare the death certificates for those rangers killed in action. He ended each report with the respectful words "rest in peace" written after his signature. He later abbreviated the phrase to "R.I.P." to save time, and, soon the men were calling Ford "Old Rip."[24] Doubts of this particular theory rest in the fact that Hays's regiment suffered few losses in the war, and rangers as a whole were notoriously lax with administrative procedures, including death certificates. Another reason for his sobriquet may have been due to his fondness for bestowing nicknames upon his men, usually based on a personal trait of the recipient. Allegedly Ford had fallen asleep on duty and some of the wits in the regiment began naming him after Rip Van Winkle. The third hypothesis revolves around his fighting spirit and his tendency to "rip" into the enemy. As historian and artist Tom Lea once observed, "He was no mere fighting man, though they did call him Rip for the way he went at it." Any of these notions could be true, and to them may be added one further piece of information. On October 15, 1846, before Hays's second regiment was even raised, Abner Squinch wrote a letter to Ford that was published in the latter's newspaper. In his missive, Squinch addressed the editor as "Rip."[25]

The next few months would offer plenty of opportunities for a fighter, regardless of his name. General Scott had taken Mexico City by September 13. Desiring reinforcements, he ordered General Patterson in late October to leave what troops were needed to garrison Vera Cruz and march the remainder to the capital. Hays was placed in charge of screening the movements of the column. The colonel's mounted riflemen numbered 580 officers and men. Most, but not all of them, were Texan recruits. On November 2, the rangers took their place in the long column of soldiers leaving the port city and rode for Mexico City, some 260 grueling miles distant. Two days later, the American troops reached Jalapa where Hays left the companies of Isaac Ferguson, Chaucer Ashton, and Preston Witt; the three officers were all ill. Sick on this occasion, Ford likewise stayed behind. Throughout his time in Mexico, he suffered through numerous bouts of an unidentified illness, probably malaria. The colonel pressed on for the town of Puebla with the companies of Jacob Roberts and Gabriel Armstrong. Jalapa was not a restful place though; rather the area was plagued with partisan bands under Zenobia, Padre Celedonio Dómeco de Jarauta, and others. On November 19, Witt's Company K launched a nighttime assault on the village of Jalcomuclo, approximately thirty miles away, and captured several *guerrillero* leaders, including two who had previously given their parole.[26]

Ford and the three companies departed Jalapa and took the road for Puebla on November 24. They rode into the high hills through rain, hail, and snow until they arrived in Perote on November 26. The rangers were exhausted by the hard march, rough roads, and raw weather, so they remained in the village for two days. They resumed their journey and traveled thirty miles before they bivouacked at Tepeyahualco. On November 30, the Texans passed Ojo de Agua, and by midafternoon were encamped under the lofty oak and pine trees around El Pinal. As dusk fell, the rangers learned partisans were slaughtering American stragglers at Tepeyahualco. One of the companies rushed back to the village with orders to show no quarter. Two hours later, the avenging riders returned and reported they had killed two *guerrilleros*, captured two unarmed but suspect Mexicans, and retrieved the corpses of two murdered Pennsylvania infantrymen. A Pennsylvania corporal, who was in the camp, slyly remarked upon the novelty of rangers taking Mexican prisoners. The rangers departed El Pinal on the morning of December 2, and reached Puebla the following evening where they rejoined their comrades in Hays's regiment. The newly arriving Texans then heard of the significant engagement Hays had led at Izúcar de Matamoros.[27]

After one night of rest, Ford and the other rangers were in the vanguard of two columns of Pennsylvania, Massachusetts, and Ohio volunteers marching for Mexico City. On December 6, the rangers followed their colonel into the environs of the capital. The ragged but heavily armed Texans drew the attention of *leperos*, cutthroats who preyed on American soldiers and Mexican residents alike. As Hays's men rode toward the central plaza, a stone hurled by a *lepero* knocked the cap off a ranger's head. The roar of a Colt six-shooter answered the rock thrower, who dropped to the cobbles with a bullet in his head. The ranger's horse walked by the fallen hat, where the Texan leaned over and picked it up without a word. A crowd of apprehensive Mexicans and curious Americans gathered in the plaza to catch a glimpse of *los Tejanos sangrientos* (the bloody Texans) as they arrived. The company officers joined Hays and his staff to learn from the billeting officer where the men would be lodged.[28]

While the rank and file waited on the southern side of the plaza, they were visited by a candy vendor, who bore his goods in a basket on his head. One of the rangers helped himself to a handful of sweets from the carrier. The Texan calmly finished the treats and took some more as the peddler seethed in indignation. The Mexican, not realizing he would be paid for his candy as Hays did not tolerate theft, picked up a pebble and hurled it at the ranger. The ranger pulled his pistol and fatally shot the vendor. The crowd, which had witnessed the killing, stampeded in panic, trampling their fellow citizens or knocking them into the gutters. The candy vendor was not the last to die that day. When the rangers rode toward their billets, one young Texan began to beat his stubborn horse with the butt of his revolver. The pistol discharged and the bullet struck a bystander in the stomach.[29]

The ensuing bloody clashes between the rangers and the citizens of Mexico City persuaded General Scott to transfer Hays's regiment to San Àngel, six miles south of the city. While Hays and eighty-four men were on an expedition to locate Jarauta, they halted in the village of San Juan Teotihuacán on January 12. The Texans bivouacked in a large building on the plaza, but foolishly failed to post guards on the perimeter. The sleepless night and the hard riding had exhausted the men and their mounts, especially Ford, who had been ill when the command began the operation. Later that morning, seventy-five lancers rushed the sleeping rangers' position and nearly captured them. Roused from their slumber, the rangers broke the horsemen with their heavy revolvers, but Padre Jarauta rallied the Mexicans to re-form the charge. Lieutenant Ephraim Merrill Daggett fired at an energetic officer, seemingly without effect. Ford also shot at the Mexican and the man dropped to the ground. Amid the incoming fire, the two rangers were arguing about who had fired the telling shot when their target leapt to his feet and fled wildly through a nearby doorway. Shortly thereafter, a well-placed bullet severely wounded the bandit party's leader, and the *guerrilleros* retreated from the town. Hays and his men returned to Mexico City that night. Ford, again suffering from illness, was ordered to his bed under a physician's care. Five days later, he was still convalescing when the regiment rode out and subsequently fought an engagement at Puebla, and a second battle at San Juan Teotihuacán.[30]

Even after the signing of the Treaty of Guadalupe Hidalgo, many *guerrilleros* were unwilling to lay down their arms, chief among them Jarauta. These villains now expanded their depredations to include not only small and isolated detachments of American troops along the Vera Cruz–Mexico City corridor, but also their fellow Mexicans who welcomed the new peace. The Texans had one last mission before their war could end. After eight p.m. on February 17, Brigadier-General Joseph Lane, five companies of rangers, two companies of the Third Dragoons, and one of the Mounted Rifles, set out to the northwest, following partisan spies who were acting as guides. Fully recovered, Ford rode with the rest of the regiment's field and staff officers at the head of the column. After they had journeyed a short way, the command moved off the Vera Cruz road and turned toward the village of Tulancingo where General Mariano Paredes y Arrillaga, a former president and current guerilla chieftain, was reported to be located. Riding through the night, the Americans reached their goal only to find their reported prey was instead the general's brother.[31]

After a forced night march on February 24 through seventy-five miles of rugged terrain, the rangers and regular troops arrived at the edge of

Mexican Guerrilleros: Mexico in 1848. Lithograph by Currier and Ives, New York City. *Courtesy Prints and Photographs Division, Library of Congress, Washington, D.C.*

Zacualtipán, where spies learned Jarauta was hiding. The Americans stormed into the town as Mexican rifle fire from a *cuartel* struck the column. Colonel Hays quickly ordered Ford and Major Truit to take a squad of fifteen to eighteen rangers and deal with the enemy there. The remainder of the assaulting force rushed to the central plaza. Truit's detachment broke open the heavy doors of the patio in front of the *cuartel* and charged inside. They were greeted with a heavy fire delivered by two companies of *guerrilleros* situated in a two-story building, with a high palisade protecting the front. A lower barricade stretched across the plaza parallel to the taller stockade. Sheltering behind the shorter wall, the sharpshooting rangers were able to drive the Mexicans from their position. The demoralized guerrillas began attempting to escape by scaling the outer wall. Spying the retreat, Ford and Private Jacob Horne of Company E scrambled atop the wall, braved the enemy fire as they ran along the top, and stopped above the doorway. Under fire from a distance of only twenty paces, the two Texans halted a large party of Mexicans striving to abandon the *cuartel*.[32]

Antonio López de Santa Anna. From New York *Illustrated News*, April 30, 1853. *Courtesy Special Collections, The University of Texas at Arlington Libraries, Arlington, Texas.*

They had just stopped the retreating party when Horne was shot high in the chest. Ford quickly judged the serious wound was not mortal and returned to his task. A party of rangers hurried to Ford's aid, while Truit rushed to the plaza where Hays was reportedly threatened by a *lancero* attack. The adjutant, leading the detachment at the *cuartel*, breached a gate, which allowed the Texans to bring enfilade fire upon the Mexican left flank and rear. Attached to the left of the stone structure was a wooden building which had been set afire. Cut off by the burning structure, the enemy was forced to surrender. Finding the lancer threat sufficiently managed, Truit returned to his detachment in time to supervise the securing of the twenty-one Mexican prisoners. The enemy's losses at the *cuartel* were eleven dead and one dying, at least four of them by Ford's hand, including a colonel. Another eleven were wounded. Horne, who would die at the Pachuca hospital on the return journey, was the only seriously wounded Texan; two others received slight injuries.[33]

The Americans left Zacualtipán on the morning of February 26, and arrived in Mexico City on March 1. The following morning, they returned to their San Àngel camp. U.S. and Mexican military commanders settled on an armistice three days later. Any further ranger operations would be conducted against *guerrillero* parties branded as outlaws by both governments.[34]

In early March, Hays was ordered to patrol the National Road toward Vera Cruz and clear out the bandits plaguing the supply trains. Methodically scouting the countryside along the road, the rangers were engaged in minor skirmishing as they rode toward Jalapa. Once they had arrived and were bivouacked two miles above the city, the rangers were informed that deposed *Presidente* Antonio López de Santa Anna would be traveling the same road on his way into exile. At once, many of the Texans resolved to assassinate the defeated dictator. Ford and Truit, the ranking officers present, decided they could not order the wrathful men to turn away from their decision. Appealing to reason and principle instead, the two acquiesced the *caudillo* had waged a savage, inhumane war on the people of Texas. But since he was under the protection of a safe conduct granted by General Scott, the act of executing him would dishonor themselves and their state. Considering the officers' point, the men declared, "Then we will not do it." Ford did deny the rangers permission to speak with their old foe, but they could take a close look at him. The rangers, numbering several hundred, lined both sides of the road as Santa Anna's convoy approached. The general, his wife, and their daughter rode in an open carriage surrounded by Mexican lancers and U.S. mounted troops. The entourage passed by as the grim Texans watched without voicing a word or moving a muscle. Major John Reese Kenly, a Maryland officer who commanded the escort, later wrote: "The Texans had behaved with great propriety, the well-disposed among them checking even an utterance of what might have been deemed disrespectful, to one under the safeguard and honor of our flag."[35]

The regiment continued scouting the road toward Vera Cruz before returning to Mexico City on April 19. Hays soon received orders to proceed to Vera Cruz once more and muster his rangers out of service. They escorted an army wagon train on the trip, and went into camp outside Vergara on April 29. By May 1, the men of the First Texas Mounted Volunteers were discharged from federal service, except for Hays, Ford, and several others. The adjutant, the colonel, and some of the men boarded the steamer *Maria Burt* bound for Port Lavaca, where ecstatic citizens held a ball for them a few days later. Originally intending to serve with Colonel Bell's regiment on the frontier, Ford changed his mind while sailing to Texas. He left Port Lavaca and traveled to the ranger camp at Enchanted Rock, where his old company under Captain Highsmith was located. There he mustered out on May 14, 1848.[36]

Ford returned to Austin and resumed his duties as editor and publisher of the *Texas Democrat*. After his experiences in Mexico, he soon found the routine chafing, and welcomed an opportunity for adventure once more. Seeking new endeavors, he and Cronican sold the newspaper to William H. Cushney, one of the previous owners of the *National Register*. At the same time, following the discovery of gold near Sacramento, a group of prominent Austin citizens were pursuing ways to establish a practical overland route to California via El Paso. In early 1849, Ford was named to a committee charged with preparing a report to present the benefits of a San Antonio–El Paso road. Colonel Hays had made an expedition to that distant town the previous year, but had been forced to turn back before reaching his goal. Ford's panel drew heavily on Hays's report.[37]

While the committee was at work, Major Robert Simpson Neighbors, long-time Indian agent in Texas, was looking at the same issue. He secured permission from military authorities in San Antonio to undertake a personal reconnaissance of the route he thought most feasible for a military and civilian wagon road. After obtaining the services of Comanche guides, he made a stop in Austin. There, at the urging of the citizens' group, Ford offered his assistance to Neighbors's exploration. The Indian agent welcomed Ford, whose medical, surveying, and rangering experiences would prove invaluable.[38]

Mounted on mules rather than horses, the expedition left the North Bosque settlement on March 23. They reached the Cross Timbers, moved on to the Colorado River, and up the Concho before striking the Horsehead Crossing of the Pecos on April 17. Making Carrizo Pass on April 24, the party, low on supplies, reached San Elizario five days later. They rested for a few days in the village before commencing the remaining twenty miles to El Paso. The explorers went back to San Elizario, where they secured supplies and a new guide, and set off on May 6. The expedition rode over the Guadalupe Mountains and followed the Pecos toward the Horsehead Crossing, which they attained on May 20. They reached the head of the Concho River four days later. After striking the San Saba on May 29, most of the Indians left the party to travel directly to the Torrey Trading House on Tehuacana Creek, while Neighbors and Ford continued on to Fredericksburg and then San Antonio on June 2.[39]

Ford and Neighbors prepared reports detailing their travels, that of the Indian agent being submitted to army department headquarters. After being celebrated by his friends in the city, Ford left San Antonio and returned home to Austin. The *Texas Democrat* published his account on June 23, which outlined the wagon road they judged to be "safe and practicable at all seasons." In his own statement, Neighbors said, "In Dr. John S. Ford I found an energetic and able assistant, the services rendered by him were important to the successful termination of the expedition. I cheerfully recommend him to your favorable notice."[40] His exploration duties over, Ford returned to his medical practice. There seemed little call for his services at that time, so, still needing to keep busy, he immersed himself in community affairs.

He joined the Austin chapter of the Sons of Temperance, but he yearned for more active pursuits.[41]

By June 1849, the theoretical federal troop strength in Texas stood at one thousand infantrymen, one hundred artillerists, and three hundred dragoons—some fourteen hundred soldiers in twenty-eight companies. The numbers were similar to those Texas had fielded when she was still a republic and was considered by Washington to be adequate. The following month, Brevet Major-General George Mercer Brooke, commander of U.S. Army forces in Texas, wrote the adjutant-general that the companies were only half full, and there were actually fewer than one thousand soldiers in Texas. As the *Texas State Gazette* editorialized, "The idea of repelling mounted Indians, the most expert horsemen in the world, with a force of foot soldiers, is here looked upon as extremely ridiculous."[42]

Article XI of the Treaty of Guadalupe Hidalgo required the United States to curtail Indian depredations into Mexico. Because the Comanche people were starving due to a decline in the bison population, suffering from an outbreak of smallpox and cholera, and facing a collapse of their trading network with the Cheyennes, Arapahos, and Osages, large numbers of war parties raided through the expanding Texas borderlands and deep into northern Mexico.[43] By the end of 1849, 171 people in the Nueces Strip were killed, seven wounded, twenty-five captured, and six thousand horses would be stolen, along with other property valued at $100,000. The article proved unenforceable and was abrogated by the Gadsden Treaty in 1853. Most of the raids would occur in the country between San Antonio and Brownsville until approximately 1857.[44] Following the war, South Texas saw an influx of muleskinners, mustangers, soldiers of fortune, filibusters, insurrectionists, army deserters, prostitutes, smugglers, scalp hunters, and slave trackers, all eager to exploit the opportunities offered by the borderlands. In addition to Comanche, Lipan, and Kiowa incursions, Mexican *bandidos* and American desperadoes plied their bloody trade upon the respectable farmers, ranchers, merchants, lawyers, traders, and missionaries who were establishing Brownsville, Eagle Pass, Edinburg, Rio Grande City, Roma, and other settlements in the lower valley. The headquarters of the Eighth Military Department was inundated with pleas for aid from those exposed to the raids. Many called for the formation of ranger companies to protect the threatened regions.[45]

General Brooke assured Governor George Tyler Wood the military could handle the problem and rangers were not necessary. He believed their "general and natural hostility to the Indians" would bring about a widespread war. The friction between the State of Texas and the federal government over the issue of frontier protection grew from the prevailing attitude behind Brooke's comments, and would have profound consequences years later. Depredations continued to mount throughout the summer and the state fielded several ranger companies to deal with them.[46]

Events forced the general to reconsider his earlier decision. On August 9, he proposed to Governor Wood one company of seventy-five men be mustered into federal service to range the Nueces Strip, but a fresh wave of raids caused him to adjust his plans. On August 11, Brooke requested the governor instead raise three companies of mounted volunteers. Each company would consist of one captain, one first and one second lieutenant, four sergeants, four corporals, two musicians, one farrier and blacksmith, and sixty-four privates. Brooke reminded the governor "the Officers should be selected with the greatest care, having in view their efficiency, sound habits and knowledge of border war, as, without the proper qualifications, they can render but little service." Using Corpus Christi as a central depot, the troops were to serve for six months and patrol from that town to Goliad to the Rio Grande. The rangers were required to furnish their own horse, saddle and bridle, and halter and lariat. The quartermaster and commissary departments were instructed to provide transportation, camp equipage, subsistence, rifles and pistols, and ammunition.[47]

The governor agreed to the general's request, and Adjutant General John Drayton Pitts tapped his good friend Rip Ford, as well as John J. Grumbles and Jerome B. McCown, two veteran ranger captains who had served during the late war. On August 23, 1849, Ford organized his recruits in Austin and, in the customary fashion, was elected captain of the company. Thomas M. Wooldridge was chosen as the first lieutenant and Jeremiah W. Robertson as the second. The command was then mustered into federal service the same day and was soon on the San Antonio road bound for South Texas.[48]

Ford's company reached Corpus Christi on September 5, where they received arms and supplies. He then led his men about eight miles south to Henry Lawrence Kinney's ranch on the Cajo del Oso. Later they relocated to another camp on the Santa Gertrudis. Through the remainder of the year, and on into 1850, the company patrolled their area of responsibility. The work was grueling and thankless, as the rangers chased raiders only to have repeated heavy rains obliterate the tracks, or some other unexpected event thwart them bringing hostile Indians to battle.[49]

Unlike Hays, Ford resembled the popular image of a ranger captain in that he stood more than six feet tall, and possessed a lean, muscular build. He had wavy, light brown hair, piercing blue eyes, high cheekbones, and an aquiline nose. He was normally quiet in his speech, but given to profanity in the midst of battle. He did not imbibe alcohol and read one passage from the Bible every day, even when campaigning.

As the company's term of service neared its end, General Brooke wrote, "The murders and robberies lately repeated by the Indians and the season now approaching when a renewal of the same atrocities may be expected, the exigencies of the cause appear to me to demand the continuance of the force already in service." He went on to compliment the rangers in the field: "In justice to the companies of Captains Ford, Grumbles, & McCown, with their officers, I take great pleasure in acknowledging their energy and perseverance in the most active scouting and pursuit of the savages, with a perfect obedience in the execution of all orders (and in connexion [*sic*]) with a due subordination of Regular troops."[50]

The rangers' six-month enlistment expired on February 23, 1850, and the company was reorganized prior to being remustered the next day for another half-year. Some, disillusioned with the privations or lack of fighting, took their discharge. They were replaced by more hardy souls. Andrew Jackson Walker was the company's new first lieutenant, and Malcijah Benjamin "Kige" Highsmith (son of veteran ranger captain Samuel Highsmith) was the second lieutenant. David M. Level was the orderly sergeant, while Doctor Phillip Noland Luckett, who had been a member of the original company, remained as surgeon.[51]

Governor Peter Hansborough Bell received a letter from citizens living in the lower Rio Grande Valley requesting the protection of a ranger company. The petitioners specifically asked that Ford be commissioned to command the outfit. Whether the request factored into army department headquarters' thinking, Ford was ordered to take a position at the abandoned *hacienda* of San Antonio Viejo on the Laredo road, approximately forty-five miles north of Ringgold Barracks, in order to more effectively deter attacks. The company erected a camp in an oak grove one-half mile south of the *hacienda's* wells before turning their attentions to active campaigning.[52]

Contrary to most other captains of the time, Ford regularly drilled his men in horsemanship, the manual of arms, and the formations necessary to successfully battle the Comanches. The captain ensured that such exercises "appealed to the pride and to the sense of honor of the men." The engagements they trained to conduct were usually running fights involving fifteen to twenty mounted men on each side. The historical record detailing the company's discipline and cohesion testifies to the success of his efforts.[53]

One such action occurred after Ford, Lieutenant Walker, and twenty-nine men left their camp on May 7 and rode along the Rio Grande. They were heading for Fort Merrill in order to procure newer pistols. Finding a Comanche arrow in a freshly killed deer on the tenth, Ford dispatched Walker and ten men to Laredo in order to deceive the Indians into thinking the whole command was returning, and to get Walker in the rear of any war party traveling upriver. Breaking camp on May 13, Ford's remaining rangers discovered a fresh Indian trail, followed the party of fifteen riders northwest some five miles, and found they were already past the Comanche Crossing of the Nueces River. Ford directed twelve rangers to dismount and move through the chaparral to the right of the crossing, while the captain took the other seven to the left. The Texans swam the river and resumed the pursuit. Eight miles later, they found the war party and charged them. The Comanches were armed with lances and bows and arrows. The rangers carried muzzle-loading Mississippi rifles; only Ford and Sergeant Level had revolvers. At fifteen feet, the clash between the two sides was almost at point-blank range. In the running fight that covered three miles, the better-mounted rangers killed four Comanches and wounded seven others before the band reached the safety of the chaparral. The only Texan casualty cited in the post-action report was a slight wound caused by a falling arrow. Ford neglected to mention the scratch across the back of his right hand from another arrow, which caused him tremendous pain. He believed the arrowhead had been coated with rattlesnake venom. The injury proved beyond treatment and his arm slowly became paralyzed, albeit temporarily, over the next five or six years. He also suffered an annual skin eruption on his hand.[54]

Trailing the Indian party, Ford and his rangers awoke on the morning of May 14 to discover the survivors of the previous fight had been reinforced by another seventy-five Comanches. The Indians had attempted to attack during the night of May 13, but Ford had posted a strong picket, and the Comanches waited for another chance. Ford kept his men formed and by brief, wary marches moved the command down the Nueces toward Fort Merrill. The Indians matched the rangers step for step. Several times they demonstrated a willingness to attack the Texans, but the company's discipline and frequent drilling invariably forced the Comanches to abandon their charges at the last minute. For more than three days, the rangers held fast to their defensive posture on the march and in camp, while the food stores dwindled. When the last of the coffee was consumed, the rangers began boiling a tea using mesquite wood and copious amounts of sugar. They did not have to drink the vile brew for long as they soon reached Fort Merrill. The post commander promptly delivered rations and forage to the rangers.[55]

The captain returned to the company's bivouac with the pistols on the evening of May 25. Later in the night, a sentry heard owl hoots all around the campsite. Ford, who believed in preparing for the worst, alerted the men to ready themselves for an attack; the camp guard was posted, additional sentinels were dispersed along the perimeter, and everywhere weapons were carefully loaded and positioned for immediate use. The air rang with the sound of a rifle volley at three a.m. and Ford's instinct for danger was vindicated. The captain called out commands as his rangers leaped to their feet, firearms in hand. While the main guard stayed to watch the campsite, other rangers rode to relieve the outer ring of sentinels whose sharp fire drove the Comanches back into the night. Once the sun rose, no Indians could be found. On May 27, Ford broke camp and ordered the company to return to San Antonio Viejo.[56]

The ride was uneventful until the rangers came across fresh Indian sign on the morning of May 29. Roque Maugricio, the company's half-Comanche, half-Mexican scout, rode along studying the tracks. Ford left a seven-man rearguard with the pack mules and ordered the other seventeen men to make ready for action. Within four miles, near the Rancho Amargosa, the Texans spied an Indian encampment in a chaparral thicket to the left. The company charged and fired on the fourteen Comanches, who mounted their horses and fled, signaling as they topped each rise. Roque explained they were indicating a need for assistance from fellow tribesmen in the area and advised the rearguard might be in danger. One ranger riding with the captain, William Gillespie (a cousin of Captain Robert Addison "Ad" Gillespie), was already down, mortally wounded by a dying Indian. Gillespie's comrades helped him to the shelter of the mesquite before continuing on with the pursuit. Ford, heeding Roque's suggestion, ordered the vanguard to reverse course and charge the enemy threatening the rear. Gillespie's companions feared he would fall prey to the Comanches if left behind and refused to move. Ford was thirty yards ahead of the command before he realized he was alone. Turning his horse, he lost his temper when he saw the men hanging back and swore at them, accusing them of cowardice. Roque rode forward to explain the situation and Ford immediately ordered Gillespie be carried to the safety of the ranks.[57]

Ford delayed the charge until the rearguard began advancing out of the chaparral. Then, riding at a diagonal to link up, the rangers opened a methodical, long-range fire. Several warriors were wounded and a number of Comanche horses were killed. The two ranger detachments charged home, striking the war party on the left flank and the rear. Otto Cuero, the war chief, alighted to the ground and gave his horse to a wounded Indian so he could lead a delaying action against the Texans. Other Comanches on horseback attempted to screen their dismounted comrades, while the entire war party slowly fell back toward the Agua Dulce, approximately one mile distant. Another ranger charge broke the maneuver and the Indians fled for the timber. Ford fired at Otto Cuero at a range of 125 yards, but the shot seemed to have no effect. The captain ordered David Steele to dismount and kill the fleeing war chief. Otto Cuero paused to look back as Steele lined up his sights and fired. The shot hammered the chief off his horse.[58]

Ford halted the pursuit once they reached the timber, and directed the rangers back to their original position. Ford and Steele tarried to recover the dead chief's arms and equipment. In inspecting the body, they found that Ford's bullet had pierced the Indian's left arm while Steele's drilled him behind the ear. Three other Comanches had been killed and four or five wounded. One of those was found by Roque in a mesquite thicket bearing several wounds. The eighteen-year-old was promised his life if he would surrender, which he promptly did. His name proved to be Carne Muerto (Dead Meat) and he was believed to be the son of the notorious war chief Santa Anna. Besides Gillespie, the only other casualty was Sergeant Level who had been wounded by a musket ball above the ankle. The sergeant was angrier that his horse had been hurt, and treated his own injury as a trifling matter. Gillespie could not ride a horse, so his fellow rangers rigged a litter for him. The company then marched down the Agua Dulce in order to meet a detachment of Grumbles's command encamped twelve miles away. Gillespie's agony forced them to halt short of their goal, and he died that night. The following morning, the rangers carried his body to the rendezvous and buried him with full military honors. Once back at San Antonio Viejo, Steele sent Otto Cuero's arms and equipment to Governor Bell, while Ford wrote his report on the May 12 action. General Brooke was delighted with the outcome.[59]

The captain was not the only ranger officer to have a brush with the Indians. Lieutenant Walker had been directed to handle the fresh raids occurring in Webb County in early June. To that end, he and twelve men engaged a horse-stealing band of Comanches at Don Basilio Benavides's ranch. Three of the seven warriors were killed in the skirmish and three more were wounded before the Comanches escaped into the chaparral.[60]

In order to provide improved protection to Webb County residents, and to freight traffic on the Laredo–San Antonio road, Ford relocated his camp from San Antonio Viejo to Los Ojuelos, approximately forty miles east of Laredo on the road between that town and Corpus Christi. Ford also reorganized the company prior to the end of the rangers' enlistments. Traveling to San Antonio, the rangers acquired arms, ammunition, and supplies, signed on fresh recruits, and marched to their new camp.[61]

The company remustered on September 24 at Laredo. Highsmith was replaced by Edward "Ed" Burleson, Jr. (the son of former general Edward Burleson) as second lieutenant. Ford spent much of the winter confined to his sickbed in Laredo. Walker and Burleson kept the company active in his absence.[62]

Walker and twenty men were patrolling northeast of Laredo on January 19, 1851, when they found an empty Comanche encampment on the Arroyo Gato. Certain the raiders would return, Walker set an ambush. Six days later, fifteen warriors rode into the kill zone, and the rangers charged them. Two Comanches were slain and two wounded. The surviving Indians left behind approximately seventy-five head of horses and mules and a stolen Mexican boy.[63]

After delivering Carne Muerto to San Antonio, Burleson and twenty men were returning to camp on January 27, when they spied three Comanches near the Nueces. Selecting eight men to accompany him, Burleson set out in pursuit. As he neared the Indians, they whirled around and were joined by another eleven dismounted Comanches who had been hidden. The eight rangers misinterpreted Burleson's orders and also dismounted, while the Indians moved to attack. The subsequent skirmish was vicious as the Texans' carbines and Colt pistols vied with the Indians' lances and bows and arrows. The Indians suddenly broke off "the most desperate fight" and ran for the nearest thickets. Ranger Baker Barton was dead, William Lackey would breathe his last a week later at Fort McIntosh, and Burleson and four others bore painful but non-life-threatening injuries. Four Comanches lay lifeless on the ground, while another eight had staggered away wounded.[64]

The company enlisted for the fourth time on March 23 at Los Ojuelos. This tour of duty provided a great deal of patrolling but little in the way of combat. Indeed, the Comanches ceased with raiding the border settlements. The only trouble came from Seminoles in Mexico and they crossed the river infrequently. With the resumption of peace, Ford did not believe General Brooke would wish to retain the rangers much longer. He and his men decided to seek their discharge when the time came. In September, Ford received orders to march the company to Fort McIntosh, where he and his rangers left federal service on the twenty-third.[65]

Ford did not take the time to reflect on a job well done. Instead he joined the revolution of José María de Jesús Carvajal and the newly formed Liberal party in Mexico. Carvajal, born in Béxar and educated in Virginia, had declared for the establishment of the *Plan de la Loba*. Advocating for constitutional reforms and a withdrawal of the Mexican national army from the northern frontier, he found support among many influential politicians and businessmen in South Texas including Charles Stillman, Mifflin Kenedy, and Richard King. In return for financial and material aid from Texas merchants, Carvajal agreed to ensure runaway slaves would have no sanctuary south of the Rio Grande, all three thousand escaped slaves then in Mexico would be returned to their owners, a free-trade zone would be established along the border, and high tariffs and other restrictions to Anglo trade would be removed.[66] Immediately following his ranger company's discharge, Ford rode to Camargo to accept the post of second-in-command of the *Liberalista* army. Accompanying him was Andrew Walker and twenty-eight former rangers. Arriving at Carvajal's camp on October 1, Ford was commissioned a colonel and placed in command of all American volunteers; his force was designated the Auxiliary Troops. Anglo backing and the presence of *gringo* soldiers of fortune led many of Carvajal's own supporters to complain their leader had become too *agringado*, or Americanized, to succeed in Mexico.[67]

On October 9, Carvajal's eleven hundred men marched toward Matamoros, ninety-odd miles downstream, to engage the forces of *Presidente* Mariano Arista's central government. The main body of *Liberalistas* arrived at the outskirts of Matamoros on October 21, and drove the *Centralistas* from Fort Paredes on the northwest perimeter of the city. The following morning, supported by a single six-pounder, Ford led five American companies, and portions of the Reynosa, Mier, and Guerrero battalions, in the main assault on the city. The Auxiliary Troops engaged the Mexicans in sharp urban combat and advanced as far as the northwest corner of the Plaza Hidalgo before they were stopped by intense fire from nine guns. In danger of being outflanked, Ford called for reinforcements, but Carvajal instead ordered a withdrawal. The Texan thought the directive unwise and refused to obey, even after two more demands. He finally complied, having had to convince his angry subordinates that good discipline was essential for a successful revolutionary army. Ford's men fell back to Fort Paredes at nightfall and spent a sleepless night in the rain.[68]

The attack was resumed on the twenty-third. Two hundred and fifty *filibusteros* once more fought their way to the plaza, and again the enemy's artillery and musket fire halted them. Seeking the positions of the concealed riflemen, Ford peered out the door of his command post. His scalp grazed by a musket ball, he sustained a concussion that became apparent a short time later when he could not form intelligible words. Ford was taken across the river to Brownsville and the home of Judge William Walradt Dunlap. An army surgeon from Fort Brown dressed his wound, and Ford remained confined to bed while the siege of Matamoros reached its ludicrous end on the thirtieth.[69]

Ford learned Carvajal had abandoned Matamoros in the face of approaching *Centralista* reinforcements. Andy Walker had assumed command of the Auxiliary Troops and led the rearguard in the retreat. His wound still unhealed, Ford rode after the *Liberalistas* but, traveling a dozen miles upstream, he still could not locate the army. He returned to Brownsville and soon discovered they had withdrawn to Reynosa, some sixty miles above Matamoros. Ford boarded the next available King & Kenedy steamboat and took passage to Carvajal's camp. Disembarking at Reynosa, he ascertained Carvajal had decided to postpone active campaigning until he replenished the troop strength lost through widespread desertions. Promoted to a brigade command, Ford was detailed to enlist more Texans. Conscious of federal neutrality laws, he traveled to Austin in late November or early December to attract volunteers for the *Liberalista* cause.[70]

His recruiting was interrupted by the death of Edward Burleson, military hero, former vice-president of the Texas republic, and state senator for the Twenty-first District. Ford was prompted by friends in Austin to stand for the special election that would fill the vacancy. He won on January 12, 1852, and took his seat in the statehouse representing Travis, Hays, and Gillespie Counties. Associates in Brownsville insisted his decision to become a candidate was to "cover his real designs" and expected him to soon return to Mexico. After the legislature adjourned on February 16, Ford did resume his duties as a *Liberalista* brigadier.[71]

During the three months Ford was in Texas, the fortunes of Carvajal's revolt had waned. He had been bloodily repulsed at Cerralvo and Camargo before withdrawing to Rio Grande City. Ford found him there and informed him there would be no more recruits from Texas. The lack of funds was the reason he gave the revolutionary leader, but he also privately believed Carvajal had failed to press the assault in Matamoros and frittered away the army's strength by using undersized, unsupported detachments.[72]

Resigning from the *Liberalista* army, Ford purchased the *South-Western American* in Austin, and managed the paper as publisher and editor. In June 1853, Ford was once again selected for the Democratic State Central Committee. His term was to end on December 8, 1854. His prominence among his neighbors increased when he was elected mayor of Austin on December 31, 1853. In early 1854, Ford ceased publishing the *American*, acquired two new partners, and opened the *Texas State Times* from the same offices. In January 1855, his mayoral term ended and Ford campaigned hard for the man who would become his successor. After a brief but ardent flirtation with the American ("Know-Nothing") Party, Ford was welcomed back into the fold of the Democratic Party in May 1857, and attended the state convention in Waco as a correspondent. While there, he was officially called to take a seat in the convention. He became a member of the Committee on Invitations of the Young Men's Democratic Association of Travis County on May 30, and a member of the finance committee on June 13. In the latter month, Ford suspended operations of the *Times* and sold his interest to other investors.[73]

The growing number of ranches and farms laid waste on the borderlands, and the shifting of federal military resources from the state, concerned the legislature. The lawmakers requested the Texas congressional delegation in Washington work to authorize a regiment of Texas Mounted Volunteers for federal service. Senator Sam Houston was a tireless champion of the Texas regiment issue. During debate on a military appropriations bill, the "Old Lion" took to the floor on February 11, 1858, and advised his colleagues: "Give us one thousand rangers, and we will be accountable for the defense of our frontier of eighteen hundred miles. We ask for no regular troops; withdraw them, if you please." In the meantime, Brevet Major-General David Emanuel Twiggs, commanding the Department of Texas, discussed with Secretary of

War John Buchanan Floyd the need for a mounted volunteer corps. Twiggs also endorsed Ford for the command of such a force if approved. Twiggs's suggestions were incorporated into House Resolution No. 313, which, after lengthy debate, was signed into law on April 7. Unfortunately, Congress made no specific appropriation for the volunteers in the measure. The president also refused to call out the regiment, as he judged the Regular Army of eighteen thousand soldiers sufficient.[74]

While politicians discussed and dithered, Governor Hardin Richard Runnels had decided to take matters into his own hands and alter the frontier policies set by his predecessors. On January 27, 1858, he signed into law "An Act for the better protection of the Frontier." He was then authorized to receive seventy thousand dollars in appropriations from the state treasury and recruit one hundred rangers for six months. The following day, the executive appointed Ford senior captain with "full and complete command" of the four companies already called out to protect the frontier, and directed him to raise the approved additional rangers. "I impress upon you the necessity of action and energy," Runnels wrote Ford in the official orders. "Follow any and all trails of hostile or suspected hostile Indians you may discover, and if possible, overtake and chastise them, if unfriendly." The governor then offered Ford's command to General Twiggs for muster into the federal service, and requested the cooperation of the army. Twiggs declined Runnels's proposition, but promised his department's assistance to the rangers.[75]

On February 8, the governor appointed Ed Burleson, Jr. first lieutenant in Ford's company, effective the fifth, as well as quartermaster and *ex officio* paymaster of the forces called out in the provisions of the legislation. William A. Pitts received a commission of second lieutenant. Robert Cotter was elected orderly sergeant and would act as battalion sergeant major, while Doctor Powhatan Jordan was contracted to be the battalion surgeon. Of the four companies working at the time of his appointment, Ford retained those of Lieutenants James Harvey Tankersley and Allison Nelson, and discharged Captain John H. Connor and Lieutenant Thomas Claiborne Frost.[76]

In March, Ford organized and commanded a campaign designed to take the fight into the *Comanchería*. In the first phase of his operation, the senior captain deployed four columns under Burleson, Nelson, Tankersley, and himself and Pitts to sweep northward through beleaguered Brown, Coleman, Palo Pinto, Comanche, Erath, Young, Buchanan (present Stephens), and Eastland Counties. Ford's route took his twenty-man detachment past Caddo Peaks to the headwaters of Hubbard Creek to the designated headquarters on the Clear Fork. Each of the rangers was armed with a muzzle-loading rifle and a brace of Colt revolvers. The *Texas State Gazette* noted the expedition was capable of firing fifteen hundred bullets before any individual would need to reload. Sixteen mule-drawn wagons followed the riders bearing the supplies and ammunition.[77]

Establishing a base of operations at Cottonwood Springs in Young County on March 19, which he named Camp Runnels in honor of the governor, Ford requested William Preston and William Nimrod Perry Marlin raise small detachments of twenty-five or thirty men and join him. He then called on Shapley Prince Ross, Indian agent at the Brazos Reservation, and enlisted 113 eager warriors from the Shawnee, Delaware, Tawakoni, Tonkawa, Caddo, Anadarko, and Waco tribes. The Indian chiefs and captains included Jim Pockmark and José Casa María of the Caddos and Anadarkos; Plácido and O'Quinn of the Tonkawas; Ah-qua-quash (Shot Arm) of the Wacos; Jim Linney of the Shawnees and Delawares; and Nid-e-wats of the Tawakonis. Keechi, the expedition's spy, had lived among the Comanches and spoke their language fluently. Tempering these welcome additions to his force was the loss of Lieutenant Burleson, who was called home on urgent business. Nevertheless, with 102 rangers under Pitts, Preston, Nelson, and Tankersley, the Indian auxiliaries personally commanded by Agent Ross, and two wagons, one ambulance, and fifteen pack mules, Ford commenced the second phase of his campaign on April 22: the invasion of the Comanche homeland.[78]

Crossing the Red River seven days later, they marched up the valley with scouts reconnoitering the country ahead. Failing to discover any sign of hostiles, they turned in the direction of the Washita River on May 7. The next day, the guides discovered a trail leading into the Antelope Hills and soon found numerous traces of their foe. On the afternoon of May 11, after the scouts discovered the possible location of a *ranchería*, Ford made camp, left a small guard behind, and took one hundred rangers and all the allied Indians in search of the enemy. Keeping to the low ground, they carefully rode until dusk when the captain sent out Indians to locate their forward scout. They missed him in the darkness and he stayed outside the camp until daylight.[79]

At seven a.m. on May 12, the expedition moved on the enemy, and a small camp of five lodges was taken and destroyed; some Comanches were also captured. Two other Indians retreated toward the Canadian River, and the entire Texan force galloped after them. After racing for three miles, the rangers and their Brazos allies beheld seventy lodges of the Kutsutuuka Comanches near Little Robe Creek. The camp's occupants included three hundred warriors led by Tahnahwah chief Pobishequasso (known as "Iron Jacket" because of his Spanish mail coat). The two running Comanches dashed amongst the lodges and gave the alarm. Captain Ross and his Reserve Indians immediately rode to the right flank of the *ranchería* and cut the surprised Comanches' line of retreat toward the Canadian. Iron Jacket, splendid in his armor and regalia, boldly issued a challenge to Ross's Shawnees to fight him man-to-man. They instead cut him down. At the same time, the rangers charged in two columns into the village itself. Ford and Pitts led the right, while Nelson commanded the left wing of his own, Tankersley's, and Preston's detachments. The right division drove through the village, while the left circled around to outflank those escaping.[80]

The battle soon became a "series of single combats" that spread over an area six miles in length and three in width. The Comanches were demoralized by their chief's death (his armor was supposed to magically render him impervious to bullets) and, sensing their despair, Ford pressed the attack. The Comanches were quickly routed, and Nelson's detachments pursued for three miles before the lieutenant called a halt. A few warriors acted as a rearguard so their families could escape, but they swiftly fell before the rangers' deadly revolvers. The shooting ceased between noon and one o'clock, and the individual squads straggled into the *ranchería*.[81]

Another Comanche encampment of one hundred lodges lay three or four miles upriver on the Canadian. The Nokonis there had heard the gunfire, and the men assembled and threatened to charge the Texans and their allies. The opposing bands of Indian warriors rode forth and attempted to goad each other into some reckless maneuver, while the rangers held themselves in support. The riding went on for a half-hour with neither gaining an advantage.

Ford decided to end matters and ordered another charge. The Comanches fell back, and Nelson's detachment used a nearby ridge to mask an oblique movement on the enemy right flank. The maneuver was partially spoiled by the impetuous charge of a party of Tonkawas, and the hostile Indians scattered in every direction. The Texans pursued as much as their jaded horses would allow. By two o'clock, after a chase of two and a half to three miles, Ford ordered the rangers to halt. The expedition returned to their camp while smoke signals were visible in numerous directions; all were interpreted as indicating flight.[82]

The Antelope Hills battle had taken seven hours and was the most successful Indian engagement fought by Texas Rangers in decades. Ford had proven the Comanches could be "followed, overtaken, and beaten" on their own ground by a disciplined, well-equipped, and determined force. His key to success lay in that he ignored county, departmental, and, indeed, state boundaries and instead pursued the enemy into their sanctuary. The victory was one of Ford's greatest triumphs and enhanced his status as the standard-bearer of the Texas Ranger tradition in the antebellum era. Sergeant Cotter shared his opinion of his captain decades later with the *Galveston Daily News*: Ford "was without any doubt one of if not the best and boldest ranger captains the state has produced. His men loved him and had implicit faith in him." Seventy-six Comanches were killed, an undetermined number were wounded, three hundred horses were seized, eighteen Indian women and children were captured, and two Mexican children were liberated. None of the horses were determined to have been stolen from Texan owners, which would lead some later historians to question the Texans' "minimal justification" for the raid. Casualties for the Texans and the Brazos Indians were two killed and three wounded.[83]

The expedition broke camp on the morning of May 13, and returned to Camp Runnels. The Texans reached Cottonwood Springs on the evening of May 21, and parted with their Indian allies. Ford spent the next day writing his report on the campaign before submitting it to the governor. Among the items he detailed was praise for the performance of Captain Ross and the Brazos Indians; the leadership of Nelson, Tankersley, and Preston; and the conduct of the rank and file rangers.[84]

As mentioned above, the Ranger Regiment failed to be called out, and Runnels directed Ford on July 6 to disband the companies when their enlistments expired on August 5. The rangers left Camp Runnels in the middle part of the month. Nelson's company marched to Stephenville to muster out, while Ford, Pitts, and Burleson (who had returned to the company) took the remainder to Lampasas. The captain and a portion of the state troops then returned to Austin, where they were the "subject of congratulation among their many friends in [the] city."[85]

Unfortunately, Ford's triumph and the Army's subsequent strikes at Rush Springs and Crooked Creek could not halt depredations occurring in Denton, Montague, Jack, Brown, and Lampasas Counties, among others. An atmosphere of fear and outrage ensued, and the governor received petitions from citizens of Wise, Lampasas, San Saba, and Cooke Counties demanding relief from Indian raids. Agitators blamed the inhabitants of the Comanche and Brazos agencies. Hostile war bands from the *Comanchería* were believed to be using the Clear Fork reservation as a base of operations, but the Brazos Indians, despite their steadfast service to Texas and the lack of evidence concerning their involvement, were considered guilty nevertheless.[86]

Ford was authorized to raise a ranger company of eighty-eight men on November 2, 1858, in order to "protect the exposed settlements, which have recently suffered from Indian depredations." The captain was further instructed that should circumstances "require the organization of an expedition to move against the Comanches in their haunts you are fully authorized and empowered to muster the requisite number of men into the State service to accomplish the object." The company was mustered on November 10, and Ford was promptly elected captain. John R. Gibbons and Aaron Burleson were chosen as first and second lieutenants, respectively. The company departed Austin in two squads on November 23 and 24, and rode into northern Comanche County. There they established Camp Leon near the junction of Mercer Creek and the South Leon River. Accompanied by a party of Shawnee and Delaware scouts, Ford led a hunt for hostile Comanches west through the Red River country. South of the Pease River, Shawnee leaders Chul-e-quah and Jim Linney diverted the rangers' line of march after finding sign of a large number of Comanches in the area. They were sure even if Ford realized the enemy was superior in numbers, he would be inclined to attack anyway.[87]

Predictably, blood was shed when seven Caddos from the Brazos agency were slain in Palo Pinto County on December 27 by a gang of white vigilantes. Another eight Indians were severely wounded in the attack.[88] Major Robert Neighbors, by this time supervising federal Indian agent for Texas, filed a complaint of murder before Judge Nicholas William Battle of the Nineteenth Judicial District in Waco against Peter Garland and seventeen other men. The suspects organized with other co-conspirators and threatened armed resistance to anyone who would hinder them. The judge issued warrants for the alleged offenders, and deputized Ford to serve them. In a letter to prosecutor Edward Jeremiah Gurley, dated January 22, 1859, the captain refused on the grounds he was a soldier, not a peace officer, and did not have permission from the governor to comply with the judge's orders. He maintained he was only legally authorized to assist, rather than directly serve, civil process, and no law officer had yet attempted an arrest. Ford defended his position in letters to the *Texas State Gazette*, which were published in the April and May issues. Gurley's rebuttals also appeared in the paper and detailed his beliefs as to why Ford should have executed the arrest warrants. Ford was correct according to a strict interpretation of the statutes, but even most of his friends thought him wrong in choosing to allow the killers to escape justice.[89]

In light of recent events, the governor clarified to Ford his policy:

> If you are called upon by any peace officer or other person deputed by Judicial authority to whom warrants have been directed for the arrest of the offenders, you will act promptly in giving all the aid in your power, and be justified in the use of all lawful means to effect the object, [t]he right of the civil authorities to call on the *military*, when resistance is made to due process of the law, cannot be questioned.[90]

On March 3, Runnels further directed Ford to "give your assistance promptly, as heretofore instructed, to the authorities for the execution of the warrants, and bring the parties before the proper tribunals for examination …"[91]

The Reserve Indians continued to be suspected of complicity in acts of violence, and even the governor and the Indian agents called for their removal from the state. The executive wrote, "Guilty or innocent there is to be no more peace as long as they remain on our soil." On April 5, Secretary of War Floyd authorized soldiers in the Department of Texas to consider any Indian found off their reservation as hostile and to engage them.[92] In the end, the federal government declared the reservation system in Texas a failure, and banished 380 Comanches and 1,050 Brazos tribesmen to Fort Cobb in the Indian Territory. Ford and his rangers were unable to bring hostile Indians to battle during their enlistment, and the company was mustered out in Austin on May 10. In the same month, a petition circulated throughout Austin calling upon Ford to run for the office of governor, but he refused to accept any nomination.[93]

Just as the reservation controversy was being settled, long-simmering tensions in the Rio Grande Valley were threatening to erupt. Juan Nepomuceno "Cheno" Cortina was the son of a wealthy *tejano* landowner, and a *ranchero* himself. He was also an indicted murderer and stock thief who stole cattle on either side of the river and sold them to the opposite. Despite his criminal proclivities, he was known as a reliable provider of Mexican votes to the "Blue Party," the Democratic political machine in Cameron County, which had emerged in the wake of the Mexican War. Ironically, he was a defender of the *tejanos* who were resentful of the very same Anglo organization. On July 13, 1859, Robert Shears, the Brownsville city marshal, was attempting to arrest Tomás Cabrera, an aging *vaquero* who had once worked for Cortina and his mother. When the *tejano* resisted, Shears began to brutally pistol-whip him. Striding forth from Gabriel Castel's cantina, Cortina shot the law officer in the shoulder and freed his former employee from custody. The two men then escaped into Matamoros, where Cortina was hailed as a defender of Mexican rights. This exploit, and the ones to come, would be recounted in numerous *corridos* (heroic border ballads) and in folklore.[94]

Later, on September 28, he and fifty to sixty of his followers descended on Brownsville so Cortina could kill several of his personal enemies. Four Americans and one Mexican were murdered, and ten or twelve prisoners were released from jail. Earlier in the year, General Twiggs had ordered

Juan N. Cortina. From *Frank Leslie's Illustrated Newspaper*, April 9, 1864. *Courtesy Prints and Photographs Division, Library of Congress, Washington, D.C.*

the garrisons at Fort Brown and Ringgold Barracks to abandon the posts and redeploy to the western frontier. Deterring Comanche and Kiowa depredations from the north was considered a greater priority than possible threats south of the Rio Grande. Left unprotected, town residents requested assistance from Matamoros authorities, and General José María Carvajal and two other prominent citizens of the latter municipality crossed the river to convince Cortina to leave. Additionally, a company of Mexican national guardsmen were deployed to the border to assist in protecting the lives and property of the Texans.[95]

In the aftermath of Cortina's invasion, the panicked Anglo citizens of Brownsville formed a Committee of Safety, which in turn raised the "Brownsville Tigers" militia company. From Matamoros, Cortina issued a fiery *pronunciamiento* on September 30 justifying his actions by denouncing "a multitude of lawyers, a secret conclave," which was bent on "despoiling the Mexicans of their lands." He also asserted he had no further designs on Brownsville, if his enemies who had survived were delivered to him. The "Cortina War" may have ended then and there if his elderly chief lieutenant, Tomás Cabrera, had not been captured on October 12 by a sheriff's posse. Instead, Cortina swore to "lay the town in ashes" if Cabrera was not released, but the townsmen refused. Cortina again crossed the river with forty men and established an encampment at Rancho del Carmen, his mother's ranch.[96]

On October 22, a motley force of twenty Brownsville Tigers, forty Mexican *rancheros*, and seventy-five militiamen from Matamoros rode out looking for a fight. Two days later, the expedition attacked Cortina's camp and pushed the *insurrectos* from their first position before being completely routed; the Texans abandoned their two 4-pound artillery pieces in the retreat. The Brownsville Tigers lost one man killed and several slightly wounded, while the *Cortinistas* reportedly lost eight killed. Stirred by Cortina's victories, *campesinos*, *vaqueros*, *rancheros*, and *bandidos* from Camargo, Reynosa, Los Cuevas, San Carlos, Victoria, and other border towns flocked to his banner, drawn by the prospects of both deliverance and plunder.[97]

Representing the state, Captain William Gerard Tobin and his company of one hundred rangers arrived in Brownsville on November 10. A successful businessman in San Antonio, Tobin had been commissioned to assist the civil authorities, but he proved to be an inept military commander. In evaluating the newly arrived captain and his rangers, Professor Walter P. Webb would comment, "On the whole these men were a sorry lot, and their conduct for the remainder of the war reflects no credit on their organization." One day after the rangers' arrival, Tomás Cabrera was dragged from his jail cell by a riotous mob and lynched in the town square. While no direct evidence implicated the rangers, the contemporary reports implied their involvement.[98]

On November 21, thirty-two Karnes County volunteers under Lieutenant John Littleton were ambushed on Palo Alto Prairie. Three rangers were killed, four wounded, and one was made a prisoner; the latter was found tortured and murdered the following day. On the twenty-second, Tobin responded by marching to Rancho del Carmen with his company and Captain Peter Tumlinson's thirty-nine Atascosa County rangers. The Texans were beaten back by a barrage of round shot, grape, and canister. Realizing the enemy held a strong position in the thick chaparral, and with *insurrectos* threatening to outflank him, Tobin ordered a withdrawal that turned into a confused retreat. The next day, Tobin advanced again, but, after observing Cortina's defensive works, the Texan officers decided that attacking would be inadvisable. Cortina issued a second *pronunciamiento* the same day, which continued his passionate and grandiose call for justice from Anglo tyranny.[99]

The whole fiasco took a turn for the better with the appearance of two men. The first to arrive on the scene was Major Samuel Peter Heintzelman, who reoccupied Fort Brown on December 5. The force he had under his command consisted of two companies of the First Infantry, three batteries of the First Artillery, and one company of the Second Cavalry. The second man to reach Brownsville was Rip Ford.[100]

Governor Runnels, doubtful of Tobin's abilities, had issued Ford a commission of major on November 17. The ranger was given the authority to raise a mounted company at Goliad and take command of all state troops on the Lower Rio Grande. While organized under the orders of the state's chief executive, the company was to function according to the army's Articles of War. The following day, the legislature passed a joint resolution authorizing the governor to call out as many volunteers as necessary to quell the

Cortina disturbances. Those men already in the field were to be retroactively accepted into the service. All were to be retained until the crisis was resolved. The fifty-five rangers Ford had recruited rode to the Rancho de los Indios, arriving on December 13, and established a strong position. That evening, since Ford was leading the expedition, they elected Joseph Walker as captain and company commander. Later in the night, a party of two hundred men, later verified to have been led by Cortina, approached within one mile of Ford's camp, then withdrew. Certain the bandit chieftain had set an ambuscade in the darkness, the major declined to go out and meet them.[101]

The company arrived in Brownsville the following morning. At the same time, Heintzelman and Tobin, with 165 federal and 120 state troops, had attacked one hundred *Cortinistas* at El Ebonal. Having arrived in the early hours, Heintzelman wanted the rangers to reconnoiter the ground, but they did not choose to move until daylight. By this time, Tobin was commanding a battalion composed of his own company and those of G. J. Hampton and Peter Tumlinson. Advancing to within sixty yards of the enemy position, the Texans beheld the Mexicans entrenched behind a breastwork built across the road. Heintzelman then ordered the advance. At first Tobin's men hesitated, but once they witnessed the solid discipline of the regulars, the rangers pressed forward. Heintzelman dismounted most of the state troops and ordered them to move through the brush to the flanks. Suddenly, the *Cortinistas* opened up with a four-pound cannon, but the American artillery unlimbered two 24-pounders and returned fire. The Mexicans attacked both of Heintzelman's flanks until the former were forced to withdraw. Twice, within four miles, the *insurrectos* made stands along the road to Rio Grande City; each time they were routed. A portion of the enemy forces was driven across the river while the remainder fled, leaving behind provisions and old firearms. Two regulars were slightly wounded and one ranger mortally. The Mexicans lost eight killed and an unknown number were wounded. Heintzelman considered the victory to be won in spite of the rangers' presence.[102]

Once the American force was back in Brownsville, Ford and Heintzelman held a discussion on the current situation. The Texan assured the regular officer he and Walker's company would cooperate fully with Heintzelman's command. There was no time to hold an election for ranger battalion commander as the army major immediately sent his mounted elements on scouting duty. The rangers under Ford and Tobin would continue to operate independently of each other. On December 17, Tobin and sixty volunteers were directed to proceed toward Point Isabel to "attack and disperse any men he may meet in a hostile attitude"; Ford took sixty men to Los Fresnos in order to "intercept any who attempt to escape in that direction;" and Captain George Stoneman, commanding Company E, Second Cavalry, rode to Las Norias for "the same purpose." Ford and Stoneman returned to camp two days later without having engaged any *Cortinistas*. Contrary to his orders, Tobin had taken approximately 150 men, and his party came back on the twentieth. While they were on patrol, some of his men had lynched an innocent Mexican *vaquero*, but Tobin refused to accept responsibility as "it was done without his orders or knowledge." An outraged Heintzelman wrote in his journal, "It will have a very bad effect."[103]

On the twenty-first, Heintzelman led 150 regulars and 198 rangers toward Rio Grande City. As he neared the town, the army major learned Cortina and five to six hundred of his partisans had taken possession of abandoned Ringgold Barracks. In the subsequent set-piece battle, on the morning of December 27, Ford, commanding the companies of Andrew Herron and Joe Walker, led eighty rangers in the attack on Cortina's line. They scattered the enemy pickets and routed the force sent to meet them at Ringgold Barracks. Bypassing the town, Ford charged a hill on which Cortina allegedly had his command post, but the bandit chieftain had fallen back to a position above the town on the Roma road. Peering through a heavy fog, Ford ascertained Cortina's right wing was positioned between the road and the river, while his left encircled a cemetery. Ford directed Tobin, who was commanding the 113 men of Hampton's and Tumlinson's companies, to take the cemetery and engage the Mexican artillery. He planned to leave the center for Heintzelman's guns.[104]

Under a hail of canister, grapeshot, and musket balls, Ford crossed the Roma road and charged the *Cortinista* right flank. Positioned beside the lane and behind a fence were two cannons (the same artillery earlier lost by the Brownsville Tigers), and Ford sent a small detachment to deal with that threat. As the guns were being silenced, Ford flanked the position, and ordered his men to dismount forty yards from the artillery and reinforce the detachment. Sixteen of his men were wounded as the rangers advanced under cover of the chaparral to take the cannons. They drove off the gunners, but a heavy musket fire forced them to take shelter before they could seize the artillery pieces themselves. Meanwhile, Tobin's men had assaulted the cemetery and failed to take the position. They then rode to rejoin Ford's command.[105]

A mounted Mexican charge burst from the mist, but a Texan volley ensured many of "Cortina's bold riders were left on the ground." The cannons escaped as the demoralized enemy force broke and fled. Arriving on the field, Heintzelman ordered Ford to press the attack and capture the artillery. The rangers regrouped and raced up the Roma road in pursuit. After a ten-mile chase, Cortina rallied his harassed men for a stand. The Mexicans fired a volley, and the Texans responded with a shout and charged the bandits. The rangers seized one gun and even turned it on the Mexicans. Abandoning the other cannon, the *Cortinistas* fled in panic toward Roma, and Ford followed closely lest the *insurrectos* loot the town. Cortina and approximately twenty men ignored Roma and swam their horses across the Rio Grande. The rest of the *Cortinistas* were harried by the rangers and Stoneman's cavalry until they scattered into the brush, abandoning arms, provisions, and baggage. The rangers suffered sixteen wounded, two of them severely. Ford himself received two contusions from grapeshot.[106]

The battle of Rio Grande City was a decisive victory, and one for which Ford and his rangers could take full credit. Tobin, despite having been present during the engagement, made little contribution and the army troops did not arrive until the fight was nearly over. Cortina's force had lost fifty to sixty in the action. He escaped but his popular revolution was finished in Texas.[107] In addition, newly inaugurated Governor Sam Houston ordered all armed bands operating along the lower Rio Grande to disperse and return to their lawful occupations. All persons owning allegiance to a foreign government were advised that if they were arrested bearing arms, they would be regarded as "bandits and invaders."[108]

Governor Runnels had bestowed a commission on William Tobin, but he soon came to regret that decision. The executive had subsequently conferred on Ford the rank of major and the duties of mustering officer. Unfortunately, the order authorizing the deployment of state troops also called for an election for the position of commanding officer. Heintzelman held no regard for Tobin's leadership and preferred Ford. "I hope all means that Ford will be elected the Major," he wrote. "He is by all odds the better man. He controls his men & Tobin is controlled by his. I would rather have Ford with 50 than Tobin with all his men." Nevertheless, the vote was held on December 31, and Tobin won by a margin of six votes. Ford likewise had scant respect for the new commander's military abilities, and he was not legally obligated to serve under him, so he decided to resign. Having enlisted for an unspecified period of time, and sharing their major's views on Tobin, Captain Walker and the rest of the company accompanied Ford to Brownsville for disbandment.[109]

Tobin's electoral victory would prove short-lived with the arrival of Robert Hall Taylor and Angel Navarro, commissioners sent by Governor Houston to "enquire into the cause, origin, and progress of the disturbances existing in that region." Taylor reported some of their conclusions to the governor on January 16: "There is nothing like command among the Rangers … The present officer [Tobin] I am told by good judges is utterly incompetent to command in the field." Four days before, Taylor and Navarro had ordered Tobin to Brownsville to be mustered out. On January 17, Ford discharged Walker's company, and the captain and about twenty men returned home. Expecting additional fighting, Ford and the rest remained in Brownsville to await developments. The commissioners enrolled Ford and thirty of his men back into service on January 20. Ford was elected captain, Matthew Nolan first lieutenant, and John James Dix and William D. Howard second lieutenants. The captain was directed to recruit another thirty-three men, and the new command was designated as Company A. On February 1, they were joined with Captain John Littleton's Company B to constitute the "Rio Grande Squadron." Taylor and Navarro further ordered that Ford, as senior officer, was subordinate to Major Heintzelman.[110]

Following his defeat at Rio Grande City, Cortina's insurrection became more akin to organized banditry. His numerous raiding parties returned from Texas with stolen livestock and other loot, and had the tacit blessing of

Mexican officials on the frontier. As Navarro reported to the governor: "It is our opinion that the authorities on the Mexican side of the river are cognizant now, and have been all the while of his movements, and that his men are armed by them, and he has been furnished ammunition, and received aid and comfort from the beginning."[111] To frustrate the designs of Cortina and his sponsors, Heintzelman deployed his horsemen along the river from Rio Grande City to Brownsville. Unfortunately, the major did not have authority to invade Mexico and eliminate Cortina's band once and for all. Ford felt himself to be under no such limitation, a fact which concerned Heintzelman.[112]

At the same time, Tobin and Tumlinson's men were marching down the Rio Grande to Brownsville to disband, and accompanying the steamer *Ranchero* to the same destination. The boat was carrying a cargo worth $200,000, including sixty thousand in specie. Cortina was rumored to be planning to intercept and steal the shipment near La Bolsa, a bend in the river thirty-five miles above Matamoros. Ford led his two companies in combing the riverbanks, while George Stoneman's regulars patrolled the road. In the early afternoon of February 4, Ford ordered an advance party under Corporal Milton A. Duty to park their wagons and pack train at a *ranchito* opposite Bolsa Bend known as Zacatel. Later in the day, the scouts engaged thirty armed *Cortinistas* in the process of crossing the border back into Mexico. Some of Tobin's men soon arrived and took positions alongside Duty's detachment. Approaching the narrow bend in the river, the *Ranchero* was caught in the crossfire of the skirmishing Mexicans and rangers as it sailed by. The *bandidos* were driven from their herd of stolen horses and booty, but ranger Fountain B. Woodruff was mortally wounded. News of the *Ranchero* incident became exaggerated and the public grew to believe Cortina, intent on plundering the cargo, had deliberately attacked the boat.[113]

Using the episode as a pretext to cross the Rio Grande, Ford led thirty-five rangers from his squadron over the border toward a nearby *rancho*. Major Tobin, Captain Tumlinson, and twelve of their men accompanied the sortie. At their intended target, Cortina had hurriedly built palisades and placed his two hundred bandits behind them. They also took cover behind the buildings and *jacales*. Ford used the river bank to mask his approach and fired on Cortina's left wing. "The rangers shot to kill: it was victory or death with them," the senior captain later wrote. The Mexicans' response was heavier but ineffective. Ford then ordered a charge around the defensive works and rolled up the flank. As night fell, Cortina's men retreated with a loss of twenty-nine killed and forty injured. In addition to the slain Private Woodruff, Ford's casualties were two wounded.[114]

The victory at Rancho La Bolsa, as well as the ongoing exchange between Governor Houston and the James Buchanan administration, compelled Secretary of War Floyd to order Lieutenant-Colonel Robert Edward Lee to assume command of the Department of Texas. Acting in his brevet rank of colonel, Lee, "an officer of great discretion and ability," was to contact Mexican authorities and deliver an ultimatum: either force Cortina to cease his depredations or U.S. regulars would cross the Rio Grande and do the task themselves.[115]

On March 13, the Mexican commandant of Matamoros alerted Heintzelman that Cortina and forty men had been at Rancho La Mesa two days previously, and proposed a joint effort. Informed at his Agua Negra camp, Ford was suspicious of the offer and suspected a trap. However, Heintzelman gave his blessing to the operation, which was composed of Stoneman's company, Lieutenant Manning Kimmel's Company G, also of the Second Cavalry, and the Rio Grande Squadron. The rangers and federal cavalry crossed the border on the early morning of March 18 and advanced on La Mesa. His scouts having found an ambush on the road, Ford encouraged avoiding the direct route. The Americans reached their objective prior to dawn, but a Mexican picket sounded the alarm. Drums quickly beat the call to arms, and enemy cavalry and infantry began forming. The U.S. regulars charged the Mexican horsemen on the left flank, the rangers rushed the foot soldiers on the right, and both rolled up the opposing line, driving it back into the village. The only casualties were a woman mistakenly killed and a Mexican soldier wounded. Instead of Cortina's partisans, the Americans' foe was discovered to be troops of the *Guardia Nacional*. Later in the morning, a second column of 150 guardsmen appeared on the main road. Ford parleyed with the senior Mexican officer who had refused to confer with Stoneman. The meeting deteriorated into an angry exchange of recriminations. When asked about the roadside ambuscade, the colonel responded evasively but boasted that had he and his *soldados* been present at La Mesa, the outcome would have been different. The ranger captain offered to fight the Mexicans with just his Texans, while Stoneman's regulars observed from the sides. His proposal was declined.[116]

The next day, after escorting the *Ranchero* downriver, the Americans received a dispatch from Heintzelman instructing them to return to United States soil. Cortina was rumored to be somewhere near Camargo or Matamoros, and the captains had hoped to pursue him. Instead, the rangers and regulars returned to Agua Negra on March 21. Colonel Lee soon arrived to take personal command and encamped near Edinburg. The Virginian officer accepted reports and advice from Heintzelman and Ford. He then dispatched a sequence of concise and uncompromising letters to Mexican officials in Reynosa and Matamoros concerning the capture of Cortina. By May 6, when Lee returned to San Antonio, Cortina remained at large in the Burgos Mountains, but the border war had more or less dwindled into the usual uneasy peace. Receiving orders from the governor, the Rio Grande Squadron rode to Goliad and was discharged on May 17.[117]

Once he settled his accounts with the state, Ford returned to Brownsville for four months. He spent time with friends and also courted Adelina Norton "Addie" Smith. Born on October 10, 1838, she was the daughter of Major Elihu Dwight Smith, a prominent merchant. As the presidential election of November 1860 neared, passions surrounding the secession controversy simultaneously intensified. Once the citizens of Texas learned of Abraham Lincoln's victory, the leading advocates for separation, Ford included, called for a special assembly to decide on the issue. On January 8, 1861, Texans voted for delegates to the Secession Convention scheduled to convene in Austin twenty days later; Ford was elected by Cameron County to be one of them.[118]

On February 1, the delegates approved an ordinance by a vote of 168 to eight to declare Texas "a separate sovereign State, and that her citizens are absolved from allegiance to the United States, or the Government thereof." The convention adjourned on February 4 and the matter was put to a popular vote on February 23. On March 2, the convention assembled to tally the votes. Two days later, the delegates publicized the count with 46,153 for secession and 14,747 opposed. Texas was declared to have withdrawn from the Union effective March 2.[119]

The Committee of Public Safety, a fifteen-member body charged with implementing the Secession Convention's military policies and protecting the frontier, appointed Ford to the rank of colonel of cavalry on February 5. His orders, which as a member of the committee he partially wrote, were to raise six hundred state troops and take command of the Military District of the Rio Grande. The area of operations encompassed "a point on the Rio Grande, half-way between Forts Duncan and McIntosh and including all forts on the Rio Grande below said point, and the entire district of country between the Nueces and Rio Grande, and at right angles with the general course of said river to the point of beginning." He was next to effect the removal of U.S. troops from his district and the securing of public property. To this end, he sent instructions to Mat Nolan, John Littleton, and John Lawrence Donelson to muster mounted companies at Corpus Christi before moving to the border. Ford then traveled to Galveston by way of Hempstead and Houston to begin organizing the arriving recruits. Commissioner Ebenezer B. Nichols went to New Orleans to secure funding and arms and returned on February 17.[120]

On the night of February 19, accompanied by Lieutenant-Colonel Hugh McLeod as second-in-command, Ford and his men sailed for the federal garrison on the island of Brazos Santiago, several miles above Brownsville. Disembarking two days later, the five hundred volunteers persuaded the thirteen regular artillerymen present to abandon the post and evacuate to the mainland. Ford, Nichols, and McLeod went to Fort Brown the next day and discussed with federal officers the surrender of the installation and its three-hundred-member garrison. Captain Bennett Hoskin Hill, the post commander, refused the Texans' request to capitulate in the late morning of February 23. He then insultingly related how only the counsel of his officers kept him from arresting Ford, Nichols, and McLeod for treason. Nichols and Ford privately decided the former would return to Galveston and bring back rifle companies to reinforce the Brazos Santiago occupying force; the commissioner departed on February 25.[121]

Ford met with his old comrade Captain George Stoneman to enlist his aid in convincing Hill to peacefully evacuate Fort Brown. Shortly thereafter,

Hill received General Twiggs's February 18 order directing the surrender of all federal posts and property in Texas. Two days later, Nichols advised the Committee of Public Safety he was dispatching an additional 325 troops to McLeod. Benjamin Franklin Terry and the battalion of reinforcements arrived on March 1. On March 19, the Secession Convention confirmed Ford in his rank when they elected him commander of the Second Texas Mounted Rifles. Two days later, the last United States troops departed Texas, and Colonel Ford, now headquartered at Fort Brown, assumed complete responsibility for protecting the lower valley from foreign invasion.[122]

Even as his military dispositions were being arranged, Ford once more took a wife. On March 31, the colonel married Addie in the Brownsville Presbyterian Church. Despite his marital good fortune, his duty became more complicated when, on April 18, he learned that Fort Sumter had been bombarded. The possible threat of Federal invasion quickly surpassed that of Indian and bandit attacks. A naval blockade of all Southern ports imposed on April 19 included those on the Gulf coast. The cordon posed a significant danger to a Confederacy that lacked an industrial capacity to supply its troops in the field. Accordingly, neutral Matamoros became the best outlet for Rebel cotton to European textile mills, which would be used to secure credit. The town also served as port of entry for firearms, sulfur, saltpeter, medical supplies, clothing, and footwear. The Brazos Santiago and Point Isabel forts at the mouth of the river could not withstand a naval assault, so Fort Brown, approximately twenty miles upriver, would be crucial to commanding the lower Rio Grande.[123]

Once the Confederate District of Texas assumed military responsibility from the Committee of Public Safety on April 12, Colonel Earl Van Dorn, the new commander, decided on two lines of defense for the western frontier. The first stretched from the Red River to the junction of the North and Main Conchos, while the second extended from Fort Inge to Forts Quitman, Davis, Stockton, Lancaster, Clark, Camp Wood, and Fort Bliss. Ford was assigned to command the latter and remain in the lower valley. His regiment of mounted riflemen, mustered into Confederate service on May 23 as the Second Texas Cavalry, was in San Antonio enrolling men to bring troop levels to full strength. His original intention had been to supplement the troopers of Nolan's Company G, Harris A. Hamner's Company H, Littleton's Company I, and Donelson's Company K. Instead, the new recruits were formed into six companies and marched to the upper Rio Grande valley under Lieutenant-Colonel John Robert Baylor to counter a possible Union incursion from New Mexico.[124]

Even while Ford and the balance of his regiment readied their defenses, Juan Cortina returned to the Rio Grande. He urged the *tejano* and *mexicano* residents of Zapata County to declare against the Confederacy, although they spurned Texas more than they favored the Union. Such a position offered *ranchero* Antonio Ochoa and his followers the opportunity to rise in opposition to the Anglo political faction in the county, and for plunder north of the border. The *pronunciados* began pillaging on both sides of the river from Brownsville to Laredo. Cortina crossed the Rio Grande on May 19, but his brigands were crushed in a series of clashes with Mat Nolan and Captain Santos Benavides, the latter commanding a company of Texas state cavalry. The deciding engagement occurred at Carrizo on May 23. After Cortina was repelled, Mexican military commanders convinced him to seek a more salubrious clime.[125]

In September 1861, Brigadier-General Paul Octave Hébert replaced Van Dorn, and Ford was ordered to take a leave of absence on November 1. He returned to San Antonio on furlough and spent time with his family. The following month, Colonel Henry McCulloch, commanding the Military Sub-District of the Rio Grande, and Ford's immediate superior, assigned him to supervise the construction of coastal defenses near Brownsville. On January 6, 1862, the Ninth Legislature proclaimed a joint resolution that the "gallant and soldierly bearing" of Colonel Ford and his men on the border entitled them to the thanks of the people of Texas. Colonel McCulloch issued Special Order No. 25 on February 17, which named Ford to once more command Fort Brown and the lower Rio Grande, effective March 5.[126]

Ford carried on attempts to keep the peace on the border and promote trade, but his involvement in disputes between Mexican officials in Tamaulipas, and his continued friendship with José Carvajal, would see him relieved of his command. In May, Brigadier-General Hamilton Prioleau Bee replaced Colonel McCulloch, and ordered Ford to San Antonio for reassignment. The Confederate Congress had enacted legislation on April 16, 1862, obliging all white male citizens between the ages of eighteen and thirty-five to register for military service. On June 2, Ford was appointed superintendent of conscripts for the Department of Texas, as well as commander of the Houston conscript camp. Ford's new position would prove to be extremely frustrating, and one ill-suited to his talents. Transferring his headquarters to Austin the following month, Ford was joined in November by his wife and their infant daughter, Mary Louise (Lula), who had been born on August 15. To add insult to injury, Bee ordered the reorganization of the Second Texas Cavalry in October, and Ford lost his colonel's commission in the subsequent election. The forfeiture of military rank would cost him the position of superintendent of conscripts as well.[127]

Oran Milo Roberts, former chairman of the Secession Convention, praised Ford for his conscription services, declaring he was "well-fitted for that position," but also acknowledged he was "the best military man we had in Texas at the time of the war." Most Texans believed him worthy of advancement to higher rank. Indeed, several Texas delegates to the Confederate Provisional Congress petitioned President Jefferson Davis on September 20, 1862, to appoint Ford a brigadier-general. John Henniger Reagan, the Confederate postmaster general, was urged to facilitate the request on November 6. Reagan dispatched the letter to Secretary of War Judah Philip Benjamin on December 1. Other prominent gentlemen in South Texas appealed to the president on December 17, requesting Ford be promoted and assigned to the Rio Grande line. Three more petitions on Ford's behalf were sent on February 16, 1863, but Davis and Benjamin decided vacancies in the grade of brigadier should be filled by officers holding Confederate commissions or, in special circumstances, by leading politicians. Ford possessed neither prerequisite so, despite the numerous entreaties, he was not selected to wear the wreath and stars of a general officer. All was not lost, though. Once the Confederate Trans-Mississippi Department was created, Ford was recalled by Major-General John Bankhead "Prince John" Magruder, on March 21, 1863, to be superintendent of conscripts for the newly established District of Texas, New Mexico, and Arizona. Even while Ford was denied a Confederate commission, and remained a civilian, Magruder openly referred to him as a colonel and authorized him to act as such. Furthermore, Ford's monthly salary from the departmental paymaster was set at the $210 rate for Confederate Army colonels.[128]

Operating without official guidance from the Conscript Bureau, Superintendent Ford framed an exemption policy that excused all those whose occupation or employment were vital to the war effort. He was determined to apply the Conscript Act impartially, and refused several bribes. He also exempted overseers, but drafted plantation owners according to his belief that those with the most to lose should fight. He furloughed able-bodied men living on the frontier who were needed to defend their families from Indian raids. Respecting the principles of those who did not support secession, he never intentionally conscripted a Union sympathizer, even after armed bands of deserters, draft dodgers, and Unionists hampered the efforts of his enrolling officers in the northern tier of counties.[129]

Even as he worked for the Conscript Bureau, military operations elsewhere were ensuring Ford's return to field duty. After the Confederate recapture of Galveston, and the ill-fated Union attack at Sabine Pass, Major-General Nathaniel Prentice Banks, commander of the Union Department of the Gulf, initiated plans to invade South Texas. He made demonstrations at Opelousas and Barre's Landing that drew all but a skeleton force of Confederates away from the Rio Grande, then launched his attack on the mouth of the river. With six thousand troops of the XIII Army Corps under Major-General Napoleon Jackson Tecumseh Dana, Banks seized Brazos de Santiago on November 2, took Brownsville four days later, and established his headquarters at Fort Brown. By the end of the month, the Union position was secure from the Gulf to Rio Grande City. The Confederate supply line from Matamoros to Brownsville was severed, and goods were forced to enter Texas at Eagle Pass or Laredo, thus increasing costs by at least half. However, the Union high command failed to capitalize upon the gains of Banks's forces and the invasion ground to a halt.[130]

While a few prominent Texans allied themselves to the federal occupation, most of the citizens on the lower Rio Grande cleaved to the Confederacy. In December, they called for assistance, naming Ford personally.

Seizing upon the chance to assume a more active role in the war, Ford made plans to recruit volunteers to liberate the valley. Although sympathetic to the goal, Magruder was reluctant to lend support to what his superiors would doubtless consider an unsanctioned operation led by a civilian, especially one who had been refused commissions by the Confederate Army. Undeterred, but still requesting official approval from Magruder, Ford enlisted Austin citizens exempted from the draft and left for San Antonio. He was sure he could raise a force on state authority, but he also knew he would need Confederate personnel to bolster his strength to meet an estimated seven thousand Union troops.[131]

On December 22, Magruder sent Ford a lengthy, confidential order that gave him command of all troops in San Antonio, and to the west and south of the town. Ford's expeditionary force, styled the "Cavalry of the West," was to be largely composed of recruits either too young or too old for Confederate military service, deserters, renegades, and soldiers of fortune. They enlisted for short terms, and were guaranteed they would not serve beyond the state's boundaries. Magruder could not reinforce the Rio Grande line as he was still facing a potential major Union thrust from Louisiana, a *ruse de guerre* Banks skillfully perpetuated to mislead Confederate opposition. The general's letter further instructed Ford to deceive Federal commanders into thinking he was marching to reinforce Indianola. The expedition's destination proved to be well-known, but the recruitment drive was nevertheless proceeding satisfactorily. Ford also planned to raise volunteers from among the Texas refugees in Matamoros, Reynosa, Camargo, and other Mexican river towns.[132]

Making his headquarters at San Antonio, Ford occupied himself in assembling his staff and the recruits, in handling the myriad logistical details, including the impressment of forage and wagons, and in directing the activities of companies already in the field. Among his staff officers were Major Anton Felix Hans Hellmuth von Blücher, chief of staff; Major Albert Walthersdorff, "instructor of tactics;" Captain Charles H. Merritt, quartermaster; Captain John Littleton, commissary of subsistence; and Captain William Giles Martin Samuel, ordnance officer. Ford also had to overcome the professional jealousy of several Confederate officers who believed they outranked the expedition commander. To counter that claim, Ford would later be commissioned a brigadier-general of state troops on March 1, 1864. By the end of winter, the Cavalry of the West was ready to go to war.[133]

On March 17, thirteen hundred volunteers rode through Alamo Plaza and out of town. Among the companies were those of Captain Thomas E. Cater, D. W. Nelson, Theophilus G. Anderson, W. W. Ferrill (succeeded by J. G. White), B. F. Fly, Samuel W. Barker, H. Scott, A. L. Doughty, and William Armstrong. Accompanying the column was Lieutenant C. B. Gardiner's section of Captain H. B. Christmas's battery. South Texas, especially the lower valley, had been suffering from a severe drought for the last four years, and the march to the Rio Grande would prove grueling. Arriving in Banquete within the week, Ford then set out on March 26 for Laredo, while Companies A, D, F, and G of the Second Texas Cavalry under Major Mat Nolan were posted near Corpus Christi to screen Ford's left flank. Captain James Alexander Ware, commanding Company F, First Texas Cavalry at San Patricio, and Captain George Henry Giddings, leading an independent battalion at Eagle Pass, each added their men to the expedition. Lieutenant-Colonel Daniel Showalter and four companies of the Fourth Cavalry, Arizona Brigade joined the column on the thirtieth. The Rio Grande Expeditionary Force marched across the bone-dry country and into Laredo on April 15, where Captain José del Refugio Benavides and his Company B of the Thirty-third Texas Cavalry attached themselves to the campaign.[134]

After a stay of less than a week in Laredo, the Cavalry of the West commenced its advance on Federal positions in the lower valley. They rode through ten days of rain before nearing their first objective, Rio Grande City, on April 23. The Texans reached Ringgold Barracks on the edge of town, only to find it abandoned by the Federals who had withdrawn downriver to Edinburg. Seeking intelligence on the Union forces around Brownsville, Ford crossed over to Matamoros and met with Mexican authorities. He would also establish cordial relations with officials in Camargo by the end of May. Meanwhile, on April 27, General Magruder had signed General Order No. 118, which received Ford into Confederate service temporarily as a brigadier-general and assigned him to command the Third District of the Western Sub-district. Welcoming the official endorsement of the expedition, Ford received the order on May 13 at Ringgold Barracks. Unfortunately, several problems, including supply procurement, difficulties with the Cotton Bureau, the expiration of ninety-day enlistments, desertions, and professional rivalries held up the march at Ringgold Barracks for six weeks.[135]

As he was resolving these complications, Ford learned the Federals had possibly evacuated Brownsville. To verify the information, on or about June 21, he led a reconnaissance-in-force of sixty cavalry troopers toward a camp at Como se Llama Ranch. Arriving on June 23, he met Colonel Showalter and 225 men of the Fourth Arizona who were also on a scout toward Brownsville. In the early morning of June 25, they rode south for the river road. Reaching it by mid-morning, the horsemen moved through the chaparral toward the Federal cavalry outpost at Las Rucias Ranch. The Union troops were expecting an attack but failed to watch the road from the south, as they believed Ford was approaching from upriver and would arrive later in the day.[136]

In the midst of a raging thunderstorm, Ford sent skirmishers under Captain James Dunn, commanding Company D of Cater's recently organized battalion, to quietly probe the enemy's position. Instead, the advance detachment was fired upon and Dunn led his men in a bold charge to meet the Yankees. Dunn fell at the head of his company, and Ford ordered Showalter's, Cater's, and Refugio Benavides's men forward. The Federals were also Texans, Companies A and C of Colonel Edmund Jackson Davis's First Texas (Union) Cavalry under Captain Philip G. Temple. Advised the Confederates would treat them as traitors, they fought frantically from the ranch's *jacales* and brick headquarters. Lieutenant Gardiner put his two guns into action, and the sharp engagement was quickly ended; out of 250 Union troopers, twenty were killed, including a number of wounded who perished while trying to escape across a small lagoon, and thirty-six were taken prisoner. The remainder fled into the cane thickets on the Mexican side of the river. The Confederates took arms, saddles, wagons, and approximately twenty horses. Only three of Ford's men were killed and four were wounded.[137]

Ford was alert to the possibility of a counterattack from the balance of Davis's regiment, so he fell back to Edinburg. He waited until June 27 before returning to Ringgold Barracks. The Federal commander at Fort Brown overestimated Ford's force to be twelve hundred men rather than the four hundred he actually commanded. Thus, the Yankee officer decided to wait for an attack where he could make good use of his infantry and artillery.[138]

The road to Brownsville was open to Ford, except for a paltry screen of cavalry pickets. The colonel had no accurate estimate of his enemy's strength, though, so he decided to proceed cautiously. He remained at Ringgold Barracks for several weeks amassing ammunition, provisions, wagons, and pack animals, and awaiting the arrival of new recruits. The transfer of men and stores to Southern forces in Louisiana complicated his arrangements. He lost his artillery when Lieutenant Gardiner's section returned to San Antonio on account of not having adequate numbers to man the guns. On July 19, his preparations at last complete, Ford led his column of fifteen hundred men toward Brownsville, one hundred miles distant.[139]

The Cavalry of the West engaged a Union picket situated behind *jacales* and a fence at the Ebonal Ranch on July 22. Ford placed half of his command in reserve and, although too sick with malaria to climb into the saddle unassisted, drove the Federals from their positions with the remainder. The enemy was forced to the Brownsville city limits, but a short-lived skirmish between Ford's rearguard and a Union scouting party caused the colonel to halt for the night. The next morning, Ford left a picket on the road and concentrated his command at Carricitos Ranch, twenty-two miles above Brownsville.[140]

The Federals seemed content to assume a defensive posture. After waiting until July 25, the Expeditionary Force marched on the town. Ford halted his troops in Dead Man's Hollow, within striking distance of the Union lines, and deployed dismounted riflemen forward to engage the defenders. The skirmishers pushed the Federals back into Brownsville, but Ford kept his main body out of the enemy's artillery range. Conversely, the Union soldiers refused to advance into the open so all of the fighting was done at long-distance with little effect. The aimless skirmishing continued until July 29 when a reconnaissance of Brownsville revealed Federal forces had abandoned the town and Fort Brown. Following a trail of discarded equipment, Giddings's battalion engaged the Yankee rearguard approximately fifteen miles below the post and drove it into the main column. Ford learned that night the Union troops were assembling on Brazos Santiago. The next morning, he raised the Stars and Bars above the fort after an absence of more than two years. Addie, Lula, and the newest Ford daughter, Addie Julia, born on July 14 in Matamoros, soon joined the colonel as illness finally forced him to his sickbed. Even while convalescing, Ford issued orders designed to consolidate Confederate control of the area, and to be kept appraised of Federal movements.[141]

Ford's liberation of Brownsville became jeopardized in late August by the war being waged in Mexico. The long-standing struggle between liberals and conservatives now embroiled the republican army of Benito Juárez and the Franco-Mexican imperial forces of Emperor Maximilian I, the Austrian archduke and pawn of Emperor Napoleon III. For some months, the parallel American and Mexican civil wars had been overlapping along the Rio Grande. While Union and Rebel forces dueled from Laredo to Brazos Santiago, fighting occurred on the Mexican side from Matamoros to Bagdad. The duplicitous Juan Cortina, who had returned to the border as the *Juárista* commander at Matamoros, and was himself facing a French-Imperialist threat, was urged by Union officials to capture Brownsville in conjunction with Federal forces on Brazos Santiago. Needing a secure line of retreat in case Matamoros fell to the *Imperialistas*, Cortina suspended all river trade with the Confederates, and positioned six cannons directly opposite Brownsville. He then dispatched six hundred Mexican *soldados*, supported by a battery, to cross upstream and push down the Rio Grande City road.[142]

The frontal attack began on September 6, when Union cavalry and artillery crossed to the mainland and engaged Showalter's Fourth Arizona and Captain Richard Taylor, commanding Company A of the Thirty-third Texas Cavalry, both positioned at Palmito Ranch. Across the Rio Grande, Cortina's cannons opened fire and the Confederate defensive line broke briefly before rallying at a new position eight miles from Fort Brown. The Union commander, unsure of Ford's strength, stalled at Palmito, while heavy rains turned the road west of Brownsville into a quagmire. That night, during the worst thunderstorm of the year, Ford saw to the safety of his family. He placed them in a Brownsville convent, but Mrs. Ford refused to leave her husband, and returned to Fort Brown to share in the danger. In the end, though, the expected attack never materialized. Cortina's inroad from Matamoros had been prevented by the river, which was swollen to flood stage by the steady rains, and by the stubborn refusal of Colonel Servando Canales and other officers to strike. Ford sent a severe message to Cortina demanding a reason for his "unprovoked and unwarranted" attack, but the *caudillo* skirted the question.[143]

With his rear and flank secured for the moment, Ford looked to his front at Palmito Hill. Giddings's two hundred Confederates positioned there maneuvered to meet the enemy's advance several miles above Palmito on September 9. At the same time, Ford prepared to defend Brownsville in case of a reversal on the battlefield. With the first light of day, William H. D. Carrington's company proceeded down the river road concealed by the chaparral until they were within two hundred yards of the Yankee position at the San Martin ranch. The skirmish continued for some five to six hours. By early afternoon, Gidding's entire battalion was on the field, and the two hundred Federals and fifty *Cortinistas* retreated approximately eight miles in the face of the Confederate counter-offensive led by captains William N. Robinson, R. W. Carr, —Saunders, J. M. Onins, and Carrington. A trail of weapons, equipment, and casualties, some eighty to ninety killed and wounded, marked the Union withdrawal. The fighting continued intermittently though September 11. The following morning, Carrington's scouts observed the Union troops retreating across the narrow channel to Brazos Island.[144]

Although Ford had cleared the lower valley of an armed Union presence, except for Brazos Santiago, efforts were made by the Confederate War Department to return control of the region to regular military authority, and to break up his ad hoc command. The Confederate soldiers he had led were obliged to obey orders, but many of the volunteers who were exempt from conscription, and had not enlisted for a definite term, were extremely reluctant to serve under another commander. The situation was initially calmed when Brigadier-General James Edwin Slaughter took command of the Western Sub-District in November, and established his headquarters at Fort Brown. He rearranged his order of battle into the Southern Division, commanded by Ford at Fort Brown; the Western Division covering the Laredo area; and the Northern Division at Corpus Christi. Throughout the winter, Slaughter laudably struggled to procure provisions and clothing for the troops. Nevertheless, the two men would soon clash over differences in policy, military strategy, and logistics. In addition, by February 1865, Slaughter had either transferred or furloughed two-thirds of Ford's remaining soldiers, leaving the colonel with 22 officers and 398 rank and file.[145]

In March 1865, Major-General Lewis "Lew" Wallace, an Indiana politician in peacetime, appeared at Brazos Santiago. Endowed with the support of President Lincoln, Secretary of State William Henry Seward, and Lieutenant-General Ulysses S. Grant, Wallace was interested in negotiating a truce between Union and Confederate forces on the lower Rio Grande. His ultimate goal, besides the fulfillment of his own personal ambitions, was to restore South Texas, indeed the entire Trans-Mississippi Department, to the Union, and raise a combined Federal-Confederate army to drive the French and *Imperialista* forces from northern Mexico. Through a civilian intermediary, Slaughter and Ford agreed to parley with Wallace at Point Isabel on March 11. The Union general proposed Confederates in the Trans-Mississippi Department end their rebellion and swear allegiance to the United States. Once these conditions were met, they would receive full amnesty, and the private property rights of the former secessionists would be honored, except for slaveholders whose chattel would be freed. Echoing Wallace's endgame, Slaughter observed the accord would be more successful if Confederate officers returned to the Union presenting several conquered Mexican states as gifts. Ford privately informed Slaughter he believed Edmund Kirby Smith was secretly negotiating with Emperor Maximilian for the annexation of Texas by Mexico. When asked his opinion on such a course, Ford replied, if necessary, he would personally lead a counter-revolution against the department commander. Since any fighting on the Rio Grande would not affect the overall outcome of the war, Wallace suggested a cease-fire. He cautioned the two Southern officers he did not possess the authority to unilaterally implement his proposals, but believed he would win approval from his government. He later reported the discussion interested Slaughter and Ford, both of whom were open to an honorable withdrawal from a losing fight. However, Major-General John George Walker, who had replaced Magruder as district commander the previous August, intercepted and opened the confidential letter outlining Wallace's proposal to Kirby Smith. He angrily publicized the contents and sent admonishing messages to Slaughter and Ford, as well as to Wallace. Walker opposed any surrender to the federal government and refused to forward the note. Wallace left Texas admitting defeat. Ford later opined the Confederate States should have accepted the offer in light of the hardships Reconstruction would produce.[146]

By the spring of 1865, furloughs, transfers, and desertions had reduced Ford's Cavalry of the West to a shadow of its former self. Under his direct command, he had two separate cavalry battalions composed of Captain Cater's three companies and Colonel Giddings's six. He also supervised five mounted companies from Colonel Santos Benavides's Thirty-third Texas Cavalry, but they were posted on the river below Ringgold Barracks. Captain O. G. Jones's Third Texas Field Artillery, as well as an independent, three-company battalion under Captain Theophilus G. Anderson, garrisoned Fort Brown. Anderson's command was comprised of his own company, and those of David M. Wilson and Frederick Bird Smith Cocke. To make matters worse, Ford had been obliged to scatter his men to areas not stricken by the continuing drought in order that the horses might graze.[147]

The truce informally agreed upon by Wallace and Slaughter lasted for two months. An area between Palo Alto Prairie and Palmito Ranch served as neutral ground between the two opposing forces. Almost five weeks after the surrender at Appomattox, and two days following President Davis's capture in Georgia, the last battle of the Civil War was fought at Palmito Ranch. This needless clash was primarily due to the Brazos garrison commander, Colonel Theodore Harvey Barrett of the Sixty-second U.S. Colored Infantry. With the war winding down, Barrett, who had seen little to no combat, was anxious to garner some measure of martial glory for himself. He requested permission to attack Fort Brown, and was unequivocally denied by his superiors. In "direct violation of orders," Barrett decided to seize the post.[148]

On the evening of May 11, following Barrett's directives, Lieutenant-Colonel David Branson, with ten white officers and 250 black infantrymen, departed Brazos Island and crossed Boca Chica Point in a driving rain. They were accompanied by fifty dismounted troopers of the Second Texas (Union) Cavalry under First Lieutenant James W. Hancock. At dawn the next morning, the Federals moved upriver through the chaparral. When they reached

Palmito at eight-thirty a.m., they were blocked by Giddings's cavalry battalion, which was distributed throughout the area. Captain William Robinson was in command while Giddings was on furlough. Robinson's 190 men offered a stiff resistance until they were forced to withdraw around noon. The doughty captain launched a counterattack in the late afternoon, and pushed the Yankees back to White's Ranch. When Ford received word of the Federal violation of the cease-fire, he recalled his dispersed cavalry companies. He reported the presence of Union troops to Slaughter, and the general responded by calling for his personal effects to be loaded onto a carriage and for a general retreat. The indomitable Ford told his superior officer in no uncertain terms: "You can retreat and go to hell if you wish. These are my men and I am going to fight."[149]

The overconfident Barrett, along with Lieutenant-Colonel Robert G. Morrison and two hundred soldiers of the Thirty-fourth Indiana, marched all night to reinforce Branson's vanguard. Upon reaching White's Ranch on the thirteenth, the colonel ordered another advance. By eleven o'clock, Ford had assembled Captain Jones's six cannons and thirty gunners, Anderson's battalion under Captain Wilson, and George A. Gibson's and A. C. Jones's mounted companies of Benavides's regiment. Standing to horse, they rode out of Fort Brown toward the sound of the guns. Four hours later, they were two miles west of Palmito Hill where they found Robinson's troopers fighting a vigorous delaying action. Commanding a total of three hundred men, Ford deployed Robinson's battalion to the left and Wilson's, Anderson's, and A. C. Jones's companies to the right to fix the Union line. A detachment from Jones's cavalry under Second Lieutenant Jesse Vineyard and two guns led by Lieutenant S. Gregory maneuvered to turn the enemy's exposed right flank. Cocke's and Gibson's companies were sent farther to strike the Yankees' extreme right and rear. Masked by brush and the terrain of Tulosa Hill, another section of artillery led by Lieutenant J. Mayrant Smith unlimbered in the center, and the last pair under Captain Jones's personal command were held in reserve three hundred yards to the rear. Almost immediately the Rebel artillery began bringing a dreadful fire down upon the two companies of the Thirty-fourth Indiana who comprised the skirmish line.[150]

Dazed by the sudden turn of events, Colonel Barrett ordered the main body of his force to retreat at the double-quick, but neglected to recall his one hundred skirmishers. Ford stood with some of his horsemen in the thicket, while balls from the Federal rifles flew past their heads. "Men, we have whipped the enemy in all previous fights," he said to his eager Texans. "We can do it again." The soldiers shouted their approval. Ford ordered the charge, and 275 cavalrymen thundered out to meet the weary and unsupported Hoosiers. The Yankee ranks had already been torn by shot and shell when the Southern horse drove into them and forced them to surrender. As the Sixty-second Colored Infantry, the surviving Indiana troops, and the Second Texas (Union) fell back the seven miles to the Boca Chica, the exhausted and heat-stricken Federals made temporary stands three times. On each occasion the Confederate artillery and the enveloping Rebel cavalry forced them to flee. At dusk, Ford halted his pursuit as the broken Billy Yanks staggered across a swampy inlet to Brazos Santiago. General Slaughter, accompanied

"Texas Rangers." From Benson John Lossing's *Harper's Encyclopedia of United States History.*

by Captain Carrington, commanding Cater's battalion, arrived on the field and needlessly harried the last of the retreating Yankees.[151]

Guarding against a counterattack, Ford withdrew to a camp ten miles below Fort Brown. Despite the heavy fighting his command had just seen, his reported losses were trifling: no dead and "five or six, wounded," one seriously. The Federal force suffered twenty-five to thirty killed and wounded. The Confederates captured 111 enlisted men and four officers. Ford later paroled all of his prisoners and allowed them to return to their units.[152]

As the war progressed toward its inevitable conclusion in the Trans-Mississippi, Slaughter sold six pieces of artillery and supplementary equipment for seventeen thousand dollars to General Tomás Mejía, an Imperialist commander who had taken Matamoros the previous September. Aspiring to "restore quiet and peace to the country," Ford quickly learned of the transaction and ordered his superior officer confined on May 25. Slaughter was released after he transferred approximately twenty thousand dollars in silver to Ford, who distributed the specie among his men for more than a year's worth of wages in arrears. Ford kept four thousand as his own pay, which was less than half of what he was owed. Slaughter issued his last order on May 26 and transferred command of the sub-district to Ford. The same day, as his men quietly took their leave for home or joined him in exile, Ford took his family to Matamoros where he had rented a house with Mejía's blessing.[153]

On June 2, General Kirby Smith surrendered all Confederate forces in the Trans-Mississippi Department. Immediately, General Magruder, who had once more taken command of the district in March, appointed Ford one of the commissioners charged with arranging the capitulation of former Confederates to the Federal authorities. The colonel worked diligently in his last assignment, orchestrating the paroles of numerous refugees in Matamoros. His own surrender became effective on July 18, but Ford remained in Matamoros for more than a month deciding on his future. He had no wish to be an expatriate in Mexico or some other foreign land. He later related how he also felt honor-bound to share with his former comrades-in-arms the difficult road ahead for Texas. At the same time, Major-General Frederick Steele, commanding Union forces on the Rio Grande, demanded the return of the battery Slaughter had sold to the Imperialists. The matter was referred to Maximilian, who complied with the ultimatum. The guns were sitting on the Fort Brown parade ground by July 10. Ford also returned to Brownsville, but the recent active campaigning had left him in poor health and he was unable to make a living. Captain Richard King, appreciative of Ford's service on the border, secretly paid the ex-colonel's rent and deposited $250 monthly into his bank account.[154]

Ford's condition gradually improved by the spring of 1866. His second son, John William, was born on April 3 of the same year. Across the river, Matamoros saw, as Professor Jerry Thompson and Lawrence Jones described the scene, "some of the most brutal and bloody fighting in the city's long and often violent history." General Mejía negotiated with José Carvajal a withdrawal from Matamoros due to reverses in the war and a loss of popular support for Maximilian. Mejía and his Imperial forces departed the city on June 24 with all honors of war, and Carvajal proclaimed himself *Juárista* governor. He immediately called on Ford to raise a volunteer force and come to his aid; he also offered him a commission of brigadier. Although Ford was interested, he requested official approval from Major-General Philip Henry Sheridan, commanding general of the Fifth Military District, before crossing into Mexico. The general opposed allowing armed ex-Confederates to travel to a foreign country. Ford responded he harbored no disloyalty or ill will toward the United States, and would not enlist any man who did. Sheridan grudgingly consented in the end.[155]

Accompanied by more than one hundred men, Ford crossed the border and took command of one of the small forts protecting Matamoros. On August 12, Ford was visiting Carvajal's headquarters when he learned a counter-revolution against the latter's rule was underway. Returning to his post, Ford was requested to confer with the uprising's leader, Servando Canales, Carvajal's foster son and an old friend. The two met and, while the bloodless *coup d'état* was really a struggle between two *caudillos* for prominence, Canales declared he remained a loyal supporter of the Juárez government. With Carvajal forced into exile in the United States, Ford accepted a commission of brigadier from Canales, now military governor of Tamaulipas. The state of affairs in Matamoros then became truly byzantine as Juárez had ordered on August 5 for Carvajal to be replaced with General Santiago Tapía. Word of the new appointment reached the city on October 2, but Canales refused to relinquish command. The situation placed Ford and his Texans in a delicate position: if they continued to support Canales, they would be forced to fight the very cause they had come to Mexico to defend. In the end, Ford reluctantly agreed to attack Canales's headquarters in the main plaza. He absented himself on the grounds of illness, and the nighttime assault, launched during a violent thunderstorm, was repulsed amid much enthusiastic, harmless firing. Afterwards, Ford oversaw the safe crossing of his men into Texas. The volunteers disbanded, content to let the Mexicans solve their own problems.[156]

Following his latest adventure south of the border, Ford continued to live and work in Brownsville. He returned to the newspaper business, being employed as editorial assistant for the *Ranchero* and later the *Courier*. On November 26, two companies of the Fourth Cavalry crossed into Matamoros to protect American lives and property while the forces of Canales and *Juárista* general Mariano Escobedo fought an internecine battle in the city. On the same day, Ford was appointed by the Fort Brown commander to lead a police force comprised of five companies of armed officers and special constables. His orders were to deter crime in the area, principally cattle theft, and safeguard the American side of the border. He served as foreman of the federal grand jury in the Brownsville district during the winter of 1866 and 1867. He dispensed advice on border conditions to a series of garrison commanders and sometimes guided cavalry companies on patrols against cattle rustlers. In 1868, he formed a partnership with Jesse E. Dougherty to publish the *Brownsville Sentinel*; Ford served as editor. He also became a director of the Rio Grande Railroad Company, which incorporated on August 13, 1870, and built a narrow-gauge line from Point Isabel to Brownsville.[157]

With congressional passage of the Amnesty Act in May 1872, and the full restoration of his citizenship rights, Ford became politically active once more in the Democratic Party. He was rewarded for his efforts by being named a delegate to the National Convention in Baltimore. In the midst of a realignment in the political party system, the Democratic leadership had declared for Horace Greeley in the upcoming presidential election, and Ford was seated with the Liberal Republican candidate's supporters on July 9. That same year, the state of Texas began to appoint cattle and hide inspectors to suppress the activities of "hide peelers," men who slaughtered and skinned cattle not their own for the hides and tallow. Ford was named the inspector for Cameron County. In the fall of 1873, Democrats regained power in the Texas statehouse and began to repeal laws enacted by the Radical Republicans. Ford also returned to political office when the citizens of Brownsville elected him their next mayor [158]

In December 1873, Ford abruptly left town for the state capital. Once there, he and several prominent Democrats observed the constitutional crisis that had erupted after Governor Edmund J. Davis, a Radical Republican, refused to abide by the results of the recent gubernatorial election. The Democratic nominee Richard Coke had won in a landslide, but Davis insisted the results were invalid; the law under which the election had been held was ruled unconstitutional. On January 13, 1874, the legislature-elect announced the Fourteenth Legislature was in session, but Davis refused to recognize them. On January 15, newly elected Speaker Guy Morrison Bryan appointed Ford, Brigadier-General William Polk "Old Gotch" Hardeman, and Colonel William N. Hardeman assistant sergeants-at-arms responsible for protecting the legislature, the public buildings, and the capitol grounds. After Davis declined to surrender the executive offices, state papers, and public property to his successor on January 16, a mob of indignant Coke supporters marched down Congress Avenue intent on seizing the armory and its garrison. Ford, the practiced orator who had once convinced his fellow rangers to not assassinate Santa Anna, persuaded the irate partisans to refrain from aggressive actions that would taint their cause. That night, Davis finally realized the futility of further obstinacy and relinquished his authority. Rumors of Radicals seizing the statehouse in the night caused Ford and the others to be retained until February 7. He departed for home after marching in the San Jacinto Day parade on April 21.[159]

Ford resumed his duties as the Brownsville mayor, but this was only to be the beginning in his new life as a statesman. His command of border Spanish gained him the additional position of official translator of the circuit court for the Eastern District of Texas in 1875. Later in the summer, he served as a delegate from the Thirtieth Senatorial District to the state constitutional convention. He and the rest of the body sought to replace the Radical Republican document with one more agreeable to the majority. Convening on September 6, the convention appointed Ford chairman of the Committee on State Affairs and a member of the committees on Suffrage, Municipal Corporations, Printing and Contingent Expenses, Apportionment, and Frontier Affairs. The convention adjourned on November 24.[160]

In January 1876, Ford was solicited for financial donations to the revolution of General Porfirio Díaz. The grizzled ranger bluntly explained the terms for his support. Juan Cortina had continued to plague Texans on the border with his sponsorship of depredations since 1868. If he were removed from the Rio Grande, then American donors would aid the revolt. Díaz gave his word and, backed by South Texas and New York business interests, he soon launched a campaign from Vera Cruz that ended in victory in Mexico City. Once firmly in power, the new ruler of Mexico recalled and arrested Cortina. The old general and bandit would live under house arrest until his death in 1894.[161]

Appreciative of his most recent services, the electorate of the Twenty-ninth District sent Ford to the state senate, where he served in the Fifteenth and Sixteenth Legislatures. He was also named to the executive committee of the state Democratic Party. Continuing to advocate for frontier defense, he traveled to Washington and appeared before the House Committee on Foreign Affairs as an expert on border conditions. Even as he was engaged in this important work, he did, however, desire a public office with more permanency, such as collector of customs at Brazos Santiago. Unfortunately, the election of ex-Union general and Republican Rutherford Birchard Hayes to the presidency in 1876 ensured no federal appointments would be his for at least the next four years.[162]

Time would, instead, bring the aging ranger some personal highs and tragic lows. At some point in 1879, the sixty-three-year-old Ford and his wife adopted Lillian Alva, who had been born on June 21, 1878. Tragically, his son, fourteen-year-old John William, a student at the Military Institute of Austin, was showing some other boys a pistol on January 8, 1880, when the weapon accidentally discharged and the bullet struck him in the left thigh. The youth seemed to be recovering until he took a turn for the worse and died on February 25. The general medical consensus for the cause of death was hemorrhage and "nervous depression." The Ford family experienced more troubles just two years later. On the evening of November 19, 1882, Lula was discovered bound and gagged on the bridge spanning the Colorado River near town. Earlier that night, she had been descending a flight of stairs outside her bedroom window when a white male and a black female seized her and bore her away. Ignoring her pleas, the kidnappers told the young woman they were taking her to meet an unknown third party. While crossing the bridge, the victim and her captors encountered a buggy driven by an elderly man. The abductors fled into the darkness under the bridge while the old-timer freed Lula from her restraints. The next morning, Colonel Ford tracked the kidnappers, but lost the trail. The incident became a matter for the police, and the case seems to have gone unsolved.[163]

On August 30, 1879, Ford submitted his resignation from the senate and assumed the superintendence of the state Deaf and Dumb Institution three days later. Henry McCulloch, the former ranger captain and Confederate general, had resigned the post following a bitter political fight and legislative subcommittee investigation. Ford, enjoying a greater degree of success, was reappointed on September 1, 1880, January 20, 1881, and January 16, 1883. In addition to learning sign language, the new superintendent made changes to the curriculum that emphasized trade skills, such as bookbinding, shoemaking, cabinetmaking, and printing. He personally subsidized the school's newspaper, the *Texas Mute Ranger*, and occasionally contributed articles on Texas history. With his "characteristic energy," he also oversaw an expansion of the campus to include a new chapel, additions to existing buildings, supplied water, and an increased enrollment to more than ninety students. Even as the demanding work began to bear fruit, he was forced to resign from the school, effective December 30, 1883, due to political strife and failing health.[164]

Ford and his family then moved to San Antonio where he spent his final years. He secured an appointment as deputy collector of internal revenue in 1885, and served until his retirement four years later. Even in his departure from public life, he remained active. He had previously been president of the Association of the Soldiers of the Mexican War in Texas, and so developed a keen interest in the state's history. He labored to complete his memoirs, a project he had started while at the Deaf and Dumb Institution, and collected information for a planned written history of Texas.

He penned numerous historical articles for San Antonio newspapers, and was an active member of the Alamo Association by 1894. His short history of the Alamo battle was published as a pamphlet in order to raise donations for a monument to the mission's fallen martyrs.[165]

Having returned to Texas sometime after 1850, Ford's oldest daughter, Fannie, had married lawyer and quartermaster Captain William Grey Thomas in San Antonio on January 28, 1862. Following the war, Grey, as he was known, returned to his law practice in Austin and served as city attorney in 1874 and 1875. He also worked as president of the Austin & Pacific Short Line Railroad and the Austin Street Railway Company. He was an active member of the Royal Arch Masons. They had one son and one daughter. Grey died on March 5, 1880, in Austin, and was interred at Oakwood Cemetery. Fannie turned her home into a boarding house before consumption took her life on August 5, 1895. She was laid to rest next to her husband.[166]

In the short time he had remaining, Ford made two final contributions to his beloved state. He was present for a meeting on March 2, 1897, that would see the founding of the Texas State Historical Society, a goal he had been championing since 1874. Secondly, in April 1892, he had penned a letter to the editor of the *San Antonio Express*, which was reprinted in other newspapers, calling for a reunion of republican and antebellum rangers. The idea would lie dormant for several years until Will Lambert, who had served under Ford on the Rio Grande, began to actively arrange such an event. The organizers of the Texas Rangers' Association met in Austin on May 12, 1897, and a constitution and bylaws were adopted on June 11. The legendary soldier and Indian fighter would be unable to attend the first formal meetings of either organization as he suffered a debilitating stroke on October 1. He fought valiantly to recover amid several relapses, but ultimately died on the evening of November 3, 1897. The following day, with his Presbyterian pastor officiating, he was buried at the United Confederate Veterans Cemetery in San Antonio.[167]

Addie lived with Lula in San Antonio and received a pension from the state as an impoverished Confederate widow. She died on February 19, 1901, of "the grippe," and was buried next to her husband.[168]

Mary Louise, Ford's first daughter born of his third marriage, married real estate dealer Joseph Warner Maddox on January 10, 1884. The couple moved to San Antonio later in the year; they had no children. Lula died on June 24, 1916, of acute nephritis. She was buried in the United Confederate Veterans Cemetery the next day.[169]

Addie Julia married Samuel Delgado De Cordova, son and business partner of land agent Phineas De Cordova, at St. Paul's Episcopal Church in Austin on January 10, 1883. They had two sons. In 1905, Sam and Addie relocated to Houston, where he became the land department manager for the trustee of the Thomas William House estate. He died of cancer on January 28, 1909, in Houston. After her husband's death, Addie lived with her sons in Houston, Corpus Christi, and Lake Charles, Louisiana. She died in the latter place on August 11, 1953.[170]

After graduating from San Antonio High School in 1897, Lillian married Robert Alonzo Votaw, Sr. on August 28, 1901, in Austin. They had one son who would die in December 1958, and one daughter. Moving to Brownsville in 1903, Lillian worked in the women's suffrage movement while her husband operated a produce business and a farm. They relocated to San Antonio prior to 1910, where Robert was employed as a salesman for the Peden Iron & Steel Company. Robert and Lillian lived with Lula and Joseph for a time before moving to Robstown in 1926. A veteran of World War I, Robert died at the U.S. Naval Hospital in Corpus Christi on August 25, 1948, and was buried in the Robstown Cemetery. Diagnosed with cerebral arteriosclerosis and senility, Lillian died at South Park Manor nursing home in Corpus Christi on May 7, 1971, of a cerebral vascular accident. After a funeral service at St. Andrews Episcopal Church, she was buried next to her husband.[171]

John S. Ford was one of the most talented men in nineteenth century Texas. He led a life of diverse occupations and experiences: doctor, surveyor, editor, explorer, soldier, legislator, and historian. While he lacked the national stature of Sam Houston or Peter Bell, he nevertheless stood at the center of nearly every important event in Texas for over a half-century. Even with his impressive list of accomplishments, perhaps his memorable achievements were to occur during his years as a Texas Ranger.

Lawrence Sullivan Ross. *Courtesy Cushing Memorial Library and Archives, Texas A&M University, College Station, Texas.*

Chapter 7

Lawrence S. Ross: "Public Duty was an Important Fixture in His Life"

Lawrence Sullivan Ross served Texas well and with devotion for over forty years. Be it as an Indian fighter, a hell-for-leather cavalry general, a statesman, or an educator, public duty was an important fixture in his life. He was well-read for his time, but he trained himself for no particular profession. Rather, he seemed to gravitate toward a military career, and his early reputation was founded upon his abilities as a fighter and leader. That his ranger service lasted less than two years is made immaterial by the renown and admiration he earned for his exploits, although that status has become stained in recent years. Proclaiming him a "superior Ranger captain," Robert Utley declared further: "Despite his youth, he commanded the respect and therefore the disciplined teamwork of his men, a quality that set such captains as Jack Hays, Ben McCulloch, and Rip Ford apart from lesser leaders." The Texan horsemen under his command in Tennessee and Georgia similarly idolized him. Returning home from the war, he championed law and order, responsible governance, and improved education, and became one of the most-revered men in the state.

He was born on September 27, 1838, in Bentonsport, Van Buren County, Iowa Territory. Shapley Prince Ross, his father, had been born in Jefferson County, Kentucky, on January 18, 1811, and Catherine Hallum (Fulkerson) Ross, his mother, in Rockingham, Virginia, on September 27, 1812. They married in St. Charles County, Missouri, on November 4, 1830. In addition to Lawrence, their children were Mary Rebecca Ross, born on September 30, 1831; Margaret Virginia Ross, on October 23, 1833; Peter Fulkerson Ross, on July 27, 1837; Anna Ross, on May 8, 1841; James Mervin Ross, on February 29, 1845; Robert Shapley Ross, on April 22, 1848; Catherine "Kate" Ross, on January 6, 1851; and William Hallum Ross, on August 18, 1853.[1]

In 1839 the Ross family migrated to Texas, first settling at Nashville in Milam County. Shapley swore an oath of allegiance to the Republic of Texas, which entitled him and his kin to a headright of 640 acres. They worked a farm, traded stock, and endured the occasional brush with hostile Indians. Two years later, the Rosses and seven or eight other families moved about thirty-five miles west to choice land on the Little River. Shapley had traded his horse herd and wagons for 640 acres there and six hundred acres in Burleson County.[2]

Desiring to provide his children with a formal education, Shapley exchanged 290 acres for a wagon and a yoke of oxen and relocated the household to Austin in 1845. Despite the move, the Ross children were said to have learned "far more from their cultured mother than in the rude classrooms of the day." While Texans were fighting in the American army in Mexico, Shapley commanded a ranger company on the Little River, Brushy Creek, the Brazos, and at Bosque Station from July 26, 1846, to February 15, 1849. Following his discharge, the family relocated at the behest of land developer Jacob De Cordova to the rich bottomlands west of the Brazos and surrounding Waco Springs, arriving on March 1. For agreeing to make the move, the elder Ross obtained from De Cordova's company four town lots in the new village of Waco, the ferry franchise, and the opportunity to purchase eighty additional acres at the special price of one dollar per acre. He subsequently bought another two hundred acres at $2.50 per acre. Shapley's house would be built in an "open hog-wallow prairie," located in the area of present South Eleventh Street and Ross Avenue, and the ferry was established at the top of modern-day Washington Street. The 1850 federal census lists Shapley as a "hotel keeper" with real estate valued at five thousand dollars and two slaves, one twenty-five-year-old male and one eighteen-year-old female.[3]

Seeking to expand on the schooling he had received while in Austin, Sul entered the Preparatory Department of Baylor University in Independence, Texas, in March 1856. He studied under Doctor Rufus Columbus Burleson, the esteemed president of the small institution. By the end of the first school term, Ross had completed the two-year program that would prepare him for future college courses. The following year, he traveled by horseback to attend Wesleyan University in Florence, Alabama. While a student at the college, Ross joined the Methodist Church.[4]

In the summer of 1858, Ross was home on summer vacation following his junior year at college. His father had been appointed Indian agent for the Brazos Reservation three years before, and a major topic of discussion was Rip Ford's recent Antelope Hills expedition in which Shapley had participated. The talk also concerned the new operation the army was organizing.[5]

Brevet Major-General David Emanuel Twiggs, commanding general of the Department of Texas, had written the War Department requesting authorization to organize a campaign of four companies and Indian guides into hostile country, even if the trail took the soldiers across departmental lines.[6] Permission was granted and army headquarters issued General Order No. 18 authorizing Twiggs to alter the dispositions of his troops to meet the needs of the service. In turn, Twiggs released Special Order No. 71 on August 9, which called for the organization of a punitive expedition. The order directed companies of the Second Cavalry to march north from Fort Belknap and establish a supply depot on Otter Creek in the Choctaw Reservation. Once the base was completed, the column was to reconnoiter the country between the Red River and the north fork of the Canadian River. Most importantly, the expedition commander was given carte blanche to pursue hostile Indians beyond the limits of the department and Texas itself.[7]

Chosen to be the officer in charge, Brevet Major Earl Van Dorn requested the presence of Shapley Ross and his Brazos Reservation allies to accompany the column. Although the Indians were anxious to meet their Comanche foes in battle, they objected to Shapley accompanying them on account of his ill health and his importance to their life on the reservation. Plácido, the same Tonkawa chief who had fought alongside republic-era rangers, appealed to the agent to instead entrust the leadership of the Indian

Earl Van Dorn. Portrait carte de visite by E. & H. T. Anthony, New York City. WICR 31608. *Courtesy Wilson's Creek National Battlefield, Republic, Missouri.*

detachment to Sul. The elder Ross gave his consent, and all of the tribesmen pledged their loyalty and unwavering faith in the twenty-year-old college student.[8]

On September 15, the soldiers marched north from Fort Belknap toward Otter Creek. The column consisted of troopers of Companies A, F, H, and K, Second Cavalry; a fifty-man detachment from Companies C and F, First Infantry; and 113 Indian auxiliaries. Led by Ross, the allied tribesmen were Wichitas of the Waco band under Tawakoni Jim and Nasthoe,

Tonkawas under Plácido, Tawakonis under Ochilas, and assorted Caddos and Delawares. Guided by Plácido and Ochilas, the troops marched northeast to the west fork of the Trinity River, then turned northwest and traversed the northwest corner of Wilbarger County. They crossed the Red River and, on September 23, arrived at Otter Creek in modern-day Tillman County, Oklahoma. Ross chose a site for the base camp on the southeast side of the creek and the soldiers began construction. The depot was named Camp Radziminski in honor of a Polish-born lieutenant from Company K who had recently died of tuberculosis.[9]

Ross's Indian scouts were dispatched to search for sign of hostile Comanches. Nasthoe (Shot-in-the-Foot) rode east with his son Wau-see-sic-an to a Wichita village on Wild Horse Creek in present Grady County to obtain information. Instead the two found a nearby village of approximately four to six hundred Comanches drawn from the Kutsutʉʉkas, Penatʉkas, and several other bands. They were led by Quohoahteme (Hair-Bobbed-on-One-Side) of the Kutsutʉʉkas, Hotowokowot (Over-the-Buttes) of the Yaparʉkas, and Potsanaquahip (Buffalo Hump), the notorious Penatʉka chief who had been an implacable foe of Texas for years.[10]

The assembled Comanches were in the area to treat with the Wichitas, Chickasaws, and Choctaws. The Comanches had believed the Wichitas were involved in Rip Ford's attack several months before, and had retaliated by stealing their horses. When they were convinced of their mistake, the Comanches sent envoys to the Wichitas, then encamped next to the village to make peace and return the stolen stock. They had also just returned from Fort Arbuckle where they had discussed a peace treaty with the post commander.[11]

Nasthoe and Wau-see-sic-an went into the Wichita village, advised the headmen of the coming attack, then returned to Camp Radziminski. After arriving on September 29, they informed Ross of their find. Buffalo Hump learned of the soldiers' presence at approximately the same time. Ross reported his scouts' information to Van Dorn who, in turn, directed his company commanders to ready their troops for a short operation. One hour after Nasthoe's arrival, the soldiers were on the move.[12]

Van Dorn expected to attack the following morning, but neither Nasthoe nor Wau-see-sic-an comprehended units of distance. The village was actually ninety miles away rather than the forty they had reported. Instead of striking at dawn, the column rode throughout the day and on into the night. Van Dorn finally ordered a halt late on the afternoon of the thirtieth at White Wolf Ford, on the south bank of Medicine Bluff Creek, to rest the horses and allow the men to make coffee. As night fell, the troops were in the saddle again. They rode through the night over rough ground until, at daybreak, they entered an undulating prairie broken by widely spaced ridges. The exhausted troopers and the auxiliaries had been on the trail for thirty-six hours, the only breaks in the last sixteen had been to water their mounts. As they moved through the foggy morning, Nasthoe and Tawakoni Jim reported the Comanche camp was nearby.[13]

The Comanches knew the soldiers were coming. Scouts had kept the troopers under observation since Otter Creek, and had followed the column every step of the way out of Camp Radziminski since the twenty-ninth. One lookout returned to the Comanche *ranchería* to inform Buffalo Hump of the soldiers' advance. The principal chief wanted to abandon the camp, but his warriors believed themselves ready for a fight. An oracle determined the omens were good, and the soldiers were no threat to the village. They were also certain their peace discussions at Fort Arbuckle meant they would be in no danger of attack. Consequently, most of the *ranchería* inhabitants had gone to bed without taking any precautions.[14]

With his scouts' reports delivered, Van Dorn ordered his men to ready themselves for the confrontation. He guarded against possible friendly fire incidents by moving all allied Indians to the right flank. The regular cavalrymen were deployed in four columns of two, each guiding on the right company. The 225 troopers alternately walked and trotted their mounts through the thinning mist toward the *ranchería*. At about seven o'clock, the columns maneuvered into line, the bugler sounded "charge," and the horses were spurred forward.[15]

The sleeping Comanches were taken completely by surprise, but they recovered and rushed to meet the oncoming cavalry. As the regulars charged, Ross and his auxiliaries galloped to stampede the enemy horse herd. After driving the ponies beyond the reach of the Comanches, Ross collected his warriors and rejoined the fight in the lower portion of the camp. Hindered by the rough terrain, the troopers broke formation and engaged the Indians in individual, close-quarters combat. The air was torn by the clamor of shouts and war cries, the crack of pistols and carbines, and the hoof beats of charging horses. Vision became obscured once the mist mixed with clouds of powder smoke. Both sides battled furiously as the soldiers and Brazos Indians pressed home the attack, and the Comanches strived to screen the escape of their noncombatants.[16]

Peering through the haze, Ross noticed a large party of fugitives fleeing the camp. Calling for assistance, he urged his horse after them. In the commotion of the battle, only three men—Lieutenant Cornelius Van Camp, Private Carroll C. Alexander, and an unnamed Caddo scout—heard him and followed in pursuit. The four men raced after the escapees only to find they were women and children. Ross ordered the others to let the Indians go until he noticed one of the girls was white. He instructed the Caddo to seize her, and the scout had to struggle to retain his hold on the dirty, terrified child. The recovery of the girl distracted Ross and his companions from the continuing fight, and they found themselves cut off from the main body of regulars by a band of approximately twenty-five enemy warriors. Loosing a volley of arrows, the Comanches charged the three white men. Van Camp was struck by one arrow, which pierced his heart, and he toppled from his saddle. Private Alexander, also hit, was seriously wounded. Ross raised his Sharps rifle to return fire, but the percussion cap snapped and the weapon misfired. In the same instant, an arrow pierced his shoulder. As he swayed from the impact, Mohee, a Comanche Ross had known since childhood, caught up Alexander's Springfield .58-caliber carbine and shot the Texan through the body at point-blank range.[17]

Tumbling to the ground with blood flowing from his wounds, Ross lay stunned until he saw the gleam of a Comanche scalping knife. With his arm and side paralyzed to some extent, and sliding into unconsciousness, he struggled to retrieve the holstered pistol pinned under his body. He was saved from certain death when an approaching body of cavalry caused the advancing Mohee to instead turn and flee. Before the warrior could make his escape, though, Lieutenant James Patrick Major cut him down with a shotgun. Caddo John, one of the allied Indians, dressed Ross's wounds and carried him back to the army surgeon accompanying the column.[18]

After nearly two hours, the superior firepower of the cavalry triumphed and the Comanches retired from the field. The Indians left fifty-six fallen warriors behind, but they had successfully covered the withdrawal of the women, children, and elderly. Also lost were two women "accidentally killed," most of the horse herd, and all the camp equipage. In Van Dorn's report, the major praised Ross who "did good and efficient service, and [was] spoken of highly by all the officers for [his] bearing during the engagement." General Twiggs published a statement to the entire department, a portion of which read: "The friendly Indians who were under Mr. Ross rendered essential service in first stampeding and afterwards securing the enemy's animals, and are deserving of like praise with the regular troops."[19]

Ross was recuperating at home in Waco when he received a letter from Brevet Lieutenant-General Winfield Scott expressing his compliments and admiration. The army's general-in-chief went on to offer Ross a direct comissioned in the cavalry, but the young student politely declined so he could complete his education. His recovery was painful, but he was sufficiently mended by December to return to Alabama and finish his senior year. He graduated in June 1859 with an *artium baccalaureus* degree and returned home.[20]

Before he had gone back to the university, Ross attempted to find any family or friends of the little white girl who had been recovered from the Comanches. His efforts proved unsuccessful, so he "adopted, reared, and educated" the child whom he named Lizzie Ross. Her namesake was Ross's fiancée Elizabeth Dorothy "Lizzie" Tinsley, whom he had known since childhood and had been courting for a time. The eldest daughter of Doctor David Augustus Richard Tinsley, a wealthy physician and planter, she had been born on November 29, 1845, in Augusta, Georgia.[21]

On March 17, 1860, Governor Houston instructed his aide-de-camp Colonel Middleton Tate Johnson to "raise a sufficient number of mounted rangers to repel, pursue and punish the Indians now ravaging the northern and northwestern settlements of Texas."[22] On April 2, Ross enlisted in a McLennan County ranger company organized by Captain Joseph M. Smith for Colonel Johnson's regiment. He was elected first lieutenant. The balance of the company was two other lieutenants, a surgeon, eight noncommissioned officers, and eighty-four privates. The command departed Waco for

Fort Belknap in Young County on the twenty-third, while Ross was granted permission to travel by another route for the purposes of unspecified personal business. He rejoined his comrades on May 2 at his father's ranch, and the company arrived at its rendezvous near Belknap the next day. Ross was immediately detailed to conduct a scout from the fort to the Big Wichita. The rangers found recent signs of activity, including three large trails leading northwest to the Wichita Mountains, before returning to camp on the eleventh. In the voting for regimental officers on the fifteenth, Johnson was elected colonel, Smith lieutenant-colonel, and William F. Fitzhugh major. Even while sick with bronchitis, Ross was elected captain without opposition five days later. The Waco company was mustered into Johnson's command on May 18. In addition to Ross, the other captains were Nicholas Henry Darnell, Tarrant County; William Middleton Woods, Fannin County; Gabriel S. Fitzhugh (Major Fitzhugh's brother), Collin County; Thomas J. Johnson (the colonel's son), Tarrant County; William Cornelius Dalrymple, Williamson County; and Edward "Ed" Burleson, Jr., Hays County. Peter Ross, Sul's older brother, organized and led a company of forty-three allied Indians from April 6 to October 16, 1860. Plácido was among them.[23]

The eight companies of Johnson's regiment were ordered to invade the *Comanchería*, but even before the operation commenced, boredom, carousing, and logistical problems plagued the outfit. The expedition proved a failure, due in no small part to its colonel. With his poor grasp of personal leadership and administrative detail, Johnson proved a poor choice to direct the regiment. He even abandoned his command on June 6 to go to Galveston to marry, leaving Lieutenant-Colonel Smith to handle preparations for the expedition, including the procuring of supplies, ammunition, and transportation.[24]

The three hundred rangers broke camp by companies and began the march into Indian country; Ross's men left on June 10. Alerted to the regiment's presence, the Indians fired the prairie and destroyed a great deal of the forage needed for the rangers' horses. The scorched earth encompassed much of northwest Texas and extended into the Indian Territory. As they rode along, the Texans found any unburned grass had already been eaten by the buffalo herds in the area. Crossing the Red River, the Waco company struck Otter Creek on June 18, and arrived at the regiment's field headquarters at

PLACIDO, CHIEF OF THE TONKAWAS.

Placido. From Homer S. Thrall's *A Pictorial History of Texas*.

Camp Radziminski. From their camp and from the Wichita Agency, the regiment conducted patrols of the country between the Red and Canadian Rivers. Peter with twenty-six Indian auxiliaries, and Lieutenants Willis L. Lang and Thomas Kelliher with thirty-one rangers, undertook a twenty-day scout to the headwaters of the Red and Washita Rivers. Realizing the regiment had failed to see any action, and concerned he would be unable to feed his mounts if he continued north, Smith suspended the expedition on July 12. Colonel Johnson arrived at Radziminski later the same day. On the thirteenth, the companies began to disperse and Ross took some sick men to the Indian agency at Fort Cobb.[25]

The campaign had cost the state fifteen hundred dollars per day without once glimpsing a hostile Indian. Governor Houston effectively cancelled the expedition on August 4 and recalled the regiment on the twenty-sixth. Before any of the governor's orders would reach him on October 13, Johnson led 180 men to the North Fork of the Red River and established a new base of operations known as Camp Louise. Given permission to return home, Ross left his men on August 29 and went on to his ranch. The remainder of the company arrived in Waco on September 7 and was mustered out of service the same day. Frustrated and angry with Johnson's failure to bring the enemy to battle, or even keep the executive informed of his activities, Houston ordered the regiment to disband on September 12.[26]

Because his father had been castigated for his role in the unpopular "Reservation War," Ross was deemed guilty by association. He also found himself blamed for the recent disastrous expedition; some in the northwestern counties even called for his lynching. The bitterness would continue through the autumn. On October 13, eighty men attending a barbecue in Palo Pinto would sign a resolution demanding Ross resign his commission and depart the frontier.[27]

Despite the Johnson campaign's embarrassing end, and the strident public criticism of the governor, Ross won gubernatorial approval for his first tenure as a ranger captain. Indeed, he was appointed by Houston to raise another company of mounted volunteers on September 11, 1860. The authorized strength was one captain, three lieutenants, four sergeants, four corporals, and sixty rank and file. The company completed its organization at Waco on

October 3 and departed town three days later. Ross and his rangers assumed their station on Elm Creek, eight miles from Fort Belknap, on October 17. Holding an election for company officers, Ross was chosen as captain, Thomas Kelliher as first lieutenant, M. W. Summerville second lieutenant, and David L. Sublett third lieutenant. The company took the field ten days later to conduct regular patrols of their district. They did not find any hostile Indians, but the scouting was seen as excellent training. Horse-stealing forays had occurred for much of the year, but the settlers in Jack, Palo Pinto, Parker, and Young Counties began to suffer in late November. In that month, Nokoni Comanches engaged in a spree of robbery and rape, and the murder of six people, five of them women.[28]

Word reached Ross from Fort Cobb in the Indian Territory that Comanches unaffiliated with the reservation there were reportedly camped on the Pease River. The ranger captain planned an attack on these hostile Indians, but believed he had too few men to achieve a significant victory. Therefore, he went to Camp Cooper and requested assistance from Captain Nathan George "Shanks" Evans, commanding Company H, Second Cavalry. Evans agreed to supply Ross with First Sergeant John W. Spangler and twenty troopers. Spangler had been the only enlisted man mentioned by name in dispatches following the Wichita village fight. The sergeant, with "cool courage, daring intrepidity, and gallant bearing," had killed six Comanches in personal combat. Captain James Jackson "Jack" Cureton and sixty-eight Palo Pinto volunteers also chose to accompany the expedition. Cureton was a Mexican War veteran, an Indian fighter of some repute, and a settler on Keechi Creek.[29]

On December 11, Ross's forty rangers and Spangler's federal troops departed Elm Creek. They met up with Cureton's volunteers at the headwaters of Salt Creek on the morning of the twelfth, and all of them set out for the Pease River on the fourteenth. They rode northwest through the frigid cold, crossed the Big Wichita River on the sixteenth, and reached the Pease the evening of the seventeenth. The scarcity of forage along the route of march affected the horses of some twenty rangers and all of Cureton's men, and they were unable to keep up with the remainder of the column. On the morning of December 19, soaked by intermittent rain, and buffeted by a harsh norther, the chilled horsemen struck a fresh Indian trail in present Foard County. They soon found a *ranchería* of fifteen to twenty-five Nokoni Comanches on Mule Creek near its junction with the Pease. The Indians were in the process of breaking camp and departing, and Ross and Spangler were forced to move quickly. The Texan took five or six of his men, and possibly three regulars, to the left side of the Indian camp, while the rest of the sergeant's detachment moved to the right. Ross and Spangler were separated from each other by a deep ravine.[30]

The surprised Comanches were overwhelmed as three Indians fell before the deadly fire of the rangers, and eleven were dispatched by the regulars' revolvers. Lieutenant Summerville attempted to charge an unnamed chief who had dismounted, "evidently determined to sell his life as dearly as possible." Summerville was leveling his gun to shoot the Indian when his horse abruptly stopped. At the same time, the chief loosed an arrow that missed as the lieutenant fell off the far side of his steed. Coming to his subordinate's aid, Ross killed the warrior in hand-to-hand combat. Several other Comanches were able to reach their horses and escape the village, but at least some of them were pursued and killed within two miles, "fighting with great desperation all the while."[31]

Lieutenant Kelliher observed a lone Comanche riding off and gave chase. Overtaking the fleeing horse, Kelliher was about to shoot when the rider halted, revealed herself to be a white woman, and displayed a small child. "*Americano*," she shrieked. The subaltern took her into custody. Lieutenant Sublett captured a small Indian boy approximately seven to twelve years old and purportedly the slain chief's son. At first, the lad expected he would be killed at any moment by the white men, but Ross took him back to Fort Belknap, then home to Waco. There he was named Pease Ross, but his actual status, whether a member of the family or a type of servant, is unclear.[32]

In the "hotly contested" engagement that lasted about a half-hour, Ross reported twelve or thirteen Indians were killed, while Spangler stated the number was fourteen. Johnathan Hamilton Baker, a member of Cureton's company, recorded in his journal one day after the fight that the bodies of only seven Comanches were found, three men and four women. In addition to the three prisoners, between forty to forty-five animals were captured, as well as all the tents and camp equipage. Articles seized, including clothes and a Bible, indicated the defeated Comanches belonged to the same band that had raided the settlements in November. The rangers and regulars suffered no injuries, except for two wounded horses. Lieutenant-Colonel Robert Edward Lee, acting commander of the Second Cavalry, afterwards described the engagement as a "Brilliant Success."[33]

The rangers and soldiers returned to their respective headquarters on December 20, while Cureton's volunteers probed the area for another five days. The white prisoner and her baby were taken to Camp Cooper. Speaking little to no English, the woman recalled she had been stolen when she was a little girl, but could not remember her Christian name or where she had once lived. Since then, she assumed the name Naudah, married a warrior known as Puhtocnocony (called Peta Nocona by white men), became a mother, and assimilated into the tribe. Isaac Parker later identified her as his long-lost niece, Cynthia Ann Parker.[34]

In the decades following the fight, the action at Pease River and the recapture of Cynthia Ann Parker would become a significant, albeit controversial, event in Texas history. The above description is largely based upon Ross's dispatch to a *Dallas Herald* correspondent written on December 23, 1860, his official report composed on January 4, 1861, Sergeant Spangler's two accounts composed on December 24, 1860, and January 16, 1861, and several newspaper articles published in the weeks following the incident. However, later recollections and eyewitness statements written up to seventy years after the fact must be taken with a reasonable degree of skepticism. While much of the forthcoming commentary will concern Ross's accounts over the years, the objective historian should also consider Spangler's two reports and their veracity. Colonel Thomas T. Smith, an author and retired army officer, addressed the issue of

> skewed estimates of Indian opponents and casualties from the soldiers writing the primary accounts … there are several factors that tend to mitigate wild exaggeration. The army in the nineteenth century, as it does today, maintained a strict code of honor, particularly in official reports to superiors, which includes most of the combat reports. Even if

Cynthia Ann Parker. Daguerreotype by A. F. Corning, Fort Worth, Texas. *Author's Collection*.

> the unit leader wanted to inflate the numbers in the public record he would face correction from other soldier-witnesses, often veterans with a keen eye for detail.[35]

One who would dismiss the sergeant's reports as falsehoods would first need to prove he and the twenty troopers of his detachment were all willing to lie to their company commander, and to every superior officer in the chain of command. As far as can be determined, not one of those soldiers later disputed the contents of the statements submitted to Captain Evans. Given the sheer volume of material that would be produced in later years, perhaps the earliest accounts are the closest history will get to the truth.

The first additions to the initial version began with a letter written by Ross that was printed in the *Galveston Daily News* in June 1875. The purpose of the correspondence was ostensibly to correct the record, but the beginnings of new and inconsistent details are found there instead. Ross first contributed to the confusion by erroneously dating the battle as occurring on December 18. In this same letter, he also identified the chief he had killed as Mohee, but a Comanche with that name had been slain at the Wichita village two years previously. In the case of these two alterations, a simple case of mistaken memory is most likely the reason for the first, while the second is admittedly perplexing.[36]

The "authorized" version, based on Ross's remembrances, was introduced in James DeShields's biography of Cynthia Ann Parker in 1886. In this work, the short skirmish became a critical battle in which: "So signal a victory had never before been gained over the fierce and war-like Comanches … The great Comanche confederacy was forever broken … The blow was a most decisive one." Additionally, Ross inserted his involvement into the description of Lieutenant Kelliher's chase, identified the Comanche chief he had fought to be Peta Nocona, and claimed the "noted warrior of great repute" was finished off by a Mexican servant who had once been a Comanche prisoner. While this story has become the most widely circulated, it has been disputed. Quanah Parker wrote to legendary frontiersman Charles Goodnight "in the winter of 1877 and 1878," and declared that his father had not perished at the Pease River. Instead, he had left the camp days previously with Quanah and his brother. The war chief who was slain was named No-bah. On July 9, 1896, Parker, in a speech at Quanah, Texas, further claimed Nocona died of illness two or three years after the engagement, and was buried near the Antelope Hills and the South Canadian River in present Lipscomb County. In the letter to Goodnight, Quanah stated he did not want to diminish "a single honor won by Gov. Ross … he was a brave and honorable foe," but the former captain had been honestly mistaken. While casting no aspersions on Quanah Parker's character, it should be noted Ross was not the only man who revised his story over time. In a speech at the 1909 State Fair, Parker identified the Comanche leader at Mule Creek as Yaqua.[37]

The early 1900s would offer reminiscences of participants that suggest the Pease River incident was not a crucial battle, or even a less glorious skirmish, but instead an outright massacre. According to Goodnight, who was with Cureton's men, and thus not actually present for the fight, women were among those shot down "nearly in a pile," and only the regular soldiers killed them, "not one of [the rangers] shot a squaw that day." Eighty-nine-year-old Hiram B. Rogers, once a private in Ross's company, recounted in an interview in 1928: "I was in the Pease River fight, but I am not very proud of it. That was not a battle at all, but just a killing of squaws." In contrast, Colonel Martin L. Crimmins, in his biographical sketch of Sergeant Spangler, stipulates that all the Indians were bundled in buffalo robes for protection from the cold weather, and identifying warriors from noncombatants would have proven difficult in the midst of battle. However, he refutes that Sergeant Spangler knowingly massacred unarmed women.[38]

In recent years, Paul H. Carlson and Tom Crum have advanced the debate in an article for the *Southwestern Historical Quarterly*, and later expounded upon their theory in a full-length book. Two of the basic purposes of both works is to "describe how Sul Ross and his friends shaped descriptions of the battle and the capture of Cynthia Ann Parker for Ross's political ends" and "analyze some of the questionable accounts, altered diaries, missing reports, and major questions that have become a part of Parker's life story and histories of the massacre." Their chief concerns were the witness statements, a different version of Johnathan Baker's diary that is archived at the Briscoe Center for American History, and Ross's after-action report that went missing from the State Archives sometime after it was reprinted in the *San Antonio Express* in 1908. Among their conclusions are that the Pease River engagement was an attack on "mostly women and children," that Sul Ross and his cronies manipulated the voting public into accepting a false description of the incident, and "missing documents, contradictory eyewitness accounts, false memory, and fictionalized diary entries explain in part the difficulty in acquiring accurate data on the event and the absence of reliable histories of what occurred."[39]

Carlson and Crum's premise has become the conventional wisdom concerning the fight at the Pease River. As a result, Sul Ross's reputation has become tarnished to the extent he is now considered the villain of the entire episode. Cynthia Ann Parker was unquestionably a tragic figure, and her life was twice heartbreakingly affected by forces beyond her control. Regardless of whether she was forcibly taken from Comanche friends and family, the reason for her even being a member of the Nokoni band—the earlier massacre of the Parker clan, and her subsequent kidnapping and captivity while an impressionable nine-year-old girl—should not be blithely overlooked. After nearly a quarter-century among the Comanches, Cynthia Ann, the little girl who had been given no choice in the matter, was long gone, and Naudah, who consequently knew no other way of life, stood in her place.

The life of a Comanche prisoner was a nightmarish existence as the examples of Rachel Plummer, Cynthia's fellow captive in 1836, and Matilda Lockhart of Council House fame, plainly demonstrate. Being knowledgeable frontiersmen, Ross and the others were sincere in their desire to liberate Cynthia from what was widely regarded as a fate worse than death. In making a moral judgement that a massacre, rather than a skirmish, occurred, Carlson and Crum cite as proof Baker's assertion that four women and three men were found dead on the site after five days of searching the area for Indian sign, as well as Hiram Rogers's 1928 interview. They also speculate those killed "in all likelihood were shot in the back," but they seem not to have considered that one or more of the women at Mule Creek may have actually been combatants. In his book, *Without Quarter: The Wichita Expedition and the Fight on Crooked Creek*, William Y. Chalfant discusses the Wichita village fight of two years earlier: "Under the circumstances of poor vision, the excitement and fear of combat, and the common appearance of hairstyles and buckskin clothing … the enemy could not be clearly seen and identified." He continued, "Comanche women had a reputation of fighting fiercely to defend their families and property, and some were possibly shot while using bows and arrows against the oncoming soldiers." Another unexplored possibility is while the white men "camped near the battle site that night," a few intrepid Comanche survivors might have returned in the darkness and retrieved some, but not all, of their dead. The disparity between Ross and Spangler's figures with those of Baker's would thus be explained. Moreover, Carlson and Crum refer several times to the slaughter of children, but the most reliable accounts do not mention youngsters being among the slain. Possibly, as Colonel Crimmins suggests, and Chalfant supports with a similar occurrence, Ross and the others were unable to determine the sex of Indians wearing buffalo robes and bearing arms while in the midst of battle. In all fairness, perhaps, after the brutal murders of six settlers the previous month, they were indeed not overly precise in identifying their targets. The blood of innocents was on the hands of white rangers and soldiers, and Indian warriors and women, in equal measures. Any fight near the dwellings of homesteaders or tribal bands was sure to touch those not directly engaged in the killing. Texas ranger Nelson Lee emphasized: "Texans had no other alternative than to return blow for blow, and to demand blood for blood." The available and reliable evidence is open to interpretation, and may allow one to blame the Texans for atrocities and excuse similar, or worse, excesses committed by Indians, or vice versa. The third option would be to realize the Texas borderlands were populated by representatives of two diametrically opposed cultures, and a bloody, fierce war of attrition for control of that same space was inevitable. As Doctor Stephen L. Hardin remarked, "Warfare in Texas was a savage, dirty pursuit, unrestrained by codes of civilized behavior."[40]

On the other hand, Carlson and Crum do clearly establish a politically ambitious Ross changed his story in order to promote himself to voters. Evidence provided below will reveal he was also not above shading the truth to conceal unpleasant personal details. Obviously not a shining example of probity, Ross the politician bears the blame for the modifications in his printed statements, but the contradictory and/or dishonest eyewitness accounts are the responsibility of those individuals alone. As documents relating to the Texas Rangers, and dating from 1920 to the early 1970s, have likewise disappeared from the State Archives, the absence of Ross's original report may not be the work of a conspiracy, but possibly nothing more sinister than simple negligence or pilfery. Since the statement was already available to the readers of the *San Antonio Express*, the theft of the original copy would not provide Ross's legacy much protection. Furthermore, Baker's dissimilar diary entries raise questions as to a possible motive for the changes, but the long-dead Ross cannot be blamed for this action. Despite the prevailing interpretation, the morass of fact and fiction that has typified the entire affair continues to ensure the absolute truth remains unknown.

Unaware of the arguments that would engage future historians, the governor was pleased with the results of the fight and with the young ranger captain. Meeting him in Waco on New Year's Day, Houston offered Ross a new commission when his current one expired. He directed Ross to discharge his men, reenlist those who wanted to remain in the service, and secure enough recruits to bring the company's strength to eighty-three. Houston assured him written orders would be forthcoming.[41]

Ross enrolled twenty men for the new company and waited several days for the promised orders, but none came. Finally, he took his recruits and returned to Fort Belknap. He discovered upon his arrival at Elm Creek that Captain William Dalrymple had been named aide-de-camp to the governor with the rank of colonel. Dalrymple's commission made him the ranking officer on the northern frontier and commander of all ranger companies posted there. Ross was organizing his new company as per the governor's stated directions when Dalrymple arrived at the post. The colonel was offended he had not been consulted and, professing to be unaware of any verbal instructions from Houston, chastised Ross for disobeying his orders. This quarrel prompted Ross to complete the organization of the company, then return to Waco to resign on February 5, 1861. Lieutenant Sublett was elected to replace him as company commander.[42]

Houston received the resignation letter on February 22. He immediately wrote Dalrymple and informed him of Ross's decision, but noted he refused to accept the notification. He also absolved the young captain of any blame

Sam Houston. *Courtesy Prints and Photographs Collection, Texas State Library and Archives Commission, Austin, Texas.*

in the misunderstanding. Houston wrote to Ross and requested the captain return to Elm Creek to take the field. In further recognition of Ross's service, the governor appointed him colonel and aide-de-camp.[43]

Events overtook the matter when the governor refused to appear before the Secession Convention on March 16 and swear allegiance to the Confederate States of America. The delegates declared his office vacant and appointed Lieutenant-Governor Edward Clark to take his place. Houston condemned the convention's actions as a usurpation of power, but chose not to use force to maintain the governorship. With sectional discord developing into outright rebellion, Ross, while no secessionist firebrand, chose to cast his fortunes with Texas and the South.[44]

In the three-month interval before Ross would go to war, he was busy with various pursuits. First, he and Elizabeth Tinsley married on May 28, 1861, in Waco. Then, cutting his honeymoon short, he accepted a commission from Governor Clark to lead a peace commission to the Indian Territory in order to secure friendly relations with the tribes across the Red River. He traveled to the Washita Agency, but found that Confederate officials had already negotiated a preliminary treaty with the Indians.[45]

Ross returned to Waco and spent several days with Lizzie before joining the cavalry company Peter was recruiting. Once the ranks were filled, the outfit was slated to join the regiment Barton Warren Stone, Jr. had been authorized to raise. Traveling to Dallas, the men had to wait almost one week before the mustering officer arrived from San Antonio. They then relocated to Camp Bartow, thirteen miles to the south near Lancaster. Returning from a short leave to Waco on September 1, Ross found that his name had been advanced for the position of major in the forthcoming election for regimental officers. In the meantime, Peter's company was enrolled into the Sixth Texas Cavalry as Company G on September 7; Sul enlisted as a private.[46]

Ross actively campaigned for the majority and defeated his two opponents in the election on September 13 by a margin of three to one. His new rank was to take effect on September 19. The other regimental field officers were Colonel Stone and Lieutenant-Colonel John Summerfield Griffith. According to family lore, Pease Ross, Sul's "ward," accompanied the major as his horse tender through all of the subsequent campaigns and "fought like the devil." Charles Goodnight later recounted, "Ross said he had no idea how many men the boy killed."[47]

The regiment took up the line of march on September 16, and Major Ross commanded the vanguard of three companies through the Indian Territory. The Texans arrived at the divisional headquarters of Brigadier-General Ben McCulloch near Maysville, Arkansas, on October 20. From there, the Sixth Texas was assigned to Colonel James McQueen McIntosh's brigade at Camp Davis. In addition to the Sixth, McIntosh's command was comprised of the Third, Ninth, and Eleventh Texas Cavalry Regiments, the First Texas Cavalry Battalion, and the First Arkansas Cavalry Battalion.[48]

The Texans had arrived at an uncertain time. The Confederate strategy in Missouri was hamstrung by "petty quarrels and jealousies" between Sterling Price and McCulloch, and by a dearth of intelligence on the enemy's location and composition. Price wanted McCulloch to join him in an all-out attack on the Union army, but the experienced ranger refused until he had more information. In order to gain knowledge of John Charles Frémont's forces, McCulloch turned to Ross, another bold Indian fighter with the suitable skills to lead a scouting detachment of five companies. Twice in the first weeks of November, Ross led reconnaissance parties around Springfield. Both times the scouts infiltrated the Union lines, gathered needed intelligence, and slipped out before Federal troops could close on them. Ross reported that Federal forces in Springfield, now under Major-General David Hunter, were awaiting orders to advance south. Before McCulloch and Price could agree on a plan of action, Hunter retreated to St. Louis on November 9.[49]

In early 1862, twelve thousand Union soldiers under Brigadier-General Samuel Ryan Curtis were marching on Springfield, forcing Price and eight thousand Missourians to evacuate the city. Retreating southward, Price joined McCulloch in the Boston Mountains country of northern Arkansas. The Federals were on Sugar Creek by February 18, near the rise in the ground known as Pea Ridge. Ascertaining the enemy supply lines were stretched dangerously thin, McCulloch gave free rein to Ross and five hundred cavalrymen from the Third, Sixth, and Ninth Texas Cavalry Regiments to raid behind the Union lines. The major's orders were to reconnoiter the Yankee positions, destroy wagon trains, and generally harass the opposing force.

Swinging around the left flank of Curtis's approaching army, Ross's ten companies rode north and west into Missouri on February 23 and slashed into the Federal rear. Three days later, seventy miles behind the lines, they swooped down on a Union supply train near Keetsville. Missing the opportunity to capture two enemy generals, the Confederates did, nevertheless, take eleven prisoners, appropriate more than sixty horses and mules, and destroy several wagonloads of commissary stores.[50]

On March 3, shortly after Ross's return, Major-General Earl Van Dorn, his old comrade from the Wichita Expedition, arrived to take personal command of the Army of the West. The new commander expressed confidence his sixteen thousand Confederate troops and one thousand Indian auxiliaries could effortlessly crush the extended Federal line. The army advanced and met the enemy at Sugar Creek. Van Dorn decided to avoid a direct assault and, instead, executed a flanking maneuver by sending McCulloch and Price up the Telegraph Road stretching from Bentonville to Springfield, and the Keetsville detour road to attack Curtis in the rear. On the fifth, the Sixth Texas advanced up a parallel road a few miles to the east in order to distract the attention of the Federals. The Third and Eleventh Texas Cavalry Regiments waited in ambush a short distance behind. After waiting in vain for several hours, Stone led his troopers to within two miles of the Yankee lines and captured thirty-six prisoners and seven wagons laden with corn.[51]

Beginning before sunrise on March 6, the movement around Pea Ridge, which took more time than expected, was discovered and Curtis was able to wheel his army to meet the threat. By daybreak of the seventh, McCulloch's division had reached the detour, but the Texan's men were separated from Price's Missourians by five miles of rough road. Thus, the Confederates were forced to fight on widely divergent fronts.[52]

Hearing the sounds of battle in the vicinity of Elkhorn Tavern, McCulloch's column readied themselves for the likelihood of fighting their way to the other wing's location. McIntosh's five cavalry regiments left the road in columns of fours and rode southwest through the heavy woods to engage potential threats. As they emerged from the growth into Wiley Foster's wheatfield, the Texans discerned the Third Iowa Cavalry and a masked battery of three guns on their right flank. The bluecoats opened fire with salvos of solid shot and, without hesitation, Colonel McIntosh ordered a daring charge on the Union guns and supporting cavalry. The Iowa horsemen rode to meet the advancing Rebels, but they were driven aside as McIntosh's troopers, shouting their loud Texas yells, overran the battery. Ross was commanding a battalion of three companies in the charge, and he reined in long enough to accept the surrender of the artillery commander. He then reformed his men and assailed the Union cavalry once more. The fighting became general near Leetown, and the other Rebel cavalry regiments were dismounted to bolster the infantry line. The Sixth Texas was ordered to constitute a mounted reserve near John Jay Good's Texas battery. While Stone's men were exposed to enemy fire as the battle ebbed and flowed, they took no further active role in the engagement.[53]

Generals McCulloch and McIntosh were both killed in the fighting. With their deaths, the Confederate effort on the west side of Pea Ridge evaporated, although Van Dorn continued the attack to the east on the morning of March 8. The endeavor failed, and Ross placed the blame squarely on Van Dorn's shoulders. The commanding general had overmarched and underfed his men before committing them to battle. He had also failed to adapt to unforeseen changes in the tactical situation, and neglected to share his plan of attack with either McCulloch or Price. With Van Dorn separating his forces, and preventing effective coordination and communications, Curtis had been able to use his interior lines to meet each Confederate wing and defeat them in detail. The Sixth Texas lost a total of nineteen killed, wounded, or missing. In a letter home, Ross remarked, "We whipped ourselves."[54]

The defeat made the chances of retaking Missouri impossible, and the Confederates were obliged to withdraw deeper into Arkansas. On March 17, Van Dorn ordered a reorganization of Colonel Thomas James Churchill's brigade, which was to be composed of the First Arkansas Mounted Rifles, and the Sixth, Ninth, and Eleventh Texas Cavalry Regiments. The brigade was to constitute a cavalry reserve under the army commander's personal direction.[55]

Later in the month, Van Dorn received orders to abandon northwestern Arkansas and move his 22,000 troops across the Mississippi. Their assignment was to reinforce General Albert Sidney Johnston in Tennessee following the latter's reverses at Forts Henry and Donelson. While on the march, the army's sixteen cavalry regiments, including the Sixth Texas, were detoured to Des Arc, Arkansas, on April 3. Arriving eleven days later, they were dismounted due to a lack of forage, and the horses were sent back to Texas. The order was a source of great resentment toward Van Dorn as the Texans considered the mounted arm their natural home.[56]

The disgruntled former cavalrymen were taken by steamboat to Memphis, arriving two weeks after the battle at Shiloh. While in the city, they learned the Confederate Congress had passed the Conscription Act of April 16 that extended the enlistments of those aged eighteen to thirty-five an additional three years. The new law also authorized a reorganization of companies, battalions, and regiments.[57]

Colonel Stone sought an appointment to brigadier general under the provisions of the act, and left his regiment to hurry to Richmond. So sure was he of success, he failed to campaign for reelection. The rank and file insisted Ross seek the office of colonel, but Lieutenant-Colonel Griffith also desired the position, and Ross was reluctant to deny him. He did, however, sign the regimental muster rolls as acting regimental commander in March and April. In the interim, the Sixth and Ninth Texas were assigned to Brigadier-General John Seldon Roane's brigade in Major-General Samuel Jones's division. The issue of the regimental command remained undecided when Roane's brigade was ordered to travel by rail to Corinth, Mississippi, a strategically vital junction of the Memphis & Charleston and Mobile & Ohio Railroads. Along with a portion of the Army of the West, they were to join the Army of Mississippi under the command of General Pierre Gustave Toutant-Beauregard, who had succeeded the slain Johnston. Once arrived, despite his protests, Ross found himself elected colonel on May 24.[58]

The situation for the Confederates in Mississippi was dire. Union Major-General Henry Wager Halleck was cautiously advancing on Corinth in overall command of Ulysses S. Grant's Army of the Tennessee, Don Carlos Buell's Army of the Ohio, and John Pope's Army of the Mississippi, totaling some 100,000 Yankee soldiers. The Sixth Texas skirmished several times with the enemy as Beauregard's 66,000 troops abandoned the town by May 30 and retreated south along the Mobile & Ohio Railroad toward Tupelo.[59]

Roane's brigade was reorganized in early June, and acting Brigadier-General Charles W. Phifer, a capable West Point-trained professional, took over the reins of leadership. Despite his misgivings over his promotion, Ross was emerging as a superb regimental commander. As General Phifer was often absent, Ross also commanded the brigade as the senior colonel. His name was recommended for promotion to brigadier himself several times during the summer of 1862. Indicative of the high regard Ross's superiors held for the young colonel, the Sixth Texas was the only regiment in the division scheduled to be remounted as soon as possible.[60]

Before the horses arrived in Mississippi, though, the regiment faced hard service on foot. General Braxton Bragg replaced Beauregard as commander of the Western Department on June 17. Van Dorn was ordered to take charge of the District of Southern Mississippi and Eastern Louisiana at Vicksburg, and "Old Pap" Price assumed leadership of the Army of the West at Tupelo. Shortly thereafter, Bragg led his force, soon to be renamed the Army of Tennessee, to Chattanooga in preparation for an invasion of Kentucky. While Bragg marched with 34,000 men to do battle with General Buell, Van Dorn and Price, with the remaining 32,000, were ordered to prevent a juncture of Grant's forces in northern Mississippi with Buell's in Middle Tennessee.[61]

The Army of the West marched toward Iuka, Mississippi, to prevent such a merger, and entered the town on September 14, on the heels of the retreating Federal garrison. The fifteen thousand hungry Rebels were able to seize a large amount of commissary stores from the Union supply depot. General Grant, wanting to relieve pressure on Buell, saw an opportunity to pin Price against the Tennessee River and destroy his army. He sent five divisions under Edward Otho Cresap Ord and William Rosecrans to attack the Missouri general before reinforcements from Van Dorn could arrive. Seeking to escape the trap, Price directed Brigadier-General Dabney Herndon Maury to fend off Ord three miles to the west while Henry Little's division sought to open the line of retreat blocked by Rosecrans south of town. However, Ord did not join in the battle on September 19, due to an oddity of nature known as an "acoustic shadow," which prevented him from hearing the sounds of battle just a few miles away. Most of the fighting occurred between Little and Rosecrans. Maury's division—including Ross's regiment—was held in reserve, and the struggle progressed without any real involvement from the Sixth Texas. After dusk, Price was able to extricate his army utilizing a road Rosecrans had failed to block.[62]

After its lucky escape from Iuka, Price's army retreated along the Mobile & Ohio rails until they reached Baldwyn on September 25. He reunited with Van Dorn at Ripley on the twenty-eighth and placed himself under the Mississippian's command. The Army of the West was reorganized as a corps under Price and formed part of Van Dorn's Army of West Tennessee.[63]

While Bragg was making his thrust into Kentucky, Van Dorn decided to recapture the crucial railroad junction of Corinth with a *coup de main*. On October 2, his 22,000 Confederates crossed the Hatchie River and, the following morning, attacked Corinth's earthworks in frontal assaults from the north and northwest. Amid stifling heat, Phifer's troops drove the Billy Yanks from their rifle pits between the two railroads to their second line of fortifications. The Sixth Texas was heavily engaged as they charged an enemy battery of nine guns supported by infantry. With their colonel in the lead, the dismounted Rebel horsemen strove bravely amidst a storm of grapeshot and shell, over *abatis* of fallen timber, and through rows of *chevaux de frise* into the redoubts from which the Union troops retreated. Once the guns were in Confederate hands, the Federals withdrew to their third and final line of defense. Enduring an hour-long bombardment from a dozen heavy cannons, the Sixth Texas was one-half mile in front of their lines and a mere three hundred yards from the enemy. Ross formed the men on the reverse slope of a hill and sent for fresh orders from General Phifer. The reply was for the Texans to hold the hill at all costs until the arrival of reinforcements. Fifteen minutes had passed when Ross discerned one thousand men moving out of the Federal breastworks and flanking his position. Seeing no fresh troops marching to his support, he reluctantly gave the order to abandon the hill.[64]

Commencing the second day of the battle, Maury's two brigades stormed Battery Robinett in the Union center amid a hailstorm of musketry and artillery fire. Ross's men charged across three hundred yards, and 150 fell before the works could be reached. Wielding bayonets and clubbed rifles, the Confederates took the stronghold from the Twenty-sixth Ohio Infantry, but were in a precarious position due to a lack of support. Despite being thrown by his

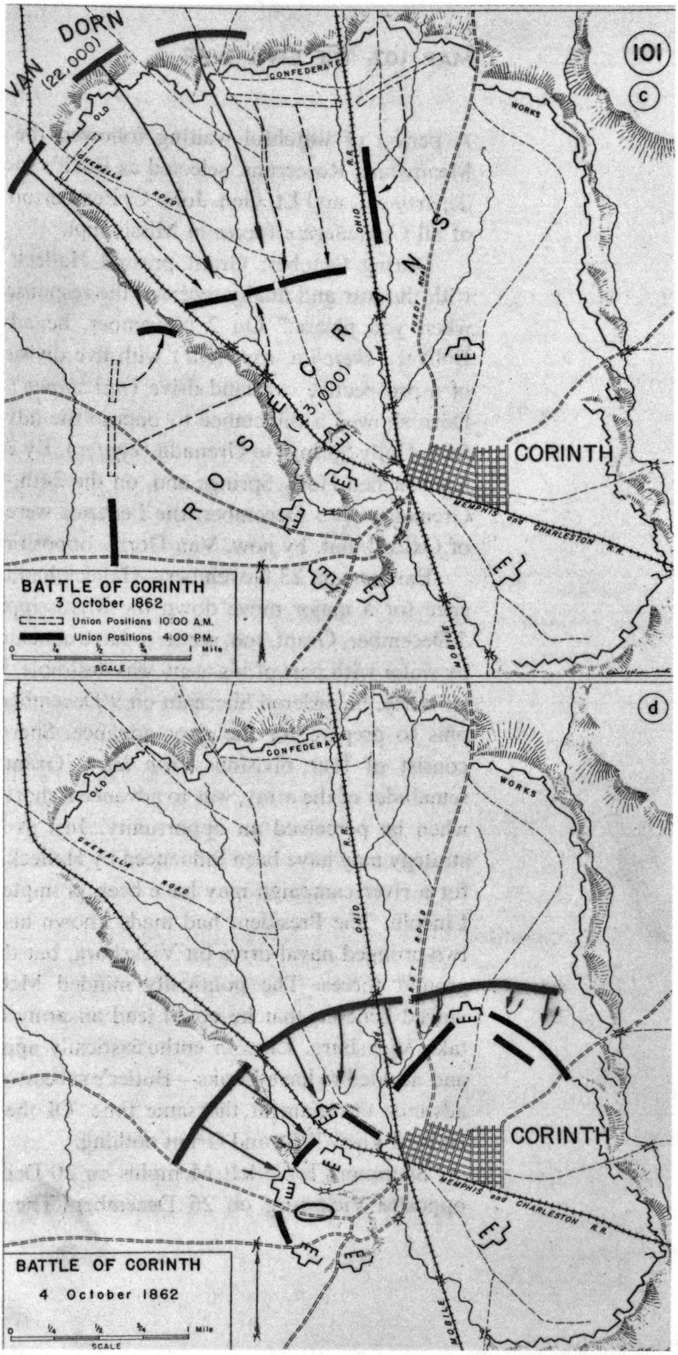

Map of Corinth. From *West Point Atlas of American Wars. Courtesy Geography and Maps Division, Library of Congress, Washington, D.C.*

panicked horse, Ross reached the parapet and was rallying his men when the Eleventh Missouri and Twenty-sixth Ohio counterattacked. The outnumbered Texans were forced to fall back, and Van Dorn soon ordered all of his forces to withdraw from Corinth. Maury's command was now a division in name only, having lost 2,527 out of the 4,800 present at the start of the battle.[65]

On the morning of October 5, the retreating Confederates arrived at Davis Bridge over the Hatchie River. They found themselves trapped between Ord's five thousand bluecoats on the opposite bank and Rosecrans's 23,000 at the Tuscumbia River bridge five miles away. While scouts searched for an alternate escape route, Van Dorn sent the surviving members of Maury's division, including the Sixth Texas, across the bridge to deter the Federal pursuers. As Phifer was ill, Ross was acting brigade commander, and he led his seven hundred troopers to support John Creed Moore's shattered brigade and six guns in attacking the Yankees. The Texans pressed the enemy for an hour, but were forced to pull back to the bluff on the opposite bank. After another crossing was discovered six miles south at Crum's Mill, Ross's men aided William Lewis Cabell's Arkansas brigade in delaying the Union pursuit. Rosecrans chose not to follow the retreating Johnny Rebs.[66]

As Van Dorn withdrew his army further into Mississippi, the Sixth Texas Cavalry was reassigned to Colonel John Wilkins Whitfield's brigade on October 23. They were joined by the Third, Ninth, and Twenty-seventh Texas Cavalry Regiments, and the long-awaited horses arrived on November 5.[67] Following a successful raid on the Union depot at Holly Springs in December, Van Dorn was appointed chief of cavalry in the Department of Mississippi and East Louisiana on January 13, 1863. Joseph Eggleston Johnston, commanding general of the western theater, made plans to detach him and his mounted troopers to Bragg's Army of Tennessee. His mission was to screen Bragg's left flank, disrupt Federal communications, and prevent the movement of enemy reinforcements from western Tennessee into the central part of the state.[68] By February 6, Van Dorn's mounted force consisted of two divisions totaling 7,455 sabers. Whitfield's brigade was part of the Second Division under Brigadier-General William Hicks "Red" Jackson. Brigadier-General Nathan Bedford Forrest's cavalry brigade was temporarily attached to Van Dorn's command.[69]

The following day, the cavalry corps made a hard march to Columbia, Tennessee, and spent the last days of the month skirmishing with small Federal detachments. On March 4, Jackson's division was moving toward Franklin on a "forced reconnaissance" when they engaged a Union infantry brigade and six hundred cavalrymen at Thompson's Station near Spring Hill. The opposing artillery batteries dueled for a time until the Yankee gunners drove off their foes. The engagement ceased for the night. The next morning, reinforced by the rest of Van Dorn's corps, Jackson's dismounted troopers were positioned along the hills overlooking the Franklin Pike. Whitfield's brigade was posted on the left flank, Frank Crawford Armstrong's on the right, and Forrest's deployed on the extreme right stretching into an open field. Whitfield placed the Third, Ninth, and Twenty-seventh Texas Cavalry Regiments along a stone wall fronting the Thirty-third Indiana Infantry's hilltop position, while the Sixth Texas and the Third Arkansas Cavalry moved ahead of the brigade beside the railroad. The Confederates charged across the valley through a fusillade of shell and canister, and assaulted the Federal line three times before they finally took the hill. Meanwhile, Forrest had moved his artillery and dismounted cavalry to the Union left flank and commenced a raking fire. The bluecoat cavalry and artillery escaped along the turnpike to Franklin, but the Rebels were able to capture twelve hundred Union infantrymen. Van Dorn's command suffered 357 casualties in total, of which the Sixth Texas's share was two killed and thirty-four wounded.[70]

On March 16, Van Dorn's cavalry corps was formally assigned to the Army of Tennessee, while his horsemen skirmished with the enemy during the third week of the same month. Ross's Texans scouted towards Franklin for enemy movement on the first of April. On the tenth, Van Dorn's 3,100 troopers conducted a reconnaissance-in-force along the Columbia–Franklin Pike. The Confederates discovered eight thousand Union soldiers and twenty guns positioned on the high ground to the north and east of the Harpeth River, principally on Figuers' Hill, and in the town of Franklin. Van Dorn sent Forrest's brigade up the Lewisburg Pike while he and Jackson's riders continued on the Columbia road. Van Dorn's column struck the town and drove the Federal garrison back to their positions north of the river. Major-General Gordon Granger, the Yankee commander, saw his chance to encircle and crush the

Rebel cavalry, but his own horsemen attacked before Forrest was fully in their net, and his infantry were too slow in surrounding Jackson. Van Dorn withdrew his men to Spring Hill before the trap could be set. While the Texas Cavalry Brigade was dismounted and fought in the battle line several times, they were mostly held in reserve.[71]

The month of May would bring a reorganization of the Confederate cavalry corps, and signal a change for Ross and his Texans. Van Dorn was murdered in his quarters at Spring Hill on the seventh by an allegedly cuckolded husband. As ranking officer, Jackson temporarily assumed command until, on May 19, he and his division were sent to support Vicksburg, then besieged by Generals Grant and William Tecumseh Sherman. Accordingly, Forrest was placed in charge of all Confederate cavalry in Tennessee.[72]

While marching to the city's rescue, Ross was embroiled in another conflict, this one over the brigade command. Before the division left for Vicksburg, Whitfield had gone to Richmond to seek promotion to brigadier. Successful in his petitioning, he returned to resume his command on May 21. Jackson thought Whitfield unfit for the role and asked General Joe Johnston, commanding the "Army of Relief" at Canton, to relieve him in favor of Ross. Johnston approved the request, and Ross formally assumed command of the Texas Cavalry Brigade on June 5, but Whitfield refused to leave the brigade's headquarters. Without delay, Whitfield appealed his case to the secretary of war, and the matter remained in question while Johnston's army sought to break through the Union cordon at Vicksburg. Ross's men were assigned to outpost duty from the Yazoo River to Baldwin's Ferry southeast of the Black River, and the colonel's headquarters was positioned near Bolton. Although Ross had proven himself the better brigade commander, and despite Whitfield's deteriorating health, the latter was officially confirmed in the command on June 17. The same day, the Sixth Texas was assigned to garrison Brownsville, Mississippi, and report on the movements of the enemy.[73]

Vicksburg fell on July 4, 1863, after forty-seven days under siege. While Johnston was forced to retreat beyond Jackson, Mississippi, the Confederate cavalry, including Ross and the rest of the Texas Brigade, steadily contested Sherman's advance into the central portions of the state. Between mid-July and mid-August, Ross led a composite detachment of the Sixth Texas combined with a battalion and a four-gun battery drawn from other outfits. Later, in order to utilize Ross's talents to the utmost, Major-General Stephen Dill Lee, the new cavalry chief in Mississippi, detached the Sixth Texas from Whitfield's brigade and, merging it with Colonel Robert Alexander Pinson's First Mississippi Cavalry, created a command expressly for Ross. Lee joined other senior officers in calling for the Texas colonel's promotion.[74]

Ross's new brigade was ordered to Pontotoc in late September, where his 894 men were reinforced to a total of eleven hundred soldiers. On the twenty-fifth, General Johnston instructed Ross, Samuel Wragg Ferguson, and James Ronald Chalmers to prepare 2,500 of their best troopers for a raid into central Tennessee. The campaign was supposed to be a coordinated effort with Major-General Joseph Wheeler targeting both Sherman's reinforcements and the railroads situated in Rosecrans's rear at Chattanooga. General Lee's horsemen were to be assisted by Philip Roddey's independent brigade in destroying railroad bridges over the Duck and Elk Rivers, but, instead, General Bragg sent Roddey's cavalry to attack a wagon train at Anderson's Crossroads. Lee arrived at the Tennessee River on October 6, where he expected to unite with Roddey for the planned raid. Instead, he met Wheeler's retreating cavalry and learned of their defeat at Farmington. Absent support from Roddey, Lee abandoned the campaign. In the end, the entire expedition was a haphazard affair that failed due to poor preparation and execution.[75]

Meanwhile, Federal columns under Sherman were moving along the Memphis & Charleston Railroad toward besieged Chattanooga. Ordered to the area to impede the Yankee advance, Jackson's four thousand men were encamped east of Tuscumbia, Alabama. While there, they skirmished several times with Union forces at Bear Creek. On October 21, at eleven a.m., the Rebels once more attacked the enemy cavalry and drove two regiments back to Cherokee Station, fourteen miles west of Tuscumbia, where the Southerners encountered two Yankee infantry divisions. From his headquarters on Cane Creek, Jackson was determined to hold the enemy and destroy the railroad as much as possible before he was obliged to withdraw. For six days, the Confederate horsemen stood their ground at Little Bear Creek against eight thousand Federals until they were outflanked and forced back to a position six miles east of town. Having occupied Tuscumbia, the Union troops were ordered to abandon their gains, leave the rails incomplete, and proceed toward Big Bear Creek. From Eastport, they were to take transports across the river. Jackson's riders attacked the rear guard at Cherokee Station on the twenty-ninth and, after a severe skirmish, retired before the main force. The Federals completed their crossing, then marched north of the river. Returning to northern Mississippi, Ross's troopers had been successful in their limited objective, but the fighting had done little to affect the overall outcome of the Chattanooga siege.[76]

Late in November, Lee's cavalry rode north from New Albany on another raid, this time to destroy the section of railroad recently rebuilt by Sherman to link the Union garrisons of Memphis and Corinth. Ross's brigade was sent after a Union raiding party on the twenty-seventh and met them at Ellistown. The Billy Yanks retreated so rapidly the Rebels could do little damage. In early December, Ross's troopers routed a numerically superior enemy force along the Memphis & Charleston Railroad at Salisbury, Tennessee, and pushed them from the town. Later in the evening, the Texans and Pinson's Mississippians tore two miles of track from the ground and burned the timbers. As the Confederates rode westward from the smoking railroad, Ross's brigade and another unit engaged four Federal cavalry regiments at Moscow, Tennessee, on December 3. The enemy brigade, commanded by Colonel Edward Hatch, was crossing a bridge over the Wolf River when the rebel horsemen struck. Attacking with great ferocity, Ross forced many of the bluecoats to spur their horses into the river to escape.[77]

Ross and the Sixth Texas were ordered back to Clinton, Mississippi, after Whitfield, whose health was steadily declining, transferred to the Trans-Mississippi Department. Colonel Hinchie Parham Mabry served as temporary brigade commander until Ross returned from Tennessee. General Lee then appointed Ross to the permanent command of the Texas Cavalry Brigade on December 16, and urged his advancement to brigadier-general. He would finally be promoted on February 5, 1864, to take effect from December 21. Until the end of the war, Ross's Brigade was comprised of the Third, Sixth, Ninth, and Twenty-seventh Texas Cavalry Regiments.[78]

Regrettably, the new brigade commander found his outfit was rife with discontent. To channel the rank and file's mutinous attitude into more positive avenues, Lee sent Ross's brigade to escort 34,000 badly needed muskets across the Mississippi River to Brigadier-General Alfred Mouton. On December 22, the brigade rode toward the vicinity of Greenville via the Yazoo Delta. The cavalry troopers slogged through freezing rain and muddy roads, while bogged wagons and cannons, not to mention the pitiful state of the draft animals, slowed their progress. Only by the superhuman efforts of the men did Ross move his artillery to Garvin's Ferry on the Sunflower River. Icy temperatures on the night of December 31 trapped the wagons in frozen mud five miles to the rear of the main body of cavalry, which made further movement impossible. Ross was not willing to abandon the mission, so each trooper took two muskets, and each officer bore three, to carry on horseback all the way to Gaines Ferry on the Mississippi. Because of Federal gunboats prowling the river, the weapons had to be conveyed across on one small boat over the span of three nights.[79]

After he accomplished this assignment, Ross set about completing his secondary objective of disrupting Union river traffic. The one artillery piece that had been able to accompany the brigade was positioned on the bank when twelve enemy vessels appeared on January 6, 1864. One transport was disabled, but it escaped to the opposite shore before the Rebels could seize it. Ross's men were suffering from exposure and hunger, and some were without footwear, so he led them back into the interior where shelter and food were more readily available.[80]

Before the Texans could go into winter quarters, Ross received instructions to take up position near Benton, Mississippi. His assignment was to guard the swollen Yazoo River and the Mississippi Central Railroad against a large enemy force concentrating at Vicksburg. The brigade reached its goal on January 20. From February 3 to the fifth, they repulsed heavy Federal assaults of cavalry and infantry supported by gunboats at Liverpool, Mechanicsburg, and Yazoo City.[81]

The enemy riverine traffic proved to be a diversion as General Sherman and 25,000 Union troops left Vicksburg on February 3 with the goal of capturing Meridian. Five days later, the Texas Cavalry Brigade rode to rejoin Jackson's division east of the Pearl River in order to protect the essential rail and supply center. Even though he had ordered his forces to contest the enemy's raid into central Mississippi, Lieutenant-General Leonidas Polk, commanding the Army of Mississippi, lost his nerve and withdrew his twenty thousand soldiers. William Wing Loring's and Samuel Gibbs French's infantry divisions fell back to Demopolis, Alabama, while Jackson's division rode north to reinforce Forrest. The movement proved unnecessary as the "Wizard of the Saddle" ably defeated a Federal cavalry column, riding out of Memphis to join Sherman, near West Point. Meanwhile, the Yankee commander occupied Meridian on February 14, and spent five days destroying railroad tracks, bridges, trestles, locomotives, and sawmills before returning to Vicksburg.[82]

Even as Sherman's men were devastating the railway, Ross's brigade checked the advance of a Federal raiding party at Marion Station near Meridian on February 17. His decision to uncover the Yazoo, although compelled by the tactical situation, exposed the country to enemy inroads, and approximately sixteen hundred white and black Union cavalrymen and foot soldiers seized Yazoo City on February 19. The bluecoats raided east toward the Mississippi Central Railroad and north to Grenada and Greenwood. They stripped the countryside of slaves, livestock, foodstuffs, and cotton before returning to Yazoo City on February 28. The same afternoon, a Texan scouting party encountered a squadron of the First Mississippi Cavalry, U.S. Colored Troops and withdrew before them to the brigade's bivouac near Benton. Ross ordered the Sixth and Ninth Texas to charge the forty black soldiers who, by then, were within three hundred yards of the campsite. The Union troops broke after the first volley and fled in "wild disorder"; eight were killed. The Confederates continued pursuing them until they neared the Federal fortifications at Yazoo City. When recovering the bodies of the First Mississippi, Union burial parties discovered six of the black soldiers "had been brutally used" after surrendering. Ross justified the murders by pointing out that two of his own men had been similarly executed at Mechanicsburg earlier in the month.[83]

After four days of haphazard skirmishing, Ross was reinforced on March 4 by Brigadier-General Robert Vinkler Richardson's brigade of 550 Tennessee cavalrymen. The following day, the thirteen hundred Confederates launched an assault that drove two thousand bluecoats from all but one

Nathan Bedford Forrest. Dry glass plate negative in the Brady-Handy Collection. *Courtesy Prints and Photographs Division, Library of Congress, Washington, D.C.*

fortification. In fierce, hand-to-hand fighting that lasted throughout the day, the Rebels took the city and captured seventeen prisoners and much needed supplies. Ross harshly demanded the surrender of the remaining redoubt on the Benton Road, then manned by the Eleventh Illinois Infantry and the First Mississippi Cavalry. The negotiations broke down when Ross would not recognize black men as legitimate soldiers. The disagreement became moot when Federal reinforcements arrived. Suddenly outnumbered, Ross prudently withdrew his troops to Benton.[84]

From there the Texas Cavalry Brigade was to move on to new battlefields. "Red" Jackson's cavalry division joined General Polk's army at Columbus, Mississippi, on April 13. Eager for a fight, Ross and his men were sent to Montavallo and then Rome, Georgia, on May 14. They were to aid General Johnston, by then commanding the Army of Tennessee, in opposing Sherman's drive through Georgia. Fielding the armies of the Tennessee, the Cumberland, and the Ohio, the Union juggernaut of 120,000 men sought to seize the vital industrial and railroad center of Atlanta, in conjunction with similar thrusts at Mobile and Richmond. Johnston was forced to withdraw to Adairsville, where Polk's cavalry united with the corps of John Bell Hood and William Joseph Hardee on the sixteenth. In the ensuing reorganization, the Army of Mississippi merged with Johnston's forces to become the Third Corps.[85] Ross's Texans were assigned to guard the crossings of the Oostanaula River above Rome and, on May 17, he received word the enemy was advancing upon the town. The brigade quickly raced for Rome and, once arrived, moved to the front. Fighting dismounted, the Confederates pushed the Yankee skirmishers back and attacked the main force, a Union infantry division. The Federal troops retreated in confusion nearly a mile, and the victorious Johnny Rebs held the field until they retired the next evening. The brigade lost fifty men killed and wounded in the encounter.[86]

For the next 112 days, while covering Johnston's progression of strategic withdrawals, the brigade was under fire almost daily. They fought in eighty-six actions at such places as Kingston, the Etowah River, Raccoon Creek, Stilesborough, Burnt Hickory, Dallas, New Hope Church, Lost Mountain, Big Muddy Creek, Sweet Water, Powder Springs, Shaw's House, Lick Skillet, and the Chattahoochee River. Many of the engagements were minor affairs, but each one cost the brigade in wounds and lives.[87] By retreating before the enemy for little to no gains, Johnston lost the confidence of President Jefferson Davis and was relieved of his command. On July 18, John Bell Hood was promoted to the temporary rank of full general, and appointed to lead the Department and Army of Tennessee.[88]

As part of his overall strategy, General Sherman directed Union cavalry to initiate a bold attack on the surviving railroad south of Atlanta. In a two-pronged movement, Brigadier-General Edward Moody McCook took four thousand troopers westward around the city, while Major-Generals George Stoneman and Kenner Garrard and five thousand horsemen went to the east side. The two wings were to rendezvous at Lovejoy's Station and together destroy the rail line from there to Macon.[89]

By July 27, Confederate army commanders were aware of the Federals' intentions. General Wheeler galloped east to intercept Stoneman and Garrard, while Jackson, with the brigades of Ross and Thomas Harrison, moved to strike McCook's column. Without informing his fellow commanders of any change in objectives, Stoneman decided to rescue Federal prisoners of war at Macon and Andersonville and so rode east and south. When Garrard reached the rendezvous point, and Stoneman failed to show, he led his troops back to their camp. Meanwhile, McCook's nine understrength regiments had a twelve-hour head start, and they were able to destroy a Confederate supply train and wreck portions of the Macon & Western and Atlanta & West Point rail lines before they could be brought to battle.[90]

On the evening of the twenty-ninth, Ross's gray-coated riders engaged the Federal troopers at Lovejoy's Station. The Eighth Iowa Cavalry struggled twice to punch through the encircling Confederates and both times were repulsed; they were successful on the third attempt and rode for the safety of the Chattahoochee River. Ross reformed his brigade and galloped after the raiders. Wheeler's column, having ridden to reinforce Jackson's two brigades, caught up with the enemy at Newnan the following day, and immediately moved to attack. Ross dismounted his brigade, sent his horses to the rear, and charged the Federals. The surrounded McCook ordered his men to cut their way through the Rebel lines. As one dismounted detachment of the Eighth Iowa fought Ross's troopers in fierce hand-to-hand combat, a greater number of men from the same regiment bore down on the brigade headquarters and captured a number of the officers, including Ross, and five hundred horses. Their detention proved short-lived as Wheeler's column counterattacked and freed the Texas general and his staff. Reclaiming their horses, the Texas Brigade rode to the rear of the enemy force and received the surrender of a sizeable portion of the Eighth Iowa. By this time, the Texans had been in the saddle and fought the enemy for three days and two nights at a cost of five killed and eleven wounded.[91]

Remaining southwest of Atlanta, Ross's understrength brigade was assigned to picket the fords of the Chattahoochee and guard the Atlanta & West Point Railroad. On August 16, a detachment of Brigadier-General Judson Kilpatrick's Federal cavalry raided the railroad depot at Fairburn and burned the building. Two days later, 4,500 Yankee horse brushed aside pickets of the Sixth Texas at Owl Rock Creek and attacked Ross's camp. Repulsed by the numerically superior enemy column, Ross remained in action, skirmishing with the Union troops until they reached Jonesborough on August 19. On the twentieth, Confederate infantry and artillery, as well as Frank Armstrong's brigade, joined Ross in confronting Kilpatrick's men at Lovejoy's Station.[92]

Kilpatrick found himself in the same predicament as McCook, and likewise had to fight to break free of the encircling Rebels. Ross's dismounted Texans blocked the escape route of two Federal brigades, and the Union commander ordered an artillery salvo that stampeded the Confederate horses. Six regiments of Yankee cavalry then charged Ross's men. The Third Texas held the line for a moment, pouring a volley into the oncoming Federals, and then, with no time to reload, retreated. Before they could reach the rear, the Union horsemen were upon the Confederates in a *mêlée* of kicking horses and hacking sabers. While the brigade was thought to have been annihilated, as soon as the Union column had ridden on, Ross ordered his bugler to sound assembly. Responding to the notes of the call, the humiliated Texans began straggling in from every direction. The brigade suffered two killed, twenty wounded, and thirty captured during the Kilpatrick raid.[93]

The Texas Brigade was back on the Atlanta & West Point line by August 22. Fighting continued until Atlanta fell on September 2, but Ross's men remained on the railroad for another three days. For much of the rest of the month, the Texans were on picket duty at Newnan and Decatur. The brigade's casualty list for the period of May 15 to September 4, 1864 included thirty-three men killed, 177 wounded, and sixty captured. On September 28, Ross temporarily assumed command of a division comprised of his brigade and that of Brigadier-General Samuel Jameson Gholson.[94]

Having lost Atlanta, the audacious Hood decided to seize the initiative from Sherman by cutting the extended Yankee supply lines to Chattanooga and Nashville, and by forcing the Federal commander to give battle on terrain favorable to the Southern cause. The Confederate commanding general and his 39,000 soldiers crossed the Chattahoochee River west of Palmetto on September 29, and the Tennessee River at Tuscumbia on November 20. Ross and the rest of Jackson's division were active in screening the advance and striking at the enemy's railways. While the plan succeeded initially, when the Army of Tennessee arrived at the place where he hoped to engage Sherman, Hood discovered his forces significantly outnumbered. Furthermore, ignoring the Confederate thrust into central Tennessee, Sherman had taken the cream of his armies and embarked on his historic march through Georgia toward the sea. Instead, Hood faced the stalwart general George Henry Thomas and seventy thousand Union soldiers.[95]

Major-General Forrest had been given command of all five thousand cavalrymen in Hood's army, including Jackson's division. Ross's brigade was part of the vanguard of the Confederate advance into Tennessee and, although the Texans only numbered 686 effectives, their fighting ability remained undiminished. On November 21, amid snow and an icy wind, Hood's troops marched north toward Columbia in order to seize Pulaski and keep Major-General John McAllister Schofield's Army of the Ohio separated from Thomas's Army of the Cumberland in Nashville. The next day, Jackson's and Brigadier-General Abraham Buford's cavalry engaged Federal forces at Lawrenceburg near Pulaski, and again at Campbellsville on the twenty-fourth. Two days later, Forrest's horsemen were at Columbia and invested the town until Stephen Lee, now commanding the Second Corps, arrived to take over. Unfortunately, the trap Hood envisioned failed to spring shut and Schofield evacuated the town on the twenty-seventh.[96]

The next day, the Texans mounted up and crossed Holland's Ford of the Duck River. They rode east on the Shelbyville Road where they repulsed a Federal brigade near Rally Hill and captured an entire company of the Seventh Ohio Cavalry. Forrest then dispatched Ross to pursue James Harrison Wilson's Union cavalry as they retreated northward toward Franklin. While following the Federal horsemen, Ross destroyed an ordnance train at Thompson's Station, and burned a railroad bridge. He turned his attention to the Columbia–Nashville Pike the next day, where his men blocked Schofield's wagon train for thirty minutes. In a nighttime raid, the Texans seized thirty-nine wagons laden with badly needed supplies. The Confederate horsemen were situated amongst Schofield and Thomas, but miscommunications between Hood and Major-General Benjamin Franklin Cheatham allowed Schofield's troops to march through Spring Hill and escape to Franklin.[97]

Ross also moved his brigade toward the latter town, arriving on November 30, just as Hood was commencing his costly frontal assaults on Schofield's fortifications. The main part of the action was centered on the outskirts of Franklin south of the Harpeth River, while Jackson's and Buford's divisions—three thousand strong—crossed the river to the east at Hughes Ford. The Texans quickly took the high ground a half-mile past the north bank and forced the Federal cavalry back upon their main body. However, Wilson had been reinforced to six thousand men, and Brigadier-General Edward Hatch's 2,800 dismounted troopers were armed with the seven-shot Spencer carbine, which they used to deadly effect. Ross sent the Ninth Texas forward, but they were repulsed with heavy losses. He was forced to put in the Third Texas to halt the Yankee counterattack. Jackson's gray-coated horsemen failed to dislodge Wilson's two divisions and, after two hours of fierce fighting, were forced back over the river. The shooting stopped all along the line late in the evening and, about three a.m., Schofield's men withdrew and marched for Nashville. Forrest's troopers were in the saddle the next morning and crossed the Harpeth in pursuit. The Texas Brigade was in front of Nashville on December 3, and picketed the Nolansville Pike until Hood's infantry arrived.[98]

Ross was not present in the field from December 5 to the twenty-third due to illness. Skirmishing with the Yankees at La Vergne and Murfreesboro,

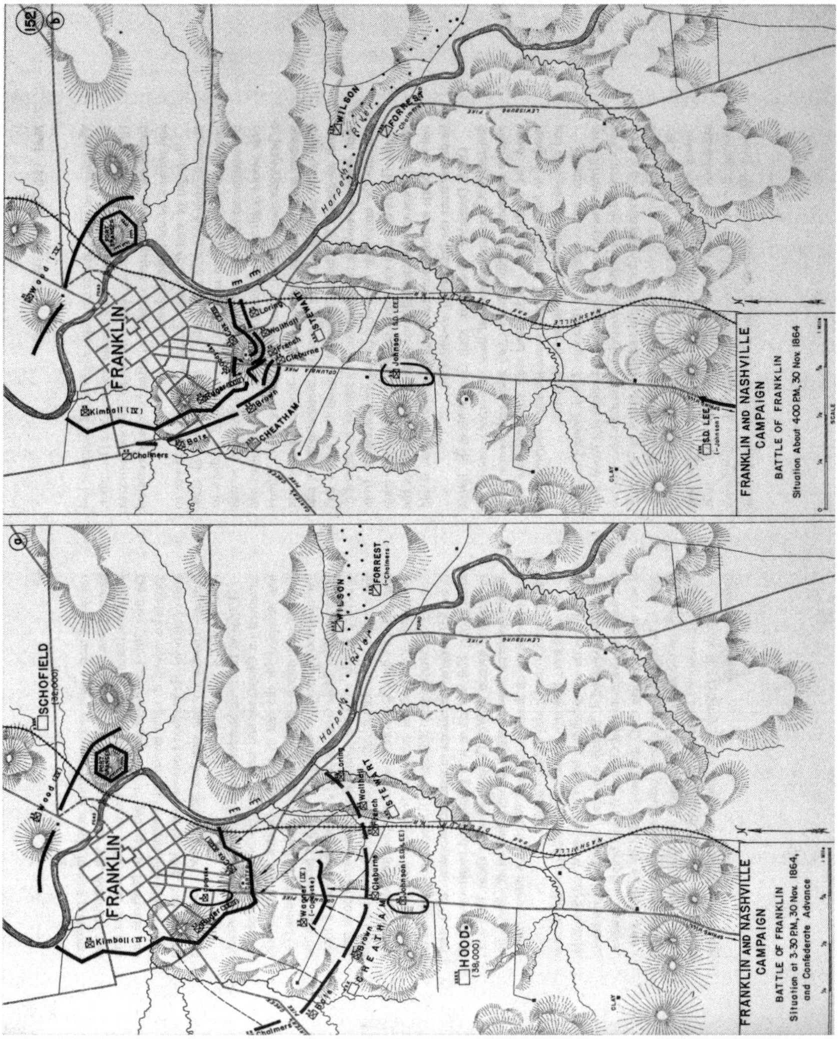

Map of Franklin. From *West Point Atlas of American Wars. Courtesy Geography and Maps Division, Library of Congress, Washington, D.C.*

the brigade under Colonel Dudley William "Dud" Jones was near the latter town on December 15 when Hood and Thomas met in battle at Nashville. Taking no part in the main encounter, the Texans instead captured a freight train of fourteen cars loaded with food and supplies. On the eighteenth, after Hood's disastrous defeat, Forrest's corps withdrew to the Columbia–Nashville Pike. They found the shattered remnants of the Army of Tennessee and provided protection from Wilson's nine thousand cavalrymen. Assigning Jackson's division and Major-General Edward Cary Walthall's eight under-strength infantry brigades to act as a rearguard, Hood led the rest of his army south in retreat on December 20. Alternating with Armstrong's brigade as the last unit in the column, Ross's men held off relentless attacks by the pursuing Union forces. The exhausted Rebels at last reached the safety of the Tennessee River on December 27. Once the Confederate army was in friendly territory, Forrest was assigned to command all cavalry in the Department of Alabama, Mississippi, and East Louisiana. The regiments of his cavalry corps took up positions across northeastern Mississippi. In this most recent campaign, the Texas Brigade had lost eighty-seven killed and wounded, and had taken 550 prisoners, nine stands of colors, and several hundred horses. In addition to the captures, the Texans were able to seize enough equipment, blankets, and coats to resupply all four regiments.[99]

On January 23, Hood was granted relief from the command of the Army of Tennessee, and he was replaced by Joe Johnston. Later in the month, and into early February, Ross's men were assigned to picket duty along the south banks of the Tennessee before being posted near Vicksburg, Canton, and finally Deasonville. For two or three days, the general took to his sickbed and had to be nursed by friends. Following this bout, he would suffer from chronic bronchitis for the rest of his life. On February 20, amid a reorganization of Jackson's division, half the brigade received sixty-day furloughs. Ross urged those returning home to recruit soldiers for the Confederacy, and to prevail upon deserters to return to the colors. The brigadier himself took ninety days of leave on March 13 and departed for Texas. Colonel Dud Jones assumed command of the brigade.[100]

Ross reached his home in Waco around the first of April. While the general was visiting family and friends, the fighting in the East was coming to an end at Appomattox Court House. By the time of General Johnston's capitulation on April 26, Ross doubtless knew the war was lost. His failing health led him to stay in Texas and recover before rejoining his men. Thus, he was not present when the Texas Cavalry Brigade surrendered at Jackson, Mississippi, on May 13.[101]

As Ross had not been present to submit his men to Federal authority, he also did not have the opportunity to secure his own parole. Due to this unfortunate circumstance, he faced possible arrest or the confiscation of his property, not to mention the loss of his civil rights, including the ability to vote and hold public office. Once his health permitted, Ross applied for amnesty in Austin on August 4, 1865. The request was approved on October 2, 1866, and Ross received his warrant of pardon the following July.[102]

By war's end, Ross had reportedly participated in 135 engagements, captured thirty stands of colors, and had five to seven horses shot from under him. Wearied by hard service and exposure, he put his uniform away and turned his energies to raising cotton, corn, cattle, and children. He owned 160 acres of rich bottomland on the South Bosque River west of Waco, and approximately five acres in town. Born to Ross and Lizzie in those early years was Mervin Hallum, on January 2, 1866; Lawrence Sullivan, Jr., on July 25, 1868; Florine, on October 3, 1870; and Harvey Bernard, on March 5, 1873.[103]

Ross was content to live a simple, quiet life on his farm and avoid political strife. His home in town sat in front of the Austin road, approximately near the intersection of Austin Avenue and South Thirteenth Street. The years after the war were hard, but his agrarian efforts proved fruitful as he was soon running a herd of ninety horses and sixty-five head of cattle. The region was abundantly fertile for wheat, cotton, and livestock, and Ross became prosperous by developing those markets. By 1874, he was overseeing 537 acres and raising thirty-five horses and ten head of cattle.[104]

Leaving his plantation for only one extended time during Reconstruction, Ross escorted his mother, his ward Lizzie, who had grown into an "accomplished and interesting woman," and other family members from Waco to Los Angeles in August 1870. Shapley and Peter had earlier traveled to California after the elder Ross had reportedly assaulted a Yankee soldier.

The Guns Were Silent. Oil on board painting by Don Stivers. *Courtesy Tracy Stivers.*

Returning home after a stay of a few weeks, Ross was working his land in 1873 when a delegation of citizens called on him to run for sheriff.[105]

Even as the county was transforming from a mainly stock-raising community to a diversified economy of agricultural production, manufacturing, and merchandising, Waco was still a wild and wooly frontier town which earned its unsavory reputation as "Six-shooter Depot." Cattle herds trailing to Kansas cowtowns began passing through the area in 1868. Over the next three years, some 600,000 to 700,000 head of steers were driven over the nearby branch of the Chisholm Trail. In 1872, the Waco Tap Railroad connected Waco to the Houston & Texas Central line in Bremond, and the town of 5,500 residents had experienced the countless saloons, gambling halls, and whorehouses accompanying either of the two events, not to mention the associated lawlessness. Across the Brazos from Waco lay the six thousand-acre Tomás de la Vega land grant. Desperadoes of every stripe hid from the law in this vast wilderness of scrub and creek bottoms. They lived by stealing timber and livestock, and previous attempts to bring them to justice had been unsuccessful. Associates of the outlaws were willing to commit perjury, or to participate in a jailbreak, while honest witnesses were intimidated from testifying.[106]

Ross agreed to run, and was elected sheriff on December 2, 1873, without having to campaign or otherwise solicit votes. Sheriff Peter McClelland vacated on January 12, 1874, and, upon taking the oath of office, Sheriff Ross began his campaign to impose law and order. His efforts were fully supported by the vigorous new county attorney, William Kendall. Ross deputized his brother Peter and several other men and set about clearing the outlaws out of the de la Vega grant. The Ross brothers arrested more than seven hundred offenders in less than two years, and, by September 1875, the McLennan County district court was reporting 455 criminal cases on the docket. The area was cleaned up by 1876.[107]

The grant was not the only source of concern for the sheriff. Among the men he and his other deputies D. C. McCowan and Robert Crowder arrested were Jack Benson, wanted for murder in Burleson County; a man named Fleming, who had fled to Hood County forfeiting his bond on a charge of cattle theft; William M. Eglin, indicted for murder and wholesaling and retailing liquor without a license; and two unnamed men charged with burglary. One noted desperado menacing the county was William Andrew Jackson "Tehuacana Bill" Posey, who was wanted for cattle rustling. Some years previously, Posey had been tried and convicted of mule theft in Judge Nicholas William Battle's court, but had escaped from his guards while walking back to the jail. The rewards for his apprehension amounted to fifteen hundred dollars. Even as Posey was on the run, his brother-in-law had been overseeing the fugitive's property and unwisely assuming ownership. In July 1873, the outlaw hung his larcenous relative from the limb of a tree and left him to slowly die of strangulation. To add to Ross's troubles, law officers brought in a badman named William A. Posey, only this second individual was proven to be not the Waco outlaw, but someone wanted in Lamar County for murder. At the end of June 1874, the Posey of McLennan County notoriety was finally captured at his farm twenty miles west of Muskogee in the Creek Nation. On July 8, the outlaw was brought to Waco under heavy guard, and the next day he was sentenced to five years in the penitentiary on the earlier conviction. Posey began his journey to Huntsville on the tenth, and Ross soon received word the notorious outlaw was securely confined.[108]

In addition to his vigorous work in McLennan County, Ross also looked for ways to improve law enforcement throughout the state. He was a leading organizer of the Sheriffs' Association of Texas, which met for the first time on August 14, 1874, at the Navarro County courthouse in Corsicana. Attended by sheriffs from sixty-five counties, the meeting was called to order by Ross. He immediately relinquished the chair to James Emerson Barkley of Dallas, who was elected permanent chairman. Ross joined the committee charged with drafting resolutions that articulated the purpose of the association. Ross publicly offered two declarations. The first was to encourage his fellow lawmen to "deprecate the spirit of mob-law, and lawlessness and crime …" and "use all the power and influence that we possess to enforce the laws and make them honored, respected and obeyed." The second was to call on the governor to pardon Constable Mathew Caldwell of Limestone County, convicted of murder five years previously, and release him from prison.[109]

In 1875, Governor Coke reasoned in his message to the Fourteenth Legislature that conditions were favorable for the successful repeal of the Constitution of 1869. During the second session, the lawmakers passed a joint resolution requiring an election be held the first Monday in August. The voters were to approve or reject the call for a convention to rewrite the document, and vote for ninety delegates, three from each senatorial district. If the meeting was approved, it was to meet on the first Monday in September in Austin. On August 2, fewer than half the registered voters went to the polls, but the convention was accepted by a majority of 29,934. On the same day, the citizens of the Nineteenth District, which at the time included Coryell, McLennan, Bosque, Hamilton, Brown, Coleman, Runnels, and Comanche Counties, elected the popular young Sheriff Ross to be one of three delegates to the convention. The other two were Indian fighter and surveyor George Bernard Erath of McLennan County and Confederate veteran James Richard Fleming of Comanche County.[110]

The delegates met in the Hall of Representatives at noon on September 6. After presenting his credentials, Ross took the oath of office. Among his preliminary committee assignments was waiting upon convention president-elect Edward Bradford Pickett and conducting him to the chair, ascertaining the officers and employees necessary to conduct business, and determining compensation for the delegates. On September 8, he was appointed to the Standing Committee on the Legislative Department. Later he was a member of committees on Revenue and Taxation, Apportionment, Frontier Affairs, Education, and public schools. Taking his duties seriously, Ross only missed five days of the sixty-five the convention was in session and cast 343 votes, missing or abstaining from voting only sixty-six times. As the convention reached its conclusion, Ross was chosen to be part of a committee to prepare an address to the citizens of Texas. When the body adjourned on November 24, Ross and his fellow committee members remained in Austin to finish their work. The constitution would be presented to the voters and overwhelmingly approved on February 15, 1876, by a count of 136,606 to 56,653.[111]

Having since returned home, Ross left the sheriff's office the same day the constitution was adopted. He resumed his life as a thriving farmer, and over the next four years exhibited scant interest in politics. His family continued to grow as Frank Ritchie was born on April 27, 1876, and Anne Elizabeth, known as "Bessie," arrived on April 24, 1878. His commercial pursuits remained prosperous as he worked not only his plantation, but also invested in numerous town lots.[112]

Ross resisted the efforts of friends to nominate him for higher public office, but he was involved in veterans' affairs. He had been instrumental in forming the Whitfield and Ross' Brigade Association and spoke at the first meeting on October 21, 1875. He also gave his support to establishing a written history of the Texas Cavalry Brigade. With the general's encouragement and financial assistance, Victor Marion Rose, a cavalryman under Ross, and later editor of the *Victoria Advocate*, published *Ross' Texas Brigade: Being a Narrative of Events Connected with Its Service in the Late War Between the States* in 1881.[113]

The general's future in politics became determined when the senatorial convention for the Twenty-second District, which comprised McLennan, Hill, and Johnson Counties, met in July 1880. The delegates were deciding between Captain Samuel Crockett Upshaw or Doctor Astyanax M. Douglass, both from Hill County, but neither man accrued the required two-thirds majority vote. After several days spent at an impasse, Ross was suggested as a compromise candidate. The committee unified on the recommendation and nominated him before adjourning. Despite his previous refusal to accept a political office, the nominee reluctantly consented to run. His opponent in the general election was Columbus Lee Wasson of Hill County, the Greenback Party candidate. Even though a contender belonging to the Democratic Party was assured a victory in the polls at that time, Ross surprised even himself when he won the election by approximately two thousand votes.[114]

Ross had just received his committee assignments and begun routine work in the Seventeenth Legislature when he received a desperate telegram from Lizzie. Their newest son, James Tinsley, born on December 30, 1880, was gravely ill. Perhaps not understanding the seriousness of the situation, Ross replied he was incapable of leaving the Senate, citing the press of his duties. Distracted by thoughts of home, he proved unable to contribute much to the session. On Sunday, he received the tragic news that James had died on February 3, 1881.[115]

Ross obtained an indefinite leave of absence and returned home. One week later, he was back in the Senate where he sought comfort from his grief through work. He served on the committees for Educational Affairs, Internal Improvements, Finance, Penitentiaries, Military Affairs, State Affairs, Contingent Expenses, Stock and Stock Raising, Agricultural Affairs, and Enrolled Bills. He was also a teller, and later in the session served on the committees involving Industries, Public Health, and the History of Texas. As reflected by his voting record, Ross was a Jeffersonian Democrat and a fiscal conservative. He introduced bills dealing with judicial and agricultural affairs, supported the placement of a prohibition amendment on the next statewide election, advocated the establishment of the University of Texas at Austin, and opposed wasteful government spending.[116]

When the legislative session adjourned, Ross hurried home in order to take Lizzie to a resort where she could recover her physical and emotional health. Afterward they returned to the plantation until the senate reconvened. Their last son, Neville Presley, would be born on March 23, 1882. Normally, the legislative houses would have waited two years before meeting again, but the State Capitol was destroyed by fire in early November 1881. The governor called for a special session, which assembled the first week of April 1882. The term lasted until May 5, and conducted extensive business concerning interim accommodations for state offices, including the state supreme court, the court of appeals, commission of appeals, and the state law library. A joint committee later examined suitable quarters for the legislature and the comptroller's and treasurer's offices. In this same session, Ross opposed land grants to railroads, supported a reduction in the poll tax, moved to destroy several unused engraved plates for state bonds, and served as chairman of the Finance Committee.[117]

Becoming more polished as a legislator, his voting record reveals he advocated simple, basic bills, and fought most amendments. He also usually opposed postponing consideration of legislation or early adjournment for the day. His endeavors could have continued when the Seventeenth Legislature met again in January 1883. Two days before the special session ended, though, the senate passed a reapportionment bill, which reduced Ross's four-year senate term to two years. Since he considered his duty to the public complete, he chose not to seek a second term. The two years Ross spent in the senate were significant in preparing him for higher office. He sharpened the political skills he had learned at the constitutional convention, furthered various alliances, and tested the mettle of his rival lawmakers. He gained considerable insight into the political process of the statehouse, and earned a reputation as an honest, hard-working statesman. Such a status would earn him popularity with his constituents in the years to come.[118] But even as Ross returned to Waco and resumed his home life, the family was again struck by tragedy. Going out into a blizzard after a doctor for his aunt, who was in labor, Mervin subsequently took sick and died of pneumonia on January 31, 1883, at the age of seventeen.[119]

Ross continued to oppose any gubernatorial nomination for himself but he maintained an interest in state affairs. Waco railroad attorney and

Democratic Party leader George Clark persisted in trying to persuade Ross to run for governor, usually by appealing to his sense of civic duty. Finally, in February 1886, Ross, to the intense satisfaction of his supporters, announced his candidacy in the upcoming election. He was opposed in the primary race by state comptroller Colonel William Jesse Swain, Lieutenant-Governor Francis Marion Martin, Major John Thomas Brackenridge of Austin, and Lieutenant-Colonel Dewitt Clinton Giddings of Brenham. The topic of Cynthia Ann Parker and her poignant life had once more begun to appear in Fort Worth newspapers in 1884 and 1885. Once Ross declared his intention to run for the governorship, articles and editorials concerning the candidate, both pro and con, were published throughout the state. Curiously, in a survey of Texas newspapers published in 1886, few were found to mention his role in the Pease River action.[120]

In an interview with the *Galveston Daily News*, Ross expressed his views on the various issues of the day. During the wide-ranging discussion, he opposed the inefficient leasing of public lands and encouraged their sale to homesteaders with minimal government regulation, favored the earmarking of monies derived from the land transactions for public education and their placement into interest-bearing securities, advocated the state penitentiary becoming as self-sufficient as possible, espoused his support for the Agricultural and Mechanical College of Texas, and disagreed with statewide prohibition, although he did endorse local option. An editorial published the following day expressed satisfaction with Ross's "broad and artistically constructed" platform and complimented the candidate on his ability to express his ideas "clearly and well."[121]

Clark, who also served as Ross's campaign manager, wrote of the candidate:

> He was a pure, loveable man, brave as a lion, but in politics quite timid. Twice during the campaign he became disheartened at the prospect and wanted to withdraw. There was nothing wrong with his candidacy and everything was progressing beautifully. Finally, he came to my office and declared his abandonment of the candidacy, but I only laughed at him for his timidity. He had no campaign committee, but left everything in my personal charge. I did not even employ an extra stenographer, but found my stenographer perfectly adequate for the work I had to do.[122]

The state convention met in Galveston on August 10, and the delegates spent the first session choosing a temporary chairman and organizing the committees. The following day the caucus nominated Ross, "the little cavalryman," by acclamation for the governorship on the first ballot. Thomas Benton Wheeler and James Stephen Hogg were selected for the offices of lieutenant-governor and attorney general, respectively, on the same ticket. In the general election on November 2, Ross was opposed by Doctor Archelaus Madison Cochran, the Republican candidate, and Prohibitionist Ebenezer Lafayette Dohoney. Despite his "timidity," Ross won 228,776 votes, while Cochran received 65,236 and Dohoney 19,186.[123]

The victor and his running mate swore their oaths of office on January 18, 1887. Shapley and Catherine were on hand for the ceremony and given places of honor from which to proudly watch their son. Later in the evening, the inaugural ball was held at the Driskill Hotel and hailed as "one of the largest and most fashionable gatherings ever assembled in a Texas ball-room." Once he assumed office, the governor quickly went to work and, among other appointments, nominated Wilburn Hill King on January 19 to be the new adjutant general. Two days after becoming chief executive of Texas, Ross gave his first address to the Twentieth Legislature and laid out his vision for the state. The speech was translated into Spanish, German, and Bohemian, an indication of the sources for Texas's recent population growth. During his four years in office, Ross remained interested in fiscal conservatism and proposed reforms in land policy and public education, advocated relief for thirty thousand people suffering from the severe drought, oversaw the construction and dedication of a new state capitol building, inhibited fence-cutting and mob rule, enforced anti-trust laws and regulation of the railroads, recommended pensions for indigent Confederate veterans, and promoted interest in Texas tourism and investment.[124]

Deciding to run for a second term, Ross was unopposed for the office by the Republicans or members of his own party. His only challenger, Marion Martin, was backed by a coalition of Prohibitionists, Knights of Labor, and radical members of the Farmers' Alliance. In the end, Ross crushed his opponent by 250,388 votes to 98,447.[125]

Ross's second inauguration was held on January 15, 1889, at the nearly completed capitol. He and Lieutenant-Governor Wheeler were announced in the chamber of the House of Representatives, where they were sworn into office by Judge Norman Goree Kittrell.[126] In his biennial message to the Twenty-first Legislature, the governor praised the Frontier Battalion, the successor to the Texas Ranger heritage he and others had helped to forge in the antebellum years:

> I have found the use of this force at my command—a most important and indispensable agency for the better protection of the laws. They have proven most excellent conservators of the peace, and of incalculable value in preserving human life and property. Whenever there has been a demonstration, having the semblance of organized resistance to the law, and an application was made by the local authority, setting forth the necessity of their use in support of civil power, these gallant men have with cheerful alacrity responded to every call made upon them, and by this exhibition of firm purpose to suppress all unlawful practices, tranquility has been maintained without the effusion of blood or loss of life.[127]

While traveling on state business to Washington and New York in the spring of 1890, Governor Ross fascinated newspapermen with his own ranger service. He was warmly received at a dinner party held at the famous Delmonico's restaurant, where, during coffee and cigars, he gave an impromptu speech. Although his central aim for the trip east was to invite former President and Mrs. Grover Cleveland to the forthcoming Texas State Fair and Dallas Exposition, he agreed to be interviewed by a *New York Herald* reporter to whom he recounted the thrilling experiences of his youth.[128] As the *Galveston Daily News* noted:

> The enforcement of the laws … the protection given property and life have been recognized, and the state is in a better condition in every way now than it has ever been in its history … [Ross] is considered a marvel in having succeeded in developing from a ranger boy into a governor … The ranger is, of course, considered … as a man who has more fight than polish, more bravery than education. So when they have seen the governor their wonder is great."[129]

Even before his second term ended at the end of January 1891, Ross was offered the presidency of the struggling Agricultural and Mechanical College at Bryan. In existence since 1876, the school had functioned without a formal president up to this point in time. Long a champion of higher education, he accepted on August 8, 1890, and formally assumed his new office on February 1, 1891. He would remain in this position for the rest of his life.[130]

Ross's tenure as president would transform the college from an obscure school to a leading institution. Due to his personal popularity in the state, enrollment in the first two years increased exponentially. The dormitories boasted 109 rooms capable of housing 250 students. By 1893, a total of 343 arrived before registration could be stopped. As journalist and author Clarence N. Ousley noted, "it is not too much to say that many parents sent their sons to Sul Ross rather than to college." New ground was broken in a series of building projects, including residences to accommodate staff members, the Ross Hall dormitory built in 1892, mechanical engineering shops constructed the same year, the first power plant and the President's Home in 1893, and a twelve-thousand-seat mess hall in 1897. Other improvements included a wood shop, blacksmithy, ice plant, steam laundry, waterworks, and natatorium. Upon Ross's recommendation, the legislature appropriated five thousand dollars for a scholarship fund. The Scott Volunteers had formed in 1887 as a ceremonial drill company of students, and the group changed its name in 1891 to the Ross Volunteers to honor the new college president. After Ross's death, the designation of the organization reflected each successive president until 1905 when the title Ross Volunteers became permanent. Since its inception, the company has served as the governor's honor guard and each executive's official escort on inauguration day.[131]

Despite the press of his collegiate duties, Ross continued to be involved in supporting his wartime comrades. On April 6, 1893, at the annual Texas United Confederate Veterans reunion in Dallas, he was elected the Texas Division's major-general. He was reelected the following two years in Houston and in Waco over his fervent objections. He was finally succeeded in the office by Colonel Hannibal Honestus Boone on May 24, 1895. That same year, Governor Charles Allen Culberson offered Ross a seat on the Railroad Commission. He accepted, but the clamor of Brazos County citizens begging him to stay was so great, he relented and remained at the helm of the college.[132]

During the Christmas break of 1897–1898, Ross, Neville, and several friends traveled to the Navasota River bottoms to hunt deer. The trip went well until the college president began suffering from acute indigestion and severe chills. Leaving the others to continue the hunt, he returned home to College Station on December 30. His condition fluctuated, and he died on January 3, 1898. The exact cause of Ross's death remains unknown, but Judith Ann Benner, his second major biographer, theorized he died of a coronary heart attack brought on by physical exertion in the chilly weather, ingestion of an indigestible meal, and the emotional stress of the hunt. Another diagnosis was that death occurred due to "acute congestion of the stomach and bowels."[133] The following morning, the body of Lawrence Sullivan Ross lay in state in the assembly hall of the college. He was then escorted to Waco by the entire student population. His comrades of the United Confederate Veterans gathered in their old gray uniforms and formed an honor guard. With five thousand mourners in attendance, he was buried next to his father in the family plot in Oakwood Cemetery.[134]

Within days of his death, various parties began to call for the erecting of a memorial to the former governor. Perhaps the most recognizable sight on the College Station campus is the statue of Ross, built by Pompeo Coppini and dedicated on May 4, 1919. Since that time, the statue, known as "Sully," has become a shrine for generations of Aggies. The university has numerous long-held traditions and a particular one is that students often place coins at Ross's feet for good luck on exams or other important activities.[135]

In 1917, an act of the Thirty-fifth Legislature created a new normal college in Alpine to train teachers. Named Sul Ross State Normal College in honor of the late Texas Ranger, Confederate general, governor, and educator, the school opened its doors on June 14, 1920. The institution currently operates as Sul Ross State University.[136]

Elizabeth returned to Waco where she lived at the family residence. The former First Lady of Texas remained popular with the public. Still mourning her loss, she was stricken with partial paralysis affecting her left side on April 26, 1905. She rallied for a time before her death at Florine's home on June 8. After a funeral service at Austin Avenue Methodist Church, she was buried in Oakwood Cemetery at her husband's side.[137]

Remaining in California, Lizzie married saloonkeeper and shooting gallery owner Pierre Loiseau in Los Angeles on June 5, 1876. Numerous sources relying on Sul Ross's accounts assert Lizzie married a prosperous merchant, but, although scant in their number, period newspaper articles suggest otherwise. By this time a political figure in Austin, Ross may have been embarrassed that his adopted daughter would wed a man who was several times a defendant in court cases alleging he had kept a disorderly house, violated the Sunday blue laws, or sold liquor without a license. On a lighter note, Pierre was also known for the cork leg he used with as much skill as a real one. Few established facts exist of Lizzie's life in California, and she and her son were thought to have both died in 1886. Her final resting place is unknown.[138]

Much of Pease Ross's life is similarly unclear and difficult to resolve. After the close of the Civil War, Ross stated his "ward" was given an education and offered the choice of returning to his people or remaining with the Ross family; he chose to stay in Waco. Pease made trips to Kansas as a trail driver, and was said to have married Texana Manning in 1878, although this last detail is most likely false. Pease and Texana were further alleged to have engaged in a romantic liaison that produced one son, although neither the relationship nor the paternity of her child can be confirmed. Public records do reveal Texana married Kisic Thomas, a black man nine years her senior, on October 3, 1878, while pregnant with a boy who was born three months later. While not absolute proof, the death certificate for her first-born child lists "Willie Ross" as the name of the father. Whether "Willie" is a name Pease assumed in his adulthood, or someone completely different remains a mystery. One theory posits the wedding occurred because Texana would have been shamed by an out-of-wedlock child fathered by an Indian. Texana's father was William "Buck" Manning, former slave of the Reverend William Manning and influential patriarch of the county's freedman community. Her honor, and that of the family, was publicly preserved by her marriage to Kisic. The possible circumstances of his failed love affair, and the peculiar place Pease would have had in Waco society, may have driven him into self-destructive behavior. Described as a "respected citizen," he nevertheless had at least one run-in with the law for fighting and drinking. The year of his death remains uncertain, possibly in 1883, 1885, or 1887.[139]

The rest of Sul's children led much more verifiable lives. Lawrence Jr. married Mary E. "Mollie" Duffield in Austin on May 19, 1891; they had no children. Living in Waco, he was engaged in the wholesale grocery business and in insurance. Moving to Harlingen in May 1909, he was president of the Harlingen State Bank, a farmer and real estate agent, and the town mayor. While traveling home on a train from Mineral Wells on October 7, 1914, he suffered a bout of paralysis and was taken to a Houston hospital. He died the next day of Bright's disease and apoplexy. His body was transported to Waco that night, and was buried in Oakwood Cemetery.[140]

Florine married Doctor Henry Hill Harrington in Bryan on August 10, 1892, and bore him one son. Her husband was a professor of chemistry and mineralogy at Texas A&M until he was elected president of the college in 1905. Harrington resigned in 1908, and went to work for the University of Texas and the Railroad Commission. Florine and Henry moved to Mercedes in 1921. Dying in August 1939 of pneumonia, he was buried at Cedarvale Cemetery in Bay City. While a patient at Matagorda General Hospital, Florine died of toxemia from ulcerative cellulitis on her arm on October 7, 1945. She was buried at Cedarvale Cemetery the following day.[141]

Harvey married Maude Lee Higdon on March 1, 1897, and fathered five children, although only two sons survived into adulthood. He supervised the family plantation, and worked as manager of the Texas Traction Company in Waco. Suffering from hypertension, he died of a cerebral hemorrhage on October 18, 1944, in Marlin, and was buried in Oakwood Cemetery.[142]

Frank attended Texas A&M at age fifteen, and the University of Virginia the following year. While a student in College Station, he enlisted in the Sixth Infantry Regiment, Texas Volunteer Guard. In 1898, he was recommended for the position of adjutant with the rank of first lieutenant. After receiving his medical degree from Tulane University, he performed postgraduate work in Vienna, Austria. He then served as second assistant physician and superintendent at the State Lunatic Asylum in Austin before becoming assistant city health officer in Houston in 1904. Among his many duties, he worked to eradicate a yellow fever outbreak, and conducted an inspection of Monterrey. He married Mary Cummins Stuart on April 30, 1907, and fathered two daughters. He was also a member of the Waco Medical Association. Frank left government service effective December 1, 1910, to pursue a private psychiatric practice. Diagnosed with a lung abscess on November 22, 1938, he died at Methodist Hospital on December 4, and was buried in Seabrook Cemetery two days later.[143]

Bessie attended Waco Female College and H. Sophie Newcomb Memorial College in New Orleans. She married businessman and rancher Frank Clarke on September 21, 1898, in Bryan, and bore him two sons and one daughter. She died of septicemia on July 25, 1932, at Providence Sanitarium, and was buried at Oakwood Cemetery the following day.[144]

Neville attended Texas A&M and Baylor University, graduating from the latter. He received a commission of second lieutenant in the Texas National Guard on June 18, 1901, and promoted to captain of Company K, Second Infantry Regiment on June 2, 1902. He engaged in the cotton industry in Waco and ranched in Midland County, where he married Dorothy Dale Patton on June 30, 1909. They would have no children. After farming in Andrews County, he worked for the Texas Power & Light Company for twenty-three years, ending his career as a right-of-way supervisor in Dallas. After suffering a nervous breakdown, he shot himself in the head on August 7, 1938. An inquest held the following day ruled his death a suicide. He was buried in Oakwood Cemetery.[145]

Lawrence S. Ross would wear the mantle of a Texas Ranger captain for only a brief time. Those same years would refine his character and hone his sense of leadership so that he could undertake a brilliant career of service to Texas. As a Confederate brigade commander, sheriff, legislator, governor, and university president, his contributions and accomplishments would bring him honor and respect, and benefit his state immeasurably.

Endnotes

Abbreviations

BCAH: Briscoe Center for American History
FTRA: Former Texas Ranger Association
HML&HC: Haley Memorial Library and History Center
NARA: National Archives and Records Administration
PPHM: Panhandle-Plains Historical Museum
RG: Record Group
SJMH: San Jacinto Museum of History
TGLO: Texas General Land Office
TRHF&M: Texas Ranger Hall of Fame and Museum
TSLAC: Texas State Library and Archives Commission

**Note: In order to abbreviate references for sources found in the Texas State Archives, this author has adopted, in part, Robert Utley's method of citing the record group followed by the box number: e.g. 401–178 denotes Record Group 401 (Adjutant General's office), box 178.

Notes for Chapter 1

1. Gregg Cantrell, *Stephen F. Austin: Empresario of Texas* (New Haven: Yale University Press, 1999), 18–22, 23–27. Cantrell has written the most authoritative biography of Stephen Austin to date, although his work deals only superficially with the Texas colony's frontier troubles. David B. Gracy II, *Moses Austin: His Life* (San Antonio: Trinity University Press, 1987), 11, 21, 22, 24, 27, 29–37, 42–43, 52, 65, 68–73, 78, 79, 117; Dudley G. Wooten, *A Comprehensive History of Texas, 1685 to 1897* (Dallas: William G. Scarff, 1898), 1: 440; James L. Haley, *Passionate Nation: The Epic History of Texas* (New York: Free Press, 2006), 67. See also George P. Garrison, "A Memorandum of M. Austin's Journey from the Lead Mines in the County of Wythe in the State of Virginia to the Lead Mines in the Province of Louisiana West of the Mississippi," *American Historical Review* 5 (April 1900): 518–542.
2. Cantrell, *Stephen F. Austin*, 30–40, 45–49; Eugene C. Barker, ed., *The Austin Papers* (Washington, D.C and Austin, 1924–1928),

1: 93–96, 195; Gracy, *Moses Austin*, 115–116, 128–132, 136–137, 165; M. Austin to S. F. Austin, April 28, 1812, Moses and Stephen F. Austin Papers, Series II, Pt. 1, Box 2Q412, BCAH.

3. Gracy, *Moses Austin*, 165; Gillum Ferguson, *Illinois in the War of 1812* (Urbana: University of Illinois Press, 2012), 136–144; Kate L. Gregg, "The War of 1812 on the Missouri Frontier," *Missouri Historical Review* 33 (January 1939): 187, 190, 196–198; Index to Compiled Service Records of Volunteer Soldiers Who Served During the War of 1812, Col. McNair's Mounted Illinois and Missouri Militia, Stephen F. Austin; *Missouri Gazette and Public Advertiser*, August 7, 1813; Frederic L. Billon, *Annals of St. Louis in its Territorial Days, from 1804 to 1821* (St. Louis, MO: Printed for the author, 1888), 48–49, 51–52.
4. Cantrell, *Stephen F. Austin*, 63–68, 69–71, 77; Eugene C. Barker, *The Life of Stephen F. Austin, Founder of Texas, 1793–1836* (New York: Da Capo Press, 1968), 23–24; Gracy, *Moses Austin*, 179–180, 181; Barker, ed., *Austin Papers*, 1: 329, 327, 330–331, 333–334, 337, 342–346, 358–359; 2: 76–78; Robert L. Jones and Pauline H. Jones, "Stephen F. Austin in Arkansas," *Arkansas Historical Quarterly* 25 (Winter 1966): 337–339, 340, 341–342, 344, 345, 347; Wilson to Bryan, March 12, 1819, Deed Agreement, June 16, 1819, Austin Papers, Series II, Pt. 2, Box 2Q412, BCAH. In 1811 and 1812, the region around the Mississippi River town of New Madrid was rocked by a series of devastating earthquakes. Owners of real estate damaged by the seismic upheaval received certificates permitting them to relinquish their New Madrid properties and relocate to other public lands. The process became rife with fraud, speculation, and litigation. For more on the New Madrid land certificates, see Conevery Bolton Valencius, *The Lost History of the New Madrid Earthquakes* (Chicago: University of Chicago Press, 2013).
5. Cantrell, *Stephen F. Austin*, 53, 68–69, 72–73, 87, 90–91; Gracy, *Moses Austin*, 182–191; Barker, ed., *Austin Papers*, 1: 93–94, 216, 218–219, 232–233, 234; Dorothy B. Dorsey, "The Panic of 1819 in Missouri," *Missouri Historical Review* 29 (January 1935): 80–83, 85; Murray N. Rothbard, *The Panic of 1819: Reactions and Policies* (New York: Columbia University Press, 1962), 84; Breckenridge Jones, "One Hundred Years of Banking in Missouri, 1820–1920," *Missouri Historical Review* 15 (January 1921): 348, 352, 353, 357, 361, 365; Billon, *Annals of St. Louis*, 85, 86, 87. See also Hattie M. Anderson, "Frontier Economic Problems in Missouri, 1815–1828," *Missouri Historical Review* 34 (January 1935): 38–70.

6. Cantrell, *Stephen F. Austin*, 71–72, 77–78; Barker, ed., *Austin Papers*, 1: 365–366; Jones and Jones, "Stephen F. Austin in Arkansas," 348, 350; *Arkansas Gazette*, February 12, July 15, October 28, 1820.
7. Cantrell, *Stephen F. Austin*, 73–75; Gracy, *Moses Austin*, 200; John Henry Brown, *History of Texas, from 1685 to 1892* (St. Louis, MO: L. E. Daniell, 1892), 1: 75–80, 101; Ed Bradley, *"We Never Retreat": Filibustering Expeditions into Spanish Texas, 1812–1822* (College Station: Texas A&M University Press, 2015), 178–196; Haley, *Passionate Nation*, 71; *Arkansas Gazette*, June 3, November 11, 1820. Years later, Stephen Austin would characterize the actions of himself and his father in 1819 and 1820 as stages in a carefully executed strategy to colonize Texas. Available evidence suggests rather that the scheme was originally all Moses's doing and Stephen was in New Orleans to escape his legal and financial troubles. Cantrell, *Stephen F. Austin*, 75–76, 78.
8. Gracy, *Moses Austin*, 3–4, 201–203; Barker, ed., *Austin Papers*, 1: 370–371; H. W. Brands, *Lone Star Nation: How a Ragged Army of Volunteers Won the Battle for Texas Independence—and Changed America* (New York: Doubleday, 2004), 19–22; Bradley, *"We Never Retreat"*, 200–208; William C. Davis, *Lone Star Rising: The Revolutionary Birth of the Texas Republic* (College Station: Texas A&M University Press, 2004), 55, 61; Pekka Hämäläinen, *The Comanche Empire* (New Haven: Yale University Press, 2008), 187, 190; Mary Austin Holley, *Texas* (Austin: Texas State Historical Association, 1985), 310. The "baron" was born Philip Hendrik Nering Bögel in Paramaribo, Dutch Guinea, on November 23, 1759. For more on this pivotal figure, see Charles A. Bacarisse, "Baron de Bastrop," *Southwestern Historical Quarterly* 58 (January 1955): 319–330. In a bitter irony, "it was the Comanches, and the Apaches, that initially destabilized the region for the young government of Mexico, and it becomes clear that the Comanches were instrumental in determining the long-term political history of the state. In this regard, Comanches were also instrumental in creating the conditions of their own defeat by opening the state to Anglo settlement." Andrew McKee Jones, "Comanches and Texans in the Making of the Comanche Nation: The Historical Anthropology of Comanche-Texan Relations, 1803–1997" (Ph.D. dissertation, University of Wisconsin-Madison, 1997), 73.
9. Cantrell, *Stephen F. Austin*, 81–82, 3–4, 87–88, 90–91; Gracy, *Moses Austin*, 205–207, 208–209, 214–215; Barker, ed., *Austin Papers*, 1: 373–374, 379–380, 381, 393, 401; *St. Louis Enquirer*, June 16, 1821;

Gregg Cantrell, "The Partnership of Stephen F. Austin and Joseph H. Hawkins," *Southwestern Historical Quarterly* 99 (July 1995): 4. Despondent after the death of her husband, Maria passed away on January 8, 1824. Barker, ed., *Austin Papers*, 1: 799–800, 854; Gracy, *Moses Austin*, 220.

10. Cantrell, *Stephen F. Austin*, 88, 91–94, 96, 98; Barker, ed., *Austin Papers*, 1: 397–398, 401–402, 427; Stephen F. Austin, "Journal of Stephen F. Austin on His First Trip to Texas, 1821," *The Quarterly of the Texas State Historical Association* 7 (April 1904): 286–288, 296; *Arkansas Gazette*, September 29, October 6, 1821; Wooten, ed., *Comprehensive History of Texas*, 1: 470–472; Brands, *Lone Star Nation*, 66, 67–68; Haley, *Passionate Nation*, 72–73. For an example of the permits Austin offered to the settlers, see Ernest W. Winkler, ed., *Manuscript Letters and Documents of Early Texians, 1821–1845* (Austin: The Steck Company, 1937), 6.
11. Cantrell, *Stephen F. Austin*, 99–101, 103, 108–109; Barker, *Life of Stephen F. Austin*, 41; Barker, ed., *Austin Papers*, 1: 428–429, 419–21, 415, 422–423, 432–433, 435–436, 2: 860–861; Cantrell, "The Partnership of Stephen F. Austin and Joseph H. Hawkins," 1, 5–7; J. H. Kuykendall, "Reminiscences of Early Texans," Pt. 3, *The Quarterly of the Texas State Historical Association* 7 (July 1903): 29; Richard V. Francaviglia, *From Sail to Steam: Four Centuries of Texas Maritime History, 1500–1900* (Austin: University of Texas Press, 1998), 87–88.
12. Cantrell, *Stephen F. Austin*, 12; Moses Austin Bryan, "Personal Recollections of Stephen F. Austin," Pt. 1, *The Texas Magazine* 3 (September 1897): 102; Brands, *Lone Star Nation*, 56.
13. Cantrell, *Stephen F. Austin*, 110–111; Barker, *Life of Stephen F. Austin*, 45–46; Barker, ed., *Austin Papers*, 1: 814, 487, 483; Randolph B. Campbell, *Gone to Texas: A History of the Lone Star State* (New York: Oxford University Press, 2003), 104; Hämäläinen, *The Comanche Empire*, 196.
14. Cantrell, *Stephen F. Austin*, 105–107, 113–114, 123–125, 152; Barker, *Life of Stephen F. Austin*, 48–49, 88; Barker, ed., *Austin Papers*, 1: 5, 815–817, 629–630, 505, 518–519, 555, 561; Wooten, ed., *Comprehensive History of Texas*, 1: 473–475; James T. DeShields, *They Sat in High Place: The Presidents and Governors of Texas* (San Antonio: The Naylor Company, 1940), 4–5; Timothy E. Anna, *Forging Mexico, 1821–1835* (Lincoln: University of Nebraska Press, 1998), 94–95; Campbell, *Gone to Texas*, 105; Holley, *Texas*, 313.

15. Cantrell, *Stephen F. Austin*, 126; Anna, *Forging Mexico*, 96–97, 138; Eugene C. Barker, "Stephen F. Austin," *Mississippi Valley Historical Review* 5 (June 1918): 23; Wooten, ed., *Comprehensive History of Texas*, 1: 475; Brands, *Lone Star Nation*, 80–81; David J. Weber, *The Mexican Frontier, 1821–1846: The American Southwest Under Mexico* (Albuquerque: University of New Mexico Press, 1982), 162; Davis, *Lone Star Rising*, 62. While waiting for his grant to be affirmed, Austin dabbled in writing a constitution for the new Republic of Mexico. Barker, ed., *Austin Papers*, 1: 601–627.
16. Cantrell, *Stephen F. Austin*, 143; Barker, *Life of Stephen F. Austin*, 102, 162, 98–99; Barker, ed., *Austin Papers*, 1: 560, 582–583; Holley, *Texas*, 285; Hämäläinen, *The Comanche Empire*, 196; Eugene C. Barker, "The Government of Austin's Colony, 1821–1831," *Southwestern Historical Quarterly* 21 (January 1918): 226–227, 233; J. H. Kuykendall, "Reminiscences of Early Texans," Pt. 1, *The Quarterly of the Texas State Historical Association* 6 (January 1903): 248; Ibid., Pt. 2 (April 1903): 31; Winkler, ed., *Manuscript Letters*, 18–22.
17. Barker, ed., *Austin Papers*, 1: 676; Tumlinson and Kuykendall to Trespalacios, January 7, 1823, Roll 073, Frames 0964–0968, Bexar Archives, BCAH; Trespalacios to Tumlinson, January 31, 1823, Frames 016–017, Tumlinson and Kuykendall to Commandant General, March 5, 1823, Frames 309–311, Morrison to Trespalacios, June 5, 1823, Frames 0932–0935, all on Roll 074, Bexar Archives, BCAH; Stephen L. Moore, *Savage Frontier: Rangers, Riflemen, and Indian Wars in Texas* (Denton: University of North Texas Press, 2002), 1: 8–9; Allen G. Hatley, *The Indian Wars in Stephen F. Austin's Texas Colony, 1822–1835* (Austin: Eakin Press, 2001), xv–xvi; Kuykendall, "Reminiscences of Early Texans," Pt. 1: 237; Robert M. Utley, *Lone Star Justice: The First Century of the Texas Rangers* (New York: Berkley Books, 2002), 15.
18. Kuykendall to Governor, July 13, 1823, Winkler, ed., *Manuscript Letters*, 28–29; Marshall E. Kuykendall, *They Slept Upon Their Rifles: The Story of the Captain Robert H. Kuykendall Family in America and the Entry of the Family with the Anglo Settlement into Mexican/Texas in Stephen F. Austin's Colony in 1821* (Fort Worth: Nortex Press, 2005), 49–50.
19. Cantrell, *Stephen F. Austin*, 134, 142–143, 146, 147; Barker, *Life of Stephen F. Austin*, 99–100, 131; Barker, ed., *Austin Papers*, 1: 677–678, 679–681, 703–704, 811–824; Baker, "Government of Austin's Colony,"

226, 236; Wooten, ed., *Comprehensive History of Texas*, 1: 476–477; Hans Peter Nielson Gammel, comp., *The Laws of Texas, 1822–1897* (Austin: The Gammel Book Company, 1898), 1: 13, 27–30, 35.

20. Barker, ed., *Austin Papers*, 1: 678–679.
21. Barker, ed., *Austin Papers*, 1: 684–685, 710–711, 688–689; Walter Prescott Webb, *The Texas Rangers: A Century of Frontier Defense* (Austin: University of Texas Press, 1965), 20; Frederick Wilkins, *The Legend Begins: The Texas Rangers, 1823–1845* (Austin: State House Press, 1996), 7; Hatley, *Indian Wars*, xviii, 26–28, 93.
22. Cantrell, *Stephen F. Austin*, 139; Barker, ed., *Austin Papers*, 1: 701–702; Kuykendall, "Reminiscences of Early Texans," Pt. 3: 31–32.
23. Cantrell, *Stephen F. Austin*, 144–145; Kenneth E. Hendrickson, *The Chief Executives of Texas: From Stephen F. Austin to John B. Connally, Jr.* (College Station: Texas A&M University Press, 1995), 6; Joseph W. McKnight, "Stephen F. Austin's Legalistic Concerns," *Southwestern Historical Quarterly* 89 (January 1986): 248; Stephen F. Austin, *Translation of the Laws, Orders, and Contracts, on Colonization, from January, 1821, Up to This Time* (San Felipe de Austin: Godwin B. Cotton, 1829), 66–67; Barker, "Government of Austin's Colony," 229–230; Wooten, ed., *Comprehensive History of Texas*, 1: 481–492.
24. Cantrell, *Stephen F. Austin*, 145; Austin, *Laws, Orders, and Contracts*, 67; McKnight, "Stephen Austin's Legalistic Concerns," 251. See also Henry W. Barton, "The Anglo-American Colonists under Mexican Militia Laws," *Southwestern Historical Quarterly* 65 (July 1961): 61–71.
25. Nathan A. Jennings, *Riding for the Lone Star: Frontier Cavalry and the Texas Way of War, 1822–1865* (Denton: University of North Texas Press, 2016), 13, 15, 31–33, 43–44, 27; Mike Cox, *The Texas Rangers: Wearing the Cinco Peso, 1821–1900* (New York: Tom Doherty Associates, 2008), 23; Gerald E. Poyo, ed., *Tejano Journey, 1770–1850* (Austin: University of Texas Press, 1996), 49–50, 52; John Grenier, *The First Way of War: American War Making on the Frontier, 1607–1814* (New York: Cambridge University Press, 2005), 1, 3, 6, 126, 128, 134–135; Barker, *Life of Stephen F. Austin*, 107–108; Barker, ed., *Austin Papers*, 1: 715–716, 838–839.
26. Cantrell, *Stephen F. Austin*, 137–138; Barker, ed., *Austin Papers*, 1: 840, 768; J. H. Kuykendall, "Reminiscences of Early Texans," Pt. 2, *The Quarterly of the Texas State Historical Association* 6 (April 1903): 35; John Henry Brown, *Indian Wars and Pioneers of Texas*

(Austin: State House Press, 1988), 7; William B. Dewees, *Letters from an Early Settler of Texas*, comp. Cara Cardelle (Louisville: Morton & Griswold, 1852), 51–52; Jesse Burnam, "Recollections of Capt. Jesse Burnam," *The Quarterly of the Texas State Historical Association* 5 (July 1901): 17–18.

27. Barker, *Life of Stephen Austin*, 105–106; Barker, ed., *Austin Papers*, 1: 885–887, 930–931; Cox, *Wearing the Cinco Peso*, 36–37; Hatley, *Indian Wars*, 44; Kuykendall, "Reminiscences of Early Texans," Pt. 2: 35–37; John Wesley Wilbarger, *Indian Depredations in Texas* (Austin: State House Press, 1985), 201–202; Henderson K. Yoakum, *History of Texas from its First Settlement in 1685 to its Annexation to the United States in 1846* (New York: Redfield, 1856), 1: 224–225.
28. Cantrell, *Stephen F. Austin*, 147; Barker, *Life of Stephen F. Austin*, 98, 131; Campbell, *Gone to Texas*, 106; Brands, *Lone Star Nation*, 92, 106; Weber, *The Mexican Frontier*, 162–163.
29. Barker, ed., *Austin Papers*, 2: 1304–1305, 1315, 1317–1319, 1323–1325, 1332–1333, 1338, 1340, 1357; Moore, *Savage Frontier*, 1: 11–12; Marshall, *They Slept Upon Their Rifles*, 207.
30. Barker, ed., *Austin* Papers, 2: 1357, 1440–1443.
31. Hatley, *Indian Wars*, 48; Stanley Noyes, *Los Comanches: The Horse People, 1751–1845* (Albuquerque: University of New Mexico Press, 1993), 136, 225.
32. Cantrell, *Stephen F. Austin*, 151, 161, 195, 203; Barker, ed., *Austin Papers*, 1: 758, 730; Davis, *Lone Star Rising*, 60–61, 63–64; Stephen L. Hardin, *Texian Iliad: A Military History of the Texas Revolution, 1835–1836* (Austin: University of Texas Press, 1994), 5; Poyo, ed., *Tejano Journey*, 128; Haley, *Passionate Nation*, 81, 84, 90; Walter Lord, *A Time to Stand* (Lincoln: University of Nebraska Press, 1978), 42; Lester G. Bugbee, "Slavery in Early Texas," *Political Science Quarterly* 13 (September 1898): 394, 399, 407–410; Ernest Wallace and David M. Vigness, eds., *Documents of Texas History* (Austin: The Steck Company, 1963), 61–62. Barker, "Stephen F. Austin," 22: "I had an ignorant, whimsical, selfish and suspicious set of rulers over me to keep good natured, a perplexed, confused colonization law to execute, and an unruly set of North American frontier republicans to controul [*sic*] who felt that they were sovereigns, for they knew that they were beyond the arm of the Govt. or of law, unless it pleased them to be controuled [*sic*]."
33. Austin, *Laws, Orders, and Contracts*, 21.

34. Weber, *The Mexican Frontier*, 31–32; Chris Frazer, *Bandit Nation: A History of Outlaws and Cultural Struggle in Mexico, 1810–1920* (Lincoln: University of Nebraska Press, 2006), 25–26; Mary Margaret McAllen Amberson, et al., *I Would Rather Sleep in Texas: A History of the Lower Rio Grande Valley and the People of the Santa Anita Land Grant* (Austin: Texas State Historical Association, 2003), 68; Hubert Howe Bancroft, *History of the North Mexican States and Texas* (San Francisco: The History Company, 1889), 2: 84–86, 94, 97.
35. Cantrell, *Stephen F. Austin*, 162, 174, 175–176, 199, 203, 223; Barker, *Life of Stephen F. Austin*, 140–143, 133, 123–124, 126; Barker, ed., *Austin Papers*, 1: 912–913, 935–936, 1087, 1106–1107, 1431–1432, 1631, 1687–1688, 1689–1698, 1353; 2: 70; Campbell, *Gone to Texas*, 107–108; Holley, *Texas*, 204–216, 222–224, 230; Mary Virginia Henderson, "Minor Empresario Contracts for the Colonization of Texas, 1825–1834," *Southwestern Historical Quarterly* 31 (April 1928): 298–299; Brown, *History of Texas*, 1: 119–120. See also Eugene C. Barker, "Descriptions of Texas by Stephen F. Austin," *Southwestern Historical Quarterly* 28 (October 1924): 98–121.
36. Cantrell, *Stephen F. Austin*, 180–187; Barker, *Life of Stephen F. Austin*, Ch. 7; Barker, ed., *Austin Papers*, 1: 1532, 1539–1541, 1558, 1527, 1570–1572, 1587–1589, 1604; Campbell, *Gone to Texas*, 109–110; Brands, *Lone Star Nation*, 107–111.
37. Kuykendall, "Reminiscences of Early Texans," Pt. 3: 39; Hatley, *Indian Wars*, 54, 133–134 n3.
38. Moore, *Savage Frontier*, 1: 12–13; Yoakum, *History of Texas*, 1: 260–261; Wilbarger, *Indian Depredations in Texas*, 206–207; Kuykendall, *They Slept Upon Their Rifles*, 208; Brown, *History of Texas*, 1: 156–158.
39. Cantrell, *Stephen F. Austin*, 176–177, 208–214, 220–225, 226–227; Barker, *Life of Stephen F. Austin*, 310, 313–314; Barker, ed., *Austin Papers*, 1: 696, 1495–1498; Weber, *The Mexican Frontier*, 166; Gifford E. White, *1830 Citizens of Texas* (Austin: Eakin Press, 1999), viii, 239; Campbell, *Gone to Texas*, 110, 113; Alleine Howren, "Causes and Origin of the Decree of April 6, 1830," *Southwestern Historical Quarterly* 16 (April 1913): 415–417; Davis, *Lone Star Rising*, 77; Paul D. Lack, *The Texas Revolutionary Experience: A Political and Social History, 1835–1836* (College Station: Texas A&M University Press, 1992), 5; Dewees, *Letters from an Early Settler*, 142; Poyo, ed., *Tejano Journey*, 41. Austin wrote an essay reviewing the history

of the Texas colony and focusing on the potential negative outcomes of the Law of April 6. He also maintained Texas would not profit by separating from Mexico. The document can be found in Austin Papers, Series III, Box 2Q413, BCAH.

40. Cantrell, *Stephen F. Austin*, 153–159, 201, 203; Barker, *Life of Stephen F. Austin*, 111–117; Barker, ed., *Austin Papers*, 1: 917, 939, 1239; Lester G. Bugbee, "Some Difficulties of a Texas Empresario," *Publications of the Southern History Association* 3 (April 1899): 99–104, 106–107; Brands, *Lone Star Nation*, 101–106; Cantrell, "Partnership of Stephen F. Austin and Joseph H. Hawkins," 6–17; Bryan, "Recollections of Austin," Pt. 1: 101; Barker, "Stephen F. Austin," 31–32. Eugene C. Barker, "Stephen F. Austin and the Independence of Texas," *The Quarterly of the Texas State Historical Association* 13 (April 1910): 260: "While never deviating from his declared motto of 'fidelity and gratitude to Mexico,' Austin stood always ready to guard the interests of the colonists."
41. Brands, *Lone Star Nation*, 218.
42. Cantrell, *Stephen F. Austin*, 242–245, 341–343; Barker, ed., *Austin Papers*, 2: 725; Rebecca Smith Lee, *Mary Austin Holley: A Biography* (Austin: University of Texas Press, 1962), 230–235, 237–238.
43. Cantrell, *Stephen F. Austin*, 229–231, 251–252; Barker, *Life of Stephen F. Austin*, 386–388, 396; Barker, ed., *Austin Papers*, 2: 452, 611, 564, 568; Weber, *The Mexican Frontier*, 246; Brands, *Lone Star Nation*, 164–167, 179–184; Haley, *Passionate Nation*, 103–106. See also Will Fowler, *Santa Anna of Mexico* (Lincoln: University of Nebraska Press, 2007).
44. Cantrell, *Stephen F. Austin*, 261–262; Barker, *Life of Stephen F. Austin*, 404–408, 410–412; Lack, *Texas Revolutionary Experience*, 7; Poyo, ed., *Tejano Journey*, 44; Campbell, *Gone to Texas*, 122; Davis, *Lone Star Rising*, 91.
45. Cantrell, *Stephen F. Austin*, 263–265, 267–285, 289–290; Barker, ed., *Austin Papers*, 2: 960–961, 954, 988–998, 1003–1005, 1007–1008, 1024, 1012–1013, 1049–1051, 1053, 1058, 1059, 1060–1061, 1066, 1072, 1075–1085, 3: 10–13, 17–18; Barker, *Life of Stephen F. Austin*, 417–421, 423, 426, 430; McKnight, "Stephen Austin's Legalistic Concerns," 264–266; Davis, *Lone Star Rising*, 99; Wallace and Vigness, eds., *Documents of Texas History*, 80–85; Barker, "Stephen F. Austin," 32; Brands, *Lone Star Nation*, 220–226; Campbell, *Gone to Texas*, 125. For accounts of his incarceration, see Stephen F. Austin, "The 'Prison Journal' of Stephen F. Austin," *The Quarterly of the Texas State*

Historical Association 2 (January 1899): 183–210; David B. Edward, *The History of Texas; or, The Emigrant's, Farmer's and Politician's Guide* (Cincinnati, OH: J. A. James & Company, 1836), 211–220; and Grayson to Lamar, February 14, 1837, Charles Adams Gulick, et al., eds., *The Papers of Mirabeau Bounaparte Lamar* (Austin: A. C. Baldwin & Sons, 1922–1927), 1: 535.

46. Cantrell, *Stephen F. Austin*, 291, 294, 296, 300; Lord, *A Time to Stand*, 63–64; Davis, *Lone Star Rising*, 113, 121–123; Lack, *Texas Revolutionary Experience*, 18; John Holmes Jenkins, ed., *The Papers of the Texas Revolution, 1835–1836* (Austin: Presidial Press, 1973), 1: 43.
47. Malcolm D. McLean, comp. and ed., *Papers Concerning Robertson's Colony in Texas* (Arlington: University of Texas at Arlington Press, 1974–1993), 10: 47, 465, 467; Noyes, *Los Comanches*, 247; Brown, *History of Texas*, 1: 287.
48. McLean, comp. and ed., *Papers Concerning Robertson's Colony*, 10: 48–49, 465–467, 503–57, 546–547; John H. Moore, Public Debt Claim No. 1346, Reel 175, Frame 141, TSLAC; Moore, *Savage Frontier*, 1: 24; Yoakum, *History of Texas*, 1: 352; Brown, *History of Texas*, 1: 287–288; "Survivors of the Texas Revolution," *The Texas Almanac for 1872* (Galveston: Richardson, Belo, & Company, 1871), 109.
49. McLean, comp. and ed., *Papers Concerning Robertson's Colony*, 10: 465–466; Gammel, comp., *Laws of Texas*, 1: 1134; Utley, *Lone Star Justice*, 19; Moore, *Savage Frontier*, 1: 204.
50. Cantrell, *Stephen F. Austin*, 305, 309, 310, 312; Barker, ed., *Austin Papers*, 3: 35–37, 73, 102, 128–129; Jodella D. Kite, "The War and Peace Parties of Pre-Revolutionary Texas, 1835–1836," *East Texas Historical Journal* 29 (March 1991): 13–14; Hendrickson, *Chief Executives of Texas*, 7; Bryan, "Recollections of Austin," Pt. 1: 106, 107, 108–109; Barker, "Stephen F. Austin and the Independence of Texas," 273–277; Brands, *Lone Star Nation*, 248; Yoakum, *History of Texas*, 1: 343. See also Jesús F. de la Teja, ed., *Tejano Leadership in Mexican and Revolutionary Texas* (College Station: Texas A&M University Press, 2010).
51. Cantrell, *Stephen F. Austin*, 312–313, 315; Barker, ed., *Austin Papers*, 3: 130; Jenkins, ed., *Papers of the Texas Revolution*, 1: 427, 455–456; *Texas Republican*, August 22, 29, September 26, 1835; Hardin, *Texian Iliad*, 7–13; Campbell, *Gone to Texas*, 129–130; Brands, *Lone Star Nation*, 253.
52. Cantrell, *Stephen F. Austin*, 313; Davis, *Lone Star Rising*, 136; Eugene C. Barker, ed., "Journal of the Permanent Council (October

11–27, 1835)," *The Quarterly of the Texas State Historical Association* 7 (April 1904): 252–278; Gammel, comp., *Laws of Texas*, 1: 512; *Journals of the Consultation Held at San Felipe de Austin, October 16, 1835* (Houston: Telegraph Power Press, 1838), 5; Jenkins, ed., *Papers of the Texas Revolution*, 2: 103.

53. Cantrell, *Stephen F. Austin*, 316–317; Barker, ed., *Austin Papers*, 3: 161; Grayson to Austin, October 11, 1835, Austin Papers, Series III, Box 2Q414, BCAH; Bryan, "Recollections of Austin," Pt. 1: 109; Noah Smithwick, *The Evolution of a State, or Recollections of Old Texas Days*, comp. Nanna Smithwick Donaldson (Austin: University of Texas Press, 1983), 74–75; Jenkins, ed., *Papers of the Texas Revolution*, 2: 31–33, 81–82, 94, 101, 108–109; Poyo, ed., *Tejano Journey*, 52–53; "General Austin's Order Book for the Campaign of 1835," *The Quarterly of the Texas State Historical Association* 11 (July 1907): 1, 3, 5, 6–7, 11; Hardin, *Texian Iliad*, 26–27.
54. Cantrell, *Stephen F. Austin*, 317; Alwyn Barr, *Texans in Revolt: The Battle for San Antonio, 1835* (Austin: University of Texas Press, 1990), 15; Hardin, *Texian Iliad*, 27; Campbell, *Gone to Texas*, 134; Jenkins, ed., *Papers of the Texas Revolution*, 2: 127–128, 138–139, 142–143, 151, 153–154, 162–163, 287–288; Poyo, ed., *Tejano Journey*, 55.
55. Cantrell, *Stephen F. Austin*, 317, 321–322; Eugene C. Barker, "The Texas Revolutionary Army," *The Quarterly of the Texas State Historical Association* 9 (April 1906): 248; "General Austin's Order Book," 32–33; Jenkins, ed., *Papers of the Texas Revolution*, 2: 205, 230, 242–243; Davis, *Lone Star Rising*, 152; Hardin, *Texian Iliad*, 27, 29–34; Regimental weekly return, October 21, 1835, Austin Papers, Series III, Box 2Q414, BCAH.
56. Moore, *Savage Frontier*, 1: 34–35, 39, 41; Barker, ed., "Journal of the Permanent Council," 260–262; Gammel, comp., *Laws of Texas*, 1: 513, 526–527; Jenkins, ed., *Papers of the Texas Revolution*, 2: 303; William C. Binkley, ed., *Official Correspondence of the Texas Revolution, 1835–1836* (New York: D. Appleton-Century Company, 1936), 1: 44; James W. Parker, Audited Claim No. 7785, Reel 80, Frame 510, TSLAC.
57. Jenkins, ed., *Papers of the Texas Revolution*, 2: 490; Daniel B. Friar, Audited Claims No. 39 and 7766, Reel 33, Frame 491, TSLAC; Moore, *Savage Frontier*, 1: 42, 46, 289–290 n28.
58. Barker, ed., "Journal of the Permanent Council," 261, 271; Gammel, comp., *Laws of Texas*, 1: 521, 526, 528.

59. Cantrell, *Stephen F. Austin*, 323; *Journals of the Consultation*, 6; Gammel, comp., *Laws of Texas*, 1: 513, 522; Jenkins, ed., *Papers of the Texas Revolution*, 2: 215–216, 346–348, 9: 260–261; Eugene C. Barker, "The Texas Declaration of Causes for Taking Up Arms Against Mexico," *The Quarterly of the Texas State Historical Association* 15 (January 1912): 182–183; Eugene C. Barker, "The Finances of the Texas Revolution," *Political Science Quarterly* 19 (December 1904): 616–617. Hereafter cited as "Texas Revolutionary Finances."
60. Cantrell, *Stephen F. Austin*, 324; *Ordinances and Decrees of the Consultation, Provisional Government of Texas, and the Convention, Which Assembled at Washington, March 1, 1836* (Houston: National Banner Office, 1838), 4–10; *Journals of the Consultation*, 43–44; Jenkins, ed., *Papers of the Texas Revolution*, 3: 247, 283–285; Campbell, *Gone to Texas*, 137.
61. Cantrell, *Stephen F. Austin*, 325; Hardin, *Texian Iliad*, 57–58, 62–63; Jenkins, ed., *Papers of the Texas Revolution*, 9: 281–282; Gammel, comp., *Laws of Texas*, 1: 543, 925, 661, 915, 991, 584, 932–934. The regular army and the militia had little opportunity to organize as volunteers were urgently needed for the capture of Béxar. Future recruiting was stymied by American volunteers refusing to submit to military discipline and citizens of Texas displaying a surprising indifference to the war. Barker, "The Texas Revolutionary Army," 229, 235–236, 237–238, 249.
62. *Journals of the Consultation*, 49; Gammel, comp., *Laws of Texas*, 1: 576–577, 916. See also *Journal of the Proceedings of the General Council of the Republic of Texas* (Houston: National Intelligencer Office, 1839), 39, 47, 49, 55, 87–88; and *Ordinances and Decrees*, 20–21.
63. Moore, *Savage Frontier* 1: 65–66; Gammel, comp., *Laws of Texas*, 1: 600–601, 924–925; *Proceedings of the General Council*, 13, 73; Jenkins, ed., *Papers of the Texas Revolution*, 3: 68, 70, 259; Smithwick, *Evolution of a State*, 82.
64. Cantrell, *Stephen F. Austin*, 326; Barker, ed., *Austin Papers*, 3: 247; Davis, *Lone Star Rising*, 177–178; Hardin, *Texian Iliad*, 54, 56; Campbell, *Gone to Texas*, 138; Brands, *Lone Star Nation*, 280–281; Barr, *Texas in Revolt*, 29, 31.
65. Cantrell, *Stephen F. Austin*, 326–327; Barker, ed., *Austin Papers*, 3: 268; William T. Austin, "Account of the Campaign of 1835 by William T. Austin, Aide to Gen. Stephen F. Austin and Gen. Edward

Burleson," *Texana* 4 (Winter 1966): 317; "General Austin's Order Book," 50, 51–53; Jenkins, ed., *Papers of the Texas Revolution*, 2: 450–451, 495–496; Moses Austin Bryan, "Personal Recollections of Stephen F. Austin," Pt. 2, *The Texas Magazine* 3 (November 1897): 165–166; Brands, *Lone Star Nation*, 282–283; Hardin, *Texian Iliad*, 61–62. For a roster of the army at that particular time, see "List of men who have this day volunteered to remain before Bexar—November 24, 1835," Austin Papers, Series III, Box 2Q414, BCAH.

66. Cantrell, *Stephen F. Austin*, 331–332; Barker, ed., *Austin Papers*, 3: 279; Barker, "Declaration of Causes," 184; Ralph W. Steen, "Analysis of the Work of the General Council, Provisional Government of Texas, 1835–1836," Pt. 1, *Southwestern Historical Quarterly* 40 (April 1937): 323–324; Gammel, comp., *Laws of Texas*, 1: 652.
67. Cantrell, *Stephen F. Austin*, 333–334; Barker, ed., *Austin Papers*, 3: 293; James P. Bevill, *The Paper Republic: The Struggle for Money, Credit, and Independence in the Republic of Texas* (Houston, TX: Bright Sky Press, 2009), 90, 91; Steen, "Analysis of Work of General Council," Pt. 1: 322; Bryan, "Recollections of Austin," 168; George P. Garrison, ed., *Diplomatic Correspondence of the Republic of Texas* (Washington, D.C.: Government Printing Office, 1908), 1: 51–54.
68. Barr, *Texans in Revolt*, 44; Hardin, *Texian Iliad*, 67–68, 78; Jenkins, ed., *Papers of the Texas Revolution*, 3: 98–99, 160–164, 186–188, 197–198, 240, 390; Poyo, ed., *Tejano Journey*, 55; Haley, *Passionate Nation*, 133; Yoakum, *History of Texas*, 2: 25–30. For the Texan order of battle, see Barr, *Texans in Revolt*, 71. See also Lois Garver, "The Life of Benjamin Rush Milam," *Southwestern Historical Quarterly* 38 (October 1934, January 1935): 79–121, 177–202.
69. Moore, *Savage Frontier*, 1: 70; Jenkins, ed., *Papers of the Texas Revolution*, 3: 230; McLean, comp. and ed., *Papers Concerning Robertson's Colony in Texas*, 13: 55–56; John J. Tumlinson, Audited Claim No. 618, Reel 106, Frame 582, TSLAC; Isaac W. Burton, Audited Claim No. 6221, Reel 14, Frame 40, TSLAC; Brown, *Indian Wars*, 89; Smithwick, *Evolution of a State*, 82.
70. Hämäläinen, *The Comanche Empire*, 196–199; Noyes, *Los Comanches*, 137; James T. DeShields, *Border Wars of Texas* (Austin: State House Press, 1993), 168–172; Brown, *Indian Wars*, 89–90; Smithwick, *Evolution of a State*, 82–87.
71. Eli Seale, Audited Claim No. 209, Reel 93, Frame 163, TSLAC; Silas M. Parker, Audited Claim No. 182, Reel 80, Frames 564–568,

TSLAC; James W. Parker, Audited Claim No. 7785, Reel 80, Frame 512, TSLAC; Daniel B. Friar, Audited Claims No. 39 & 7766, Reel 33, Frame 491, TSLAC; Moore, *Savage Frontier*, 1: 66.

72. Duncan W. Robinson, *Judge Robert McAlpin Williamson: Texas' Three-Legged Willie* (Austin: Texas State Historical Association, 1948), 129, 132, 135; Jenkins, ed., *Papers of the Texas Revolution*, 4: 249; Binkley, ed., *Official Correspondence*, 1: 387–388, 453–454; Stephen L. Moore, *Eighteen Minutes: The Battle of San Jacinto and the Texas Independence Campaign* (Dallas: Republic of Texas Press, 2004), 81; Smithwick, *Evolution of a State*, 87–88. A number of other volunteer ranger companies were raised independent of Williamson's battalion, including those under Sterling Clack Robertson, Louis B. Franks, Stephen Townsend, Thomas Hudson Barron, and William C. Wilson. Moore, *Savage Frontier*, 1: 72–73, 82–83, 84, 93–95, 96.
73. Cantrell, *Stephen F. Austin*, 334, 337–338, 339–343; Barker, ed., *Austin Papers*, 3: 297–298, 314, 317; Jenkins, ed., *Papers of the Texas Revolution*, 3: 432–436, 4: 51, 331, 377, 497–498; Bevill, *The Paper Republic*, 94, 96; Barker, "Texas Revolutionary Finances," 630; Binkley, ed., *Official Correspondence*, 2: 286–291, 571–573, 1086; Barker, "Stephen F. Austin and the Independence of Texas," 282–283; Davis, *Lone Star Rising*, 204; *New York Evening Star*, February 1, 1836; Garrison, ed., *Diplomatic Correspondence*, 1: 72–73. For the text of Austin's address at Louisville, see Holley, *Texas*, 253–280.
74. Lack, *Texas Revolutionary Experience*, 50–51, 53–54; Jenkins, ed., *Papers of the Texas Revolution*, 3: 237–239, 458–460, 4: 17–26, 50, 63–65, 68–69, 77, 91–92, 108, 117–118, 121–124, 128–130; Brands, *Lone Star Nation*, 315–317, 318; W. Roy Smith, "The Quarrel Between Governor Smith and the Council of the Provisional Government of the Republic," *The Quarterly of the Texas State Historical Association* 5 (April 1902): 283, 309, 312–335.
75. Jenkins, ed., *Papers of the Texas Revolution*, 4: 493–497, 9: 289–291, 293–304, 305, 309–310, 313, 325–339, 519–520; Lack, *Texas Revolutionary Experience*, 87, 89–93. The rapid progress the delegates made in just sixteen days is noteworthy. If nothing else, the Convention gave clarity to the Texian cause, empowered a single civil administration, and established a unified military command structure. Davis, *Lone Star Rising*, 242.

76. Cantrell, *Stephen F. Austin*, 343; Barker, *Life of Stephen F. Austin*, 500; Barker, ed., *Austin Papers*, 3: 341–342, 328–330; Garrison, ed., *Diplomatic Correspondence*, 1: 79–82; Lord, *A Time to Stand*, 171; *Philadelphia Inquirer and Daily Courier*, April 1, 9, 1836.
77. Jenkins, ed., *Papers of the Texas Revolution*, 3: 379–380, 4: 501, 9: 366–367; Hardin, *Texian Iliad*, 127–149, 164–174; *New York Evening Post*, April 11, 19, May 4, June 9, 1836; Haley, *Passionate Nation*, 154–161, 172–177; Lord, *A Time to Stand*, 169–174. For a solid account of the events at the Alamo, see James Donovan, *The Blood of Heroes: The 13-Day Struggle for the Alamo—and the Sacrifice That Forged a Nation* (New York: Little, Brown & Company, 2012). For a frank discussion of the Goliad atrocity, see Jay A. Stout, *Slaughter at Goliad: The Mexican Massacre of 400 Texas Volunteers* (Annapolis, MD: Naval Press Institute, 2008).
78. Cantrell, *Stephen F. Austin*, 335, 343–345; Barker, ed., *Austin Papers*, 3: 340; Barker, "Texas Revolutionary Finances," 633; *New York Commercial Advertiser*, April 27, 1836; *New York Evening Post*, April 27, May 30, 1836; Bevill, *The Paper Republic*, 120; *Philadelphia Inquirer and Daily Courier*, May 3, 1836; Binkley, ed., *Official Correspondence*, 2: 1086.
79. Barker, ed., *Austin Papers*, 3: 344–348.
80. For examples of the geographic breadth of Austin's post, see *Baltimore Gazette and Daily Advertiser*, May 10, 1836; *Richmond Enquirer*, May 17, 1836; and *St. Louis Daily Commercial Bulletin*, June 3, 1836.
81. Cantrell, *Stephen F. Austin*, 345–347; *New York Commercial Advertiser*, May 7, 1836; Jenkins, ed., *Papers of the Texas Revolution*, 6: 308, 327, 93; Campbell, *Gone to Texas*, 160–161; *Baltimore Gazette and Daily Advertiser*, May 25, 1836; Garrison, ed., *Diplomatic Correspondence*, 1: 98–99; Bevill, *The Paper Republic*, 130.
82. Cantrell, *Stephen F. Austin*, 348–349; Barker, ed., *Austin Papers*, 3: 372–373, 380–383, 384–385; Jenkins, ed., *Papers of the Texas Revolution*, 7: 279, 334, 354–358, 365–366, 8: 282; Garrison, ed., *Diplomatic Correspondence*, 1: 100–101, 106–107; *Telegraph and Texas Register*, August 30, 1836; Brands, *Lone Star Nation*, 471, 477. For the terms of the two Treaties of Velasco, see *Stanley Siegel, A Political History of the Texas Republic, 1836–1845* (Austin: University of Texas Press, 1956), 24–26.

83. Cantrell, *Stephen F. Austin*, 350–353; Barker, ed., *Austin Papers*, 3: 411–414, 416, 418–421, 428; *Telegraph and Texas Register*, August 9, 16, 23, 30, 1836; Jenkins, ed., *Papers of the Texas Revolution*, 8: 104–105, 114, 166–167, 241, 282, 300–301; Davis, *Lone Star Rising*, 297.
84. Cantrell, *Stephen F. Austin*, 355, 359; Barker, ed., *Austin Papers*, 3: 428, 438; *Siegel, Political History of the Texas Republic*, 55; Lack, *Texas Revolutionary Experience*, 260; Campbell, *Gone to Texas*, 162; Haley, *Passionate Nation*, 206.
85. Cantrell, *Stephen F. Austin*, 360–361; Barker, *Life of Stephen F. Austin*, 517–519; Barker, ed., *Austin Papers*, 3: 438–439, 444, 449; Amelia W. Williams and Eugene C. Barker, ed., *Writings of Sam Houston* (Austin: University of Texas Press, 1938–43), 1: 457–458, 462; Garrison, ed., *Diplomatic Correspondence*, 1: 127–143, 149–151; Barker, "Stephen F. Austin," 32.
86. Binkley, ed., *Official Correspondence*, 2: 879; Robinson, *Robert McAlpin Williamson*, 151; John J. Tumlinson, Audited Claim No. 618, Reel 106, Frame 582, TSLAC; Moore, *Savage Frontier*, 1: 173; Ben C. Stuart, "Texas Indian Fighters and Frontier Rangers" (MS, 1916), TSLAC, 4.
87. Mike Cox, *Texas Ranger Tales II* (Plano: Republic of Texas Press, 1999), 2–3, 4–5; John W. Crain, "Isaac Watts Burton: The Glorious Years, 1832–1843," *Southwestern Historical Quarterly* 109 (October 2005): 177–181; Francaviglia, *From Sail to Steam*, 116; Haley, *Passionate Nation*, 201; Binkley, ed., *Official Correspondence*, 2: 816–817; *Telegraph and Texas Register*, August 2, 1836.
88. Cantrell, *Stephen F. Austin*, 363–367, 377; Brands, *Lone Star Nation*, 474, 479; DeShields, *They Sat in High Place*, 11; Bryan, "Recollections of Austin," Pt. 2: 172; General Orders Concerning Austin's Death, December 27, 1836, Williams and Barker, eds., *Writings of Sam Houston*, 2: 28–29. Reprinted in *Telegraph and Texas Register*, December 27, 1836. *San Antonio Daily Express*, *Houston Post*, and *Dallas Morning News*, all dated October 20, 1910. For a fuller description of Austin's final hours, see George L. Hammeken, "Recollections of Stephen Austin," *Southwestern Historical Quarterly* 20 (April 1917): 378–380. See also *Telegraph and Texas Register*, December 27, 1836; and Alexander W. Terrell, "Stephen F. Austin: A Memorial Address," *The Quarterly of the Texas State Historical Association* 14 (January 1911): 182–197.

Notes for Chapter 2

1. James Kimmins Greer, *Texas Ranger: Jack Hays in the Frontier Southwest* (College Station: Texas A&M University Press, 1993), 15; Dumas Malone, ed., *Dictionary of American Biography* (New York: Charles Scribner's Sons, 1932), 8: 463; John C. Caperton, "Sketch of Colonel John C. Hays, the Texas Rangers, Incidents in Texas and Mexico, Etc." Box 2R35, John Coffee Hays Collection, BCAH, 1; Francis B. Heitman, *Historical Register and Dictionary of the United States Army from its Organization, September 29 1789, to March 2 1903* (Washington, D.C.: Government Printing Office, 1903), 1: 516. The two most common, albeit unverifiable, assertions for Harmon's middle name are Atkins or Archibald.

   There has been some dispute over the identity of Harmon's father. The prevailing theory has been he was Colonel Robert Hays, the man who had built Fort Haysboro in Davidson County, Tennessee. Actually, genealogical evidence compiled by the late Madelon Wright Smith, former president of the Mount Juliet-West Wilson County Historical Society, proves Harmon was the son of John and Rebecca Maxwell (Thompson) Hays, who were living in Wilson County by 1800. Mrs. Smith's research further establishes John and Robert were brothers, which may have contributed to the confusion. Madelon Smith, "The Family of 'John Jack Hays'," Madelon Wright Smith Memorial Archives, Mount Juliet-West Wilson County Historical Society Collection, 1–2, 7. One interesting side note is John and Robert's father owned a gristmill in Rockbridge County, Virginia. He might have been a neighbor of Bigfoot Wallace's family, who also lived in the area. Oren F. Morton, *A History of Rockbridge County, Virginia* (Staunton, VA: The McClure Company, 1920), 55, 56, 169, 346, 456.

   Besides Harmon's service, the Hays family enjoyed close personal connections to General Jackson. Indeed, Rachel Donelson Jackson, his wife, was a sister-in-law to Harmon's uncle, Robert, who was also Jackson's adjutant during the war. The future president was said to have purchased the land on which The Hermitage was later built from Robert, but, in fact, Jackson purchased the initial tract from Nathaniel Hays in 1804. The latter's exact connection to Harmon's family line remains unconfirmed. Madelon Smith, "Notes on the Hays Family," Madelon Wright Smith Memorial Archives, 1; H. W. Brands, *Andrew Jackson: His Life and Times* (New York: Anchor Books, 2005), 99, 148.

2. Smith, "Family of 'John Jack Hays'," 7; Smith, "Notes on the Hays Family," 3; Jay Guy Cisco, *Historic Sumner County, Tennessee* (Nashville: Folk-Keelin Printing Company, 1909), 196; Malone, ed., *Dictionary of American Biography*, 8: 461.
3. *Fourth U.S. Census*, Wilkinson County, Mississippi; *Fifth U.S. Census*, Wilson County, Tennessee; Smith, "Family of 'John Jack Hays'," 7.
4. Greer, *Texas Ranger*, 16–17, 18–20; Smith, "Family of 'John Jack Hays'," 1; Dixon Merritt, *The History of Wilson County: Its Land and Its Life* (Nashville: Benson Printing Company, 1961), 312; Isaac Dunbar Affleck, "History of John C. Hayes," Pt. I, Box 2Q401, Isaac Dunbar Affleck Papers, BCAH, 8; Paul K. Conkin, *Peabody College: From a Frontier Academy to the Frontiers of Teaching and Learning* (Nashville: Vanderbilt University Press, 2002), 1–5, 16–17, 34–35. Through a series of name changes and mergers, remnants of the University of Nashville are now part of Vanderbilt University. The Vanderbilt library does not possess any pre-1850 catalogs, which might have contained student lists, nor do any of the early account books mention Hays.
5. Greer, *Texas Ranger*, 22–24; Caperton, "Sketch of Colonel John C. Hays," 6; Affleck, "History of John C. Hayes," Pt. I: 17; Cage to Houston, November 29, 1837, Document No. 1436, Box 2–22/165, Andrew Jackson Houston Collection, TSLAC; Heitman, *Historical Register and Dictionary of the United States Army*, 1: 545; Bexar County Clerk, Return of Certificates No. 10, August-November 1839, File No. 16, TGLO; Hans Peter Nielson Gammel, comp., *The Laws of Texas, 1822–1897* (Austin: The Gammel Book Company, 1898), 1: 1414, 2: 35; *Telegraph and Texas Register*, April 11, 1837. For more on the traditional version, see Cleburne Huston, *Deaf Smith: Incredible Texas Spy* (Waco: Texian Press, 1973), 112–113, 115.
6. Greer, *Texas Ranger*, 25; Rena Maverick Green, ed., *Memoirs of Mary A. Maverick, Arranged by Mary A. Maverick and Her Son George Madison Maverick* (San Antonio: Alamo Printing Co., 1921), 29; Caperton, "Sketch of Colonel John C. Hays," 3; J. Marvin Hunter, ed., "Jack Hays, the Intrepid," *Old West* 1 (Summer 1965): 68; Pekka Hämäläinen, *The Comanche Empire* (New Haven: Yale University Press, 2008), 215; Stephen Hardin, *Texas Rangers* (Oxford, UK: Osprey History, 2000), 6; James T. DeShields, "Hays as a Surveyor," "Sketches Concerning the Life of John C. Hays," James Thomas DeShields Papers, BCAH, 2–3.

7. Greer, *Texas Ranger*, 28; John Henry Brown, *Indian Wars and Pioneers of Texas* (Austin: State House Press, 1988), 50–51; James T. DeShields, *Border Wars of Texas* (Austin: State House Press, 1993), 239; *Telegraph and Texas Register*, September 1, 1838; Thomas W. Kavanagh, *Comanche Political History: An Ethnohistorical Perspective, 1706–1875* (Lincoln: University of Nebraska Press, 1996), 260. A party of Comanches visited Bastrop on September 6, and expressed "much dissatisfaction" with the recent skirmish. *Telegraph and Texas Register*, September 15, 1838.
8. Greer, *Texas Ranger*, 28; Frederick Wilkins, *The Legend Begins: The Texas Rangers, 1823–1845* (Austin: State House Press, 1996), 72; DeShields, *Border Wars of Texas*, 242–243; Colonel Harry McCorry Henderson, *Colonel Jack Hays, Texas Ranger* (San Antonio: The Naylor Company, 1954), 6.
9. Greer, *Texas Ranger*, 33. He purportedly led a small, informal group of eight to ten volunteers beginning in February. No muster roll exists of their service, but Charles Wilkins Webber claims to have been a member of this band. *Tales of the Southern Border* (Philadelphia: Lippincott, Grambo & Co., 1853), 47–70.
10. Stephen L. Moore, *Savage Frontier: Rangers, Riflemen, and Indian Wars in Texas*, 2: 228; Juan N. Seguin, Unpaid Claim, Reel 256, Frame 219, TSLAC; John James, Unnumbered Claim, Reel 164, Frames 349–350, 353–354, 360, 362–366, 368, TSLAC; *Houston Daily Post*, November 7, 1897. Miles Squier Bennet wrote a series of articles on the early days of Texas for the *Post* and the *Cuero Star*. These writings, which include an account of this campaign, were drawn from his narrative diary and notes contained within the Valentine Bennet Scrapbook, which is archived in the Briscoe Center for American History, the University of Texas at Austin. Moore, *Savage Frontier*, 2: 228, 380 n30, n33. Greer has Hays commanding the expedition, albeit one much smaller. He may have mistaken Karnes's campaign for the foray Hays led to Cañon de Uvalde two years later. *Texas Ranger*, 35.
11. *Houston Daily Post*, November 7, 1897; Green, ed., *Memoirs of Mary A. Maverick*, 29–30.
12. Greer, *Texas Ranger*, 36; J. W. Benedict, "Diary of a Campaign against the Comanches," *Southwestern Historical Quarterly* 32 (April 1929): 300, 307–308; Muster and Pay Rolls, José M. Gonzales, 401–718, TSLAC; John James, Unnumbered Claim, Reel 164, Frames 350–351, 355, 357–358, TSLAC; *Telegraph and Texas Register*, September 18, 1839; Hays to Lamar, n.d., Charles Adams Gulick, et al., eds.,

The Papers of Mirabeau Bounaparte Lamar (Austin: A. C. Baldwin & Sons, 1922–1927), 4: 231–232. Hereafter cited as *Lamar Papers*. Gerald S. Pierce, *Texas Under Arms: The Camps, Forts, and Military Towns of the Republic of Texas, 1836–1846* (Austin: Encino Press, 1969), 137–138.

13. Greer, *Texas Ranger*, 36; Benedict, "Diary of a Campaign against the Comanches," 308–309; Nathan A. Jennings, *Riding for the Lone Star: Frontier Cavalry and the Texas Way of War, 1822–1865* (Denton: University of North Texas Press, 2016), 141.
14. Greer, *Texas Ranger*, 36; Hays to Lamar, n.d., Gulick, et al., eds., *Lamar Papers*, 4: 232; Benedict, "Diary of a Campaign against the Comanches," 309; *Telegraph and Texas Register*, December 11, 1839; Henderson, *Jack Hays*, 14; *Niles' National Register* 57 (January 11, 1840): 306.
15. Moore, *Savage Frontier* (Denton: University of North Texas Press, 2002–2010), 2: 334–336; Benedict, "Diary of a Campaign against the Comanches," 309–310; *Telegraph and Texas Register*, December 11, 1839; Muster and Pay Rolls, José M. Gonzales, 401–718, TSLAC; Pierce, *Texas Under Arms*, 138. Karnes was in the midst of planning another campaign against the Comanches when he died on August 16, 1840. *Telegraph and Texas Register*, July 1, 15, September 2, 1840.
16. Greer, *Texas Ranger*, 37, 40; Van Ness to Lamar, February 15, 1840, Gulick, et al., eds., *Lamar Papers*, 3: 333. For an account of the Council House Fight, see Stanley Noyes, *Los Comanches: The Horse People, 1751–1845* (Albuquerque: University of New Mexico Press, 1993), 280–286.
17. Greer, *Texas Ranger*, 39; Donaly E. Brice, *The Great Comanche Raid: Boldest Attack of the Texas Republic* (Austin: Eakin Press, 1987), 3–4, 64, 69; James L. Haley, *Passionate Nation: The Epic History of Texas* (New York: Free Press, 2006), 227–228; Moore, *Savage Frontier*, 3: 104; Caperton, "Sketch of Colonel John C. Hays," 8. See also Donaly E. Brice, "Participants in the Battle of Plum Creek," *Plum Creek Almanac* 2 (Fall 1984): 99.
18. Gammel, comp., *The Laws of Texas*, 2: 475–476. Reprinted in *Telegraph and Texas Register*, February 10, 1841. Muster and Pay Rolls, Captain John C. Hays, Company of Spies, 401–718, Captain John T. Price, Company of Spies, -719, Captain Antonio Pérez, Spy Company, -719, TSLAC; *Telegraph and Texas Register*, January 6, 1841. Past authors,

including Greer, Roger Conger, and Frederick Wilkins, have presented Hays's first legitimate commission date as occurring in early 1840. As Stephen L. Moore has correctly noted, a comprehensive review of after-action reports, correspondence, and audited claims reveals Hays did not begin commanding officially sanctioned ranger companies until January 1841. The confusion probably began with Hays himself. In a letter written to Mirabeau Lamar in 1844, he noted the various engagements his first company had been involved in as transpiring in 1840. The events he described to the former president match the details given in his previous, properly dated reports. Moore, *Savage Frontier*, 3: 180; Hays to Lamar, n.d., Gulick, et al., eds., *Lamar Papers*, 4: 232. Further, Hays provided the same erroneous year to his biographer, John Caperton, some three decades later. "Sketch of Colonel John C. Hays," 8.

19. John Henry Brown, *History of Texas, from 1685 to 1892* (St. Louis, MO: L. E. Daniell, 1893), 2: 211; Mike Cox, *The Texas Rangers: Wearing the Cinco Peso, 1821–1900* (New York: Tom Doherty Associates, 2008), 78; Webber, *Tales of the Southern Border*, 55; Caperton, "Sketch of Colonel John C. Hays," 47; Samuel C. Reid, Jr., *The Scouting Expeditions of McCulloch's Texas Rangers; or, the Summer and Fall Campaigns of the Army of the United States in Mexico—1846* (Philadelphia: G. B. Zieber and Company, 1847), 108; Green, ed., *Memoirs of Mary A. Maverick*, 29.
20. Caperton, "Sketch of John C. Hays," 10.
21. Price to Archer, January 23, 1841, *Journals of the House of Representatives of the Republic of Texas: Fifth Congress, First Session*, Appendix, 444; Moore, *Savage Frontier*, 3: 185; Hays to Lamar, n.d., Gulick, et al., eds., *Lamar Papers*, 4: 232; Joseph B. Wilkinson, *Laredo and the Rio Grande Frontier: A Narrative* (Austin: Jenkins Publishing Co., 1975), 175–176; Seb S. Wilcox, "Laredo during the Texas Republic," *Southwestern Historical Quarterly* 42 (October 1938): 99. Based on the faulty information previously discussed, Greer inadvertently placed the Laredo episode one year earlier than its actual occurrence. *Texas Ranger*, 37.
22. John A. Adams, Jr., *Conflict and Commerce on the Rio Grande: Laredo, 1755–1955* (College Station: Texas A&M University Press, 2008), 60–62; Hämäläinen, *The Comanche Empire*, 198–199; J. Frank Dobie and John D. Young, *A Vaquero of the Brush Country: The Life and Times of John D. Young* (Austin: University of Austin Press, 1998), 45; Bell to Archer, October 4, 1841, *Journals of the Sixth Congress*,

ed. Harriet Smither, 3: 432–433; *Telegraph and Texas Register*, June 9, 1841; Wilcox, "Laredo during the Texas Republic," 98; Cox, *Wearing the Cinco Peso*, 82.

23. Greer, *Texas Ranger*, 45; Joseph Milton Nance, *After San Jacinto: The Texas-Mexican Frontier, 1836–1841* (Austin: University of Texas Press, 1963), 410; Hays to Archer, April 14, 1841, *Journals of the Sixth Congress*, 3: 411. Reprinted in *Texas Sentinel*, April 22, 1841; and *Telegraph and Texas Register*, April 28, 1841. DeShields, "Frontier Sketches," "Sketches Concerning the Life of John C. Hays," 1–2.
24. Greer, *Texas Ranger*, 45; Nance, *After San Jacinto*, 411; Hays to Archer, April 14, 1841, *Journals of the Sixth Congress*, 3: 411; Hays to Lamar, n.d., Gulick, et al., eds., *Lamar Papers*, 4: 232; Sylvia Villarreal Bisnar, *P. L. Buquor, Indian Fighter, Texas Ranger, Mayor of San Antonio* (Bloomington, IN: AuthorHouse, 2009), 40; Affleck, "History of John C. Hayes," Pt. I: 148; Henderson, *Jack Hays*, 26–27.
25. Greer, *Texas Ranger*, 46; Moore, *Savage Frontier*, 3: 214–215; Bisnar, *P. L. Buquor*, 40–41; Caperton, "Sketch of Colonel John C. Hays," 14; Hays to Archer, April 14, 1841, *Journals of the Sixth Congress*, 3: 411; Hays to Lamar, n.d., Gulick, et al., eds., *Lamar Papers*, 4: 232–233; Affleck, "History of John C. Hayes," Pt. I: 152–153.
26. Greer, *Texas Ranger*, 46; Nance, *After San Jacinto*, 414; Moore, *Savage Frontier*, 3: 216; Affleck, "History of John C. Hayes," Pt. I: 153–154.
27. Nance, *After San Jacinto*, 414; *Telegraph and Texas Register*, June 9, 1841; *Texas Sentinel*, May 27, 1841; Affleck, "History of John C. Hayes," Pt. I: 155.
28. Hays to Lamar, n.d., Gulick, et al., eds., *Lamar Papers*, 4: 233; Nance, *After San Jacinto*, 415; Muster and Pay Rolls, John C. Hays, 401–718, TSLAC.
29. Gammel, comp., *Laws of Texas*, 2: 646–648, 574; Pierce, *Texas Under Arms*, 141; Muster and Pay Rolls, Captain John C. Hays, 401–718, TSLAC; John C. Hays, Public Debt Claim No. 998, Reel 160, Frame 472, Reel 199, Frame 411, TSLAC. Companies were approved for Bastrop, Béxar, Bowie, Fannin, Goliad, Gonzales, Harrison, Houston, Lamar, Milam, Montgomery, Nacogdoches, Panola, Paschal, Red River, Refugio, Robertson, San Patricio, Travis, and Victoria Counties.
30. *Telegraph and Texas Register*, June 9, 1841; Green, ed., *Memoirs of Mary A. Maverick*, 55–56.
31. Greer, *Texas Ranger*, 46–47; Hays to the Secretary of War, July 1, 1841, *Journals of the Sixth Congress*, 3: 422. Reprinted in the *Austin*

City Gazette, July 7, 1841. A typescript of the article can be found in Box 3F176, Hays Collection, BCAH. John C. Hays, Public Debt Claim No. 996, Reel 160, Frames 379–482, TSLAC; Hays to Lamar, n.d., Gulick, et al., eds., *Lamar Papers*, 4: 233–234.

32. Greer, *Texas Ranger*, 47; Caperton, "Sketch of John C. Hays," 16–18; Hays to Lamar, n.d., Gulick, et al., eds., *Lamar Papers*, 4: 234; Hunter, ed., "Jack Hays, the Intrepid," 72–73; Jess Arnold, "Captain Jack," *True West* 2 (December 1954-January 1955): 15.
33. Hays to the Secretary of War, July 1, 1841, *Journals of the Sixth Congress*, 3: 422; *Telegraph and Texas Register*, July 14, 1841; Hays to Lamar, n.d., Gulick, et al., eds., *Lamar Papers*, 4: 234.
34. Greer, *Texas Ranger*, 50; Moore, *Savage Frontier*, 3: 278; Hays to the Secretary of War, July 1, 1841, *Journals of the Sixth Congress*, 3: 422–423; Muster and Pay Rolls, John C. Hays, 401–718, TSLAC; Caperton, "Sketch of Col. John C. Hays," 22–23; John Wesley Wilbarger, *Indian Depredations in Texas* (Austin: State House Press, 1985), 79.
35. Greer, *Texas Ranger*, 50; Hays to Archer, August 13, 1841, *Journals of Sixth Congress*, 3: 423–424; Caperton, "Sketch of John C. Hays," 18; *Telegraph and Texas Register*, August 4, 1841; Hunter, ed., "Jack Hays, the Intrepid," 73; Hays to Lamar, n.d., Gulick, et al., eds., *Lamar Papers*, 4: 234. Sherry Robinson, *I Fought a Good Fight: A History of the Lipan Apaches* (Denton: University of North Texas Press, 2013), 197.
36. Gulick, et al., eds., *Lamar Papers*, 4: 235.
37. Greer, *Texas Ranger*, 51; Hays to Archer, August 13, 1841, *Journals of Sixth Congress*, 3: 424; Hays to Lamar, n.d., Gulick, et al., eds., *Lamar Papers*, 4: 234–235; F. Todd Smith, *From Dominance to Disappearance: The Indians of Texas and the Near Southwest, 1786–1859* (Lincoln: University of Nebraska Press, 2005), 176; Muster and Pay Rolls, John C. Hays, 401–718, TSLAC; John C. Hays, Public Debt Claim No. 998, Reel 160, Frame 472, Reel 199, Frame 411, TSLAC.
38. Greer, *Texas Ranger*, 51–52; J. Marvin Hunter, "Jack Hays: The Famous Texas Ranger," *Frontier Times* 1 (October 1923): 1.
39. Muster and Pay Rolls, John C. Hays, 401–718, TSLAC; John C. Hays, Public Debt Claim No. 996, Reel 160, Frames 379, 439, TSLAC; Pierce, *Texas Under Arms*, 142–143; *Telegraph and Texas Register*, December 8, 1841; Lamar to Hays, October 2, 1841, Record

of Executive Documents from the 10th December 1838 to the 14th December 1841, Executive Record Books, Reel No. 3472/353.91, TSLAC, 250–251. Hays would finally be able to settle his accounts after May 5, 1846, when the First Legislature authorized him to draw and disburse the monies due the men of his old minute company. Gammel, comp., *Laws of Texas*, 2: 1484.

40. Moore, *Savage Frontier*, 3: 344. For other discussions of the battle, see Greer, *Texas Ranger*, 52–53; C. L. Douglas, *The Gentlemen in the White Hats: Dramatic Episodes in the History of the Texas Rangers* (Dallas: South-West Press, 1934), 28–29; Roger N. Conger, et al., *Rangers of Texas* (Waco: Texian Press, 1969), 13–14; Hardin, *Texas Rangers*, 12–13; Charles M. Robinson III, *The Men Who Wear the Star: The Story of the Texas Rangers* (New York: The Modern Library, 2001), 65–66; Wilkins, *The Legend Begins*, 202–204; Michael L. Collins, *Texas Devils: Rangers and Regulars on the Lower Rio Grande, 1846–1861* (Norman: University of Oklahoma Press, 2008), 24–25; and Jennings, *Riding for the Lone Star*, 160–161.
41. Haley, *Passionate Nation*, 231; James P. Bevill, *The Paper Republic: The Struggle for Money, Credit, and Independence in the Republic of Texas* (Houston, TX: Bright Sky Press, 2009), 250; William Carey Crane, *Life and Select Literary Remains of Sam Houston of Texas* (Philadelphia: J. B. Lippincott & Co., 1884), 296; Stanley Siegel, *A Political History of the Texas Republic, 1836–1845* (Austin: University of Texas Press, 1956), 120, 145, 187.
42. Houston to the House of Representatives, January 6, 1842, Amelia W. Williams and Eugene C. Barker, ed., *Writings of Sam Houston* (Austin: University of Texas Press, 1938–1943) 2: 423; Hockley to Houston, January 25, 1842, *Journals of the Sixth Congress*, 1: 303–304; *Telegraph and Texas Register*, December 15, 1841; Jennings, *Riding for the Lone Star*, 164–165; Gerald Swetnam Pierce, "The Army of the Texas Republic, 1836–1845" (Ph.D. dissertation, University of Mississippi, 1963), 234–235; Gammel, comp., *Laws of Texas*, 2: 746.
43. *Telegraph and Texas Register*, February 23, March 9, 1842; Joseph Milton Nance, *Attack and Counterattack: The Texas-Mexican Frontier, 1842* (Austin: University of Texas Press, 1964), 9–11, 12, 14; Green, ed., *Memoirs of Mary A. Maverick*, 60; Brown, *History of Texas*, 2: 211; Gammel, comp., *Laws of Texas*, 2: 770–771.
44. Greer, *Texas Ranger*, 64–65; Robert M. Utley, *Lone Star Justice: The First Century of the Texas Rangers* (New York: Berkley Books,

2002), 42; Robinson, *Men Who Wear the Star*, 321; *Telegraph and Texas Register*, March 16, 23, April 27, 1842; Nance, *Attack and Counterattack*, 23, 30, 26–27; Nance, *After San Jacinto*, 47–48, 52; Raúl A. Ramos, *Beyond the Alamo: Forging Mexican Ethnicity in San Antonio, 1821–1861* (Chapel Hill: University of North Carolina Press, 2008), 186; Brown, *History of Texas*, 2: 214–215.

45. Nance, *Attack and Counterattack*, 52; John H. Jenkins and Kenneth Kesselus, *Edward Burleson: Texas Frontier Leader* (Austin: Jenkins Publishing Company, 1990), 298; Harry A. Gailey, Jr., "Sam Houston and the Texas War Fever, March-August 1842," *Southwestern Historical Quarterly* 62 (July 1958): 38–39; John C. Hays, Unnumbered Audited Claim, Reel 43, Frame 42, TSLAC; Brown, *History of Texas*, 2: 215–216; Address of Edward Burleson to Citizen Volunteer Soldiers, April 2, 1842, *Journals of the Sixth Congress*, 3: 46–47. Reprinted in *Telegraph and Texas Register*, April 20, 1842.
46. Nance, *Attack and Counterattack*, 114, 116; Catherine W. McDowell, ed., *Now You Hear My Horn: The Journal of James Wilson Nichols, 1820–1887* (Austin: University of Texas Press, 1967), 76; *Northern Standard*, September 3, 1842.
47. Greer, *Texas Ranger*, 48; McDowell, ed., *Now You Hear My Horn*, 77; Moore, *Savage Frontier* 4: 33–36; Clifford R. Caldwell, *A Day's Ride from Here: Noxville, Texas* (Charleston, SC: The History Press, 2011), 25–26; Mike Cox, *Gunfights and Sites in Texas Ranger History* (Charleston, SC: The History Press, 2015), 57–58; Andrew Jackson Sowell, *Texas Indian Fighters: Early Settlers and Indian Fighters of Southwest Texas* (Austin: State House Press, 1986), 20–24, 317–321, 809–810; Creed Taylor, Republic Pensions, Reel 241, Frames 174–178, TSLAC. Sowell wrote "The Battle of Bandera Pass," which appeared in *San Antonio Light*, September 21, 1921, and was reprinted in *Frontier Times* 2 (May 1925): 22–23. In the article, he dated the fight as occurring in 1842.

    For examples of how these mistakes have gained credibility with otherwise reliable authors, see Charles M. Robinson III, "The Forgotten Fight at Bandera Pass," *True West* 39 (June 1992): 22–24; and Bill O'Neal, *Fighting Men of the Indian Wars: A Biographical Encyclopedia of the Mountain Men, Soldiers, Cowboys, and Pioneers Who Took Up Arms During America's Westward Expansion* (Stillwater, OK: Barbed Wire Press, 1991), 139.

48. Greer, *Texas Ranger*, 49; McDowell, ed., *Now You Hear My Horn*, 77; Sowell, *Texas Indian Fighters*, 22; Creed Taylor, "Jack Hays Fight on the Guadalupe," Box 3F176, Hays Collection, BCAH.
49. Greer, *Texas Ranger*, 49; McDowell, ed., *Now You Hear My Horn*, 77–78; Wilbarger, *Indian Depredations in Texas*, 73–74; Taylor, "Jack Hays Fight on the Guadalupe."
50. Greer, *Texas Ranger*, 65; Report of the Secretary of War and Marine, November 12, 1842, *Journals of the House of Representatives of the Seventh Congress*, Appendix, 30; *Telegraph and Texas Register*, June 15, 1842; Gammel, comp., *Laws of Texas*, 2: 816. Another company was authorized to range the Trinity and Navasota Rivers country. Houston to the Texas Senate, July 18, 1842, Williams and Barker, eds., *Writings of Sam Houston*, 3: 106; Nance, *Attack and Counterattack*, 280, 291.
51. Report of the Secretary of War and Marine, November 12, 1842, *Journals of the House, Seventh Congress*, Appendix, 30–31. Reprinted in *Telegraph and Texas Register*, January 4, 1843.
52. Greer, *Texas Ranger*, 65; Wilkins, *The Legend Begins*, 124; Nance, *Attack and Counterattack*, 280–281; *Telegraph and Texas Register*, September 7, 1842. Captain Ephraim W. McLean was also ordered to raise a company and patrol the country west of the San Antonio River, but he too had trouble finding a sufficient number of men to recruit. *Morning Star*, August 6, 1842; *Telegraph and Texas Register*, August 10, 1842.
53. Greer, *Texas Ranger*, 69; Houston to Hays, September 14, 1842, Williams and Barker, eds., *Writings of Sam Houston*, 4: 144–146; Hays to the Citizens of Texas, September 12, 1842, Hutchinson, et al. to the Citizens of Gonzales County, September 10, 1842, *Journals of the House, Seventh Congress*, Appendix, 21–22, 18–19; Diary of Judge Anderson Hutchinson, September 10, 1842, Ernest William Winkler, "The Béxar and Dawson Prisoners," *The Quarterly of the Texas State Historical Association* 13 (April 1910): 294; Nance, *Attack and Counterattack*, 306–307.
54. Hays to the Secretary of War, September 12, 1842, *Journals of the House, Seventh Congress*, Appendix, 16; Bisnar, *P. L. Buquor*, 66; Ramos, *Beyond the Alamo*, 186, 188, 189; Brazos, *Life of Robert Hall: Indian Fighter and Veteran of Three Great Wars* (Austin: State House Press, 1992), 70; Joseph M. Nance, trans. and ed., "Brigadier General Adrian Woll's Report of His Expedition into Texas in 1842," *Southwestern Historical Quarterly* 58 (April 1955): 525, 527, 535–538; Nance,

Attack and Counterattack, 306–307, 318. Anderson Hutchinson's diary stated Hays left San Antonio for his scouting mission with six men. Winkler, "Béxar and Dawson Prisoners," 294.

55. Greer, *Texas Ranger*, 70–71; Hays to the Citizens of Texas, September 12, 1842, Caldwell to Hamilton, September 18, 1842, *Journals of the House, Seventh Congress*, Appendix, 21–22, 16; Bisnar, *P. L. Buquor*, 66–67; Sowell, *Texas Indian Fighters*, 24; Nance, *Attack and Counterattack*, 322, 346; John C. Hays, Unnumbered Audited Claim, Reel 43, Frame 44, Public Debt Claim No. 1561, Reel 160, Frames 483–491, TSLAC; Z. N. Morrell, *Flowers and Fruits from the Wilderness* (Boston: Gould & Lincoln, 1872), 163–165, 166; Brazos, *Life of Robert Hall*, 71; *Nelson* Lee, *Three Years Among the Comanches: The Narrative of Nelson Lee, the Texas Ranger* (Norman: University of Oklahoma Press, 1991), 54; *Telegraph and Texas Register*, September 21, 1842.
56. Morrell, *Flowers and Fruits*, 167; *Telegraph and Texas Register*, October 22, November 2, 1842; Green, ed., *Memoirs of Mary A. Maverick*, 72.
57. Greer, *Texas Ranger*, 71–73; Caldwell to Hamilton, September 18, 1842, *Journals of the House, Seventh Congress*, Appendix, 17; McDowell, ed., *Now You Hear My Horn*, 98; Morrell, *Flowers and Fruits*, 167–169; Sowell, *Texas Indian Fighters*, 24; Brown, *History of Texas*, 2: 224; Lee, *Three Years Among the Comanches*, 55; *Telegraph and Texas Register*, October 22, November 2, 1842; Nance, *Attack and Counterattack*, 358. Woll reported he sent 130 horsemen to pursue Hays's detachment. He further stated he crossed the Salado lower from the Texian position and formed his troops in two lines at their rear. Nance, trans. and ed., "Adrian Woll's Report," 543.
58. Greer, *Texas Ranger*, 73; Nance, *Attack and Counterattack*, 357, 359–360; McDowell, ed., *Now You Hear My Horn*, 99; Morrell, *Flowers and Fruits*, 170; Brown, *History of Texas*, 2: 225; Henderson, *Jack Hays*, 42.
59. Greer, *Texas Ranger*, 73; A. J. Sowell, *Rangers and Pioneers of Texas* (Austin: State House Press, 1991), 215; Utley, *Lone Star Justice*, 46; Brazos, *Life of Robert Hall*, 72; Caldwell to Hamilton, September 18, 1842, *Journals of the House, Seventh Congress,* Appendix, 17; Nance, *Attack and Counterattack*, 360; *Telegraph and Texas Register*, September 28, October 12, 1842. Sowell maintained Wilson Randle killed Córdova, while Brown and Ford argued John Lowe fired the

fatal shot. Sowell, *Texas Indian Fighters*, 25; Brown, *Indian Wars*, 56–57, 66; John S. Ford, "John C. Hayes in Texas," Box 2Q512, John Salmon Ford Papers, BCAH, 10. Morrell claimed Woll later admitted losing six hundred soldiers during the invasion. *Flowers and Fruits*, 179. Another person stated one hundred Mexicans were killed on the battlefield and one hundred wounded, of which twenty-three had died by the following day. *Telegraph and Texas Register*, October 26, 1842. Woll's self-serving report counted his losses at twenty-nine killed and fifty-eight wounded, claimed "considerable" Texian casualties of 180 killed, and asserted the survivors had fled through the woods. He further maintained his own withdrawal was caused by concern that Texian forces might be marching on his rear. Nance, trans. and ed., "Adrian Woll's Report," 541, 544.

60. Greer, *Texas Ranger*, 73; Caldwell to Hamilton, September 18, 1842, *Journals of the House, Seventh Congress*, Appendix, 17. Caperton related the story of how Hays and Ben McCulloch infiltrated Woll's camp on the Medina to determine the Mexican general's numbers. "Sketch of Colonel John C. Hays," 26–27.

61. Greer, *Texas Ranger*, 73–78; Caldwell to Hamilton, September 18, 1842, *Journals of the House, Seventh Congress*, Appendix, 17; Affleck, "History of John C. Hayes," Pt. I: 254–255, 259–261; *Telegraph and Texas Register*, October 22, 1842; McDowell, ed., *Now You Hear My Horn*, 109–110; Nance, trans. and ed., "Adrian Woll's Report," 549; Caperton, "Sketch of John C. Hays," 28; Sowell, *Texas Indian Fighters*, 25–28; Green, ed., *Memoirs of Mary A. Maverick*, 75–76; Brazos, *Life of Robert Hall*, 72. Perhaps wishing to sully his enemy's honor, Woll recounted: "Captain Hays, presented himself on horseback on the other side of the arroyo at the edge of the forest, and, taking off his hat, hailed me. He called me by my name and title, requesting that I approach to speak to him. Notwithstanding the remarks of my aides-de-camp who implored me not to believe these friendly demonstrations, I advanced; and taking off my hat to reply to the salute, I had gone a distance of about 30 yards, which is the breadth of the arroyo, when two Texans hidden behind some trees aimed and discharged their rifles at me. Fate determined that they would not hit their mark, and the whistling balls passed over my head; then the aforesaid Hays projected himself precipitately into the most dense [part] of the forest, defaming God and insulting me and calling me a coward." Nance, trans. and ed., "Adrian Woll's Report,"

549–550. No other account, written by either a Texian or a Mexican, has been found to substantiate Woll's dubious claim.

62. Houston to Somervell, October 3, 1842, Williams and Barker, eds., *Writings of Sam Houston*, 3: 170. Reprinted in *Telegraph and Texas Register*, October 12, 1842. Brown, *History of Texas*, 2: 233.
63. Houston to Somervell, October 3, 1842, *Journals of the House, Seventh Congress*, Appendix, 4.
64. Greer, *Texas Ranger*, 79–80, 81; Hamilton to Somervell, October 19, 1842, Hamilton to Somervell, November 19, 1842, Williams and Barker, eds., *Writings of Sam Houston*, 3: 188, 197–199; Affleck, "History of John C. Hayes," Pt. I: 270; Hamilton to Somervell, November 7, 1842, Hamilton to Somervell, November 19, 1842, Hemphill to Hamilton, November 21, 1842, *Journals of the House, Seventh Congress*, Appendix, 7–14; *Telegraph and Texas Register*, November 2, 1842; Nance, *Attack and Counterattack*, 458; General Thomas J. Green, *Journal of the Texian Expedition against Mier* (New York: Harper & Brothers, 1845), 41, 44–45; Sterling Brown Hendricks, "The Somervell Expedition to the Rio Grande, 1842," *Southwestern Historical Quarterly* 23 (October 1919): 116–118; Ernest William Winkler, ed., "The Bryan-Hayes Correspondence," Pt. 1, ibid. 25 (October 1921): 104.
65. Greer, *Texas Ranger*, 82–83; John Holland Jenkins, *Recollections of Early Texas: The Memoirs of John Holland Jenkins*, ed. John Holmes Jenkins III (Austin: University of Texas Press, 2003), 107; Brown, *History of Texas*, 2: 234, 236; Hendricks, "Somervell Expedition," 116, 117, 120, 119; Robinson, *I Fought a Good Fight*, 205; *Telegraph and Texas Register*, January 11, 1843; Noah Smithwick, *The Evolution of a State, or Recollections of Old Texas Days*, comp. Nanna Smithwick Donaldson (Austin: University of Texas Press, 1983), 160; Green, *Journal of the Texian Expedition against Mier*, 44–46, 53; Henderson, *Jack Hays*, 49.
66. Hendricks, "Somervell Expedition," 119–120.
67. Nance, *Attack and Counterattack*, 514–515, 521; Thomas W. Bell, *A Narrative of the Capture and Subsequent Suffering of the Mier Prisoners in Mexico* (Waco: Texian Press, 1964), 9. Hereafter cited as *Mier Expedition Narrative*. Adams, *Conflict and Commerce on the Rio Grande*, 69; *Telegraph and Texas Register*, January 4, 18, 1843; *Morning Star*, January 17, 1843; William Preston Stapp, *The Prisoners of Perote* (Austin: University of Texas Press, 1977), 18–19; Winkler, ed., "Bryan-Hayes Correspondence," Pt. 1: 105; Green, *Journal of the*

Texian Expedition against Mier, 56–57; Joseph D. McCutchan, *Mier Expedition Diary: A Texan Prisoner's Account*, ed. Joseph Milton Nance (Austin: University of Texas Press, 1978), 25–26; Wilcox, "Laredo during the Texas Republic," 101–102.

68. Sam W. Haynes, *Soldiers of Misfortune: The Somervell and Mier Expeditions* (Austin: University of Texas Press, 1990), 57–58, 51; Jennings, *Riding for the Lone Star*, 177.
69. Nance, *Attack and Counterattack*, 529–530, 554–555; *Telegraph and Texas Register*, January 18, 1843; Hendricks, "Somervell Expedition," 130; McCutchan, *Mier Expedition Diary*, 29; Randolph B. Campbell, *Gone to Texas: A History of the Lone Star State* (New York: Oxford University Press, 2003), 179; Adele B. Looscan, ed., "Journal of Lewis Birdsall Harris, 1836–1842," *Southwestern Historical Quarterly* 25 (January 1922): 189.
70. Nance, *Attack and Counterattack*, 557; Winkler, ed., "Bryan-Hayes Correspondence," Pt. 1: 105; Stapp, *Prisoners of Perote*, 30; *Morning Star*, January 17, 1843; Lucy A. Erath, ed., "Memoirs of Major George Bernard Erath," Pt. 3, *Southwestern Historical Quarterly* 27 (July 1923): 43; Looscan, ed., "Journal of Lewis Birdsall Harris," 193; Hendricks, "Somervell Expedition," 139; Robinson, *I Fought a Good Fight*, 206–207. Affleck and Greer claim Hays remained to command the rangers who stayed behind. "History of John C. Hays," Pt. I: 296–299; *Texas Ranger*, 88–89. Haynes follows suit in *Soldiers of Misfortune*, 63.

    For contemporary mentions of Flacco's murder, see Gulick, et al., eds., *Lamar Papers*, 6: 297; *Telegraph and Texas Register*, March 29, April 26, 1843; and Affleck, "History of John C. Hayes," Pt. I: 299–300. Due in no small part to this tragedy, the Lipans thereafter became deadly foes of the Texans. For more on the Lipan people, see Thomas A. Britten, *The Lipan Apaches: People of Wind and Lightning* (Albuquerque: University of New Mexico Press, 2009).
71. Greer, *Texas Ranger*, 89; Gammel, comp., *Laws of Texas*, 2: 848, 865; *Annual Report of the Secretary of War, November 25, 1843*, 401–1215, TSLAC; Houston to Lewis and Others, May 18, 1843, Williams and Barker, eds., *Writings of Sam Houston*, 3: 391; Bisnar, *P. L. Buquor*, 71.
72. Muster and Pay Rolls, John C. Hays, 401–718, TSLAC.
73. Greer, *Texas Ranger*, 90; Moore, *Savage Frontier*, 4: 130; *Telegraph and Texas Register*, April 26, May 10, 1843; *Morning Star*, April 20, 1843; Affleck, "History of John C. Hayes," Pt. I: 309.
74. Greer, *Texas Ranger*, 90–91; Proclamation by the President, April 27, 1843, Williams and Barker, eds., *Writings of Sam Houston*, 3:

366–367. Reprinted in *Telegraph and Texas Register*, May 17, 1843, *Red-Lander*, May 20, 1843, and *Civilian and Galveston Gazette*, May 31, 1843. Bisnar, *P. L. Buquor*, 71; Anson Jones, *Memoranda and Official Correspondence Relating to the Republic of Texas, Its History and Annexation* (New York: D. Appleton and Company, 1859), 252; *Telegraph and Texas Register*, July 12, 1843.

75. Greer, *Texas Ranger*, 91–92; *Telegraph and Texas Register*, May 31, September 27, November 22, 1843; Muster and Pay Rolls, John C. Hays, 401–718, TSLAC; *Morning Star*, September 21, 1843; Houston to Raymond, September 26, 1843, Williams and Barker, eds., *Writings of Sam Houston*, 3: 431.
76. Greer, *Texas Ranger*, 93; *Telegraph and Texas Register*, November 1, 29, 1843, January 3, 1844; *Annual Report of the Secretary of War, November 25, 1843*, 401–1215, TSLAC; Hays to Hill, November 12, 1843, 401–1308, TSLAC; Wilkins, *The Legend Begins*, 173; John C. Hays, Audited Claim No. 994, Reel 43, Frames 57–58, Unnumbered Audited Claim, Reel 43, Frames 39–40, TSLAC. The Eighth Congress passed a joint resolution on December 19 to reimburse the rangers whose pay was in arrears, and the merchants who had supplied them, the combined sum of $6,450. Gammel, comp., *Laws of Texas*, 2: 915.
77. Greer, *Texas Ranger*, 93–94; *Telegraph and Texas Register*, November 29, 1843; Ella Foy O'Gorman, *Descendants of Virginia Calverts* (Los Angeles: s. n., 1947), 200.
78. *Telegraph and Texas Register*, February 7, 14, 1844; Gammel, comp., *Laws of Texas*, 2: 943–944.
79. Greer, *Texas Ranger*, 99; Gammel, comp., *Laws of Texas*, 2: 961–963; Patsy McDonald Spaw, ed., *The Texas Senate* (College Station: Texas A&M University Press, 1990), 1: 134.
80. Greer, *Texas Ranger*, 99; Muster and Pay Rolls, John C. Hays, 401–791, TSLAC; Moore, *Savage Frontier*, 4: 141; *Telegraph and Texas Register*, February 28, March 6, 1844.
81. Greer, *Texas Ranger*, 99; Hamilton to Houston, November 30, 1844, *Journals of the House of Representatives of the Ninth Congress of the Republic of Texas*, Appendix, 28; *Telegraph and Texas Register*, March 20, April 17, 24, May 1, 15, 1844; Muster and Pay Rolls, John C. Hays, 401–791, TSLAC; *Morning Star*, April 13, 1844.
82. Greer, *Texas Ranger*, 104–105; Houston to Henderson, February 20, 1844, Williams and Barker, eds., *Writings of Sam Houston*, 4: 269. Houston also described Hays as a colonel and volunteer aide-de-camp on the presidential staff. John W. Lockhart, "Jack Hays Visit to Washington,"

Hays Collection, Box 3F176, BCAH; Richard B. McCaslin, *Washington on the Brazos: Cradle of the Texas Republic* (Austin: Texas State Historical Association, 2016), 32, 74; *Morning Star*, May 9, 1844. See also Mrs. Jonnie Lockhart Wallis and Lawrence L. Hill, eds., *Sixty Years on the Brazos: The Life and Letters of Dr. John Washington Lockhart, 1824–1900* (Waco: Texian Press, 1967).

83. Robert M. Utley, "The Texas Ranger Tradition Established: Jack Hays and Walker Creek," *Montana: The Magazine of Western History* 52 (Spring 2002): 2–11; Hardin, *Texas Rangers*, 12; Kavanagh, *Comanche Political History*, 269.
84. *Journals of the Fourth Congress of the Republic of Texas*, ed. Harriet Smither, 2: 124–125; Robert Lawrence Wilson, *Colt: An American Legend* (New York: Abbeville Press, 1985), 18; Downing to Thompson, n.d., *Report from the Secretary of the Navy*, Senate Document No. 503, 26th Congress, 1st Session, 13. Reprinted in *Army and Navy Chronicle* 10 (1840), Appendix: 13.
85. John E. Parsons, ed., *Samuel Colt's Own Record of Transactions with Captain Walker and Eli Whitney, Jr. in 1847* (Hartford: Connecticut Historical Society, 1949), 9; Jennings, *Riding for the Lone Star*, 28, 182–183; Hardin, *Texas Rangers*, 11–12; Extract of Letter from Commodore E. W. Moore, *Memorial of Samuel Colt*, Senate Report No. 296, 30th Congress, 2nd Session, 11; Wilkins, *The Legend Begins*, 177.
86. Hays to Secretary of War and Marine, June 16, 1844, *Journals of the House, Ninth Congress*, Appendix, 32. Reprinted in *Texas National Register*, December 14, 1844. Kenneth F. Neighbours, "The Battle of Walker's Creek," *West Texas Historical Association Yearbook* 41 (1965): 123; Ford, "John C. Hayes in Texas," 19. Using at least five sources, Greer extracted details of the Walker's Creek fight and inserted them into his narrative as three separate engagements. *Texas Ranger*, 96–98, 102, 103, 105–108. Bisnar makes the same error in *P. L. Buquor*, 76–77
87. Hays to Secretary of War and Marine, June 16, 1844, *Journals of the House, Ninth Congress*, Appendix, 32; Neighbours, "Battle of Walker's Creek," 123–124; *Morning Star*, June 29, 1844; Caperton, "Sketch of John C. Hays," 21–22; Ford, "John C. Hayes in Texas," 20; Utley, *Lone Star Justice*, 10–11; Lee, *Three Years Among the Comanches*, 24–25.
88. Hays to Secretary of War and Marine, June 16, 1844, *Journals of the House, Ninth Congress*, Appendix, 32–33; *Telegraph and Texas Register*,

July 3, 1844; Sowell, *Texas Indian Fighters*, 333; Affleck, "History of John C. Hayes," Pt. I: 350; Wilbarger, *Indian Depredations in Texas*, 76.

89. Hays to Secretary of War and Marine, June 16, 1844, *Journals of the House, Ninth Congress*, Appendix, 33; Ford, "John C. Hayes in Texas," 22; Wilbarger, *Indian Depredations in Texas*, 78. The captain reported a number of Wacos and Mexicans had accompanied the Comanche war party. *Morning Star*, June 29, 1844; Green, ed., *Memoirs of Mary A. Maverick*, 82–83; Moore, *Savage Frontier*, 4: 155; Muster and Pay Rolls, John C. Hays, 401–718, TSLAC.
90. Muster and Pay Rolls, John C. Hays, 401–718, TSLAC; *Telegraph and Texas Register*, December 18, 1844. On February 3, 1845, Congress passed a joint resolution for the financial relief of Hays and his company. The captain's accounts were audited and settled for the sum of $405. Gammel, comp., *Laws of Texas*, 2: 1147.
91. Greer, *Texas Ranger*, 113, 115; Gammel, comp., *Laws of Texas*, 2: 1124–1125; Spaw, ed., *Texas Senate*, 1: 152; Bevill, *The Paper Republic*, 278; *Telegraph and Texas Register*, March 12, April 30, 1845; Muster and Pay Rolls, John C. Hays, 401–718, -791, TSLAC; Pierce, *Army of the Texas Republic*, 329.
92. Charles D. Spurlin, *Texas Volunteers in the Mexican War* (Austin: Eakin Press, 1998), 2–3; Marcy to Taylor, May 28, 1845, Bancroft to Taylor, June 15, 1845, *Mexican War Correspondence*, House Executive Document No. 60, 30th Congress, 1st Session, 79–81; Steven E. Woodworth, *Manifest Destinies: America's Westward Expansion and the Road to the Civil War* (New York: Vintage Books, 2010), 143–144; Z. T. Fulmore, "The Annexation of Texas and the Mexican War," *The Quarterly of the Texas State Historical Association* 5 (July 1901): 38–39.
93. Greer, *Texas Ranger*, 116; Compiled Service Records of Volunteer Soldiers, Hays' Texas Mounted Rangers, John C. Hays; *Daily Picayune*, September 25, 1845; *Telegraph and Texas Register*, October 15, 1845; Taylor to Adjutant General, September 14, 1845, *Mexican War Correspondence*, 107; Wilkins, *The Legend Begins*, 196; Robinson, *Men Who Wear the Star*, 73; K. Jack Bauer, *The Mexican War, 1846–1848* (Lincoln: University of Nebraska Press, 1992), 33; Frank Leon Jones III, *With Zachary Taylor in Texas* (M.S. thesis, Texas A&M University-Kingsville, 1995), 20, 33.
94. Affleck's original article was reprinted as "Great Battle at Painted Rock," *Frontier Times* 1 (January 1924): 40–43.

95. See Mike Cox, "Battle of the Painted Rocks: Scraping off the Layers," *West Texas Historical Association Yearbook* (2002): 151–169; and Moore, *Savage Frontier*, 4: 201–203. See also Greer, *Texas Ranger*, 118–123; Hunter, ed., "Jack Hays, the Intrepid," 86–87; Conger, et al., *Rangers of Texas*, 11–12; Gregory F. Michno and Susan J. Michno, *Forgotten Fights: Little-Known Raids and Skirmishes on the Frontier, 1823 to 1890* (Missoula, MT: Mountain Press Publishing Company, 2008), 73–74; and Wayne R. Austerman, "Ambush and Siege at Paint Rock," and "Fog of Three Battles," both in *Wild West* 22 (April 2010): 44–49.
96. *Journals of the Senate of the First Legislature of the State of Texas* (Clarksville: Standard Office, 1848), 87.
97. Fulmore, "The Annexation of Texas and the Mexican War," 40; *Daily Union*, December 31, 1845. For a more complete account, see Campbell, *Gone to Texas*, 182–186.
98. Woodworth, *Manifest Destinies*, 155–156; Theophilus F. Rodenbough, comp., *From Everglade to Canyon with the Second United States Cavalry* (Norman: University of Oklahoma Press, 2000), 99–101; General Samuel G. French, *Two Wars: An Autobiography of Gen. Samuel G. French* (Nashville: Confederate Veteran, 1901), 46; Hardee to Taylor, April 26, 1846, *Correspondence with General Taylor*, House Executive Document No. 119, 29th Congress, 2nd Session, 19–21; Polk to the Congress, May 11, 1846, *Mexican War Correspondence*, 8; *Congressional Globe*, 29th Congress, 1st Session, 795. See also Taylor to Adjutant General, April 26, 1846, Thornton to Bliss, April 27, 1846, *Mexican War Correspondence*, 141, 298.
99. Greer, *Texas Ranger*, 129–130; Compiled Service Records of Volunteer Soldiers, First Texas Mounted Rifles, John C. Hays; Frederick Wilkins, *The Highly Irregular Irregulars: Texas Rangers in the Mexican War* (Austin: Eakin Press, 1990), 36–37; *Daily Picayune*, June 5, 1846; Special Orders No. 113, July 28, 1846, *Mexican War Correspondence*, 241; *Daily Delta*, August 15, 1846; Henry W. Barton, *Texas Volunteers in the Mexican War* (Waco: Texian Press, 1970), 29–34; Dudley G. Wooten, ed., *A Comprehensive History of Texas, 1685 to 1897* (Dallas: William G. Scarff, 1898), 2: 337.

    The Second Texas Mounted Rifles, commanded by Colonel George T. Wood, also served with distinction, but his men, recruited from East Texas counties, lacked the specialized frontier skills and panache exhibited by Hays's regiment. *Niles' National Register* 70 (August 15, 1846): 372; Wilkins, *The Highly Irregular Irregulars*, 42–43.

The departure of Hays and so many of his veteran rangers left the defense of the frontier severely weakened. Brevet Colonel William S. Harney, commanding at San Antonio, was authorized to call on the acting governor of Texas for mounted volunteers, if deemed necessary. Taylor to Adjutant General, July 29, 1846, *Correspondence with General Taylor*, 117–118. For a detailed summary of this often overlooked portion of the war, see William C. Holden, "Five Texas Frontier Companies during the Mexican War," *Southwestern Historical Quarterly* 66 (July 1962): 17–30.

100. Greer, *Texas Ranger*, 130–132; Jennings, *Riding for the Lone Star*, 200; Captain William Seaton Henry, *Campaign Sketches of the War with Mexico* (New York: Harper & Brothers, 1847), 125–126; *Niles' National Register* 71 (September 5, 1846): 2, 70 (August 29, 1846): 416; *Texas Democrat*, January 27, 1847; James Buckner Barry, *Buck Barry, Texas Ranger and Frontiersman*, ed. James K. Greer (Lincoln: University of Nebraska Press, 1984), 33; Taylor to Adjutant General, August 25, 1846, *Mexican War Correspondence*, 413; Ford, "John C. Hayes in Texas," 27.
101. *Daily Delta*, September 6, 1846; Henry, *Campaign Sketches*, 160; George Wilkins Kendall, *The War Between the United States and Mexico, Illustrated* (New York: D. Appleton & Company, 1851), 5; Order No. 129, August 27, 1846, *Mexican War Correspondence*, 526.
102. Wilkins, *The Highly Irregular Irregulars*, 77; Taylor to Adjutant General, August 25, 1846, *Mexican War Correspondence*, 412–413; Charles D. Spurlin, comp., *Texas Veterans in the Mexican War: Muster Rolls of Texas Military Units* (Victoria, TX: privately printed, 1984), 17–34.
103. Greer, *Texas Ranger*, 134–135, 137–141; Taylor to Adjutant General, September 12, 1846, *Mexican War Correspondence*, 421; Jennings, *Riding for the Lone Star*, 200; James K. Holland, "Diary of a Texan Volunteer in the Mexican War," *Southwestern Historical Quarterly* 30 (July 1926): 23, 24, 25; Luther Giddings, *Sketches of the Campaign in Northern Mexico* (New York: George P. Putnam & Co., 1853), 139–140, 142, 152; Thomas Bangs Thorpe, *Our Army at Monterey* (Philadelphia: Carey and Hart, 1848), 156; Walter Prescott Webb, *The Texas Rangers in the Mexican War* (Austin: Jenkins Garrett Press,

1975), 35; Hays to Worth, September 25, 1846, Gulick, et al., eds., *Lamar Papers*, 4: 138–139. Reprinted in *The Historical Magazine* 3 (January 1874): 8–10. Kendall, *War Between the United States and Mexico*, 6; *Niles' National Register* 71 (November 7, 1846): 155; Jimmy L. Bryan, Jr., *More Zeal Than Discretion: The Westward Adventures of Walter P. Lane* (College Station: Texas A&M University Press, 2008), 52.

104. Greer, *Texas Ranger*, 139, 143–144; James M. McCaffrey, *Army of Manifest Destiny: The American Soldier in the Mexican War, 1846–1848* (New York: New York University Press, 1992), 132; Hays to Worth, September 25, 1846, Gulick, et al., eds., *Lamar Papers*, 4: 139; *Daily Picayune*, February 17, 1847; Ford, "John C. Hayes in Texas," 31–32; Spurlin, *Texas Volunteers*, 83–84; *American Flag*, October 7, 1846; Christopher D. Dishman, *A Perfect Gibraltar: The Battle for Monterrey, Mexico, 1846* (Norman: University of Oklahoma Press, 2010), 154–155.
105. Greer, *Texas Ranger*, 145–146; Hays to Worth, September 25, 1846, Gulick, et al., eds., *Lamar Papers*, 4: 139–140; Spurlin, *Texas Volunteers*, 86; Affleck, "History of John C. Hayes," Pt. II, Box 2Q402, Affleck Papers, 537–539; Justin H. Smith, *The War with Mexico* (New York: The Macmillan Company, 1919), 1: 246–247.
106. Greer, *Texas Ranger*, 146–148; *Texas Democrat*, January 27, 1847; Hays to Worth, September 25, 1846, Gulick, et al., eds., *Lamar Papers*, 4: 140; Arnold, "Captain Jack," 40; John S. D. Eisenhower, *So Far from God: The U.S. War with Mexico, 1846–1848* (Norman: University of Oklahoma Press, 2000), 139–140; *American Flag*, October 7, 1846; Giddings, *Sketches of the Campaign*, 196; *Daily Picayune*, October 4, 1846.
107. Greer, *Texas Ranger*, 148–152; Hays to Worth, September 25, 1846, Gulick, et al., eds., *Lamar Papers*, 4: 140; *Texas Democrat*, January 27, 1847; Ford, "John C. Hayes in Texas," 37; Stephen B. Oates, "Los Diablos Tejanos," *The American West* 2 (Summer 1965): 43–44; Eisenhower, *So Far from God*, 142; Reid, *Scouting Expeditions*, 192; Robert H. Ferrell, ed., *Monterrey Is Ours!: The Mexican War Letters of Lieutenant Dana, 1845–1847* (Lexington: University Press of Kentucky, 1990), 137–138; Barry, *A Texas Ranger*, 38–39. Justin Smith wrote that Hays, presumably in the aftermath of the Mier Expedition, had once been a prisoner in the Monterey post office, and vowed to bed down for the night in that particular building or

in hell. *War with Mexico*, 1: 258. While a dramatic tale, this episode never happened as Hays had turned back before Fisher's column reached Mier. He had also never been taken prisoner in that or any other action.

108. Holland, "Diary of a Texan Volunteer in the Mexican War," 27; Giddings, *Sketches of the Campaign*, 212; *Daily Picayune*, November 4, 1846; *Democratic Telegraph and Texas Register*, October 21, 1846; James K. Polk, *The Diary of James K. Polk*, ed. Milton M. Quaife (Chicago: A. C. McClurg & Company, 1910), 2: 181; Order No. 124, October 1, 1846, *Mexican War Correspondence*, 508; Compiled Service Records of Volunteer Soldiers, First Texas Mounted Rifles; Taylor to Adjutant General, October 6, 1846, *Correspondence with General Taylor*, 146; Bauer, *Mexican War*, 101–102. Taking swift action in one incident, Hays investigated the murder of a Mexican lancer by a Texas ranger and turned the culprit over to military authorities. *Civilian and Galveston Gazette*, August 17, 1848. See eyewitness testimony, certified by the colonel, in Statement of Lieutenant W. B. P. Gaines, October 6, 1846, *Correspondence with General Taylor*, 147; Worth to Bliss, September 28, 1846, *Report of the Secretary of War, 1846*, 107. Reprinted in *Texas Democrat*, October 28, 1846.
109. Greer, *Texas Ranger*, 155–158; Wilkins, *The Highly Irregular Irregulars*, 113; *Texas Democrat*, November 11, December 16, 1846, January 6, March 6, 1847; *Daily Picayune*, January 24, February 8, 1847. In May 1852, Hays requested from the Senate Committee on Military Affairs financial compensation for the period during which he raised and organized the regiment. The committee denied the allowance. *Petition of John C. Hays*, Senate Report No. 221, 32nd Congress, 1st Session, 1.
110. Greer, *Texas Ranger*, 158–160; Henderson to Polk, February 18, 1847, Dorman H. Winfrey and James M. Day, eds., *The Indian Papers of Texas and the Southwest* (Austin: Texas State Historical Association, 1995), 5: 26–27; *Democratic Telegraph and Texas Register*, March 8, 1847; Hays to Polk, March 20, 1847, April 16, 1847, Letters Received by the Office of the Adjutant General, M567, RG 94, NARA. Hereafter cited as Letters Received, Adjutant General's Office. Barton, *Texas Volunteers*, 88; *Daily Picayune*, March 31, 1847.
111. Greer, *Texas Ranger*, 160–162; Green, ed., *Memoirs of Mary A. Maverick*, 94; Hunter, "Famous Texas Ranger," 2; *Democratic Telegraph and Texas Register*, March 22, April 12, 1847.

112. Greer, *Texas Ranger*, 163; Compiled Service Records of Volunteer Soldiers, First Texas Mounted Volunteers (Six Months), John C. Hays; *Democratic Telegraph and Texas Register*, March 22, April 12, May 17, 1847; *Daily Picayune*, May 29, June 15, 1847; Taylor to Adjutant General, April 21, 1847, May 27, 1847, June 8, 1847, Orders No. 60, May 27, 1847, *Mexican War Correspondence*, 1131, 1145–1146, 1175.
113. Greer, *Texas Ranger*, 166; Hays to Jones, August 9, 1847, Hays to Taylor, July 13, 1847, Box 2B36, Peter Hansborough Bell Papers, BCAH; Order No. 5, July 13, 1847, Henderson to Jones, July 10, 1847, Letters Received, Adjutant General's Office, NARA; Spurlin, *Texas Volunteers*, 122–123; Compiled Service Records of Volunteer Soldiers, First Texas Mounted Volunteers (Twelve Months), John C. Hays, Peter H. Bell.
114. Greer, *Texas Ranger*, 166–168; Taylor to Adjutant General, July 27, 1847, *Mexican War Correspondence*, 1185–1186; Hays to Taylor, July 13, 1847, Hays to Jones, August 11, 1847, Box 2B36, Bell Papers, BCAH; *Daily Picayune*, July 27, 1847; Henderson to Marcy, August 22, 1847, Letters Received, Adjutant General's Office, NARA; Spurlin, *Texas Veterans*, 91–102, 105–111; *American Flag*, September 1, 1847.
115. Greer, *Texas Ranger*, 168; Henderson to Lamar, August 21, 1847, Gulick, et al., eds., *Lamar Papers*, 4: 177–178; Marcy to Taylor, July 17, 1847, *Mexican War Correspondence*, 1194; *Niles' National Register* 73 (September 18, 1847): 38, 40. Despite orders to join Scott's army, the Texans were not to participate in the general's brilliant overland campaign to Mexico City. For more on this vain, pompous, and gifted American commander, see Timothy D. Johnson, *Winfield Scott: The Quest for Military Glory* (Lawrence: University Press of Kansas, 1998).
116. Greer, *Texas Ranger*, 168; Scott to Taylor, April 24, 1847, *Mexican War Correspondence*, 1171; Proclamation, April 21, 1847, *Correspondence Between the Secretary of War and Generals Scott and Taylor, and Between General Scott and Mr. Trist*, House Executive Document No. 56, 30th Congress, 1st Session, 141; Irving W. Levinson, *Wars within War: Mexican Guerrillas, Domestic Elites, and the United States of America, 1846–1848* (Fort Worth: Texas Christian University Press, 2005), 16, 41–42; Eric W. Knapp, "'War Without Pity': Guerrilla Conflict in the Mexican War" (M.A. thesis, University of Nebraska, 1995), 26, 35; Polk,

Diary of James K. Polk, 3: 89; Marcy to Scott, October 6, 1847, *Mexican War Correspondence*, 1007.

117. Greer, *Texas Ranger*, 170; Ford, "John C. Hayes in Texas," 61; Pancoast to Parents, September 22, 1847, Frederick C. Chabot, *Texas Letters* (San Antonio: Yanaguana Society, 1940), 93; *Daily Delta*, October 10, 1847; Wilson to Jones, October 20, 1847, Letters Received, Adjutant General's Office, NARA.
118. Greer, *Texas Ranger*, 170, 172; Ford, "John C. Hayes in Texas," 67. The manner in which the rangers received the new weapons is discussed in Chapter 5. See also Robert Lawrence Wilson, *Colt: An American Legend* (New York: Abbeville Press, 1985), 23–28. Extract of Letter from Colonel Jack Hays, *Memorial of Samuel Colt*, 11: "I have had a good opportunity of testing the utility of Colt's pistols during the late Mexican war, and feel no hesitation in saying they are superior (in my opinion) to any other now known for cavalry."
119. Greer, *Texas Ranger*, 173–175; *Daily Picayune*, December 9, 1847; Ford, "John C. Hayes in Texas," 78; Marcy to Scott, October 6, 1847, Lane to Scott, October 18, 1847, *Correspondence Between the Secretary of War and Generals Scott and Taylor*, 198, 220–221; Lane to the Secretary of War, October 13, 1847, Letters Received, Adjutant General's Office, NARA; Bauer, *Mexican War*, 329–331; Knapp, "'War Without Pity'," 52.
120. Greer, *Texas Ranger*, 176; Lane to Adjutant General, December 1, 1847, *Annual Report of the Secretary of War*, House Executive Document No. 1, 30th Congress, 2nd Session, 86. Hereafter cited as *Annual Report of the Secretary of War, 1848*. The letter was reprinted in *American Flag*, February 12, 1848. Albert G. Brackett, *General Lane's Brigade in Central Mexico* (Cincinnati, OH: H.W. Derby & Co., 1854), 188–189.
121. Greer, *Texas Ranger*, 176; Lane to Adjutant General, December 1, 1847, *Annual Report of the Secretary of War, 1848*, 86; Bauer, *Mexican War*, 334; Collins, *Texas Devils*, 29; Campbell, *Gone to Texas*, 120; Henderson, *Jack Hays*, 83.
122. Greer, *Texas Ranger*, 177–178; Lane to Adjutant General, December 1, 1847, *Annual Report of the Secretary of War, 1848*, 87–89; Ford, "John C. Hayes in Texas," 80–81; Spencer C. Tucker, ed., *The Encyclopedia of the Mexican-American War: A Political, Social, and Military History* (Santa Barbara, CA: ABC-CLIO, 2013), 1: 258.
123. Greer, *Texas Ranger*, 180–182, 184; Collins, *Texas Devils*, 30–32; *Niles' National Register* 73 (January 8, 1848): 304; Levinson,

Wars within War, 61, 63; Edward S. Wallace, "The United States Army in Mexico City," *Military Affairs* 13 (Autumn 1949): 161; Oates, "Los Diablos Tejanos," 47. Colonel Ebenezer Dumont of the Fourth Indiana Volunteers wrote a letter to the *Indiana Register* describing the Texans' entry into Mexico City. The dispatch was reprinted in *Democratic Telegraph and Texas Register*, February 24, 1848. On October 22, 1847, General Scott had ordered that all liquor shops be closed after six p.m. in the hopes of reducing the number of drunken soldiers murdered by *leperos*. Jacob Oswandel, *Notes of the Mexican War, 1846–47–48* (Philadelphia: n.p., 1885), 456.

124. Greer, *Texas Ranger*, 183–184; *Democratic Telegraph and Texas Register*, February 24, 1848; Caperton, "Sketch of Colonel John C. Hays," 61; Lee, *Three Years Among the Comanches*, 75–76.
125. William J. Hughes, *Rebellious Ranger: Rip Ford and the Old Southwest* (Norman: University of Oklahoma Press, 1964), 46; Levinson, *Wars within War*, 37, 40, 139 n61. Jarauta had been involved in the *Carlista* guerrilla movement before becoming an ordained priest. He later left Spain and served at the cathedral in Vera Cruz. Once the war in Mexico began, he deserted his parish to answer the Mexican government's call for partisan leaders. Tucker, ed., *Encyclopedia of the Mexican-American War*, 1: 326.
126. Scott to Secretary of War, January 13, 1848, *Mexican War Correspondence*, 1067; J. M. Wynkoop, ed., *Anecdotes and Incidents: Comprising Daring Exploits, Personal and Amusing Adventures of the Officers and Privates of the Army, and Thrilling Incidents of the Mexican War* (Pittsburgh, PA: 1848), *104–105; Daily Picayune*, January 29, 1848; Knapp, "'War Without Pity'," 57. Daggett is known as the "Father of Fort Worth." For more on this Texas pioneer, see Richard F. Selcer, "On the Trail of the Young Ephraim Merrill Daggett: A Photo Essay," *Southwestern Historical Quarterly* 115 (April 2012): 378–395.
127. Greer, *Texas Ranger*, 187; Spurlin, *Texas Volunteers*, 132; Oswandel, *Notes of the Mexican War*, 449; Scott to Secretary of War, January 13, 1848, *Mexican War Correspondence*, 1067.
128. Greer, *Texas Ranger*, 187; *Niles' National Register* 73 (February 19, 1848): 387; Isaac George, *Heroes and Incidents of the Mexican War* (Greensburg, PA: Review Publishing Co., 1903), 211–212.
129. Greer, *Texas Ranger*, 187–189; Spurlin, *Texas Volunteers*, 132; Wynkoop, ed., *Anecdotes and Incidents*, *100–101; Daily Picayune*, January 29, 1848; Charles F. Hinds, "Mexican War Journal of Leander M. Cox,"

The Register of the Kentucky Historical Society 56 (January 1958): 49; Scott to Secretary of War, January 13, 1848, *Mexican War Correspondence*, 1067; *Niles' National Register* 73 (February 19, 1848): 387; Oswandel, *Notes of the Mexican War*, 457, 464.

130. Greer, *Texas Ranger*, 190–192; Lane to Secretary of War, February 10, 1848, Letters Received, Adjutant General's Office, NARA; Ford, "John C. Hayes in Texas," 106–108; Pancoast to Sister, March 2, 1848, Chabot, ed., *Texas Letters*, 97; Wynkoop, ed., *Anecdotes and Incidents*, 38; George, *Heroes and Incidents of the Mexican War*, 220; *Niles' National Register* 73 (February 26, 1848): 407; Heitman, *Historical Register and Dictionary of the United States Army*, 1: 796, 2: 40.

131. Greer, *Texas Ranger*, 192–194; Lane to Secretary of War, February 10, 1848, Letters Received, Adjutant General's Office, NARA; Brackett, *General Lane's Brigade*, 237–240; *Democratic Telegraph and Texas Register*, March 9, 1848; Wynkoop, ed., *Anecdotes and Incidents, 38–39;* John R. Kenly, *Memoirs of a Maryland Volunteer: War with Mexico, in the Years 1846–7–8* (Philadelphia: J. P. Lippincott & Co., 1873), 397; Affleck, "History of John C. Hayes," Pt. II: 674–677.

132. Greer, *Texas Ranger*, 194–197; Pancoast to Sister, March 2, 1848, Chabot, ed., *Texas Letters*, 97; Lane to Secretary of War, February 10, 1848, Letters Received, Adjutant General's Office, NARA; Brackett, *General Lane's Brigade*, 240–247.

133. Greer, *Texas Ranger*, 185–186; McCaffrey, *Army of Manifest Destiny*, 201; Ford, "John C. Hayes in Texas," 94, 95–98; Jenkins, *Recollections of Early Texas*, 149–150; Charles M. Robinson III, *Texas and the Mexican War: A History and a Guide* (Austin: Texas State Historical Association, 2004), 91; Harold J. Weiss, Jr., "The Bloody Texans in the Mexican War: The Reasons Why," *The Westerners Brand Book, New York Posse* 16 (1969): 4. The German-born Alsans had reportedly been a veteran of Napoleon Bonaparte's cavalry. *Daily Picayune*, March 8, 1848.

134. Greer, *Texas Ranger*, 198–201; Pancoast to Sister, March 2, 1848, Chabot, ed., *Texas Letters*, 97; Lane to Adjutant General, March 2, 1848, Hays to Lane, March 1, 1848, *Annual Report of the Secretary of War, 1848*, 95–96, 98–99; R. S. Ripley, *The War with Mexico* (New York: Harper & Brothers, 1849), 2: 635; *Texas Democrat*, April 22, 1848.

135. Greer, *Texas Ranger*, 201; Lane to Adjutant General, March 2, 1848, Hays to Lane, March 1, 1848, *Annual Report of the Secretary of War,*

1848, 96–97, 99; *Texas Democrat*, April 22, 1848; *Daily Picayune*, March 21, 22, 1848.

136. Lane to Adjutant General, March 2, 1848, Hays to Lane, March 1, 1848, Polk to Hays, March 2, 1848, *Annual Report of the Secretary of War, 1848*, 97, 99–100, 101; Ethan Allen Hitchcock, *Fifty Years in Camp and Field: Diary of Major-General Ethan Allen Hitchcock, U.S.A.*, ed. William Augustus Croffut (New York: G. P. Putnam's Sons, 1909), 322; Oates, "Los Diablos Tejanos," 48; *Daily Picayune*, March 23, 1848.
137. Greer, *Texas Ranger*, 202; Ripley, *War with Mexico*, 2: 637; Oates, "Los Diablos Tejanos," 48. Jarauta refused to lay down his arms and allied with Mariano Paredes in continued opposition to the peace treaty. On July 18, 1848, while fighting the forces of Anastacio Bustamante, he was captured at Valencia and executed by firing squad the next day. Tucker, ed., *Encyclopedia of the Mexican-American War*, 1: 326; Levinson, *Wars within War*, 41, 113.
138. Greer, *Texas Ranger*, 204–209; Ford, "John C. Hayes in Texas," 158–159, 167; *Texian Advocate*, May 4, 18, 1848; Kenly, *Memoirs of a Maryland Volunteer*, 392, 394–395; Wooten, ed., *Comprehensive History of Texas*, 2: 338; Compiled Service Records of Volunteer Soldiers, First Texas Mounted Volunteers (Twelve Months), John C. Hays.
139. James K. Greer, *Colonel Jack Hays, Texas Frontier Leader and California Builder* (College Station: Texas A&M University Press, 1987), 214–215; Gammel, comp., *Laws of Texas*, 3: 48–49; *Texas Democrat*, June 10, 1848; Compiled Service Records of Volunteer Soldiers, First Texas Mounted Volunteers (Twelve Months), John C. Hays. The two ranger companies on the frontier under Lieutenant-Colonel Bell had been joined by several others, and they were reorganized into a new regiment on July 11, 1848. Bell was elected the outfit's colonel. *Democratic Telegraph and Texas Register*, August 10, 1848; Wooten, ed., *Comprehensive History of Texas*, 2: 338.
140. Greer, *Colonel Jack Hays*, 217–226; "Jack Hays' Expedition to El Paso and California, 1849," Box 3F176, Hays Collection, BCAH, n. pag.; Rena Maverick Green, ed., *Samuel Maverick, Texan: 1803–1870* (San Antonio: privately printed, 1952), 333–342; William S. Speer and John Henry Brown, eds., *The Encyclopedia of the New West* (Marshall, TX: United States Biographical Publishing Company, 1881), 237; Thomas T. Smith, *The U.S. Army and the Texas Frontier Economy, 1845–1900* (College Station: Texas A&M University Press, 1999), 138–139; *Western Texian*, January 12, 1849;

Democratic Telegraph and Texas Register, December 28, 1848; *Texas Democrat*, August 16, 30, September 20, 1848, February 10, 1849; Ralph P. Bieber, "The Southwestern Trails to California in 1849," *The Mississippi Valley Historical Review* 12 (December 1925): 353; A. B. Bender, "Opening Routes across West Texas, 1848–1850," *Southwestern Historical Quarterly* 37 (October 1933) : 117–119. See also Hays to Marcy, December 13, 1848, *Annual Report of the Secretary of War*, Senate Executive Document No. 32, 32nd Congress, 1st Session, 64–65; *Democratic Telegraph and Texas Register*, November 23, 1848; and *Daily Picayune*, December 29, 1848. While preparations for the expedition were underway, Hays had also been elected surveyor of the Bexar District. He soon resigned the office. *Texas Democrat*, August 16, 1848.

141. Greer, *Colonel Jack Hays*, 228, 229–230; Medill to Hays, April 11, 1849, Brown to Hays, July 26, 1849, *Presidential Message Transmitting Information on California and New Mexico*, House Executive Document No. 17, 30th Congress, 1st Session, 230–232; *Daily Alta California*, December 7, 1884.

142. Greer, *Colonel Jack Hays*, 232–236; "Jack Hays' Expedition to El Paso and California, 1849," n. pag.; Thomas B. Eastland and Joseph G. Eastland, "To California through Texas and Mexico: The Diary and Letters of Thomas B. Eastland and Joseph G. Eastland, His Son," ed. Douglas S. Watson and Dorothy H. Huggins, *California Historical Society Quarterly* 18 (June 1939): 101–121, 132; Robert Eccleston, *Overland to California on the Southwestern Trail 1849*, ed. George P. Hammond and Edward H. Howes (Berkeley: University of California Press, 1950), ii–iii, v, 22, 25–26, 65, 88, 92, 103, 113, 131; Report of Captain J. E. Johnston, December 28, 1849, Report of Captain S. G. French, December 21, 1849, *Reconnaissance of Routes from San Antonio to El Paso*, Senate Executive Document No. 64, 31st Congress, 1st Session, 26–28, 40–41; *The Argonaut*, March 9, 16, 1878. John Nugent, one of Hays's companions, and the founder of the *San Francisco Herald*, wrote "Scraps of Early History," a series of six articles for the *Argonaut* that described his journey to California. See also John Boessenecker, *Gold Dust and Gunsmoke: Tales of Gold Rush Outlaws, Gunfighters, Lawmen, and Vigilantes* (New York: John Wiley & Sons, 1999), 209–213.

In February 1849, Lieutenants William Farrar Smith of the Topographical Engineers and William Henry Chase Whiting of the Corps of Engineers were dispatched by the War Department to blaze a practical road to El Paso for "military and commercial purposes." Their return route, which was used by Hays and his party, became known as the "Lower" or "Military" road. Report of Lieutenant W. H. C. Whiting, *Annual Report of the Secretary of War*, House Executive Document No. 5, 31st Congress, 1st Session, 281–293; Joseph Carroll McConnell, *The West Texas Frontier: or, A Descriptive History of Early Times in Western Texas* (Jacksboro, TX: Gazette Print, 1933), 1: 59–60.

143. Greer, *Colonel Jack Hays*, 240–252; *The Argonaut*, March 16, 23, 1878; Robinson, *I Fought a Good Fight*, 223; Annie Heloise Abel, ed., *The Official Correspondence of James S. Calhoun* (Washington, D.C.: Government Printing Office, 1915), 34–35; Eccleston, *Overland to California on the Southwestern Trail*, vi–viii, 138, 165, 172, 174–202, 232. John Nugent lent his journal of the excursion to Lieutenant John Grubb Parke, who conducted the survey for a potential transcontinental railroad along the thirty-second parallel. The trail would become the Butterfield Overland Mail stage road and, later, the Southern Pacific railway. Captain Andrew Atkinson Humphreys, the commander of the Pacific Railroad Surveys, credited Nugent's notes with aiding in the mapping of the route, which, consequently, was sometimes called Nugent's Wagon Road. Nugent's Pass and Nugent's Springs also bore his name. Report of Captain A. A. Humphreys, November 26, 1856, *Annual Report of the Secretary of War*, House Executive Document No. 1, 34th Congress, 3rd Session, 206–209.

144. Greer, *Colonel Jack Hays*, 253–255; Walter T. Durham, *Volunteer Forty-Niners: Tennesseans and the California Gold Rush* (Nashville: Vanderbilt University Press, 1997), 47, 132; Henderson, *Jack Hays*, 99; *The Argonaut*, March 30, 1878; *Daily Alta California*, January 24, 25, February 1, March 18, 1850.

145. Greer, *Colonel Jack Hays*, 257; Green, ed., *Memoirs of Mary A. Maverick*, 108–109; *Oakland Tribune Magazine*, December 2, 1923; Stephanie C. Shulsinger, "Colonel Jack Hays in California," *Real West* 16 (February 1973): 28; *Daily Alta California*, February 1, 1850.

146. Greer, *Colonel Jack Hays*, 258–260; Durham, *Volunteer Forty-Niners*, 133; Philip J. Ethington, *The Public City: The Political Construction of Urban Life in San Francisco, 1850–1900* (Berkeley: University of California Press, 2001), 68; *Oakland Tribune Magazine*, December 2, 1923; Pioneer, "Some Amended Historic Data," *The Overland Monthly* 10 (August 1887): 221–222; *Daily Alta California*, March 25, 26, 1850.

147. Greer, *Colonel Jack Hays*, 260–263; Durham, *Volunteer Forty-Niners*, 13–134; Ethington, *The Public City*, 68–70; William Benemann, ed., *A Year of Mud and Gold: San Francisco in Letters and Diaries, 1849–1850* (Lincoln: University of Nebraska Press, 2003), 163, 178–179, 182; *Oakland Tribune Magazine*, December 2, 1923; Shulsinger, "Colonel Jack Hays in California," 28.
148. Greer, *Colonel Jack Hays*, 263–264; Kevin J. Mullen, *Let Justice Be Done: Crime and Politics in Early San Francisco* (Reno: University of Nevada Press, 1989), 102; *Daily Alta California*, April 1, 4, 6, 10, 1850; Hunter, ed., "Jack Hays, the Intrepid," 95; Charles P. Kimball, *The San Francisco City Directory, September 1, 1850* (San Francisco: Journal of Commerce Press, 1850), 123.
149. Gordon Morris Bakken, ed., *Law in the Western United States* (Norman: University of Oklahoma Press, 2000), 82–83; James P. Delgado, "Gold Rush Jail: The Prison Ship 'Euphemia'," *California History Magazine* 60 (Summer 1981): 136, 138–139; Mary Floyd Williams, *History of the San Francisco Committee of Vigilance of 1851: A Study of Social Control on the California Frontier in the Days of the Gold Rush* (Berkeley: University of California Press, 1921), 246–247. Hereafter cited as *Vigilance Committee of 1851*. Theodore H. Hittell, *History of California* (San Francisco: N. J. Stone & Company, 1897), 4: 119; Hubert Howe Bancroft, *Popular Tribunals* (San Francisco: The History Company, 1887), 1: 305.
150. Greer, *Colonel Jack Hays*, 266–267, 281–282; Kimball, *San Francisco City Directory*, 56; *Seventh U.S. Census*, Guadalupe County, Texas; Gilbert Richards, *Crossroads: People and Events of The Redwoods of San Mateo County* (Woodside, CA: Gilbert Richards Publications, 1973), 42–43, 53; Frank Merriman Stanger, *Sawmills in the Redwoods: Logging on the San Francisco Peninsula, 1849–1967* (San Mateo, CA: San Mateo County Historical Association, 1967), 37–38; Roscoe D. Wyatt, *Days of the Dons: On the Spanish and Mexican Ranchos of the San Francisco Peninsula and in the Santa Clara Valley* (Redwood City, CA: San Mateo County Title Company, 1949), 49; Frank Merriman Stanger, *History of San Mateo County* (San Mateo, CA: Arthur H. Cawston, 1938), 92; Shulsinger, "Colonel Jack Hays in California," 29; *Alameda Sun*, August 4, 2008.
151. Mullen, *Let Justice Be Done*, 42, 175–176, 108–109, 113; Charles Wollenberg, *Golden Gate Metropolis: Perspectives on Bay Area History* (Berkeley: Institute of Governmental Studies, University

of California, 1985), 75–76, 80; H. W. Brands, *The Age of Gold: The California Gold Rush and the New American Dream* (New York: Anchor Books, 2003), 259–264, 323–324; Williams, *Vigilance Committee of 1851*, 142–145, 248–249; Mary Floyd Williams, ed., *Papers of the San Francisco Committee of Vigilance of 1851* (Berkeley: University of California Press: 1919), 32, 93, 157–160, 177, 266, 602–603, 622, 729. Hereafter cited as *Committee of Vigilance Papers*. Kenneth M. Johnson, ed., *San Francisco as It Is: Gleanings from the Picayune* (Georgetown, CA: Talisman Press, 1964), 146–147; Bancroft, *Popular Tribunals*, 1: 305–306, 401–402.

152. Boessenecker, *Gold Dust and Gunsmoke*, 35; Brands, *The Age of Gold*, 266–267; *Daily Alta California*, June 12, 14, 1851; Mullen, *Let Justice Be Done*, 165.
153. Greer, *Colonel Jack Hays*, 272–273; M. W. Wood, *History of Alameda County, California* (Oakland: Pacific Press, 1883), 902; Arnold, "Captain Jack," 42. For the story of this career ship's captain, see Edgar Wakeman, *The Log of an Ancient Mariner. Being the Life and Adventures of Captain Edgar Wakeman*, ed. Minnie L. Wakeman-Curtis (San Francisco: A. L. Bancroft & Co., 1878).
154. Greer, *Colonel Jack Hays*, 276–278; Brands, *The Age of Gold*, 268; Ethington, *The Public City*, 109–111; Johnson, ed., *San Francisco as It Is*, 177–178, 195–196; Williams, *Vigilance Committee of 1851*, 295; *Daily Alta California*, August 21, 1851; Williams, ed., *Committee of Vigilance Papers*, 524–526, 528–530, 533–534; Bancroft, *Popular Tribunals*, 1: 351, 2: 388; Shulsinger, "Colonel Jack Hays in California," 29.
155. Greer, *Colonel Jack Hays*, 266, 278–279, 283–284; *Daily Alta California*, September 7, 1851; Peter Thomas Conmy, *The Beginnings of Oakland, California, A.U.C.* (Oakland: Oakland Public Library, 1961), 34–36; Mel Scott, *The San Francisco Bay Area: A Metropolis in Perspective* (Berkeley: University of California Press, 1985), 33–35; C. Raymond Clar, "Pioneer Among the Argonauts," Pt. 3, *The Pacific Historian* 6 (May 1962): 59, 60–62; Wollenberg, *Golden Gate Metropolis*, 90–92, 95; W. W. Robinson, *Land in California: The Story of Mission Lands, Ranchos, Squatters, Mining Claims, Railroad Grants, Land Scrip, Homesteads* (Berkeley: University of California Press, 1979), 116; Annalee Allen, "Colonel Jack Hays of Fernwood," *Oakland Heritage Alliance News* 12 (Spring 1993): 3; Wyatt, *Days of the Dons*, 50; *Oakland Tribune Magazine*, December 2, 1923; *Journals of Senate and Assembly of the Twentieth Session of the Legislature*

of the State of California, Appendix, 4: 129–130, 162. Among Hays' partners in the land purchase were Caperton, John Clar, Joseph K. Irving, Jacob A. Cost, and B. De la Barra. Hays and Caperton initially each held a one-third interest in the venture, and would later buy out a few of the principals to obtain quarter-interests. Wood, *History of Alameda County*, 486.

156. Greer, *Colonel Jack Hays*, 285–286, 294, 298; *Find A Grave*, s.v. "John Caperton Hays" and "Richard 'Dick' Hays"; Smith, "Family of 'John Jack Hays'," n. pag.
157. Greer, *Colonel Jack Hays*, 286–288; Hittell, *History of California*, 4: 132; Pierce to the Senate of the United States, March 16, 1853, *Journal of the Executive Proceedings of the Senate*, 9: 77, 81; John Hays Hammond, *The Autobiography of John Hays Hammond* (New York: Farrar & Rinehart, 1935), 1: 25; *Sacramento Daily Union*, June 15, 1853; C. Raymond Clar, "Pioneer Among the Argonauts," Pt. 4, *The Pacific Historian* 6 (June 1962): 111; Hunter, "Famous Texas Ranger," 3; *Evening Star*, March 19, 1853. Deputy Thomas P. Johnson was appointed interim sheriff and sworn into office on June 17. *Daily Alta California*, June 18, 1853.
158. Greer, *Colonel Jack Hays*, 290–291; Howard R. Lamar, *Texas Crossings: The Lone Star State and the American Far West, 1836–1986* (Austin: University of Texas Press, 1991), 33; Clar, "Pioneer Among the Argonauts," Pt. 3, 57; Gordon Morris Bakken, "Mexican and American Land Policy: A Conflict of Cultures," *Southern California Quarterly* 75 (Fall/Winter 1993): 241–242; Paul W. Gates, *Land and Law in California: Essays on Land Policies* (Ames: Iowa State University Press, 1991), 186; Conmy, *The Beginnings of Oakland*, 29–34; Wollenberg, *Golden Gate Metropolis*, 92–96; Linda Ferguson Browne, ed., *J. Ross Browne: His Letters, Journals, and Writings* (Albuquerque: University of New Mexico Press, 1969), 175; *Evening Star*, October 28, 1854; Richards, *Crossroads*, 53; Stanger, *Sawmills in the Redwoods*, 37–38; *Moore & DePue's Illustrated History of San Mateo County, California—1878* (Woodside, CA: Gilbert Richards Publications, 1974), 16.
159. Greer, *Colonel Jack Hays*, 301–302; Durham, *Volunteer Forty-Niners*, 135; *Annual Report of the Commissioner of the General Land Office*, Senate Executive Document No. 1, 35th Congress, 2nd Session, 131; *Daily Alta California*, August 15, 1857; *Evening Star*, March 21, April 4, July 13, 23, 1857.

160. Greer, *Colonel Jack Hays*, 307–309, 311; *Sacramento Daily Union*, October 7, 1857; *Daily Alta California*, August 17, 1857; *Evening Star*, October 10, 1857, June 17, 1858; Shulsinger, "Colonel Jack Hays in California," 30.
161. Greer, *Colonel Jack Hays*, 310; *Daily Alta California*, May 15, 1858; *Find A Grave*, s.v. "Kitty Hays"; Smith, "Family of 'John Jack Hays'," n. pag.
162. Greer, *Colonel Jack Hays*, 328–329; Richards, *Crossroads*, 43; Wyatt, *Days of the Dons*, 50; Wood, *History of Alameda County*, 905.
163. Hammond, *Autobiography of John Hays Hammond*, 1: 26. The land where the property once lay is near present Mountain Boulevard and Thornhill Drive in the Montclair District of Oakland.
164. Ferol Egan, *Sand in a Whirlwind: The Paiute Indian War of 1860* (Reno: University of Nevada Press, 2003), 95, 114–115, 135–155; Sarah Winnemucca Hopkins, *Life Among the Paiutes: Their Wrongs and Claims*, ed. Mrs. Horace Mann (Reno: University of Nevada Press, 1994), 71; *Sacramento Daily Union*, May 9, 11, 14, 15, 21, 1860; Sally Zanjani, *Devils Will Reign: How Nevada Began* (Reno: University of Nevada Press, 2006), 131–134; Robert Wooster, *The American Military Frontiers: The United States Army in the West, 1783–1900* (Albuqueque: University of New Mexico Press, 2009), 158; William C. Miller, "The Pyramid Lake Indian War of 1860," *Nevada Historical Society Quarterly* 1 (September 1957): 38, 40–46.
165. Greer, *Colonel Jack Hays*, 313–314; Clarke to Scott, May 11, 1860, Clarke to Cooke, May 14, 1860, Hays to Cummings, June 12, 1860, *Annual Report of the Secretary of War*, Senate Executive Document No. 1, 36th Congress, 2nd Session, 107, 109, 89. Hereafter cited as *Annual Report of the Secretary of War, 1860. Daily Alta California*, May 24, 26, 1860.
166. Greer, *Colonel Jack Hays*, 315–318; Egan, *Sand in a Whirlwind*, 193–194, 200–206; Zanjani, *Devils Will Reign*, 135; *San Francisco Daily Evening Bulletin*, May 28, 29, May 30, June 5, 7, 1860; *Marysville Daily Appeal*, June 9, 1860; Gregory F. Michno, *Encyclopedia of Indian Wars: Western Battles and Skirmishes, 1850–1890* (Missoula, MT: Mountain Press Publishing Company, 2003), 74–75; *Sacramento Daily Union*, May 25, 26, June 5, 1860; *Daily Alta California*, June 7, 1860.
167. Greer, *Colonel Jack Hays*, 320–321; Hays to Cummings, June 12, 1860, Stewart to Clarke, June 3, 1860, Floyd to the President,

December 3, 1860, *Annual Report of the Secretary of War, 1860*, 90–91, 113, 4; Wooster, *American Military Frontiers*, 158; *San Francisco Daily Evening Bulletin*, May 30, June 7, 8, 16, 1860; *Sacramento Daily Union*, June 12, 1860.

168. Greer, *Colonel Jack Hays*, 321–322; Hays to Cummings, June 12, 1860, Stewart to Clarke, June 3, 1860, *Annual Report of the Secretary of War, 1860*, 91, 113–114; *San Francisco Daily Evening Bulletin*, June 16, 1860; *Daily Alta California*, June 9, 1860.
169. Greer, *Colonel Jack Hays*, 322–327; Hays to Cummings, June 12, 1860, Stewart to Clarke, June 3, 1860, *Annual Report of the Secretary of War, 1860*, 91–92, 114; Wooster, *American Military Frontiers*, 158; *San Francisco Daily Evening Bulletin*, June 8, 1860.
170. Greer, *Colonel Jack Hays*, 329–330, 332–333; *Sacramento Daily Union*, June 12, 13, 1861; Bailey Millard, *History of the San Francisco Bay Region* (Chicago: American Historical Society, 1924), 35; Shulsinger, "Colonel Jack Hays in California," 31; William Halley, *The Centennial Year Book of Alameda County, California* (Oakland: William Halley, 1876), 155. His brother, Harry, would serve the Confederacy as a general officer in the Army of Northern Virginia. Ezra J. Warner, *Generals in Gray: Lives of the Confederate Commanders* (Baton Rouge: Louisiana State University Press, 2008), 130. For more on the sectional divide in California, see Leonard L. Richards, *The California Gold Rush and the Coming of the Civil War* (New York: Alfred A. Knopf, 2007); and Monika Trobits, *Antebellum and Civil War San Francisco: A Western Theater for Northern and Southern Politics* (Charleston, SC: The History Press, 2014).
171. Greer, *Colonel Jack Hays*, 339–347, 349–352, 336; Allen, "Colonel Jack Hays of Fernwood," 4; *Eighth* and *Ninth U.S. Census*, Alameda County, California; Conmy, *The Beginnings of Oakland*, 41; Henderson, *Jack Hays*, 104; *Alameda Sun*, September 4, 2008; *Oakland Tribune*, April 20, 1875; Wood, *History of Alameda County*, 763, 796; Davis, *History of Political Conventions*, 360–361; Halley, *Centennial Year Book of Alameda County*, 433. The asylum was later renamed the California School for the Deaf and Blind.
172. Greer, *Colonel Jack Hays*, 333, 358, 339, 355–356, 340; *Find A Grave*, s.v. "Harry Hays," "Richard 'Dick' Hays," "Mary Susan 'Susie' Hays," "Elizabeth Brenham 'Betty' Hays"; *San Francisco Daily Evening Bulletin*, August 28, 1877;

173. Greer, *Colonel Jack Hays*, 337, 365, 369, 372, 357, 365, 369, 371–372; *Oakland Tribune*, April 23, 24, 1883; *Daily Alta California*, April 23, 1883. Coincidentally, April 21 is celebrated in Texas as San Jacinto Day.
174. *Alameda Sun*, September 4, 2008; *Twelfth U. S. Census*, Arapahoe County, Colorado; *Thirteenth U. S. Census*, Alameda County, California; *San Francisco Call* and *San Francisco Chronicle*, both dated May 20, 1913. Dingee partitioned a segment of the estate into five- and ten-acre lots and marketed them to people wishing suburban homes. The house and Dingee's extensive art collection was completely destroyed by a fire in October 1889. Eight years later, the remaining forty-five acres were sold to investors who subdivided the tract into lots. *Daily Alta California*, September 15, 17, 1886; *San Francisco Call*, October 19, 1899, January 19, 1907.
175. *Oakland Tribune*, November 4, 1880; *Twelfth U. S. Census*, Alameda County, California; *Thirteenth U. S. Census*, Tulare County, California; *San Francisco Call*, June 14, 16, 1911; Millard, *San Francisco Bay Region*, 36, 336–338. The patriarch of the McMullen family was Captain John McMullen, who had served in the Mier Expedition and the Mexican War, and had accompanied Hays to California. The two families had shared a deep friendship for years even before the children married.
176. Millard, *San Francisco Bay Region*, 36; *Daily Alta California*, January 8, 1888; *Twelfth U. S. Census*, Arapahoe County, Colorado; Frederick Evans, comp., *After Twenty-five Years, Class of 1886* (Princeton: Princeton University Press, 1911), 71–72, 111, 116; *Oakland Tribune*, January 12, 1903, February 1, 1944; *San Francisco Call*, October 3, 1908; *Thirteenth* and *Fourteenth U. S. Census*, Alameda County, California.

Notes for Chapter 3

1. Thomas W. Cutrer, *Ben McCulloch and the Frontier Military Tradition* (Chapel Hill: University of North Carolina Press, 1993), 10–11; William H. Bailey, Sr., *The Genealogy of the Latham-Hill-Montfort-Littlejohn-McCulloch-Campbell and Brownrigg Families* (Knoxville: American Historical Books, 1899), 41; Homer Pittard, "From Jefferson to Elkhorn Tavern: The Story of Ben McCulloch," *Rutherford County Historical Society Publication* 11 (Summer 1978): 7–8; *The National Cyclopaedia of American Biography* (New York: James T. White and

Company, 1895), 4: 104; Thomas W. Cutrer, "'The Tallapoosa Might Truly Be Called the River of Blood': Major Alexander McCulloch and the Battle of Horseshoe Bend, March 27, 1813," *Alabama Historical Review* 43 (January 1990): 35–39. Alexander died after a lengthy illness in Dyer County on August 6, 1846. *Nashville Christian Advocate*, August 12, 1846. Frances died near Maypearl, Texas, on May 10, 1866, and was reburied in the State Cemetery on May 27, 1938, next to Ben's grave. Ben McCulloch biographical sketch, Louis Wiltz Kemp Papers, SJMH; *San Antonio Express*, 25, 28, 1938.

2. Cutrer, *Ben McCulloch*, 11–13; Dumas Malone, ed., *Dictionary of American Biography* (New York: Charles Scribner's Sons, 1933), 12: 5; *Dallas Morning News*, April 17, 1921. Professor Walter Webb wrote an article entitled "Exploits of the Texas Rangers—Ben McCulloch, Fighting Man" for the paper's Sunday magazine section. This piece has been incorrectly dated in other works as April 19.
3. Cutrer, *Ben McCulloch*, 13, 15–16; Victor M. Rose, *The Life and Services of Gen. Ben McCulloch* (Austin: The Steck Company, 1958), 40–41; *Dallas Morning News*, April 17, 1921; H. W. Brands, *Lone Star Nation: How a Ragged Army of Volunteers Won the Battle for Texas Independence—and Changed America* (New York: Doubleday, 2004), 329–332; Jack W. Gunn, "Ben McCulloch: A Big Captain," *Southwestern Historical Quarterly* 58 (July 1954): 1; L. E. Daniell, comp., *Personnel of the Texas State Government* (Austin: Press of the City Printing Company, 1887), 225.
4. Stephen L. Moore, *Eighteen Minutes: The Battle of San Jacinto and the Texas Independence Campaign* (Dallas: Republic of Texas Press, 2004), 43, 58–59, 75–76, 114–115, 147–149, 183–184; William C. Davis, *Lone Star Rising: The Revolutionary Birth of the Texas Republic* (College Station: Texas A&M University Press, 2004), 243–248; Gerald E. Poyo, ed., *Tejano Journey, 1770–1850* (Austin: University of Texas Press, 1996), 58; Eugene C. Barker, "The San Jacinto Campaign," *The Quarterly of the Texas State Historical Association* 4 (April 1901): 43–244; John Holmes Jenkins, ed., *The Papers of the Texas Revolution, 1835–1836* (Austin: Presidial Press, 1973), 5: 83; H. M. Henderson, "A Critical Analysis of the San Jacinto Campaign," *Southwestern Historical Quarterly* 59 (January 1956): 344–347.
5. Ben McCulloch, Audited Claim No. 1224, Reel 67, Frame 189, TSLAC; William Hester Patton, James Clinton Neill, and Isaac N. Moreland biographical sketches, Kemp Papers, SJMH; Brands,

Lone Star Nation, 441; Colonel John M. Swisher, *The Swisher Memoirs*, ed. Rena Maverick Green (San Antonio: The Sigmund Press, 1932), 38; Ernest William Winkler, "The 'Twin Sisters' Cannon, 1836–1865," *Southwestern Historical Quarterly* 21 (July 1917): 61–63; Henderson K. Yoakum, *History of Texas from its First Settlement in 1685 to its Annexation to the United States in 1846* (New York: Redfield, 1856), 2: 300.

6. Stephen L. Hardin, *Texian Iliad: A Military History of the Texas Revolution, 1835–1836* (Austin: University of Texas Press, 1994), 183–184, 192, 199–202; Moore, *Eighteen Minutes*, 212, 222–225, 233–234, 242, 251–235, 258–259; Davis, *Lone Star Rising*, 264–266; Jenkins, ed., *Papers of the Texas Revolution*, 5: 504–505; Swisher, *Swisher Memoirs*, 40; Jimmy L. Bryan, Jr., *More Zeal Than Discretion: The Westward Adventures of Walter P. Lane* (College Station: Texas A&M University Press, 2008), 17.
7. Hardin, *Texan Iliad*, 202–205; Brands, *Lone Star Nation*, 444–446; Jenkins, ed., *Papers of the Texas Revolution*, 5: 513; Swisher, *Swisher Memoirs*, 41; Barker, "San Jacinto Campaign," 284; Walter P. Lane, *The Adventures and Recollections of General Walter P. Lane: A San Jacinto Veteran, Containing Sketches of the Texan, Mexican, and Late Wars* (Austin: Jenkins Publishing Company, 1970), 12–13; N. D. Labadie, "San Jacinto Campaign," *The Texas Almanac for 1859* (Galveston: Richardson and Company, 1858), 51–53; "Compendium of the History of Texas," *The Texas Almanac for 1860* (Galveston: Richardson and Company, 1859), 63. For more on the Twin Sisters and the San Jacinto battlefield, see Dana L. Pertermann and Holly Kathryn Norton, eds., *The Archaeology of Engagement: Conflict and Revolution in the United States* (College Station: Texas A&M University Press, 2015).
8. Cutrer, *Ben McCulloch*, 20–21; Rose, *Gen. Ben McCulloch*, 42; Moore, *Eighteen Minutes*, 303–308, 313, 316–317, 318–325, 329–330, 333–337, 344–350, 353–354; Hardin, *Texan Iliad*, 207–215; Poyo, ed., *Tejano Journey*, 59–60; Ernest Wallace and David M. Vigness, eds., *Documents of Texas History* (Austin: The Steck Company, 1963), 113; George Washington Hockley biographical sketch, Kemp Papers, SJMH; Swisher, *Swisher Memoirs*, 39, 44; Barker, "San Jacinto Campaign," 255–256; Lucy A. Erath, ed., "Memoirs of Major George Bernard Erath," Pt. 2, *Southwestern Historical Quarterly* 26 (April 1923): 263; Amelia W. Williams and Eugene C. Barker, ed., *Writings of*

Sam Houston (Austin: University of Texas Press, 1938–1943), 7: 325; *Galveston Daily News*, March 6, 1893; "Compendium of the History of Texas," 64, 66–67. For more on Santa Anna's capture, his signing of the two Treaties of Velasco, and his release to disturb Texas once more, see Davis, *Lone Star Rising*, 272–273, 280–281, 282–283, 285–286, 289–290, 303.

9. Cutrer, *Ben McCulloch*, 21; Rose, *Gen. Ben McCulloch*, 42–43; Ben McCulloch biographical sketch, Kemp Papers, SJMH; Gunn, "Ben McCulloch," 2.
10. Rose, *Gen. Ben McCulloch*, 43.
11. Gregg J. Dimmick, *Sea of Mud: The Retreat of the Mexican Army After San Jacinto, An Archaeological Investigation* (Austin: Texas State Historical Association, 2004); Moore, *Eighteen Minutes*, 408; Hardin, *Texian Iliad*, 216, 245–246.
12. Cutrer, *Ben McCulloch*, 21, 26; Rose, *Gen. Ben McCulloch*, 44–46; *Muster Rolls of the Texas Revolution* (Austin: Daughters of the Republic of Texas, 1986), 72. Robbins's company was in service from April 25 to August 13, 1836. Moore, *Savage Frontier*, 1: 125, 168; Ben McCulloch, Audited Claim No. 1224, Reel 67, Frames 189, 191, TSLAC; *Memorial and Genealogical Record of Southwest Texas* (Easley, SC: Southern Historical Press, 1978), 579; Daniell, comp., *Personnel of the Texas State Government*, 225–226; Gerald S. Pierce, *Texas Under Arms: The Camps, Forts, and Military Towns of the Republic of Texas, 1836–1846* (Austin: Encino Press, 1969), 61; Brazos, *Life of Robert Hall: Indian Fighter and Veteran of Three Great Wars* (Austin: State House Press, 1992), xii.
13. Nathan Boone Burkett, "Early Days in Texas," ed. Wallace L. McKeehan, *Sons of DeWitt Colony Texas*, 2008; Brazos, *Life of Robert Hall*, 39–40; Lockhart to Barton, March 30, 1839, Frederick C. Chabot, ed., *Texas Letters* (San Antonio: Yanaguana Society, 1940), 78; Gregory and Susan Michno, *A Fate Worse Than Death: Indian Captivities in the West, 1830–1885* (Caldwell, ID: Caxton Press, 2009), 55.
14. Cutrer, *Ben McCulloch*, 28; Rose, *Gen. Ben McCulloch*, 46; Noah Smithwick, *The Evolution of a State, or Recollections of Old Texas Days*, comp. Nanna Smithwick Donaldson (Austin: University of Texas Press, 1983), 154–157; John Wesley Wilbarger, *Indian Depredations in Texas* (Austin: State House Press, 1985), 144–146, 288; John Henry Brown, *Indian Wars and Pioneers of Texas* (Austin: State House Press, 1988), 73–74; James T. DeShields, *Border Wars of Texas* (Austin: State

House Press, 1993), 263–264; A. J. Sowell, *Rangers and Pioneers of Texas* (Austin: State House Press, 1991), 181.

15. Cutrer, *Ben McCulloch*, 29; Rose, *Gen. Ben McCulloch*, 47; Brown, *Indian Wars*, 74; Wilbarger, *Indian Depredations in Texas*, 288–289.
16. Cutrer, *Ben McCulloch*, 29; Rose, *Gen. Ben McCulloch*, 47; Brown, *Indian Wars*, 74; DeShields, *Border Wars of Texas*, 264.
17. Cutrer, *Ben McCulloch*, 29; Rose, *Gen. Ben McCulloch*, 47–48; Brown, *Indian Wars*, 74; Wilbarger, *Indian Depredations in Texas*, 289, 610; DeShields, *Border Wars of Texas*, 264.
18. *Dallas Weekly Herald*, August 22, 1874; *National Cyclopaedia of American Biography*, 4: 104; *Memorial and Genealogical Record of Southwest Texas*, 579; Hilton R. Greer, "The Code of Honor under the Lone Star," *The Scrap Book* 6 (October 1908): 578.
19. Burleson to Lamar, April 4, 1839, Charles Adams Gulick, et al., eds., *The Papers of Mirabeau Bounaparte Lamar* (Austin: A. C. Baldwin & Sons, 1922–1927), 2: 49–50. Hereafter cited as *Lamar Papers*. *Telegraph and Texas Register*, April 10, 1839; *Morning Star*, April 11, 1839; Poyo, ed., *Tejano Journey*, 104; Andrew Jackson Sowell, *Texas Indian Fighters: Early Settlers and Indian Fighters of Southwest Texas* (Austin: State House Press, 1986), 15; Wilbarger, *Indian Depredations in Texas*, 153–156; Sowell, *Rangers and Pioneers of Texas*, 189–190.
20. Cutrer, *Ben McCulloch*, 35; Rose, *Gen. Ben McCulloch*, 48–49; Hans Peter Nielson Gammel, comp., *The Laws of Texas, 1822–1897* (Austin: The Gammel Book Company, 1898), 2: 44; Muster and Pay Rolls, Mathew Caldwell, 401–717, TSLAC; Message to Congress, January 4, 1839, Robinson to Lamar, February 24, 1839, Gulick, et al., eds., *Lamar Papers*, 2: 402, 468; Brown, *Indian Wars*, 64; Joseph Milton Nance, *After San Jacinto: The Texas-Mexican Frontier, 1836–1841* (Austin: University of Texas Press, 1963), 128; *Morning Star*, April 23, 1839.
21. Cutrer, *Ben McCulloch*, 35; Rose, *Gen. Ben McCulloch*, 50–51; Poyo, ed., *Tejano Journey*, 104; *Telegraph and Texas Register*, May 1, 1839; DeShields, *Border Wars of Texas*, 273–274.
22. Cutrer, *Ben McCulloch*, 36–37; Rose, *Gen. Ben McCulloch*, 52–53; Greer, "Code of Honor under the Lone Star," 578; Jack Kenny Williams, *Dueling in the Old South: Vignettes of Social History* (College Station: Texas A&M University Press, 1980), 44. Bruce Collins, *White Society in the Antebellum South* (New York: Longman Group, 1985), 162:

"[The Southern culture] retained an anachronistic code of behavior, rooted in ideas of personal and family honour and promoting a readiness among individuals to take direct charge of and responsibility for their fate … this code stimulated family loyalty, self-reliance and self-respect … it [also] encouraged arrogance, vigilantism, duelling, brawling and a general disinclination to abide by the canons of a formal and impersonal body of law."

23. Moore, *Savage Frontier*, 2: 198–199; Brown, *Indian Wars*, 65; *Telegraph and Texas Register*, May 15, 21, 1839; Muster and Pay Rolls, Mathew Caldwell, 401–717, TSLAC.
24. Cutrer, *Ben McCulloch*, 34, 37; Rose, *Gen. Ben McCulloch*, 53; Frank Brown, "Annals of Travis County and of the City of Austin: From the Earliest Times to the Close of 1875," Ch. 6: 60; Greer, "Code of Honor under the Lone Star," 579; "From Capt. Benj. Hill," *Lamar Papers*, 6: 135; Williams, *Dueling in the Old South*, 26, 27, 56; Bertram Wyatt-Brown, *Southern Honor: Ethics and Behavior in the Old South* (New York: Oxford University Press, 2007), 360, 355, 352–353. Until his death in 2012, Wyatt-Brown was the recognized expert on the role of honor in Southern society. He also wrote *Honor and Violence in the Old South* (New York: Oxford University Press, 1986); and *The Shaping of Southern Culture: Honor, Grace, and War, 1760s–1880s* (Chapel Hill: University of North Carolina Press, 2001). See also John Lyde Wilson, *Code of Honor; or Rules for the Government of Principals and Seconds in Duelling* (Charleston, SC: Thomas J. Eccles, 1838).
25. Cutrer, *Ben McCulloch*, 37–38; Rose, *Gen. Ben McCulloch*, 54–55; *Galveston Daily News*, August 21, 1874.
26. *Journals of the Fourth Congress of the Republic of Texas*, ed. Harriet Smither, 2: 13, 27, 36, 39, 40, 42, 43, 46, 57, 70, 75, 80, 85, 86, 87, 88, 183, 186, 187, 188, 189, 190, 192, 193, 196, 200, 201; *Telegraph and Texas Register*, October 28, 1840; Ernest R. Lindley, comp., and Elizabeth LeNoir Jennett, ed., *Biographical Directory of the Texan Conventions and Congresses, 1832–1845* (Austin: Book Exchange, 1941), 29, 129.
27. Cutrer, *Ben McCulloch*, 38; Mike Cox, *The Texas Rangers: Wearing the Cinco Peso, 1821–1900* (New York: Tom Doherty Associates, 2008), 81. Henry killed a drunken and boorish Ross at a party on Christmas Day, 1839. Sweitzer died in a private affray with Robert S. Neighbors in 1841. Nance, *After San Jacinto*, 235–236; *Civilian and Galveston Gazette*, January 18, 1840.

28. Michno, *A Fate Worse Than Death*, 58–60; Rupert Norval Richardson, *The Comanche Barrier to South Plains Settlement* (Glendale, CA: The Arthur H. Clark Company, 1933), 109–111; David La Vere, *Contrary Neighbors: Southern Plains and Removed Indians in Indian Territory* (Norman: University of Oklahoma Press, 2000), 95–96; James L. Haley, *Passionate Nation: The Epic History of Texas* (New York: Free Press, 2006), 227–228.
29. Donaly E. Brice, *The Great Comanche Raid: Boldest Indian Attack of the Texas Republic* (Austin: Eakin Press, 1987), 28–29. Brice, now retired from the Texas State Archives, has written the most influential work on the Plum Creek episode. For a condensed version, see "The Great Comanche Raid of 1840: Its Causes and Results," *South Texas Studies* 7 (1996): 75–99. Thomas W. Kavanagh, *Comanche Political History: An Ethnohistorical Perspective, 1706–1875* (Lincoln: University of Nebraska Press, 1996), 264; Ben C. Stuart, "Texas Indian Fighters and Frontier Rangers" (MS, 1916), TSLAC, 17; *Telegraph and Texas Register*, August 19, September 9, 1840; Wilbarger, *Indian Depredations in Texas*, 29.
30. DeShields, *Border Wars of Texas*, 299; Mildred Mayhall, *Indian Wars of Texas* (Waco: Texian Press, 1965), 31, 34; *Austin City Gazette*, September 2, 1840.
31. Brice, *Great Comanche Raid*, 29–31; Brown, *Indian Wars*, 79–80; John Holland Jenkins, *Recollections of Early Texas: The Memoirs of John Holland Jenkins*, ed. John Holmes Jenkins III (Austin: University of Texas Press, 2003), 61; John J. Linn, *Reminiscences of Fifty Years in Texas* (Austin: State House Press, 1986), 338–339; Mayhall, *Indian Wars of Texas*, 31–32; Haley, *Passionate Nation*, 229; *Telegraph and Texas Register*, September 9, 1840.
32. Brice, *Great Comanche Raid*, 32–33; Catherine W. McDowell, ed., *Now You Hear My Horn: The Journal of James Wilson Nichols, 1820–1887* (Austin: University of Texas Press, 1967), 57; Stanley Noyes, *Los Comanches: The Horse People, 1751–1845* (Albuquerque: University of New Mexico Press, 1993), 287–288; Kerr to Moore, August 9, 1840, Gulick, et al., eds., *Lamar Papers*, 3: 428–429.
33. Brice, *Great Comanche Raid*, 33; Brown, *Indian Wars*, 80; Yoakum, *History of Texas*, 2: 301.
34. Moore, *Savage Frontier*, 3: 92–93; Ernest W. Winkler, ed., *Manuscript Letters and Documents of Early Texians, 1821–1845* (Austin: The Steck Company, 1937), 237; Linn, *Fifty Years in Texas*, 342; *Austin City Gazette*, September 2, 1840.

35. Cutrer, *Ben McCulloch*, 41; Rose, *Gen. Ben McCulloch*, 56; Linn, *Fifty Years in Texas*, 342; Yoakum, *History of Texas*, 2: 302; *Telegraph and Texas Register*, September 9, 1840.
36. Brice, *Great Comanche Raid*, 34. McCulloch's three companions were Alsey S. Miller, Archibald Gipson, and Barney Randell. Rose, *Gen. Ben McCulloch*, 56; John H. Jenkins and Kenneth Kesselus, *Edward Burleson: Texas Frontier Leader* (Austin: Jenkins Publishing Company, 1990), 248; Wilbarger, *Indian Depredations in Texas*, 29; Stuart, "Texas Indian Fighters and Frontier Rangers," 19.
37. Cutrer, *Ben McCulloch*, 42; Rose, *Gen. Ben McCulloch*, 56; Brice, *Great Comanche Raid*, 35–36; Moore, *Savage Frontier*, 3: 98–99; Jenkins, *Recollections of Early Texas*, 63; Stuart, "Texas Indian Fighters and Frontier Rangers," 19; Huston to Archer, August 12, 1840, *Journals of the House of Representatives of the Republic of Texas: Fifth Congress, First Session*, Appendix, 141. Reprinted in *Telegraph and Texas Register*, August 26, 1840.
38. Cutrer, *Ben McCulloch*, 42; Rose, *Gen. Ben McCulloch*, 56, 62–63; Brazos, *Life of Robert Hall*, 54; McDowell, ed., *Now You Hear My Horn*, 60; Huston to Archer, August 12, 1840, *Journals of the House, Fifth Congress*, Appendix, 141.
39. Brice, *Great Comanche Raid*, 39; Huston to Archer, August 12, 1840, *Journals of the House, Fifth Congress*, Appendix, 141; Brown, *Indian Wars*, 81; Mayhall, *Indian Wars of Texas*, 35.
40. Cutrer, *Ben McCulloch*, 42–43; Rose, *Gen. Ben McCulloch*, 56; Brown, *Indian Wars*, 81; Jenkins, *Recollections of Early Texas*, 63–64; Huston to Archer, August 12, 1840, *Journals of the House, Fifth Congress*, Appendix, 141.
41. Brice, *Great Comanche Raid*, 41; Mayhall, *Indian Wars of Texas*, 36–37; Jenkins, *Recollections of Early Texas*, 65; Huston to Archer, August 12, 1840, *Journals of the House, Fifth Congress*, Appendix, 141–142; Z. N. Morrell, *Flowers and Fruits from the Wilderness* (Boston: Gould & Lincoln, 1872), 129.
42. Rose, *Gen. Ben McCulloch*, 57; Wilbarger, *Indian Depredations in Texas*, 32; Sowell, *Texas Indian Fighters*, 418. Writing sixteen years previously, Sowell claimed Alonzo Sweitzer and Ben McCulloch, rather than Henry, saved each other's lives at the battle. *Rangers and Pioneers of Texas*, 207.
43. Brice, *Great Comanche Raid*, 41; Cutrer, *Ben McCulloch*, 43; Rose, *Gen. Ben McCulloch*, 57–58; Brown, *Indian Wars*, 82; DeShields, *Border Wars of Texas*, 300–301; Wilbarger, *Indian Depredations in Texas*, 31.

44. Brice, *Great Comanche Raid*, 42–47; Cutrer, *Ben McCulloch*, 44; Rose, *Gen. Ben McCulloch*, 58–59; McDowell, ed., *Now You Hear My Horn*, 62; Brown, *History of Texas*, 2: 181; Huston to Archer, August 12, 1840, *Journals of the House, Fifth Congress*, Appendix, 142; Sowell, *Rangers and Pioneers of Texas*, 209; Daniell, comp., *Personnel of the Texas State Government*, 229.
45. Brice, *Great Comanche Raid*, 48, 44–45, 100 n38; Huston to Archer, August 12, 1840, Huston to Archer, September 28, 1840, *Journals of the House, Fifth Congress*, Appendix, 142, 143–144. The second letter was reprinted in *Telegraph and Texas Register*, October 14, 1840. Brazos, *Life of Robert Hall*, 55, 58; *Telegraph and Texas Register*, September 9, 1840; *Austin City Gazette*, August 19, 1840.
46. *Telegraph and Texas Register*, October 7, 14, 21, 28, 1840.
47. Moore, *Savage Frontier*, 3: 145–155; *Telegraph and Texas Register*, September 9, November 18, 1840; Jenkins, *Recollections of Early Texas*, 171–174; Nathan A. Jennings, *Riding for the Lone Star: Frontier Cavalry and the Texas Way of War, 1822–1865* (Denton: University of North Texas Press, 2016), 150–152; Stuart, "Texas Indian Fighters and Frontier Rangers," 6–7.
48. Moore, *Savage Frontier*, 3: 137; *Telegraph and Texas Register*, September 2, 1840; Letter to Citizens of Victoria and Texana Respecting Indian Expedition, September 9, 1840, Dorman H. Winfrey and James M. Day, eds., *The Indian Papers of Texas and the Southwest* (Austin: Texas State Historical Association, 1995), 1: 115; *Texas Sentinel*, November 28, 1840.
49. Moore, *Savage Frontier*, 3: 137; *Texas Sentinel*, November 28, 1840; *Telegraph and Texas Register*, October 21, 1840; Jenkins, *Recollections of Early Texas*, 187.
50. *Texas Sentinel*, November 28, 1840.
51. Moore, *Savage Frontier*, 3: 141–143; *Texas Sentinel*, November 28, 1840; Jenkins, *Recollections of Early Texas*, 187–188; Wilbarger, *Indian Depredations in Texas*, 374–375.
52. Gammel, comp., *Laws of Texas*, 2: 137–139.
53. Cutrer, *Ben McCulloch*, 48; Rose, *Gen. Ben McCulloch*, 66; DeShields, *Border Wars of Texas*, 324; Brown, *Indian Wars*, 84; Wilbarger, *Indian Depredations in Texas*, 289.
54. Cutrer, *Ben McCulloch*, 48; Rose, *Gen. Ben McCulloch*, 66; Moore, *Savage Frontier*, 3: 337; Frederick Wilkins, *The Legend Begins: The Texas Rangers, 1823–1845* (Austin: State House Press, 1996), 99;

Brown, *Indian Wars*, 84–85; DeShields, *Border Wars of Texas*, 324; "Callahan's Body Taken to Austin," *Frontier Times* 8 (March 1931): 247.

55. Cutrer, *Ben McCulloch*, 48; Forrest Daniell, "Texas Pioneer Surveyors and Indians," *Southwestern Historical Quarterly* 60 (April 1957): 501.
56. Gunn, "Ben McCulloch," 5; Benjamin McCulloch, Unnumbered Public Debt Claim, Reel 171, Frame 457, TSLAC. Fourteen years later, Callahan led an unsanctioned strike into Mexico, in pursuit of either depredating Indians or runaway slaves. For more details, see Michael L. Collins, *Texas Devils: Rangers and Regulars on the Lower Rio Grande, 1846–1861* (Norman: University of Oklahoma Press, 2008), 74–88.
57. Cutrer, *Ben McCulloch*, 50–51; Rose, *Gen. Ben McCulloch*, 66–67; Ralph A. Wooster, "Texas Military Operations against Mexico, 1842–1843," *Southwestern Historical Quarterly*, 67 (April 1964): 466; Jerry D. Thompson, *Sabers on the Rio Grande* (Austin: Presidial Press, 1974), 103–104; Brown, *History of Texas*, 2: 212; William S. Speer and John Henry Brown, eds., *The Encyclopedia of the New West* (Marshall, TX: United States Biographical Publishing Company, 1881), 295; Rena Maverick Green, ed., *Memoirs of Mary A. Maverick, Arranged by Mary A. Maverick and Her Son George Madison Maverick* (San Antonio: Alamo Printing Co., 1921), 62. McCulloch would receive compensation for his service in the Woll invasion in which he held the rank of major. Benjamin McCulloch, Public Debt Claim No. 1565, Reel 171, Frames 464–466, 474, TSLAC.
58. *Journals of the Sixth Congress of the Republic of Texas, 1841–1842*, ed. Harriet Smither, 3: 69, 125–127, 165–167. The "War bill" was reprinted in *Telegraph and Texas Register*, July 20, 1842. Houston to Senate and House of Representatives, June 27, 1842, Houston to House of Representatives, July 22, 1842, Williams and Barker, eds., *Writings of Sam Houston*, 3: 83, 116–124; Stanley Siegel, *A Political History of the Texas Republic, 1836–1845* (Austin: University of Texas Press, 1956), 198–199.
59. Cutrer, *Ben McCulloch*, 54; Houston to McCulloch, June 18, 1842, Williams and Barker, eds., *Writings of Sam Houston*, 3: 71–72; Hockley to McCulloch, July 21, 1842, Box 2-22/181, Andrew Jackson Houston Collection, TSLAC; *Civilian and Galveston Gazette*, July 24, 1842; George P. Garrison, ed., *Diplomatic Correspondence of the Republic of Texas* (Washington, D.C.: Government Printing Office, 1908), 1: 581.
60. Cutrer, *Ben McCulloch*, 54–55; Rose, *Gen. Ben McCulloch*, 67; Francis R. Lubbock, *Six Decades in Texas, or Memoirs of Francis*

Richard Lubbock: Governor of Texas in War-Time, 1861–63, ed. C. W. Raines (Austin: Ben C. Jones & Co., 1900), 145; Orders to the Country, September 16, 1842, Houston to Hamilton, September 16, 1842, Williams and Barker, eds., *Writings of Sam Houston*, 7: 6–7, 3: 159–160; *Telegraph and Texas Register*, September 21, 28, 1842; George R. Nielsen, "Mathew Caldwell," *Southwestern Historical Quarterly* 63 (April 1961): 496–498; Burkett, "Early Days in Texas."

61. Cutrer, *Ben McCulloch*, 55–56; Moore, *Savage Frontier*, 4: 88–89; Joseph Milton Nance, *Attack and Counterattack: The Texas-Mexican Frontier, 1842* (Austin: University of Texas Press, 1964), 386–388; Jenkins, *Recollections of Early Texas*, 99; Brown, *History of Texas*, 2: 228; *Telegraph and Texas Register*, September 28, 1842; *The Planter*, September 23, 1843.
62. Cutrer, *Ben McCulloch*, 56; Nance, *Attack and Counterattack*, 390–391; Jenkins, *Recollections of Early Texas*, 99; Morrell, *Flowers and Fruits*, 174; General Thomas J. Green, *Journal of the Texian Expedition against Mier* (New York: Harper & Brothers, 1845), 34–35; Daniell, comp., *Personnel of the Texas State Government*, 231.
63. Cutrer, *Ben McCulloch*, 63; Nance, *Attack and Counterattack*, 393–394; Morrell, *Flowers and Fruits*, 176–177; Brown, *History of Texas*, 2: 229; McDowell, ed., *Now You Hear My Horn*, 109–110; *Telegraph and Texas Register*, September 28, October 12, 1842; *Civilian and Galveston City Gazette*, October 1, 1842.
64. Wilkins, *The Legend Begins*, 141; Nance, *Attack and Counterattack*, 394–395; *The Planter*, September 23, 1843; Morrell, *Flowers and Fruits*, 177–178; McDowell, ed., *Now You Hear My Horn*, 112; *Telegraph and Texas Register*, October 26, 1842.
65. Cutrer, *Ben McCulloch*, 56; Morrell, *Flowers and Fruits*, 178; McDowell, ed., *Now You Hear My Horn*, 109, 113; Daniell, comp., *Personnel of the Texas State Government*, 231; *Houston Post*, January 16, 1898. Caldwell was blamed for the abortive outcome of the campaign by those who sought to replace him. Despite the unfair criticism, he conscientiously accepted full responsibility. He returned home and died on December 28, 1842. Caldwell to Hamilton, September 18, 1842, *Journals of the House of Representatives of the Seventh Congress of the Republic of Texas*, Appendix, 18; Nielsen, "Mathew Caldwell," 501.
66. Houston to Somervell, October 3, 1842, *Journals of the House, Seventh Congress*, Appendix, 3–4.

67. Cutrer, *Ben McCulloch*, 57; Nance, *Attack and Counterattack*, 423; Somervell to Houston, November 14, 1842, *Journals of the House, Seventh Congress*, Appendix, 11–12; Ben McCulloch, Public Debt Claim No. 671, Reel 171, Frame 461, TSLAC; Daniell, comp., *Personnel of the Texas State Government*, 231; Sterling Brown Hendricks, "The Somervell Expedition to the Rio Grande, 1842," *Southwestern Historical Quarterly* 23 (October 1919): 113.
68. Thomas W. Bell, *A Narrative of the Capture and Subsequent Suffering of the Mier Prisoners in Mexico* (Waco: Texian Press, 1964), 8. Hereafter cited as *Mier Expedition Narrative*. Rena Maverick Green, ed., *Samuel Maverick, Texan: 1803–1870* (San Antonio: privately printed, 1952), 204; McCutchan, *Mier Expedition Diary*, 17; Report of the Secretary of War, December 14, 1842, *Journals of the House, Seventh Congress*, Appendix, 10–11; Lucy A. Erath, ed., "Memoirs of Major George Bernard Erath," Pt. 3, *Southwestern Historical Quarterly* 27 (July 1923): 39–40.
69. Cutrer, *Ben McCulloch*, 59; Nance, *Attack and Counterattack*, 507; Thompson, *Sabers on the Rio Grande*, 122; Brown, *History of Texas*, 2: 237–238; Hendricks, "Somervell Expedition," 120; McCutchan, *Mier Expedition Diary*, 24; Green, *Journal of the Texian Expedition Against Mier*, 54–55; *Morning Star*, January 7, 1843; Erath, ed., "Memoirs of Major George Bernard Erath," Pt. 3: 40.
70. Cutrer, *Ben McCulloch*, 59; Erath, ed., "Memoirs of Major George Bernard Erath," Pt. 3: 41; Green, *Journal of the Texian Expedition against Mier*, 61–62; Thompson, *Sabers on the Rio Grande*, 129; William Preston Stapp, *The Prisoners of Perote* (Austin: University of Texas Press, 1977), 24–26; Bell, *Mier Expedition Narrative*, 10; John Warren Hunter, "Adventures of a Mier Prisoner," *Frontier Times* 2 (April 1925): 18.
71. Cutrer, *Ben McCulloch*, 60–61; Nance, *Attack and Counterattack*, 566; Joseph B. Wilkinson, *Laredo and the Rio Grande Frontier: A Narrative* (Austin: Jenkins Publishing Co., 1975), 179; McCutchan, *Mier Expedition Diary*, 31, 33–35; Jenkins, *Recollections of Early Texas*, 108; Bell, *Mier Expedition Narrative*, 11–13; Hunter, "Adventures of a Mier Prisoner," 18; Green, *Journal of the Texian Expedition against Mier*, 74; *Southern Intelligencer*, September 16, 1857; Marilyn McAdams Sibley, ed., *Samuel H. Walker's Account of the Mier Expedition* (Austin: Texas State Historical Association, 1978), 34; Daniell, comp., *Personnel of the Texas State Government*, 232–233; Wilbarger, *Indian Depredations in*

Texas, 612; Ben McCulloch, Public Debt Claim No. 671, Reel 171, Frame 461, TSLAC. See also "Abstract of the Muster-Rolls of the Companies Comprising the Army on the South-Western Frontier," *Journals of the House of Representatives of the Ninth Congress of the Republic of Texas*, Appendix, 75.

72. Cutrer, *Ben McCulloch*, 64; Rose, *Gen. Ben McCulloch*, 67; Wilkins, *The Legend Begins*, 189; Nance, *Attack and Counterattack*, 417; Muster and Pay Rolls, John C. Hays, 401–718, -791, TSLAC; *Northern Standard*, July 10, 1844.
73. Cutrer, *Ben McCulloch*, 65; Rose, *Gen. Ben McCulloch*, 68; Anson Jones, *Memoranda and Official Correspondence Relating to the Republic of Texas, Its History and Annexation* (New York: D. Appleton and Company, 1859), 493; Williams and Barker, eds., *Writings of Sam Houston*, 4: 269; Compiled Service Records of Volunteer Soldiers, Gillespie's Company, Texas Mounted Rangers, Ben McCulloch; *Telegraph and Texas Register*, December 31, 1845; Ernest R. Lindley, ed., *Members of the Legislature of the State of Texas from 1846 to 1939* (Austin: State of Texas, 1939), 4; *Journals of the House of Representatives of the First Legislature of the State of Texas*, 4, 22; *Northern Standard*, March 11, 1846; Gammel, comp., *Laws of Texas*, 3: 1415.
74. *Democratic Telegraph and Texas Register*, May 13, 1846. The Militia Acts of May 2, 1792, and February 28, 1795 authorized three-month enlistments for militia, while the Act of May 13, 1846, specified six months for militia and twelve months for volunteers. *The Public Statutes at Large of the United States of America*, 1: 264, 424–425, 9: 9–10.
75. Cutrer, *Ben McCulloch*, 67–68; Rose, *Gen. Ben McCulloch*, 69–70; Samuel C. Reid, Jr., *The Scouting Expeditions of McCulloch's Texas Rangers; or, the Summer and Fall Campaigns of the Army of the United States in Mexico—1846* (Philadelphia: G. B. Zieber and Company, 1847), 38, 40–41; *Democratic Telegraph and Texas Register*, May 6, 1846; *Daily Picayune*, June 3, 1846; Compiled Service Records of Volunteer Soldiers, First Texas Mounted Rifles, Ben McCulloch.
76. Cutrer, *Ben McCulloch*, 70, 68; Rose, *Gen. Ben McCulloch*, 70; John Duff Brown, "Reminisces of Jno. Duff Brown," *The Quarterly of the Texas State Historical Association* 12 (April 1909): 304–305; Compiled Service Records of Volunteer Soldiers, First Texas Mounted Rifles, Ben McCulloch; Taylor to Adjutant General, August 31, 1846, *Mexican War Correspondence*, House Executive Document No. 60, 30th Congress, 1st Session, 322–323. The reason Taylor accepted

McCulloch's men for three months, rather than the six or twelve required by the most recent congressional act, is unknown. Henry W. Barton observed enlistments of Texas ranger companies, such as those commanded by John T. Price and Sam Walker, were ending. He surmised the general was in desperate need of mounted troops and willing to overlook the niceties of the law in the name of expediency. *Texas Volunteers in the Mexican War* (Waco: Texian Press, 1970), 29.

77. Reid, *Scouting Expeditions*, 23.
78. Cutrer, *Ben McCulloch*, 70; Rose, *Gen. Ben McCulloch*, 70; *Niles' National Register* 71 (September 26, 1846): 55, 70 (July 4, 1846): 273; Special Order No. 85, June 15, 1846, Taylor to Adjutant General, June 17, 1846, *Mexican War Correspondence*, 523, 550–551; *Daily Picayune*, June 24, 1846.
79. Cutrer, *Ben McCulloch*, 70–71; Reid, *Scouting Expeditions*, 44–52; *Daily Picayune*, July 7, 1846; Walter Prescott Webb, *The Texas Rangers: A Century of Frontier Defense* (Austin: University of Texas Press, 1965), 95–96; *Niles' National Register* 70 (August 1, 1846): 342.
80. Cutrer, *Ben McCulloch*, 73; Rose, *Gen. Ben McCulloch*, 75; Reid, *Scouting Expeditions*, 53; Walter Prescott Webb, *The Texas Rangers in the Mexican War* (Austin: Jenkins Garrett Press, 1975), 24.
81. Rose, *Gen. Ben McCulloch*, 78; *Daily Picayune*, July 8, 1846; John S. D. Eisenhower, *So Far from God: The U.S. War with Mexico, 1846–1848* (Norman: University of Oklahoma Press, 2000), 63, 64–65.
82. Reid, *Scouting Expeditions*, 56–57.
83. Charles M. Robinson III, *The Men Who Wear the Star: The Story of the Texas Rangers* (New York: The Modern Library, 2001), 84; Frederick Wilkins, *The Highly Irregular Irregulars: Texas Rangers in the Mexican War* (Austin: Eakin Press, 1990), 55.
84. Reid, *Scouting Expeditions*, 23; Compiled Service Records of Volunteer Soldiers, First Texas Mounted Rifles, Samuel C. Reid.
85. Reid, *Scouting Expeditions*, 26.
86. Cutrer, *Ben McCulloch*, 71, 75; Rose, *Gen. Ben McCulloch*, 86; Reid, *Scouting Expeditions*, 78–83; *Daily Picayune*, July 17, 19, August 1, 9, 25, 1846; Adjutant General's Office, *Official Army Register, Corrected to August 31, 1847*, 8; McCulloch to Taylor, July 20, 1846, McCulloch to Bliss, July 23, 1846, Box 3G37, McCulloch Family Papers, BCAH; Brown, "Reminiscences of Jno. Duff Brown," 305; Taylor to Adjutant General, August 10, 1846, *Mexican War Correspondence*, 408; *Niles' National Register* 71 (September 5, 1846): 2.

87. Cutrer, *Ben McCulloch*, 75; Reid, *Scouting Expeditions*, 91, 92, 96, 101, 102–103; Special Orders No. 119, August 11, 1846, *Mexican War Correspondence*, 534; *Daily Picayune*, August 15, 28, 1846.
88. Compiled Service Records of Volunteer Soldiers, First Texas Mounted Rifles, Ben McCulloch, William H. Kelley, James S. Allen; Christopher D. Dishman, *A Perfect Gibraltar: The Battle for Monterrey, Mexico, 1846* (Norman: University of Oklahoma Press, 2010), 74; Captain William Seaton Henry, *Campaign Sketches of the War with Mexico* (New York: Harper & Brothers, 1847), 155–156.
89. Cutrer, *Ben McCulloch*, 76–77; Rose, *Gen. Ben McCulloch*, 94–95; Reid, *Scouting Expeditions*, 105, 113, 118, 126–129; *Daily Picayune*, September 12, 22, November 19, October 6, 1846; *New York Herald*, October 3, 1846; Lubbock, *Six Decades in Texas*, 182; Charles Spurlin, "Texas Volunteers in the Monterrey Campaign," Pt. 1, *Military History of Texas and the Southwest* 16 (1980): 6; S. Compton Smith, *Chile Con Carne; or, The Camp and the Field* (New York: Miller & Curtis, 1857), 57; Henry, *Campaign Sketches*, 182; *Niles' National Register* 71 (October 31, 1846): 131.
90. Cutrer, *Ben McCulloch*, 79; Reid, *Scouting Expeditions*, 141–143; *Daily Picayune*, November 19, 1846; Justin H. Smith, *The War with Mexico* (New York: The Macmillan Company, 1919), 1: 237; Henry, *Campaign Sketches*, 190–191; Major George Deas, "Reminiscences of the Campaign on the Rio Grande," Pt. 3, *The Historical Magazine* 7 (April 1870): 238; Spurlin, "Texas Volunteers in the Monterrey Campaign," Pt. 1: 9; Lane, *Adventures and Recollections*, 43.
91. Cutrer, *Ben McCulloch*, 79, 82; Reid, *Scouting Expeditions*, 156; Spurlin, "Texas Volunteers in the Monterrey Campaign," Pt. 1: 13; Eisenhower, *So Far from God*, 131; Dishman, *A Perfect Gibraltar*, 87–89; Felice Flanery Lewis, *Trailing Clouds of Glory: Zachary Taylor's Mexican War Campaign and His Emerging Civil War Leaders* (Tuscaloosa: University of Alabama, 2010), 130, 134–135.
92. Cutrer, *Ben McCulloch*, 82–83; Reid, *Scouting Expeditions*, 157; Robert M. Utley, *Lone Star Justice: The First Century of the Texas Rangers* (New York: Berkley Books, 2002), 68–69; R. S. Ripley, *The War with Mexico* (New York: Harper & Brothers, 1849), 1: 216–217; Smith, *War with Mexico*, 1: 243; George Wilkins Kendall, *The War Between the United States and Mexico, Illustrated* (New York: D. Appleton & Company, 1851), 6; *Daily Picayune*, February 17, 1847; John S. Ford, "John C. Hayes in Texas," Box 2Q512, John Salmon Ford Papers, BCAH, 29.

93. Cutrer, *Ben McCulloch*, 83; Reid, *Scouting Expeditions*, 157–158; Lewis, *Trailing Clouds of Glory*, 135; Eisenhower, *So Far from God*, 131; Smith, *War with Mexico*, 1: 243; *Northern Standard*, November 7, 1846; Lane, *Adventures and Recollections*, 44.
94. Cutrer, *Ben McCulloch*, 83–87; Rose, *Gen. Ben McCulloch*, 106, 107–108, 109–110; Reid, *Scouting Expeditions*, 160–165, 181–186, 190–194; *General Taylor and His Staff* (Philadelphia: Grigg, Elliott & Co., 1848), 203; *Northern Standard*, October 24, 1846; *Texas Democrat*, November 25, 1846.
95. Major Ian B. Lyles, "Mixed Blessing: The Role of the Texas Rangers in the Mexican War, 1846–1848" (MMAS thesis, Fort Leavenworth, 2003), 48–49.
96. Taylor to Adjutant General, September 25, 1846, Terms of Capitulation of the city of Monterey, September 24, 1846, *Annual Report of the Secretary of War*, House Executive Document No. 4, 29th Congress, 2nd Session, 78–79, 80–81.
97. Cutrer, *Ben McCulloch*, 88; Rose, *Gen. Ben McCulloch*, 110; Reid, *Scouting Expeditions*, 225, 232–233; Compiled Service Records of Volunteer Soldiers, First Texas Mounted Rifles, Ben McCulloch; *Niles' National Register* 71 (November 21, 1846): 181; *Texas Democrat*, October 21, 1846.
98. Eisenhower, *So Far from God*, 149–150; Charles M. Robinson III, *Texas and the Mexican War: A History and a Guide* (Austin: Texas State Historical Association, 2004), 72, 74; Marcy to Taylor, October 13, 1846, Taylor to Santa Anna, November 5, 1846, Taylor to Adjutant General, November 9, 1846, Order No. 139, November 8, 1846, Taylor to Adjutant General, November 24, 1846, *Mexican War Correspondence*, 355, 437, 361–362, 377–378.
99. Scott to Taylor, December 20, 1846, Scott to Taylor, January 3, 1847, Taylor to Scott, two letters dated January 15, 1847, *Mexican War Correspondence*, 839–840, 848–850, 861–864; Smith, *War with Mexico*, 1: 362; James K. Polk, *The Diary of James K. Polk*, ed. Milton M. Quaife (Chicago: A. C. McClurg & Company, 1910), 2: 236; Richard Bruce Winders, *Mr. Polk's Army: The American Military Experience in the Mexican War* (College Station: Texas A&M University Press, 1997), 33–34. For more on Taylor as both soldier and president, see John S. D. Eisenhower, *Zachary Taylor* (New York: Times Books, 2008).
100. Cutrer, *Ben McCulloch*, 92; Rose, *Gen. Ben McCulloch*, 111; Utley, *Lone Star Justice*, 78–79; Webb, *Texas Rangers*, 112; *Niles' National*

Register 72 (July 17, 1847): 308; *Daily Picayune*, January 27, 1847; *Northern Standard*, November 28, 1846, March 6, 1847; Barton, *Texas Volunteers in the Mexican War*, 81; Brazos, *Life of Robert Hall*, 78; Taylor to Adjutant General, June 8, 1847, *Mexican War Correspondence*, 1176; Compiled Service Records of Volunteer Soldiers, McCulloch's Company, Texas Mounted Volunteers (Spies), Benjamin McCulloch. For more on Texas rangers in Tamaulipas, Nuevo León, Coahuila, Chihuahua, and Zacatecas, see Bryan, *More Zeal Than Discretion*, 60–73; and Collins, *Texas Devils*, 12–16.

101. Scott to Taylor, January 26, 1847, Taylor to Adjutant General, February 4, 1847, Taylor to Adjutant General, February 7, 1847, Taylor to Scott, February 7, 1847, *Mexican War Correspondence*, 864–865, 1109–1111, 1162–1163; James M. McCaffrey, *Army of Manifest Destiny: The American Soldier in the Mexican War, 1846–1848* (New York: New York University Press, 1992), 141; Isaac Ingalls Stevens, *Campaigns of the Rio Grande and of Mexico* (New York: D. Appleton and Company, 1851), 39, 42–43; Grady McWhiney and Sue McWhiney, eds., *To Mexico with Taylor and Scott, 1845–1847* (Waltham, MA: Blaisdell Publishing Company, 1969), 81, 84; Eisenhower, *So Far from God*, 175–176. See also Scott to Taylor, January 3, 1847, Taylor to Scott, January 26, 1847, *Mexican War Correspondence*, 849–850, 890–891.
102. Cutrer, *Ben McCulloch*, 94–95; Rose, *Gen. Ben McCulloch*, 112–113; Reid, *Scouting Expeditions*, 233–234; Brazos, *Life of Robert Hall*, 81; Taylor to Adjutant General, March 6, 1847, *Annual Report of the Secretary of War*, House Executive Document No. 8, 30th Congress, 1st Session, 132. Hereafter cited by *Annual Report of the Secretary of War, 1847*. Pat B. Clark, *The History of Clarksville and Old Red River County* (Dallas: Mathis, Van Nort & Co., 1937), 248–249; Henry, *Campaign Sketches*, 310; *General Taylor and His Staff*, 204.
103. Cutrer, *Ben McCulloch*, 95–99; Rose, *Gen. Ben McCulloch*, 113–116; Reid, *Scouting Expeditions*, 234–236; Clark, *Red River County*, 250–255; James Henry Carleton, *The Battle of Buena Vista, with the Operations of the "Army of Occupation" for One Month* (New York: Harper and Brothers, 1848), 12, 19–20; *Democratic Telegraph and Texas Register*, April 5, 1847; Luther Giddings, *Sketches of the Campaign in Northern Mexico* (New York: George P. Putnam & Co., 1853), 287; Kendall, *War Between the United States and Mexico*, 11. For the Mexican order of battle, see Stephen A. Carney, *Desperate*

Stand: The Battle of Buena Vista (Washington, D.C.: U.S. Army Center of Military History, 2010), 17–18.

104. Taylor to Adjutant General, March 6, 1847, *Annual Report of the Secretary of War, 1847*, 132; *Democratic Telegraph and Texas Register*, April 5, 1847; McCaffrey, *Army of Manifest Destiny*, 142; John R. Kenly, *Memoirs of a Maryland Volunteer: War with Mexico, in the Years 1846–7–8* (Philadelphia: J. P. Lippincott & Co., 1873), 259–260; Carleton, *Buena Vista*, 20–21, 27.
105. Cutrer, *Ben McCulloch*, 99–100; Clark, *Red River County*, 255–256; Lewis, *Trailing Clouds of Glory*, 203; K. Jack Bauer, "General John E. Wool's Memoranda of the Battle of Buena Vista," *Southwestern Historical Quarterly* 77 (July 1973): 115; Taylor to Adjutant General, February 24, 1847, *Annual Report of the Secretary of War, 1847*, 97, 132–133, 140; Carney, *Desperate Stand*, 23.
106. Clark, *Red River County*, 256–259; Taylor to Adjutant General, March 6, 1847, *Annual Report of the Secretary of War, 1847*, 133–137; Taylor to Scott, March 1, 1847, *Correspondence Between the Secretary of War and Generals Scott and Taylor, and Between General Scott and Mr. Trist*, House Executive Document No. 56, 30th Congress, 1st Session, 358; McCaffrey, *Army of Manifest Destiny*, 144–145; Brazos, *Life of Robert Hall*, 82; Carleton, *Buena Vista*, 64; McWhiney and McWhiney, ed., *To Mexico with Taylor and Scott*, 82. See also Richard Bruce Winders, *Panting For Glory: The Mississippi Rifles in the Mexican War* (College Station: Texas A&M University Press, 2016).
107. Taylor to Adjutant General, June 8, 1847, *Mexican War Correspondence*, 1176; Wool to Bliss, March 4, 1847, Bissell to Wool, February 28, 1847, Trail to Wool, February 28, 1847, *Annual Report of the Secretary of War, 1847*, 144–153, 175–178, 178–180; Carney, *Desperate Stand*, 35.
108. Cutrer, *Ben McCulloch*, 102; Brazos, *Life of Robert Hall*, 84, 86; Carleton, *Buena Vista*, 146; Taylor to Adjutant General, March 6, 1847, *Annual Report of the Secretary of War, 1847*, 137.
109. Cutrer, *Ben McCulloch*, 103; Compiled Service Records of Volunteer Soldiers, McCulloch's Company, Texas Mounted Volunteers (Spies), Benjamin McCulloch; Taylor to Adjutant General, June 8, 1847, Taylor to Adjutant General, August 3, 1847, *Correspondence Between the Secretary of War and Generals Scott and Taylor*, 366, 377; *Democratic Telegraph and Texas Register*, June 21, 1847; Bliss

to Adjutant General, June 16, 1847, Letters Received by the Office of the Adjutant General, M567, RG 94, NARA. Hereafter cited as Letters Received, Adjutant General's Office. *American Flag*, June 19, 30, 1847; Muster and Pay Rolls, Ben McCulloch, 401–794, TSLAC.

110. Taylor to Adjutant General, June 16, 1847, *Mexican War Correspondence*, 1178. Lyles, "Mixed Blessing," 78–81, 96–97, 99; Jimmy L. Bryan, Jr., "Agents of Destiny: Texas Rangers and the Dilemma of the Conquest Narrative," *The Martial Imagination: Cultural Aspects of American Warfare*, ed. Jimmy L. Bryan, Jr. (College Station: Texas A&M University Press, 2013), 58–59. Irving W. Levinson, *Wars within War: Mexican Guerrillas, Domestic Elites, and the United States of America, 1846–1848* (Fort Worth: Texas Christian University Press, 2005), 27: "The ongoing adventurism and lack of discipline within the ranks of volunteers contributed to the aggravation of tension between the invading army and Mexican civilians. " For further discussion on the violent excesses of regulars and volunteers, see Paul Foos, *Short, Offhand, Killing Affair: Soldiers and Social Conflict During the Mexican-American War* (Chapel Hill: University of North Carolina Press, 2002), 83–134.

    Collins, *Texas Devils*, 12: "during the campaigns of 1846 and 1847, roaming gangs of Mexican banditti raided ranchos, ransacked villages, and pillaged the properties of peasants and landlords alike; their misdeeds were sometimes wrongfully assigned to *los malvados Tejanos*, 'the evil Texans. '"

111. Cutrer, *Ben McCulloch*, 104–106; Rose, *Gen. Ben McCulloch*, 117, 121; Francis B. Heitman, *Historical Register and Dictionary of the United States Army from its Organization, September 29 1789, to March 2 1903* (Washington, D.C.: Government Printing Office, 1903), 1: 661; Gunn, "Ben McCulloch," 8–9; *Daily National Intelligencer*, January 15, 1848; *Congressional Globe*, 31st Congress, 1st Session, 2073; *Texas State Gazette*, November 30, 1850.

112. Cutrer, *Ben McCulloch*, 106–108; Rose, *Gen. Ben McCulloch*, 122; Walter T. Durham, *Volunteer Forty-Niners: Tennesseans and the California Gold Rush* (Nashville: Vanderbilt University Press, 1997), 41; *Daily Picayune*, August 22, 1849; *San Antonio Ledger*, July 8, 1852; *Texas State Gazette*, September 1, 22, November 24, 1849; *Placer Times*, December 8, 1849; *Daily Alta California*, December 10, 1849.

113. Cutrer, *Ben McCulloch*, 113–115; Mark A. Eifler, *Gold Rush Capitalists: Greed and Growth in Sacramento* (Albuquerque: University

of New Mexico Press, 2002), 132–160; W. W. Robinson, *Land in California: The Story of Mission Lands, Ranchos, Squatters, Mining Claims, Railroad Grants, Land Scrip, Homesteads* (Berkeley: University of California Press, 1979), 114–115; *Placer Times*, May 1, 5, 1850; *Sacramento Daily Transcript*, August 15, 19, 31, 1850, January 21, 1851; *Northern Standard*, September 21, 1850; *Daily Alta California*, August 15, 19, 23, 1850; Pittard, "From Jefferson to Elkhorn Tavern," 21.

114. Cutrer, *Ben McCulloch*, 115–117; Rose, *Gen. Ben McCulloch*, 122; Sacramento *Daily Transcript*, August 23, 24, September 2, 4, 9, December 2, 19, 1850; Howard R. Lamar, *Texas Crossings: The Lone Star State and the American Far West, 1836–1986* (Austin: University of Texas Press, 1991), 15; Durham, *Volunteer Forty-Niners*, 135; George Harwood Philips, *"Bringing Them Under Subjection": California's Tejón Indian Reservation and Beyond, 1852–1864* (Lincoln: University of Nebraska Press, 2004), 21–22, 26–35; H. W. Brands, *The Age of Gold: The California Gold Rush and the New American Dream* (New York: Anchor Books, 2003), 310.
115. Cutrer, *Ben McCulloch*, 118; Rose, *Gen. Ben McCulloch*, 122; Gunn, "Ben McCulloch," 11; *Daily Alta California*, October 15, 1851; *Sacramento Daily Union*, January 13, 1852.
116. Cutrer, *Ben McCulloch*, 120–124; Rose, *Gen. Ben McCulloch*, 122; *Alexandria Gazette and Virginia Advertiser*, March 9, 1853; *Northern Standard*, May 7, 1853; *Texas State Gazette*, April 16, 1853; Virgil D. White, *Index of U.S. Marshals, 1789–1960* (Waynesboro, TN: National Historical Publishing Company, 1988), 58; *Daily Union*, April 1, 1853.
117. Cutrer, *Ben McCulloch*, 125–130; *Telegraph and Texas Register*, April 22, 1853; *Congressional Globe*, 35th Congress, 2nd Session, 773–784; *Texas State Gazette*, April 16, June 25, August 13, October 1, 1853, May 13, December 9, 1854; Robert E. May, *Manifest Destiny's Underworld: Filibustering in Antebellum America* (Chapel Hill: University of North Carolina Press, 2002), 117–119, 166; Joseph E. Chance, *José María de Jesús Carvajal: The Life and Times of a Mexican Revolutionary* (San Antonio: Trinity University Press, 2006), 146–147, 158, 162–163; Joseph A. Stout, Jr., *Schemers and Dreamers: Filibustering in Mexico, 1848–1921* (Fort Worth: Texas Christian University Press, 2002), 23; *Western Texan*, November 24, 1853; *Galveston Weekly News*, January 3, 1854. The list of unindicted co-conspirators in the Carvajal episode is lengthy and includes merchant Charles Stillman, Richard

King, Mifflin Kenedy, Henry Clay Davis, and John S. Ford. For more on the disreputable Watrous, see Walace Hawkins, *The Case of John C. Watrous: United States Judge for Texas, A Political Story of High Crimes and Misdemeanors* (Dallas: University Press, 1950).

118. Cutrer, *Ben McCulloch*, 126–127, 130; Frederick S. Calhoun, *The Lawmen: United States Marshals and Their Deputies, 1789–1989* (Washington, D.C.: Smithsonian Institution Press, 1989), 54–55, 56–57.

119. Robert M. Utley, *Frontiersmen in Blue: The United States Army and the Indian, 1848–1865* (Lincoln: University of Nebraska Press, 1981), 3, 11, 18–21; James R. Arnold, *Jeff Davis's Own: Cavalry, Comanches, and the Battle for the Texas Frontier* (New York: John Wiley & Sons, 2000), 19; Albert G. Brackett, *History of the United States Cavalry, From the Formation of the Federal Government to the 1st of June, 1863* (New York: Harper & Brothers, 1865), 140; George F. Price, *Across the Continent with the Fifth Cavalry* (New York: Antiquarian Press, 1959), 16–17; *The Statutes at Large and Treaties of the United States of America*, 10: 639; *Congressional Globe*, 33rd Congress, 2nd Session, Appendix, 399–400.

120. Cutrer, *Ben McCulloch*, 127–128, 132–134; Rose, *Gen. Ben McCulloch*, 121, 122–123, 125–126; Speer and Brown, eds., *Encyclopedia of the New West*, 296; *Memorial and Genealogical Record of Southwest Texas*, 580; William Preston Johnston, *The Life of Albert Sidney Johnston* (Austin: State House Press, 1997), 184; B. M. Hord, "Gen. Ben McCulloch," *Confederate Veteran* 12 (February 1904): 67; Charles P. Roland, *Albert Sidney Johnston: Soldier of Three Republics* (Lexington: University Press of Kentucky, 2001), 169–170.

121. Cutrer, *Ben McCulloch*, 134–136; Rose, *Gen. Ben McCulloch*, 125–126; Emory M. Thomas, *Robert E. Lee: A Biography* (New York: W. W. Norton & Company, 1997), 161; *Texas State Times*, March 24, April 7, 1855; Speer and Brown, eds., *Encyclopedia of the New West*, 296; Brackett, *History of the United States Cavalry*, 142; Harold B. Simpson, *Cry Comanche: The 2nd U.S. Cavalry in Texas, 1855–1861* (Hillsboro, TX: Hill Junior College Press, 1979), 23; *Daily National Intelligencer*, March 12, 30, 1855; Gammel, comp., *Laws of Texas*, 4: 487–488. Although 116 captains and lieutenants were appointed to the four new regiments from civilian life, McCulloch was the only such individual to be nominated for a field-grade commission. Utley, *Frontiersmen in Blue*, 34.

122. Cutrer, *Ben McCulloch*, 137, 139, 144; White, *Index of U.S. Marshals*, 58; *The Texas Almanac for 1857* (Galveston: Richardson and Company, 1856), 103; *Texas State Gazette*, January 24, May 2, 7, 1857.

123. Cutrer, *Ben McCulloch*, 144–145; David L. Bigler and Will Bagley, *The Mormon Rebellion: America's First Civil War, 1857–1858* (Norman: University of Oklahoma Press, 2011), 132, 148–150, 157–162; William P. MacKinnon, ed., *At Sword's Point: A Documentary History of the Utah War to 1858* (Norman, OK: The Arthur H. Clark Company, 2008), 173–174; *Message from the President*, December 8, 1857, House Executive Document No. 2, 35th Congress, 1st Session, 24; *Second Message to Congress*, House Executive Document No. 2, 35th Congress, 2nd Session, 10; George Rollie Adams, *General William S. Harney: Prince of Dragoons* (Lincoln: University of Nebraska Press, 2001), 170; General Orders No. 1, July 15, 1857, Floyd to McCulloch, July 8, 1857, McCulloch to Floyd, July 21, 1857, Letters Received, Adjutant General's Office, NARA; Lay to Harney, June 29, 1857, McDowell to Johnston, August 28, 1857, *Annual Report of the Secretary of War*, House Executive Document No. 2, 35th Congress, 1st Session, 21–24; Roland, *Albert Sidney Johnston*, 185–197; *Southern Intelligencer*, September 16, 1857. For more on Sumner's operations, see William Y. Chalfant, *Cheyennes and Horse Soldiers: The 1857 Expedition and the Battle of Solomon's Fork* (Norman: University of Oklahoma Press, 1989).

Indicative of the dangers facing emigrants in Utah, a wagon train of over one hundred Arkansas pioneers was effectively wiped out at Mountain Meadows on September 11, 1857. The seventy-odd murderers were local Mormon militiamen and Paiute warriors. Seventeen orphaned children were spared and returned to their home state three years later. For more details, see Juanita Brooks, *The Mountain Meadows Massacre* (Norman: University of Oklahoma Press, 1991); and Will Bagley, *Blood of the Prophets: Brigham Young and the Massacre at Mountain Meadows* (Norman: University of Oklahoma Press, 2004).

124. Cutrer, *Ben McCulloch*, 151, 145–146; Rose, *Gen. Ben McCulloch*, 124–125, 127–128; MacKinnon, ed., *At Sword's Point*, 173; *Civilian and Gazette*, May 12, June 9, 1857; *Galveston Weekly News*, September 1, 1857; *Northern Standard*, October 17, 1857.

125. *San Antonio Ledger*, September 12, 1857.

126. Cutrer, *Ben McCulloch*, 147–150; *Congressional Globe*, 35th Congress, 1st Session, Pt. 1: 492–497, 1175; Stephen L. Hardin, "'Valor, Wisdom, and Experience': Early Texas Rangers and the Nature of Frontier Leadership," *Tracking the Texas Rangers: The Nineteenth Century*, ed. Bruce A. Glasrud and Harold J. Weiss, Jr. (Denton: University of North Texas Press, 2012), 56; Dunbar Rowland, ed., *Jefferson Davis, Constitutionalist: His Letters, Papers and Speeches* (Jackson: Mississippi Department of Archives and History, 1923), 1: 449–450, 467–468; *Civilian and Gazette*, June 1, 1858. For the law authorizing the Texas regiment, see *The Statutes at Large and Treaties of the United States of America*, 11: 262–263.
127. Cutrer, *Ben McCulloch*, 151–153; Bigler and Bagley, *Mormon Rebellion*, 180–187, 298–299; Floyd to Powell and McCulloch, April 12, 1858, Powell and McCulloch to Floyd, April 25, 1858, May 3, 1858, June 1, 1858, *Annual Report of the Secretary of War*, House Executive Document No. 2, 35th Congress, 2nd Session, 160–162, 163–167. Hereafter cited as *Annual Report of the Secretary of War, 1858*. *Civilian and Gazette*, April 13, 1858.
128. Cutrer, *Ben McCulloch*, 154–158; Bigler and Bagley, *Mormon Rebellion*, 313–314, 324–325; Donald R. Moorman with Gene A. Sessions, *Camp Floyd and the Mormons: The Utah War* (Salt Lake City: University of Utah Press, 2005), 42, 43–46, 53; Powell and McCulloch to Johnston, June 12, 1858, June 26, 1858, July 3, 1858, August 24, 1858, Johnston to Powell and McCulloch, July 14, 1858, General Orders No. 30, June 16, 1858, Powell and McCulloch to Floyd, July 3, 1858, Johnston to McDowell, July 8, 1858, *Annual Report of the Secretary of War, 1858*, 167–172, 175–177, 120–121, 119, 122.
129. Cutrer, *Ben McCulloch*, 160, 161–163; White, *Index of U.S. Marshals*, 58; Speer and Brown, eds., *Encyclopedia of the New West*, 296; Scott A. Silverstone, *Divided Union: The Politics of War in the Early American Republic* (Ithaca: Cornell University Press, 2004), 245; John Basset Moore, ed., *The Works of James Buchanan* (Philadelphia: J. B. Lippincott Company, 1910), 10: 354; *Civilian and Gazette*, December 7, 1858, January 4, 25, March 15, 1859; *Evening Star*, January 6, 1859; *Daily Globe*, February 22, 1859; Gunn, "Ben McCulloch," 14.
130. Cutrer, *Ben McCulloch*, 164–165, 173, 174–175; Gunn, "Ben McCulloch," 16–17; George D. Moller, *American Military Shoulder Arms* (Albuquerque: University of New Mexico Press, 2011), 3: 30–31, 95–97, 171, 173, 175–177; *Offers and Contracts for Carrying the Mails, &c*, House

Executive Document No. 86, 36th Congress, 1st Session, 461, 462; *Evening Star* and *New York Times*, both dated March 24, 1858; H. Parker Johnson, "Coraville, Denver's First Post Office," *The Colorado Magazine* 24 (January 1947): 38–39.

131. Cutrer, *Ben McCulloch*, 173–174; *Congressional Globe*, 35th Congress, 1st Session, Pt. 1: 716, Pt. 2: 1679–1682; Favoring a Protectorate Over Mexico, April 20, 1858, Houston to McCulloch, February 13, 1860, Williams and Baker, eds., *Writings of Sam Houston*, 7: 85–99, 473–474; Houston to Mann, August 27, 1860, Houston to McCulloch, August 28, 1860, ibid., 8: 126–128; Webb, *Texas Rangers*, 197–215; Stout, *Schemers and Dreamers*, 49; Collins, *Texas Devils*, 103–106, 179, 181–185, 213–225; Carl Coke Rister, *Robert E. Lee in Texas* (Norman: University of Oklahoma Press, 2004), 102–106. McCulloch's recall to Texas, and the anticipation of decisive action on the border, was widely covered in the newspapers. For examples, see *Evening Star*, March 8, 1860; *Daily National Intelligencer*, March 20, 1860; *Southern Intelligencer*, February 15, 1860; and *Dallas Herald*, February 29, April 4, 1860.

132. Cutrer, *Ben McCulloch*, 177–186; Rose, *Gen. Ben McCulloch*, 129; Ernest William Winkler, ed., *Journal of the Secession Convention of Texas in 1861* (Austin: Austin Printing Company, 1912), 24, 125, 264–265, 267, 269, 271, 272, 274, 276–286, 297; Walter L. Buenger, *Secession and the Union in Texas* (Austin: University of Texas Press, 1984), 153–154, 157; Randolph B. Campbell, *Gone to Texas: A History of the Lone Star State* (New York: Oxford University Press, 2003), 243; "General Twiggs's Surrender to the Texans," *Harper's Weekly* 5 (March 23, 1861): 182; *The War of the Rebellion: A Compilation of the Official Records of the Union and Confederate Armies*, Series I, I: 503–504, 517–522, 581–582, 584, 590, 634, Series II, I: 11–12, 28–29. Hereafter cited as *OR*; all references are to Series I unless otherwise indicated. Robert Underwood Johnson and Clarence Clough Buel, eds., *Battles and Leaders of the Civil War* (Secaucus, NJ: Castle Books, 1982), 1: 35; R. H. Williams, *With the Border Ruffians: Memories of the Far West, 1852–1868* (New York: E. P. Dutton and Company, 1907), 162–164; *San Antonio Herald*, February 23, 1861; *Texas State Gazette*, March 9, 1861.

Included in McCulloch's volunteer force were 150 Knights of the Golden Circle. As with any secret society, numerous conspiracy theories have been advanced as to the degree the Knights were active in the opening days of secession. Kenneth W. Howell, ed., *The Seventh Star of the Confederacy: Texas during the Civil War*

(Denton: University of North Texas Press, 2009), 52–67. Anna Irene Sandbo, "The First Session of the Secession Convention of Texas," *Southwestern Historical Quarterly* 18 (October 1914): 175: "To what extent … the order influenced the secession convention, directly or indirectly, must remain a matter of surmise. The most that one can safely say is that probably the order encouraged secession and the extension of slavery, and that it was a factor of some importance in forming and uniting public opinion at this time."

133. Cutrer, *Ben McCulloch*, 188–190; Rose, *Gen. Ben McCulloch*, 129; Winkler, ed., *Journal of the Secession Convention*, 265–266, 269, 274, 276, 366–367, 217, 274–277, 372; Clement A. Evans, ed., *Confederate Military History* (Atlanta: Confederate Publishing Company, 1899), 11: 42–43; Daniell, comp., *Personnel of the Texas State Government*, 251–252; *OR*, I: 609–610, 617–618, 621–622, II: 680; *Daily Picayune*, April 4, 18, 25, 1861; J. K. P. Blackburn, "Reminiscences of the Terry Rangers," *Southwestern Historical Quarterly* 22 (July 1918): 38–39; "A Texan Ranger," *Harper's Weekly* 5 (July 6, 1861): 430; "General Ben M'Culloch," ibid. (September 7, 1861): 571; *Evening Star*, January 10, 1861; Speer and Brown, eds., *Encyclopedia of the New West*, 296.

The "very high military qualities" of McCulloch were recommended to Secretary Walker by several notable individuals, including Howell Cobb and John Hemphill. Hemphill to Walker, March 16, 1861, Saunders to Walker, March 18, 1861, Cobb to Walker, April 8, 1861, Letters Received, Adjutant General's Office, M619, NARA.

For more on Henry McCulloch's efforts on the northwestern frontier, see David Paul Smith, *Frontier Defense in the Civil War: Texas' Rangers and Rebels* (College Station: Texas A&M University Press, 1992).

134. Cutrer, *Ben McCulloch*, 190–193; Rose, *Gen. Ben McCulloch*, 129; *Northern Standard*, May 18, 1861; *Weekly Ledger and Texan*, March 16, 1861; Winkler, ed., *Journal of the Secession Convention*, 125, 132, 277; *OR*, Series IV, I: 721; Stephen B. Oates, *Confederate Cavalry West of the River* (Austin: University of Texas Press, 1961), 63; Evans, ed., *Confederate Military History*, 11: 34, 50, 56; McCulloch to Walker, March 20, 1861, Letters Received, Adjutant General's Office, M619, NARA. For more on George Morse and his role in the Confederacy, see Gordon L. Jones, *Confederate Odyssey: The George W. Wray Jr. Civil War Collection at the Atlanta History*

Center (Athens: University of Georgia Press, 2014), 272–273, 291–322

135. Cutrer, *Ben McCulloch*, 194–195; Rose, *Gen. Ben McCulloch*, 129; *OR*, III: 575; Compiled Service Records of Confederate General and Staff Officers, Benjamin McCulloch; Davis to the Congress, May 11, 1861, *Journal of the Confederate Congress*, Senate Document No. 234, 58th Congress, 2nd Session, 1: 213; John H. Eicher and David J. Eicher, *Civil War High Commands* (Stanford: Stanford University Press, 2001), 376, 796, 872; Ezra J. Warner, *Generals in Gray: Lives of the Confederate Commanders* (Baton Rouge: Louisiana State University Press, 2008), 200. See also James M. McPherson, *Embattled Rebel: Jefferson Davis and the Confederate Civil War* (New York: Penguin Book, 2014).

    The first Confederate general officer to be appointed without a West Point education, McCulloch was initially outranked by only four other field commanders: Albert Sidney Johnston, Joseph E. Johnston, P. G. T. Beauregard, and Braxton Bragg. He also bore the same date of commissioning as General Robert E. Lee. Hord, "Gen. Ben McCulloch," 67. Moreover, McCulloch was the first Texan to be named a general, and was the earliest of the aforementioned (and fourth Confederate general) to die in combat. Ralph A. Wooster, *Lone Star Generals in Gray* (Austin: Eakin Press, 2000), 145–146, 279 n109.

136. Cutrer, *Ben McCulloch*, 198–200, 202–205; Oates, *Confederate Cavalry West of the River*, 64; *OR*, III: 575–576, 583, 587–588, 590–591, 595–597, 602, 603, 614, 622–623, Series IV, I: 513–527, 542–554, 579–581, 582, 636–666, 669–687; *Dallas Herald*, June 5, 12, 19, 1861; Mary Jane Warde, *When the Wolf Came: The Civil War and the Indian Territory* (Fayetteville: University of Arkansas Press, 2013), 52–56; Neal Terry Bullock, "The Confederate Services of General Ben McCulloch" (M.A. thesis, University of Arkansas, 1957), 101–102; James McPherson, *Battle Cry of Freedom: The Civil War Era* (New York: Oxford University Press, 1988), 351; Jay Monaghan, *Civil War on the Western Border, 1854–1865* (Lincoln: University of Nebraska Press, 1984), 214, 216.

137. William Garrett Piston and Richard W. Hatcher III, *Wilson's Creek: The Second Battle of the Civil War and the Men Who Fought It* (Chapel Hill: University of North Carolina Press, 2000), 95–96, 98; *OR*, III: 576, 581, 582, 583, 587, LIII: 687, 691; *Dallas Herald*, May 12, July 24, 1861; Nicholas Bart Pearce, "Price's Campaign of 1861,"

Publications of the Arkansas Historical Association 4 (1917): 334–335; Alwyn Barr, "Confederate Artillery in Arkansas," *Arkansas Historical Quarterly* 22 (Autumn 1963): 238–239; E. I. Stirman, "Career of Gen. Ben McCulloch," *Confederate Veteran* 21 (April 1913): 173; Stephen B. Oates, "Recruiting Confederate Cavalry in Texas," *Southwestern Historical Quarterly* 64 (April 1961): 469; Bruce S. Allardice, *Confederate Colonels: A Biographical Register* (Columbia: University of Missouri Press, 2008), 415, 425.

138. William Watson, *Life in the Confederate Army: Being the Observations and Experiences of an Alien in the South during the Civil War* (Baton Rouge: Louisiana State University Press, 1995), 179.

139. Cutrer, *Ben McCulloch*, 206–207, 208–214, 220–221; Rose, *Gen. Ben McCulloch*, 130–132, 135; *OR*, III: 39–40, 94, 98, 599–600, 603, 606–608, 610–612, 616, 622–623, 743–745, Series II, I: 179–180; Thomas W. Cutrer, *Theater of a Separate War: The Civil War West of the Mississippi River, 1861–1865* (Chapel Hill: University of North Carolina Press, 2017), 41; Piston and Hatcher, *Wilson's Creek*, 101–104; Eric Ethier, "The Battle of Wilson's Creek," *Civil War Times* 44 (December 2005): 45; *Dallas Herald*, July 10, 24, August 7, 1861; Pearce, "Price's Campaign of 1861," 336–338; Franz Sigel, "The Military Operations in Missouri in the Summer and Autumn of 1861," *Missouri Historical Review* 26 (July 1932): 356; Evans, ed., *Confederate Military History*, 10: 23; Johnson and Buel, eds., *Battles and Leaders*, 1: 270.

140. Cutrer, *Ben McCulloch*, 221–225; Rose, *Gen. Ben McCulloch*, 135; *OR*, III: 102–103, 98–99, 622, 746, 672, LIII: 720, 727; Edwin C. Bearss, *The Battle of Wilson's Creek* (Springfield, MO: Wilson's Creek National Battleground Foundation, 1992), 24–26, 31; Pearce, "Price's Campaign of 1861," 338–339; Watson, *Life in the Confederate Army*, 191. For more on the Missouri general, see Albert Castel, *General Sterling Price and the Civil War in the West* (Baton Rouge: Louisiana State University Press, 1993).

141. Cutrer, *Ben McCulloch*, 225, 216; Rose, *Gen. Ben McCulloch*, 135; Louis S. Gerteis, *The Civil War in Missouri: A Military History* (Columbia: University of Missouri Press, 2012): 62; Major George E. Knapp, *The Wilson's Creek Staff Ride and Battlefield Tour* (Fort Leavenworth: Combat Studies Institute, 1993), 9; Tom Cagley and Parke Pierson, "The Civil War in Arkansas," *America's Civil War* 18 (July 2005): 41; Eicher and Eicher, *Civil War High Commands*, 892; Douglas Hale, *The Third Texas Cavalry in the Civil War* (Norman:

University of Oklahoma Press, 1993), 57; Speer and Brown, eds., *Encyclopedia of the New West*, 297.

142. Cutrer, *Ben McCulloch*, 225–229, 231; Rose, *Gen. Ben McCulloch*, 137; *OR*, III: 65, 94, 99, 104, 745–746, LIII: 720–721; Watson, *Life in the Confederate Army*, 200, 201–210; Knapp, *Wilson's Creek Staff Ride*, 9, 11; Gerteis, *Civil War in Missouri*, 62–63; Pearce, "Price's Campaign of 1861," 340, 341–343; Johnson and Buel, eds., *Battles and Leaders*, 1: 271; *Dallas Herald*, August 14, 1861.

143. Cutrer, *Ben McCulloch*, 229–232, 233; Rose, *Gen. Ben McCulloch*, 137–139; Piston and Hatcher, *Wilson's Creek*, 196–212; Dee Brown, "Wilson's Creek," *Civil War Times Illustrated* 11 (April 1972): 11, 13; Willard E. Wight, ed., "An Unofficial Account of the Battle of Wilson Creek, August 10, 1861," *Arkansas Historical Quarterly* 15 (Winter 1956): 362–363; Monaghan, *Civil War on the Western Border*, 170–172; *Dallas Herald*, August 28, September 18, 1861.

144. Cutrer, *Ben McCulloch*, 232–233; Rose, *Gen, Ben McCulloch*, 138, 139–140; *OR*, III: 105; Gerteis, *Civil War in Missouri*, 68; W. E. Woodruff, Jr., *With the Light Guns in '61–'65: Reminiscences of Eleven Arkansas, Missouri, and Texas Light Batteries, in the Civil War* (Little Rock, AR: Central Printing Company, 1903), 41–42; Knapp, *Wilson's Creek Staff Ride*, 12; Watson, *Life in the Confederate Army*, 213–214; William H. Tunnard, *A Southern Record: The History of the Third Regiment Louisiana Infantry* (Dayton, OH: Morningside Bookshop, 1970), 51–52.

145. Cutrer, *Ben McCulloch*, 233–234; Rose, *Gen. Ben McCulloch*, 138, 140–142; *OR*, III: 106, 120; Piston and Hatcher, *Wilson's Creek*, 222–231, 246–261; Bearss, *Battle of Wilson's Creek*, 66, 86–91; Gerteis, *Civil War in Missouri*, 69; Monaghan, *Civil War on the Western Border*, 177; Watson, *Life in the Confederate Army*, 217–221; Brown, "Wilson's Creek," 15; Wight, ed., "Battle of Wilson Creek," 363.

146. Cutrer, *Ben McCulloch*, 236–237, 242–243; Rose, *Gen. Ben McCulloch*, 142; *OR*, III: 67–69, 106–107, 688, 689, 691–692, 694, LIII: 736; Knapp, *Wilson's Creek Staff Ride*, 60; Monaghan, *Civil War on the Western Border*, 178–181; Johnson and Buel, eds., *Battles and Leaders*, 1: 303; Evans, ed., *Confederate Military History*, 10: 32–33, 9: 62; Wight, ed., "Battle of Wilson Creek," 364; Ethier, "Battle of Wilson's Creek," 49, 65; Speer and Brown, eds., *Encyclopedia of the New West*, 297; Watson, *Life in the Confederate Army*, 232–233.

147. *Journal of the Confederate Congress*, 1: 376. See also *OR*, III: 130, LIII: 731.
148. Cutrer, *Ben McCulloch*, 246–251, 254; Rose, *Gen. Ben McCulloch*, 177–178; *OR*, III: 691–692, 747, 672, LIII: 727; Cutrer, *Theater of a Separate War*, 61; Bullock, "Confederate Services of General Ben McCulloch," 103; Monaghan, *Civil War on the Western Border*, 204, 229; Watson, *Life in the Confederate Army*, 243–244; Woodruff, *With the Light Guns*, 54–56.
149. Cutrer, *Ben McCulloch*, 259–261, 250–251, 256–257, 270, 276; Rose, *Gen. Ben McCulloch*, 180–182, 192; *OR*, III: 689, 690, 691–692, 694, 700, 708–709, 715–716, 722, 733–738, 742–743, 748–749, LIII: 735–736, 753–755, VIII: 699, 701–702, 718–719, Series IV, I: 627, 628, 630, 631; Cutrer, *Theater of a Separate War*, 61; Woodruff, *With the Light Guns*, 54; Speer and Brown, eds., *Encyclopedia of the New West*, 298–299; Watson, *Life in the Confederate Army*, 242–244; *Dallas Herald*, September 4, December 18, 1861; Tunnard, *A Southern Record*, 154; Bullock, "Confederate Services of General Ben McCulloch," 56, 66, 68, 72–73.
150. Cutrer, *Ben McCulloch*, 273, 277, 280; Rose, *Gen. Ben McCulloch*, 192; *OR*, XIII: 830, 7: 826, VIII: 283, 750–752, 734, 745–746, 748–749, III: 575; Jackson to Davis, November 5, 1861, *Journal of the Confederate Congress*, 1: 480–481; Speer and Brown, eds., *Encyclopedia of the New West*, 299; Arthur B. Carter, *The Tarnished Cavalier: Major General Earl Van Dorn, C.S.A.* (Knoxville: University of Tennessee Press, 1999), 40, 42–44; Johnston, *Albert Sidney Johnston*, 523; Eicher and Eicher, *Civil War High Commands*, 884.
151. Cutrer, *Ben McCulloch*, 281–285; Rose, *Gen. Ben McCulloch*, 197–199; *OR*, VIII: 59, 61, 462, 513–514, 516, 525, 550–551, 553, 283, 305, 554, 555, 559, 563, 750–752, 753, 756–757, 763; Monaghan, *Civil War on the Western Border*, 229; *Houston Telegraph* and *San Antonio Herald*, both dated March 1, 1862; Washington Lafayette Gammage, *The Camp, the Bivouac, and the Battle Field* (Little Rock: Arkansas Southern Press, 1958), 22; Cagley and Pierson, "Civil War in Arkansas," 41.
152. Bullock, "Confederate Services of General Ben McCulloch," 105.
153. Cutrer, *Ben McCulloch*, 288, 290–291; Rose, *Gen. Ben McCulloch*, 200; *OR*, VIII: 755, 763–764, 283; James R. Knight, *The Battle of Pea Ridge: The Civil War Fight for the Ozarks* (Charleston, SC: The History Press, 2012), 58; John Henry Brown, "'The Paths of Glory':

The War-Time Diary of John Henry Brown, C.S.A.," ed. W. J. Lemke, *Arkansas Historical Quarterly* 15 (Winter 1956): 347; Michael A. Hughes, "A Forgotten Battle in a Region Ignored: Pea Ridge or Elkhorn Tavern, Arkansas, March 7–8, 1862," *Blue and Gray Magazine* 5 (January 1988): 14; Richard H. Owens, "Battle of Pea Ridge: Deciding the Fate of Missouri," *America's Civil War* 12 (January 2000): 46; Cagley and Pierson, "Civil War in Arkansas," 41.

154. Cutrer, *Ben McCulloch*, 285; Rose, *Gen. Ben McCulloch*, 200–201; *OR*, VIII: 728, 746, 763, 819–820, 283; William L. Shea and Earl J. Hess, *Pea Ridge: Civil War Campaign in the West* (Chapel Hill: University of North Carolina Press, 1992), 23, 57; D. Alexander Brown, "Pea Ridge: Gettysburg of the West," *Civil War Times Illustrated* 6 (October 1967): 6; Speer and Brown, eds., *Encyclopedia of the New West*, 299; Warde, *When the Wolf Came*, 60, 95–96; Barr, "Confederate Artillery in Arkansas," 241–242.

155. Cutrer, *Ben McCulloch*, 291–293; Rose, *Gen. Ben McCulloch*, 200–202; *OR*, VIII: 191, 196–198, 209–210, 283, 592, 287; Brown, "Paths of Glory," 348; Johnson and Buel, eds., *Battles and Leaders*, 1: 319; Gammage, *The Camp, the Bivouac, and the Battle Field*, 23; Owens, "Battle of Pea Ridge," 46; Dabney H. Maury, "Recollections of General Earl Van Dorn," *Southern Historical Society Papers* 19 (January 1891): 193; Walter Lee Brown, "Pea Ridge: Gettysburg of the West," *Arkansas Historical Quarterly* 15 (Spring 1956): 10; Edwin C. Bearss, "The First Day at Pea Ridge, March 7, 1862," *Arkansas Historical Quarterly* 17 (Summer 1958): 132.

156. Cutrer, *Ben McCulloch*, 294–297; *OR*, VIII: 281, 283–284, 317, 287, 305, 307; Carter, *Tarnished Cavalier*, 55–57; Knight, *Battle of Pea Ridge*, 66–67; Johnson and Buel, eds., Battles *and Leaders*, 1: 320; Hughes, "Forgotten Battle," 18; Cagley and Pierson, "Civil War in Arkansas," 42; Gammage, *The Camp, the Bivouac, and the Battle Field*, 24; Warde, *When the Wolf Came*, 97; Owens, "Battle of Pea Ridge," 47; Bearss, "First Day at Pea Ridge," 133.

157. *OR*, VIII: 191–192, 199, 281, 283, 284; Shea and Hess, *Pea Ridge*, 120, 195–198; Monaghan, *Civil War on the Western Border*, 239; Johnson and Buel, eds., *Battles and Leaders*, 1: 320.

158. Cutrer, *Ben McCulloch*, 298–307; Rose, *Gen. Ben McCulloch*, 203–210; *OR*, VIII: 217–218, 226, 231, 233–234, 246–247, 283–284, 287–290, 293–294, 306; *Tri-Weekly Telegraph*, August 11, 1862; Watson, *Life in the Confederate Army*, 292–303; Gammage,

The Camp, the Bivouac, and the Battle Field, 25; D. A. Brown, "Pea Ridge," 8, 9; Warde, *When the Wolf Came*, 97–98; Owens, "Battle of Pea Ridge," 48; Shelby Foote, *The Civil War: A Narrative* (New York: Vintage Books, 1986), 1: 286–291; McPherson, *Battle Cry of Freedom*, 405. Some early accounts erroneously credited scout and gunfighter James Butler "Wild Bill" Hickok with killing McCulloch. For further discussion, see Joseph G. Rosa, *They Called Him Wild Bill: The Life and Adventures of James Butler Hickok* (Norman: University of Oklahoma Press, 1964), 56. Although Private Peter Pelican of the Thirty-sixth Illinois has been acknowledged as having shot McCulloch, the actual Yankee who fired the fatal bullet remains unknown. Pelican was merely the first to reach the general's body and subsequently took his pocket watch, which he later gave or sold to his colonel. Knight, *Battle of Pea Ridge*, 89.

159. Cutrer, *Ben McCulloch*, 311–313; Rose, *Gen. Ben McCulloch*, 206, 249; Brown, "Paths of Glory," 348–349, 354, 358–359; *Texas State Gazette*, April 12, 1862; Lindley, comp., and Jennett, ed., *Biographical Directory of the Texan Conventions and Congresses*, 129. Brown described how he secured the general's Colt Navy pistol and gave the weapon to Andrew McCulloch, eldest son of John McCulloch, who was serving in Parson's regiment. Brown also confirmed Ben McCulloch never carried a sword due to the old wound he received in the duel with Rueben Ross. *Tri-Weekly Telegraph*, August 11, 1862.

160. House Resolution —, *Journal of the Confederate Congress*, 5: 283, 285.

Notes for Chapter 4

1. George Selden Wallace, *Wallace: Genealogical Data Pertaining to the Descendants of Peter Wallace and Elizabeth Woods, His Wife* (Charlottesville, VA: Michie Company, 1927), 164–165, 327; Ruth Petracek, *The Wallace Collection* (Santa Anna, CA: Petracek, 1979), 1: 13; George W. Diehl, *Rockbridge County, Virginia Notebook*, comp. A. Maxim Coppage III (Utica, KY: McDowell Publications, 1982), 96; Dorthie and Edwin C. Kirkpatrick, *Rockbridge County Marriages, 1778–1850* (Athens, GA: Iberian Publishing Company, 1985), 217; "Wallace Family: Ten Children of Andrew Wallace and Jane Blair," *In and Around Rockbridge* 16 (Winter 2009): 666; William Harris Miller, *History and Genealogies of the Families of Miller, Woods, Harris, Wallace, Maupin, Oldham, Kavanaugh, Brown* (Richmond,

KY: privately printed, 1907), 375–376; *Fourth U.S. Census*, Rockbridge County, Virginia. Andrew died on September 13, 1846.

2. Samuel Wallace, Unnumbered Audited Claim, Reel 109, Frame 105, TSLAC; H. W. Brands, *Lone Star Nation: How a Ragged Army of Volunteers Won the Battle for Texas Independence—and Changed America* (New York: Doubleday, 2004), 390–407; Stephen L. Moore, *Eighteen Minutes: The Battle of San Jacinto and the Texas Independence Campaign* (Dallas: Republic of Texas Press, 2004), 128–133; *Richmond Enquirer*, May 13, June 7, 1836; Harbert Davenport, *Notes from an Unfinished Study of Fannin and His Men, 1936*, ed. H. David Maxey, 2008. See also Jewel Davis Scarborough, "The Georgia Battalion in the Texas Revolution: A Critical Study," *Southwestern Historical Quarterly* 63 (April 1960): 511–532.
3. Andrew Jackson Sowell, *Life of "Big Foot" Wallace: The Great Ranger Captain* (Austin: State House Press, 1989), 10–12; Stanley Vestal, *Bigfoot Wallace: Texas Indian Fighter* (Cambridge: Riverside Press, 1942), 24; Charles Haven Ladd Johnston, *Famous Frontiersmen and Heroes of the Border* (Boston: L. C. Page & Company, 1913), 226.

   Much of what is known of Wallace's time in Texas comes by way of two biographies drawn from the memories of the aging frontiersman himself. There are two major drawbacks to both works. First, in addition to Wallace's acknowledged inclination for embellishment, his recollections were told quite a few decades after the actual events. Second, neither author made any attempt to verify his reminiscences with independent evidence. In 1870, John C. Duval's *The Adventures of Big-Foot Wallace* was published to great acclaim; a second edition appeared in 1872. Wallace did not like the book and, wanting to set the record straight, would later agree to work with another writer. A second printing of the second edition was issued in 1873, followed by a third edition in 1885. The fourth and last edition appeared in 1921. The Steck Company of Austin produced a facsimile of the final edition in 1935, which sold 14,500 copies in one year. Mabel Major and Rebecca Smith Lee edited the fourth issuance in 1936 and published it with Tardy Publishing Company of Dallas.

   In 1899, Texas historian and former ranger A. J. Sowell published his *Life of "Big Foot" Wallace: The Great Ranger Captain*, which featured accounts "gathered … from the old frontiersman himself." Wallace declared it to be a faithful and accurate telling of his life's story. J. Marvin Hunter's *Frontier Times* printed Sowell's work in unrevised installments in 1927 and once more in pamphlet form in 1934. The Steck Company issued a facsimile edition in 1957.

Borrowing heavily from Sowell's work, Stanley Vestal published *Bigfoot Wallace: Texas Indian Fighter* in 1942. Although other uncited sources were used, many of the errors in Sowell's book found their way into the later work. For more on the difficulties in confirming the facts of Wallace's life, see Mark Boardman, "On the Trail of Bigfoot," *True West* 61 (August 2014): 28–31.

4. Bill O'Neal, *Fighting Men of the Indian Wars: A Biographical Encyclopedia of the Mountain Men, Soldiers, Cowboys, and Pioneers Who Took Up Arms during America's Westward Expansion* (Stillwater, OK: Barbed Wire Press, 1991), 219; Hilory G. Bedford, *Texas Indian Troubles* (Dallas: Hargreaves Publishing Company, 1905), 103–104.
5. Sowell, *Life of "Big Foot" Wallace*, 16; Hans Peter Nielson Gammel, comp., *The Laws of Texas, 1822–1897* (Austin: The Gammel Book Company, 1898), 1: 654, 982; Bounty Warrant No. 1399, December 28, 1837, File No. 602, TGLO. Wallace also received the pay due his brother from March 23, 1836, to his death. Samuel P. Wallace, Unnumbered Audited Claim, Reel 109, Frame 105, TSLAC.
6. John C. Duval, *The Adventures of Big-Foot Wallace*, ed. Mabel Major and Rebecca Smith Lee (Lincoln: University of Nebraska Press, 1966), 99–109; Wilbarger, *Indian Depredations in Texas*, 130–138; Bedford, *Texas Indian Troubles*, 121, 127–128. See also J. Frank Dobie, *Rattlesnakes* (Austin: University of Texas Press, 1965), 134–140.
7. Sowell, *Life of "Big Foot" Wallace*, 17–18; Vestal, *Bigfoot Wallace*, 35–38; O'Neal, *Fighting Men of the Indian Wars*, 219; Andrew Jackson Sowell, *Texas Indian Fighters: Early Settlers and Indian Fighters of Southwest Texas* (Austin: State House Press, 1986), 54. O'Neal claimed six men were with Wallace and Black, while Sowell and Vestal specified four.
8. Sowell, *Life of "Big Foot" Wallace*, 47–48; Moore, *Savage Frontier*, 3: 169–170; John H. Jenkins and Kenneth Kesselus, *Edward Burleson: Texas Frontier Leader* (Austin: Jenkins Publishing Company, 1990), 182–185; John Henry Brown, *Indian Wars and Pioneers of Texas* (Austin: State House Press, 1988), 61–62; John Holland Jenkins, *Recollections of Early Texas: The Memoirs of John Holland Jenkins*, ed. John Holmes Jenkins, III (Austin: University of Texas Press, 2003), 56–60. Five-year-old Thomas Coleman was taken captive by the raiders and held until he had almost reached manhood. After his rescue,

"unable to adapt himself to civilized life," he went back to the Comanches and disappeared into history. Gregory and Susan Michno, *A Fate Worse Than Death: Indian Captivities in the West, 1830–1885* (Caldwell, ID: Caxton Press, 2009), 63, 65–66. Among the dead at Brushy Creek were Jacob Burleson, James Gilleland, Lemuel Blakey, and John Walters. For Edward Burleson's report of the fight, see *Telegraph and Texas Register*, April 17, 1839.

9. Sowell, *Life of "Big Foot" Wallace*, 27–28; Shannon Garst, *Big Foot Wallace of the Texas Rangers* (New York: Julian Messner, 1951), 58; Frank Brown, "Annals of Travis County and of the City of Austin: From the Earliest Times to the Close of 1875," Ch. 6: 68.
10. Vestal, *Bigfoot Wallace*, 48, 51; George U. Hubbard, *The Humor and Drama of Early Texas* (Lanham, MD: Republic of Texas Press, 2003), 228.
11. Sowell, *Life of "Big Foot" Wallace*, 3; Stephen L. Moore, "Texas Ranger William A. A. "Bigfoot" Wallace (1817–1899)," *The Texas Ranger Dispatch* 12 (Winter 2003): 17.
12. Vestal, *Bigfoot Wallace*, 51–52; Hubbard, *Humor and Drama of Early Texas*, 229. Chief Bigfoot would later kill Fox in the suburbs of town. Wallace followed the Indian's trail numerous times, but was never able to catch sight of him. Vestal, *Bigfoot Wallace*, 56–57. Edward Dixon Westfall was said to have killed him on the Llano. Sowell, *Texas Indian Fighters*, 55. Actually, the notorious Indian was killed by Daniel Monroe, Franklin Bryant, Shapley Ross, and R. S. Woolfolk in late August 1842 on the Little River. *Telegraph and Texas Register*, September 28, 1842; Clarke, "Life of Sul Ross," 12. See also *Northern Standard*, October 15, 1842; DeWitt Clinton Baker, comp., *A Texas Scrap-Book* (New York City: A. S. Barnes & Company, 1875), 124; and "Capt. Shapley P. Ross Kills Old Big Foot," *Frontier Times* 6 (November 1928): 57–58.
13. O'Neal, *Fighting Men of the Indian Wars*, 219.
14. Donaly E. Brice, *The Great Comanche Raid: Boldest Indian Attack of the Texas Republic* (Austin: Eakin Press, 1987), 36–37, 42; Z. N. Morrell, *Flowers and Fruits from the Wilderness* (Boston: Gould & Lincoln, 1872), 128–129, 130; Jenkins and Kesselus, *Edward Burleson*, 250–251; James L. Haley, *Passionate Nation: The Epic History of Texas* (New York: Free Press, 2006), 229–230; Bedford, *Texas Indian Troubles*, 45–46; Pekka Hämäläinen, *The Comanche Empire* (New Haven: Yale University Press, 2008), 223, 231; David Paul Smith, *Frontier*

Defense in the Civil War: Texas' Rangers and Rebels (College Station: Texas A&M University Press, 1992), 130–135. See also Donaly E. Brice, "The Battle of Plum Creek," *Plum Creek Almanac* 1 (Fall 1983). Numerous sources, including Sowell and Vestal, have claimed Wallace served in Jack Hays's ranger company at Plum Creek. As discussed in Chapter 2, Hays did not officially command rangers until early 1841. Moreover, Wallace's name does not appear on the muster and pay rolls for Hays's company in that particular year.

15. F. E. Harris, "Last Range of Big-Foot Wallace," *Frontier Times* 20 (March 1943): 91–92; August Santleben, *A Texas Pioneer: Early Staging and Overland Freighting Days on the Frontiers of Texas and Mexico*, ed. Isaac Dunbar Affleck (New York: The Neale Publishing Company, 1910), 251; Tax Rolls, Medina, County, 1845–1866.
16. William A. A. Wallace, Public Debt Claim No. 1532, Reel 193, Frames 557–558. Wallace's name also appears on the March 11, 1842, muster roll of Captain Washington D. Miller's volunteer company. Joseph Milton Nance, *Attack and Counterattack: The Texas-Mexican Frontier, 1842* (Austin: University of Texas Press, 1964), 589; Gerald Swetnam Pierce, "The Army of the Texas Republic, 1836–1845" (Ph.D. dissertation, University of Mississippi, 1963), 247; Henderson K. Yoakum, *History of Texas from Its First Settlement in 1685 to Its Annexation to the United States in 1846* (New York: Redfield, 1856), 2: 351, 354; Houston to Somervell, March 10, 1842, Houston to Somervell, March 18, 1842, Houston to Morehouse, March 18, 1842, Amelia W. Williams and Eugene C. Barker, ed., *Writings of Sam Houston* (Austin: University of Texas Press, 1938–1943), 2: 492–493, 509–511; Anson Jones, *Memoranda and Official Correspondence Relating to the Republic of Texas, Its History and Annexation* (New York: D. Appleton and Company, 1859), 173.
17. John Forester, *Memoirs of John Forester: Soldier, Indian Fighter, and Texas Ranger in the Republic of Texas* (Austin: Pemberton Press, 1969), 12.
18. Vestal, *Bigfoot Wallace*, 69; Sowell, *Texas Indian Fighters*, 58–59; Charles M. Robinson III, *The Men Who Wear the Star: The Story of the Texas Rangers* (New York: The Modern Library, 2001), 67; *Telegraph and Texas Register*, September 7, 1844; William A. A. Wallace, Public Debt Claim No. 1532, Reel 193, Frame 558, TSLAC; Nance, *Attack and Counterattack*, 303–304, 336–337.
19. Haley, *Passionate Nation*, 238; Nance, *Attack and Counterattack*, 347–348; Yoakum, *History of Texas*, 2: 364; John Henry Brown,

History of Texas, from 1685 to 1892 (St. Louis, MO: L. E. Daniell, 1893), 2: 223.

20. Sowell, *Life of "Big Foot" Wallace*, 61; Nance, *Attack and Counterattack*, 350–351; Frederick Wilkins, *The Legend Begins: The Texas Rangers, 1823–1845* (Austin: State House Press, 1996), 133; Yoakum, *History of Texas*, 2: 364; Jenkins, *Recollections of Early Texas*, 96.
21. Vestal, *Bigfoot Wallace*, 74; Yoakum, *History of Texas*, 2: 364; General Thomas J. Green, *Journal of the Texian Expedition against Mier* (New York: Harper & Brothers, 1845), 31; Sowell, *Texas Indian Fighters*, 59–60; Nance, *Attack and Counterattack*, 361. Sowell and Vestal both claimed Wallace killed the Mexican who had tried to shoot him. Garst maintained Ben McCulloch, who would not be present on the battlefield for several more hours, shot him. *Big Foot Wallace*, 90.
22. Sowell, *Life of "Big Foot" Wallace*, 65–68; Vestal, *Bigfoot Wallace*, 77; Harriet Smither, ed., "Diary of Adolphus Sterne," Pt. 18, *Southwestern History Quarterly* 34 (January 1931): 260; Gerald S. Pierce, *Texas Under Arms: The Camps, Forts, and Military Towns of the Republic of Texas, 1836–1846* (Austin: Encino Press, 1969), 146; Brazos, *Life of Robert Hall: Indian Fighter and Veteran of Three Great Wars* (Austin: State House Press, 1992), 73; E. L. Zoltan, "Big Foot Wallace of Texas," *Golden West* 4 (May 1968): 24.
23. Haley, *Passionate Nation*, 239; O'Neal, *Fighting Men of the Indian Wars*, 220; Brown, "Annals of Travis County," Ch. 9: 25–27; Bedford, *Texas Indian Troubles*, 114–117; Wilbarger, *Indian Depredations in Texas*, 124–126.
24. William A. A. Wallace, Public Debt Claim No. 1360, Reel 193, Frame 546, TSLAC.
25. Duval, *Big-Foot Wallace*, 171.
26. Joseph D. McCutchan, *Mier Expedition Diary: A Texan Prisoner's Account*, ed. Joseph Milton Nance (Austin: University of Texas Press, 1978), 14–20; *Telegraph and Texas Register*, February 22, 1843; *Morning Star*, February 18, 1843; William Preston Stapp, *The Prisoners of Perote* (Austin: University of Texas Press, 1977), 27; Houston Wade, comp., *Notes and Fragments of the Mier Expedition* (La Grange: La Grange Journal, 1936–1937), 1: 119, 2: 41; William A. A. Wallace, Republic Pensions, Reel 244, Frame 101, TSLAC; Brown, *Indian Wars*, 140; Andrew Jackson Sowell, *History of Fort Bend County* (Waco: W. M. Morrison, 1964), 187.

27. Green, *Journal of the Texian Expedition against Mier*, 82, 83–84; John Warren Hunter, "Adventures of a Mier Prisoner," *Frontier Times* 2 (April 1925): 19; Wade. comp., *Notes and Fragments*, 2: 125–127; James M. Day, ed., "Diary of James A. Glasscock, Mier Man," *Texana* 1 (Spring 1963): 89; Stapp, *Prisoners of Perote*, 32; McCutchan, *Mier Expedition Diary*, 42–44; *Morning Star*, February 9, 1843; *Daily National Intelligencer*, March 6, 1843.
28. McCutchan, *Mier Expedition Diary*, 44–45; Green, *Journal of the Texian Expedition Against Mier*, 86–88; Stapp, *Prisoners of Perote*, 32–33; "When a Handful of Americans Invaded Mexico," *Frontier Times* 6 (March 1929): 247; Wade, comp., *Notes and Fragments*, 2: 128–129; Day, ed., "Diary of James A. Glasscock," 89; *Northern Standard*, September 21, 1843.
29. Sowell, *Life of "Big Foot" Wallace*, 74; Vestal, *Bigfoot Wallace*, 102–103.
30. McCutchan, *Mier Expedition Diary*, 45–46; Thomas W. Bell, *A Narrative of the Capture and Subsequent Sufferings of the Mier Prisoners in Mexico* (Waco: Texian Press, 1964), 15. Hereafter cited as *Mier Expedition Narrative*. Wade, comp., *Notes and Fragments*, 2: 129–130, 131; Green, *Journal of the Texian Expedition Against Mier*, 89, 91–93; Brazos, *Life of Robert Hall*, 111; *Telegraph and Texas Register*, August 2, 1843; Stapp, *Prisoners of Perote*, 33.
31. Vestal, *Bigfoot Wallace*, 104–105, 107; Garst, *Big Foot Wallace*, 100; McCutchan, *Mier Expedition Diary*, 46, 60; Stapp, *Prisoners of Perote*, 33–34; *Niles' National Register* 64 (March 11, 1843): 18; *Morning Star*, February 9, 1843; Hunter, "Adventures of a Mier Prisoner," 19; Johnston, *Famous Frontiersmen*, 234.
32. Sowell, *Life of "Big Foot" Wallace*, 79–80; Vestal, *Bigfoot Wallace*, 122–124; Sam W. Haynes, *Soldiers of Misfortune: The Somervell and Mier Expeditions* (Austin: University of Texas Press, 1990), 76; McCutchan, *Mier Expedition Diary*, 52; Joseph Milton Nance, *Dare-Devils All: The Texas Mier Expedition, 1842–1844*, ed. Archie P. McDonald (Austin: Eakin Press, 1998), 64–72; Day, ed., "Diary of James A. Glasscock," 90; *Telegraph and Texas Register*, August 2, 1843; Green, *Journal of the Texian Expedition Against Mier*, 107; William A. A. Wallace, Audited Claim No. 2995, Reel 109, Frames 110, 112, TSLAC; Duval, *Big-Foot Wallace*, 181. For the terms of surrender, see *Morning Star*, January 31, 1843; and *Telegraph and*

Texas Register, February 1, 1843. See also *Daily Picayune*, February 8, 1843; *Telegraph and Texas Register*, February 22, 1843; and *Northern Standard*, September 21, 1843.

The reports of Mexican casualties varied widely. Originally the Texians estimated more than six hundred Mexicans were killed and two hundred wounded. Later the butcher's bill was revised to more than nine hundred killed and wounded. In the United States, the approximation was 420 killed and 130 wounded. Green claimed Mexican officers told him the combined figure was over seven hundred. The U.S. consul in Matamoros and several American and British citizens there reported more than eight hundred killed and wounded. The only consensus seems to be that Mexican losses far exceeded those of the Texians. Nance, *Dare-Devils All*, 92.

33. Stapp, *Prisoners of Perote*, 53–54, 64–65; McCutchan, *Mier Expedition Diary*, 82–83; Day, ed., "Diary of James A. Glasscock," 93–94; James M. Day, ed., "Israel Canfield in the Mier Expedition," *Texas Military History* 3 (Fall 1963): 174–175; *Northern Standard*, March 2, 1843; Duval, *Big-Foot Wallace*, 199. For a discussion of the "notorious" Canales, see Joseph Benjamin Ridout, "An Anti-National Disorder: Antonio Canales and Northeastern Mexico, 1836–1852" (M.A. thesis, University of Texas at Austin, 1994).
34. Duval, *Big-Foot Wallace*, 208–209, 215–216; Vestal, *Bigfoot Wallace*, 148–149; "Letters from 'Big Foot Wallace'," *Frontier Times* 8 (June 1931): 417; McCutchan, *Mier Expedition Diary*, 84; Wade, comp., *Notes and Fragments*, 1: 69–70, 72–82; Day, ed., "Diary of James A. Glasscock," 95–97; Stapp, *Prisoners of Perote*, 81–86; Nance, *Dare-Devils All*, 279.
35. Vestal, *Bigfoot Wallace*, 151; Zoltan, "Big Foot Wallace of Texas," 25.
36. Duval, *Big-Foot Wallace*, 232–234; Vestal, *Bigfoot Wallace*, 162; Haynes, *Soldiers of Misfortune*, 119; Haley, *Passionate Nation*, 239; A. Russell Buchanan, ed., "George Washington Trahern: Texas Cowboy Soldier from Mier to Buena Vista," *Southwestern Historical Quarterly* 58 (July 1954): 65–66; Day, ed., "Diary of James A. Glasscock," 101–102.
37. Vestal, *Bigfoot Wallace*, 174–175; Garst, *Big Foot Wallace*, 125; Nance, *Dare-Devils All*, 308, 320–321; Stapp, *Prisoners of Perote*, 117; *Telegraph and Texas Register*, August 16, 1843; Wade, comp., *Notes and Fragments*, 2: 29; *Daily Picayune*, April 5, 1843.
38. Bell, *Mier Expedition Narrative*, 53, 54–55, 58–59; Haynes, *Soldiers of Misfortune*, 166; Manton to Dear Friend, September 22, 1843,

Frederick C. Chabot, ed., *Texas Letters* (San Antonio: Yanaguana Society, 1940), 47; Day, ed., "Diary of James A. Glasscock," 107–110; Stapp, *Prisoners of Perote*, 153, 158–159; Yoakum, *History of Texas*, 2: 398–399; McCutchan, *Mier Expedition Diary*, 106; Day, ed., "Israel Canfield in the Mier Expedition," 189, 191; Duval, *Big-Foot Wallace*, 244–245; Wade, comp., *Notes and Fragments*, 2: 29–30; William F. Wilson, "Two Letters from a Mier Prisoner," *The Quarterly of the Texas State Historical Association* 2 (January 1899): 234.

For a description of the prison, see J. J. McGrath and Walace Hawkins, "Perote Fort—Where Texans Were Imprisoned," *Southwestern Historical Quarterly* 48 (January 1945): 340–345. For a list of the 248 prisoners held by the Mexicans in early 1843, see *Civilian and Galveston Gazette*, February 8, 1843. See also *Northern Standard*, February 10, 1844; and L. U. Spellman, "Letters of the 'Dawson Men' from Perote Prison," *Southwestern Historical Quarterly* 38 (April 1935): 246–249.

39. Nance, *Dare-Devils All*, 378; Bell, *Mier Expedition Narrative*, 74; McCutchan, *Mier Expedition Diary*, 143–144; Green, *Journal of the Texian Expedition Against Mier*, 477; James M. Day, ed., "Diary of James A. Glasscock, Mier Man—Second Book," *Texana* 1 (Summer 1963): 237. Wallace's claim to the government mistakenly indicated he was a prisoner until the general release on September 15. William A. A. Wallace, Public Debt Claim No. 1360, Reel 193, Frame 549, TSLAC.
40. Sowell, *Life of "Big Foot" Wallace*, 111–112; Buchanan, ed., "George Washington Trahern," 68; *Daily Picayune*, September 19, October 1, 1844; *Telegraph and Texas Register*, October 30, 1844; William A. A. Wallace, Public Debt Claim No. 1360, Reel 193, Frame 546, TSLAC. On December 3, 1849, a joint resolution was introduced in the Third Legislature for the relief of Wallace and another member of Captain Hays's 1842 spy company who had been taken prisoner in Mexico. After being referred to the committees of engrossment and military affairs, the measure was approved on February 8, 1850, and Wallace was awarded $487 for past service and losses. The following day, all of the volunteers captured at Mier and Santa Fé were entitled to receive $22.50 per month, from the time they mustered into service until one month after the general release of the prisoners. *Journals of the House of Representatives of the State of Texas, Third Legislature*, 220, 302, 315; Gammel, comp., *Laws of Texas*, 3: 754, 594–595; William A. A. Wallace, Public Debt Claim No. 1360, Reel 193, Frame 548, TSLAC.

41. Haynes, *Soldiers of Misfortune*, 202; *Daily Picayune*, November 5, 1844.
42. Sowell, *Life of "Big Foot" Wallace*, 120; Vestal, *Bigfoot Wallace*, 221–222; Garst, *Big Foot Wallace*, 136; Muster and Pay Rolls, John C. Hays, 401–718, -791.
43. *Texas National Register*, October 9, 1845; Compiled Service Records of Volunteer Soldiers, Gillespie's Company, Texas Mounted Volunteers, W. A. A. Wallace; *Democratic Telegraph and Texas Register*, November 16, 1846; *Texas Democrat*, January 21, 1846; Henry W. Barton, *Texas Volunteers in the Mexican War* (Waco: Texian Press, 1970), 8.
44. Compiled Service Records of Volunteer Soldiers, Gillespie's Company, Texas Mounted Volunteers, W. A. A. Wallace and G. H. Nelson; *Daily Picayune*, July 7, August 11, 1846; Taylor to Adjutant General, August 3, 1846, *Mexican War Correspondence*, House Executive Document No. 60, 30th Congress, 1st Session, 402; Robert W. Johannsen, *To the Halls of the Montezumas: The Mexican War in the American Imagination* (New York: Oxford University Press, 1985), 38; Michael L. Collins, *Texas Devils: Rangers and Regulars on the Lower Rio Grande, 1846–1861* (Norman: University of Oklahoma Press, 2008), 12; Barton, *Texas Volunteers*, 44; Mike Cox, *The Texas Rangers: Wearing the Cinco Peso, 1821–1900* (New York: Tom Doherty Associates, 2008), 110; Paul Foos, *Short, Offhand, Killing Affair: Soldiers and Social Conflict During the Mexican-American War* (Chapel Hill: University of North Carolina Press, 2002), 120–121; *Democratic Telegraph and Texas Register*, July 29, 1846; Zachary Taylor, *Letters of Zachary Taylor from the Battle-Fields of the Mexican War* (Rochester, NY: William K. Bixby, 1908), 22.
45. Special Order No. 134, September 1, 1846, Order No. 115, September 11, 1846, *Mexican War Correspondence*, 536, 504–505; John S. D. Eisenhower, *So Far from God: The U.S. War with Mexico, 1846–1848* (Norman: University of Oklahoma Press, 2000), 123.
46. Order No. 119, September 17, 1846, Order No. 120, September 18, 1846, *Mexican War Correspondence*, 506; Frederick Wilkins, *The Highly Irregular Irregulars: Texas Rangers in the Mexican War* (Austin: Eakin Press, 1990), 82; Christopher D. Dishman, *A Perfect Gibraltar: The Battle for Monterrey, Mexico, 1846* (Norman: University of Oklahoma Press, 2010), 85.
47. Charles M. Robinson III, *Texas and the Mexican War* (Austin: Texas State Historical Association, 2004), 64; Charles Spurlin, "Texas Volunteers in the Monterrey Campaign," Pt. 1, *Military History of Texas*

and the Southwest 16 (1980): 10; Luther Giddings, *Sketches of the Campaign in Northern Mexico* (New York: George P. Putnam & Co., 1853), 143–144; Captain William Seaton Henry, *Campaign Sketches of the War with Mexico* (New York: Harper & Brothers, 1847), 192; John R. Kenly, *Memoirs of a Maryland Volunteer: War with Mexico, in the Years 1846–7–8* (Philadelphia: J. P. Lippincott & Co., 1873), 97; *Daily Picayune*, October 6, 1846.

48. Felice Flanery Lewis, *Trailing Clouds of Glory: Zachary Taylor's Mexican War Campaign and His Emerging Civil War Leaders* (Tuscaloosa: University of Alabama Press, 2010), 128; Justin H. Smith, *The War with Mexico* (New York: The Macmillan Company, 1919), 1: 239; Dishman, *A Perfect Gibraltar*, 97, 101, 103.
49. Worth to Bliss, September 28, 1846, *Report of the Secretary of War*, House Executive Document No. 4, 29th Congress, 2nd Session, 102. Reprinted in *Democratic Telegraph and Texas Register*, January 4, 1847. Robert H. Ferrell, ed., *Monterrey Is Ours!: The Mexican War Letters of Lieutenant Dana, 1845–1847* (Lexington: University Press of Kentucky, 1990), 129; Charles D. Spurlin, *Texas Volunteers in the Mexican War* (Austin: Eakin Press, 1998), 76; Justin, *War with Mexico*, 1: 242; Major Ian B. Lyles, "Mixed Blessing: The Role of the Texas Rangers in the Mexican War, 1846–1848" (MMAS thesis, Fort Leavenworth, 2003), 37.
50. Lewis, *Trailing Clouds of Glory*, 137–138; Dishman, *A Perfect Gibraltar*, 150; R. S. Ripley, *The War with Mexico* (New York: Harper & Brothers, 1849), 1: 219–220; Thomas Bangs Thorpe, *Our Army at Monterey* (Philadelphia: Carey and Hart, 1848), 174; Spurlin, "Texas Volunteers in the Monterrey Campaign," Pt. 1: 16. *Texas Democrat*, November 4, 1846.
51. Smith, *War with Mexico*, 1: 244–246; Persifor F. Smith, "The Second Brigade at Monterey," *The Historical Magazine* 3 (March 1874): 138; K. Jack Bauer, *The Mexican War, 1846–1848* (Lincoln: University of Nebraska Press, 1992), 94; Henry, *Campaign Sketches*, 202; Ripley, *War with Mexico*, 1: 221–222; George Wilkins Kendall, *The War Between the United States and Mexico, Illustrated* (New York: D. Appleton & Company, 1851), 7; *Niles' National Register* 71 (October 24, 1846): 115; Charles Spurlin, "With Taylor and McCulloch Through the Battle of Monterey," *Texas Military History* 6 (Fall 1967): 217.
52. Sowell, *Life of "Big Foot" Wallace*, 122–123; Thorpe, *Our Army at Monterey*, 70, 175; Henry, *Campaign Sketches*, 205; Lewis, *Trailing*

Clouds of Glory, 152; Giddings, *Sketches of the Campaign*, 193–194; Ripley, *War with Mexico*, 1: 224–225; Dishman, *A Perfect Gibraltar*, 155; Noah Smithwick, *The Evolution of a State, or Recollections of Old Texas Days*, comp. Nanna Smithwick Donaldson (Austin: University of Texas Press, 1983), 212; Wilkins, *The Highly Irregular Irregulars*, 94; Walter P. Lane, *The Adventures and Recollections of General Walter P. Lane: A San Jacinto Veteran, Containing Sketches of the Texan, Mexican, and Late Wars* (Austin: Jenkins Publishing Company, 1970), 46–47; *Texas Democrat*, October 28, 1846; Franklin Smith, *The Mexican War Journal of Captain Franklin Smith*, ed. Joseph E. Chance (Jackson: University of Mississippi Press, 1991), 28, 150–151; Spurlin, *Texas Volunteers*, 90.

53. Robinson, *Texas and the Mexican War*, 67–68; Spurlin, *Texas Volunteers*, 91; Dishman, *A Perfect Gibraltar*, 194; Sowell, *Texas Indian Fighters*, 84–85.
54. Sowell, *Life of "Big Foot" Wallace*, 123; *Northern Standard*, December 19, 1846.
55. *Daily Picayune*, October 21, 1846; Compiled Service Records of Volunteer Soldiers, Gillespie's Company, Texas Mounted Volunteers, W. A. A. Wallace.
56. Giddings, *Sketches of the Campaign*, 221–222.
57. Compiled Service Records of Volunteer Soldiers, Bell's Regiment of Texas Mounted Volunteers, William Wallace; *Texas Democrat*, September 4, 1847, July 19, 1848; *Democratic Telegraph and Texas Register*, December 14, 1848.
58. First Class Warrant No. 535, Bandera County, patented June 21, 1856, File No. 604, Patents No. 351 and 352, Kerr County, patented May 2, 1848, File No. 602, TGLO; J. Marvin Hunter, *Pioneer History of Bandera County: Seventy-five Years of Intrepid History* (Bandera, TX: Hunter's Printing House, 1922), 100. Wallace Creek is a northern branch of the Medina River near the tiny village of Bluff. Kerr County Deed Records, Book D, 109–110; Tax Rolls, Bexar County, 1849–1852; Dot Ferguson Hatfield, *Medina's Early Days* (Medina, TX: privately published, 1995), 6.
59. Sowell, *Life of "Big Foot" Wallace*, 126–133; Sherry Robinson, *I Fought a Good Fight: A History of the Lipan Apaches* (Denton: University of North Texas Press, 2013), 224–225; Thomas T. Smith, *Fort Inge: Sharps, Spurs, and Sabers on the Texas Frontier, 1849–1869* (Austin: Eakin Press, 1993), 21. For more on Westfall,

see Kathryn and Irwin Sexton, "Edward Dixon Westfall: Early Texas Climatologist, Philosopher, and Philanthropist," *Southwestern Historical Quarterly* 68 (July 1964): 1–13.

60. *Journals of the House, Third Legislature*, 13–14; *Texas State Gazette*, August 25, 1849, March 9, 1850; Wood to Crawford, December 14, 1849, Brooke to Bell, March 6, 1850, *Annual Report of the Secretary of War*, Senate Executive Document No. 1, Pt. 10, 31st Congress, 2nd Session, 13–14, 30–31. Hereafter cited as *Annual Report of the Secretary of War, 1850*. Foster, et al. to Bell, March 6, 1850, Dorman H. Winfrey and James M. Day, eds., *The Indian Papers of Texas and the Southwest* (Austin: Texas State Historical Association, 1995), 5: 89. Hereafter cited as *Texas Indian Papers*. *Democratic Telegraph and Texas Register*, May 23, 1850.
61. Carded Records Showing Military Service of Soldiers Who Fought in Volunteer Organizations During the Indian Wars, Texas Mounted Volunteers, William A. A. Wallace. Hereafter cited as Carded Records … Indian Wars. Deas to Bell, March 6, 1850, Winfrey and Day, eds., *Texas Indian Papers*, 5: 88; *Texas State Gazette*, April 20, 1850. The mustering officer who enrolled Wallace's company into the service was Brevet Captain William Steele, Second Dragoons, who would become adjutant general of Texas some twenty years hence.
62. Orders No. 27, June 4, 1850, 301–18, TSLAC; Hardee to Deas, September 14, 1850, *Annual Report of the Secretary of War, 1850*, 56–59; *Nueces Valley*, July 13, 1850; Joseph Indus Lambert, *One Hundred Years with the Second Cavalry* (Topeka: Press of the Capper Printing Co., 1939), 48; Smith, *Fort Inge*, 40–44, 49; Mike Cox, *Texas Ranger Tales II* (Plano: Republic of Texas Press, 1999), 32–34; Robinson, *I Fought a Good Fight*, 228; "Big Foot Wallace's Fight on the Nueces," *Frontier Times* 3 (May 1926): 9–11. See also *Texas State Gazette*, August 31, 1850; and *Democratic Telegraph and Texas Register*, September 11, 1850.
63. Carded Records … Indian Wars, Texas Mounted Volunteers, William A. A. Wallace; *Seventh U.S. Census*, Bexar County, Texas; Smith, *Fort Inge*, 49–50, 189–190. Henry McCulloch received a commission from Governor Bell to raise a ranger company for federal service with an organization date set for November 5, 1850. *Texas State Gazette*, October 26, 1850.
64. *Democratic Telegraph and Texas Register*, September 18, October 23, 1850; Orders No. 39, September 17, 1850, *Annual Report of the*

Secretary of War, 1850, 62–63; Carded Records … Indian Wars, Texas Mounted Volunteers, William A. A. Wallace.

65. *San Antonio Ledger*, February 6, 1851; Brooke to Bell, February 7, 1851, 301–18, TSLAC; *Western Texan*, March 6, 1851; *Victoria Advocate*, March 20, 1851; Carded Records … Indian Wars, Texas Mounted Volunteers, William A. A. Wallace.
66. *San Antonio Ledger* and *Western Texan*, July 17, 1851; *Texas State Gazette*, July 26, 1851; *Civilian and Galveston Gazette*, July 29, 1851; *Victoria Advocate*, July 31, 1851.
67. Sowell, *Life of "Big Foot" Wallace*, 163; Vestal, *Bigfoot Wallace*, 267; Carded Records … Indian Wars, Texas Mounted Volunteers, William A. A. Wallace; John Hope Franklin and Loren Schweninger, *Runaway Slaves: Rebels on the Plantation* (New York: Oxford University Press, 1999), 25, 115, 151; Kenneth W. Howell, ed., *The Seventh Star of the Confederacy: Texas during the Civil War* (Denton: University of North Texas Press, 2009), 37. The classic work on the subject of the Fugitive Slave Act and its legal and social ramifications remains Stanley W. Campbell, *The Slave Catchers: Enforcement of the Fugitive Slave Law, 1850–1860* (Chapel Hill: University of North Carolina Press, 2011). See also Randolph B. Campbell, *An Empire for Slavery: The Peculiar Institution in Texas, 1821–1865* (Baton Rouge: Louisiana State Press, 1991); and Frederick Law Olmsted, *A Journey Through Texas, or A Saddle-Trip on the Southwestern Frontier* (New York: Dix, Edwards & Co., 1857), 327.
68. Wayne R. Austerman, *Sharps Rifles and Spanish Mules: The San Antonio–El Paso Mail, 1851–1881* (College Station: Texas A&M University Press, 1985), 21–22, 315; Smith, *Fort Inge*, 51; Robert N. Mullin, "Stagecoach Pioneers of the Southwest," *Southwestern Studies* 71 (1983): 3; *Letter from the Postmaster General Transmitting a Report on Mail Contracts, &c*, House Executive Document No. 56, 32nd Congress, 1st Session, 391; *Daily National Intelligencer*, September 22, 1851; *San Antonio Ledger*, August 19, 1852.
69. Thomas T. Smith, *The U.S. Army and the Texas Frontier Economy, 1845–1900* (College Station: Texas A&M University Press, 1999), 156; James Day, "Big Foot Wallace in Trans-Pecos Texas," *West Texas Historical Association Yearbook* 55 (1979): 72, 74; Olmsted, *Journey Through Texas*, 287; A. C. Greene, *900 Miles on the Butterfield Trail* (Denton: University of North Texas Press, 2006), 232–233; Austerman, *Sharps Rifles and Spanish Mules*, 28; W. H. Timmons, *El Paso:*

A Borderlands History (El Paso: Texas Western Press, 1990), 139; Robert H. Thonhoff, "San Antonio Stage Lines, 1847–1881," *Southwestern Studies* 29 (1971): 10.

70. Austerman, *Sharps Rifles and Spanish Mules*, 51, 58–59; Greene, *900 Miles on the Butterfield Trail*, 232; Thonhoff, "San Antonio Stage Lines," 14–17; Emmie Giddings W. Mahon and Chester V. Kielman, "George H. Giddings and the San Antonio-San Diego Mail Line," *Southwestern Historical Quarterly* 61 (October 1957): 228–229; Basil C. Pearce, "Pioneer Overland Route," *Western Express* 12 (April 1962): 4–5; "The Overland Mail Line," *Frontier Times* 8 (February 1931): 227. After Birch's death, the contract was awarded to Giddings and Doyle on March 3, 1858. Their San Antonio–San Diego route became the famous "Jackass Line" which ran until April 1861. Ralph Moody, *Stagecoach West* (Lincoln: University of Nebraska Press, 1998), 84–88.
71. First Class Certificate No. 506, Kerr County, patented December 19, 1851, File No. 715, TGLO; Kerr County Deed Records, Book D, 110–111. Harrisburg County changed its name to Harris County in 1839.
72. Gregory F. Michno and Susan J. Michno, *Forgotten Fights: Little-Known Raids and Skirmishes on the Frontier, 1823 to 1890* (Missoula, MT: Mountain Press Publishing Company, 2008), 118–119; *San Antonio Ledger*, September 23, 1852; *Texas State Gazette* and *Texian Advocate*, both dated September 25, 1852; *Daily National Intelligencer*, December 2, 1852. Sowell asserted this incident occurred in 1850, but Wallace did not begin driving a stagecoach until late 1851. Sowell, *Life of "Big Foot" Wallace*, 138–139. See also Garst, *Big Foot Wallace*, 151; and Austerman, *Sharps Rifles and Spanish Mules*, 315.
73. Sowell, *Life of "Big Foot" Wallace*, 140; O'Neal, *Fighting Men of the Indian Wars*, 220–221; *Daily Picayune*, September 28, 1852; John Russell Bartlett, *Personal Narrative of Explorations and Incidents in Texas, New Mexico, California, Sonora, and Chihuahua* (New York: D. Appleton & Company, 1854), 2: 397.
74. A. J. Sowell, "The Life of Bigfoot Wallace," *Frontier Times* 5 (January 1928): 166; Vestal, *Bigfoot Wallace*, 257–258; *San Antonio Ledger* and *Western Texan*, both dated May 12, 1853; Austerman, *Sharps Rifles and Spanish Mules*, 316.
75. *San Antonio Ledger*, January 12, 1854; *Texas State Gazette*, January 24, 1854; Glenn Sample Ely, *The Texas Frontier and the Butterfield*

Overland Mail, 1858–1861 (Norman: University of Oklahoma Press, 2016), 319; *New York Daily Times*, February 1, April 17, 1854.

76. Sowell, *Life of "Big Foot" Wallace*, 140–141; Garst, *Big Foot Wallace*, 152–153; Ely, *Texas Frontier and the Butterfield Overland Mail*, 287; Robert Wooster, *History of Fort Davis, Texas* (Santa Fe: Southwest Region, National Park Service, 1990), 92. *Ojo del Muerto*, the Spring of the Dead, was called "Dead Man's Hole" by Wallace.
77. *San Antonio Ledger*, September 6, 8, 29, 1855; *San Antonio Texan*, October 4, 1855.
78. Sowell, *Texas Indian Fighters*, 86; *San Antonio Herald*, April 19, 1856; Santleben, *A Texas Pioneer*, 13; Hunter, *Pioneer History of Bandera County*, 26; "Captured an Indian Near Bandera," *Frontier Times* 1 (July 1924): 21.
79. J. C. Wood, *Report to Hon. A. V. Brown, Postmaster-General, on the Opening and Present Condition of the United States Overland Mail Route between San Antonio, Texas, and San Diego, California* (Washington, D.C., 1858), 4, 7; *San Antonio Ledger*, August 8, 1857; *Civilian and Gazette*, August 18, 1857.
80. Wood, *Report to Hon. A. V. Brown*, 7–8; Austerman, *Sharps Rifles and Spanish Mules*, 95–96; Returns from U.S. Military Posts, 1800–1916, Fort Clark, July 1857, Camp Hudson, July 1857, M617, NARA; *Galveston Weekly News*, September 1, 1857; *San Antonio Ledger*, August 22, 1857.
81. Sowell, *Life of "Big Foot" Wallace*, 153–154; Harris, "Last Range of Big-Foot Wallace," 91, 92; *San Antonio Ledger*, November 14, December 5, 12, 1857. Wallace received bounty warrant No. 2058 for 960 acres on account of his brother's service. A survey was made in Medina County but not patented. Instead, the warrant was rejected by the court of claims on October 23, 1860. Written on the document are the words: "Rejected because I have evidence that he escaped the massacre and that he has already received 960 acres of land. W. S. Hotchkiss." Whatever proof Hotchkiss, the Commissioner of Claims for the General Land Office, believed he possessed remains unknown. Bounty Warrant No. 2058, Medina County, August 17, 1855, File No. 1323, TGLO. See also Thomas Lloyd Miller, *Bounty and Donation Land Grants of Texas, 1835–1888* (Austin: University of Texas Press, 1967), 661.
82. Sowell, *Life of "Big Foot" Wallace*, 154–155; *San Antonio Texan*, April 22, 1858.

83. Vestal, *Bigfoot Wallace*, 268–271; *Eighth U.S. Census*, Wythe County, Virginia. Wallace supposedly could have claimed a sizeable inheritance in Virginia, but he refused the legacy, saying he was "tolerably well satisfied" with his life as it was. Wharton J. Green, *Recollections and Reflections: An Auto of Half a Century and More* (Raleigh, NC: Edwards and Broughton Printing Company, 1906), 129–130.
84. *San Antonio Herald*, November 2, 1861; Hunter, *Pioneer History of Bandera County*, 95–96; Brazos, *Life of Robert Hall*, 119; Smith, *Fort Inge*, 133. Ross Kennedy had led a party of eleven volunteers up the Sabinal the previous year. The events of his foray share similarities with the description of the Sabinal Canyon fight in Sowell's book. There is a possibility some conflating of the two accounts may have occurred. *San Antonio Ledger and Texan*, March 31, April 7, 1860; Sowell, *Life of "Big Foot" Wallace*, Ch. 28. See also Sowell, *Texas Indian Fighters*, 108–109, 224–225, 306–307, 660–661; *San Antonio Light*, March 24, 1929; Vestal, *Bigfoot Wallace*, 272–278, 280–281. Garst, *Big Foot Wallace*, 166; A. J. Sowell, *Rangers and Pioneers of Texas* (Austin: State House Press, 1991), 88–91; and A. J. Durham, "Life History of a Pioneer Citizen of Sabinal," *Frontier Times* 1 (July 1924): 10–11. For a Wallace tale set during the war, see Charles T. Carlton, "Bigfoot Wallace Stuffed with Hickory Nuts," *Frontier Times* 1 (January 1924): 37–38.
85. Tax Rolls, Medina County, 1866–1867. Stephen Lapp, director of the Medina County Museum, provided the author with a city map of Devine that shows a parcel of land east of the Chacon known as the "Bigfoot Tracts." Wilbarger, *Indian Depredations in Texas*, 127–129; Bedford, *Texas Indian Troubles*, 118–120; James Cox, *Historical and Biographical Record of the Cattle Industry and the Cattlemen of Texas and Adjacent Territory* (St. Louis: Woodward & Tiernan Printing Co., 1894), 282–283.
86. Tax Rolls, Medina County, 1867–1870, 1872–1878; *Ninth U.S. Census*, Medina County, Texas; Kerr County Deed Records, Book C, 226–228, 391–393, Book D, 107–109, 111–113, 337–338, 412–413; Bandera County Deed Records, Book B, No. 2, 33–35, 369–370.
87. William A. A. Wallace, Republic Pensions, Reel 244, Frames 99–101, 106, 109, TSLAC; Wilbarger, *Indian Depredations in Texas*, 113–114; *Galveston Daily News*, March 18, 1880; Tax Rolls, Medina County, 1879–1880; *Tenth U.S. Census*, Frio County, Texas; *Austin Weekly Statesman*, April 29, 1880; M. P. Lehman, "Big Foot Wallace: A Legend

in His Own Time," *Real West* 17 (February 1974): 73; Brazos, *Life of Robert Hall*, 108.

88. Harris, "Last Range of Big-Foot Wallace," 92–93; Frances Bramlette Farris, *From Rattlesnakes to Road Agents*, ed. C. L. Sonnichsen (Fort Worth: Texas Christian University Press, 1985), 35; Cox, *Texas Ranger Tales II*, 25; Sowell, *Texas Indian Fighters*, 398; Crawford Laxson, "Personal Recollections of Big-Foot Wallace," *Frontier Times* 12 (January 1935): 169.
89. *Austin Weekly Statesman*, February 7, 1889; Gammel, comp., *Laws of Texas*, 9: 1396–1397; Donation Certificate No. 2864, Galveston County, filed January 7, 1899, File No. 32, Donation Certificate No. 1483, Galveston County, issued July 6, 1899, File No. 502, Donation Certificate No. 2790, Galveston County, patented September 26, 1889, File No. 29, Donation Certificate No. 2794, Galveston County, patented August 30, 1890, File No. 30, Donation Certificate No. 27/139, Aransas County, issued March 31, 1890, File No. 170, TGLO; Farris, *From Rattlesnakes to Road Agents*, 46–47; *Galveston Daily News*, September 21, 22, 1889.
90. Cox, *Texas Ranger Tales II*, 36–37; Farris, *From Rattlesnakes to Road Agents*, 46, 47, 49; Laxson, "Personal Recollections of Big-Foot Wallace," 169; *Dallas Morning News*, April 8, October 5, 1898; *San Antonio Daily Express*, January 8, 1899; *Brownsville Daily Herald*, January 11, 1899; Gammel, comp., *Laws of Texas*, 11: 46–47.

Notes for Chapter 5

1. Samuel H. Walker, "The Walkers of Toaping Castle, Md." (MS, 1883) 4, 5–6, 16–17. The author of this manuscript was the son of Johnathan Walker, not the subject of this chapter. According to Carol Borchardt, Registrar of the Prince George's County Genealogical Society, the name of Bear Garden Branch was later changed to Indian Creek. *Evening Star*, October 13, 1883; Gaius Marcus Brumbaugh, *Maryland Records—Colonial, Revolutionary, County, & Church* (Lancaster, PA: Lancaster Press, 1928), 2: 516; Henry C. Peden, Jr., *Revolutionary Patriots of Prince George's County, 1775–1783* (Westminster, MD: Family Line Publications, 1997), 314; Samuel H. Walker, "Florida and Seminole Wars," Box 1982/47, Samuel Hamilton Walker Papers, TSLAC, 1. Unless otherwise indicated, all references to the Walker Papers derive from Box 1982/47. *Prince Georges Post*, April 13, 1967; Helen W. Brown, *Index of*

Marriage Licenses, Prince George's County, Maryland, 1777–1886 (College Park, MD: privately printed, 1971), 226; Adelaide B. Baggerly Chase, "Baggerly Family Records," *National Genealogical Society Quarterly* 31 (December 1943): 102; Edmund L. Dana, "Incidents in the Life of Capt. Samuel H. Walker, Texan Ranger," *Proceedings of the Wyoming Historical and Geological Society* 3 (1882): 44. There has been some confusion as to Walker's actual birth year. His gravestone bears the date 1815. *The Handbook of Texas* in its print and online versions gives it as 1817. Webb believed it to be 1810. *Texas Rangers*, 84.

Samuel Walker's grandfather, Isaac, received a land patent for sixty-four acres from Frederick Calvert, Sixth Baron Baltimore on September 29, 1757. The tract was named in the original grant as "Toping Castle." Peter Wilson Coldham, *Settlers of Maryland, 1679–1783* (Baltimore, MD: Genealogical Publishing Company, 2010), 1: 686. The elder Nathan died at Toaping Castle on December 28, 1842. *Daily National Intelligencer*, January 3, 1843. A letter from Jennie E. Beall to Florida Walker found in the Walker Papers, dated December 8, 1860, indicates Elizabeth died in April 1860. The estate is now part of the Golden Triangle Business Park in the town of Greenbelt, while the family cemetery is all that remains of the property. A Prince George's County Historical Society marker designates the site.

2. *Fourth* and *Sixth U.S. Census*, Prince George's County, Maryland; Shirley Langdon Wilcox, ed., *1828 Tax List, Prince George's County, Maryland* (Bowie, MD: Prince George's County Genealogical Society, 1985), 22–23.
3. Walker, "Florida and Seminole Wars," 2; John K. Mahon, *History of the Second Seminole War, 1835–1842* (Gainesville: University Press of Florida, 1985), 75–85, 95, 98–102, 104–106, 138; John T. Ellisor, *The Second Creek War: Interethnic Conflict and Collusion on a Collapsing Frontier* (Lincoln: University of Nebraska Press, 2010), 12, 18–21, 142–143; *American State Papers: Military Affairs*, 6: 622–623; *Army and Navy Chronicle* 2 (February 4, 1836): 74, 75, (February 25, 1836): 120, 124, (March 31, 1836): 196–199; *Niles' Weekly Register* 50 (May 21, 1836): 205–206, (May 28, 1836): 217; *Letter from the Secretary of War*, House Document No. 115, 24th Congress, 1st Session. For the various treaties by which the United States acquired Creek and Seminole lands, see Charles J. Kappler, comp. and ed., *Indian Affairs: Laws and Treaties* (Washington, D.C.: Government Printing Office, 1904), 2: 107–110, 155–156, 195–198, 214–217, 264–268, 284–286,

341–345, 388–391, 394–395, 398–400. See also *American State Papers: Military Affairs*, 6: 1026–1069.

4. *American State Papers: Military Affairs*, 6: 807, 812, 1051, 7: 799; *Daily National Intelligencer*, May 25, 31, 1836; Carded Records Showing Military Service of Soldiers Who Fought in Volunteer Organizations During the Indian Wars, *1817–1858*, Irwin's Company, Samuel H. Walker. Hereafter cited as Carded Records ... Indian Wars. Beall to Cass, June 6, 1836, Letters Received by the Office of the Adjutant General, M567, RG 94, NARA. Hereafter cited as Letters Received, Adjutant General's Office. Francis B. Heitman, *Historical Register and Dictionary of the United States Army from its Organization, September 29 1789, to March 2 1903* (Washington, D.C.: Government Printing Office, 1903), 1: 202; Charles K. Gardner, *A Dictionary of All Officers: Who Have Been Commissioned, or Have Been Appointed and Served, in the Army of the United States* (New York: D. Van Nostrand, 1860), 385.
5. *Army and Navy Chronicle* 2 (June 16, 1836): 382, (June 23, 1836): 397; *Daily National Intelligencer*, June 16, July 1, 29, 1836.
6. Robinson to Jones, July 11, 1836, Walker to Jones, August 17, 1836, Jones to Cass, September 19, 1836, Letters Received, Adjutant General's Office, NARA; Returns from U.S. Military Posts, 1800–1916, Fort Mitchell, September-October 1836, Fort Brooke, October 1836, M617, NARA. Hereafter cited as Post Returns. Walker, "Florida and Seminole Wars," 1–7; Jimmy L. Bryan, Jr., "The Patriot-Warrior Mystique: John S. Brooks, Walter P. Lane, Samuel H. Walker and the Adventurous Quest for Renown," *Texans and War: New Interpretations of the State's Military History*, ed. Alexander Mendoza and Charles Davis Grear (College Station: Texas A&M University Press, 2012), 115; *Daily National Intelligencer*, October 1, 1836; S. H. Walker to J. T. Walker, October 2, 1836, Walker Papers, TSLAC; Heitman, *Historical Register and Dictionary of the U.S. Army*, 1: 573; *Army and Navy Chronicle* 3 (October 27, 1836): 269; *American State Papers: Military Affairs*, 7: 863.
7. Walker, "Florida and Seminole Wars," 7; John and Mary Lou Missall, comps. and eds., *This Miserable Pride of a Soldier: The Letters and Journals of Col. William S. Foster in the Second Seminole War* (Tampa: University of Florida Press, 2005), 40–49, 51; Michael G. Schene, "Fort Foster: A Second Seminole War Fort," *Florida Historical Quarterly* 54 (January 1976): 320; Post Returns, Fort Brooke, November-

December 1836; McClintock to Jesup, November 27, 1836, Foster to Jones, December 8, 1836, Letters Received, Adjutant General's Office, NARA; Gardner, *Dictionary of All Officers*, 247; *Army and Navy Chronicle* 5 (August 17, 1837): 106; Frank Laumer, "This Was Fort Dade," *Florida Historical Quarterly* 45 (July 1966): 3. Redeeming himself, Robinson was commended for his "gallantry and good conduct" during the fighting in the Wahoo swamp between November 17 and the twenty-first. *Daily National Intelligencer*, December 21, 1836.

8. Post Returns, Fort Brooke, December 1836; Walker, "Florida and Seminole Wars," 9; Mahon, *The Second Seminole War*, 199, 200, 203–204; Laumer, "This Was Fort Dade," 7.
9. S. H. Walker to J. T. Walker, March 5, 1837, Walker Papers, TSLAC.
10. Post Returns, Fort Brooke, May 1837; *Daily National Intelligencer*, February 24, June 23, 1837; *Army and Navy Chronicle* 5 (July 6, 1837): 8, 10, 4 (June 22, 1837): 394; Irwin to Poinsett, October 18, 19, 1837, Letters Received, Adjutant General's Office, NARA. Irwin led another company of sixty-seven volunteers back to Florida in late October 1837. *Army and Navy Chronicle* 5 (October 26, 1837): 270.
11. Carded Records … Indian Wars, Irwin's Company, Samuel H. Walker; S. H. Walker to J. T. Walker, May 10, 1837, July 7, 1837, July 13, 1837, January 17, 1840, S. H. Walker to C. E. Walker, October 21, 1838, February 16, 1839, Walker to Mother and Father, April 20, 1839, Walker Papers, TSLAC; Malcolm J. Rohrbough, *Trans-Appalachian Frontier: People, Societies, and Institutions, 1775–1850* (Bloomington: Indiana University Press, 2008), 376, 377, 380; James Owens Knauss, "St. Joseph, an Episode of the Economic and Political History of Florida," *Florida Historical Society Quarterly* 6 (July 1927): 11–12; Walker, "Walkers of Toaping Castle," 6.
12. Walker, "Florida and Seminole War," 1–12; S. H. Walker to J. T. Walker, February 24, 1840, March 7, 1840, April 20, 1840, June 16, 1841, Taylor to Walker and Nevarro, March 15, 1840, Taylor to Walker, March 17, 1840, Walker to Mehnew, August 8, 1841, Walker to Bass, August 22, 1841, Walker Papers, TSLAC. After he achieved renown, accounts inaccurately reported Walker had served as a scout for Lieutenant-Colonel William S. Harney's expedition into the Everglades in November 1840. For the apocryphal tale, see Fayette Robinson, "Captain Samuel Walker," *Graham's American Magazine Monthly* 32 (June 1848): 301. For more on Harney's campaign, see George Rollie

Adams, *General William S. Harney: Prince of Dragoons* (Lincoln: University of Nebraska Press, 2001), 75–77.

13. S. H. Walker to A. H. Walker, January 22, 1842, March 10, 1842, Box 1989/080-1, Walker Papers, TSLAC; Bryan, "The Patriot-Warrior Mystique," 119; *Daily Union*, May 21, 1846; Jesse Billingsley, Public Debt Claim No. 1287, Reel 137, Frames 280–285, TSLAC. For more on Billingsley, see Jesse Billingsley biographical sketch, Louis Wiltz Kemp Papers, SJMH.
14. James C. Wilson, *Address on the Occasion of Removing the Remains of Captains Walker and Gillespie* (San Antonio: Published by a committee of citizens, 1856), 16; Dana, "Capt. Samuel H. Walker," 57–58.
15. Marilyn McAdams Sibley, ed., *Samuel H. Walker's Account of the Mier Expedition* (Austin: Texas State Historical Association, 1978), 25–26; Joseph Milton Nance, *Attack and Counterattack: The Texas-Mexican Frontier, 1842* (Austin: University of Texas Press, 1964), 368; *Telegraph and Texas Register*, October 5, 26, 1842, May 3, 1843; Rena Maverick Green, ed., *Memoirs of Mary A. Maverick, Arranged by Mary A. Maverick and Her Son George Madison Maverick* (San Antonio: Alamo Printing Co., 1921), 73–74; Ralph A. Wooster, "Texas Military Operations against Mexico, 1842–1843," *Southwestern Historical Quarterly* 67 (April 1964): 470–472; Catherine W. McDowell, ed., *Now You Hear My Horn: The Journal of James Wilson Nichols, 1820–1887* (Austin: University of Texas Press, 1967), 108.
16. John H. Jenkins and Kenneth Kesselus, *Edward Burleson: Texas Frontier Leader* (Austin: Jenkins Publishing Company, 1990), 317; Sylvia Villarreal Bisnar, *P. L. Buquor, Indian Fighter, Texas Ranger, Mayor of San Antonio* (Bloomington, IN: AuthorHouse, 2009), 68–69; Nance, *Attack and Counterattack*, 406; *Telegraph and Texas Register*, September 14, October 12, 1842; *Civilian and Galveston Gazette*, October 12, November 2, 1842.
17. Sibley, ed., *Samuel H. Walker's Account*, 32–33, 35; Sam W. Haynes, *Soldiers of Misfortune: The Somervell and Mier Expeditions* (Austin: University of Texas Press, 1990), 53–54; Houston Wade, comp., *Notes and Fragments of the Mier Expedition* (La Grange: La Grange Journal, 1936–1937), 1: 134; Wooster, "Texas Military Operations Against Mexico," 475; Samuel H. Wallace, Audited Claim No. 2917, Reel 108, Frame 621, TSLAC; Llerena B. Friend, "Sidelights and

Supplements on the Perote Prisoners," *Southwestern Historical Quarterly* 69 (October 1965): 227–228.

18. Sibley, ed., *Samuel H. Walker's Account*, 35–36; Lucy A. Erath, ed., "Memoirs of Major George Bernard Erath," Pt. 3, *Southwestern Historical Quarterly* 27 (July 1923): 44–46; James M. Day, ed., "Diary of James A. Glasscock, Mier Man," *Texana* 1 (Spring 1963): 88; Frederick C. Chabot, *The Perote Prisoners: Being the Diary of James L. Trueheart* (San Antonio: The Naylor Company, 1944), 71; Joseph B. Wilkinson, *Laredo and the Rio Grande Frontier: A Narrative* (Austin: Jenkins Publishing Co., 1975), 180; Thomas W. Bell, *A Narrative of the Capture and Subsequent Sufferings of the Mier Prisoners in Mexico* (Waco: Texian Press, 1964), 14. Hereafter cited as *Mier Expedition Narrative*. Samuel H. Walker, Audited Claim No. 2917, Reel 108, Frame 623, TSLAC. Three years later, Walker designated Jack Hays to act as his agent in the matter of his claim to the Texas government. See also Andrew Jackson Sowell, *Texas Indian Fighters: Early Settlers and Indian Fighters of Southwest Texas* (Austin: State House Press, 1986), 61.
19. Sibley, ed., *Samuel H. Walker's Account*, 36–37. In the aftermath of the battle, General Woll was appointed commander of the Army of the North on January 30, 1843. Ampudia was likewise named second-in-command. Nance, *Dare-Devils All*, 84.
20. Sibley, ed., *Samuel H. Walker's Account*, 38–40; James M. Day, ed., "Israel Canfield in the Mier Expedition," *Texas Military History* 3 (Fall 1963): 171, 173; Day, ed., "Diary of James A. Glasscock," 91–92; William Preston Stapp, *The Prisoners of Perote* (Austin: University of Texas Press, 1977), 44–45; General Thomas J. Green, *Journal of the Texian Expedition against Mier* (New York: Harper & Brothers, 1845), 118–123; John Warren Hunter, "Adventures of a Mier Prisoner," *Frontier Times* 2 (April 1925): 21.
21. Sibley, ed., *Samuel H. Walker's Account*, 44–45, 47–53; S. H. Walker to A. M. Walker, May 6, 1843, Box 1989/080-1, Walker Papers, TSLAC; Chabot, *The Perote Prisoners*, 72–73; Hunter, "Adventures of a Mier Prisoner," 22–23; *Telegraph and Texas Register*, November 29, 1843; Stapp, *Prisoners of Perote*, 69, 72, 75; Bell, *Mier Expedition Narrative*, 27–33; Wade, comp., *Notes and Fragments*, 2: 87–88.
22. Sibley, ed., *Samuel H. Walker's Account*, 57–61; S. H. Walker to A. M. Walker, May 6, 1843, Box 1989/080-1, Walker Papers, TSLAC; Bell, *Mier Expedition Narrative*, 35, 38–40; Wade, comp., *Notes and*

Fragments, 2: 28; *Daily Picayune*, April 5, 1843; Stapp, *Prisoners of Perote*, 91–93; Day, ed., "Israel Canfield in the Mier Expedition," 180–181; Haynes, *Soldiers of Misfortune*, 129–130; Wilkinson, *Laredo and the Rio Grande Frontier*, 177; *Niles' National Register* 64 (May 13, 1843): 176.

23. Stapp, *Prisoners of Perote*, 107, 113; Bell, *Mier Expedition Narrative*, 44, 47–48; Day, ed., "Diary of James A. Glasscock," 106; Day, ed., "Israel Canfield in the Mier Expedition," 184–185; Nance, *Dare-Devils All*, 322; Sibley, ed., *Samuel H. Walker's Account*, 65–67; Dana, "Capt. Samuel H. Walker," 45. A common story portrays Walker as having been a captive in Perote castle. Another relates how he placed a dime under a flagpole he was forced to erect. According to the legend, he swore to return for it one day and subsequently fulfilled his promise when he joined the invading American army. Neither account can be substantiated by existing evidence. Jacob Oswandel, *Notes of the Mexican War, 1846–47–48* (Philadelphia: n.p., 1885), 176–177, 182. Allen G. Hatley perpetuates the apocryphal tale in "Samuel Walker: Valiant Warrior," *True West* 47 (May 2000): 34, but he corrects the record in "Sam Walker," *The Texas Ranger Dispatch* 2 (Winter 2000): 10.
24. *Niles' National Register* 65 (September 2, 1843): 4; *Daily Picayune*, August 25, 1843; *Northern Standard*, October 14, 1843.
25. Sibley, ed., *Samuel H. Walker's Account*, 76–81; Wade, comp., *Notes and Fragments*, 1: 134; 2: 142–144; Day, ed., "Israel Canfield in the Mier Expedition," 187–188; McCutchan *Mier Expedition Diary*, 123; Green, *Journal of the Texian Expedition Against Mier*, 446; *Northern Standard*, October 14, 1843; S. H. Walker to A. M. Walker, May 6, 1843, Box 1989/080-1, Walker Papers, TSLAC. Wilson's account of the escape can be found in *Daily Picayune*, October 12, 1843; and *Northern Standard*, November 18, 1843.
26. Houston to Elliot, January 24, 1843, Amelia W. Williams and Eugene C. Barker, ed., *Writings of Sam Houston* (Austin: University of Texas Press, 1938–1943), 3: 300; *Niles' National Register* 64 (May 6, 1843): 146; Walker to Houston, October 28, 1843, Green to Walker, November 8, 1843, Walker to Green, November 9, 1843, Thomas J. Green Papers, Southern Historical Collection, Wilson Library, University of North Carolina at Chapel Hill. Reprinted in the *Telegraph and Texas Register*, December 13, 1843. Green, *Journal of the Texian Expedition against Mier*, 453; Kuykendall, *Sketches of Early Texians*, 8. Houston defended his actions in a letter

to Hamilton Stuart, which was reprinted in Wade, comp., *Notes and Fragments*, 2: 11–17.

T. J. Green, a bitter personal enemy of Houston, fervently believed the president had disavowed the Mier prisoners, which led to the decimation at Salado. Green, *Journal of the Texian Expedition against Mier*, 216–217, 456–460. Originally published in 1845, Green's book was most notable for two things: the author's passionate hatred for Sam Houston and his penchant for making himself the hero of the whole episode. For another example of his vitriol, see *Telegraph and Texas Register*, December 13, 1843.

27. James T. DeShields, "The Life and Adventures of Colonel John C. Hays," "Sketches Concerning the Life of John C. Hays," James Thomas DeShields Papers, BCAH, 10; Thomas W. Kavanagh, *Comanche Political History: An Ethnohistorical Perspective, 1706–1875* (Lincoln: University of Nebraska Press, 1996), 268–269; John Holland Jenkins, *Recollections of Early Texas: The Memoirs of John Holland Jenkins*, ed. John Holmes Jenkins III (Austin: University of Texas Press, 2003), 145–146; Nathan A. Jennings, *Riding for the Lone Star: Frontier Cavalry and the Texas Way of War, 1822–1865* (Denton: University of North Texas Press, 2016), 184–185; Dana, "Capt. Samuel H. Walker," 47–49.
28. Western to Houston, June 16, 1844, Dorman H. Winfrey and James M. Day, eds., *The Indian Papers of Texas and the Southwest* (Austin: Texas State Historical Association, 1995), 1: 72–73; "The Battle of Walker Creek, June 8, 1844" (MS, n.d.), Walker Vertical File, TRHF&M, 1, 12, 21; Frederick C. Chabot, *With the Makers of San Antonio* (San Antonio: Artes Graficas, 1937), 289–291.
29. James Kimmins Greer, *Texas Ranger: Jack Hays in the Frontier Southwest* (College Station: Texas A&M University Press, 1993), 113; Muster and Pay Rolls, John C. Hays, 401–718, -791, TSLAC; *Telegraph and Texas Register*, April 2, 1845; *Texas National Register*, May 1, 8, 1845.
30. Richard Bruce Winders, *Crisis in the Southwest: The United States, Mexico, and the Struggle Over Texas* (Lanham, MD: SR Books, 2004), 92; Thomas to Taylor, September 17, 1844, *Annual Report of the Secretary of State*, House Executive Document No. 2, 28th Congress, 1st Session, 37; Charles M. Robinson III, *Texas and the Mexican War: A History and a Guide* (Austin: Texas State Historical Association, 2004), 9.

31. Bancroft to Taylor, June 15, 1845, Taylor to Adjutant General, June 30, 1845, Taylor to Adjutant General, July 28, 1845, Taylor to Adjutant General, August 30, 1845, *Mexican War Correspondence*, House Executive Document No. 60, 30th Congress, 1st Session, 81–82, 801, 97, 104–105; Henry W. Barton, *Texas Volunteers in the Mexican War* (Waco: Texian Press, 1970), 6; Justin H. Smith, *The War with Mexico* (New York: The Macmillan Company, 1919), 1: 141–142; Major George Deas, "Reminiscences of the Campaign on the Rio Grande," Pt. 1, *The Historical Magazine* 7 (January 1870): 19; Frank Leon Jones III, "With Zachary Taylor in Texas" (M.S. thesis, Texas A&M University-Kingsville, 1995), 9.
32. Taylor to Jones, August 16, 1845, *Mexican War Correspondence*, 101, 106.
33. S. H. Walker to A. M. Walker, August 26, 1845, Box 1989/080-1, Walker Papers, TSLAC; Michael L. Collins, *Texas Devils: Rangers and Regulars on the Lower Rio Grande, 1846–1861* (Norman: University of Oklahoma Press, 2008), 16; Wilson, *Address*, 14–15.
34. Compiled Service Records of Volunteer Soldiers, First Texas Mounted Rifles, Samuel H. Walker; *Texas Democrat*, September 9, 1846; Frederick Wilkins, *The Highly Irregular Irregulars: Texas Rangers in the Mexican War* (Austin: Eakin Press, 1990), 24; Barton, *Texas Volunteers*, 7; Voucher No. 2, October 24, 1845, 401–1152, TSLAC.
35. Marcy to Taylor, January 13, 1846, Order No. 30, March 8, 1846, Taylor to Adjutant General, March 25, 1846, Taylor to Adjutant General, March 29, 1846, Taylor to Adjutant General, April 6, 1846, *Mexican War Correspondence*, 90–91, 120, 129–130, 132–134; K. Jack Bauer, *The Mexican War, 1846–1848* (Lincoln: University of Nebraska Press, 1992), 37, 38–40; John S. D. Eisenhower, *So Far from God: The U.S. War with Mexico, 1846–1848* (Norman: University of Oklahoma Press, 2000), 51–54; Steven E. Woodworth, *Manifest Destinies: America's Westward Expansion and the Road to the Civil War* (New York: Vintage Books, 2010), 144, 151; Captain William Seaton Henry, *Campaign Sketches of the War with Mexico* (New York: Harper & Brothers, 1847), 63; Smith, *War with Mexico*, 1: 145–146, 148; George Wilkins Kendall, *The War Between the United States and Mexico, Illustrated* (New York: D. Appleton & Company, 1851), 1.
36. Henry, *Campaign Sketches*, 74–75; Ampudia to Taylor, April 12, 1846, Taylor to Ampudia, April 12, 1846, Taylor to Adjutant General,

April 15, 1846, *Mexican War Correspondence*, 138–140; Deas, "Reminiscences of the Campaign," Pt. 1: 21.

37. Mike Cox, *The Texas Rangers: Wearing the Cinco Peso, 1821–1900* (New York: Tom Doherty Associates, 2008), 103; Henry, *Campaign Sketches*, 85; Compiled Service Records of Volunteer Soldiers, Walker's Company, Texas Mounted Rangers, Samuel H. Walker; *Texas Democrat*, May 6, 1846.
38. Douglas A. Murphy, *Two Armies on the Rio Grande: The First Campaign of the US-Mexican War* (College Station: Texas A&M University Press, 2015), 145; Charles T. Haven and Frank A. Belden, *A History of the Colt Revolver* (New York: Bonanza Books, 1940), 272; Charles D. Spurlin, *Texas Volunteers in the Mexican War* (Austin: Eakin Press, 1998), 26; Barton, *Texas Volunteers*, 11; James E. Hicks, *Notes on United States Ordnance* (Mount Vernon, NY: privately printed, 1940), 1: 59, 61–62; Kendall, *War Between the United States and Mexico*, 1.
39. *Niles' National Register* 70 (May 23, 1846): 180; *Daily National Intelligencer*, May 18, 1846; *New York Herald*, May 19, 1846; Charles D. Spurlin, comp., *Texas Veterans in the Mexican War: Muster Rolls of Texas Military Units* (Victoria, TX: privately printed, 1984), 212–214; Clifford R. Caldwell and Ron DeLord, *Texas Lawmen, 1835–1899: The Good and the Bad* (Charleston, SC: The History Press, 2011), 280; Barton, *Texas Volunteers*, 12; Taylor to Adjutant General, May 3, 1846, *Mexican War Correspondence*, 289–290; Haven and Belden, *History of the Colt Revolver*, 273. The given number of rangers at each engagement varies according to the source. Smith stated Walker's detachment was twenty strong. *War with Mexico*, 1: 160. Walter Webb claimed the number was seventy-five. *The Texas Rangers in the Mexican War* (Austin: Jenkins Garrett Press, 1975), 11. The *Congressional Globe* concurred that Walker had twenty-four men at his skirmish. *Congressional Globe*, 29th Congress, 2nd Session, 149. A later volume of the same publication maintained Radcliffe had thirty men. Ibid., 30th Congress, 1st Session, 87. George W. Trahern recounted seven or eight rangers were at Radcliffe's camp and two were killed in the attack. A. Russell Buchanan, ed., "George Washington Trahern: Texas Cowboy Soldier from Mier to Buena Vista," *Southwestern Historical Quarterly* 58 (July 1954): 71.
40. Taylor to Adjutant General, May 3, 1846, *Mexican War Correspondence*, 289; *Daily Union*, May 18, 1846; *General Taylor and His*

Staff (Philadelphia: Grigg, Elliott & Co., 1848), 181; Felice Flanery Lewis, *Trailing Clouds of Glory: Zachary Taylor's Mexican War Campaign and His Emerging Civil War Leaders* (Tuscaloosa: University of Alabama Press, 2010), 68; *Nelson* Lee, *Three Years Among the Comanches: The Narrative of Nelson Lee, the Texas Ranger* (Norman: University of Oklahoma Press, 1991), 71. While the audacity attributed to Walker was consistent with his personality, Lee's claims cannot be fully substantiated as his name does not appear in the *Compiled Service Records* for Walker's company.

41. Woodworth, *Manifest Destinies*, 157; Taylor to Adjutant General, May 3, 1846, Orders No. 55, May 1, 1846, *Mexican War Correspondence*, 289–290, 486; *General Taylor and His Staff*, 181; Eisenhower, *So Far from God*, 71; Bauer, *Mexican War*, 49; Jones, "With Zachary Taylor in Texas," 118.
42. Robinson, *Texas and the Mexican War*, 31; Henry, *Campaign Sketches*, 88; *Niles' National Register* 71 (October 3, 1846): 67.
43. Taylor to Adjutant General, May 5, 1846, Brown to Taylor, May 4, 1846, *Mexican War Correspondence*, 292–294; Murphy, *Two Armies on the Rio Grande*, 180–182; J. M. Wynkoop, ed., *Anecdotes and Incidents: Comprising Daring Exploits, Personal and Amusing Adventures of the Officers and Privates of the Army, and Thrilling Incidents of the Mexican War* (Pittsburgh, PA: n.p., 1848), 53–54; Thomas Bangs Thorpe, *Our Army on the Rio Grande* (Philadelphia: Carey and Hart, 1846), 59, 61–62; *Democratic Telegraph & Texas Register*, May 13, 20, 1846; *Niles' National Register* 71 (September 12, 1846): 25; Dana, "Capt. Samuel H. Walker," 51–52.
44. Lewis, *Trailing Clouds of Glory*, 73; Orders No. 58, May 7, 1846, *Mexican War Correspondence*, 487; Barton, *Texas Volunteers*, 13. The post opposite Matamoros would later be renamed Fort Brown in honor of Major Brown, who was slain in the shelling. Thomas T. Smith, *The Old Army in Texas: A Research Guide to the U.S. Army in Nineteenth-Century Texas* (Austin: Texas State Historical Association, 2000), 56.
45. Taylor to Adjutant General, May 9, 1846, McIntosh to Bliss, December 2, 1846, *Mexican War Correspondence*, 295, 1103; Taylor to Adjutant General, May 16, 1846, *Congressional Globe*, 29th Congress, 1st Session, Appendix, 675–676; Steven A. Carney, *Guns Along the Rio Grande: Palo Alto and Resaca de la Palma* (Washington, D.C.: U.S. Army Center of Military History, 2005), 17, 18–20; Murphy, *Two Armies on the Rio Grande*, 193–194, 200–201; E. Kirby Smith, *To Mexico with Scott: Letters*

of Captain E. Kirby Smith to His Wife (Cambridge, MA: Harvard University Press, 1917), 48–49; *Niles' National Register* 70 (June 20, 1846): 251, (June 27, 1846): 263; Major George Deas, "Reminiscences of the Campaign on the Rio Grande," Pt. 2, *The Historical Magazine* 7 (February 1870): 101; Larnard to Hitchcock, May 14, 1846, Frederick C. Chabot, ed., *Texas Letters* (San Antonio: Yanaguana Society, 1940), 119. Eisenhower, *So Far from God*, 379: "American artillery at the time of the Mexican War was the equal if not the superior of any artillery in the world." For more on the first major battle of the conflict, including the bombardment of Fort Texas, see Charles M. Haecker and Jeffrey G. Mauck, *On the Prairie of Palo Alto: Historical Archaeology of the U.S.-Mexican War Battlefield* (College Station: Texas A&M University Press, 1997).

46. Walter Prescott Webb, *The Texas Rangers in the Mexican War* (Austin: Jenkins Garrett Press, 1975), 14.
47. Taylor to the Adjutant General, May 9, 1846, *Mexican War Correspondence*, 295–296; James M. McCaffrey, *Army of Manifest Destiny: The American Soldier in the Mexican War, 1846–1848* (New York: New York University Press, 1992), 11; Grady McWhiney and Sue McWhiney, eds., *To Mexico with Taylor and Scott, 1845–1847* (Waltham, MA: Blaisdell Publishing Company, 1969), 36; Kendall, *War Between the United States and Mexico*, 3; Taylor to Adjutant General, May 17, 1846, Staniford to Taylor and Ridgely to Taylor, both dated May 10, 1846, Twiggs to Taylor, May 11, 1846, McCall to Bliss, May 13, 1846, *Congressional Globe*, 29th Congress, 1st Session, Appendix, 676–681; *Niles' National Register* 70 (June 20, 1846): 253; Thomas D. Roberts, "Resaca de la Palma: A Traditional Episode in the History of the Second Cavalry," *The Journal of the American Military History Foundation* 1 (Autumn 1937): 103.
48. Spurlin, *Texas Volunteers*, 15; *Daily Picayune*, May 13, 1846; *Niles' National Register* 73 (November 20, 1847): 181; Henry, *Campaign Sketches*, 97; Theophilus F. Rodenbough, comp., *From Everglade to Canyon with the Second United States Cavalry* (Norman: University of Oklahoma Press, 2000), 108; Roberts, "Resaca de la Palma," 105; Taylor to Adjutant General, May 17, 1846, Twiggs to Taylor, May 11, 1846, *Congressional Globe*, 29th Congress, 1st Session, Appendix, 676–678. May's dragoons also captured General Rómulo Díaz de la Vega, the Mexican artillery commander who had been gallantly leading his cannon crews in person. Eisenhower, *So Far from God*, 84.

49. Deas, "Reminiscences of the Campaign," Pt. 2: 103; Murphy, *Two Armies on the Rio Grande*, 226; Spurlin, *Texas Volunteers*, 16; Wilkins, *The Highly Irregular Irregulars*, 33; Robinson, *Texas and the Mexican War*, 46; Taylor to Adjutant General, May 17, 1846, *Congressional Globe*, 29th Congress, 1st Session, Appendix, 676; *Texas Democrat*, May 27, June 10, 1846; Jones, "With Zachary Taylor in Texas," 40; *Daily Union*, May 23, 1846; Taylor to Adjutant General, May 18, 1846, *Mexican War Correspondence*, 297–298.
50. Henry, *Campaign Sketches*, 115; *Niles' National Register* 70 (June 27, 1846): 263, (May 30, 1846): 201–202, 73 (November 20, 1847): 181; *Daily Picayune*, May 14, 16, 1846; *Daily Union*, May 21, 1846; *New York Herald*, May 19, 20, 1846; Bryan, "The Patriot-Warrior Mystique," 120; Carol Clark, *Charles Deas and 1840s America* (Norman: University of Oklahoma Press, 2009), 30, 105, 201; Taylor to Adjutant General, May 17, 1846, *Congressional Globe*, 29th Congress, 1st Session, Appendix, 676. For more examples of Walker's national reputation, see *Louisville Daily Courier*, May 21, 1846; *Mississippi Free Trader*, May 14, 1846; *Baltimore Sun*, June 6, 1846; and *New York Tribune*, May 26, 1846.
51. Taylor to Adjutant General, May 18, 1846, *Mexican War Correspondence*, 297–298; Henry, *Campaign Sketches*, 108; Thorpe, *Our Army on the Rio Grande*, 123–124; *Daily Picayune*, May 29, 1846; *Niles' National Register* 70 (June 13, 1846): 228.
52. Compiled Service Records of Volunteer Soldiers, First Texas Mounted Rifles, and Walker's Company, Texas Mounted Rangers, Samuel H. Walker; *Democratic Telegraph and Texas Register*, July 1, 1846; John Henry Brown, *History of Texas, from 1685 to 1892* (St. Louis, MO: L. E. Daniell, 1893), 2: 322; Captain Ralph C. Deibert and Colonel Harry N. Cootes, *A History of the Third United States Cavalry: The Regiment of Mounted Riflemen, the First Regiment of Mounted Riflemen, the Third United States Cavalry* (Harrisburg, PA: Telegraph Press, 1933), 2–3; *Niles' National Register* 70 (August 1, 1846): 338–339; Walker to Jones, two letters dated June 30, 1846, Letters Received, Adjutant General's Office, NARA. The remainder of Walker's ranger company was discharged on July 16. *Daily Picayune*, August 9, 1846. Walker's promotion caused at least seven Regular Army lieutenants serving in Texas and Mexico to petition Congress protesting his advancement at their expense. Walker Papers, TSLAC.

A detachment of Walker's mounted rifle company under Second Lieutenant George McLane was ordered to embark from Baltimore for Point Isabel on September 3. Once in Mexico, McLane's men were to be attached to the Second Infantry and serve as foot soldiers until they could be supplied with horses. Jones to Taylor, August 31, 1846, *Correspondence with General Taylor*, 181.

53. *Niles' National Register* 70 (August 1, 1846): 352; Spurlin, *Texas Volunteers*, 57–58; Charles D. Spurlin, "Ranger Walker in the Mexican War," *Military History of Texas and the Southwest* 9 (1971): 268.
54. Major George Deas, "Reminiscences of the Campaign on the Rio Grande," Pt. 5, *The Historical Magazine* 7 (May 1870): 311; Luther Giddings, *Sketches of the Campaign in Northern Mexico* (New York: G. P. Putnam & Co., 1853), 158–159; Barton, *Texas Volunteers*, 54; *Daily Picayune*, December 4, 1846; Worth to Bliss, September 28, 1846, *Report of the Secretary of War*, House Executive Document No. 4, 29th Congress, 2nd Session, 102. Hereafter cited as *Report of the Secretary of War, 1846*. Zachary Taylor, *Letters of Zachary Taylor from the Battle-Fields of the Mexican War* (Rochester, NY: William K. Bixby, 1908), 59–60; Eisenhower, *So Far from God*, 127–128.
55. Eisenhower, *So Far from God*, 128–129; Worth to Bliss, September 28, 1846, *Report of the Secretary of War, 1846*, 103; Robert H. Ferrell, ed., *Monterrey Is Ours!: The Mexican War Letters of Lieutenant Dana, 1845–1847* (Lexington: University Press of Kentucky, 1990), 131; Thomas Bangs Thorpe, *Our Army at Monterey* (Philadelphia: Carey and Hart, 1848), 64; Albert G. Brackett, *History of the United States Cavalry, From the Formation of the Federal Government to the 1st of June, 1863* (New York: Harper & Brothers, 1865), 63–64.
56. Worth to Bliss, September 28, 1846, *Report of the Secretary of War, 1846*, 103–104; *Daily Picayune*, December 4, 1846; Giddings, *Sketches of the Campaign*, 154, 191–192; John S. Ford, "John C. Hayes in Texas," Box 2Q512, John Salmon Ford Papers, BCAH, 30; Eisenhower, *So Far from God*, 133; Ferrell, ed., *Monterrey Is Ours*, 132; James Buckner Barry, *Buck Barry, Texas Ranger and Frontiersman*, ed. James K. Greer (Lincoln: University of Nebraska Press, 1984), 35–36.
57. Kendall, *War Between the United States and Mexico*, 8; Lewis, *Trailing Clouds of Glory*, 152; Christopher D. Dishman, *A Perfect Gibraltar: The Battle for Monterrey, Mexico, 1846* (Norman: University of Oklahoma Press, 2010), 158–159; Ford, "John C. Hayes in Texas," 33; *Daily Picayune*, November 19, December 4, 1846;

Worth to Bliss, September 28, 1846, *Report of the Secretary of War, 1846*, 104–105; Thorpe, *Our Army at Monterey*, 71; Deas, "Reminiscences of the Campaign," Pt. 5: 313.

58. John R. Kenly, *Memoirs of a Maryland Volunteer: War with Mexico, in the Years 1846–7–8* (Philadelphia: J. P. Lippincott & Co., 1873), 121; Barry, *A Texas Ranger*, 37; *Northern Standard*, December 5, 1846; Worth to Bliss, September 28, 1846, *Report of the Secretary of War, 1846*, 105; Lewis, *Trailing Clouds of Glory*, 153; S. Compton Smith, *Chile Con Carne; or, The Camp and the Field* (New York: Miller & Curtis, 1857), 91–92.
59. Worth to Bliss, September 28, 1846, *Report of the Secretary of War, 1846*, 105–106; Kendall, *War Between the United States and Mexico*, 9; McCaffrey, *Army of Manifest Destiny*, 134; Spurlin, "Ranger Walker in the Mexican War," 269; Buchanan, ed., "George Washington Trahern," 72; Smith, *Chile Con Carne*, 93–94; Ford, "John C. Hayes in Texas," 38.
60. Ford, "John C. Hayes in Texas," 38–39; Walter P. Lane, *The Adventures and Recollections of General Walter P. Lane: A San Jacinto Veteran, Containing Sketches of the Texan, Mexican, and Late Wars* (Austin: Jenkins Publishing Company, 1970), 47; Webb, *Texas Rangers in the Mexican War*, 57; Eisenhower, *So Far from God*, 144; Lewis, *Trailing Clouds of Glory*, 154.
61. Samuel C. Reid, Jr., *The Scouting Expeditions of McCulloch's Texas Rangers; or, the Summer and Fall Campaigns of the Army of the United States in Mexico—1846* (Philadelphia: G. B. Zieber and Company, 1847), 200–201; Kendall, *War Between the United States and Mexico*, 9; Spurlin, *Texas Volunteers*, 96; Ford, "John C. Hayes in Texas," 39–40.
62. Jimmy L. Bryan, Jr., *More Zeal Than Discretion: The Westward Adventures of Walter P. Lane* (College Station: Texas A&M University Press, 2008), 56; Heitman, *Historical Register and Dictionary of the U.S. Army*, 1: 736; *Northern Standard*, December 5, 1846; DeWitt Clinton Baker, comp., *A Texas Scrap-Book* (New York City: A. S. Barnes & Company, 1875), 173–174; Ford, "John C. Hayes in Texas," 40–41; Lane, *Adventures and Recollections*, 48.
63. Ampudia to Taylor, September 23, 1846, Taylor to Ampudia, September 24, 1846, *Mexican War Correspondence*, 348–349; McCaffrey, *Army of Manifest Destiny*, 134–135; R. S. Ripley, *The War with Mexico* (New York: Harper & Brothers, 1849), 1: 244.

64. *Northern Standard*, November 7, 1846.
65. Special Order No. 148, October 1, 1846, *Mexican War Correspondence*, 538; Compiled Service Records of Volunteer Soldiers, First Texas Mounted Rifles, Samuel H. Walker; Robert M. Utley, *Lone Star Justice: The First Century of the Texas Rangers* (New York: Berkley Books, 2002), 74; Jimmy L. Bryan, Jr., "Agents of Destiny: Texas Rangers and the Dilemma of the Conquest Narrative," *The Martial Imagination: Cultural Aspects of American Warfare*, ed. Jimmy L. Bryan, Jr. (College Station: Texas A&M University Press, 2013), 57; *Democratic Telegraph and Texas Register*, November 9, 1846; *Texas Democrat*, October 28, 1846; *Niles' National Register* 71 (November 28, 1846): 208. For examples of the Texas Rangers' hard-won national reputation, see *Democratic Telegraph and Texas Register*, December 28, 1846; *Daily Picayune*, November 13, 1846; and *New York Herald*, November 6, 1846.
66. *Daily National Intelligencer*, November 25, December 11, 1846, July 24, 1847; James K. Polk, *The Diary of James K. Polk*, ed. Milton M. Quaife (Chicago: A. C. McClurg & Company, 1910), 2: 252; Harvey W. Crews, ed., *Centennial History of the City of Washington, D.C.* (Dayton: United Brethren Publishing House, 1892), 235; John E. Parsons, ed., *Samuel Colt's Own Record of Transactions with Captain Walker and Eli Whitney, Jr. in 1847* (Hartford: Connecticut Historical Society, 1949), 7–10, 11–12, 16–17, 24–27, 29, 39–40, 46–48, 81, 88–89; Waldo Emerson Rosebush, *Frontier Steel: The Men and Their Weapons* (Appleton, WI: C. C. Nelson Publishing Company, 1958), 52–53; Hicks, *Notes on United States Ordnance*, 1: 76–78, 2: 134–136; *Daily Picayune*, January 16, 29, July 24, 1847. Extract of Report of Military Affairs Committee, *Memorial of Samuel Colt*, Senate Report No. 296, 30th Congress, 2nd Session, 2: "Colt's repeating pistols are the most efficient arm, for mounted men and frontier troops, now known or used; and that it is highly expedient for the government to introduce them into extensive use for these purposes."
67. Parsons, ed., *Samuel Colt's Own Record*, 54, 56, 60–64, 72, 97–98; *Daily Union*, January 18, February 6, 15, 1847; Paul Foos, *Short, Offhand, Killing Affair: Soldiers and Social Conflict During the Mexican-American War* (Chapel Hill: University of North Carolina Press, 2002), 114; Jesup to Walker, January 28, 1847, Walker to Jones, February 9, 1847, March 1, 1847, March 24, 1847, Letters Received, Adjutant

General's Office, NARA; Haven and Belden, *History of the Colt Revolver*, 49, 50, 285–286, 292–293; *Daily National Intelligencer*, February 16, April 10, 1847; Rosebush, *Frontier Steel*, 65, 67, 69–71; Gregory J. W. Urwin, *The United States Cavalry: An Illustrated History: 1776–1944* (Norman: University of Oklahoma Press, 2003), 86. See the Roll of Enlistment for the United States Mounted Riflemen, January 22, 1847, Walker Papers, TSLAC. See also Hicks, *Notes on United States Ordnance*, 2: 136–141.

68. Walker to Jones, May 3, 1847, Letters Received, Adjutant General's Office, NARA; *Niles' National Register* 72 (May 29, 1847), 198, (June 19, 1847), 250; *Daily Picayune*, May 19, 20, 1847. Companies C and I were the only two troops mounted in the entire regiment. The others would fight on foot. "Reminiscences of the War with Mexico, as Told by Col. Thomas Claiborne," *The Vedette* 7 (April 1886): 13.
69. Claiborne to Andrews, November 18, 1847, Walker Papers, TSLAC. As Company C's first lieutenant, Claiborne was well-situated to witness Walker's exploits.
70. Oswandel, *Notes of the Mexican War*, 171–172.
71. Ibid., 172.
72. Adams, *William S. Harney*, 101; Robinson, *Texas and the Mexican War*, 87; Scott to Marcy, May 20, 1847, *Correspondence Between the Secretary of War and Generals Scott and Taylor, and Between General Scott and Mr. Trist*, House Executive Document No. 56, 30th Congress, 1st Session, 154; Claiborne to Andrews, November 18, 1847, Walker Papers, TSLAC.
73. "Reminiscences of the War with Mexico," 13; Dana, "Capt. Samuel H. Walker," 56; Oswandel, *Notes of the Mexican War*, 186–190; *Niles' National Register* 72 (August 7, 1847): 359. See also Cadwalader to Scott, July 12, 1847, Walker to Wynkoop, June 21, 1847, and Wynkoop to Scott, June 23, 1847, *Annual Report of the Secretary of War*, House Executive Document No. 8, 30th Congress, 1st Session, Appendix, 19, 23, 22.
74. Childs to Hooker, July 12, 1847, Wynkoop to Scott, June 23, 1847, Walker to Wynkoop, June 21, 1847, *Annual Report of the Secretary of War, 1847*, Appendix, 21–25; "Reminiscences of the War with Mexico," 13; Claiborne to Andrews, November 18, 1847, Walker Papers, TSLAC; Dana, "Capt. Samuel H. Walker," 56–57; Irving W. Levinson, *Wars within War: Mexican Guerillas, Domestic Elites, and the United States of America, 1846–1848* (Fort Worth:

Texas Christian University Press, 2005), 44; *Niles' National Register* 72 (August 7, 1847): 359; Oswandel, *Notes of the Mexican War*, 190–192; Spencer C. Tucker, ed., *The Encyclopedia of the Mexican-American War: A Political, Social, and Military History* (Santa Barbara, CA: ABC-CLIO, 2013), 1: 344.

75. Claiborne to Andrews, November 18, 1847, Walker Papers, TSLAC; Wilkins, *The Highly Irregular Irregulars*, 155; Robinson, *Texas and the Mexican War*, 87. Written nearly forty years after the fact, Claiborne's account of Walker's detention in the *Vedette* was somewhat different. In the later version, Wynkoop led a force of four infantry companies and Walker's mounted rifles to Juan de Soto. The colonel accused the *alcalde* of concealing a weapons cache of eight hundred firearms, and threatened to destroy the town unless the guns were produced. The Mexican, who denied knowing the location of any rifles, begged Walker for help. The Texan accepted the *alcalde's* word and advised Wynkoop not to shell Jalapa. Resenting his subordinate's interference, Wynkoop ordered Walker to fire a house. The captain refused the illegal order, and he was promptly placed under arrest. "Reminiscences of the War with Mexico," 13–14.
76. Smith, *War with Mexico*, 2: 173–175; Report of Colonel Childs, October 13, 1847, *Report of the Secretary of War, 1847*, 471–475; Tucker, ed., *Encyclopedia of the Mexican-American War*, 1: 529–530.
77. Albert G. Brackett, *General Lane's Brigade in Central Mexico* (Cincinnati, OH: H.W. Derby & Co., 1854), 46–47, 113–116; Kenly, *Memoirs of a Maryland Volunteer*, 300–308, 320; Smith, *War with Mexico*, 2: 176; Ripley, *War with Mexico*, 2: 505; Claiborne to Andrews, November 18, 1847, S. H. Walker to J. T. Walker, October 5, 1847, Walker Papers, TSLAC; "Reminiscences of the War with Mexico," 14; *Niles' National Register* 73 (November 13, 1847): 176; Bauer, *Mexican War*, 330; Heitman, *Historical Register and Dictionary of the United States Army*, 2: 45, 58.
78. Brackett, *General Lane's Brigade*, 88–89, 92; Wynkoop, ed., *Anecdotes and Incidents*, 61–64; Smith, *War with Mexico*, 2: 176–177; Lane to Adjutant General, October 18, 1847, *Annual Report of the Secretary of War, 1847*, 477–479; Ripley, *War with Mexico*, 2: 505–506; "Reminiscences of the War with Mexico," 14; *Niles' National Register* 73 (November 13, 1847): 176, (November 20, 1847): 206, 209; Robert W. Johannsen, *To the Halls of the Montezumas: The Mexican War in the American Imagination* (New York: Oxford University Press, 1985), 36; Eric W. Knapp,

"'War Without Pity': Guerrilla Conflict in the Mexican War" (M.A. thesis, University of Nebraska, 1995), 49–50; Steven A. Carney, *The Occupation of Mexico, May 1846-July 1848* (Washington, D.C.: U.S. Army Center of Military History, [2005]), 37. See also Robinson, *Texas and the Mexican War*, 88; Oswandel, *Notes of the Mexican War*, 345, 350; *General Taylor and His Staff*, 185–195; and *Northern Standard*, November 27, December 4, 1847. Claiborne later asserted Walker, before his death, had saved the lives of sixty prisoners at Huamantla who the former believed might have otherwise received no quarter. Claiborne to Andrews, November 18, 1847, Walker Papers, TSLAC.

Speaking at Walker's interment ceremony in 1856, James C. Wilson cited other two phrases Walker may have uttered: "I am dying boys, you can do nothing for me now; I'll never see Texas again. Carry me back to San Antonio, and bury me with Ad Gillespie" and "I am gone boys. Never surrender! Never surrender! Hand me my six-shooter!" Wilson, *Address*, 8.

79. Lane to Adjutant General, October 18, 1847, *Annual Report of the Secretary of War, 1847*, 479.
80. *Niles' National Register* 73 (November 20, 1847): 192, 206; Brackett, *General Lane's Brigade*, 94, 96–97; "Reminiscences of the War with Mexico," 15; Wynkoop, ed., *Anecdotes and Incidents, 65–66; Daily Picayune*, November 30, December 11, 15, 21, 1847; Frank Brown, "Annals of Travis County and of the City of Austin: From the Earliest Times to the Close of 1875," Ch. 13: 13; *Texas Democrat*, January 12, 1848; Wilson, *Address*, 16. See also Mike Cox, *Texas Ranger Tales: Stories That Need Telling* (Plano: Republic of Texas Press, 1997), 12–16.
81. Hans Peter Nielson Gammel, comp., *The Laws of Texas, 1822–1897* (Austin: The Gammel Book Company, 1898), 5: 753. See also Paul E. Sturdevant, "Robert John Walker and Texas Annexation: A Lost Champion," *Southwestern Historical Quarterly* 109 (October 2005): 189–202.

Notes for Chapter 6

1. Richard B. McCaslin, *Fighting Stock: John S. "Rip" Ford of Texas* (Fort Worth: Texas Christian University Press, 2011), 1, 3; John Salmon Ford, *Rip Ford's Texas*, ed. Stephen B. Oates (Austin: University of Texas Press, 1998), xviii, 5, 8–9; Catherine Robertson Sheils, "Salmon Family," *"Kith and Kin" Genealogical Bulletin* 2 (January 1973): 44;

Third U.S. Census, Greenville District, South Carolina; Plats and Surveys, Series 3, Book 32, RG 50, Tennessee State Library and Archives, 291; Surveyor's Entry Book, Series 2, Book 3, ibid., 553; Middle Tennessee Land Grants, Book 5, ibid., 894; Middle Tennessee Land Grants, Book 14, ibid., 240, 270; Helen Crawford Marsh and Timothy Richard Marsh, comps., *Lincoln County, Tennessee Tax List, 1829–1832* (Shelbyville, TN: Marsh Historical Publications, 1981), 32; *Fourth U.S. Census*, Lincoln County, Tennessee; Charles L. Martin, "The Last of the Ranger Chieftains," *The Texas Magazine* 6 (January 1898): 34–35; Captain John A. Barksdale, comp., *Barksdale Family History and Genealogy (with Collateral Lines)* (Richmond, VA: William Byrd Press, 1940), 270. Harriet died in Tennessee in 1845, while William died in Travis County, Texas, on October 15, 1866. Ford, *Rip Ford's Texas*, 8–9; Frank Brown, "Annals of Travis County and of the City of Austin: From the Earliest Times to the Close of 1875," Ch. 13: 40; *Southern Intelligencer*, October 25, 1866.

2. McCaslin, *Fighting Stock*, 4; Ford, *Rip Ford's Texas*, xviii; *Find A Grave*, s.v. "Fannie Ford Thomas"; George Henry Davis, *Genealogy of Thomas Davis (1782–1846) and His Descendants* (New York: Scarborough Press, 1949), Appendix A. The Davis genealogical record was transcribed from the inner pages of Thomas Davis's family Bible. *Seventh U.S. Census*, Rutherford and Lincoln Counties, Tennessee. Genealogist Carolyn Bausinger was responsible for recognizing Mary Thomas Davis's identity and making the appropriate connections to Ford.
3. McCaslin, *Fighting Stock*, 4–6; Ford, *Rip Ford's Texas*, xviii, 9–10, 25, 27; Martin, "The Last of the Ranger Chieftains," 35; Colonel John M. Swisher, *The Swisher Memoirs*, ed. Rena Maverick Green (San Antonio: The Sigmund Press, 1932), 56; *Telegraph and Texas Register*, December 16, 1837.
4. Dianna Everett, *The Texas Cherokees: A People Between Two Fires, 1819–1840* (Norman: University of Oklahoma Press, 1995), 90–91; Córdova to Flores, July 19, 1838, Dorman H. Winfrey and James M. Day, eds., *The Indian Papers of Texas and the Southwest* (Austin: Texas State Historical Association, 1995), 1: 15–16, 36. Hereafter cited as *Texas Indian Papers*. Gerald E. Poyo, ed., *Tejano Journey, 1770–1850* (Austin: University of Texas Press, 1996), 96–98, 99–100; James T. DeShields, *Border Wars of Texas* (Austin: State House Press, 1993), 245, 246, 270–271; James L. Haley, *Passionate Nation: The Epic History of*

Texas (New York: Free Press, 2006), 224; Dorman H. Winfrey, "Chief Bowles of the Texas Cherokee," *Chronicles of Oklahoma* 32 (Spring 1954): 36. For Brigadier-General Valentín Canalizo's instructions to Córdova, see Canalizo to Córdova, February 27, 1838, *Encroachment of the Indians of the United States upon the territories of Mexico*, Senate Executive Document No. 14, 32nd Congress, 2nd Session, 33–34.

5. Ford, *Rip Ford's Texas*, 34–35; *Telegraph and Texas Register*, September 29, 1838; Muster and Pay Rolls, Henry W. Augustine, 401–717, TSLAC; John S. Ford, Unnumbered Audited Claim, Reel 128, Frame 147, TSLAC; John Henry Brown, *Indian Wars and Pioneers of Texas* (Austin: State House Press, 1988), 63; Mary Whatley Clarke, *Thomas J. Rusk: Soldier, Statesman, Jurist* (Austin: Jenkins Publishing Company, 1971), 110–111; Gerald Swetnam Pierce, "The Army of the Texas Republic, 1836–1845" (Ph.D. dissertation, University of Mississippi, 1963), 134.
6. McCaslin, *Fighting Stock*, 7; Ford, *Rip Ford's Texas*, 35–37; Everett, *The Texas Cherokees*, 94–95; Gerald S. Pierce, *Texas Under Arms: The Camps, Forts, and Military Towns of the Republic of Texas, 1836–1846* (Austin: Encino Press, 1969), 86; Poyo, ed., *Tejano Journey*, 101; Jimmy L. Bryan, Jr., *More Zeal Than Discretion: The Westward Adventures of Walter P. Lane* (College Station: Texas A&M University Press, 2008), 35; Clarke, *Thomas J. Rusk, 112–113;* Winfrey, "Chief Bowles of the Texas Cherokee," 36; Muster and Pay Rolls, Henry W. Augustine, 401–717, TSLAC.
7. Treaty, September 2, 1838, Winfrey and Day, eds., *Texas Indian Papers*, 1: 53; Annual Report of the Secretary of War, November 1839, *Journals of the Fourth Congress of the Republic of Texas*, ed. Harriet Smither, 3: 77; Everett, *The Texas Cherokees*, 96, 103–104; Albert Woldert, "The Last of the Cherokees in Texas, and the Life and Death of Chief Bowles," *Chronicles of Oklahoma* 1 (June 1923): 202–203; Message to the Senate and House of Representatives, December 20, 1838, *Journal of the House of Representatives of the Republic of Texas, Regular Session of the Third Congress*, 174; Lamar to Bowles, May 26, 1839, Charles Adams Gulick, et al., eds., *The Papers of Mirabeau Bounaparte Lamar* (Austin: A. C. Baldwin & Sons, 1922–1927), 2: 590–594. Reprinted in *Telegraph and Texas Register*, July 10, 1839. DeShields, *Border Wars of Texas*, 224. See also John Boyd Trollinger, "The Indian Policy of Mirabeau B. Lamar, President of the Republic of Texas, 1838–1841" (M.A. thesis, Texas Tech University, 1996),

28–34; and Stephen L. Moore, *Last Stand of the Texas Cherokees: Chief Bowles and the 1839 Cherokee War in Texas* (Garland, TX: RAM Books, 2009).

8. Lamar to Burnet, June 27, 1839, Douglass to Johnston, July 16, 1839, Winfrey and Day, eds., *Texas Indian Papers*, 1: 67–70, 76–77; Annual Report of the Secretary of War, November 1839, *Journals of the Fourth Congress*, 3: 78; Everett, *The Texas Cherokees*, 104–107; Charles P. Roland, *Albert Sidney Johnston: Soldier of Three Republics* (Lexington: University Press of Kentucky, 2001), 92; Clarke, *Thomas J. Rusk*, 128–132; Stanley Siegel, *A Political History of the Texas Republic, 1836–1845* (Austin: University of Texas Press, 1956), 108–109; Pierce, *Texas Under Arms*, 79–80; *Telegraph and Texas Register*, July 24, August 7, 14, 1839; Brown, *Indian Wars*, 67; "Trouble with the Cherokee Tribe," *Frontier Times* 1 (January 1924): 10.
9. McCaslin, *Fighting Stock*, 7; Ford, *Rip Ford's Texas*, 29–30; Muster and Pay Rolls, William Kimbro, 401–719, TSLAC; Douglass to Johnston, n.d., *Journals of the Fourth Congress*, 3: 106; *Telegraph and Texas Register*, July 31, August 7, 1839; DeShields, *Border Wars of Texas*, 277; John Wesley Wilbarger, *Indian Depredations in Texas* (Austin: State House Press, 1985), 171–172; A. J. Sowell, *Rangers and Pioneers of Texas* (Austin: State House Press, 1991), 52; John H. Reagan, "The Expulsion of the Cherokees from East Texas," *The Quarterly of the Texas State Historical Association* 1 (July 1897): 45–46. See also Anna Muckleroy, "The Indian Policy of the Republic of Texas," Ch. 5, *Southwestern Historical Quarterly* 26 (October 1922): 147.
10. McCaslin, *Fighting Stock*, 8–9; Ford, *Rip Ford's Texas*, xix, 19; Muster and Pay Rolls, William Kimbro, 401–719, TSLAC; *Red-Lander*, September 9, 1841, May 19, 26, July 7, 1842, October 7, 1843.
11. McCaslin, *Fighting Stock*, 10; Ford, *Rip Ford's Texas*, 32; Ralph Widener, "John S. 'Rip' Ford, Colonel, C.S.A.," *The United Daughters of the Confederacy Magazine* 47 (May 1984): 19; *Journals of the House of Representatives of the Ninth Congress of the Republic of Texas*, 3–4, 6, 17, 18, 26, 40–41, 85–86, 93–97, 181–183, 378, 385–387; Ernest R. Lindley, comp., and Elizabeth LeNoir Jennett, ed., *Biographical Directory of the Texan Conventions and Congresses, 1832–1845* (Austin: Book Exchange, 1941), 39, 84–85; *Texas National Register*, December 7, 14, 28, 1844, January 4, 11, 25, March 22, 1845.

12. McCaslin, *Fighting Stock*, 11–12; Ford, *Rip Ford's Texas*, xx, 49, 50–51; Steven E. Woodworth, *Manifest Destinies: America's Westward Expansion and the Road to the Civil War* (New York: Vintage Books, 2010), 141; Siegel, *Political History of the Texas Republic*, 245, 253; *Texas National Register*, June 19, 1845; James P. Bevill, *The Paper Republic: The Struggle for Money, Credit, and Independence in the Republic of Texas* (Houston, TX: Bright Sky Press, 2009), 289; *Journals of the House, Extra Session, Ninth Congress*, 5, 41, 48, 50–51; John S. Ford, Audited Claim No. 2483, Reel 32, Frame 291. For a thorough examination of Texas's path to statehood, and the resulting growth of sectionalism, see Joel H. Silbey, *Storm Over Texas: The Annexation Controversy and the Road to Civil War* (New York: Oxford University Press, 2005).
13. McCaslin, *Fighting Stock*, 12; Ford, *Rip Ford's Texas*, xx; Randolph B. Campbell, *Gone to Texas: A History of the Lone Star State* (New York: Oxford University Press, 2003), 186; *Texas National Register*, July 24, October 2, 1845.
14. McCaslin, *Fighting Stock*, 12–13; Ford, *Rip Ford's Texas*, xx, xxi, 54–55; Brown, "Annals of Travis County," Ch. 11: 44–45; *Texas National Register*, January 3, 1846; *Texas Democrat*, January 21, March 7, April 15, May 6, 1846; Francis R. Lubbock, *Six Decades in Texas, or Memoirs of Francis Richard Lubbock: Governor of Texas in War-Time, 1861–63*, ed. C. W. Raines (Austin: Ben C. Jones & Co., 1900), 185. On March 20, 1848, a joint resolution authorized the appropriation of $359.89 to Ford and Cronican for their services as public printers. Hans Peter Nielson Gammel, comp., *The Laws of Texas, 1822–1897* (Austin: The Gammel Book Company, 1898), 3: 421–422.
15. McCaslin, *Fighting Stock*, 15; Ford, *Rip Ford's Texas*, xxi–xxii; *Texas Democrat*, May 27, June 10, August 26, 1846. Louisa's headstone is engraved with a death date of August 5, 1846, but her obituary, written by her husband, gives the date as August 21. *Find A Grave*, s.v. "Louisa Ford."
16. McCaslin, *Fighting Stock*, 15–16; Ford, *Rip Ford's Texas*, 60, xxii; *Texas Democrat*, December 9, 1846, July 24, 1847; Compiled Service Records of Volunteer Soldiers, First Texas Mounted Volunteers, John S. Ford.
17. McCaslin, *Fighting Stock*, 16; Ford, *Rip Ford's Texas*, 61–62; Henderson to Marcy, August 22, 1847, Winfrey and Day, eds., *Texas Indian Papers*, 5: 32–33; *American Flag*, September 22, 1847.

18. McCaslin, *Fighting Stock*, 16; Ford, *Rip Ford's Texas*, 65–66; *American Flag*, September 8, 11, 1847; John S. Ford, "John C. Hayes in Texas," Box 2Q512, John Salmon Ford Papers, BCAH, 62–63; *Daily Picayune*, October 29, 1847. Robert Selph Henry theorized Zenobia was actually Padre Celedonio Dómeco de Jarauta. The confusion was allegedly because the guerrilla's "operations were so active and so wide-spread that he appears in most of the contemporary American accounts as two persons." *The Story of the Mexican War* (New York: Da Capo Press, 1989), 373.
19. McCaslin, *Fighting Stock*, 17; Ford, *Rip Ford's Texas*, 67; Ford, "John C. Hayes in Texas," 63; *Daily Picayune*, October 29, 1847.
20. McCaslin, *Fighting Stock*, 17; Ford, *Rip Ford's Texas*, 67; Ford, "John C. Hayes in Texas," 64; *Civilian and Galveston Gazette*, November 6, 1847.
21. McCaslin, *Fighting Stock*, 17; Ford, *Rip Ford's Texas*, 68; Ford, "John C. Hayes in Texas," 64–65; *Democratic Telegraph and Texas Register*, November 4, 11, 1847.
22. McCaslin, *Fighting Stock*, 17; Ford, *Rip Ford's Texas*, 72–73; Martin, "The Last of the Ranger Chieftains," 36. Following the war, the murderous Glanton would acquire a notorious and bloody reputation in Chihuahua as a scalp hunter. Dan L. Thrapp, *Encyclopedia of Frontier Biography* (Lincoln: University of Nebraska Press, 1991), 2: 564.
23. Ford, *Rip Ford's Texas*, 76; William J. Hughes, *Rebellious Ranger: Rip Ford and the Old Southwest* (Norman: University of Oklahoma Press, 1964), 30.
24. Ford, *Rip Ford's Texas*, xxiii; Walter Prescott Webb, *The Texas Rangers: A Century of Frontier Defense* (Austin: University of Texas Press, 1965), 124 n65; Mike Cox, *Texas Ranger Tales II* (Plano: Republic of Texas Press, 1999), 43; James L. Haley, *Passionate Nation: The Epic History of Texas* (New York: Free Press, 2006), 267. Cowen, Fannie's grandson, contributed to the portions of Walter Webb's *Texas Rangers* concerning Colonel Ford's career. See also *Brownsville Herald*, November 8, 1902, January 12, 1958, January 9, 1964.
25. McCaslin, *Fighting Stock*, xv–xvi, 37; Robert M. Utley, *Lone Star Justice: The First Century of the Texas Rangers* (New York: Berkley Books, 2002), 318 n6; Martin, "Last of the Ranger Chieftains," 40; Tom Lea, *The King Ranch* (Boston: Little, Brown and Company, 1957), 1: 164; *Texas Democrat*, November 4, 1846.

26. McCaslin, *Fighting Stock*, 24; Ford, *Rip Ford's Texas*, xxiii, 75–77; *Democratic Telegraph and Texas Register*, November 4, 1847; Stephen B. Oates, "Los Diablos Tejanos," *The American West* 2 (Summer 1965): 46; J. Jacob Oswandel, *Notes of the Mexican War, 1846–47–48* (Philadelphia: n.p., 1885), 382.
27. Hughes, *Rebellious Ranger*, 33–34; Oswandel, *Notes of the Mexican War*, 397–398.
28. Ford, *Rip Ford's Texas*, xxiii, 81–82; Hughes, *Rebellious Ranger*, 37–38; Oswandel, *Notes of the Mexican War*, 401; *Daily Picayune*, December 29, 1847; Ethan Allen Hitchcock, *Fifty Years in Camp and Field: Diary of Major-General Ethan Allen Hitchcock, U.S.A.*, ed. William Augustus Croffut (New York: G. P. Putnam's Sons, 1909), 310.
29. Ford, *Rip Ford's Texas*, 81–82; Hughes, *Rebellious Ranger*, 38–39; Harold J. Weiss, Jr., "The Bloody Texans in the Mexican War: The Reasons Why," *The Westerners Brand Book, New York Posse* 16 (1969): 3; Mark E. Nackman, "The Making of the Texan Citizen Solider, 1835–1860," *Southwestern Historical Quarterly* 78 (January 1975): 243.
30. McCaslin, *Fighting Stock*, 19–20; Ford, *Rip Ford's Texas*, 82–90; Frederic Remington, "How the Law Got into the Chaparral," *Crooked Trails* (New York: Harper and Brothers, 1898), 5–6.
31. McCaslin, *Fighting Stock*, 20–22; Ford, *Rip Ford's Texas*, 91–92; Irving W. Levinson, *Wars within War: Mexican Guerrillas, Domestic Elites, and the United States of America, 1846–1848* (Fort Worth: Texas Christian University Press, 2005), 88, 89, 99.
32. McCaslin, *Fighting Stock*, 22; Ford, *Rip Ford's Texas*, 91–95; Truit to Ford, March 2, 1848, *Annual Report of the Secretary of War*, House Executive Document No. 1, 30th Congress, 2nd Session, 102. Hereafter cited as *Annual Report of the Secretary of War, 1848*. Reprinted in *Civilian and Galveston Gazette*, April 28, 1848.
33. McCaslin, *Fighting Stock*, 22; Ford, *Rip Ford's Texas*, 94–95; Truit to Ford, March 2, 1848, *Annual Report of the Secretary of War, 1848*, 102–103.
34. Hughes, *Rebellious Ranger*, 50–51; Oswandel, *Notes of the Mexican War*, 508.
35. McCaslin, *Fighting Stock*, 23; Ford, *Rip Ford's Texas*, 99, 102, 103–104; Oates, "Los Diablos Tejanos," 49; Utley, *Lone Star Justice*, 85–86; John R. Kenly, *Memoirs of a Maryland Volunteer: War with

Mexico, in the Years 1846–7–8 (Philadelphia: J. P. Lippincott & Co., 1873), 397.

36. McCaslin, *Fighting Stock*, 23; Ford, *Rip Ford's Texas*, xxiii, 106–107; *Democratic Telegraph and Texas Register*, May 25, 1848; Oates, "Los Diablos Tejanos," 49; Compiled Service Records of Volunteer Soldiers, First Texas Mounted Volunteers, John S. Ford. Historians have had to rely a great deal on the personal accounts of rangers in the Mexican War that were written years after the fact. As adjutant, Ford would have amassed a treasure trove of contemporaneous information, but his wartime letters to the *Texas Democrat*, intended for publication, were instead thrown away, and the regimental papers were accidentally left aboard the *Maria Burt*. McCaslin, *Fighting Stock*, 24.
37. McCaslin, *Fighting Stock*, 24–25; Ford, *Rip Ford's Texas*, xxiii, xxiv, 108–109, 113; Brown, "Annals of Travis County," Ch. 11: 44; *Texas Democrat*, February 24, 1849; *Corpus Christi Star*, December 5, 23, 30, 1848, January 20, 1849; Howard R. Lamar, *Texas Crossings: The Lone Star State and the American Far West, 1836–1986* (Austin: University of Texas Press, 1991), 6; Joseph Carroll McConnell, *The West Texas Frontier: or, A Descriptive History of Early Times in Western Texas* (Jacksboro, TX: Gazette Print, 1933), 1: 54–56.
38. McCaslin, *Fighting Stock*, 25–26; Ford, *Rip Ford's Texas*, xxiv–xxv, 113–114; Kenneth F. Neighbours, "The Expedition of Major Robert S. Neighbors to El Paso in 1849," *Southwestern Historical Quarterly* 58 (July 1954): 36, 37, 38; A. B. Bender, "Opening Routes across West Texas, 1848–1850," *Southwestern Historical Quarterly* 37 (October 1933): 119–120; Thomas W. Kavanagh, *Comanche Political History: An Ethnohistorical Perspective, 1706–1875* (Lincoln: University of Nebraska Press, 1996), 324.
39. McCaslin, *Fighting Stock*, 26–29; Ford, *Rip Ford's Texas*, 122; *Texas Democrat*, June 16, 23, 1849; Neighbours, "Expedition of Major Robert S. Neighbors," 49, 52; Robert S. Neighbors, "The Report of the Expedition of Major Robert S. Neighbors to El Paso in 1849," ed. Kenneth F. Neighbours, *Southwestern Historical Quarterly* 60 (April 1957): 529; W. H. Timmons, *El Paso: A Borderlands History* (El Paso: Texas Western Press, 1990), 137; Stephen B. Oates, *Visions of Glory: Texans on the Southwestern Frontier* (Norman: University of Oklahoma Press, 1970), 62–63; Bender, "Opening Routes across West Texas," 120; *Corpus Christi Star*, June 16, 1849.

40. McCaslin, *Fighting Stock*, 29–30; Ford, *Rip Ford's Texas*, xxv, 129; *Texas Democrat*, June 16, 23, 1849; Neighbors, "Report of the Expedition of Major Robert S. Neighbors," 532. See also C. L. Greenwood, "Opening Routes to El Paso, 1849," *Southwestern Historical Quarterly* 48 (October 1944): 262–268.

    Later in the year, Lieutenant Francis Theodore Bryan of the Topographical Engineers was ordered to confirm the practicality of the route Ford and Neighbors had used on their return trip. Report of Lieutenant Francis T. Bryan, October 3, 1849, *Reconnaissance of Routes from San Antonio to El Paso*, Senate Executive Document No. 64, 31st Congress, 1st Session, 13–24. The "Upper" or "Emigrant" road blazed by Ford and Neighbors continued as the major southern overland trail to California for two decades until the arrival of the railroad. Neighbours, "Expedition of Major Robert S. Neighbors," 57, 58; *Texas Democrat*, August 4, 1849. See also Mabelle Eppard Martin, "California Emigrant Roads through Texas," *Southwestern Historical Quarterly* 28 (April 1925): 287–301.
41. McCaslin, *Fighting Stock*, 30–31; Ford, *Rip Ford's Texas*, xxvi; *Texas Democrat*, July 7, 21, 1849.
42. Crawford to Brooke, June 4, 1849, Brooke to Jones, July 14, 1849, *Annual Report of the Secretary of War*, Senate Executive Document No. 1, 31st Congress, 1st Session, 138–140. Hereafter cited as *Annual Report of the Secretary of War, 1849. Texas State Gazette*, October 27, 1849. See also Lena Clara Koch, "The Federal Indian Policy in Texas, 1845–1860," Ch. 3, *Southwestern Historical Quarterly* 29 (July 1925): 19–35.
43. Francis Paul Prucha, *The Great Father: The United States and the American Indians* (Lincoln: University of Nebraska Press, 1995), 355–357; Pekka Hämäläinen, *The Comanche Empire* (New Haven: Yale University Press, 2008), 296–301, 306; Kavanagh, *Comanche Political History*, 331. See also George D. Harmon, "The United States Indian Policy in Texas," *The Mississippi Valley Historical Review* 17 (December 1930): 381; and J. Fred Rippy, "The Indians of the Southwest in the Diplomacy of the United States and Mexico, 1848–1853," *Hispanic American Historical Review* 2 (August 1919): 363–396. For more on the Indian menace in Mexico's northern borderlands, see Brian DeLay, *War of a Thousand Deserts: Indian Raids and the U.S.-Mexican War* (New Haven: Yale University Press, 2008).

44. Wood to Gentleman of the Senate, November 30, 1849, 301–18, TSLAC; Ben C. Stuart, "Texas Indian Fighters and Frontier Rangers" (MS, 1916), TSLAC, 52; Oscar J. Martínez, *Troublesome Border* (Tucson: University of Arizona Press, 2006), 19, 20, 51, 54, 57; Michael L. Collins, *Texas Devils: Rangers and Regulars on the Lower Rio Grande, 1846–1861* (Norman: University of Oklahoma Press, 2008), 38.
45. J. Fred Rippy, "Border Troubles Along the Rio Grande, 1848–1860," *Southwestern Historical Quarterly* 23 (October 1919): 92, 93; Collins, *Texas Devils*, 239, 53–56; John A. Adams, Jr., *Conflict and Commerce on the Rio Grande: Laredo, 1755–1955* (College Station: Texas A&M University Press, 2008), 79–81; Mary Margaret McAllen Amberson, et al., *I Would Rather Sleep in Texas: A History of the Lower Rio Grande Valley and the People of the Santa Anita Land Grant* (Austin: Texas State Historical Association, 2003), 119.
46. Brooke to Wood, July 11, 1849, 301–18, TSLAC; Brooke to Adjutant General, August 31, 1849, *Annual Report of the Secretary of War, 1849*, 143; *Democratic Telegraph and Texas Register*, November 16, 1848. Captain Jacob Roberts was mustered into state service for twelve months on October 20, 1848, and took station on the Rio Blanco; Henry McCulloch, on October 25, 1848, at Hamilton's Valley; James S. Sutton, on October 27, 1849, near Corpus Christi; Ben F. Hill, on October 27, 1848, on the Medina; Shapley P. Ross, on November 19, 1848, at Bosque Station; Charles Blackwell, on June 10, 1849, near Corpus Christi; and Isaac W. Johnson, on July 7, 1849, on the San Antonio River. Gammel, comp., *Laws of Texas*, 3: 465–468. Reprinted in *Texas State Gazette*, March 2, 1850. Report of the Adjutant General, November 1, 1849, *Journals of the Senate of the State of Texas, Third Session*, 62.
47. Deas to Wood, August 9, 1849, 301–18, TSLAC; Brooke to Wood and Order No. 53, both dated August 11, 1849, Winfrey and Day, eds., *Texas Indian Papers*, 5: 43–46; Brooke to Wood and Orders No. 57, both dated August 19, 1849, 301–18, TSLAC; *Democratic Telegraph and Texas Register*, August 30, 1849.
48. McCaslin, *Fighting Stock*, 35; Ford, *Rip Ford's Texas*, xxvii, 142; Frederick Law Olmsted, *A Journey Through Texas, or A Saddle-Trip on the Southwestern Frontier* (New York: Dix, Edwards & Co., 1857), 300; Report of the Adjutant General, November 1, 1849, *Journals of*

the Senate, Third Session, 63; *Texas Democrat*, August 18, 25, 1849. The *Texas State Gazette* for August 25 and *Corpus Christi Star* for September 1 named the three company commanders as Ford, Grumbles, and Henry Smock. Brown also mentions the latter individual as a captain. "Annals of Travis County," Ch. 13: 61. In the end, Smock did not receive the commission and served instead as the second lieutenant of McCown's company. *Democratic Telegraph and Texas Register*, September 27, 1849; *Texas State Gazette*, September 15, 1849.

49. McCaslin, *Fighting Stock*, 35; Ford, *Rip Ford's Texas*, 143–144, 147; Oates, *Visions of Glory*, 68, 70; Collins, *Texas Devils*, 42.
50. Brooke to Bell, January 30, 1850, 301–19, TSLAC.
51. Ford, *Rip Ford's Texas*, 149; Ranger Service Records, John S. Ford, 401–29, TSLAC; Carded Records Showing Military Service of Soldiers Who Fought in Volunteer Organizations During the Indian Wars, *1817–1858*, Texas Mounted Volunteers, John S. Ford. Hereafter cited as Carded Records … Indian Wars.
52. McCaslin, *Fighting Stock*, 38; Ford, *Rip Ford's Texas*, 150; Petition from the Citizens of Rio Grande to P. H. Bell [1850], Winfrey and Day, eds., *Texas Indian Papers*, 3: 138; Brooke to Bell, March 6, 1850, *Annual Report of the Secretary of War*, Senate Executive Document No. 1, Pt. 10, 31st Congress, 2nd Session, 27. Hereafter cited as *Annual Report of the Secretary of War, 1850.*
53. Ford, *Rip Ford's Texas*, 145; Hughes, *Rebellious Ranger*, 80; Oates, *Visions of Glory*, 70; Utley, *Lone Star Justice*, 91, 93.
54. McCaslin, *Fighting Stock*, 38–39; Ford, *Rip Ford's Texas*, 150–153; Ford to Deas, May 21, 1850, *Annual Report of the Secretary of War, 1850*, 36–38. Reprinted in *Democratic Telegraph and Texas Register*, June 13, 1850. Oates, *Visions of Glory*, 74–76; Collins, *Texas Devils*, 43; *Nueces Valley*, May 25, 1850.
55. McCaslin, *Fighting Stock*, 39; Ford, *Rip Ford's Texas*, 155–156; Oates, *Visions of Glory*, 77.
56. McCaslin, *Fighting Stock*, 39; Ford, *Rip Ford's Texas*, 156–158; Oates, *Visions of Glory*, 77–78.
57. McCaslin, *Fighting Stock*, 39–40, 37; Ford, *Rip Ford's Texas*, 158–160; Ford to Deas, May 30, 1850, *Annual Report of the Secretary of War, 1850*, 41; Collins, *Texas Devils*, 42–43.
58. McCaslin, *Fighting Stock*, 40; Ford, *Rip Ford's Texas*, 160; Ford to Deas, May 30, 1850, *Annual Report of the Secretary of War, 1850*, 41; Kavanagh, *Comanche Political History*, 335; Andrew Jackson Sowell,

Texas Indian Fighters: Early Settlers and Indian Fighters of Southwest Texas (Austin: State House Press, 1986), 820–821.

59. Ford, *Rip Ford's Texas*, 161; Ford to Deas, May 30, 1850, *Annual Report of the Secretary of War, 1850*, 41; *Texas State Gazette*, December 12, 1857; Oates, *Visions of Glory*, 79.
60. McCaslin, *Fighting Stock*, 41; Ford, *Rip Ford's Texas*, 162–163; Walker to Ford, June 19, 1850, *Annual Report of the Secretary of War, 1850*, 47–48; *Texas State Gazette*, December 12, 1857.
61. McCaslin, *Fighting Stock*, 42; Ford, *Rip Ford's Texas*, 167–168; *Texas State Gazette*, December 12, 1857.
62. McCaslin, *Fighting Stock*, 42; Ford, *Rip Ford's Texas*, 169, 170, 174; Carded Records … Indian Wars, Texas Mounted Volunteers, John S. Ford; Ranger Service Records, John S. Ford, 401–29, TSLAC; *Texas State Gazette*, December 12, 1857.
63. McCaslin, *Fighting Stock*, 43; Ford, *Rip Ford's Texas*, 174–177; Sowell, *Texas Indian Fighters*, 399, 822–824; *San Antonio Ledger*, February 6, 1851; *Democratic Telegraph and Texas Register*, February 21, 1851; *Northern Standard*, March 15, 1851.
64. McCaslin, *Fighting Stock*, 43; Ford, *Rip Ford's Texas*, 173–175, 177–179; Collins, *Texas Devils*, 53; Remington, "How the Law Got into the Chaparral," 6–8; Stuart, "Texas Indian Fighters and Frontier Rangers," 56–57; *Western Texan*, February 6, 1851; *Texas State Gazette*, December 12, 1857; John Henry Brown, *History of Texas, from 1685 to 1892* (St. Louis, MO: L. E. Daniell, 1893), 2: 359–361. See also "Rangers' Desperate Battle with Indians," *Frontier Times* 13 (February 1936): 270–272.
65. McCaslin, *Fighting Stock*, 44; Ford, *Rip Ford's Texas*, 185–187; Carded Records … Indian Wars, Texas Mounted Volunteers, John S. Ford; Ranger Service Records, John S. Ford, 401–29, TSLAC; Joseph B. Wilkinson, *Laredo and the Rio Grande Frontier: A Narrative* (Austin: Jenkins Publishing Co., 1975), 260; *Texas State Gazette*, April 19, 1851. The amount required to pay the members of Ford's company for services from September 24, 1850, to March 23, 1851, was estimated to be $14,956. *Additional Estimate*, House Executive Document No. 31, 32nd Congress, 1st Session, 2. The rangers would not receive their wages until after the first of September, 1852. *Texas State Gazette*, September 1, 1852.
66. McCaslin, *Fighting Stock*, 44–45; Ford, *Rip Ford's Texas*, xxvii, 195–196; Joseph E. Chance, *José María de Jesús Carvajal: The Life and Times of*

a Mexican Revolutionary (San Antonio: Trinity University Press, 2006), 104–105; Joseph A. Stout, Jr., *Schemers and Dreamers: Filibustering in Mexico, 1848–1921* (Fort Worth: Texas Christian University Press, 2002), 17–19; Amberson, et al., *I Would Rather Sleep in Texas*, 116, 135–136; *Reports of the Committee of Investigation Sent in 1873 by the Mexican Government to the Frontier of Texas* (New York: Baker & Goodwin, 1875), 189. Hereafter cited as *Reports of the Committee of Investigation*. Ernest C. Shearer, "The Carvajal Disturbances," *Southwestern Historical Quarterly* 55 (October 1951): 208; Brown, "Annals of Travis County," Ch. 15: 19.

67. McCaslin, *Fighting Stock*, 46; Ford, *Rip Ford's Texas*, 196–197; *Reports of the Committee of Investigation*, 188, 189; Shearer, "Carvajal Disturbances," 209; *San Antonio Ledger*, October 23, 1851; *Texas State Gazette*, October 4, 1851; Amberson, et al., *I Would Rather Sleep in Texas*, 136.
68. McCaslin, *Fighting Stock*, 46; Ford, *Rip Ford's Texas*, 197–199; *Reports of the Committee of Investigation*, 189; *Daily Picayune*, November 3, 18, 19, December 6, 1851; Stout, *Schemers and Dreamers*, 20–21; Shearer, "Carvajal Disturbances," 213; *Western Texan*, November 20, 1851; Milo Kearney and Anthony Knopp, *Boom and Bust: The Historical Cycles of Matamoros and Brownsville* (Austin: Eakin Press, 1991), 95–96. The Texans commanding companies in Ford's assault force were Andy Walker, Joseph Davis Howell, — Edmunson, Edward R. Hord, and — Shilling. *Telegraph and Texas Register*, November 28, 1851.
69. McCaslin, *Fighting Stock*, 46–47; Ford, *Rip Ford's Texas*, 200; Chance, *José María de Jesús Carvajal*, 117; Kearney and Knopp, *Boom and Bust*, 96; *Western Texan*, November 20, 1851; *Daily Picayune*, November 19, 1851.
70. McCaslin, *Fighting Stock*, 47–48; Ford, *Rip Ford's Texas*, 201, 203–204; *Daily Picayune*, November 19, December 6, 1851, January 3, 1852; Stout, *Schemers and Dreamers*, 21; Hubert Howe Bancroft, *History of Mexico* (San Francisco: A. L. Bancroft & Company, 1885), 5: 604; *Reports of the Committee of Investigation*, 189; Shearer, "Carvajal Disturbances," 221.
71. McCaslin, *Fighting Stock*, 48–49; Ford, *Rip Ford's Texas*, xxvii–xxviii, 206–207; John H. Jenkins and Kenneth Kesselus, *Edward Burleson: Texas Frontier Leader* (Austin: Jenkins Publishing Company, 1990), 384; *Texas State Gazette*, December 27, 1851, January 17, 1852; *Daily Picayune*, February 13, 20, 1852; Brown, "Annals of Travis County," Ch. 15: 31.

72. McCaslin, *Fighting Stock*, 49–50; Ford, *Rip Ford's Texas*, 204–205; *San Antonio Ledger*, May 27, 1852; Chance, *José María de Jesús Carvajal*, 125–127, 141–144; Kearney and Knopp, *Boom and Bust*, 96–97; *Daily Picayune*, December 6, 19, 24, 26, 1851, January 3, March 8, 9, 1852; *Telegraph and Texas Register*, February 20, 1852; *Reports of the Committee of Investigation*, 190; Bancroft, *History of Mexico*, 5: 605.
73. McCaslin, *Fighting Stock*, 50–62; Ford, *Rip Ford's Texas*, xxviii, xxix–xxx, xxxi, xxxii, 207–208, 211, 214–215, 218; *South-Western American*, November 17, 1852, June 25, 1853; *Texas State Gazette*, November 13, 1852, June 25, 1853, May 16, 23, June 6, 1857; *Texas State Times*, January 7, 1854, February 24, March 17, April 28, May 19, June 2, 1855, March 1, 1856, April 4, 11, May 16, 23, 1857; Brown, "Annals of Travis County," Ch. 15: 42, 11: 46; Widener, "John S. 'Rip' Ford," 19.
74. McCaslin, *Fighting Stock*, 63; Ford, *Rip Ford's Texas*, 220–221; Hämäläinen, *The Comanche Empire*, 310; Nathan A. Jennings, *Riding for the Lone Star: Frontier Cavalry and the Texas Way of War, 1822–1865* (Denton: University of North Texas Press, 2016), 259; Gammel, comp., *Laws of Texas*, 4: 1137; *Congressional Globe*, 35th Congress, 1st Session, 1187, 1239, 1297, 1425, 1433, 1473–1474, 1507, 3042, 36th Congress, 1st Session, 936–944, 1060–1063, 1142–1144, 1146, 1193–1238, 1539, 1783–1813, 2309, 2383, Appendix, 240–244. In the event the Texas regiment had been called out, Governor Runnels had already decided on his choices for officers: Ford; Henry McCulloch, Guadalupe County; William G. Tobin, Bexar County; Edward A. Palmer, Harris County; E. R. Hord, Starr County; Allison Nelson, Bosque County; Alfred Truit, Shelby County; E. A. Carroll, Henderson County; James Harrison Rogers, Cass County; and Samuel Bogart, Collin County. *Texas State Gazette*, May 22, 1858; *Congressional Globe*, 35th Congress, 1st Session, 672.
75. McCaslin, *Fighting Stock*, 63–64; Ford, *Rip Ford's Texas*, xxxii, 223–224; Gammel, comp., *Laws of Texas*, 4: 949–950, 1138; Muster and Pay Rolls, John S. Ford, 401–724, TSLAC; *Texas State Gazette*, January 30, 1858; Runnels to Ford, January 28, 1858, Winfrey and Day, eds., *Texas Indian Papers*, 3: 272–273; Runnels to Twiggs, February 2, 1858, Twiggs to Runnels, February 7, 1858, *Protection of the Frontier of Texas*, House Executive Document No. 27, 35th Congress, 2nd Session, 14, 15–16.

76. McCaslin, *Fighting Stock*, 64; Ford, *Rip Ford's Texas*, 224–225; Muster and Pay Rolls, John S. Ford, 401–724, TSLAC; Commissions of Edward Burleson and William A. Pitts, both dated February 8, 1858, 401–1153, TSLAC; Runnels to Ford, March 10, 1858, 301–27, TSLAC.
77. McCaslin, *Fighting Stock*, 64–65; Ford, *Rip Ford's Texas*, 225–226; Ford to Runnels, February 27, 1858, 301–27, TSLAC; Ford to Runnels, March 11, 1858, Winfrey and Day, eds., *Texas Indian Papers*, 3: 276; Cox, *Texas Ranger Tales II*, 46; *Texas State Gazette*, May 22, 1858.
78. McCaslin, *Fighting Stock*, 67, 69, 71–72; Ford, *Rip Ford's Texas*, xxxii, 226–227, 229, 231, 241; Ford to Runnels, March 31, 1858, Winfrey and Day, eds., *Texas Indian Papers*, 3: 280; Ford to Runnels, April 7, 1858, April 26, 1858, 301–27, TSLAC.
79. McCaslin, *Fighting Stock*, 72; Ford, *Rip Ford's Texas*, 229–232; Ford to Runnels, May 22, 1858, Winfrey and Day, eds., *Texas Indian Papers*, 5: 233–234; F. Todd Smith, *From Dominance to Disappearance: The Indians of Texas and the Near Southwest, 1786–1859* (Lincoln: University of Nebraska Press, 2005), 229; *Texas State Gazette*, May 29, 1858.
80. McCaslin, *Fighting Stock*, 72–73; Ford, *Rip Ford's Texas*, xxxiii, 232–233; Ford to Runnels, May 22, 1858, Nelson to Ford, May 21, 1858, Winfrey and Day, eds., *Texas Indian Papers*, 5: 234–235, 231; *Southern Intelligencer*, June 2, 1858; Hämäläinen, *The Comanche Empire*, 310; Rupert Norval Richardson, *The Comanche Barrier to South Plains Settlement* (Glendale, CA: The Arthur H. Clark Company, 1933), 235; Utley, *Lone Star Justice*, 101; Mike Cox, *The Texas Rangers: Wearing the Cinco Peso, 1821–1900* (New York: Tom Doherty Associates, 2008), 399 n36. Declaring it "about the hardest fight I was ever in," Major Fred Kirk, a participant in the battle, claimed Bill Terry and Bob Green fired the shots that killed Iron Jacket. *Dallas Morning News*, April 12, 1897.
81. McCaslin, *Fighting Stock*, 73; Ford, *Rip Ford's Texas*, 234; Ford to Runnels, May 22, 1858, Nelson to Ford, May 21, 1858, Winfrey and Day, eds., *Texas Indian Papers*, 5: 235, 231–232; Utley, *Lone Star Justice*, 101; Brown, *History of Texas*, 2: 375; Ben C. Stuart, "The Battle of Antelope Hills," *Frontier Times* 3 (August 1926): 10. Reprinted from *Dallas Morning News*, January 17, 1905.
82. McCaslin, *Fighting Stock*, 73; Ford, *Rip Ford's Texas*, 234–236; Ford to Runnels, May 22, 1858, Nelson to Ford, May 21, 1858, Winfrey

and Day, eds., *Texas Indian Papers*, 5: 235–238, 232; *Galveston Daily News*, August 7, 1892; Cox, *Wearing the Cinco Peso*, 147; Brown, *History of Texas*, 2: 375–376; *Texas State Gazette*, May 29, 1858.

83. McCaslin, *Fighting Stock*, 73; Ford, *Rip Ford's Texas*, 236; Ford to Runnels, May 22, 1858, Winfrey and Day, eds., *Texas Indian Papers*, 5: 237–238; Richardson, *Comanche Barrier*, 235–236; *Galveston Daily News*, August 7, 1892; Kavanagh, *Comanche Political History*, 365; Utley, *Lone Star Justice*, 101; Cox, *Wearing the Cinco Peso*, 147–148.
84. McCaslin, *Fighting Stock*, 73; Ford, *Rip Ford's Texas*, 237; Ford to Runnels, May 22, 1858, Winfrey and Day, eds., *Texas Indian Papers*, 5: 233–238; *Southern Intelligencer*, June 2, 1858.
85. McCaslin, *Fighting Stock*, 75, 77–78; Ford, *Rip Ford's Texas*, xxxii, 238; Muster and Pay Rolls, John S. Ford, 401–724, TSLAC; Runnels to Ford, July 6, 1858, Winfrey and Day, eds., *Texas Indian Papers*, 3: 292; *Texas State Gazette*, August 7, 1858.
86. Robert Wooster, *The American Military Frontiers: The United States Army in the West, 1783–1900* (Albuquerque: University of New Mexico Press, 2009), 156–157; Bishop to Runnels, September 26, 1858, Citizens of Lampasas County to Runnels, September 28, 1858, Citizens of San Saba County, September 29, 1858, Palmer to Runnels, October 4, 1858, Winfrey and Day, eds., *Texas Indian Papers*, 5: 274–280, 283; William C. Holden, "Frontier Defense, 1846–1860," *West Texas Historical Association Yearbook* 6 (1930): 55; Prucha, *The Great Father*, 364; Hämäläinen, *The Comanche Empire*, 310, 311; George Klos, "'Our People Could Not Distinguish One Tribe from Another': The 1859 Expulsion of the Reserve Indians from Texas," *Southwestern Historical Quarterly* 97 (April 1994): 605; Runnels to Floyd, August 9, 1858, Letters Received by the Office of the Adjutant General, M567, RG 94, NARA. See also Clara Lena Koch, "The Federal Indian Policy in Texas," Ch. 4, *Southwestern Historical Quarterly* 29 (October 1925): 98–127.
87. McCaslin, *Fighting Stock*, 79; Ford, *Rip Ford's Texas*, xxxii, 242; Muster and Pay Rolls, John S. Ford, 401–793, TSLAC; Runnels to Ford, November 2, 1858, Winfrey and Day, eds., *Texas Indian Papers*, 3: 304; Commissions of Ford, November 2, 1858, and Gibbons, November 10, 1858, 401–1153, TSLAC; Runnels to Ford and Runnels to Gibbons, both dated November 10, 1858, *Letter from the Secretary of War*, Senate Executive Document No. 19, 45th Congress, 2nd Session, 134. Hereafter cited as *Letter from the Secretary of War,*

1860. Texas State Gazette, November 13, 27, 1858; T. R. Havins, *Camp Colorado: A Decade of Frontier Defense* (Brownwood, TX: Brown Press, 1964), 76; William C. Yancey, "In Justice to Our Indian Allies: The Government of Texas and Her Indian Allies, 1836–1867" (M.A. thesis, University of North Texas, 2008),113. Lieutenant Burleson was the son of Jacob Burleson, who fell at Brushy Creek in 1839, and a cousin of Ed Burleson, Jr.

88. McCaslin, *Fighting Stock*, 80; Ford, *Rip Ford's Texas*, xxxiii, 247; Sturm to Ross, December 28, 1858, December 30, 1858, January 15, 1859, *Annual Report of the Commissioner of Indian Affairs*, Senate Executive Document No. 2, 36th Congress, 1st Session, 588–590, 598–600. Hereafter cited as *Annual Report of the Commissioner of Indian Affairs, 1860*. Smith, *From Dominance to Disappearance*, 232–233.
89. McCaslin, *Fighting Stock*, 80–81; Ford, *Rip Ford's Texas*, xxxiii–xxxiv, 247, 250–259; Neighbors to Denver, January 15, 1860, Ford to Gurley, January 22, 1859, *Annual Report of the Commissioner of Indian Affairs, 1860*, 590–591, 606; Battle to Runnels, February 14, 1859, Ford to Runnels, February 16, 1859, Winfrey and Day, eds., *Texas Indian Papers*, 5: 308–313. See also Neighbors to Denver, February 14, 1859, *Annual Report of the Commissioner of Indian Affairs, 1860*, 603–605; *E. J. Gurley*, House Report No. 804, 44th Congress, 1st Session, 1–2; and *Dallas Herald*, January 12, February 23, May 18, 1859.
90. Runnels to Ford, February 11, 1859, Winfrey and Day, eds., *Texas Indian Papers*, 5: 307–308.
91. Runnels to Ford, March 3, 1859, Winfrey and Day, eds., *Texas Indian Papers*, 3: 317.
92. Neighbors to Denver, February 22, 1859, *Annual Report of the Commissioner of Indian Affairs, 1860*, 620–621; Runnels to Hemphill, February 25, 1859, Winfrey and Day, eds., *Texas Indian Papers*, 5: 315; Adjutant General to Twiggs, April 13, 1859, *Annual Report of the Secretary of War*, Senate Executive No. 2, 36th Congress, 1st Session, 357–358. Hereafter cited as *Annual Report of the Secretary of War, 1859*.
93. McCaslin, *Fighting Stock*, 8–82; Ford, *Rip Ford's Texas*, xxxiii–xxxiv, 247; Smith, *From Dominance to Disappearance*, 236, 241–244; Koch, "The Federal Indian Policy in Texas," Ch. 4: 119–122; Yancey, "In Justice to Our Indian Allies," 188; S. C. Gwynne, *Empire of the Summer Moon* (New York: Scribner, 2010), 165; Hämäläinen,

The Comanche Empire, 312; Havins, *Camp Colorado*, 83; Muster and Pay Rolls, John S. Ford, 401–793, TSLAC; Brown, "Annals of Travis County," Ch. 19: 20.

94. Heintzelman to Lee, March 1, 1860, *Troubles on Texas Frontier*, House Executive Document No. 81, 36th Congress, 1st Session, 2–3; Affidavit of William W. Nelson, January 17, 1860, Reyburn to Hatch, November 21, 1859, *Difficulties on Southwestern Frontier*, House Executive Document No. 52, 36th Congress, 1st Session, 123, 65–66; Kearney and Knopp, *Boom and Bust*, 110; Will and John Gorenfeld, "Chasing Juan Cortina," *Wild West* 28 (February 2016): 48; Field Roebuck, "Cheno Cortina: Red Robber of the Rio Grande," *True West* 36 (September 1989): 17. J. Frank Dobie and John D. Young, *A Vaquero of the Brush Country: The Life and Times of John D. Young* (Austin: University of Austin Press, 1998), 49: "... Juan Nepomuceno Cortina, 'the Red Robber of the Rio Grande,' the most striking, the most powerful, the most insolent, and the most daring as well as the most elusive Mexican bandit … that ever wet his horse in the muddy waters of the Rio Bravo." For a survey of the various papers written about the bandit-hero, see Jerry D. Thompson, "The Many Faces of Juan Nepomuceno Cortina," *South Texas Studies* 2 (1991): 85–98.

95. Larharn to Twiggs, September 28, 1859, *Annual Report of the Secretary of War, 1859*, 378–379; Webb, et al. to Runnels, October 2, 1859, Reyburn to Hatch, November 21, 1859, Report of Cameron County Grand Jury, November, 1859, *Difficulties on Southwestern Frontier*, 20–23, 66–68, 92–93; Heintzelman to Lee, March 1, 1860, *Troubles on Texas Frontier*, 3–4; Adjutant General to Twiggs, January 19, 1859, General Order No. 1, February 5, 1859, *Annual Report of the Secretary of War, 1859*, 355, 359; Jerry D. Thompson, *Cortina: Defending the Mexican Name in Texas* (College Station: Texas A&M University Press, 2007), 38; *Reports of the Committee of Investigation*, 128.

    Anxious the two bodies of troops be retained at the forts, concerned citizens in Brownsville appealed to Secretary of War Floyd. The petitioners cited the multitude of *soldados* and *bandidos* across the border engaged in wholesale plundering and murder. They also referenced the economic impact to the region since trade with parties in northern Mexico worth millions of dollars would be at risk. Citizens of Brownsville to Floyd, March 9, 1859, *Difficulties on Southwestern Frontier*, 12–14.

96. Hale to Floyd, November 7, 1859, Cortina Proclamation, September 30, 1859, Cortina to Friend, October 26, 1859, Thompson to Powers and

Brown, October 25, 1859, *Difficulties on Southwestern Frontier*, 42, 70–73, 69–70; Kearney and Knopp, *Boom and Bust*, 112–113, 114; Jerry D. Thompson, *Juan Cortina and the Texas-Mexico Frontier, 1859–1877* (El Paso: Texas Western Press, 1994), 12, 14–18; Rippy, "Border Troubles Along the Rio Grande," 106; Heintzelman to Lee, March 1, 1860, *Troubles on Texas Frontier*, 4–5.

97. Hale to Floyd, November 7, 1859, Brownsville *American Flag*, October 25, 1859, *Difficulties on Southwestern Frontier*, 42–47; Thompson, *Cortina*, 47; Rippy, "Border Troubles Along the Rio Grande," 106; Heintzelman to Lee, March 1, 1860, *Troubles on Texas Frontier*, 4–5; Collins, *Texas Devils*, 121; Gorenfeld, "Chasing Juan Cortina," 49.

98. Frederick Wilkins, *Defending the Borders: The Texas Rangers, 1848–1861* (Austin: State House Press, 2001), 104; Reyburn to Hatch, November 21, 1859, *Difficulties on Southwestern Frontier*, 64–68; Webb, *Texas Rangers*, 181; Heintzelman to Withers, March 1, 1860, *Troubles on Texas Frontier*, 5; Thompson, *Cortina*, 63; *Texas State Gazette*, November 26, 1859; Collins, *Texas Devils*, 124–125. For Tobin's commission and instructions, see Runnels to Tobin, October 13, 1859, 401–1153, TSLAC.

99. Proclamation, November 23, 1859, *Herald—Extra*, n.d., *San Antonio Ledger and Texan—Extra*, December 4, 1859, *Difficulties on Southwestern Frontier*, 79–85; Thompson, *Cortina*, 64–65; Heintzelman to Withers, March 1, 1860, *Troubles on Texas Frontier*, 6; Milton M. Dodson, "Fought Cortina and His Raiders," *Frontier Times* 7 (October 1929): 48; Thompson, *Juan Cortina and the Texas-Mexico Frontier*, 23–28.

100. Jerry D. Thompson, *Fifty Miles and a Fight: Major Samuel Peter Heintzelman's Journal of Texas and the Cortina War* (Austin: Texas State Historical Association, 1998), 131–132; Special Orders No. 103, November 12, 1859, Washington to Adjutant General, December 16, 1859, *Difficulties on Southwestern Frontier*, 54–55, 86–87; Heintzelman to Lee, March 1, 1860, *Troubles on the Texas Frontier*, 7; Tobin to Runnels, December 16, 1859, 301–29, TSLAC; *Daily Picayune*, December 30, 1859. General Twiggs vacillated between overstating and diminishing the Cortina threat, and sent an array of contradictory orders. He went on sick leave, named Lieutenant-Colonel Washington Seawell as acting commander, and clarity returned to the department's command structure. See Twiggs's

various reports and orders in *Difficulties on Southwestern Frontier*, 41, 54–59, 72–74, 86.

101. McCaslin, *Fighting Stock*, 85; Ford, *Rip Ford's Texas*, xxxiv, 265–267; Governor Runnels wrote three letters to Ford on November 17, 1859 with the necessary authorization and instructions. 301–29, TSLAC. Reprinted in *Claims Against the United States*, Senate Executive Document No. 74, 46th Congress, 2nd Session, 143–144. Gammel, comp., *Laws of Texas*, 4: 1502; Patsy McDonald Spaw, ed., *The Texas Senate* (College Station: Texas A&M University Press, 1990), 1: 305; *San Antonio Ledger and Texan*, December 10, 1859; Ford to Runnels, December 16, 1859, 301–29, TSLAC.
102. McCaslin, *Fighting Stock*, 86; Ford, *Rip Ford's Texas*, 267; Thompson, *Fifty Miles and a Fight*, 138–141; Heintzelman to Adjutant General, December 16, 1859, December 18, 1859, December 27, 1859, *Difficulties on Southwestern Frontier*, 87–90, 97–98; Heintzelman to Withers, March 1, 1860, Field Return of the troops of the Brownsville Expedition, December 14, 1860, *Troubles on Texas Frontier*, 7–8, 74; Tobin to Runnels, December 16, 1859, 301–29, TSLAC; Colonel Martin L. Crimmins, "Colonel Robert E. Lee's Report on Indian Combats in Texas," *Southwestern Historical Quarterly* 39 (July 1935): 25; Wilkins, *Defending the Borders*, 109, 179 n18; Gorenfeld, "Chasing Juan Cortina," 50. The Gorenfelds have transcribed the journal of Private William Antes, Company C, First Artillery, who was an eyewitness to events on the border. Like his commanding officer, the private was not impressed with Tobin or his men. The two authors plan to publish a full-length work in the near future. See also Field & Staff, [1st] Battalion of Texas Mounted Volunteers October 19, 1859–February 10, 1860, and Field & Staff, [1st] Battalion of Texas Mounted Volunteers January 11, 1860 (organization list), both in 401–725, TSLAC.
103. McCaslin, *Fighting Stock*, 86; Ford, *Rip Ford's Texas*, 268–269; Ford to Runnels, December 16, 1859, 301–29, TSLAC; Thompson, *Fifty Miles and a Fight*, 143–144, 146–148; Collins, *Texas Devils*, 138–139; *Daily Picayune*, December 30, 1859.
104. McCaslin, *Fighting Stock*, 86–87; Ford, *Rip Ford's Texas*, 269–272; Heintzelman to Twiggs and Heintzelman to Adjutant General, both dated December 27, 1859, *Difficulties on Southwestern Frontier*, 96, 97; Heintzelman to Lee, March 1, 1860, *Troubles on Texas Frontier*, 8, 9, 10; Thompson, *Fifty Miles and a Fight*, 155; *Texas State Gazette*, January 14, March 26, 1860.

105. McCaslin, *Fighting Stock*, 87; Ford, *Rip Ford's Texas*, 272–273; Lea, *The King Ranch*, 1: 165; Heintzelman to Adjutant General, December 27, 1859, *Difficulties on Southwestern Frontier*, 97; Heintzelman to Lee, March 1, 1860, *Troubles on Texas Frontier*, 9; Roebuck, "Cheno Cortina," 21.
106. McCaslin, *Fighting Stock*, 87–88; Ford, *Rip Ford's Texas*, 273–274; Heintzelman to Lee, March 1, 1860, *Troubles on Texas Frontier*, 9; Heintzelman to Twiggs and Heintzelman to Adjutant General, both dated December 27, 1859, *Difficulties on Southwestern Frontier*, 97–98; Thompson, *Fifty Miles and a Fight*, 156; Gorenfeld, "Chasing Juan Cortina," 51; Crimmins, "Colonel Robert E. Lee's Report," 25; List of the Wounded in the Battle of Rio Grande City, December 27, 1858, 401–1153, TSLAC. Reprinted in *Daily Picayune*, January 22, 1860.
107. Ford, *Rip Ford's Texas*, 275; Heintzelman to Twiggs and Heintzelman to Adjutant General, both dated December 27, 1859, *Difficulties on Southwestern Frontier*, 97, 98; Heintzelman to Lee, March 1, 1860, *Troubles on Texas Frontier*, 10. See also Field Return of the Troops of the Brownsville Expedition, December 27, 1860, *Troubles on Texas Frontier*, 72.
108. Proclamation Ordering Armed Bands within the State to Disperse, December 28, 1859, Amelia W. Williams and Eugene C. Barker, ed., *Writings of Sam Houston* (Austin: University of Texas Press, 1938–1943), 7: 389.
109. McCaslin, *Fighting Stock*, 88; Ford, *Rip Ford's Texas*, 276–278; Runnels to Ford, November 17, 1859, 301–29, TSLAC; Thompson, *Fifty Miles and a Fight*, 142, 164; *San Antonio Ledger and Texan*, January 14, 1860; Certification of election, December 31, 1859, 401–1153, TSLAC. Ford asserted several times that his personal relations with Tobin "were always friendly and agreeable, and were never otherwise." Ford, *Rip Ford's Texas*, 286. Captain Herron's company also chose to leave on January 2. Thompson, *Fifty Miles and a Fight*, 164–165.
110. McCaslin, *Fighting Stock*, 88–89; Ford, *Rip Ford's Texas*, 278–280; Orders to Angel Navarro and Robert H. Taylor, January 2, 1860, Williams and Barker, eds., *Writings of Sam Houston*, 7: 395–396; Navarro and Taylor to Tobin, January 12, 1860, Navarro to Houston, February 15, 1860, Navarro to Heintzelman, Heintzelman to Navarro and Taylor, Navarro and Taylor to Ford, all dated February 2, 1860, *Difficulties on Southwestern Frontier*, 116, 120–122, 118–119; Muster

and Pay Rolls, John S. Ford, 401–793, TSLAC. Governor Houston subsequently certified Ford's company had been called out by competent authority and was eligible for pay under the act of January 27, 1858. Houston Proclamation, January 25, 1861, *Letter from the Secretary of War, 1860*, 144.

111. Lea, *The King Ranch*, 1: 166; *Daily Picayune*, January 22, 1860; Navarro to Houston, February 15, 1860, *Hostilities on the Rio Grande*, Senate Executive Document No. 21, 36th Congress, 1st Session, 9; Heintzelman to Seawell, January 29, 1860, *Difficulties on Southwestern Frontier*, 106–107. Houston to the Legislature, January 13, 1860, *Journals of the House of Representatives: Eighth Legislature*, 391: "Mexico is in a continual state of anarchy, her population feel none of the influences of a stable government. Lawless chieftains plunder them with impunity, and light the torch of civil war with pleasure. Riot, murder and revolution reign above law and order."

112. McCaslin, *Fighting Stock*, 90; Ford, *Rip Ford's Texas*, 281; Heintzelman to Lee, March 1, 1860, *Troubles on Texas Frontier*, 10; Heintzelman to Navarro and Taylor, February 6, 1860, *Hostilities on the Rio Grande*, 8; Heintzelman to Adjutant General, March 7, 1860, *Difficulties on Southwestern Frontier*, 137; Thompson, *Fifty Miles and a Fight*, 189, 222. In his memoirs, Ford described a meeting at this time with Doña María Estéfana de Cortina, Cheno's widowed mother, whom he found to be a lady of great dignity. A Southern gentleman of the old school, he chivalrously offered the *señora* his protection and ordered that she was not to be disturbed in any manner. Ford, *Rip Ford's Texas*, 281–282.

113. McCaslin, *Fighting Stock*, 90–91; Ford, *Rip Ford's Texas*, 282–283; *Texas State Gazette*, February 18, March 26, 1860; Thompson, *Cortina*, 83–84; Collins, *Texas Devils*, 169–170; Clifford R. Caldwell and Ron DeLord, *Texas Lawmen, 1835–1899: The Good and the Bad* (Charleston, SC: The History Press, 2011), 309.

114. McCaslin, *Fighting Stock*, 91; Ford, *Rip Ford's Texas*, 283–286; Heintzelman to Lee, March 1, 1860, Ford to Heintzelman, February 4, 1860, Tobin to Houston, February 6, 1860, Heintzelman to Angeielis, February 9, 1860, Heintzelman to Arquilles, February 9, 1860, *Troubles on Texas Frontier*, 11, 95–98, 68–70.

115. Houston to Floyd, February 13, 1860, Houston to Floyd, February 15, 1860, Williams and Baker, eds., *Writings of Sam Houston*, 7: 474–476, 478–479; Floyd to Houston, February 28, 1860, *Letter from the Secretary of War, 1860*, 141; Houston to Floyd, February 20,

1860, Adjutant General to Lee, February 24, March 2, 3, 1860, *Difficulties on Southwestern Frontier*, 131, 133–135; Carl Coke Rister, *Robert E. Lee in Texas* (Norman: University of Oklahoma Press, 2004), 102; Lee to Treviño, April 2, 1860, *Troubles on Texas Frontier*, 84–85. On February 24, Senator Louis Trezevant Wigfall of Texas introduced a joint resolution that requested the president call out the Regiment of Texas Volunteers authorized by the act of 1858. On March 1, the senator proposed an amendment appropriating one million dollars for the regiment's support. The matter was referred to the Committee of Military Affairs and ultimately failed to pass. "Domestic Intelligence," *Harper's Weekly* 4 (March 3, 1860): 94, (March 10, 1860): 150; Floyd to Davis, March 3, 1860, *Hostilities on the Rio Grande*, 19.

116. McCaslin, *Fighting Stock*, 92–93; Ford, *Rip Ford's Texas*, 290–295; Thompson, *Fifty Miles and a Fight*, 212; George F. Price, *Across the Continent with the Fifth Cavalry* (New York: Antiquarian Press, 1959), 87; Stoneman and Ford to Heintzelman, March 18, 1860, *Troubles on Texas Frontier*, 80–81; Thompson, *Cortina*, 85; *Texas State Gazette*, March 31, 1860; *Daily Ledger and Texan*, March 26, 1860.

117. McCaslin, *Fighting Stock*, 93–95, 98; Ford, *Rip Ford's Texas*, 298, 307–308; Heintzelman to Stoneman, March 19, 1860, Heintzelman to Adjutant General, March 25, 1860, Lee to Military and Civil Authorities of Reynosa, April 7, 1860, Lee to Garcia, April 12, 1860, *Troubles on Texas Frontier*, 81, 82–83, 84–85, 102–103; Heintzelman to Withers, February 29, 1860, *Difficulties on Texas Frontier*, 137–138; Houston to Ford, March 24, 1860, Williams and Barker, eds., *Writings of Sam Houston*, 7: 541; Rister, *Robert E. Lee in Texas*, 121–127; Collins, *Texas Devils*, 210; Muster and Pay Rolls, John S. Ford, 401–793, TSLAC. Heintzelman wrote that Littleton departed Fort Brown on May 2 and Ford left two days later. Thompson, *Fifty Miles and a Fight*, 242. Littleton would later be killed in the early stages of the Sutton-Taylor feud. *Galveston Daily News*, December 25, 1868.

Summarizing the entire episode, Major Heintzelman reported that fifteen Americans and eighty friendly Mexicans had been killed. Cortina was thought to have lost 151 killed; the major had no idea of the number of wounded. The country from Brownsville to Rio Grande City—a distance of 120 miles—had been laid waste, and commerce as far upriver as Laredo had been disrupted. The claims for damages submitted to the federal government exceeded $336,000. Colonel Lee observed those *ranchos* spared by Cortina were burned by Texans. Heintzelman to Lee, March 1, 1860, Lee to Adjutant General, April 11, 1860, *Troubles on Texas Frontier*, 13, 84.

118. McCaslin, *Fighting Stock*, 98–99, 102–106; Ford, *Rip Ford's Texas*, xxxv, 314–317; Benjamin Woodbridge Dwight, *The History of the Descendants of Elder John Strong, of Northampton, Mass* (Albany, NY: Joel Munsell, 1871), 184; Walter L. Buenger, *Secession and the Union in Texas* (Austin: University of Texas Press, 1984), 113, 2, 123, 125, 142–50; *Texas State Gazette*, August 11, 25, September 1, November 10, 17, 24, December 1, 8, 15, 22, 29, 1860; Anna Irene Sandbo, "The First Session of the Succession Convention of Texas, 1861," *Southwestern Historical Quarterly* 18 (October 1914): 179–180; Dudley G. Wooten, ed., *A Comprehensive History of Texas, 1685–1897* (Dallas: William G. Scarff, 1898), 2: 88; Lubbock, *Six Decades in Texas*, 310. See also Ralph A. Wooster, "An Analysis of the Membership of the Texas Secession Convention," *Southwestern Historical Quarterly* 62 (January 1959): 322–335.
119. Ernest William Winkler, ed., *Journal of the Secession Convention of Texas in 1861* (Austin: Austin Printing Company, 1912), 47–49, 88–97, 317–318; Buenger, *Secession and the Union in Texas*, 2, 150–153, 174.
120. McCaslin, *Fighting Stock*, 106–107; Ford, *Rip Ford's Texas*, xxxvii, 318; *The War of the Rebellion: A Compilation of the Official Records of the Union and Confederate Armies*, Series I, LIII: 622, 650–651. Hereafter cited as *OR*; all references are to Series I unless otherwise indicated. Lubbock, *Six Decades in Texas*, 309; Winkler, ed., *Journal of the Secession Convention*, 24, 28, 317–324; Clement A. Evans, ed., *Confederate Military History* (Atlanta: Confederate Publishing Company, 1899), 11: 21, 38; Ralph A. Wooster, *Texas and Texans in the Civil War* (Austin: Eakin Press, 1995), 15; Confederate Muster Roll Abstract Records, John S. Ford, Mat Nolan, TSLAC. For the distribution of federal forces in Texas throughout the first four months of 1861, see *OR*, Series III, I: 24–25.
121. McCaslin, *Fighting Stock*, 107–109; Ford, *Rip Ford's Texas*, 318–319; *OR*, I: 536–540, 591–592, LIII: 619–620, 646–652, 655, 658–661; *Civilian and Gazette*, March 5, 1861; Dudley G. Wooten, ed., *A Comprehensive History of Texas, 1685–1897* (Dallas: William G. Scarff, 1898), 2: 520; Winkler, ed., *Journal of the Secession Convention*, 324–325, 336, 337–342; Richard T. Marcum, "Fort Brown, Texas: The History of a Border Post" (Ph.D. dissertation, Texas Technological

College, 1964), 138. Ford's captains were Henry Van Buren, Galveston Artillery; Nahor Biggs Yard, Galveston Rifles; William H. Redwood, Lone Star Rifles; Samuel Boyer Davis, Lone Star Coast Guards; William Edwards, Milam Rifles; Frederick H. Odlum, Davis Guards; and Daniel A. Conner, Fort Bend Rifles. *Texas State Gazette*, March 2, 23, 1861.

122. McCaslin, *Fighting Stock*, 109–111, 113; Ford, *Rip Ford's Texas*, 319, 320–321, 324–326; *OR*, I: 540, 574–575, 591–592, LIII: 619–620, 652–656, 660–665; Winkler, ed., *Journal of the Secession Convention*, 324–334, 345; Alwyn Barr, "Texas Coastal Defense, 1861–1865," *Southwestern Historical Quarterly* 65 (July 1961): 3; McLeod to Ford, March 2, 1861, John S. Ford Papers, TCM94.1.0691, HML&HC; *Texas State Gazette*, March 23, 1861; "Affairs in Texas," *Harper's Weekly*, 5 (March 23, 1861): 183; Carded Records and Correspondence Re: John S. Ford, War Department Collection of Confederate Records, RG 109, NARA; Bruce S. Allardice, *Confederate Colonels: A Biographical Register* (Columbia: University of Missouri Press, 2008), 151; *Dallas Herald*, June 12, 1861. Terry's battalion was composed of Alfred C. McKeen, Galveston Rifles; W. D. Williams, Liberty Guard; W. G. Moseley, Brazoria Volunteers; Edwin Waller, Jr., Houston Volunteers; and Isaac C. Stafford, Gentry Volunteers. *Galveston Weekly News*, March 16, 1861.

123. McCaslin, *Fighting Stock*, 113; Ford, *Rip Ford's Texas*, xxxvii, 325–327; Brown, "Annals of Travis County," Ch. 21: 43; Confederate Pension Application, Addie N. Ford, No. 356, TSLAC; Robert P. Weinert, "Confederate Border Troubles with Mexico," *Civil War Times Illustrated* 3 (October 1964): 37; Robert W. Delaney, "Matamoros, Port for Texas during the Civil War," *Southwestern Historical Quarterly* 58 (April 1955): 474, 475; Amberson, et al., *I Would Rather Sleep in Texas*, 187, 190; James A. Irby, *Backdoor at Bagdad: The Civil War on the Rio Grande* (El Paso: Western Texas Press, 1977), 8, 18–19; Bruce A. Cheeseman, "'Let Us Have 500 Good Determined Texans': Richard King's Account of the Union Invasion of South Texas, November 12, 1863, to January 20, 1864," *Southwestern Historical Quarterly* 101 (July 1997): 78; Kearney and Knopp, *Boom and Bust*, 120–121. The best account of Matamoros as a commercial center during the war remains James W. Daddysman, *The Matamoros Trade: Confederate Commerce, Diplomacy, and Intrigue* (Newark: University of Delaware Press, 1984). See also Robert M. Browning, Jr., *Lincoln's Trident: The West Gulf*

Blockading Squadron During the Civil War (Tuscaloosa: University of Alabama Press, 2015).

124. Ford, *Rip Ford's Texas*, 325–326; *OR*, I: 574–575, 577–578, 623, 628, 630–631; Compiled Service Records of Confederate Soldiers, Second Texas Mounted Rifles, John S. Ford; Winkler, ed., *Journal of the Secession Convention*, 400–403; Janet B. Hewett, ed., *Texas Confederate Soldiers, 1861–1865* (Wilmington, NC: Broadfoot Publishing Company, 1997),1: 388, 216, 314, 140.
125. McCaslin, *Fighting Stock*, 116–118; Ford, *Rip Ford's Texas*, 324–325; Thompson, *Cortina*, 97–101; Jerry D. Thompson, *Sabers on the Rio Grande* (Austin: Presidial Press, 1974), 200–201; Bruce S. Allardice, *More Generals in Gray* (Baton Rouge: Louisiana State University Press, 1995), 36; Jerry Thompson and Lawrence T. Jones III, *Civil War and Revolution on the Rio Grande Frontier: A Narrative and Photographic History* (Austin: Texas State Historical Association, 2004), 35–36; Irby, *Backdoor at Bagdad*, 20; *Civilian and Gazette*, May 7, 21, 1861.
126. McCaslin, *Fighting Stock*, 122–123; Ford, *Rip Ford's Texas*, 329, 331; *OR*, IX: 700, 706; Compiled Service Records of Confederate Soldiers, Second Texas Mounted Rifles, John S. Ford; Stephen B. Oates, "John S. 'Rip' Ford: Prudent Cavalryman, C.S.A.," *Southwestern Historical Quarterly* 64 (January 1961): 295; Evans, ed., *Confederate Military History*, 11: 49, 69; Gammel, comp., *Laws of Texas*, 5: 578.
127. McCaslin, *Fighting Stock*, 128–130, 133, 139; Ford, *Rip Ford's Texas*, xxxviii, 332; *OR*, IX: 708–709, XV: 826, 880–881, XXVI, Pt. 2: 21–22, 47, 73; Chance, *José María de Jesús Carvajal*, 173–177; Amberson, et al., *I Would Rather Sleep in Texas*, 194; Ralph A. Wooster, *Lone Star Generals in Gray* (Austin: Eakin Press, 2000), 116; *Semi-Weekly News*, May 22, 1862; *Tri-Weekly Telegraph*, May 21, June 27, October 1, 1862; Albert Burton Moore, *Conscription and Conflict in the Confederacy* (Columbia: University of South Carolina Press, 1996), 13; Oates, "John S. 'Rip' Ford," 296; Evans, ed., *Confederate Military History*, 11: 69; Stephen B. Oates, "Texas Under the Secessionists," *Southwestern Historical Quarterly* 67 (October 1963): 195.
128. McCaslin, *Fighting Stock*, 139–141; Ford, *Rip Ford's Texas*, 332, 341; OR, XXVI, Pt. 2: 42, 65, 382, 517; Oates, "John S. 'Rip' Ford," 297; Moore, et al. to Davis, September 20, 1862, Moore to Reagan, November 6, 1862, Reagan to Benjamin, December 1, 1862, Petition

to Senators and Representatives and Guinn, et al. to Randolph, both dated February 16, 1863, Unnumbered General Orders, March 21, 1863, Pay Vouchers, Carded Records and Correspondence Re: John S. Ford; Allardice, *Confederate Colonels*, 151; Widener, "John S. 'Rip' Ford," 20.

129. McCaslin, *Fighting Stock*, 137–138, 143–144; Ford, *Rip Ford's Texas*, 332, 333, 341; *OR*, XXVI, Pt. 2: 119–120; *Tri-Weekly Telegraph*, July 4, 1862; Oates, "John S. 'Rip' Ford," 297; Oates, "Texas Under the Secessionists," 197–201. For more on conscription in the Confederacy, see Moore, *Conscription and Conflict*, 16, 34, 53, 67–68, 140, 185–186, 202, 224, 247–248.

130. Ford, *Rip Ford's Texas*, xxxviii, 342; *OR*, XXVI, Pt. 1: 3–4, 18–21, 290–292, 397–399, 413–415, 423–425, 529–532, 876–878, Pt. 2: 218, 399–400, XXXIV, Pt. 4: 467, Pt. 2: 277–278, 888–890; *Official Records of the Union and Confederate Navies in the War of the Rebellion*, Series I, XIX: 217–224, XX: 647–649; Banks to Lincoln, November 9, 1863, *Army and Navy Official Gazette*, 1: 342; Kearney and Knopp, *Boom and Bust*, 126, 129; William Riley Brookshear, *War Along the Bayous: The 1864 Red River Campaign in Louisiana* (Washington, D.C.: Brassey's, 1998), 23; Thompson and Jones, *Civil War and Revolution on the Rio Grande Frontier*, 66.

131. McCaslin, *Fighting Stock*, 145; *OR*, XXVI, Pt. 2: 415, 530; Kearney and Knopp, *Boom and Bust*, 129–130; Cheeseman, "Let Us Have 500 Good Determined Texans," 86, 92; *Texas State Gazette*, December 23, 1863.

132. Ford, *Rip Ford's Texas*, 343; *OR*, XXVI, Pt. 1: 525–526, 543–544, Pt. 2: 524, 525, 530, 534–535l, XXXIV, Pt. 2: 835, LIII: 922; Robert L. Kerby, *Kirby Smith's Confederacy: The Trans-Mississippi South, 1863–1865* (New York: Columbia University Press, 1972), 194, 365–366; Wilkinson, *Laredo and the Rio Grande Frontier*, 294–295; Allardice, *Confederate Colonels*, 151; Confederate Muster Roll Abstract Records, John S. Ford, TSLAC.

133. McCaslin, *Fighting Stock*, 148, 150; Ford, *Rip Ford's Texas*, 344–346; *OR*, LIII: 922–923, XXXIV, Pt. 2: 232, 295, 906, 936, 946–949, 961–962, 968–969, 979–980, 1004–1005, 1011, 1039, XXVI, Pt. 2: 516–517, 540, 543–544, 560–561, LIII: 952–953, 966–968, 969; Oates, "John S. 'Rip' Ford," 299; Benavides to Ford, January 10, 1864, Ford to Benavides and Ford to Carr, both dated February 27, 1864, TCM94.1.0296, TCM94.1.0313, TCM94.1.0353, Ford Papers, HML&HC; Ford to Turner, January 27, 1864, Carded Records and

Correspondence Re: John S. Ford; Compiled Service Records of Confederate General and Staff Officers, Albert Walthersdorff, Charles H. Merritt, W. G. M. Samuels. Blücher was the grandnephew of Field Marshal Gebhard Leberecht von Blücher, the Prussian commander at the Battle of Waterloo. *Corpus Christi Caller-Times*, May 11, 1952.

134. McCaslin, *Fighting Stock*, 150; Ford, *Rip Ford's Texas*, 346; *OR*, XXXIV, Pt. 1: 643–644, 647–649, Pt. 2: 947, 1074, 1069, 1106–1107, 1081–1082, Pt. 3: 129–130, 176, 754, 775–776, 808, Pt. 4: 677, XLI, Pt. 2: 995, 1001, LIII: 922; Thompson and Jones, *Civil War & Revolution on the Rio Grande Frontier*, 77; *Weekly State Gazette*, August 31, 1864; Evans, ed., *Confederate Military History*, 11: 123; Compiled Service Records of Confederate Soldiers, Second Texas Cavalry, Regimental Return, July 1864, Miscellaneous, C. B. Gardiner, First Texas Cavalry, James A. Ware. Gardiner is listed in the service records under the name Sardiner. *San Antonio Daily Express*, May 11, 1902; Marcus J. Wright, comp., *Texas in the War, 1861–1865*, ed. Harold B. Simpson (Hillsboro, Texas: Hill Junior College Press, 1965), 33, 126 n280, 127 n281.

The captains of Giddings's battalion were William N. Robinson, Company A; J. M. Onins, Company B; R. W. Carr, Company C; and J. W. Maddox, Company D. Lieutenant Albert H. Wood served as adjutant. The captains are scattered throughout the two miscellaneous rolls of the Compiled Service Records of Confederate Soldiers while Wood is in Compiled Service Records of Confederate General and Staff Officers. See also Hewett, ed., *Texas Confederate Soldiers*, 1: 396, 84, 417, 344, 587, 2: 272–274.

While serving as sheriff of Nueces County, Mat Nolan was killed in the line of duty on December 22, 1864, by a pair of Unionist brothers. Caldwell and DeLord, *Texas Lawmen*, 179–180.

One interesting side note occurred in April when a pregnant Mrs. Ford and Lula took the stage from San Antonio to Matamoros by way of Eagle Pass and the Mexican side of the river. Intending to visit her mother in Brownsville, she was warned by her sister that Federal authorities meant to arrest her if she crossed the border. Unexpectedly, she was visited by her husband's old nemesis, Juan Cortina, now military governor of Tamaulipas, who offered her his assistance. Mrs. Ford politely declined, but Cortina repeatedly extended her every courtesy. The general was able to gain permission from Union officers at Fort Brown, with whom he was on good terms, for Mrs. Ford to cross into Brownsville. He discussed the incident later with Ford and mentioned he had not forgotten the ranger's gallant behavior toward his own mother during the Cortina War. McCaslin, *Fighting Stock*, 161–163.

135. Ford, *Rip Ford's Texas*, 360; *OR*, XXXIV, Pt. 3: 789–790, 807–808, Pt. 4: 684–685, 695, Pt. 2: 647–649, 1053–1054, 1068, LIII: 994, 998–999, XLI, Pt. 2: 994–996, 1001; Oates, "John S. 'Rip' Ford," 303; Stephen A. Townsend, *The Yankee Invasion of Texas* (College Station: Texas A&M University Press, 2006), 100; Compiled Service Records of Confederate Soldiers, Second Texas Mounted Rifles, John S. Ford; Ford to Slaughter, May 27, 1864, Carded Records and Correspondence Re: John S. Ford; Descriptive List of Deserters, Tate's Company, Cater's Battalion, May 29, 1864, TCM94.40.1, Ford Expeditionary Forces Records, Texas Confederate Museum Collection, HML&HC.

136. McCaslin, *Fighting Stock*, 164–165; Ford, *Rip Ford's Texas*, 362; *OR*, LIII: 1001, XXXIV, Pt. 1: 1053–1056, Pt. 4: 685; Ford to Tobin, July 15, 1864, Carded Records and Correspondence Re: John S. Ford; Compiled Service Records of Confederate Soldiers, Fourth Regiment, Arizona Brigade, Regimental Return, June 1864; Ralph A. Wooster, *Civil War Texas: A History and a Guide* (Austin: Texas State Historical Association, 1999), 48–49; Wooten, ed., *Comprehensive History of Texas*, 2: 551.

137. McCaslin, *Fighting Stock*, 165–166; Ford, *Rip Ford's Texas*, 362–363; *OR*, XXXIV, Pt. 1: 1053–1056; Compiled Service Records of Confederate Soldiers, Miscellaneous, James Dunn, and Fourth Regiment, Arizona Brigade, Regimental Return, June 1864; Hewett, ed., *Texas Confederate Soldiers*, 1: 147; Wooten, ed., *Comprehensive History of Texas*, 2: 551; *Compiled Service Records of Volunteer Union Soldiers*, First Cavalry, Philip G. Temple; Wright, comp., and Simpson, ed., *Texas in the War*, 66, 162. Two months later, the captains of Cater's battalion were Theophilus G. Anderson, David M. Wilson, Henry Clay Davis, William H. D. Carrington, and Dan Grady. Return of Capt. T. E. Cater's Battalion, August 1864, TCM94.40.1, Ford Expeditionary Forces Records, HML&HC.

138. Ford, *Rip Ford's Texas*, 363; *OR*, XXXIV, Pt. 1: 1054, 1056, Pt. 4: 559–560; Kerby, *Kirby Smith's Confederacy*, 366.

139. McCaslin, *Fighting Stock*, 167–168; *OR*, XLI, Pt. 2: 989–990, 1001, XXXIV, Pt. 4: 669; Townsend, *Yankee Invasion of Texas*, 100.

140. McCaslin, *Fighting Stock*, 168; Ford, *Rip Ford's Texas*, 363–364; Townsend, *Yankee Invasion of Texas*, 103; *Weekly State Gazette*, August 24, 1864.
141. McCaslin, *Fighting Stock*, 168–169; Ford, *Rip Ford's Texas*, xxxix, 364–365, 367, 368; *OR*, XLI, Pt. 1: 185–186, Pt. 2: 1069–1070, Pt. 3: 3; Cave to Ford, July 29, 1864, Cave to Ford, July 31, 1864, TCM94.1.399, TCM94.1.0402a, Ford Papers, HML&HC; *Weekly State Gazette*, August 24, 31, 1864; Oates, "John S. 'Rip' Ford," 304–305; Wooten, ed., *Comprehensive History of Texas*, 2: 552; *Brownsville Herald*, August 12, 1953.
142. McCaslin, *Fighting Stock*, 173–174; Ford, *Rip Ford's Texas*, 370–371; *OR*, XLI, Pt. 2: 1088–1089, Pt. 3: 909, 911–912; Amberson, et al., *I Would Rather Sleep in Texas*, 216; Thompson, *Cortina*, 138–139, 141; Kearney and Knopp, *Boom and Bust*, 134; Irby, *Backdoor at Bagdad*, 37, 39; Thompson and Jones, *Civil War and Revolution on the Rio Grande Frontier*, 86.
143. McCaslin, *Fighting Stock*, 174–176; Ford, *Rip Ford's Texas*, 371–373; *OR*, XVI, Pt. 1: 742, Pt. 3: 946–947; Compiled Service Records of Confederate Soldiers, Thirty-third Texas Cavalry, Richard Taylor; *Weekly State Gazette*, September 21, October 19, 1864; *Dallas Herald*, October 1, 1864; Thompson, *Cortina*, 141, 143; Oates, "John S. 'Rip' Ford," 306–307; Irby, *Backdoor at Bagdad*, 39.
144. McCaslin, *Fighting Stock*, 178; Ford, *Rip Ford's Texas*, 372, 374–375; *OR*, XLI, Pt. 1: 742, Pt. 3: 184, 947; *Weekly State Gazette*, September 28, October 19, 1864; Oates, "John S. 'Rip' Ford," 307; *Victoria Advocate*, October 1, 1864; Carrington to Ford, September 15, 1864, Carrington to Giddings, n.d., TCM94.1.0362.a, TCM94.1.0547, Ford Papers, HML&HC.
145. McCaslin, *Fighting Stock*, 185–187, 188, 189; Ford, *Rip Ford's Texas*, 383–386; *OR*, LIII: 1021–1022, XLI, Pt. 4: 1109, 1085, 1138, Pt. 1: 1312, XLVIII, Pt. 1: 1358, 1407; Giddings to Murrah, October 21, 1864, Box 2014/022-3, Pendleton Murrah Papers, TSLAC; *Victoria Advocate*, October 17, 1864; Oates, "John S. 'Rip' Ford," 309–310; Townsend, *Yankee Invasion of Texas*, 116; Amberson, et al., *I Would Rather Sleep in Texas*, 256–258; Special Order No. 24, January 28, 1865, Special Order No. 32, February 7, 1865, Special Order No. 36, February 11, 1865, Special Order No. 27, February 13, 1865, Cater to Ford, December 1, 1864, Anderson to Ford, December 1, 1864, TCM94.1.0218, TCM94.1.0326, TCM94.1.274, TCM94.1.0584, TCM94.1.0379, TCM94.1.0264, Ford Papers, HML&HC.

In Giddings's battalion, the companies of J. W. Maddox and J. G. White consolidated on January 13, and Edward L. James was elected the new captain. Giddings to Ford, January 13, 1864, TCM94.1.0565, Ford Papers, HML&HC.

146. McCaslin, *Fighting Stock*, 192–195; Ford, *Rip Ford's Texas*, 388–389; *OR*, XLVIII, Pt. 1: 201, 512, 1275–1282, 1448, Pt. 2: 201, 457–463, 37, 122, XLI, Pt. 2: 1039, 1068–1069, 1277; Lew Wallace, *Lew Wallace: An Autobiography* (New York: Harper and Brothers, 1906), 814–815, 821–822, 828–831. Wallace wrote the novel *Ben-Hur: A Tale of the Christ*, which was published in 1880. Wooten, ed., *Comprehensive History of Texas*, 2: 556; J. Fred Rippy, "Mexican Projects of the Confederates," *Southwestern Historical Quarterly* 22 (April 1919): 296–298; *Galveston Daily News*, April 4, 1865; Oates, *John S. "Rip" Ford*, 310; *Tri-Weekly Telegraph*, April 5, 1865. On February 1, Kirby Smith tendered his services to Maximilian in the event of a Confederate defeat. *OR*, XLVIII, Pt. 1: 1167, 1359.

147. *OR*, XLVIII, Pt. 1: 1354–1355, 1358, 1456–1457, Pt. 2: 17–18; Phillip Thomas Tucker, *The Final Fury: Palmito Ranch, The Last Battle of the Civil War* (Mechanicsburg, PA: Stackpole Books, 2001), 57, 58–59; Ralph A. Wooster, *Lone Star Regiments in Gray* (Austin: Eakin Press, 2002), 278; Confederate Muster Roll Abstract Records, T. G. Anderson, D. M. Wilson, F. B. S. Cocke, TSLAC; William Marvel, "Last Hurrah at Palmetto Ranch," *Civil War Times* 44 (January 2006): 68–69. The company commanders of Cater's battalion were Cater, Carrington, and Lorenzo Trevino. The captains of Giddings's battalion were W. N. Robinson, Company A; J. M. Onins, Company B; R. W. Carr, Company C; Miller H. Pickrell, Company D; W. J. Weisiger, Company E; and E. L. James, Company F. Returns of Capt. T. E. Cater's Battalion and Lt. Col. G. H. Giddings's Battalion, both dated January 1865, TCM94.40.1, Ford Expeditionary Forces Records, HML&HC. All of these officers, except for Trevino, were also carried on the rolls of those surrendered by General Kirby Smith on May 26. Compiled Service Records of Confederate Soldiers, T. E. Cater, W. H. D. Carrington, Giddings's Battalion. At this time, Major Albert Walthersdorff was the garrison commander of Fort Brown.

148. McCaslin, *Fighting Stock*, 198; Irby, *Backdoor to Bagdad*, 47; *New York Times*, June 18, 1865; Tucker, *Final Fury*, 63–67; Pierre Comtois, "War's Last Battle," *America's Civil War* 5 (July 1992): 52; *Tri-Weekly Telegraph*, April 24, 28, May 24, June 9, 1865.

149. McCaslin, *Fighting Stock*, 199; Ford, *Rip Ford's Texas*, 389, 394–395; *OR*, XLVIII, Pt. 1: 265–266, 267–268; Stephen B. Oates, *Confederate Cavalry West of the River* (Austin: University of Texas Press, 1961), 156; Evans, ed., *Confederate Military History*, 11: 126; *San Antonio Daily Express*, October 10, 1890; Henry I. Kurtz, "Last Battle of the War," *Civil War Times Illustrated* 1 (April 1962): 32; *Galveston Daily News*, June 13, 1875; Noah Andre Trudeau, "The Last Gun Had Been Fired," *Civil War Times Illustrated* 29 (August 1990): 61–62; Luther Conyer, "Last Battle of the War," *Southern Historical Society Papers* 24 (January-December 1896): 309.
150. McCaslin, *Fighting Stock*, 199–200; Ford, *Rip Ford's Texas*, 390–391; *OR*, XLVIII, Pt. 1: 266, 268, 1456–1457; *New York Times*, June 18, 1865; Compiled Service Records of Confederate Soldiers, Ragsdale's Battalion, George A. Gibson, Thirty-third Texas Cavalry, Jones' Company, Texas Light Artillery; Hewett, ed., *Texas Confederate Soldiers*, 1:191; Jeffrey William Hunt, *The Last Battle of the Civil War: Palmetto Ranch* (Austin: University of Texas Press, 2002), 90–91, 105; D. M. Wilson, "Another Account," *Confederate Veteran* 18 (July 1910): 324; *Galveston Daily News*, June 13, 1875; *Houston Post*, August 31, 1916; Oates, "John S. 'Rip' Ford," 311–312; Wooster, *Texas and Texans in the Civil War*, 180; Marvel, "Last Hurrah at Palmetto Ranch," 71; Brown, *History of Texas*, 2: 432, 435–436; Wooten, ed., *Comprehensive History of Texas*, 2: 560. There is some indication that French artillerymen volunteered to man Captain Jones's guns. Thompson and Jones, *Civil War and Revolution on the Rio Grande Frontier*, 92.
151. McCaslin, *Fighting Stock*, 200; Ford, *Rip Ford's Texas*, 391; OR, XLVIII, Pt. 1: 266–267, 268–269; Evans, ed., *Confederate Military History*, 11: 127–128; Oates, "John S. 'Rip' Ford," 312–313; G. C. Goodwin, "The Last Battle of the War," *Confederate Veteran* 18 (July 1910): 324; Conyer, "Last Battle of the War," 313–314; Trudeau, "The Last Gun Had Been Fired," 62; Wooten, ed., *Comprehensive History of Texas*, 2: 560; Wooster, *Civil War Texas*, 60; Brown, *History of Texas*, 2: 432–433. Slaughter later claimed to have commanded at the battle and took credit for the Confederate victory. He made no mention of Ford. "The Last Battle of the War," *Southern Historical Society Papers* 21 (January-December 1893): 227. Private Ferdinand Gerring is believed to be the last Confederate killed in action in the Civil War. Private John Jefferson Williams, Company B, Thirty-fourth Indiana, is considered to

be the last fatality from either side. Perry D. Jamieson, *Spring 1865: The Closing Campaigns of the Civil War* (Lincoln: University of Nebraska Press, 2015), 212.

152. McCaslin, *Fighting Stock*, 201; Ford, *Rip Ford's Texas*, 392; Widener, "John S. 'Rip' Ford," 22; Evans, ed., *Confederate Military History*, 11: 128–129; *New York Times*, June 18, 1865; Brown, *History of Texas*, 2: 434–435. Captain Robinson submitted a report on his battalion's casualties, which concurs with Ford's tally. The statement also confirms the companies of Onins, Carr, and Weisiger were present at the battle. Robinson to Ford, May 17, 1865, TCM94.1.1248, Ford Papers, HML&HC.

    Colonel Barrett was relieved of his post, but subsequently assigned to a brigade command. Seeking to escape blame for the disaster, he scapegoated Morrison and preferred charges against him. During Morrison's court-martial, which convened July 21 and adjourned August 28, Ford testified for the defense. Due in no small part to his attorney, Cameron County Judge Israel Bonaparte Bigelow, a fervent secessionist, the lieutenant-colonel was found not guilty of all charges and specifications. *Flake's Daily Bulletin*, August 4, 1865; Hunt, *Last Battle of the Civil War*, Ch. 13.

153. McCaslin, *Fighting Stock*, 203–204; Ford, *Rip Ford's Texas*, xl, 376, 398, 401; *OR*, XLVIII, Pt. 2: 1313–1314, 564–565, 727–728, 813–814, 827–828, 841, 858; *Weekly State Gazette*, June 9, 1865; *Tri-Weekly Telegraph*, June 26, 1865; *New York Herald*, July 29, 1865; Slaughter to Ford, May 26, 1865, TCM94.1.879, Ford Papers, HML&HC.

    Due to the unsanctioned transfer of the battery to the Imperialists, Slaughter faced charges for violating the terms of the surrender. He confiscated 630 bales of cotton at Ringgold Barracks and sold them in Camargo for twenty-five dollars per bale. He then brazenly crossed into Mexico, his self-imposed exile made easier by his ill-gotten gains. *OR*, XLVIII, Pt. 2: 1196; Thompson and Jones, *Civil War and Revolution on the Rio Grande Frontier*, 96. See also Brad R. Clampitt, "The Breakup: The Collapse of the Confederate Trans-Mississippi Army in Texas, 1865," *Southwestern Historical Quarterly* 108 (April 2005): 498–534.

154. McCaslin, *Fighting Stock*, 207, 208, 213; Ford, *Rip Ford's Texas*, xl, 402–403; *OR*, XLVIII, Pt. 1: 1455, Pt. 2: 600–601, 727–728; *Tri-Weekly Telegraph*, June 5, 1865; Parole of Honor, July 18, 1865, Carded Records and Correspondence Re: John S. Ford; Allardice, *Confederate*

Colonels, 151; *San Antonio Daily Express*, April 15, 1885; *New York Herald*, July 29, 1865.

155. McCaslin, *Fighting Stock*, 209–210, 213; Ford, *Rip Ford's Texas*, xl, 404–405; *Find A Grave*, s.v. "John W. Ford"; Thompson and Jones, *Civil War and Revolution on the Rio Grande Frontier*, 18; *Galveston Daily News*, July 8, 1866; Kearney and Knopp, *Boom and Bust*, 146; Wilkinson, *Laredo and the Rio Grande Frontier*, 305.
156. McCaslin, *Fighting Stock*, 210–211; Ford, *Rip Ford's Texas*, 405–407; Chance, *José María de Jesús Carvajal*, 197; Amberson, et al., *I Would Rather Sleep in Texas*, 284; Bancroft, *History of Mexico*, 6: 255 n56; *Reports of the Committee of Investigation*, 202; *Flake's Weekly Bulletin*, August 22, 1866; *Southern Intelligencer*, September 6, 1866; Kearney and Knopp, *Boom and Bust*, 147. See also Ernst Pitner, *Maximilian's Lieutenant: A Personal History of the Mexican Campaign, 1864–67*, trans. and ed. Gordon Etherington-Smith (Albuquerque: University of New Mexico Press, 1993).
157. McCaslin, *Fighting Stock*, 212–216; Ford, *Rip Ford's Texas*, xl–xli, 434–435, 465, 468; Returns from U.S. Military Posts, 1800–1916, Fort Brown, November 1866, M617, NARA; Amberson, et al., *I Would Rather Sleep in Texas*, 286, 314; James Robert Crews, "Reconstruction in Brownsville, Texas" (M.A. thesis, Texas Tech University, 1969), 82; Kearney and Knopp, *Boom and Bust*, 154; *Message of the President of the United States and Accompanying Documents*, House Executive Document No. 1, 40th Congress, 2nd Session, 498; Martin, "The Last of the Ranger Chieftains," 40; Gammel, comp., *Laws of Texas*, 5: 707–710; Anna Cora Petz, "History of the Rio Grande Railroad," *Frontier Times* 14 (December 1936): 93.
158. McCaslin, *Fighting Stock*, 220; Ford, *Rip Ford's Texas*, xlii; Heather Cox Richardson, *West from Appomattox: The Reconstruction of America After the Civil War* (New Haven: Yale University Press, 2007), 125; Ernest William Winkler, ed., *Platforms of Political Parties in Texas* (Bulletin of the University of Texas, No. 53: September 20, 1916), 143–147; *Houston Telegraph*, June 20, 1872; Andrew L. Slap, *The Doom of Reconstruction: The Liberal Republicans in the Civil War Era* (New York: Fordham University Press, 2006), 164; Dobie and Young, *Vaquero of the Brush Country*, 24–25; *Weekly Democratic Statesman*, December 25, 1873.
159. McCaslin, *Fighting Stock*, 220–224; Ford, *Rip Ford's Texas*, xliii, 417–426, 434; James L. Haley, *The Texas Supreme Court:*

A Narrative History, 1836–1986 (Austin: University of Texas Press, 2013), 83–87; *Galveston Daily News*, December 4, 1874; *Weekly Democratic Statesman*, January 15, 22, 1874; Wooten, ed., *A Comprehensive History of Texas*, 2: 207. See also George E. Shelley, "The Semicolon Court of Texas," *Southwestern Historical Quarterly* 48 (April 1945): 449–468.

160. McCaslin, *Fighting Stock*, 225, 227–229; Ford, *Rip Ford's Texas*, xliii; *Texas Frontier Troubles*, House Report No. 343, 44th Congress, 1st Session, 126, 132, 133, 134, 136; Carl H. Moneyhon, *Texas After the Civil War: The Struggle of Reconstruction* (College Station: Texas A&M University Press, 2004), 199; Randolph B. Campbell, *Grass-Roots Reconstruction in Texas, 1865–1880* (Baton Rouge: Louisiana State University Press, 1997), 215; *Journal of the Constitutional Convention of the State of Texas, Begun and Held at the City of Austin, September 6, 1875*, 4, 15, 16, 23, 36, 77–78, 149–150, 158–161, 199, 202, 290, 327–328, 363–364, 371, 395, 470–471, 514–516, 698–699. Before a reorganization of districts during the convention, the Thirtieth District was composed of Cameron, Nueces, Hidalgo, Starr, Zapata, Duval, Encinal, Webb, McMullen, La Salle, Dimmitt, Maverick, Zavalla, Frio, Medina, Uvalde, Kinney, El Paso, Presidio, and Pecos Counties, and the Bexar District. Gammel, comp., *Laws of Texas*, 7: 499. See also J. E. Ericson, "The Delegates to the Convention of 1875: A Reappraisal," *Southwestern Historical Quarterly* 67 (July 1963): 22–27.
161. McCaslin, *Fighting Stock*, 229–231; Ford, *Rip Ford's Texas*, 412; Testimony of John S. Ford, January 24, 1878, *Relations of the United States with Mexico*, House Report No. 701, Pt. 2, 45th Congress, 2nd Session, 69–70; Thompson, *Cortina*, 231; John Mason Hart, *Empire and Revolution: The Americans in Mexico since the Civil War* (Berkeley: University of California Press, 2002), 66–67.
162. McCaslin, *Fighting Stock*, 232, 227, 244; Ford, *Rip Ford's Texas*, xliii–xliv; Martin, "Last of the Ranger Chieftains," 40; William S. Speer and John Henry Brown, eds., *The Encyclopedia of the New West* (Marshall, TX: United States Biographical Publishing Company, 1881), 359; *Galveston Daily News*, January 5, 15, 22, 23, 1878; *Weekly Democratic Statesman*, January 23, March 6, 1879; Testimony of John S. Ford, January 21, 24, 1878, *Relations of the United States with Mexico*, 62–64, 66–69, 164–170. See also Patsy McDonald Spaw, ed., *The Texas Senate* (College Station: Texas A&M University Press, 1999),

2: 233–236. As a senator, Ford represented Cameron, Hidalgo, Starr, Zapata, Webb, Maverick, Kinney, Uvalde, Medina, Nueces, San Patricio, Live Oak, Frio, Duval, Encinal, McMullen, LaSalle, Dimmitt, and Zavala Counties. John Cardwell, *Fifteenth Legislature: Sketches of Legislators and State Officers, 1876–1878* (Austin: Democratic Statesman Steam Print, 1876), 49.

163. McCaslin, *Fighting Stock*, 241; John W. Leonard, ed., *Woman's Who's Who of America* (New York: American Commonwealth Company, 1914), 842; *Austin Daily Democratic Statesman*, January 10, February 26, March 2, 1880; *Galveston Daily News*, February 27, 1880, November 21, 1882.

164. McCaslin, *Fighting Stock*, 239–241, 242–244; Ford, *Rip Ford's Texas*, xliv; *Journal of House of Representatives of the Sixteenth Legislature of the State of Texas, Extra Session*, 35–39; *Journal of the Senate of Texas: Being the First Session of the Seventeenth Legislature of the State of Texas*, 28, 31, 35, 99; *Journal of the Senate of Texas: Being the Regular Session of the Eighteenth Legislature of the State of Texas*, 36, 39, 223; *Galveston Daily News*, September 2, 3, 16, 1879, January 1, March 19, 1880, January 22, 1881, June 17, August 26, December 1, 1883; Brown, "Annals of Travis County," Ch. 25: 23; *Journal of the Senate of Texas: Being a Special Session of the Seventeenth Legislature of the State of Texas*, 59, 84, 90; *Journal of the Senate of Texas: Being the Called Session of the Eighteenth Legislature of the State of Texas*, 106; *Austin Daily Statesman*, November 19, 1880; *Dallas Weekly Herald*, March 29, April 19, November 29, 1883; Swisher, *Swisher Memoirs*, 59. The institution has since been renamed the Texas School for the Deaf.

165. McCaslin, *Fighting Stock*, 245, 248–265, 269; *Official Register of the United States, 1885*, 1: 127; Ibid., *1887*, 1: 130; Ibid., *1889*, 1: 137; *Austin Daily Democratic Statesman*, May 10, 1874; Martin, "Last of the Ranger Chieftains," 39.

166. *Tri-Weekly Telegraph*, July 29, August 10, 12, 17, 1863; *Ninth U.S. Census*, Travis County, Texas; *Mercantile and General City Directory of Austin, Texas—1872–73* (Austin: S. A. Gray, 1872), 22; *Mooney & Morrison's General Directory of the City of Austin, Texas, for 1877–78* (Austin: Eugene von Boeckmann, 1877), 26, 51, 67, 212; *Morrison & Fourmy's General Directory of the City of Austin, for 1881 and 1882* (Austin: E. W. Swindells, 1881), 161; Ibid., *1885 and 1886* (Austin: E. W. Swindells, 1885), 208; Ibid., *1889–90* (Galveston: Morrison &

Fourmy, 1889), 220; *Galveston Daily News*, March 7, 1880, August 7, 1895; *Find A Grave*, s.v. "William Grey Thomas" and "Fannie Ford Thomas."

167. McCaslin, *Fighting Stock*, 252–258, 260–261, 266–269, 249, 272–273; Ford, *Rip Ford's Texas*, xlvi–xlvii; Bride Neill Taylor, "The Beginnings of the State Historical Association," *Southwestern Historical Quarterly* 33 (July 1929): 1–17; *Galveston Daily News*, April 10, 24, 1892, May 12, 1897; *Brownsville Daily Herald*, June 17, 1897; *Houston Daily Post*, October 4, 5, November 4, 5, 1897; *Austin Daily Statesman*, November 4, 7, 1897. The Former Texas Ranger Association traces its lineage from the early body that Ford envisioned and Lambert initiated. See also "The Organization and Objects of the Texas State Historical Association," *The Quarterly of the Texas State Historical Association* 1 (July 1897): 71–74.
168. *Twelfth U.S. Census*, Bexar County, Texas; Confederate Pension Application, Addie N. Ford, No. 356, TSLAC; *San Antonio Daily Express* and *Houston Daily Post*, both dated February 20, 1901.
169. Ford, *Rip Ford's Texas*, 332; *Twelfth* and *Thirteenth U.S. Census*, Bexar County, Texas; *San Antonio Express*, June 25, 1916; Death Certificate, Mary Louise Ford Maddox, June 25, 1916, File No. 13507. Joseph's death certificate misidentifies his first name as "John."
170. *Weekly Democratic Statesman*, January 18, 1883; *Twelfth U.S. Census*, Travis County, Texas; *Morrison & Fourmy's General Directory of the City of Austin, 1897–98* (Galveston: Morrison & Fourmy, 1897), 126; *Galveston Daily News* and *Houston Daily Post*, both dated January 29, 1909; *Thirteenth U.S. Census*, Harris County, Texas; *Sixteenth U.S. Census*, Calcasieu Parish, Louisiana; *Brownsville Herald*, August 12, 1953.
171. McCaslin, *Fighting Stock*, 264–265, 272, 274; *San Antonio Daily Express*, December 27, 1903; *Thirteenth U.S. Census*, Bexar County, Texas; Leonard, ed., *Woman's Who's Who of America*, 842; *Appler's General Directory and Blue Book of Greater San Antonio, 1910* (San Antonio: Jules A. Appler, 1910), 1056; *Sixteenth U.S. Census*, Nueces County, Texas; *Corpus Christi Times*, December 26, 1958; Death Certificates, Robert Alonzo Votaw, Sr., August 27, 1948, File No. 3375, Lillian Alva Votaw, May 14, 1971, File No. 36108; *Corpus Christi Caller*, May 9, 1971. Lilian was also preceded in death by a grandson. *Corpus Christi Times*, February 1, 1960.

Notes for Chapter 7

1. Judith Ann Benner, *Sul Ross, Soldier, Statesman, Educator* (College Station: Texas A&M University Press, 1983), 3–5; *The National Cyclopaedia of American Biography* (New York: James T. White and Company, 1899), 9: 75; Karen Stein Daniel, *Three Generations of Descendants of Shapley Prince Ross: An Early Texas Pioneer* (Spartanburg, SC: The Reprint Company, 1994), 7; Buckley B. Paddock, *A History of Central and Western Texas* (Chicago: The Lewis Publishing Company, 1911), 1: 276–277; Raymond L. Dillard, "A History of the Ross Family and Its Most Distinguished Member, Lawrence Sullivan Ross" (M.A. thesis, Baylor University, 1931), 7–8; John Henry Brown, *Indian Wars and Pioneers of Texas* (Austin: State House Press, 1988), 315, 317, 318. Catherine died on September 22, 1886, and Shapley on September 17, 1889; both were buried in Oakwood Cemetery in Waco. *Galveston Daily News*, September 23, 1886, September 18, 1899.
2. Benner, *Sul Ross*, 5–6; Elizabeth Ross Clarke, "Life of Sul Ross," Boxes 5 and 6, Ross Family Papers, The Texas Collection, Baylor University, 4, 9. A condensed version of the manuscript can be found at the Clayton Library in Houston under the title *Biography of Lawrence Sullivan Ross* (United States: n.s., 1920?). Brown, *Indian Wars*, 316.
3. Benner, *Sul Ross*, 9–11; Clarke, "Life of Sul Ross," 29–31, 33, 35; *Waco Tribune-Herald*, October 30, 1949; Compiled Service Records of Volunteer Soldiers Who Served During the Mexican War in Organizations from Texas, Ross's Company and Bell's Regiment Texas Mounted Volunteers, Shapley P. Ross; Patricia Ward Wallace, *Waco: A Sesquicentennial History* (Virginia Beach, VA: The Donning Company, 1999), 11, 19, 20; Sharon Bracken, ed. *Historic McLennan County: An Illustrated History* (San Antonio: Historical Publishing Network, 2010), 7; William O. Wilkes, M.D., *History of the Waco Medical Association with Reminiscences and Irrelevant Comments* (Waco, TX: privately printed, 1931), 23, 35; *Seventh U.S. Census*, McLennan County, Texas (Free and Slave Schedules). Shapley became a substantial property owner as he acquired over a thousand acres on Elm Creek and the Brazos and Bosque Rivers. He also obtained another three slaves. Tax Rolls, McLennan County, 1851–1856. He maintained the ferry business until the suspension bridge was built over the Brazos in 1870. Howard J. Erlichman, *Camino Del Norte: How a Series of*

Watering Holes, Fords, and Dirt Trails Evolved into Interstate 35 in Texas (College Station: Texas A&M University Press, 2006), 84, 131.

4. Benner, *Sul Ross*, 14–21; *Fourth Annual Catalogue of the Trustees, Professors, and Students of Baylor University* (Galveston: Civilian Book and Job Company, 1856), 8; *National Cyclopaedia of American Biography*, 9: 75; Dillard, "History of the Ross Family," 30–32.
5. Benner, *Sul Ross*, 22–23; William C. Yancey, "In Justice to Our Indian Allies: The Government of Texas and Her Indian Allies, 1836–1867" (M.A. thesis, University of North Texas, 2008), 96, 107–110; Fannie McAlpine Clarke, "A Chapter in the History of Young Territory," *The Quarterly of the Southwestern Historical Association* 9 (July 1905): 56; *Dallas Herald*, August 21, 1858.
6. Twiggs to Thomas, July 6, 1858, Twiggs to Thomas, August 4, 1858, *Annual Report of the Secretary of War*, House Executive Document No. 2, 35th Congress, 2nd Session, 258–259, 261. Hereafter cited as *Annual Report of the Secretary of War, 1858*. Twiggs to Thomas, July 27, 1858, Dorman H. Winfrey and James M. Day, eds., *The Indian Papers of Texas and the Southwest* (Austin: Texas State Historical Association, 1995), 5: 255; Twiggs to Runnels, September 9, 1858, 301–28, TSLAC.
7. McDowell to Twiggs, July 22, 1858, *Protection of the Frontier of Texas*, House Executive Document No. 27, 35th Congress, 2nd Session, 26; *Northern Standard*, August 28, 1858; George F. Price, *Across the Continent with the Fifth Cavalry* (New York: Antiquarian Press, 1959), 64, 67–68; Durwood Ball, *Army Regulars on the Western Frontier, 1848–1861* (Norman: University of Oklahoma Press, 2001), 48.
8. Benner, *Sul Ross*, 24; Robert M. Utley, *Frontiersmen in Blue: The United States Army and the Indian, 1848–1865* (Lincoln: University of Nebraska Press, 1981), 130; *Waco Tribune-Herald*, October 30, 1949; *San Antonio Daily Express*, November 22, 1908; *Dallas Herald*, September 29, 1858; Myrtle Whiteside, "The Life of Lawrence Sullivan Ross" (M.A. thesis, University of Texas, 1938), 13–14.
9. Benner, *Sul Ross*, 25; William Y. Chalfant, *Without Quarter: The Wichita Expedition and the Fight on Crooked Creek* (Norman: University of Oklahoma Press, 1991), 37–40; Arthur B. Carter, *The Tarnished Cavalier: Major General Earl Van Dorn, C.S.A.* (Knoxville: University of Tennessee Press, 1999), 17; F. Todd Smith, *From Dominance to Disappearance: The Indians of Texas and the Near Southwest, 1786 to 1859* (Lincoln: University of

Nebraska Press, 2006), 231; Harold B. Simpson, *Cry Comanche: The 2nd U.S. Cavalry in Texas, 1855–1861* (Hillsboro, TX: Hill Junior College Press, 1979), 109; J. W. Williams, "The Van Dorn Trails," *Southwestern Historical Quarterly* 44 (January 1941): 321–325; Van Dorn to Withers, September 26, 1858, *Annual Report of the Secretary of War, 1858*, 268–269.

10. Price, *Across the Continent*, 68; Wilbur Sturtevant Nye, *Carbine and Lance: The Story of Old Fort Sill* (Norman: University of Oklahoma Press, 1969), 19; Ben C. Stuart, "Texas Indian Fighters and Frontier Rangers" (MS, 1916), TSLAC, 86. Thomas W. Kavanagh notes the disagreement concerning whether Potsanaquahip, or Quohoahteme and Hotowokowot, was in charge of the camp. *Comanche Political History: An Ethnohistorical Perspective, 1706–1875* (Lincoln: University of Nebraska Press, 1996), 375. For a description of the Wichita village as observed six years prior, see Randolph B. Marcy, *Thirty Years of Army Life on the Border* (New York: Harper & Brothers, 1866), 159–160.
11. Chalfant, *Without Quarter*, 40–41; Hobert D. Ragland, *The History of Rush Springs* (Rush Springs, OK: Gazette Publishing Company, 1952), 15; Rupert Norval Richardson, *The Comanche Barrier to South Plains Settlement* (Glendale, CA: The Arthur H. Clark Company, 1933), 240; David La Vere, *Contrary Neighbors: Southern Plains and Removed Indians in Indian Territory* (Norman: University of Oklahoma Press, 2000), 160.
12. Benner, *Sul Ross*, 26; Clarke, "Life of Sul Ross," 49; Nye, *Carbine and Lance*, 20; Ball, *Army Regulars*, 48; Whiting to Withers, October 2, 1858, *Annual Report of the Secretary of War, 1858*, 269; *Southern Intelligencer*, November 3, 1858.
13. Chalfant, *Without Quarter*, 41–42; James R. Arnold, *Jeff Davis's Own: Cavalry, Comanches, and the Battle for the Texas Frontier* (New York: John Wiley & Sons, 2000), 198; Williams, "Van Dorn Trails," 326–327; Van Dorn to Withers, October 5, 1858, *Annual Report of the Secretary of War, 1858*, 272. Reprinted in *Dallas Herald*, September 29, November 3, 1858. Albert G. Brackett, *History of the United States Cavalry, From the Formation of the Federal Government to the 1st of June, 1863* (New York: Harper & Brothers, 1865), 192.
14. Nye, *Carbine and Lance*, 20–21; Arnold, *Jeff Davis's Own*, 200; Richardson, *Comanche Barrier*, 240; Ragland, *History of Rush Springs*, 70, 75. French naturalist Jean Louis Berlandier had earlier noted Comanches habitually refused to post camp guards, even when

on the war path in enemy territory. Stanley Noyes, *Los Comanches: The Horse People, 1751–1845* (Albuquerque: University of New Mexico Press, 1993), 288.

15. Nye, *Carbine and Lance*, 21; Ball, *Army Regulars*, 48; Brackett, *History of the United States Cavalry*, 192; *Southern Intelligencer*, November 3, 1858; Simpson, *Cry Comanche*, 111–112.
16. Benner, *Sul Ross*, 28; Clarke, "Life of Sul Ross," 49–50; Chalfant, *Without Quarter*, 43–44; La Vere, *Contrary Neighbors*, 160; Yancey, "In Justice to Our Indian Allies," 112; Mildred Mayhall, *Indian Wars of Texas* (Waco: Texian Press, 1965), 110; Whiteside, "Life of Lawrence Sullivan Ross," 15–16; Van Dorn to Withers, October 5, 1858, Twiggs to Thomas, November 1, 1858, *Annual Report of the Secretary of War, 1858*, 272–274, 274–275.
17. Benner, *Sul Ross*, 28–29; Clarke, "Life of Sul Ross," 50–51; John Wesley Wilbarger, *Indian Depredations in Texas* (Austin: State House Press, 1985), 330; Price, *Across the Continent*, 665, 70–71; Arnold, *Jeff Davis's Own*, 205–206; Brown, *Indian Wars*, 112, 317; *Southern Intelligencer*, November 3, 1858.
18. Benner, *Sul Ross*, 29–30; Clarke, "Life of Sul Ross," 51–52; Utley, *Frontiersmen in Blue*, 131; Nye, *Carbine and Lance*, 22; Williams, "The Van Dorn Trails," 327; Ragland, *History of Rush Springs*, 77.
19. Chalfant, *Without Quarter*, 43–44; Ball, *Army Regulars*, 48–49; Pekka Hämäläinen, *The Comanche Empire* (New Haven: Yale University Press, 2008), 311; Van Dorn to Withers, October 5, 1858, Twiggs to Thomas, November 1, 1858, Orders No. 25, October 19, 1858, *Annual Report of the Secretary of War, 1858*, 272–274, 274–275, 278. The orders were reprinted in *Southern Intelligencer*, October 27, 1858. Williams, "The Van Dorn Trails," 327.
20. Benner, *Sul Ross*, 33–34; Clarke, "Life of Sul Ross," 53–54; Whiteside, "Life of Lawrence Sullivan Ross," 10, 18, 21, 23; *Dallas Herald*, November 10, 1858; *San Antonio Daily Express*, November 22, 1908; Stuart, "Texas Indian Fighters and Frontier Rangers," 89.
21. Benner, *Sul Ross*, 37; Clarke, "Life of Sul Ross," 46; Clarke, "Chapter in the History of Young Territory," 56–57; Mary D. Farrell and Elizabeth Silverthorne, *First Ladies of Texas: The First One Hundred Years, 1836–1936* (Belton: Stillhouse Hollow Publishers, 1976), 181–183. Benner, Elizabeth Clarke, and Farrell and Silverthorne all assert Elizabeth Tinsley attended Miss Susan Corner Lambdin's private academy for young ladies, but that school, located on Tenth

Street and Austin Avenue, was not established until 1870. *Waco Daily Examiner*, September 1, 1878.

22. Houston to Johnson, March 17, 1860, Amelia W. Williams and Eugene C. Barker, ed., *Writings of Sam Houston* (Austin: University of Texas Press, 1938–1943), 7: 525; *Northern Standard*, April 14, 1860. The legislature had authorized the ranger regiment Johnson was to command on January 2, 1860. Hans Peter Nielson Gammel, comp., *The Laws of Texas, 1822–1897* (Austin: The Gammel Book Company, 1898), 4: 1376–1377.
23. Benner, *Sul Ross*, 38–40; Benjamin Franklin Gholson, "Recollections of B. F. Gholson," transcript of interview with J. A. Rikard, August 1928, Gholson (B. F.) Reminiscences, 1832–1860, BCAH, 53–54; Discharge Roll of the Field and Staff Officers of the Mounted Rangers, January 1, 1861, 401–794, TSLAC; Ross to Johnson, May 11, 1860, Johnson to Houston, May 16, 1860, Johnson to Houston, May 16, 1860, 301–32, TSLAC; Thomas W. Cutrer, ed., "My Wild Hunt After Indians: The Journal of Willis L. Lang, 23 April-7 September 1860," *Military History of the Southwest* 21 (Spring 1991): 25–30, 32; William Carey Crane, *Life and Select Literary Remains of Sam Houston of Texas* (Philadelphia: J. B. Lippincott & Co., 1884), 633. Hereafter cited as *Houston's Literary Remains*. Muster and Pay Rolls, Peter F. Ross, 401–795, TSLAC; David Paul Smith, *Frontier Defense in the Civil War: Texas' Rangers and Rebels* (College Station: Texas A&M University Press, 1992), 22.
24. Johnson to Houston, May 30, 1860, 301–32, TSLAC; Smith to Houston, July 13, 1860, Box 2014/109-3, TSLAC; Cutrer, ed., "My Wild Hunt After Indians," 34; Nathan A. Jennings, *Riding for the Lone Star: Frontier Cavalry and the Texas Way of War, 1822–1865* (Denton: University of North Texas Press, 2016), 277.
25. Benner, *Sul Ross*, 42–43; Gholson, "Recollections of B. F. Gholson," 54; Cutrer, ed., "My Wild Hunt After Indians," 34–36, 40–45; Dalrymple to Houston, June 25, 1860, Smith to Houston, July 13, 1860, Johnson to Houston, July 15, 1860, Smith to Johnson, July 19, 1860, Box 2014/109-3, TSLAC; Ross to Johnson, July 28, 1860, Box 2014/109-4, TSLAC.
26. Benner, *Sul Ross*, 44–45; Houston to Johnson, August 4, 1860, Houston to Johnson, September 12, 1860, Williams and Barker, eds., *Writings of Sam Houston*, 8: 113–114, 142; *Texas State Gazette*, July 21, August 18, 1860; Johnson to Houston, August 26, 1860, Johnson to Houston, September 2, 1860, Johnson to Houston, October 14, 1860,

Box 2014/109-4, TSLAC; Cutrer, ed., "My Wild Hunt After Indians," 54–55, 56.

27. Benner, *Sul Ross*, 45, 47; John M. Elkins and Frank W. McCarty, *Indian Fighting on the Texas Frontier* (Amarillo: Russell & Cockrell, 1929), 32; Jonathan Hamilton Baker Diary, October 13, 1860, Tarrant County Archives, Tarrant County Historical Commission; *Weekly Telegraph*, October 30, 1860.
28. Benner, *Sul Ross*, 47–49; *Texas State Gazette*, July 7, 28, 1860, January 5, 1861; Houston to Ross, September 11, 1860, Williams and Barker, eds., *Writings of Sam Houston*, 8: 139–140; Ross to Houston, September 18, 1860, 301–33, TSLAC; Muster and Pay Rolls, L. S. Ross, 401–725, TSLAC; Crane, *Houston's Literary Remains*, 633; Doyle Marshall, *A Cry Unheard: The Story of Indian Attacks in and Around Parker County, Texas, 1858–1872* (Aledo, TX: Annetta Valley Farm Press, 1990), 29–35; Ida Lasater Huckabay, comp., *Ninety-Four Years in Jack County, 1854–1948* (Austin: The Steck Company, 1949), 60–64; Clarke, "Chapter in the History of Young Territory," 58–59; Ty Cashion, *A Texas Frontier: The Clear Fork Country and Fort Griffin, 1849–1887* (Norman: University of Oklahoma Press, 1996), 40–41; S. C. Gwynne, *Empire of the Summer Moon* (New York: Scribner, 2010), 155–158.
29. Benner, *Sul Ross*, 50; Clarke, "Life of Sul Ross," 56; Ross to Houston, December 8, 1860, 301–33, TSLAC; Returns from U.S. Military Posts, 1800–1916, Camp Cooper, December 1860, M617, NARA. Hereafter cited as Post Returns. Elkins and McCarty, *Indian Fighting on the Texas Frontier*, 31–32; Joseph Carroll McConnell, *The West Texas Frontier: or, A Descriptive History of Early Times in Western Texas* (Palo Pinto, TX: Texas Legal Bank & Book Co., 1939), 2: 32–33; Marshall, *A Cry Unheard*, 43–44; Colonel Martin L. Crimmins, "First Sergeant John W. Spangler, Company H, Second United States Cavalry," *West Texas Historical Association Yearbook* 26 (1950): 74; Chalfant, *Without Quarter*, 111, 126–127, 135–136.

    Cureton's volunteers have been variously described as numbering seventy, eighty, or ninety-two men. J. Marvin Hunter, comp. and ed., *Trail Drivers of Texas* (Austin: University of Texas Press, 1985), 788–790; Ernest Wallace, *Texas in Turmoil: The Saga of Texas, 1849–1875* (Austin: Steck-Vaughn Company, 1965), 27; Spangler to Evans, December 24, 1860, Letters Received by the Office of the Adjutant General, M567, RG 94, NARA.

Hereafter cited as Letters Received, Adjutant General's Office. *Civilian and Gazette*, January 15, 1861.

30. Paul H. Carlson and Tom Crum, *Myth, Memory, and Massacre: The Pease River Capture of Cynthia Ann Parker* (Lubbock: Texas Tech University Press, 2010), 131, 138–139; *San Antonio Express*, February 23, 1908; *San Antonio Ledger and Texan*, February 2, 1861; McConnell, *West Texas Frontier*, 2: 34; Huckabay, comp., *Ninety-Four Years in Jack County*, 5; Marshall, *A Cry Unheard*, 44; *Dallas Herald*, January 2, 1861; *Civilian and Gazette*, January 15, 1861; Spangler to Evans, December 24, 1860, Letters Received, Adjutant General's Office, NARA; John R. Erickson, *Prairie Gothic: The Story of a West Texas Family* (Denton: University of North Texas Press, 2005), 28–29; Baker Diary, December 16–18, 1860.
31. *San Antonio Ledger and Texan*, February 2, 1861; *Civilian and Gazette*, January 15, 1861; *San Antonio Express*, February 23, 1908; Spangler to Evans, December 24, 1860, Letters Received, Adjutant General's Office, NARA; *Dallas Herald*, January 2, 1861.
32. Clarke, "Life of Sul Ross," 61; *Civilian and Gazette*, January 8, 15, 1861; *Dallas Herald*, January 2, 1861; J. Evetts Haley, "Charles Goodnight's Indian Recollections," *Panhandle-Plains Historical Review* 1 (1928): 24; Lawrence T. Jones, "Cynthia Ann Parker and Pease Ross—The Forgotten Photographs," *Southwestern Historical Quarterly* 93 (January 1990): 382; Richard Selcer, "One Little Indian Boy," *Wild West* 28 (February 2016): 56.
33. *Dallas Herald*, January 2, 1861; Baker Diary, December 20, 1860; *Civilian and Gazette*, January 8, 15, 1861; *San Antonio Express*, February 23, 1908; Spangler to Evans, December 24, 1860, Letters Received, Adjutant General's Office, NARA; Post Returns, Camp Cooper, December 1860; Erickson, *Prairie Gothic*, 28–29; Crimmins, "First Sergeant John W. Spangler," 75; Baker Diary, December 19, 20, 1860.
34. McConnell, *West Texas Frontier*, 2: 37; Marshall, *A Cry Unheard*, 45; *Civilian and Gazette*, January 15, 1861; *Dallas Herald*, January 2, January 30, 1861; Cashion, *A Texas Frontier*, 47; Jo Ella Powell Exley, *Frontier Blood: The Saga of the Parker Family* (College Station: Texas A&M University Press, 2009), 136. For more on Cynthia's abduction as a child in 1836, her life with the Nokoni Comanches, and her sad end in 1870, see Margaret Schmidt Hacker, *Cynthia Ann Parker: The Life and the Legend* (El Paso: Texas Western Press, 1990). For the

subsequent life of Cynthia's son, Quanah Parker, see Bill Neeley, *The Last Comanche Chief: The Life and Times of Quanah Parker* (New York: John Wiley & Sons, 1995).

35. Thomas T. Smith, *The Old Army in Texas: A Research Guide to the U.S. Army in Nineteenth-Century Texas* (Austin: Texas State Historical Association, 2000), 14.

For the subsequent interpretations that added details to the story, either accurate, conflicting, or embellished, see *Galveston Daily News*, June 3, 1890; Brown, *Indian Wars*, 317; Clarke, "Chapter in the History of Young Territory," 59–60; Augusta Houghton Antony, "Lawrence Sullivan Ross, Soldier and Statesman," *The Texas Magazine* 6 (September 1912): 430–431; "Remarkable Life of Quanah Parker," *Frontier Times* 1 (October 1923): 28–30; "Ben Dragoo Tells of the Capture of Cynthia Ann Parker," ibid. (December 1923): 25–27; "The Killing of Chief Peta Nouona," *Frontier Times* 4 (December 1926): 42–43; Haley, "Charles Goodnight's Indian Recollections," 3–29; "Ben Dragoo Has Colorful History," *Frontier Times* 5 (February 1928): 216–217; Gholson, "Recollections of B. F. Gholson," 29–32; Elkins and McCarty, *Indian Fighting on the Texas Frontier*, 33–36; Rogers, "Recollections of Ranger H. B. Rogers," 69–72; J. Marvin Hunter, "'Uncle' Ben Dragoo, A Texas Ranger," *Frontier Times* 6 (April 1929): 287–291; Francis M. Peveler, "Reminiscences," interview with J. Evetts Haley, October 14, 1932, HML&HC; Clarke, "Life of Sul Ross," 58–61; J. Marvin Hunter, ed., "The Capture of Cynthia Ann Parker," *Frontier Times* 16 (May 1939): 364–365; Benner, *Sul Ross*, 51–57. See also Price, *Across the Continent*, 93; Dudley G. Wooten, ed., *A Comprehensive History of Texas, 1685 to 1897* (Dallas: William G. Scarff, 1898), 2: 342–343; C. L. Douglas, *The Gentlemen in the White Hats: Dramatic Episodes in the History of the Texas Rangers* (Dallas: South-West Press, 1934), 62–67; Rupert Norval Richardson, *The Frontier of Northwest Texas, 1846 to 1876* (Glendale: The Arthur H. Clark Company, 1963), 210–211; Frederick Wilkins, *Defending the Borders: The Texas Rangers, 1848–1861* (Austin: State House Press, 2001), 150–154; Robert M. Utley, *Lone Star Justice: The First Century of the Texas Rangers* (New York: Berkley Books, 2002), 122; Arnold, *Jeff Davis's Own*, 291–295; Jack K. Selden, *Return: The Parker Story* (Palestine, TX: Clacton Press, 2006); and Glenn Frankel, *The Searchers: The Making of an American Legend* (New York: Bloomsbury, 2013).

36. Tom Crum, "Folklorization of the Battle on Pease River," *West Texas Historical Association Yearbook* 72 (1996): 71–72; *Galveston Daily News*, June 3, 1875; *Dallas Daily Herald*, June 11, 1875. The date of December 18 is found on the Texas Centennial Marker placed at the site in 1936. The articles concerning Peta Nocona and *Cynthia* Ann Parker in both the printed and online versions of the *Handbook of Texas* also carry the incorrect date.
37. James T. DeShields, *Cynthia Ann Parker: The Story of Her Capture* (Dallas: Chama Press, 1991), 44–45. For accounts that support the "official" version, see *San Saba News and Star*, July 19, 1889; *Austin Daily Statesman*, June 1, 1890; *San Antonio Daily Express*, November 22, 1908; and Wilbarger, *Indian Depredations in Texas*, 335–338. Haley, "Charles Goodnight's Indian Recollections," 25–26. The undated message Parker wrote to Goodnight was reprinted in the *Canyon News*, June 29, 1975, while the original can be found in the Charles Goodnight Papers at the Panhandle-Plains Historical Museum. Rupert Norval Richardson, "The Death of Peta Nocona and the Recovery of Cynthia Ann Parker," *Southwestern Historical Quarterly* 46 (July 1942): 18; *Dallas Morning News*, October 27, 1909. See also Mayhall, *Indian Wars of Texas*, 115–118; *Dallas Daily Times Herald*, October 27, 1909; *Semi-Weekly Farm News*, October 29, 1909; *Dallas Morning News*, October 25, 1910; Araminta McClellan Taulman, "The Capture of Cynthia Ann Parker," *Frontier Times* 6 (May 1929): 311–312; Paul I. Wellman, "Cynthia Ann Parker," *Chronicles of Oklahoma* 12 (June 1932): 163–170; Wallace, *Texas in Turmoil*, 28; and William T. Hagan, *Quanah Parker, Comanche Chief* (Norman: University of Oklahoma Press, 1993), 6.

    For the oft-cited arguments that the Comanche killed by Ross was indeed Nocona, see Robert H. Williams, "The Case for Peta Nocona," *Texana* 10 (1972): 55–72. See also Utley, *Lone Star Justice*, 324 n36; and Gwynne, *Empire of the Summer Moon*, 194–195, 334 n2.
38. Haley, "Charles Goodnight's Indian Recollections," 22, 23; "Recollections of Ranger H. B. Rogers of the Capture of Cynthia Ann Parker," transcript of interview with J. A. Rikard, n.d., BCAH, 70; Crimmins, "First Sergeant John W. Spangler," 74. Smith, *The Old Army in Texas*, 37: "Although the Comanche and Lipan routinely killed enemy women and children and did not return soldier prisoners alive, only three army reports mention Indian women being killed in battle, and all three incidents appear to have been accidents. It is possible that the

soldiers considered the death of an Indian noncombatant too insignificant to mention, and the officers were certainly aware that their reports became a matter of public record, but primary accounts from soldiers of the era indicate it was not the policy of the regular army in Texas to kill women."

Charles Goodnight, then twenty-four-years-old, was an eyewitness to some aspects of the campaign. After serving on the northwestern frontier as a scout and ranger, he would blaze the Goodnight-Loving Trail and forge a cattle ranching empire in the Palo Duro country. J. Evetts Haley, *Charles Goodnight: Cowman and Plainsman* (Norman: University of Oklahoma Press, 1989).

Benjamin Franklin Gholson and Benjamin C. Dragoo also offered their recollections, but these are so riddled with inconsistencies, errors, and exaggerations as to be generally unusable.

39. Paul H. Carlson and Tom Crum, "The 'Battle' of Pease River and the Question of Reliable Sources in the Recapture of Cynthia Ann Parker," *Southwestern Historical Quarterly* 113 (July 2009): 35–52; Carlson and Crum, *Myth, Memory, and Massacre*, xv–xvi, 131–153.
40. Hämäläinen, *The Comanche Empire*, 253–254; Noyes, *Los Comanches*, 249–259; Kavanagh, *Comanche Political History*, 250; Gregory and Susan Michno, *A Fate Worse Than Death: Indian Captivities in the West, 1830–1885* (Caldwell, ID: Caxton Press, 2009), 35–39, 57–59. While accurately portraying the brutalities inflicted upon Comanche captives, the Michnos rely on the standard treatment concerning the Pease River engagement. Stephen L. Hardin, "'Valor, Wisdom, and Experience': Early Texas Rangers and the Nature of Frontier Leadership," *Tracking the Texas Rangers: The Nineteenth Century*, ed. Bruce A. Glasrud and Harold J. Weiss, Jr. (Denton: University of North Texas Press, 2012), 59, 58; Carlson and Crum, *Myth, Memory, and Massacre*, xiv, 5, 26, 74; Chalfant, *Without Quarter*, 94. See also Rachel Plummer, *Narrative of the Capture and Subsequent Sufferings of Mrs. Rachel Plummer During a Captivity of Twenty-one Months Among the Cumanche Indians* (Louisville: Morning Courier Office, 1839); and James W. Parker, *Narrative of the Perilous Adventures, Miraculous Escapes and Sufferings of Rev. James W. Parker: During a Frontier Residence in Texas, of Fifteen Years* (Louisville: Morning Courier Office, 1844). Gwynne, *Empire of the Summer Moon*, 19: "The logic of Comanche raids was straightforward: All the men were killed, and any men who were captured alive were tortured to death as

a matter of course, some more slowly than others; the captive women were gang-raped. Some were killed, some tortured. But a portion of them, particularly if they were young, would be spared … Babies were invariably killed, while preadolescents were often adopted by Comanches or other tribes."

41. Benner, *Sul Ross*, 58; Clarke, "Life of Sul Ross," 67–68; Wilbarger, *Indian Depredations in Texas*, 339; Ross to Houston, February 12, 1861, 301–34, TSLAC; Gholson, "Recollections of B. F. Gholson," 40–41.
42. Benner, *Sul Ross*, 59; Ross to Houston, February 12, 1861, Dalrymple to Houston, February 15, 1861, 301–34, TSLAC; Houston to Dalrymple, December 29, 1860, Box 2014/109-4, TSLAC; Muster and Pay Rolls, L. S. Ross, 401–795, TSLAC.
43. Benner, *Sul Ross*, 60; Houston to Dalrymple, February 22, 1861, 401–382, TSLAC; Wilkins, *Defending the Borders*, 160; L. E. Daniell, comp., *Personnel of the Texas State Government* (Austin: Press of the City Printing Company, 1887), 8. While the dispute was unfolding, Dalrymple was effecting the surrender of Camp Cooper and its federal garrison. Dalrymple to Houston, February 23, 1860, Box 2014/109-5, TSLAC.
44. Benner, *Sul Ross*, 60–61; Wooten, ed., *Comprehensive History of Texas*, 2: 125; James L. Haley, *Sam Houston* (Norman: University of Oklahoma Press, 2002), 390; Randolph B. Campbell, *Gone to Texas: A History of the Lone Star State* (New York: Oxford University Press, 2003), 244.
45. Benner, *Sul Ross*, 63, 64–66; Clarke, "Life of Sul Ross," 69; Victor M. Rose, *Ross' Texas Brigade: Being a Narrative of Events Connected with Its Service in the Late War Between the States* (Louisville: Courier-Journal Book and Job Rooms, 1881), 162–163; Ross to Clark, May 23, 1861, 301–36, TSLAC; Vine Deloria, Jr. and Raymond J. DeMallie, *Documents of American Indian Diplomacy, Treaties, Agreements, and Conventions, 1775–1979* (Norman: University of Oklahoma Press, 1999), 1: 587–680.
46. Benner, *Sul Ross*, 63–64, 67–68; Clarke, "Life of Sul Ross," 69, 79; Farrell and Silverthorne, *First Ladies of Texas*, 185; *Dallas Herald*, August 14, 28, September 4, 11, 25, 1861; Perry Wayne Shelton, comp., and Shelly Morrison, ed., *Personal Civil War Letters of General Lawrence Sullivan Ross, with Other Letters* (Austin: Shelly and Richard Morrison, 1994), 1, 2–3; Compiled Service Records of Confederate Soldiers, Sixth Texas Cavalry, Lawrence S. Ross.

47. Benner, *Sul Ross*, 68; Compiled Service Records of Confederate Soldiers, Sixth Texas Cavalry, Lawrence S. Ross; Bruce S. Allardice, *Confederate Colonels: A Biographical Register* (Columbia: University of Missouri Press, 2008), 359; Marcus J. Wright, comp., *Texas in the War, 1861–1865*, ed. Harold B. Simpson (Hillsboro, TX: Hill Junior College Press, 1965), 24, 112; Jones, "Cynthia Ann Parker and Pease Ross," 382; Selcer, "One Little Indian Boy," 56; Haley, "Charles Goodnight's Indian Recollections," 24.
48. Benner, *Sul Ross*, 68–69; Rose, *Ross' Texas Brigade*, 37; *Dallas Herald*, September 25, October 9, 30, 1861; Homer L. Kerr, ed., *Fighting with Ross' Texas Cavalry Brigade, C.S.A.* (Hillsboro, TX: Hill Junior College Press, 1976), 1–11; Max S. Lale and Hobart Key, Jr., eds., *The Civil War Letters of David R. Garrett: Detailing the Adventures of the 6th Texas Cavalry* (Marshall, TX: Port Caddo Press, 1963), 25, 27, 31, 33; Ralph A. Wooster, *Lone Star Regiments in Gray* (Austin: Eakin Press, 2002), 73; Wright, comp., and Simpson, ed., *Texas in the War*, 24–25, 28, 34, 112, 114–115.
49. Benner, *Sul Ross*, 70, 71; Clarke, "Life of Sul Ross," 80–82; *The War of the Rebellion: A Compilation of the Official Records of the Union and Confederate Armies*, Series I, III: 730–731. Hereafter cited as *OR*; all references are to Series I. William L. Shea and Earl J. Hess, *Pea Ridge: Civil War Campaign in the West* (Chapel Hill: The University of North Carolina Press, 1992), 19; Shelton, comp., and Morrison, ed., *Personal Civil War Letters*, ix, 18–19; Robert Underwood Johnson and Clarence Clough Buel, eds., *Battles and Leaders of the Civil War* (Secaucus, NJ: Castle Books, 1982), 1: 314; *Dallas Herald*, December 11, 1861.
50. Benner, *Sul Ross*, 72–73; Rose, *Ross' Texas Brigade*, 55, 164; *OR*, VIII: 74–75, 302; Johnson and Buel, eds., *Battles and Leaders*, 1: 314–317; Dabney H. Maury, "Recollections of the Elkhorn Campaign," *Southern Historical Society Papers* 2 (October 1876): 181; Shelton, comp., and Morrison, ed., *Personal Civil War Letters*, ix–x, 19–20; Newton A. Keen, *Living and Fighting with the Texas 6th Cavalry* (Gaithersburg, MD: Butternut Press, 1986), 23–25; A. W. Sparks, *The War Between the States as I Saw It: Reminiscent, Historical, and Personal* (Tyler, TX: Lee & Burnet, 1901), 51–52, 171; Kerr, ed., *Fighting with Ross' Texas Cavalry*, 13.
51. Benner, *Sul Ross*, 73; Carter, *Tarnished Cavalier*, 48; *Dallas Herald*, February 19, 1862; Johnson and Buel, eds., *Battles and Leaders*, 1:

319, 334, 337; Shea and Hess, *Pea Ridge*, 63; James C. Bates, *A Texas Cavalry Officer's Civil War: The Diary and Letters of James C. Bates*, ed. Richard Lowe (Baton Rouge: Louisiana State University Press, 1999), 75–76; Shelton, comp., and Morrison, ed., *Personal Civil War Letters*, x, 22; Maury, "Recollections of the Elkhorn Campaign," 186–187.

52. Bates, *Texas Cavalry Officer's Civil War*, 78; Johnson and Buel, eds., *Battles and Leaders*, 1: 320–322; Carter, *Tarnished Cavalier*, 58.
53. Benner, *Sul Ross*, 74–75; Rose, *Ross' Texas Brigade*, 56–57; *OR*, VIII: 217, 206–208, 232–235, 298–299, 301, 303, 304; Shelton, comp., and Morrison, ed., *Personal Civil War Letters*, 23; Johnson and Buel, eds., *Battles and Leaders*, 1: 321; Samuel B. Barron, *Lone Star Defenders: A Chronicle of the Third Texas Cavalry, Ross' Brigade* (New York: The Neale Company, 1908), 67–68; Martha L. Crabb, *All Afire to Fight: The Untold Tale of the Civil War's Ninth Texas Cavalry* (New York: Post Road Press, 2000), 74–75; Keen, *Living and Fighting*, 27–28; Walter P. Lane, *The Adventures and Recollections of General Walter P. Lane: A San Jacinto Veteran, Containing Sketches of the Texan, Mexican, and Late Wars* (Austin: Jenkins Publishing Company, 1970), 91; Sparks, *War Between the States*, 53, 174; Lale and Key, eds., *Letters of David R. Garrett*, 49; Edwin C. Bearss, "The First Day at Pea Ridge," *Arkansas Historical Quarterly* 17 (Summer 1958): 149; Shea and Hess, *Pea Ridge*, 102, 109. For more on Good's battery, see Andrew F. Lang, "Lone Star Pride: The Good-Douglas Texas Battery, CSA, 1861–1865," *East Texas Historical Journal* 45 (October 2007): 26–40.
54. Benner, *Sul Ross*, 75–76; *OR*, VIII: 202–203, 299; Maury, "Recollections of the Elkhorn Campaign," 187–189; Barron, *Lone Star Defenders*, 73; Bates, *Texas Cavalry Officer's Civil War*, 81–82; Albert Castel, "A New View of the Battle of Pea Ridge," *Missouri Historical Review* 62 (January 1968): 148; Shelton, comp., and Morrison, ed., *Personal Civil War Letters*, x, 22, 24, 25–26.
55. *OR*, LIII: 796–797; Johnson and Buel, eds., *Battles and Leaders*, 1: 277.
56. Rose, *Ross' Texas Brigade*, 63–64; *OR*, X, Pt. 2: 354, 405, XIII: 813–816, LIII: 784; Stephen B. Oates, *Confederate Cavalry West of the River* (Austin: University of Texas Press, 1961), 36–37; Kerr, ed., *Fighting with Ross' Texas Cavalry*, 16–17, 35; Crabb, *All Afire to Fight*, 85.

57. Kerr, ed., *Fighting with Ross' Texas Cavalry*, 38; Crabb, *All Afire to Fight*, 86–88; Albert Burton Moore, *Conscription and Conflict in the Confederacy* (Columbia: University of South Carolina Press, 1996), 14.
58. Benner, *Sul Ross*, 78–79; *OR*, X, Pt. 2: 437, 462, 489, 548–551; Shelton, comp., and Morrison, ed., *Personal Civil War Letters*, 27–28, x; Compiled Service Records of Confederate Soldiers, Sixth Texas Cavalry, Lawrence S. Ross; Keen, *Living and Fighting*, 32; John H. Eicher and David J. Eicher, *Civil War High Commands* (Stanford: Stanford University Press, 2001), 888; Barron, *Lone Star Defenders*, 80–83; Douglas Hale, *The Third Texas Cavalry in the Civil War* (Norman: University of Oklahoma Press, 1993), 108; Wright, comp., and Simpson, ed., *Texas in the War*, 24, 91; Wooster, *Lone Star Regiments in Gray*, 77.
59. Steven E. Woodworth, *Nothing but Victory: The Army of the Tennessee, 1861–1865* (New York: Alfred A. Knopf, 2005), 206–208; *OR*, X, Pt. 1: 762–765, XIII: 831–832; Dabney H. Maury, "Recollections of General Earl Van Dorn," *Southern Historical Society Papers* 19 (January 1891): 194.
60. Benner, *Sul Ross*, 80; Rose, *Ross' Texas Brigade*, 164; Sparks, *War Between the States*, 273–274; Bruce S. Allardice, *More Generals in Gray* (Baton Rouge: Louisiana State University Press, 1995), 181; Bates, *Texas Cavalry Officer's Civil War*, 155; Shelton, comp., and Morrison, ed., *Personal Civil War Letters*, x, 31, 33, 34, 39, 41, 42, 43, 44–45, 50.
61. Steven E. Woodworth, *Jefferson Davis and His Generals: The Failure of Confederate Command in the West* (Lawrence: University Press of Kansas, 1990), 106; *OR*, XVII, Pt. 1: 120–121, 376, Pt. 2: 62–140, 599, 606, 613, 614, 636, 656, 664–666, 675, X, Pt. 2: 655–657, LII, Pt. 2: 330–332; Eicher and Eicher, *Civil War High Command*, 542, 881, 892; William H. Tunnard, *A Southern Record: The History of the Third Regiment Louisiana Infantry* (Dayton: Morningside Bookshop, 1970), 174; Johnson and Buel, eds., *Battles and Leaders*, 2: 725–727, 730; James McPherson, *Battle Cry of Freedom: The Civil War Era* (New York: Oxford University Press, 1988), 515–516. See also Stuart W. Sanders, "Carnage in Kentucky's Hills," *Civil War Times* 51 (October 2012): 52–59, 80.
62. *OR*, XVII, Pt. 1: 121–123, 136–137, Pt. 2: 690, 693, 695–697, 701–706, 709, 733; Peter Cozzens, *The Darkest Days of the War: The Battles of Iuka and Corinth* (Chapel Hill: The University of North Carolina

Press, 1997), 52–55, 63–65, 68–73, 78, 123, 129–130; Robert Collins Suhr, "Small but Savage Battle of Iuka," *America's Civil War* 12 (May 1999): 44–49; Stanley F. Horn, *The Army of Tennessee: A Military History* (Norman: University of Oklahoma Press, 1993), 174; Shelby Foote, *The Civil War: A Narrative* (New York: Vintage Books, 1986), 1: 717–720; McPherson, *Battle Cry of Freedom*, 522–523; Shelton, comp., and Morrison, ed., *Personal Civil War Letters*, x, 46; Barron, *Lone Star Defenders*, 108; Sparks, *War Between the States*, 274.

63. *OR*, XVII, Pt. 2: 707–709, 710, 711–712, 714, 715, 717, 729, Pt. 1: 374–375; Tunnard, *A Southern Record*, 190–191; Hale, *Third Texas Cavalry*, 129.
64. Benner, *Sul Ross*, 83–85; Rose, *Ross' Texas Brigade*, 72; *OR*, XVII, Pt. 1: 375, 378, 385–387, 393–394, Pt. 2: 377, 710; Carter, *Tarnished Cavalier*, 91–92, 95–100; Cozzens, *Darkest Days of the War*, 136, 140–143, 149, 161, 208; Glenn W. Sunderland, "The Bloody Battle of Corinth," *Civil War Times Illustrated* 6 (April 1967): 30, 32; Johnson and Buel, eds., *Battles and Leaders*, 2: 738, 743, 745–746; Keen, *Living and Fighting*, 38–40; *Dallas Herald*, November 8, 1862.
65. Benner, *Sul Ross*, 85–86; Clarke, "Life of Sul Ross," 87–88; *OR*, XVII, Pt. 1: 169–170, 377, 379–380, 383, 387, 394; Cozzens, *Darkest Days of the War*, 255, 266–267, 273; Carter, *Tarnished Cavalier*, 101–104; Sunderland, "Bloody Battle of Corinth," 33, 36; "General and Governor Ross, of Texas," *Confederate Veteran* 2 (June 1894): 169; *Dallas Herald*, November 8, 1862; Kerr, ed., *Fighting with Ross' Texas Cavalry*, 46; Sparks, *War Between the States*, 193, 275; Johnson and Buel, eds., *Battles and Leaders*, 3: 751.
66. Benner, *Sul Ross*, 87; Ross, *Ross' Texas Brigade*, 74; *OR*, XVII, Pt. 1: 170, 376, 380–381, 388, 394–395, 399, 403; Cozzens, *Darkest Days of the War*, 278–279, 282–286, 289; Keen, *Living and Fighting*, 41–42; Barron, *Lone Star Defenders*, 121–122; Bates, *Texas Cavalry Officer's Civil War*, 188–189; Maury, "Recollections of General Earl Van Dorn," 196–197; *Dallas Herald*, November 8, 1862. See also Peter Cozzens, "Blunder at the Bridge," *Civil War Times* 49 (October 2010): 60–63.
67. Benner, *Sul Ross*, 88, 89; *OR*, XVII, Pt. 2: 741, 738; Keen, *Living and Fighting*, 44; Ross to Maury, October 21, 1862, Compiled Service Records of Confederate General and Staff Officers, Lawrence S. Ross; Harry McCorry Henderson, *Texas in the Confederacy* (San Antonio: The Naylor Company, 1955), 81, 124–126, 127.

68. *OR*, XVII, Pt. 1: 503, 539–541, Pt. 2: 811–812, 832, 833, 835, 838, 757–758, XXIII, Pt. 2: 646; A. F. Brown, "Van Dorn's Operations in Northern Mississippi—Recollections of a Cavalryman," *Southern Historical Society Papers* 5 (October 1878): 154–161; Carter, *Tarnished Cavalier*, 161, 163; Thomas Lawrence Connelly, *Autumn of Glory: The Army of Tennessee, 1862–1865* (Baton Rouge: Louisiana State University Press, 2001), 116; Foote, *Civil War*, 2: 176.
69. *OR*, XXIV, Pt. 3: 592, 614, XVII, Pt. 2: 592, 844, 846–847, LII, Pt. 2: 418, XXIII, Pt. 2: 650; Wright, comp., and Simpson, ed., *Texas in the War*, 96, 128–129; Kerr, ed., *Fighting with Ross' Texas Cavalry*, 48, 55, 57; Barron, *Lone Star Defenders*, 127; Robert Selph Henry, *First with the Most: Nathan Bedford Forrest* (New York: Mallard Press, 1991), 128.
70. Benner, *Sul Ross*, 89; Rose, *Ross' Texas Brigade*, 92–94; *OR*, XXIII, Pt. 1: 75, 77–78, 80, 84, 85–86, 90, 113–114, 116–125, 641, LII, Pt. 2: 425; Lale and Key, eds., *Letters of David R. Garrett*, 73; Kerr, ed., *Fighting with Ross' Texas Cavalry*, 59–60; Barron, *Lone Star Defenders*, 144, 148–149; Henry, *First with the Most*, 129–131; Robert C. Cheeks, "Federal Fiasco at Thompson's Station," *America's Civil War* 12 (November 1999): 28–31; Carter, *Tarnished Cavalier*, 167–170; Brian Steel Wills, *The Confederacy's Greatest Cavalryman: Nathan Bedford Forrest* (Lawrence: University Press of Kansas, 1998), 81–82.
71. Benner, *Sul Ross*, 90; *OR*, XXIII, Pt. 1: 222–227, 230–231, Pt. 2: 701, LII, Pt. 2: 450; Eicher and Eicher, *Civil War High Commands*, 543, 891; Bates, *Texas Cavalry Officer's Civil War*, 236–237; Hale, *Third Texas Cavalry*, 168–169; Carter, *Tarnished Cavalier*, 173–175; Henry, *First with the Most*, 136–138; General Thomas Jordan and J. P. Pryor, *The Campaigns of General Nathan Bedford Forrest and of Forrest's Cavalry* (New York: Da Capo Press, 1996), 245–248; Robert L. Willett, Jr., "The First Battle of Franklin," *Civil War Times Illustrated* 7 (February 1969): 16, 17–23. Joseph Wheeler was placed in command of the II Cavalry Corps of the Army of Tennessee. Mark Mayo Boatner III, *The Civil War Dictionary* (New York: David McKay Company, 1988), 187.
72. *OR*, LII, Pt. 2: 467–468, 472, 473, XXIV, Pt. 3: 947; Carter, *Tarnished Cavalier*, Ch. 10; Connelly, *Autumn of Glory*, 125; Kerr, ed., *Fighting with Ross' Texas Cavalry*, 66; Dudley G. Wooten, ed., *A Comprehensive History of Texas, 1685–1897* (Dallas: William G. Scarff, 1898), 2: 620–621; John Allan Wyeth, *That Devil Forrest: Life of General*

Nathan Bedford Forrest (Baton Rouge: Louisiana State University Press, 1989), 199, 200.

73. Benner, *Sul Ross*, 89, 91; Rose, *Ross' Texas Brigade*, 103; *OR*, LII, Pt. 2: 473, 490, 494, 497, XXIV, Pt. 1: 225, Pt. 3: 947, 955–956, 959, Pt. 2: 440, 226–227; Shelton, comp., and Morrison, ed., *Personal Civil War Letters*, x, 49, 53–54; William C. Davis, ed., *The Confederate General* (Harrisburg, PA: National Historical Society, 1991), 6: 131; Hale, *Third Texas Cavalry*, 178–181; Kerr, ed., *Fighting with Ross' Texas Cavalry*, 66, 69, 80, 98 n92.
74. Benner, *Sul Ross*, 92; Rose, *Ross' Texas Brigade*, 109–110; *OR*, XXX, Pt. 4: 576, 517, 656, 99, XXIV, Pt. 2: 535, 659–660, 1027, Pt. 3: 1041, 1048, XXXI, Pt. 3: 865; Crabb, *All Afire to Fight*, 168–169; Barron, *Lone Star Defenders*, 125, 162–163; Kerr, ed., *Fighting with Ross' Texas Cavalry*, 117–118, 80; Allardice, *Confederate Colonels*, 307; Shelton, comp., and Morrison, ed., *Personal Civil War Letters*, x–xi, 97.
75. Benner, *Sul Ross*, 92–93; Rose, *Ross' Texas Brigade*, 111, 121; *OR*, XXX, Pt. 4: 147, 704, 724; Shelton, comp., and Morrison, ed., *Personal Civil War Letters*, xi, 56; Boatner, *Civil War Dictionary*, 911; Peter Cozzens, *The Shipwreck of their Hopes: The Battles for Chattanooga* (Urbana: University of Illinois Press, 1994), 34; Wiley Sword, *Mountains Touched with Fire: Chattanooga Besieged, 1863* (New York: St. Martin's Press, 1995), 68–69. For more on Wheeler's foray, see Colonel Robert W. Black, *Cavalry Raids of the Civil War* (Mechanicsburg, PA: Stackpole Books, 2004), 54–57.
76. Benner, *Sul Ross*, 93; Rose, *Ross' Texas Brigade*, 121–122; *OR*, XXXI, Pt. 1: 25–31, Pt. 3: 605, 607–610; Lale and Key, eds., *Letters of David R. Garrett*, 87–88.
77. Benner, *Sul Ross*, 93–94; *OR*, XXXI, Pt. 1: 588–590, 586, Pt. 3: 277, 765–766; Lale and Key, eds., *Letters of David R. Garrett*, 88; Shelton, comp., and Morrison, ed., *Personal Civil War Letters*, 57, 58.
78. Benner, *Sul Ross*, 94, 96–97; Rose, *Ross' Texas Brigade*, 103, 112, 147–148; *OR*, LII, Pt. 2: 577, XXXI, Pt. 3: 794, 866, 727, 746; Boggess to Graham, December 5, 1863, Graham to Davis, December 21, 1863, Compiled Service Records of Confederate General and Staff Officers, Lawrence S. Ross; Shelton, comp., and Morrison, ed., *Personal Civil War Letters*, xi, 58–59; Kerr, ed., *Fighting with Ross' Texas Cavalry*, 103; Hale, *Third Texas Cavalry*, 196; Eicher and Eicher, *Civil War High Commands*, 462; Wright, comp., and Simpson, ed., *Texas in*

the War, 86; Allardice, *More Generals in Gray*, 146; Crabb, *All Afire to Fight*, 191.

79. Benner, *Sul Ross*, 97–98; *OR*, XXXII, Pt. 3: 877–879, Pt. 2: 823–824, XXXI, Pt. 3: 841–842, 879–880, XXXIV, Pt. 2: 810–811, 815–816, 862, 885, 999, LIII: 925–926; Barron, *Lone Star Defenders*, 146, 173–174; Crabb, *All Afire to Fight*, 187–188; Kerr, ed., *Fighting with Ross' Texas Cavalry*, 103–105; Sparks, *War Between the States*, 72, 232; W. A. Callaway, "Hard Service with Ross' Cavalry," *Confederate Veteran* 28 (September 1920): 328.
80. Benner, *Sul Ross*, 98; *OR*, XXXII, Pt. 1: 66–67, LIII: 926; Joe M. Scott, "Crossing the Mississippi in 1864," *Confederate Veteran* 29 (February 1921): 64–65; Kerr, ed., *Fighting with Ross' Texas Cavalry*, 106–107; Barron, *Lone Star Defenders*, 176.
81. Benner, *Sul Ross*, 98–99; Rose, *Ross' Texas Brigade*, 104–105, 169; *OR*, XXXII, Pt. 1: 178, 315–317, 321–322, 357, 365, 369, 387–389, Pt. 2: 513–514, 550, 585, 824–833, 862, LII, Pt. 2: 640–641; Janet B. Hewett, ed., *Supplement to the Official Records of the Union and Confederate Armies* (Wilmington, NC: Broadfoot Publishing Company, 1994–2001), Pt. II, IXX: 303. Hereafter cited as *Supplement to OR*. Shelton, comp., and Morrison, ed., *Personal Civil War Letters*, xi, 60–61; Stephen D. Lee, "Operations of the Cavalry in Mississippi, from January to March, 1864—Report of General S. D. Lee," *Southern Historical Society Papers* 9 (March 1881): 97; Kerr, ed., *Fighting with Ross' Texas Cavalry*, 109–110; Barron, *Lone Star Defenders*, 177.
82. Benner, *Sul Ross*, 99; *OR*, XXXII, Pt. 1: 174–176, 358, 366, 370, 389–390, Pt. 2: 340–341, 693; Kerr, ed., *Fighting with Ross' Texas Cavalry*, 111; Boatner, *Civil War Dictionary*, 543–544; Eicher and Eicher, *Civil War High Commands*, 888; Foote, *Civil War*, 2: 923–934; Barron, *Lone Star Defenders*, 178, 180; Henry, *First with the Most*, 222–225, 217–233.
83. Benner, *Sul Ross*, 99–100; Rose, *Ross' Texas Brigade*, 105; *OR*, XXXII, Pt. 1: 390, 322–323, 326–327, 363, 367, 757, 332; *Supplement to OR*, Pt. II, LXXVIII: 75; Kerr, ed., *Fighting with Ross' Texas Cavalry*, 111–113; Lee, "Operations of the Cavalry in Mississippi," 100–101; Barron, *Lone Star Defenders*, 181–182.
84. Benner, *Sul Ross*, 100–101; *OR*, XXXII, Pt. 1: 208, 323–325, 343, 367, 383–387, 390–391; Kerr, ed., *Fighting with Ross' Texas Cavalry*, 113; Barron, *Lone Star Defenders*, 182–183; Ross to McKee and McKee to

Ross, both dated March 5, 1863, *Army and Navy Official Gazette*, 1: 708; Lee, "Operations of the Cavalry in Mississippi," 101.

85. Benner, *Sul Ross*, 102–103; *OR*, XXXVIII, Pt. 4: 661–663, 691, 704, Pt. 3: 615, 646, 653, 660, 666, 675–677, 980, LII, Pt. 2: 659–660; Barron, *Lone Star Defenders*, 186; Kerr, ed., *Fighting with Ross' Texas Cavalry*, 138–142, 175–176; Winston Groom, *Shrouds of Glory: Atlanta to Nashville: The Last Great Campaign of the Civil War* (New York: Atlantic Monthly Press, 1995), 15, 16, 18; Woodworth, *Nothing but Victory*, 490; Albert Castel, *Decision in the West: The Atlanta Campaign of 1864* (Lawrence: University Press of Kansas, 1992), 127, 196; Connelly, *Autumn of Glory*, 314; Bromfield L. Ridley, *Battles and Sketches of the Army of Tennessee* (Mexico, MO: Missouri Printing & Publishing Company, 1906), 344.
86. Benner, *Sul Ross*, 103; *OR*, XXXVIII, Pt. 3: 899, 962–963; Kerr, ed., *Fighting with Ross' Texas Cavalry*, 143; Barron, *Lone Star Defenders*, 193; General Samuel G. French, *Two Wars: An Autobiography of Gen. Samuel G. French* (Nashville: Confederate Veteran, 1901), 194.
87. Benner, *Sul Ross*, 103–104; *OR*, XXXVIII, Pt. 3: 616, 983, 985–987, Pt. 4: 729, 731–732, 734, 737, 764–767, 779–780, 783, 786–787, 790, 792–793, 799–801, Pt. 5: 859–861, 863–864, 866, 872, 878, 884, 886, 911–912, 915, LII, Pt. 2: 678–679; Shelton, comp., and Morrison, ed., *Personal Civil War Letters*, xi, 68; Kerr, ed., *Fighting with Ross' Texas Cavalry*, 143–159; Barron, *Lone Star Defenders*, 194; Keen, *Living and Fighting*, 56–64; Sparks, *War Between the States*, 83–100, 234–235; Castel, *Decision in the West*, 205, 219; Philip L. Secrist, "The Role of Cavalry in the Atlanta Campaign, 1864," *Georgia Historical Quarterly* 56 (Winter 1972): 515–520. See also R. G. Childress, "Gen. Ross's Scouts in Georgia Campaign," *Confederate Veteran* 11 (December 1903): 552–553.
88. *OR*, XXXVIII, Pt. 3: 618, 630, Pt. 5: 889; Castel, *Decision in the West*, 360–363; Eicher and Eicher, *Civil War High Commands*, 882, 890; Richard M. McMurry, *John Bell Hood and the War for Southern Independence* (Lincoln: University of Nebraska Press, 1992), 121–122; Jeffrey D. Wert, "The Atlanta Campaign: Hood Replaces Johnston," *Civil War Times* 44 (June 2005): 8, 23. Hood had a reputation in both armies for personal bravery and a bold fighting spirit. An aggressive and able combat commander at the brigade and division level, he lacked the self-discipline and the careful attention to administrative detail necessary for effective army leadership. Woodworth, *Jefferson Davis*

and His Generals, 271, 288. See also Steven M. Hood, *John Bell Hood: The Rise, Fall, and Resurrection of a Confederate General* (El Dorado Hills, CA: Savas Beatie, 2013); and Brian Miller, *John Bell Hood and the Fight for Civil War Memory* (Knoxville: University of Tennessee, 2010).

89. *OR*, XXXVIII, Pt. 1: 75; Secrist, "Cavalry in the Atlanta Campaign," 521–522; John W. Rowell, "McCook's Raid," *Civil War Times Illustrated* 13 (July 1974): 5; John Bell Hood, *Advance and Retreat: Personal Experiences in the United States and Confederate States Armies* (Lincoln: University of Nebraska Press, 1996), 193–194, 196; Ridley, *Battles and Sketches*, 382.
90. *OR*, XXXVIII, Pt. 1: 75–77, Pt. 2: 761–762, Pt. 3: 632, 688, 954, 963, Pt. 5: 897, 901–902, 907, 923, 927; Kerr, ed., *Fighting with Ross' Texas Cavalry*, 159; Rowell, "McCook's Raid," 5; Secrist, "Cavalry in the Atlanta Campaign," 522; Barron, *Lone Star Defenders*, 199; Ridley, *Battles and Sketches*, 383–384.
91. Benner, *Sul Ross*, 105–106; Rose, *Ross' Texas Brigade*, 107; *OR*, XXXVIII, Pt. 3: 688–689, 955, 963–965, Pt. 2: 762–763, 776–777, Pt. 5: 932; Kerr, ed., *Fighting with Ross' Texas Cavalry*, 160–162; Barron, *Lone Star Defenders*, 200–204; Keen, *Living and Fighting*, 64–65; Stephen Z. Starr, *The Union Cavalry in the Civil War* (Baton Rouge: Louisiana State Press, 1985), 3: 471–473; Clement A. Evans, ed., *Confederate Military History* (Atlanta: Confederate Publishing Company, 1899), 6: 340; Rowell, "McCook's Raid," 45; Wilbur S. Nye, "Cavalry Operations Around Atlanta," *Civil War Times Illustrated* 3 (July 1964): 49.
92. Benner, *Sul Ross*, 106; Rose, *Ross' Texas Brigade*, 108; *OR*, XXXVIII, Pt. 3: 673, Pt. 1: 79–80, Pt. 2: 813–814, 824–825, 858–859, Pt. 5: 968, 971, 976, 978, 981–982, LII, Pt. 2: 724; Kerr, ed., *Fighting with Ross' Texas Cavalry*, 164–165; Barron, *Lone Star Defenders*, 205–208, 217, 222–223; Keen, *Living and Fighting*, 68–71; Secrist, "Cavalry in the Atlanta Campaign," 525–526; Jerry Keenan, "Final Cavalry Operations," *Civil War Times Illustrated* 3 (July 1964): 50.
93. Benner, *Sul Ross*, 106; *OR*, XXXVIII, Pt. 2: 814–815, 825–826, 859, 863–864, LII, Pt. 2: 725; Keenan, "Final Cavalry Operations," 50; Castel, *Decision in the West*, 473; Barron, *Lone Star Defenders*, 208–215, 222–227; Kerr, ed., *Fighting with Ross' Texas Cavalry*, 165–167; Hale, *Third Texas Cavalry*, 238–244; Crabb, *All Afire to Fight*, 249; Starr, *Union Cavalry in the Civil War*, 3: 478–479.

94. Benner, *Sul Ross*, 107; *OR*, XXXVIII, Pt. 5: 995–996, LII, Pt. 2: 733, 747, 860, Pt. 3: 693–694, XXXIX, Pt. 2: 881; *Supplement to OR*, Pt. III, III: 509–513; Shelton, comp., and Morrison, ed., *Personal Civil War Letters*, xi, 66–68; Kerr, ed., *Fighting with Ross' Texas Cavalry*, 166–169, 170–172; Barron, *Lone Star Defenders*, 228–230; Hale, *Third Texas Cavalry*, 249–252.
95. Benner, *Sul Ross*, 108; *OR*, LII, Pt. 2: 749–751, 754, 759, 760–761, 768, XLV, Pt. 1: 32–34, 767–768. Ross' entire report was reprinted in J. A. Creager, "Ross's Brigade of Cavalry," *Confederate Veteran* 28 (August 1920): 290–292. Hood, *Advance and Retreat*, 254, 255, 258–259, 264; McMurry, *John Bell Hood*, 159–167; Benjamin Franklin Cooling, *To the Battles of Franklin and Nashville and Beyond: Stabilization and Reconstruction in Tennessee and Kentucky, 1864–1866* (Knoxville: University of Tennessee, 2011), 270–272, 276, 277–278; Wiley Sword, *The Confederacy's Last Hurrah: Spring Hill, Franklin, and Nashville* (Lawrence: University Press of Kansas, 1993), 46; Groom, *Shrouds of Glory*, 59, 123–124.
96. Benner, *Sul Ross*, 109; *OR*, XLV, Pt. 1: 575–576, 752, 768–769, 687, 731; Kerr, ed., *Fighting with Ross' Texas Cavalry*, 189; Henry, *First with the Most*, 384, 385–389; Jordan and Pryor, *Campaigns of Forrest*, 611–612; Johnson and Buel, eds., *Battles and Leaders*, 4: 429; Callaway, "Hard Service with Ross' Cavalry," 329; Thomas A. Wigginton, "Cavalry Operations in the Nashville Campaign," *Civil War Times Illustrated* 3 (December 1964): 40; Wyeth, *That Devil Forrest*, 471; John R. Lundberg, *The Finishing Stroke: Texans in the 1864 Tennessee Campaign* (Abilene, TX: McWhiney Foundation Press, 2002), 75–76. Thomas Connelly and Richard McMurry maintain Hood's objective was Nashville, rather than Pulaski, although his plan was not fully formed. Connelly, *Autumn of Glory*, 490–491; McMurry, *John Bell Hood*, 169.
97. Benner, *Sul Ross*, 109–110; *OR*, XLV, Pt. 1: 148, 604, 657, 752–753, 769–770; Cooling, *To the Battles of Franklin and Nashville*, 285–287; Horn, *Army of Tennessee*, 385–393; Henry, *First with the Most*, 394; Jordan and Pryor, *Campaigns of Forrest*, 619–620; Kerr, ed., *Fighting with Ross' Texas Cavalry*, 191; Wigginton, "Cavalry Operations in the Nashville Campaign," 40–41; Johnson and Buel, eds., *Battles and Leaders*, 4: 431; Groom, *Shrouds of Glory*, 143–148; Sparks, *War Between the States*, 281.
98. Benner, *Sul Ross*, 110–111; Rose, *Ross' Texas Brigade*, 118–119; *OR*, XLV, Pt. 1: 576, 770–771, 769–770, 754, 35; McMurry, *John Bell Hood*,

174–176; Kerr, ed., *Fighting with Ross' Texas Cavalry*, 191–193; Hale, *Third Texas Cavalry*, 260; Sparks, *War Between the States*, 283–284; Wyeth, *That Devil Forrest*, 480–482; Wigginton, "Cavalry Operations in the Nashville Campaign," 41; Sword, *Confederacy's Last Hurrah*, 241, 278; Groom, *Shrouds of Glory*, 175–176; Lundberg, *Finishing Stroke*, 97–98; Johnson and Buel, eds., *Battles and Leaders*, 4: 435; Henry, *First with the Most*, 401; Crabb, *All Afire to Fight*, 270, 402 n43.

Despite the fact that Hood held the field, the Pyrrhic victory at Franklin cost his army an official total of 6,252 dead, wounded, captured, and missing. The real sum might have been as high as seven thousand. Among the casualty figures were fifty-five regimental commanders *hors de combat*, five general officers killed, one mortally wounded, and another seven generals wounded and one captured. James R. Knight, *Hood's Tennessee Campaign: The Desperate Venture of a Desperate Man* (Charleston, SC: The History Press, 2014), 93–94.

99. Benner, *Sul Ross*, 111; *OR*, XLV, Pt. 1: 38, 42, 620–621, 755–758, 771–772, 567, 603, 726–728, Pt. 2: 726, 730, 748, 756; W. A. Callaway, "Hard Times with Ross' Cavalry," *Confederate Veteran* 28 (December 1920): 447; Kerr, ed., *Fighting with Ross' Texas Cavalry*, 193–196; Wills, *The Confederacy's Greatest Cavalryman*, 291–293; Henry, *First with the Most*, 390, 404–405, 407, 411–412; McMurry, *John Bell Hood*, 177, 179; Connelly, *Autumn of Glory*, 512; Jordan and Pryor, *Campaigns of Forrest*, 645–646; Lundberg, *Finishing Stroke*, 119; Crabb, *All Afire to Fight*, xxxi, 278–283; Barron, *Lone Star Defenders*, 251–253; Wyeth, *That Devil Forrest*, 502, 504–507; Wigginton, "Cavalry Operations in the Nashville Campaign," 43; Henderson, *Texas in the Confederacy*, 93. See also Steven E. Woodworth and Charles D. Grear, eds., *The Tennessee Campaign of 1864* (Carbondale: Southern Illinois University Press, 2016); and Anne J. Bailey, *The Chessboard of War: Sherman and Hood in the Autumn Campaigns of 1864* (Lincoln: University of Nebraska Press, 2000).

From September 1863 to April 1864, Ross had experienced a fever and chills nearly every three days. Despite suffering from a likely case of malaria, he had never gone on sick leave. Jack D. Welsh, *Medical Histories of Confederate Generals* (Kent, OH: Kent State University Press, 1995), 189.

100. Benner, *Sul Ross*, 112–113; *OR*, XLV, Pt. 2: 748, 757, 762, 771, 784, 805, XLVIII, Pt. 1: 973–974, 1198, 1218, 1394–1395, XLIX, Pt. 1: 952,

953, 971, 972, 995–996, 998–999, 1033, LII, Pt. 2: 811–812; McMurry, *John Bell Hood*, 183; Eicher and Eicher, *Civil War High Commands*, 323; Welsh, *Medical Histories of Confederate Generals*, 189; Barron, *Lone Star Defenders*, 267–270, 274; Wooten, ed., *Comprehensive History of Texas*, 2: 627; Lale and Key, eds., *Letters of David R. Garrett*, 90; *Dallas Herald*, May 11, 1865; Bates, *Texas Cavalry Officer's Civil War*, 330; Henderson, *Texas in the Confederacy*, 89.

101. Benner, *Sul Ross*, 113, 115; Clarke, "Life of Sul Ross," 102–103; Sparks, *War Between the States*, 117; *Dallas Herald*, May 11, 1865; Wooten, ed., *Comprehensive History of Texas*, 2: 627.

102. Benner, *Sul Ross*, 116–117; Eicher and Eicher, *Civil War High Commands*, 462; L. S. Ross, Texas Applications for Special Pardons, Box 2006/07J-5, TSLAC; *Message of President Transmitting Names of Persons Pardoned, Who Have Been Engaged in Rebellion*, House Executive Document No. 31, 39th Congress, 2nd Session, 12; Case Files of Applications from Former Confederates for Presidential Pardons ("Amnesty Papers"), 1865–1867, Microfilm No. 1003, RG 94, NARA.

Even after his pardon application wound its way through the bureaucracy, the First Reconstruction Act of March 2, 1867, disqualified from voting all state or federal officers who had sworn to uphold the United States Constitution, then supported the Confederacy. Believing the law was not broad enough, Congress passed the Supplementary Reconstruction Act twenty-one days later. The latter act barred any man who had held state or federal office and later supported the Rebellion, including former ranger captain Sul Ross. These restrictions remained in place even after Radical Republicans in Texas failed to write the disqualifications into the state constitution in 1869. Disfranchisement continued under the directives of the Fourteenth Amendment until the Democrats returned to power in 1872. Carl H. Moneyhon, *Texas After the Civil War: The Struggle of Reconstruction* (College Station: Texas A&M University Press, 2004), 69–70; Carl H. Moneyhon, *Republicanism in Reconstruction Texas* (College Station: Texas A&M University Press, 1980), 58–59.

103. Benner, *Sul Ross*, 117–118 n18; Clarke, "Life of Sul Ross," 102–103; Wright, comp., and Simpson, ed., *Texas in the War*, 91; Clarke, "Chapter in the History of Young Territory," 61; Ezra J. Warner, *Generals in Gray: Lives of the Confederate Commanders* (Baton Rouge: Louisiana State University Press, 2008), 264; Tax Rolls, McLennan County, 1865; Daniel, *Descendants of Shapley Prince Ross*, 19–20; Dumas Malone,

ed., *Dictionary of American Biography* (New York: Charles Scribner's Sons, 1935), 16: 179.

104. Benner, *Sul Ross*, 120–122; Clarke, "Life of Sul Ross," 103; Malone, ed., *Dictionary of American Biography*, 16: 179; Wilkes, *Waco Medical Association*, 36; Tax Rolls, McLennan County, 1866–1874; Bracken, *Historic McLennan County*, 10; Wallace, *Waco*, 46; John Sleeper and J. C. Hutchins, comps., *Waco and McLennan County, Texas* (Waco: Examiner Steam Job Establishment, 1876), 25–26, 28, 31; Dayton Kelley, ed., *The Handbook of Waco and McLennan County, Texas* (Waco: Texian Press, 1972), 233.
105. Benner, *Sul Ross*, 122–123, 126; Shelton, comp., and Morrison, ed., *Personal Civil War Letters*, 71; Kelley, ed., *Handbook of Waco and McLennan County*, 233; Stuart, "Texas Indian Fighters and Frontier Rangers," 90; *Dallas Herald*, August 20, 1870; *El Paso Times*, August 28, 1886; *Waco Tribune-Herald*, October 30, 1949.
106. Wallace, *Waco*, 45–46; Bracken, *Historic McLennan County*, 10–11; Roger N. Conger, "Waco: Cotton and Culture on the Brazos," *Southwestern Historical Quarterly* 75 (July 1971): 56–57, 55; Richard Maxwell Brown, *Strain of Violence: Historical Studies of American Violence and Vigilantism* (New York: Oxford University Press, 1975), 280–281; *Austin Daily Democratic Statesman*, March 27, 1875; Roger N. Conger, "The Tomás de la Vega Eleven-League Grant on the Brazos," *Southwestern Historical Quarterly* 71 (January 1958): 381; Sleeper and Hutchins, comps., *Waco and McLennan County*, 35.
107. Benner, *Sul Ross*, 126; Sammy Tise, *Texas County Sheriffs* (Albuquerque: Oakwood Printing, 1989), 365; *Waco Tribune-Herald*, October 30, 1949; *Waco Daily Examiner*, April 21, 1874; Conger, "Tomás de la Vega Eleven-League Grant," 381; Sleeper and Hutchins, comps., *Waco and McLennan County*, 35; *Journal of the Constitutional Convention of the State of Texas, Begun and Held at the City of Austin, September 6, 1875*, 131.
108. Benner, *Sul Ross*, 127; *Waco Daily Examiner*, April 21, March 13, 25, 27, 1874; *Galveston Daily News*, July 1, 1873, March 24, July 9, 11, 15, 16, 1874. One of the men who took Posey into custody in Indian Territory was Sherman County Deputy Sheriff Lee Hall, who in a few short years would succeed L. H. McNelly as leader of the Special State Troops.

    Posey and another accomplice overpowered their guard and escaped from prison. The former visited relatives in Limestone County, secured money and a horse, and disappeared into the Nations. Believing he would end his days at the hands of a lynch mob, Posey was instead killed by the Creek Lighthorse in June 1877. *Dallas Daily Herald*, March 11, 1876; *Austin Weekly Statesman*, April 20, 1876; *Arkansas City Traveler*, July 11, 1877.

During his tenure as sheriff, Ross also arrested Myra Maybelle Shirley Reed, who was in the company of a man wanted for murder in Arkansas. Reed would become better known to history as Belle Starr. *Galveston Daily News*, May 1, 1875.

109. Benner, *Sul Ross*, 128–129; *Austin Daily Democratic Statesman*, August 26, 1874; *Dallas Daily Herald* and *Waco Daily Examiner*, both dated August 18, 1874; *Galveston Daily News*, August 15, 27, 1874. For more on State of Texas v. Caldwell, see A. W. Terrell and A. S. Walker, *The Texas Reports: Cases Argued and Decided in the Supreme Court of the State of Texas* (St. Louis: Gilbert Book Company, 1883), 41: 86–98. The Sheriff's Association continues to exist to this day.
110. Benner, *Sul Ross*, 129–130; Moneyhon, *Texas After the Civil War*, 199; Gammel, comp., *Laws of Texas*, 8: 573–777, 7: 497; *Austin Daily Democratic Statesman*, August 5, 20, December 10, 1875; *Waco Tribune-Herald*, October 30, 1949; Kelley, ed., *Handbook of Waco and McLennan County*, 233; *Journal of the Constitutional Convention*, 4; Randolph B. Campbell, *Grass-Roots Reconstruction in Texas, 1865–1880* (Baton Rouge: Louisiana State University Press, 1997), 188.
111. Benner, *Sul Ross*, 131–138; *Austin Daily Democratic Statesman*, August 20, 1875; *Journal of the Constitutional Convention*, 3–4, 8, 15, 31, 35, 228, 339, 395, 404–405, 802–807; *Austin State Gazette*, November 25, 1875; *Galveston Daily News*, October 12, November 28, 1875, February 16, 17, 18, 19, 20, 1876; *Waco Daily Examiner*, October 5, 21, 24, 26, December 2, 1875; Moneyhon, *Texas After the Civil War*, 200.
112. Benner, *Sul Ross*, 140, 118; Tise, *Texas County Sheriffs*, 365; Whiteside, "Life of Lawrence Sullivan Ross," 56; Tax Rolls, McLennan County, 1880–1887.
113. Benner, *Sul Ross*, 140–141; Whiteside, "Life of Lawrence Sullivan Ross," 69; *Waco Daily Examiner*, October 23, 1875; Shelton, comp., and Morrison, ed., *Personal Civil War Letters*, 74–76, 78–79, 85–88.
114. Benner, *Sul Ross*, 141–142; Clarke, "Life of Sul Ross," 104; Whiteside, "Life of Lawrence Sullivan Ross," 69–70; Norman G. Kittrell, *Governors*

Who Have Been, and Other Public Men of Texas (Houston, TX: Dealy-Adey-Elgin Co., 1921), 97; *A Memorial and Biographical History of Johnson and Hill Counties* (Chicago: Lewis Publishing Company, 1892), 473–475, 639–640; *Dallas Daily Herald*, July 9, November 4, 5, 1880; William Clark Griggs, *The Elusive Eden: Frank McMullan's Confederate Colony in Brazil* (Austin: University of Texas Press, 1987), 138; *Galveston Daily News*, November 5, 1880; *Austin Daily Democratic Statesman*, November 6, 1880, January 9, 1881. See also Patsy McDonald Spaw, *The Texas Senate* (College Station: Texas A&M University Press, 1999), 2: 280–281.

115. Benner, *Sul Ross*, 143; Ernest R. Lindley, ed., *Members of the Legislature of the State of Texas from 1846 to 1939* (Austin: State of Texas, 1939), 103; *Austin Daily Democratic Statesman*, February 8, 1881.
116. Benner, *Sul Ross*, 143–145; *Austin Daily Democratic Statesman*, February 13, 1881; *Journal of the Senate of the State of Texas: Being the First Session of the Seventeenth Legislature*, 79, 104, 20, 21, 38, 51–52, 64, 72, 98, 100, 116, 129, 137, 158, 161, 173–174, 191–192, 215, 229, 265, 276, 308.
117. Benner, *Sul Ross*, 145–147; Daniel, *Descendants of Shapley Prince Ross*, 20; *Journal of the Senate of the State of Texas: Being a Special Session of the Seventeenth Legislature*, 16, 52–54, 9–11, 15, 17–19, 33, 34, 35, 43, 45, 71, 77, 84; Spaw, ed., *Texas Senate*, 2: 293.
118. Benner, *Sul Ross*, 147; Texas Constitution, Art. III, Sec. 3 and 28; Gammel, comp., *Laws of Texas*, 9: 269–270; Kittrell, *Governors Who Have Been*, 97.
119. Benner, *Sul Ross*, 143 n12; Daniel, *Descendants of Shapley Prince Ross*, 19; *Waco Daily Examiner*, January 25, February 1, 1883.
120. Benner, *Sul Ross*, 148–150; *Fort Worth Daily Gazette*, May 26, June 9, 23, 1884, May 18, 1885; *Waco Tribune-Herald*, October 26, 1975; *Waco Daily Examiner*, May 9, 1884, February 25, 1886; *Galveston Daily News*, May 6, 1884, January 10, 18, February 25, May 9, 12, 13, 15, June 16, 28, August 13, 1886; Alwyn Barr, *Reconstruction to Reform: Texas Politics, 1876–1906* (Dallas: Southern Methodist University Press, 2000), 96–97; Daniell, comp., *Personnel of the Texas State Government*, 16; *Austin Weekly Statesman*, May 13, 1886; *McKinney Gazette*, August 19, 1886; *Taylor County News*, August 20, 1886; *El Paso Times*, August 28, 1886.
121. Benner, *Sul Ross*, 150–152; *Galveston Daily News*, January 17, February 25, 26, 1886; Barr, *Reconstruction to Reform*, 83, 96, 90.

See also Ernest William Winkler, *Platforms of Political Parties in Texas* (Bulletin of the University of Texas, No. 53: September 20, 1916), 237–240.

122. Waco *Tribune-Herald*, October 26, 1975.
123. Benner, *Sul Ross*, 154–157; *Waco Daily Examiner*, August 13, 1886; *Galveston Daily News*, August 11, 13, 1886; Barr, *Reconstruction to Reform*, 98, 88; Dudley M. Wooten, ed., *A Comprehensive History of Texas, 1685–1897* (Dallas: William G. Scarff, 1898), 2: 265–266; Winkler, *Platforms of Political Parties*, 237; Kenneth E. Hendrickson, *The Chief Executives of Texas: From Stephen F. Austin to John B. Connally Jr.* (College Station: Texas A&M University Press, 1995), 116.
124. Benner, *Sul Ross*, 157–197; *Galveston Daily News*, January 19, 20, 1887; *Waco Tribune-Herald*, October 30, 1949; Spaw, ed., *Texas Senate*, 2: 358; *Governor's Messages, Coke to Ross, 1874–1891* (Austin: Texas State Library, 1916), 565–569, 581–582, 583–584, 629–632; Gammel, comp., *Laws of Texas*, 9: 805, 800–802, 881–889, 1005, 1078–1081, 1169–1170; Hendrickson, *Chief Executives of Texas*, 116; *Journal of the House of Representatives of the Twentieth Legislature, State of Texas*, 64–72, 75, 84–96, 762, 876, 1138, 1160, 1199. See also Dede Weldon Casad, "The Lives and Legacies of Two Texas Governors, Richard Coke and Lawrence Sullivan Ross, Two Governors: A Comparative Study" (Ph.D. dissertation, University of Texas at Dallas, 2001); and Juanita Oliver Webb, "The Administration of Governor L. S. Ross, 1887–1891" (M.A. thesis, University of Texas at Austin, 1935).
125. Benner, *Sul Ross*, 169; *Austin Daily Statesman*, March 31, May 23, July 25, 1888; Barr, *Reconstruction to Reform*, 105; Winkler, *Platforms of Political Parties*, 253, 254–257, 260–262, 272–273; *Texas Almanac and State Industrial Guide, 1978–1979* (Dallas: A. H. Belo Corporation, 1977), 530.
126. Benner, *Sul Ross*, 170–171; *Austin Daily Statesman*, January 16, 1889.
127. *Journal of the House of Representatives, Being the Regular Session, Twenty-first Legislature*, 27.
128. Benner, *Sul Ross*, 173, 174–175; *Evening Star*, May 20, 1890; *Galveston Daily News*, *New York Herald*, and *Austin Daily Statesman*, all dated May 25, 1890.
129. *Galveston Daily News*, May 27, 1890.
130. Benner, *Sul Ross*, 202; Clarence Ousley, "History of the Agricultural and Mechanical College of Texas," *Bulletin of the Agricultural and*

Mechanical College of Texas 6 (December 1935): 58–59, 158, 159; *Texas Aggie*, March 15, 1932; *Galveston Daily News*, July 6, 7, 12, 1890, March 31, 1892; *Austin Daily Statesman*, July 10, August 9, 1890; *Journal of the House of Representatives of the State of Texas, Twenty-second Legislature, Regular Session*, 37.

131. Benner, *Sul Ross*, 206–208, 218–220; James T. DeShields, *They Sat in High Place: The Presidents and Governors of Texas* (San Antonio: The Naylor Company, 1940), 337–338; Austin E. Burges, *A Local History of A&M College, 1876–1915* (Bryan, TX: n.p., 1915), 13; Ousley, "History of the Agricultural and Mechanical College of Texas," 60, 159; *Texas Aggie*, March 15, 1932; David Brooks Cofer, *Second Five Administrators of Texas A&M College, 1890–1905* (College Station: Association of the Former Students of Texas A&M College, 1954), 62–63; *The Olio* (Columbus, OH: A. C. Berlin & Co., 1895), 65–66; John A. Adams, Jr., *Keepers of the Spirit: The Corps of Cadets at Texas A&M University, 1876–2001* (College Station: Texas A&M University Press, 2001), 55–56. See also *San Antonio Light*, April 6, 1969; and *Waco News-Tribune*, October 30, 1969.
132. Benner, *Sul Ross*, 229–230; Clarke, "Life of Sul Ross," 121; *Galveston Daily News*, April 7, 1892, April 21, 25, 1893, April 7, 9, 1894, May 25, 1895; "The Texas Reunion at Houston," *Confederate Veteran* 1 (May 1893): 154; Cofer, *Second Five Administrators*, 70; Malone, ed., *Dictionary of American Biography*, 16: 179.
133. Benner, *Sul Ross*, 231–232 n47; *Austin Daily Statesman*, *Galveston Daily News*, and *Bryan Daily Eagle*, all dated January 4, 1898; Welsh, *Medical Histories of Confederate Generals*, 189.
134. Benner, *Sul Ross*, 232; Clarke, "Life of Sul Ross," 134–135, 136–137; *San Antonio Daily Express* and *Dallas Morning News*, both dated January 5, 1898; *Galveston Daily News*, January 4, 5, 6, 1898.
135. *Galveston Daily News*, January 10, 1898; *Texas Aggie* (July/August 2007), 30.
136. Benner, *Sul Ross*, 233–234; Malone, ed., *Dictionary of American Biography*, 16: 179; Clifford B. Casey, *Sul Ross State University: The Cultural Center of Trans-Pecos Texas, 1917–1975* (Seagraves, TX: Pioneer Book Publishers, 1976), 9, 17, 18–22.
137. Farrell and Silverthorne, *First Ladies of Texas*, 191–192; *San Antonio Daily Light*, June 8, 1905; *Bryan Daily Eagle* and *Galveston Daily News*, both dated June 9, 1905.

138. "General and Governor Ross, of Texas," 169; Los Angeles County Record of Marriages, 4 (1875–1877): 220; *Los Angeles Herald*, June 10, 11, 1876, October 9, 1880, April 7, 1881, March 28, September 16, December 30, 1886; *National Cyclopaedia of American Biography*, 9: 75; Whiteside, "Life of Lawrence Sullivan Ross," 19.
139. Benner, *Sul Ross*, 55 n29; Gholson, "Recollections of B. F. Gholson," 32–33; Selcer, "One Little Indian Boy," 57–59; McLennan County Marriage Records, Book B (1878–1881): 43; Kelley, ed., *Handbook of Waco and McLennan County*, 233; Bracken, ed. *Historic McLennan County*, 80; Death Certificate, Samuel David Ross, July 15, 1949, File No. 34747; *Waco Daily Examiner*, December 10, 1881; Jones, "Cynthia Ann Parker and Pease Ross," 382. For more on Pease, see Rick Selcer, *Pease Ross: Third Captive from the Battle of the Pease River*, a videotaped 2012 lecture at Fort Worth Public Library available on Youtube.com.
140. Daniel, *Descendants of Shapley Prince Ross*, 19–20; *Valley Morning Star*, November 28, 2007; *Galveston Daily News*, October 9, 1914; Death Certificate, Mr. L. S. Ross, Jr., October 8, 1914, File No. 20716; *Find A Grave*, s.v. "Lawrence Sullivan Ross, Jr."
141. Benner, *Sul Ross*, 230; *Fifteenth U.S. Census*, Travis County, Texas; *Valley Star-Monitor-Herald*, August 20, 1939; Death Certificates, Henry Hill Harrington, August 17, 1939, Registrar's No. 69, Florine Ross Harrington, October 8, 1945, File No. 632; *Wichita Daily Times*, *Big Spring Daily Herald*, and *Paris News*, all dated October 8, 1945.
142. Benner, *Sul Ross*, 230; *Austin Daily Statesman*, January 4, 1898; Birth Certificate, Harvey Bernard Ross, Jr., November 4, 1942, File No. 3361; Death Certificate, Harvey B. Ross, October 20, 1944, File No. 200.
143. Benner, *Sul Ross*, 230; Texas Volunteer Guard Service Records, F. R. Ross, 401–210, TSLAC; *Twelfth U.S. Census*, Travis County, Texas; *Houston Post*, April 1, May 14, 1904, April 21, 30, May 1, 1907, November 26, 1910; *Fourteenth U.S. Census*, Harris County, Texas; *Galveston Daily News*, May 2, 1907; Wilkes, *Waco Medical Association*, 318; *Galveston Daily News*, *Dallas Morning News*, and *San Antonio Express*, all dated December 6, 1938; Death Certificate, Dr. Frank Ritchie Ross, December 6, 1938, File No. 55684.

144. Benner, *Sul Ross*, 230; *Daily Eagle*, September 22, 1898; *Victoria Advocate*, July 27, 1932; Death Certificate, Elizabeth Ross Clarke, July 29, 1932, Registrar's No. 425.
145. Daniel, *Descendants of Shapley Prince Ross*, 20; Midland County Marriage Records, 2 (June 1909-April 1911): 78; *Galveston Daily News*, June 30, 1901, January 13, 1903; *Thirteenth U.S. Census*, Andrews County, Texas; *Corsicana Daily Sun*, August 8, 1938; *San Antonio Express*, August 9, 1938; Death Certificate, Neville P. Ross, August 13, 1938, File No. 36192.

Bibliography

Affleck, Isaac Dunbar. "History of John C. Hays." Two parts. Typescript. Boxes 2Q401 and 2Q402, Isaac Dunbar Affleck Papers. Research and Collections Division, Briscoe Center for American History, The University of Texas at Austin.

Austin, Moses and Stephen F., Papers, 1676, 1765–1889. Research and Collections Division, Briscoe Center for American History, The University of Texas at Austin.

Baker, Jonathan Hamilton, Diary. Transcript. Tarrant County Archives, Tarrant County Historical Commission, Fort Worth, Texas.

Bell, Peter Hansborough, Papers, 1847–1898. Research and Collections Division, Briscoe Center for American History, The University of Texas at Austin.

Bexar Archives. Research and Collections Division, Briscoe Center for American History, The University of Texas at Austin.

Brown, Frank. "Annals of Travis County and of the City of Austin: From the Earliest Times to the Close of 1875." Typescript. Austin History Center, Austin, Texas. The original of this unpublished manuscript is archived at the Briscoe Center for American History, The University of Texas at Austin, while photocopies are kept at the Austin History Center.

Caperton, John C. "Sketch of Colonel John C. Hays, the Texas Rangers, Incidents in Texas and Mexico, Etc. from materials furnished by Col. Hays and Major John Caperton." Typescript. The original copy was prepared in 1879 and is archived at the Bancroft Library, University of California at Berkeley. A copy was obtained from the University of California in 1922 and is currently stored in Box 2R35, John Coffee Hays Collection, Research and Collections Division, Briscoe Center for American History, The University of Texas at Austin. The manuscript was reprinted as "Jack Hays, the Intrepid Texas Ranger," *Frontier Times* 4 (February-May 1927).

Clarke, Elizabeth Ross. "Life of Sul Ross." Typescript. Boxes 5 and 6, Ross Family Papers. The Texas Collection, Baylor University, Waco, Texas.

Confederate Muster Roll Abstract Records. Texas Adjutant General's Department. Archives and Information Services Division, Texas State Library and Archives Commission, Austin, Texas.

DeShields, James Thomas. "Sketches Concerning the Life of John C. Hays." Typescript. James Thomas DeShields Papers. Research and Collections

Division, Briscoe Center for American History, The University of Texas at Austin.

Early Tennessee/North Carolina Land Records, 1783–1931. Record Group 50. Tennessee State Library and Archives, Nashville, Tennessee. Online at Ancestry.com.

Ford Expeditionary Forces Records. Texas Confederate Museum Collection. Haley Memorial Library & History Center, Midland, Texas.

Ford, John S. "John C. Hayes in Texas." Typescript. Box 2Q512, John Salmon Ford Papers. Research and Collections Division, Briscoe Center for American History, The University of Texas at Austin.

Ford, John S. "Rip," Papers. Texas Confederate Museum Collection. Haley Memorial Library & History Center, Midland, Texas.

Gholson, Benjamin Franklin. "Recollections of B. F. Gholson." Transcript of interview with J. A. Rikard, August 1928. Gholson (B. F.) Reminiscences, 1832–1860. Research and Collections Division, Briscoe Center for American History, The University of Texas at Austin.

Green, Thomas J., Papers. Southern Historical Collection. Louis Round Wilson Special Collections Library, University of North Carolina at Chapel Hill.

Houston, Andrew Jackson, Collection. Archives and Information Services Division, Texas State Library and Archives Commission, Austin, Texas

"Jack Hays' Expedition to El Paso and California, 1849." MS. Box 3F176, John Coffee Hays Collection. Research and Collections Division, Briscoe Center for American History, The University of Texas at Austin.

Kemp, Louis Wiltz, Papers. Albert and Ethel Herzstein Library, San Jacinto Museum of History, La Porte, Texas. The collection includes biographical sketches of all participants of the battle of San Jacinto. Online at www.sanjacinto-museum.org.

Lockhart, John W. "Jack Hays Visit to Washington." MS. Box 3F176, John Coffee Hays Collection. Research and Collections Division, Briscoe Center for American History, The University of Texas at Austin. The manuscript was copied from a "Frontier Sketches" article found in the *Dallas News*, May 14, 1893.

McCulloch, Ben and Henry Eustace, Family Papers, 1798–1961. Research and Collections Division, Briscoe Center for American History, The University of Texas at Austin.

Rogers, Hiram B. "Recollections of Ranger H. B. Rogers of the Capture of Cynthia Ann Parker." Transcript of interview with J. A. Rikard, n.d. Filed with "Recollections of B. F. Gholson," Gholson (B. F.) Reminiscences,

1832–1860. Research and Collections Division, Briscoe Center for American History, The University of Texas at Austin.

Smith, Madelon Wright (Mrs. Gillon). "The Family of 'John Jack Hays'." Madelon Wright Smith Memorial Archives. Mt. Juliet-West Wilson County Historical Society Collection. Copy provided to the author by the Mt. Juliet-Wilson County Public Library, Mt. Juliet, Tennessee.

Smith, Madelon Wright (Mrs. Gillon). "Notes on the Hays Family." Madelon Wright Smith Memorial Archives. Mt. Juliet-West Wilson County Historical Society Collection. Copy provided to the author by the Mt. Juliet-Wilson County, Tennessee, Public Library.

Taylor, Creed. "Jack Hays Fight on the Guadalupe." MS. Box 3F176, John Coffee Hays Collection. Research and Collections Division, Briscoe Center for American History, The University of Texas at Austin.

Texas Adjutant General's Department. Record Group 401. Archives and Information Services Division, Texas State Library and Archives Commission, Austin, Texas.

Texas Applications for Special Pardons. Archives and Information Services Division, Texas State Library and Archives Commission, Austin, Texas.

Texas Comptroller of Public Accounts. Republic Claims, 1835–1846. Archives and Information Services Division, Texas State Library and Archives Commission, Austin, Texas. Online at www.tsl.texas.gov.

Texas Comptroller's Office. Confederate Pension Applications, 1899–1975. Archives and Information Services Division, Texas State Library and Archives Commission, Austin, Texas. Online at Ancestry.com.

———. Texas County Tax Rolls. Archives and Information Services Division, Texas State Library and Archives Commission, Austin, Texas.

Texas General Land Office. Land Grants. Archives and Records Program, General Land Office, Austin, Texas. Online at www.glo.texas.gov.

Texas Governors' Papers and Records. Record Group 301. Archives and Information Services Division, Texas State Library and Archives Commission, Austin, Texas.

Texas Secretary of State. Executive Record Books, 1835–1917. Archives and Information Services Division, Texas State Library and Archives Commission, Austin, Texas.

Walker, Samuel Hamilton, Papers. Archives and Information Services Division, Texas State Library and Archives Commission, Austin, Texas.

United States Bureau of the Census. *Third* through *Sixteenth Census of the United States*. Record Group 29: Records of the Bureau of the Census, Microfilm Publications M252, M33, M19, M704, M432,

M653, M593, T9, T623, T624, T625, T626, T627, T1134. National Archives and Records Administration, Washington, D.C. Online at Ancestry.com.

United States Department of War. Carded Records and Correspondence Re: John S. Ford, 2nd Regiment Texas Cavalry (2nd Texas Mounted Rifles) (Confederate). Record Group 109: War Department Collection of Confederate Records. National Archives and Records Administration, Washington, D. C. Copies provided to the author by the Historical Research Center, Texas Heritage Museum, Hill College, Hillsboro, Texas.

United States Department of War. Carded Records Showing Military Service of Soldiers Who Fought in Volunteer Organizations During the Indian Wars, 1817–1858. Record Group 94: Records of the Adjutant General's Office, 1780s–1917. National Archives and Records Administration, Washington, D. C.

———. Case Files of Applications from Former Confederates for Presidential Pardons ("Amnesty Papers"), 1865–1867. Record Group 94: Records of the Adjutant General's Office, 1780s–1917, Microfilm Publication M1003. National Archives and Records Administration, Washington, D. C.

———. Compiled Service Records of Volunteer Soldiers Who Served During the Mexican War in Organizations from the State of Texas. Record Group 94: Records of the Adjutant General's Office, 1780s–1917, Microfilm Publication M278. National Archives and Records Administration, Washington, D. C. Online at Fold3.com.

———. Index to Compiled Service Records of Volunteer Soldiers Who Served During the War of 1812. Record Group 94: Records of the Adjutant General's Office, 1780s–1917, Microfilm Publication M602. National Archives and Records Administration, Washington, D. C. Online at Fold3.com.

———. Letters Received by the Office of the Adjutant General, 1805–1889. Record Group 94: Records of the Adjutant General's Office, 1780s–1917, Microfilm Publication M567. National Archives and Records Administration, Washington, D. C. Online at Fold3.com.

———. Returns from U.S. Military Posts, 1800–1916. Record Group 94: Records of the Adjutant General's Office, 1780's–1917, Microfilm Publication M617. National Archives and Records Administration, Washington, D.C. Online at Ancestry.com.

Vertical Files. Armstrong Texas Ranger Research Center. Texas Ranger Hall of Fame and Museum, Waco, Texas.

Articles

"Affairs in Texas." *Harper's Weekly* 5, no. 221 (March 23, 1861).

Allen, Annalee. "Colonel Jack Hays of Fernwood." *Oakland Heritage Alliance News* 12, no. 4 (Spring 1993).

Arnold, Jess. "Captain Jack." *True West* 2, no. 3 (December 1954-January 1955).

"A Texan Ranger." *Harper's Weekly* 5, no. 236 (July 6, 1861).

Austin, Stephen F. "Journal of Stephen F. Austin on His First Trip to Texas, 1821." *The Quarterly of the Texas State Historical Association* 7, no. 4 (April 1904).

Austin, William T. "Account of the Campaign of 1835 by William T. Austin, Aide to Gen. Stephen F. Austin and Gen. Edward Burleson." *Texana* 4, no. 4 (Winter 1966).

Bakken, Gordon Morris. "Mexican and American Land Policy: A Conflict of Cultures." *Southern California Quarterly* 75, no. 3/4 (Fall/Winter 1993).

Barker, Eugene C. "The Finances of the Texas Revolution." *Political Science Quarterly* 19, no. 4 (December 1904).

———. "The Government of Austin's Colony, 1821–1831." *Southwestern Historical Quarterly* 21, no. 3 (January 1918).

———. "The San Jacinto Campaign." *The Quarterly of the Texas State Historical Association* 4, no. 4 (April 1901).

———. "Stephen F. Austin." *Mississippi Valley Historical Review* 5, no. 1 (June 1918).

———. "Stephen F. Austin and the Independence of Texas." *The Quarterly of the Texas State Historical Association* 13, no. 4 (April 1910).

———. "The Texas Declaration of Causes for Taking Up Arms Against Mexico." *The Quarterly of the Texas State Historical Association* 15, no. 3 (January 1912).

———. "The Texas Revolutionary Army." *The Quarterly of the Texas State Historical Association* 9, no. 4 (April 1906).

———, editor. "Journal of the Permanent Council (October 11–27, 1835)." *The Quarterly of the Texas State Historical Association* 7, no. 4 (April 1904).

Barr, Alwyn. "Confederate Artillery in Arkansas." *Arkansas Historical Quarterly* 22, no. 3 (Autumn 1963).

———. "Texas Coastal Defense, 1861–1865." *Southwestern Historical Quarterly* 65, no. 1 (July 1961).

Bauer, K. Jack. "General John E. Wool's Memoranda of the Battle of Buena Vista." *Southwestern Historical Quarterly* 77, no. 1 (July 1973).

Bearss, Edwin C. "The First Day at Pea Ridge, March 7, 1862." *Arkansas Historical Quarterly* 17, no. 2 (Summer 1958).

Bender, A. B. "Opening Routes across West Texas, 1848–1850." *Southwestern Historical Quarterly* 37, no. 2 (October 1933).

Benedict, J. W. "Diary of a Campaign against the Comanches." *Southwestern Historical Quarterly* 32, no. 4 (April 1929).

Bieber, Ralph P. "The Southwestern Trails to California in 1849." *The Mississippi Valley Historical Review* 12, no. 3 (December 1925).

"Big Foot Wallace's Fight on the Nueces." *Frontier Times* 3, no. 8 (May 1926).

Blackburn, J. K. P. "Reminiscences of the Terry Rangers." *Southwestern Historical Quarterly* 22, no. 1 (July 1918).

Brown, A. F. "Van Dorn's Operations in Northern Mississippi—Recollections of a Cavalryman." *Southern Historical Society Papers* 5, no. 4 (October 1878).

Brown, Dee Alexander. "Pea Ridge: Gettysburg of the West." *Civil War Times Illustrated* 6, no. 1 (October 1967).

———. "Wilson's Creek." *Civil War Times Illustrated* 11, no. 1 (April 1972).

Brown, John Duff. "Reminisces of Jno. Duff Brown." *The Quarterly of the Texas State Historical Association* 12, no. 4 (April 1909).

Brown, John Henry. "'The Paths of Glory:' The War-Time Diary of John Henry Brown, C.S.A." Edited by W. J. Lemke. *Arkansas Historical Quarterly* 15, no. 4 (Winter 1956).

Brown, Walter Lee. "Pea Ridge: Gettysburg of the West." *Arkansas Historical Quarterly* 15, no. 1 (Spring 1956).

Bryan, Moses Austin. "Personal Recollections of Stephen F. Austin." Two parts. *The Texas Magazine* 3, no. 3 (September 1897), no. 5 (November 1897).

Buchanan, A. Russell, editor. "George Washington Trahern: Texas Cowboy Soldier from Mier to Buena Vista." *Southwestern Historical Quarterly* 58, no. 1 (July 1954).

Bugbee, Lester G. "Some Difficulties of a Texas Empresario." *Publications of the Southern History Association* 3, no. 2 (April 1899).

———. "Slavery in Early Texas." *Political Science Quarterly* 13, no. 3 (September 1898).

Burnam, Jesse. "Recollections of Capt. Jesse Burnam." *The Quarterly of the Texas State Historical Association* 5, no. 1 (July 1901).

Cagley, Tom, and Parke Pierson. "The Civil War in Arkansas." *America's Civil War* 18, no. 3 (July 2005).

"Callahan's Body Taken to Austin." *Frontier Times* 8, no. 6 (March 1931).

Callaway, W. A. "Hard Service with Ross' Cavalry." *Confederate Veteran* 28, no. 9 (September 1920).

———. "Hard Times with Ross' Cavalry." *Confederate Veteran* 28, no. 12 (December 1920).

Cantrell, Gregg. "The Partnership of Stephen F. Austin and Joseph H. Hawkins." *Southwestern Historical Quarterly* 99, no. 1 (July 1995).

"Captured an Indian Near Bandera." *Frontier Times* 1, no. 10 (July 1924).

Castel, Albert. "A New View of the Battle of Pea Ridge." *Missouri Historical Review* 67, no. 2 (January 1968).

Chase, Adelaide B. Baggerly. "Baggerly Family Records." *National Genealogical Society Quarterly* 31, no. 4 (December 1943).

Cheeks, Robert C. "Federal Fiasco at Thompson's Station." *America's Civil War* 12, no. 5 (November 1999).

Cheeseman, Bruce A. "'Let Us Have 500 Good Determined Texans': Richard King's Account of the Union Invasion of South Texas, November 12, 1863, to January 20, 1864." *Southwestern Historical Quarterly* 101, no. 1 (July 1997).

Clar, C. Raymond. "Pioneer Among the Argonauts." Parts Three and Four. *The Pacific Historian* 6, no. 2 (May 1962), no. 3 (June 1962).

Clarke, Fannie McAlpine. "A Chapter in the History of Young Territory." *The Quarterly of the Texas State Historical Association* 9, no. 1 (July 1905).

Comtois, Pierre. "War's Last Battle." *America's Civil War* 5, no. 2 (July 1992).

Conger, Roger N. "The Tomás de la Vega Eleven-League Grant on the Brazos." *Southwestern Historical Quarterly* 61, no. 3 (January 1958).

———. "Waco: Cotton and Culture on the Brazos." *Southwestern Historical Quarterly* 75, no. 1 (July 1971).

Conyer, Luther. "Last Battle of the War." *Southern Historical Society Papers* 24 (January-December 1896).

Crain, John W. "Isaac Watts Burton: The Glorious Years, 1832–1843." *Southwestern Historical Quarterly* 109, no. 2 (October 2005).

Crimmins, Colonel Martin L. "Colonel Robert E. Lee's Report on Indian Combats in Texas." *Southwestern Historical Quarterly* 39, no. 1 (July 1935).

———. "First Sergeant John W. Spangler, Company H, Second United States Cavalry." *West Texas Historical Association Yearbook* 26 (1950).

Cutrer, Thomas W. "'The Tallapoosa Might Truly Be Called the River of Blood': Major Alexander McCulloch and the Battle of Horseshoe Bend, March 27, 1813." *Alabama Review* 43, no. 1 (January 1990).

———, editor. "My Wild Hunt After Indians: The Journal of Willis L. Lang, 23 April-7 September 1860." *Military History of the Southwest* 21, no. 1 (Spring 1991). The original typescript of "Captain Lang's Diary" is archived at the Research and Collections Division, Briscoe Center for American History, The University of Texas at Austin.

Dana, Edmund L. "Incidents in the Life of Capt. Samuel H. Walker, Texan Ranger." *Proceedings of the Wyoming Historical and Geological Society* No. 3 (1882).

Daniell, Forrest. "Texas Pioneer Surveyors and Indians." *Southwestern Historical Quarterly* 60, no. 4 (April 1957).

Day, James M. "Big Foot Wallace in Trans-Pecos Texas." *West Texas Historical Association Yearbook* 55 (1979).

———, editor. "Diary of James A. Glasscock, Mier Man." *Texana* 1, no. 2 (Spring 1963), no. 3 (Summer 1963).

———. "Israel Canfield in the Mier Expedition," *Texas Military History* 3, no. 3 (Fall 1963).

Deas, Major George. "Reminiscences of the Campaign on the Rio Grande." Four parts. *The Historical Magazine* 7 (Second Series), no. 1 (January 1870), no. 2 (February 1870), no. 4 (April 1870), no. 5 (May 1870).

Delaney, Robert W. "Matamoros, Port for Texas during the Civil War." *Southwestern Historical Quarterly* 58, no. 4 (April 1955).

Delgado, James P. "Gold Rush Jail: The Prison Ship 'Euphemia'." *California History Magazine* 60, no. 2 (Summer 1981).

Dodson, Milton M. "Fought Cortina and His Raiders." *Frontier Times* 7, no. 1 (October 1929).

"Domestic Intelligence." *Harper's Weekly* 4, no. 166 (March 3, 1860).

"Domestic Intelligence." *Harper's Weekly* 4, no. 167 (March 10, 1860).

Dorsey, Dorothy B. "The Panic of 1819 in Missouri." *Missouri Historical Review* 29, no. 2 (January 1935).

Eastland, Thomas B., and Joseph G. Eastland. "To California through Texas and Mexico: The Diary and Letters of Thomas B. Eastland and Joseph G. Eastland, His Son." Edited by Douglas S. Watson and Dorothy H. Huggins. *California Historical Society Quarterly* 18, no. 2 (June 1939).

Ethier, Eric. "The Battle of Wilson's Creek." *Civil War Times* 44, no. 5 (December 2005).

Erath, Lucy A. "Memoirs of Major George Bernard Erath." *Southwestern Historical Quarterly* 26, no. 3 (January 1923), no. 4 (April 1923); 27, no. 1 (July 1923), no. 2 (October 1923).

Friend, Llerena B. "Sidelights and Supplements on the Perote Prisoners." *Southwestern Historical Quarterly* 69, no. 2 (October 1965).

Fulmore, Z. T. "The Annexation of Texas and the Mexican War." *The Quarterly of the Texas State Historical Association* 5, no.1 (July 1901).

Gailey, Harry A., Jr. "Sam Houston and the Texas War Fever, March-August 1842." *Southwestern Historical Quarterly* 62, no. 1 (July 1958).

"General Austin's Order Book for the Campaign of 1835." *The Quarterly of the Texas State Historical Association* 11, no. 1 (July 1907).

"General and Governor Ross, of Texas." *Confederate Veteran* 2, no. 6 (June 1894).

"General Ben M'Culloch." *Harper's Weekly* 5, no. 245 (September 7, 1861).

"General Twiggs's Surrender to the Texans." *Harper's Weekly* 5, no. 221 (March 23, 1861).

Goodwin, G. C. "The Last Battle of the War." *Confederate Veteran* 18, no. 7 (July 1910).

Gorenfeld, Will and John. "Chasing Juan Cortina." *Wild West* 28, no. 5 (February 2016).

Greer, Hilton R. "The Code of Honor under the Lone Star." *The Scrap Book* 6, no. 4 (October 1908).

Gregg, Kate L. "The War of 1812 on the Missouri Frontier." *Missouri Historical Review* 33, no. 2 (January 1939).

Gunn, Jack W. "Ben McCulloch: A Big Captain." *Southwestern Historical Quarterly* 58, no. 1 (July 1954).

Haley, J. Evetts. "Charles Goodnight's Indian Recollections." *Panhandle-Plains Historical Review* 1, no. 1 (1928).

Harris, F. E. "Last Range of Big-Foot Wallace." *Frontier Times* 20, no. 6 (March 1943).

Hatley, Allen G. "Sam Walker." *The Texas Ranger Dispatch* 2 (Winter 2000).

———. "Samuel Walker: Valiant Warrior." *True West* 47, no. 4 (May 2000).

Henderson, H. M. "A Critical Analysis of the San Jacinto Campaign." *Southwestern Historical Quarterly* 59, no. 3 (January 1956).

Henderson, Mary Virginia. "Minor Empresario Contracts for the Colonization of Texas, 1825–1834." *Southwestern Historical Quarterly* 31, no. 4 (April 1928).

Hendricks, Sterling Brown. "The Somervell Expedition to the Rio Grande, 1842." *Southwestern Historical Quarterly* 23, no. 2 (October 1919).

Hinds, Charles F. "Mexican War Journal of Leander M. Cox." *The Register of the Kentucky Historical Society* 56, no. 1 (January 1958).

Holden, William C. "Frontier Defense, 1846–1860." *West Texas Historical Association Yearbook* 6 (1930).

Holland, James K. "Diary of a Texan Volunteer in the Mexican War." *Southwestern Historical Quarterly* 30, no. 1 (July 1926).

Hord, B. M. "Gen. Ben McCulloch." *Confederate Veteran* 12, no. 2 (February 1904).

Howren, Alleine. "Causes and Origin of the Decree of April 6, 1830." *Southwestern Historical Quarterly* 16, no. 4 (April 1913).

Hughes, Michael A. "A Forgotten Battle in a Region Ignored: Pea Ridge or Elkhorn Tavern, Arkansas, March 7–8, 1862." *Blue and Gray Magazine* 5, no. 3 (January 1988).

Hunter, J. Marvin. "Jack Hays: The Famous Texas Ranger." *Frontier Times* 1, no. 1 (October 1923).

———, editor. "Jack Hays, the Intrepid." *Old West* 1, no. 4 (Summer 1965).

Hunter, John Warren. "Adventures of a Mier Prisoner." *Frontier Times* 2, no. 7 (April 1925).

Johnson, H. Parker. "Coraville, Denver's First Post Office." *The Colorado Magazine* 24, no. 1 (January 1947).

Jones, Breckenridge. "One Hundred Years of Banking in Missouri, 1820–1920." *Missouri Historical Review* 15, no. 2 (January 1921).

Jones, Lawrence T, III. "Cynthia Ann Parker and Pease Ross—The Forgotten Photographs." *Southwestern Historical Quarterly* 93, no. 3 (January 1990).

Jones, Robert L., and Pauline H. Jones. "Stephen F. Austin in Arkansas." *Arkansas Historical Quarterly* 25, no. 4 (Winter 1966).

Keenan, Jerry. "Final Cavalry Operations." *Civil War Times Illustrated* 3, no. 4 (July 1964).

Kite, Jodella D. "The War and Peace Parties of Pre-Revolutionary Texas, 1832–1835." *East Texas Historical Journal* 29, no. 1 (March 1991).

Klos, George. "'Our People Could Not Distinguish One Tribe from Another': The 1859 Expulsion of the Reserve Indians from Texas." *Southwestern Historical Quarterly* 97, no. 4 (April 1994).

Knauss, James Owens. "St. Joseph, an Episode of the Economic and Political History of Florida." *Florida Historical Society Quarterly* 6, no. 1 (July 1927).

Koch, Lena Clara. "The Federal Indian Policy in Texas, 1845–1860." *Southwestern Historical Quarterly* 28, no. 3 (January 1925), no. 4 (April 1925); 29, no. 1 (July 1925), no. 2 (October 1925).

Kurtz, Henry I. "Last Battle of the War." *Civil War Times Illustrated* 1, no. 1 (April 1962).

Kuykendall, J. H. "Reminiscences of Early Texans." Three parts. *The Quarterly of the Texas State Historical Association* 6, no. 3 (January 1903), no. 4 (April 1903); 7, no. 1 (July 1903).

Laumer, Frank. "This Was Fort Dade." *Florida Historical Quarterly* 45, no. 1 (July 1966).

Laxson, Crawford. "Personal Recollections of Big-Foot Wallace." *Frontier Times* 12, no. 4 (January 1935).

Lee, Stephen D. "Operations of the Cavalry in Mississippi, from January to March, 1864—Report of General S. D. Lee." *Southern Historical Society Papers* 9, no. 3 (March 1881).

Lehman, M. P. "Big Foot Wallace: A Legend in His Own Time." *Real West* 17, no. 124 (February 1974).

"Letters from 'Big Foot Wallace'." *Frontier Times* 8, no. 9 (June 1931).

Looscan, Adele B., editor. "Journal of Lewis Birdsall Harris, 1836–1842." *Southwestern Historical Quarterly* 25, no. 1 (July 1921), no. 2 (October 1921), no. 3 (January 1922).

McKnight, Joseph W. "Stephen F. Austin's Legalistic Concerns." *Southwestern Historical Quarterly* 89, no. 3 (January 1986).

Mahon, Emmie Giddings W., and Chester V. Kielman. "George H. Giddings and the San Antonio-San Diego Mail Line." *Southwestern Historical Quarterly* 61, no. 2 (October 1957).

Martin, Charles L. "The Last of the Ranger Chieftains." *The Texas Magazine* 4, no. 1 (January 1898).

Marvel, William "Last Hurrah at Palmetto Ranch." *Civil War Times* 44, no. 6 (January 2006).

Maury, Dabney H. "Recollections of General Earl Van Dorn." *Southern Historical Society Papers* 19 (January 1891).

———. "Recollections of the Elkhorn Campaign." *Southern Historical Society Papers* 2, no. 4 (October 1876).

Miller, William C. "The Pyramid Lake Indian War of 1860." *Nevada Historical Society Quarterly* 1, no. 1 (September 1957).

Mullin, Robert N. "Stagecoach Pioneers of the Southwest." *Southwestern Studies*, no. 71 (1983).

Nackman, Mark E. "The Making of the Texan Citizen Solider, 1835–1860." *Southwestern Historical Quarterly* 78, no. 3 (January 1975).

Nance, Joseph M., translator and editor. "Brigadier General Adrian Woll's Report of His Expedition into Texas in 1842." *Southwestern Historical Quarterly* 58, no. 4 (April 1955).

Neighbors, Robert S. "The Report of the Expedition of Major Robert S. Neighbors to El Paso in 1849." Edited by Kenneth F. Neighbours. *Southwestern Historical Quarterly* 60, no. 4 (April 1957).

Neighbours, Kenneth F. "The Battle of Walker's Creek." *West Texas Historical Association Yearbook* 41 (1965).

———. "The Expedition of Major Robert S. Neighbors to El Paso in 1849." *Southwestern Historical Quarterly* 58, no. 1 (July 1954).

Nielsen, George R. "Mathew Caldwell." *Southwestern Historical Quarterly* 64, no. 4 (April 1961).

Nye, Wilbur S. "Cavalry Operations Around Atlanta." *Civil War Times Illustrated* 3, no. 4 (July 1964).

Oates, Stephen B. "John S. 'Rip' Ford: Prudent Cavalryman, C.S.A." *Southwestern Historical Quarterly* 64, no. 3 (January 1961).

———. "Los Diablos Tejanos." *The American West* 2, no. 3 (Summer 1965).

———. "Recruiting Confederate Cavalry in Texas." *Southwestern Historical Quarterly* 64, no. 4 (April 1961).

———. "Texas Under the Secessionists." *Southwestern Historical Quarterly* 67, no. 2 (October 1963).

Ousley, Clarence. "History of the Agricultural and Mechanical College of Texas." *Bulletin of the Agricultural and Mechanical College of Texas* 6, no. 8 (December *1935*).

Owens, Richard H. "Battle of Pea Ridge: Deciding the Fate of Missouri." *America's Civil War* 12, no. 6 (January 2000).

Pearce, Basil C. "Pioneer Overland Route." *Western Express* 12 (April 1962).

Pearce, Nicholas Bart. "Price's Campaign of 1861." *Publications of the Arkansas Historical Association* 4 (1917).

Petz, Anna Cora. "History of the Rio Grande Railroad." *Frontier Times* 14, no. 3 (December 1936).

Pioneer. "Some Amended Historic Data." *The Overland Monthly* 10 (Second Series), no. 56 (August 1887).

Pittard, Homer. "From Jefferson to Elkhorn Tavern: The Story of Ben McCulloch." *Rutherford County Historical Society Publication*, no. 11 (Summer 1978).

Reagan, John H. "The Expulsion of the Cherokees from East Texas." *The Quarterly of the Texas State Historical Association* 1, no. 1 (July 1897).

"Reminiscences of the War with Mexico, as Told by Col. Thomas Claiborne." *The Vedette* 7 (April 1886).

Richardson, Rupert Norval. "The Death of Peta Nocona and the Recovery of Cynthia Ann Parker." *Southwestern Historical Quarterly* 46, no. 1 (July 1942).

Rippy, J. Fred. "Border Troubles Along the Rio Grande, 1848–1860." *Southwestern Historical Quarterly* 23, no. 2 (October 1919).

———. "Mexican Projects of the Confederates." *Southwestern Historical Quarterly* 22, no. 4 (April 1919).

Roberts, Thomas D. "Resaca de la Palma: A Traditional Episode in the History of the Second Cavalry." *The Journal of the American Military History Foundation* 1, no. 3 (Autumn 1937).

Roebuck, Field. "Cheno Cortina: Red Robber of the Rio Grande." *True West* 36, no. 9 (September 1989).

Rowell, John W. "McCook's Raid." *Civil War Times Illustrated* 13, no. 4 (July 1974).

Sandbo, Anna Irene. "The First Session of the Succession Convention of Texas, 1861." *Southwestern Historical Quarterly* 18, no. 2 (October 1914).

Schene, Michael G. "Fort Foster: A Second Seminole War Fort." *Florida Historical Quarterly* 54, no. 3 (January 1976).

Scott, Joe M. "Crossing the Mississippi in 1864." *Confederate Veteran* 29, no. 2 (February 1921).

Secrist, Philip L. "The Role of Cavalry in the Atlanta Campaign, 1864." *Georgia Historical Quarterly* 56, no. 4 (Winter 1972).

Selcer, Richard. "One Little Indian Boy." *Wild West* 28, no. 5 (February 2016)

Shearer, Ernest C. "The Carvajal Disturbances." *Southwestern Historical Quarterly* 55, no. 2 (October 1951).

Sheils, Catherine Robertson. "Salmon Family." *"Kith and Kin" Genealogical Bulletin* 2, no. 3 (January 1973).

Shulsinger, Stephanie C. "Colonel Jack Hays in California." *Real West* 16, no. 112 (February 1973).

Sigel, Franz. "The Military Operations in Missouri in the Summer and Autumn of 1861." *Missouri Historical Review* 26, no. 4 (July 1932).

Smith, Persifor F. "The Second Brigade at Monterey." *The Historical Magazine* 3 (Third Series), no. 3 (March 1874).

Smith, W. Roy. "The Quarrel Between Governor Smith and the Council of the Provisional Government of the Republic." *The Quarterly of the Texas State Historical Association* 5, no. 4 (April 1902).

Smither, Harriet, ed. "Diary of Adolphus Sterne." Part Eighteen. *Southwestern Historical Quarterly* 34, no. 3 (January 1931).

Sowell, A. J. "The Life of Bigfoot Wallace." *Frontier Times* 5, no. 4 (January 1928).

Spurlin, Charles. "Ranger Walker in the Mexican War." *Military History of Texas and the Southwest* 9, no. 4 (1971).

———. "Texas Volunteers in the Monterrey Campaign." Two parts. *Military History of Texas and the Southwest* 16, nos. 1 and 2 (1980).

———. "With Taylor and McCulloch Through the Battle of Monterey." *Texas Military History* 6, no. 3 (Fall 1967).

Steen, Ralph W. "Analysis of the Work of the General Council, Provisional Government of Texas, 1835–1836." *Southwestern Historical Quarterly* 40, no. 4 (April 1937).

Stirman, E. I. "Career of Gen. Ben McCulloch." *Confederate Veteran* 21, no. 4 (April 1913).

Stuart, Ben C. "The Battle of Antelope Hills." *Frontier Times* 3, no. 11 (August 1926). Reprinted from *Dallas Morning News*, January 17, 1905.

Suhr, Robert Collins. "Small but Savage Battle of Iuka." *America's Civil War* 12, no. 2 (May 1999).

Sunderland, George W. "The Bloody Battle of Corinth." *Civil War Times Illustrated* 6, no. 1 (April 1967).

Taylor, Bride Neill. "The Beginnings of the State Historical Association." *Southwestern Historical Quarterly* 33, no. 1 (July 1929).

"The Last Battle of the War." *Southern Historical Society Papers* 21 (January-December 1893).

"The Overland Mail Line." *Frontier Times* 8, no. 5 (February 1931).

"The Texas Reunion at Houston." *Confederate Veteran* 1, no. 5 (May 1893).

Thonhoff, Robert H. "San Antonio Stage Lines, 1847–1881." *Southwestern Studies,* no. 29 (1971).

"Trouble with the Cherokee Tribe." *Frontier Times* 1, no. 4 (January 1924).

Trudeau, Noah Andre. "The Last Gun Had Been Fired." *Civil War Times Illustrated* 29, no. 3 (August 1990).

Utley, Robert M. "The Texas Ranger Tradition Established: Jack Hays and Walker Creek." *Montana: The Magazine of Western History* 52, no. 1 (Spring 2002).

Wallace, Edward S. "The United States Army in Mexico City." *Military Affairs* 13, no. 3 (Autumn 1949).

"Wallace Family: Ten Children of Andrew Wallace and Jane Blair." *In and Around Rockbridge* 16, no. 1 (Winter 2009).

Weinert, Robert P. "Confederate Border Troubles with Mexico." *Civil War Times Illustrated* 3, no. 6 (October 1964).

Weiss, Harold J., Jr. “The Bloody Texans in the Mexican War: The Reasons Why.” *The Westerners Brand Book, New York Posse* 16, no. 1 (1969).

Wert, Jeffrey D. “The Atlanta Campaign: Hood Replaces Johnston.” *Civil War Times* 44, no. 2 (June 2005).

“When a Handful of Americans Invaded Mexico.” *Frontier Times* 6, no. 6 (March 1929).

Widener, Ralph. “John S. ‘Rip’ Ford, Colonel, C.S.A.” *The United Daughters of the Confederacy Magazine* 47, no. 5 (May 1984). Reprinted in *Confederate Veteran* (May-June 1993).

Wigginton, Thomas A. “Cavalry Operations in the Nashville Campaign.” *Civil War Times Illustrated* 3, no. 8 (December 1964).

Wight, Willard E., editor. “An Unofficial Account of the Battle of Wilson Creek, August 10, 1861.” *Arkansas Historical Quarterly* 15, no. 4 (Winter 1956).

Wilcox, Seb S. “Laredo during the Texas Republic.” *Southwestern Historical Quarterly* 42, no. 2 (October 1938).

Willett, Robert L., Jr. “The First Battle of Franklin.” *Civil War Times Illustrated* 7, no. 10 (February 1969).

Williams, J. W. “The Van Dorn Trails.” *Southwestern Historical Quarterly* 44, no. 3 (January 1941).

Wilson, D. M. “Another Account.” *Confederate Veteran* 18, no. 7 (July 1910).

Wilson, William F. “Two Letters from a Mier Prisoner.” *The Quarterly of the Texas State Historical Association* 2, no. 3 (January 1899).

Winfrey, Dorman H. “Chief Bowles of the Texas Cherokee.” *Chronicles of Oklahoma* 32, no. 1 (Spring 1954).

Winkler, Ernest William “The Béxar and Dawson Prisoners.” *The Quarterly of the Texas State Historical Association* 13, no. 4 (April 1910).

———, ed. The Bryan-Hayes Correspondence.” *Southwestern Historical Quarterly* 25, no. 2–30, no. 1 (October 1921-July 1926).

———. “The ‘Twin Sisters’ Cannon, 1836–1865.” *Southwestern Historical Quarterly* 21, no. 1 (July 1917).

Woldert, Albert. “The Last of the Cherokees in Texas, and the Life and Death of Chief Bowles.” *Chronicles of Oklahoma* 1, no. 3 (June 1923).

Wooster, Ralph A. “Texas Military Operations against Mexico, 1842–1843.” *Southwestern Historical Quarterly* 67, no. 4 (April 1964).

Zoltan, E. L. “Big Foot Wallace of Texas.” *Golden West* 4, no. 4 (May 1968).

Books and Book Chapters

Abel, Annie Heloise, editor. *The Official Correspondence of James S. Calhoun*. Washington, D.C.: Government Printing Office, 1915.

Adams, George Rollie. *General William S. Harney: Prince of Dragoons*. Lincoln: University of Nebraska Press, 2001.

Adams, John A., Jr. *Conflict and Commerce on the Rio Grande: Laredo, 1755–1955*. College Station: Texas A&M University Press, 2008.

———. *Keepers of the Spirit: The Corps of Cadets at Texas A&M University, 1876–2001*. College Station: Texas A&M University Press, 2001.

Alexander, Bob. *Winchester Warriors: Texas Rangers of Company D, 1874–1901*. Denton: University of North Texas Press, 2009.

Allardice, Bruce S. *Confederate Colonels: A Biographical Register*. Columbia: University of Missouri Press, 2008.

———. *More Generals in Gray*. Baton Rouge: Louisiana State University Press, 1995.

Amberson, Mary Margaret McAllen, et al. *I Would Rather Sleep in Texas: A History of the Lower Rio Grande Valley and the People of the Santa Anita Land Grant*. Austin: Texas State Historical Association, 2003.

Appler's General Directory and Blue Book of Greater San Antonio, 1910. San Antonio: Jules A. Appler, 1910.

Arnold, James R. *Jeff Davis's Own: Cavalry, Comanches, and the Battle for the Texas Frontier*. New York: John Wiley & Sons, 2000.

Austerman, Wayne R. *Sharps Rifles and Spanish Mules: The San Antonio–El Paso Mail, 1851–1881*. College Station: Texas A&M University Press, 1985.

Austin, Stephen F. *Translation of the Laws, Orders, and Contracts, on Colonization, from January, 1821, Up to This Time*. San Felipe de Austin: Godwin B. Cotton, 1829.

Bailey, William H., Sr. *The Genealogy of the Latham-Hill-Montfort-Littlejohn-McCulloch-Campbell and Brownrigg Families*. Knoxville: American Historical Books, 1899.

Bakken, Gordon Morris, editor. *Law in the Western United States*. Norman: University of Oklahoma Press, 2000.

Ball, Durwood. *Army Regulars on the Western Frontier, 1848–1861*. Norman: University of Oklahoma Press, 2001.

Bancroft, Hubert Howe. *History of Mexico*. Volumes Five and Six. San Francisco: A. L. Bancroft & Company, 1885. These books comprise Volumes Thirteen and Fourteen of *The Works of Hubert Howe Bancroft*.

———. *History of the North Mexican States and Texas*. Volume Two. San Francisco: The History Company, 1889. This book comprises Volume Sixteen of *The Works of Hubert Howe Bancroft*.

———. *Popular Tribunals*. Volumes One and Two. San Francisco: The History Company, 1887. These books comprise Volumes Thirty-six and Thirty-seven of *The Works of Hubert Howe Bancroft*.

Barker, Eugene C. *The Life of Stephen F. Austin, Founder of Texas, 1793–1836*. Nashville: Cokesbury Press, 1925; rpt. New York: Da Capo Press, 1968.

———, editor. *The Austin Papers*. Volumes One and Two. Washington, D.C.: Government Printing Office, 1924–1928. The first two volumes were originally published in the *Annual Report of the American Historical Association* for 1919 and 1922. Volume Three. Austin: University of Texas Press, 1926.

Barksdale, Captain John A., compiler. *Barksdale Family History and Genealogy (with Collateral Lines)*. Richmond, VA: William Byrd Press, 1940.

Barr, Alwyn. *Reconstruction to Reform: Texas Politics, 1876–1906*. Austin: University of Texas Press, 1971; rpt. Dallas: Southern Methodist University Press, 2000.

———. *Texans in Revolt: The Battle for San Antonio, 1835*. Austin: University of Texas Press, 1990.

Barron, Samuel B. *Lone Star Defenders: A Chronicle of the Third Texas Cavalry, Ross' Brigade*. New York: The Neale Company, 1908.

Barry, James Buckner. *Buck Barry, Texas Ranger and Frontiersman*. Edited by James K. Greer. Waco: Friends of the Moody Texas Ranger Library, 1978; rpt. Lincoln: University of Nebraska Press, 1984.

Bartlett, John Russell. *Personal Narrative of Explorations and Incidents in Texas, New Mexico, California, Sonora, and Chihuahua*. Volume Two. New York: D. Appleton & Company, 1854.

Barton, Henry W. *Texas Volunteers in the Mexican War*. Waco: Texian Press, 1970.

Bates, James C. *A Texas Cavalry Officer's Civil War: The Diary and Letters of James C. Bates*. Edited by Richard Lowe. Baton Rouge: Louisiana State University Press, 1999.

Bauer, K. Jack. *The Mexican War, 1846–1848*. New York: Macmillan, 1974; rpt. Lincoln: University of Nebraska Press, 1992.

Bearss, Edwin C. *The Battle of Wilson's Creek*. Fourth Edition. Springfield, MO: Wilson's Creek National Battleground Foundation, 1992.

Bedford, Hilory G. *Texas Indian Troubles*. Dallas: Hargreaves Publishing Company, 1905.

Bell, Thomas W. *A Narrative of the Capture and Subsequent Suffering of the Mier Prisoners in Mexico*. DeSoto County, MS: R. Morris & Co., 1845; rpt. Waco: Texian Press, 1964.

Benemann, William, editor. *A Year of Mud and Gold: San Francisco in Letters and Diaries, 1849–1850*. Lincoln: University of Nebraska Press, 1998; rpt. 2003.

Benner, Judith Ann. *Sul Ross, Soldier, Statesman, Educator*. College Station: Texas A&M University Press, 1983.

Bevill, James P. *The Paper Republic: The Struggle for Money, Credit, and Independence in the Republic of Texas*. Houston, TX: Bright Sky Press, 2009.

Bigler, David L., and Will Bagley. *The Mormon Rebellion: America's First Civil War, 1857–1858*. Norman: University of Oklahoma Press, 2011.

Billon, Frederic L. *Annals of St. Louis in its Territorial Days, from 1804 to 1821*. St. Louis: printed for the author, 1888.

Binkley, William C., editor. *Official Correspondence of the Texas Revolution, 1835–1836*. Two volumes. New York: D. Appleton-Century Company, 1936.

Bisnar, Sylvia Villarreal. *P. L. Buquor, Indian Fighter, Texas Ranger, Mayor of San Antonio*. Bloomington IN: AuthorHouse, 2009.

Boatner, Mark Mayo, III. *The Civil War Dictionary*. Revised Edition. New York: David McKay Company, 1988.

Boessenecker, John. *Gold Dust and Gunsmoke: Tales of Gold Rush Outlaws, Gunfighters, Lawmen, and Vigilantes*. New York: John Wiley & Sons, 1999.

Bracken, Sharon, editor. *Historic McLennan County: An Illustrated History*. San Antonio: Historical Publishing Network, 2010.

Brackett, Albert G. *General Lane's Brigade in Central Mexico*. Cincinnati, OH: H.W. Derby & Co., 1854.

———. *History of the United States Cavalry, From the Formation of the Federal Government to the 1st of June, 1863*. New York: Harper & Brothers, 1865.

Bradley, Ed. *"We Never Retreat": Filibustering Expeditions into Spanish Texas, 1812–1822*. College Station: Texas A&M University Press, 2015.

Brands, H. W. *The Age of Gold: The California Gold Rush and the New American Dream*. New York: Anchor Books, 2003.

———. *Andrew Jackson: His Life and Times*. New York: Anchor Books, 2005.

———. *Lone Star Nation: How a Ragged Army of Volunteers Won the Battle for Texas Independence—and Changed America*. New York: Doubleday, 2004.

Brazos. *Life of Robert Hall: Indian Fighter and Veteran of Three Great Wars*. Austin: Ben C. Jones & Company, 1898; rpt. Austin: State House Press, 1992.

Brice, Donaly E. *The Great Comanche Raid: Boldest Indian Attack of the Texas Republic*. Austin: Eakin Press, 1987.

Brookshear, William Riley. *War Along the Bayous: The 1864 Red River Campaign in Louisiana*. Washington, D.C.: Brassey's, 1998.

Brown, Helen W. *Index of Marriage Licenses, Prince George's County, Maryland, 1777–1886*. College Park, MD: privately printed, 1971.

Brown, John Henry. *History of Texas, from 1685 to 1892*. Two volumes. St. Louis: L. E. Daniell, 1892–1893.

———. *Indian Wars and Pioneers of Texas*. Austin: L. E. Daniell, ca. 1896; rpt. Austin: State House Press, 1988.

Brown, Robert Maxwell. *Strain of Violence: Historical Studies of American Violence and Vigilantism*. New York: Oxford University Press, 1975.

Browne, Linda Ferguson, editor. *J. Ross Browne: His Letters, Journals, and Writings*. Albuquerque: University of New Mexico Press, 1969.

Brumbaugh, Gaius Marcus. *Maryland Records—Colonial, Revolutionary, County, and Church*. Volume Two. Lancaster, PA: Lancaster Press, 1928.

Bryan, Jimmy L., Jr. "Agents of Destiny: Texas Rangers and the Dilemma of the Conquest Narrative." *The Martial Imagination: Cultural Aspects of American Warfare*. Edited by Jimmy L. Bryan, Jr. College Station: Texas A&M University Press, 2013.

———. *More Zeal Than Discretion: The Westward Adventures of Walter P. Lane*. College Station: Texas A&M University Press, 2008.

———. "The Patriot-Warrior Mystique: John S. Brooks, Walter P. Lane, Samuel H. Walker and the Adventurous Quest for Renown." *Texans and War: New Interpretations of the State's Military History*. Edited by Alexander Mendoza and Charles Davis Grear. College Station: Texas A&M University Press, 2012.

Buenger, Walter L. *Secession and the Union in Texas*. Austin: University of Texas Press, 1984.

Burges, Austin E. *A Local History of A&M College, 1876–1915*. Bryan, TX: n.p., 1915.

Caldwell, Clifford R., and Ron DeLord. *Texas Lawmen, 1835–1899: The Good and the Bad*. Charleston, SC: The History Press, 2011.

Calhoun, Frederick S. *The Lawmen: United States Marshals and Their Deputies, 1789–1989*. Washington, D.C.: Smithsonian Institution Press, 1989.

Campbell, Randolph B. *Gone to Texas: A History of the Lone Star State*. New York: Oxford University Press, 2003.

———. *Grass-Roots Reconstruction in Texas, 1865–1880*. Baton Rouge: Louisiana State University Press, 1997.

Cantrell, Gregg. *Stephen F. Austin: Empresario of Texas*. New Haven: Yale University Press, 1999.

Carleton, James Henry. *The Battle of Buena Vista, with the Operations of the "Army of Occupation" for One Month*. New York: Harper and Brothers, 1848.

Cardwell, John. *Fifteenth Legislature: Sketches of Legislators and State Officers, 1876–1878*. Austin: Democratic Statesman Steam Print, 1876.

Carney, Stephen A. *Desperate Stand: The Battle of Buena Vista*. Washington, D.C.: U.S. Army Center of Military History, 2010.

———. *Guns Along the Rio Grande: Palo Alto and Resaca de la Palma*. Washington, D.C.: U.S. Army Center of Military History, 2005.

———. *The Occupation of Mexico, May 1846-July 1848*. Washington, D.C.: U.S. Army Center of Military History, [2005].

Carter, Arthur B. *The Tarnished Cavalier: Major General Earl Van Dorn, C.S.A.* Knoxville: University of Tennessee Press, 1999.

Casey, Clifford B. *Sul Ross State University: The Cultural Center of Trans-Pecos Texas, 1917–1975*. Seagraves, TX: Pioneer Book Publishers, 1976.

Cashion, Ty. *A Texas Frontier: The Clear Fork Country and Fort Griffin, 1849–1887*. Norman: University of Oklahoma Press, 1996.

Castel, Albert. *Decision in the West: The Atlanta Campaign of 1864*. Lawrence: University Press of Kansas, 1992.

Chabot, Frederick C. *The Perote Prisoners: Being the Diary of James L. Trueheart*. San Antonio: The Naylor Company, 1944.

———. *With the Makers of San Antonio*. San Antonio: Artes Graficas, 1937.

———, editor. *Texas Letters*. San Antonio: Yanaguana Society, 1940.

Chalfant, William Y. *Without Quarter: The Wichita Expedition and the Fight on Crooked Creek*. Norman: University of Oklahoma Press, 1991.

Chance, Joseph E. *José María de Jesús Carvajal: The Life and Times of a Mexican Revolutionary*. San Antonio: Trinity University Press, 2006.

Cisco, Jay Guy. *Historic Sumner County, Tennessee*. Nashville: Folk-Keelin Printing Company, 1909.

Clark, Carol. *Charles Deas and 1840s America*. Norman: University of Oklahoma Press, 2009.

Clark, Pat B. *The History of Clarksville and Old Red River County*. Dallas: Mathis, Van Nort & Co., 1937.

Clarke, Mary Whatley. *Thomas J. Rusk: Soldier, Statesman, Jurist*. Austin: Jenkins Publishing Company, 1971.

Cofer, David Brooks. *Second Five Administrators of Texas A&M College, 1890–1905*. College Station: Association of the Former Students of Texas A&M College, 1954.

Coldham, Peter Wilson. *Settlers of Maryland, 1679–1783*. Consolidated Edition, Volume One. Baltimore, MD: Genealogical Publishing Company, 2010.

Collins, Bruce. *White Society in the Antebellum South*. New York: Longman Group, 1985.

Collins, Michael L. *Texas Devils: Rangers and Regulars on the Lower Rio Grande, 1846–1861*. Norman: University of Oklahoma Press, 2008.

Conkin, Paul K. *Peabody College: From a Frontier Academy to the Frontiers of Teaching and Learning*. Nashville: Vanderbilt University Press, 2002.

Conmy, Peter Thomas. *The Beginnings of Oakland, California, A.U.C.* Oakland: Oakland Public Library, 1961.

Connelly, Thomas Lawrence. *Autumn of Glory: The Army of Tennessee, 1862–1865*. Baton Rouge: Louisiana State University Press, 1971; rpt. 2001.

Cooling, Benjamin Franklin. *To the Battles of Franklin and Nashville and Beyond: Stabilization and Reconstruction in Tennessee and Kentucky, 1864–1866*. Knoxville: University of Tennessee Press, 2011.

Cox, James. *Historical and Biographical Record of the Cattle Industry and the Cattlemen of Texas and Adjacent Territory*. St. Louis: Woodward & Tiernan Printing Co., 1894.

Cox, Mike. *Gunfights and Sites in Texas Ranger History*. Charleston, SC: The History Press, 2015.

———. *Texas Ranger Tales II*. Plano: Republic of Texas Press, 1999.

———. *The Texas Rangers: Wearing the Cinco Peso, 1821–1900*. New York: Tom Doherty Associates, 2008.

Cozzens, Peter. *The Darkest Days of the War: The Battles of Iuka and Corinth*. Chapel Hill: University of North Carolina Press, 1997.

———. *The Shipwreck of their Hopes: The Battles for Chattanooga*. Urbana: University of Illinois Press, 1994.

Crabb, Martha L. *All Afire to Fight: The Untold Tale of the Civil War's Ninth Texas Cavalry*. New York: Post Road Press, 2000.

Crane, William Carey. *Life and Select Literary Remains of Sam Houston of Texas*. Philadelphia: J. B. Lippincott & Co., 1884.

Crews, Harvey W., editor. *Centennial History of the City of Washington, D.C.* Dayton, OH: United Brethren Publishing House, 1892.

Cutrer, Thomas W. *Ben McCulloch and the Frontier Military Tradition*. Chapel Hill: University of North Carolina Press, 1993.

———. *Theater of a Separate War: The Civil War West of the Mississippi River, 1861–1865*. Chapel Hill: University of North Carolina Press, 2017.

Daniel, Karen Stein. *Three Generations of Descendants of Shapley Prince Ross: An Early Texas Pioneer*. Spartanburg, SC: The Reprint Company, 1994.

Daniell, L. E., compiler. *Personnel of the Texas State Government*. Austin: Press of the City Printing Company, 1887.

Davis, George Henry. *Genealogy of Thomas Davis (1782–1846) and His Descendants*. New York: Scarborough Press, 1949.

Davis, William C. *Lone Star Rising: The Revolutionary Birth of the Texas Republic*. New York: Free Press, 2004; rpt. College Station: Texas A&M University Press, 2004.

———, editor. *The Confederate General*. Volume Six. Harrisburg, PA: National Historical Society, 1991.

Deibert, Captain Ralph C., and Colonel Harry N. Cootes. *A History of the Third United States Cavalry: The Regiment of Mounted Riflemen, the First Regiment of Mounted Riflemen, the Third United States Cavalry*. Harrisburg, PA: Telegraph Press, 1933.

Deloria, Vine, Jr., and Raymond J. DeMallie. *Documents of American Indian Diplomacy, Treaties, Agreements, and Conventions, 1775–1979*. Volume One. Norman: University of Oklahoma Press, 1999

DeShields, James T. *Border Wars of Texas*. Tioga, TX: The Herald Company, 1912; rpt. Austin: State House Press, 1993. Pagination refers to the 1993 edition.

———. *Cynthia Ann Parker: The Story of Her Capture*. St. Louis: Printed for the author, 1886; rpt. Dallas: Chama Press, 1991.

———. *They Sat in High Place: The Presidents and Governors of Texas*. San Antonio: The Naylor Company, 1940.

Dewees, William B. *Letters from an Early Settler of Texas*. Compiled by Cara Cardelle. Louisville, KY: Morton & Griswold, 1852.

Diehl, George W. *Rockbridge County, Virginia Notebook*. Compiled by A. Maxim Coppage III. Utica, KY: McDowell Publications, 1982.

Dimmick, Gregg J. *Sea of Mud: The Retreat of the Mexican Army after San Jacinto, An Archeological Investigation*. Austin: Texas State Historical Association, 2004.

Dishman, Christopher D. *A Perfect Gibraltar: The Battle for Monterrey, Mexico, 1846*. Norman: University of Oklahoma Press, 2010.

Dobie, J. Frank, and John D. Young. *A Vaquero of the Brush Country: The Life and Times of John D. Young*. Dallas: Southwest Press, 1929; rpt. Austin: University of Texas Press, 1998.

Durham, Walter T. *Volunteer Forty-Niners: Tennesseans and the California Gold Rush*. Nashville: Vanderbilt University Press, 1997.

Duval, John C. *The Adventures of Big-Foot Wallace*. Edited by Mabel Major and Rebecca Smith Lee. Macon, GA: J. W. Burke & Co., 1870; rpt. Lincoln: University of Nebraska Press, 1966. Pagination refers to the 1966 edition.

Dwight, Benjamin Woodbridge. *The History of the Descendants of Elder John Strong, of Northampton, Mass*. Albany, NY: Joel Munsell, 1871.

Eccleston, Robert. *Overland to California on the Southwestern Trail 1849*. Edited by George P. Hammond and Edward H. Howes. Berkeley: University of California Press, 1950.

Egan, Ferol. *Sand in a Whirlwind: The Paiute Indian War of 1860*. Reno: University of Nevada Press, 1972; rpt. 2003.

Eicher, John H., and David J. Eicher. *Civil War High Commands*. Stanford, CA: Stanford University Press, 2001.

Eifler, Mark A. *Gold Rush Capitalists: Greed and Growth in Sacramento*. Albuquerque: University of New Mexico Press, 2002.

Eisenhower, John S. D. *So Far from God: The U.S. War with Mexico, 1846–1848*. New York: Random House, 1989; rpt. Norman: University of Oklahoma Press, 2000.

Elkins, John M., and Frank W. McCarty. *Indian Fighting on the Texas Frontier*. Amarillo: Russell & Cockrell, 1929.

Ellisor, John T. *The Second Creek War: Interethnic Conflict and Collusion on a Collapsing Frontier*. Lincoln: University of Nebraska Press, 2010.

Ely, Glenn Sample. *The Texas Frontier and the Butterfield Overland Mail, 1858–1861*. Norman: University of Oklahoma Press, 2016.

Erickson, John R. *Prairie Gothic: The Story of a West Texas Family*. Denton: University of North Texas Press, 2005.

Erlichman, Howard J. *Camino Del Norte: How a Series of Watering Holes, Fords, and Dirt Trails Evolved into Interstate 35 in Texas*. College Station: Texas A&M University Press, 2006.

Ethington, Philip J. *The Public City: The Political Construction of Urban Life in San Francisco, 1850–1900*. Berkeley: University of California Press, 2001.

Evans, Clement A., editor. *Confederate Military History*. Twelve volumes. Atlanta: Confederate Publishing Company, 1899.

Evans, Frederick, compiler. *After Twenty-five Years, Class of 1886*. Princeton: Princeton University Press, 1911.

Everett, Dianna. *The Texas Cherokees: A People Between Two Fires, 1819–1840*. Norman: University of Oklahoma Press, 1990; rpt. 1995.

Exley, Jo Ella Powell. *Frontier Blood: The Saga of the Parker Family*. College Station: Texas A&M University Press, 2009.

Farrell, Mary D., and Elizabeth Silverthorne. *First Ladies of Texas: The First One Hundred Years, 1836–1936*. Belton, TX: Stillhouse Hollow Publishers, 1976.

Farris, Frances Bramlette. *From Rattlesnakes to Road Agents*. Edited by C. L. Sonnichsen. Fort Worth: Texas Christian University Press, 1985.

Ferguson, Gillum. *Illinois in the War of 1812*. Urbana: University of Illinois Press, 2012.

Ferrell, Robert H., editor. *Monterrey Is Ours!: The Mexican War Letters of Lieutenant Dana, 1845–1847*. Lexington: University Press of Kentucky, 1990.

Foos, Paul. *Short, Offhand, Killing Affair: Soldiers and Social Conflict During the Mexican-American War*. Chapel Hill: University of North Carolina Press, 2002.

Foote, Shelby. *The Civil War: A Narrative*. Three volumes. New York: Random House, 1958; rpt. 1986.

Ford, John Salmon. *Rip Ford's Texas*. Edited by Stephen B. Oates. Austin: University of Texas Press, 1963; rpt. 1998.

Fourth Annual Catalogue of the Trustees, Professors, and Students of Baylor University. Galveston: Civilian Book and Job Company, 1856.

Francaviglia, Richard V. *From Sail to Steam: Four Centuries of Texas Maritime History, 1500–1900*. Austin: University of Texas Press, 1998.

Franklin, John Hope, and Loren Schweninger. *Runaway Slaves: Rebels on the Plantation*. New York: Oxford University Press, 1999.

Frazer, Chris. *Bandit Nation: A History of Outlaws and Cultural Struggle in Mexico, 1810–1920*. Lincoln: University of Nebraska Press, 2006.

French, General Samuel G. *Two Wars: An Autobiography of Gen. Samuel G. French*. Nashville: Confederate Veteran, 1901.

Gammage, Washington Lafayette. *The Camp, the Bivouac, and the Battle Field*. Selma, AL: Cooper & Kimball, 1864; rpt. Little Rock: Arkansas Southern Press, 1958.

Gammel, Hans Peter Nielson, compiler. *The Laws of Texas, 1822–1897*. Ten volumes. Austin: The Gammel Book Company, 1898.

Gardner, Charles K. *A Dictionary of All Officers: Who Have Been Commissioned, or Have Been Appointed and Served, in the Army of the United States*. New York: D. Van Nostrand, 1860.

Garrison, George P., editor. *Diplomatic Correspondence of the Republic of Texas*. Volume One. Washington, D.C.: Government Printing Office, 1908. Published as the *Annual Report of the American Historical Association for the Year 1907*.

Garst, Shannon. *Big Foot Wallace of the Texas Rangers*. New York: Julian Messner, 1952.

Gates, Paul W. *Land and Law in California: Essays on Land Policies*. Ames: Iowa State University Press, 1991.

George, Isaac. *Heroes and Incidents of the Mexican War*. Greensburg, PA: Review Publishing Co., 1903.

Gerteis, Louis S. *The Civil War in Missouri: A Military History*. Columbia: University of Missouri Press, 2012.

Giddings, Luther. *Sketches of the Campaigns in Northern Mexico*. New York: George P. Putnam & Co., 1853.

Governor's Messages, Coke to Ross, 1874–1891. Edited by and for the Archive and History Department. Austin: Texas State Library, 1916.

Gracy, David B., II. *Moses Austin: His Life*. San Antonio: Trinity University Press, 1987.

Green, Rena Maverick, editor. *Memoirs of Mary A. Maverick. Arranged by Mary A. Maverick and Her Son George Madison Maverick*. San Antonio: Alamo Printing Co., 1921.

———. *Samuel Maverick, Texan: 1803–1870*. San Antonio: privately printed, 1952.

Green, General Thomas J. *Journal of the Texian Expedition against Mier*. New York: Harper & Brothers, 1845.

Green, Wharton J. *Recollections and Reflections: An Auto of Half a Century and More*. Raleigh, NC: Edwards and Broughton Printing Company, 1906.

Greene, A. C. *900 Miles on the Butterfield Trail*. Denton: University of North Texas Press, 2006.

Greer, James Kimmins. *Colonel Jack Hays, Texas Frontier Leader and California Builder*. New York: E. P. Dutton & Company, 1952; rpt. College Station: Texas A&M University Press, 1987.

———. *Texas Ranger: Jack Hays in the Frontier Southwest*. College Station: Texas A&M University Press, 1993. This book is an abridged version of *Colonel Jack Hays* and ends with Hays's departure from Texas.

Grenier, John. *The First Way of War: American War Making on the Frontier, 1607–1814*. New York: Cambridge University Press, 2005.

Griggs, William Clark. *The Elusive Eden: Frank McMullan's Confederate Colony in Brazil*. Austin: University of Texas Press, 1987.

Groom, Winston. *Shrouds of Glory: Atlanta to Nashville: The Last Great Campaign of the Civil War*. New York: Atlantic Monthly Press, 1995.

Gulick, Charles Adams, et al. *The Papers of Mirabeau Bounaparte Lamar*. Six volumes. Austin: A. C. Baldwin & Sons, 1921–1922, Austin: Von Boeckmann-Jones Co., 1923–1927.

Gwynne, S. C. *Empire of the Summer Moon*. New York: Scribner, 2010.

Hale, Douglas. *The Third Texas Cavalry in the Civil War*. Norman: University of Oklahoma Press, 1993.

Haley, James L. *Passionate Nation: The Epic History of Texas*. New York: Free Press, 2006.

———. *Sam Houston*. Norman: University of Oklahoma Press, 2002.

———. *The Texas Supreme Court: A Narrative History, 1836–1986*. Austin: University of Texas Press, 2013.

Halley, William. *The Centennial Year Book of Alameda County, California*. Oakland: William Halley, 1876.

Hämäläinen, Pekka. *The Comanche Empire*. New Haven: Yale University Press, 2008.

Hammond, John Hays. *The Autobiography of John Hays Hammond*. Volume One. New York: Farrar & Rinehart, 1935.

Hardin, Stephen L. *Texian Iliad: A Military History of the Texas Revolution, 1835–1836*. Austin: University of Texas Press, 1994.

———. *Texas Rangers*. Oxford, UK: Osprey History, 2000.

———. "'Valor, Wisdom, and Experience': Early Texas Rangers and the Nature of Frontier Leadership." *Tracking the Texas Rangers: The Nineteenth Century*. Edited by Bruce A. Glasrud and Harold J. Weiss, Jr. Denton: University of North Texas Press, 2012.

Hart, John Mason. *Empire and Revolution: The Americans in Mexico since the Civil War*. Berkeley: University of California Press, 2002.

Hatfield, Dot Ferguson. *Medina's Early Days*. Medina, TX: self-published, 1995.

Hatley, Allen G. *The Indian Wars in Stephen F. Austin's Texas Colony, 1822–1835*. Austin: Eakin Press, 2001.

Haven, Charles T., and Frank A. Belden. *A History of the Colt Revolver*. New York: Bonanza Books, 1940.

Havins, T. R. *Camp Colorado: A Decade of Frontier Defense*. Brownwood, TX: Brown Press, 1964.

Haynes, Sam W. *Soldiers of Misfortune: The Somervell and Mier Expeditions*. Austin: University of Texas Press, 1990.

Heitman, Francis B. *Historical Register and Dictionary of the United States Army from its Organization, September 29 1789, to March 2 1903*. Two volumes. Washington, D.C.: Government Printing Office, 1903.

Henderson, Colonel Harry McCorry. *Colonel Jack Hays, Texas Ranger*. San Antonio: The Naylor Company, 1954.

———. *Texas in the Confederacy*. San Antonio: The Naylor Company, 1955.

Hendrickson, Kenneth E. *The Chief Executives of Texas: From Stephen F. Austin to John B. Connally, Jr.* College Station: Texas A&M University Press, 1995.

Henry, Robert Selph. *First with the Most: Nathan Bedford Forrest*. New York: Mallard Press, 1991.

———. *The Story of the Mexican War*. Indianapolis, IN: Bobbs-Merrill Company, 1950; rpt. New York: Da Capo Press, 1989.

Henry, Captain William Seaton. *Campaign Sketches of the War with Mexico*. New York: Harper & Brothers, 1847.

Hewett, Janet B., editor. *Supplement to the Official Records of the Union and Confederate Armies*. One hundred volumes. Wilmington, NC: Broadfoot Publishing Company, 1994–2001.

———. *Texas Confederate Soldiers, 1861–1865*. Two volumes. Wilmington, NC: Broadfoot Publishing Company, 1997.

Hicks, James E. *Notes on United States Ordnance*. Two volumes. Mount Vernon, NY: privately printed, 1940.

Hitchcock, Ethan Allen. *Fifty Years in Camp and Field: Diary of Major-General Ethan Allen Hitchcock, U.S.A.* Edited by William Augustus Croffut. New York: G. P. Putnam's Sons, 1909.

Hittell, Theodore H. *History of California*. Volume Four. San Francisco: N. J. Stone & Company, 1897.

Holley, Mary Austin. *Texas*. Lexington, KY: J. Clarke & Co., 1836; rpt. Austin: Texas State Historical Association, 1985.

Hood, John Bell. *Advance and Retreat: Personal Experiences in the United States and Confederate States Armies*. New Orleans: G. T. Beauregard, 1880; rpt. Lincoln: University of Nebraska Press, 1996.

Hopkins, Sarah Winnemucca. *Life Among the Paiutes: Their Wrongs and Claims*. Edited by Mrs. Horace Mann. New York: G. P. Putnam's Sons, 1883; rpt. Reno: University of Nevada Press, 1994.

Horn, Stanley F. *The Army of Tennessee: A Military History*. Indianapolis: Bobbs-Merrill Company, 1941; rpt. Norman: University of Oklahoma Press, 1993.

Howell, Kenneth W., editor. *The Seventh Star of the Confederacy: Texas during the Civil War*. Denton: University of North Texas Press, 2009.

Hubbard, George U. *The Humor and Drama of Early Texas*. Lanham, MD: Republic of Texas Press, 2003.

Huckabay, Ida Lasater, compiler, *Ninety-Four Years in Jack County, 1854–1948*. Austin: The Steck Company, 1949.

Hughes, William J. *Rebellious Ranger: Rip Ford and the Old Southwest*. Norman: University of Oklahoma Press, 1964.

Hunt, Jeffrey William. *The Last Battle of the Civil War: Palmetto Ranch*. Austin: University of Texas Press, 2002.

Hunter, John Marvin. *Pioneer History of Bandera County: Seventy-five Years of Intrepid History*. Bandera, TX: Hunter's Printing House, 1922.

———, compiler and editor. *Trail Drivers of Texas*. Nashville: Cokesbury Press, 1925; rpt. Austin: University of Texas Press, 1985.

Irby, James A. *Backdoor at Bagdad: The Civil War on the Rio Grande*. El Paso: Western Texas Press, 1977.

Jamieson, Perry D. *Spring 1865: The Closing Campaigns of the Civil War*. Lincoln: University of Nebraska Press, 2015.

Jenkins, John Holland. *Recollections of Early Texas: The Memoirs of John Holland Jenkins*. Edited by John Holmes Jenkins III. Austin: University of Texas Press, 1958; rpt. 2003.

Jenkins, John Holmes, and Kenneth Kesselus. *Edward Burleson: Texas Frontier Leader*. Austin: Jenkins Publishing Company, 1990.

Jenkins, John Holmes, editor. *The Papers of the Texas Revolution, 1835–1836*. Ten volumes. Austin: Presidial Press, 1973.

Jennings, Nathan A. *Riding for the Lone Star: Frontier Cavalry and the Texas Way of War, 1822–1865*. Denton: University of North Texas Press, 2016.

Johannsen, Robert W. *To the Halls of the Montezumas: The Mexican War in the American Imagination*. New York: Oxford University Press, 1985.

Johnson, Kenneth M., editor. *San Francisco as It Is: Gleanings from the Picayune*. Georgetown, CA: Talisman Press, 1964.

Johnson, Robert Underwood, and Clarence Clough Buel, editors. *Battles and Leaders of the Civil War*. Four volumes. New York: The Century Company, 1884–1888; rpt. Secaucus, NJ: Castle Books, 1982.

Johnston, Charles Haven Ladd. *Famous Frontiersmen and Heroes of the Border*. Boston: L. C. Page & Company, 1913.

Johnston, William Preston. *The Life of Albert Sidney Johnston: Embracing His Services in the Armies of the United States, the Republic of Texas, and the Confederate States*. New York: D. Appleton and Company, 1878; rpt. Austin: State House Press, 1997.

Jones, Anson. *Memoranda and Official Correspondence Relating to the Republic of Texas, Its History and Annexation*. New York: D. Appleton and Company, 1859.

Jordan, General Thomas, and J. P. Pryor. *The Campaigns of General Nathan Bedford Forrest and of Forrest's Cavalry*. New Orleans: Blelock & Co., 1868; rpt. New York: Da Capo Press, 1996. Originally published as *The Campaigns of Lieut.-Gen. N. B. Forrest and of Forrest's Cavalry*.

Kappler, Charles J., compiler and editor. *Indian Affairs: Laws and Treaties*. Volume Two. Washington, D.C.: Government Printing Office, 1904.

Kavanagh, Thomas W. *Comanche Political History: An Ethnohistorical Perspective, 1706–1875*. Lincoln: University of Nebraska Press, 1996.

Kearney, Milo, and Anthony Knopp. *Boom and Bust: The Historical Cycles of Matamoros and Brownsville*. Austin: Eakin Press, 1991.

Keen, Newton A. *Living and Fighting with the Texas 6th Cavalry*. Gaithersburg, MD: Butternut Press, 1986.

Kelley, Dayton, ed. *The Handbook of Waco and McLennan County, Texas*. Waco: Texian Press, 1972.

Kendall, George Wilkins. *The War Between the United States and Mexico, Illustrated*. New York: D. Appleton & Company, 1851.

Kenly, John R. *Memoirs of a Maryland Volunteer: War with Mexico, in the Years 1846–7–8*. Philadelphia: J. P. Lippincott & Co., 1873.

Kerby, Robert L. *Kirby Smith's Confederacy: The Trans-Mississippi South, 1863–1865*. New York: Columbia University Press, 1972.

Kerr, Homer L., editor. *Fighting with Ross' Texas Cavalry Brigade, C.S.A.* Hillsboro, TX: Hill Junior College Press, 1976.

Kimball, Charles P. *The San Francisco City Directory, September 1, 1850.* San Francisco: Journal of Commerce Press, 1850.

Kirkpatrick, Dorthie, and Edwin C. *Rockbridge County Marriages, 1778–1850.* Athens, GA: Iberian Publishing Company, 1985.

Kittrell, Norman G. *Governors Who Have Been, and Other Public Men of Texas*. Houston, TX: Dealy-Adey-Elgin Co., 1921.

Knapp, Major George E. *The Wilson's Creek Staff Ride and Battlefield Tour*. Fort Leavenworth: Combat Studies Institute, 1993.

Knight, James R. *The Battle of Pea Ridge: The Civil War Fight for the Ozarks*. Charleston, SC: The History Press, 2012.

———. *Hood's Tennessee Campaign: The Desperate Venture of a Desperate Man*. Charleston, SC: The History Press, 2014.

Kuykendall, Marshall E. *They Slept Upon Their Rifles: The Story of the Captain Robert H. Kuykendall Family in America and the Entry of the Family with the Anglo Settlement into Mexican/Texas in Stephen F. Austin's Colony in 1821*. Fort Worth: Nortex Press, 2005.

Lack, Paul D. *The Texas Revolutionary Experience: A Political and Social History, 1835–1836*. College Station: Texas A&M University Press, 1992.

Lale, Max S., and Hobart Key, Jr. editors. *The Civil War Letters of David R. Garrett: Detailing the Adventures of the 6th Texas Cavalry*. Marshall, TX: Port Caddo Press, 1963.

Lamar, Howard R. *Texas Crossings: The Lone Star State and the American Far West, 1836–1986*. Austin: University of Texas Press, 1991.

Lambert, Joseph Indus. *One Hundred Years with the Second Cavalry*. Topeka: Press of the Capper Printing Co., 1939.

Lane, Walter P. *The Adventures and Recollections of General Walter P. Lane: A San Jacinto Veteran, Containing Sketches of the Texan, Mexican, and Late Wars*. Marshall, TX: Tri-Weekly Herald Job Print, 1887; rpt. Austin: Jenkins Publishing Company, 1970.

La Vere, David. *Contrary Neighbors: Southern Plains and Removed Indians in Indian Territory*. Norman: University of Oklahoma Press, 2000.

Lea, Tom. *The King Ranch*. Volume One. Boston: Little, Brown and Company, 1957.

Lee, Nelson. *Three Years Among the Comanches: The Narrative of Nelson Lee, the Texas Ranger*. Albany, NY: Baker Taylor, 1859; rpt. Norman: University of Oklahoma Press, 1991.

Lee, Rebecca Smith. *Mary Austin Holley: A Biography*. Austin: University of Texas Press, 1962.

Leonard, John W., editor. *Woman's Who's Who of America*. New York: American Commonwealth Company, 1914.

Levinson, Irving W. *Wars Within War: Mexican Guerrillas, Domestic Elites, and the United States of America, 1846–1848*. Fort Worth: Texas Christian University Press, 2005.

Lewis, Felice Flanery. *Trailing Clouds of Glory: Zachary Taylor's Mexican War Campaign and His Emerging Civil War Leaders*. Tuscaloosa: University of Alabama Press, 2010.

Lindley, Ernest R., editor. *Members of the Legislature of the State of Texas from 1846 to 1939*. Austin: State of Texas, 1939.

Lindley, Ernest R., compiler, and Elizabeth LeNoir Jennett, editor. *Biographical Directory of the Texan Conventions and Congresses, 1832–1845*. Austin: Book Exchange, 1941.

Linn, John J. *Reminiscences of Fifty Years in Texas*. New York: D. & J. Sadlier & Co., 1883; rpt. Austin: State House Press, 1986.

Lord, Walter. *A Time to Stand*. New York: Harper & Row, 1961; rpt. Lincoln: University of Nebraska Press, 1978.

Lubbock, Francis R. *Six Decades in Texas, or Memoirs of Francis Richard Lubbock: Governor of Texas in War-Time, 1861–63*. Edited by C. W. Raines. Austin: Ben C. Jones & Co., 1900.

Lundberg, John R. *The Finishing Stroke: Texans in the 1864 Tennessee Campaign*. Abilene, TX: McWhiney Foundation Press, 2002.

MacKinnon, William P., editor. *At Sword's Point: A Documentary History of the Utah War to 1858*. Norman, OK: The Arthur H. Clark Company, 2008. This book comprises Volume Ten of *Kingdom in the West: The Mormons and the American Frontier*.

McCaffrey, James M. *Army of Manifest Destiny: The American Soldier in the Mexican War, 1846–1848*. New York: New York University Press, 1992.

McCaslin, Richard B. *Fighting Stock: John S. "Rip" Ford of Texas*. Fort Worth: Texas Christian University Press, 2011.

———. *Washington on the Brazos: Cradle of the Texas Republic*. Austin: Texas State Historical Association, 2016.

McConnell, Joseph Carroll. *The West Texas Frontier: or, A Descriptive History of Early Times in Western Texas*. Volume One, Jacksboro, TX: Gazette Print, 1933; Volume Two, Palo Pinto, TX: Texas Legal Bank & Book Co., 1939.

McCutchan, Joseph D. *Mier Expedition Diary: A Texan Prisoner's Account*. Edited by Joseph Milton Nance. Austin: University of Texas Press, 1978.

McDowell, Catherine W., editor. *Now You Hear My Horn: The Journal of James Wilson Nichols, 1820–1887*. Austin: University of Texas Press, 1967.

McLean, Malcolm D., compiler and editor. *Papers Concerning Robertson's Colony in Texas*. Nineteen volumes. Arlington: University of Texas at Arlington Press, 1974–1993.

McMurry, Richard M. *John Bell Hood and the War for Southern Independence*. Lincoln: University of Nebraska Press, 1982; rpt. 1992.

McPherson, James. *Battle Cry of Freedom: The Civil War Era*. New York: Oxford University Press, 1988.

McWhiney, Grady, and Sue McWhiney, editors. *To Mexico with Taylor and Scott, 1845–1847*. Waltham, MA: Blaisdell Publishing Company, 1969.

Mahon, John K. *History of the Second Seminole War, 1835–1842*. Revised Edition. Gainesville: University Press of Florida, 1967; rpt. 1985.

Malone, Dumas, editor. *Dictionary of American Biography*. Twenty-two volumes. New York: Charles Scribner's Sons, 1928–1958.

Marsh, Helen Crawford, and Timothy Richard Marsh, compilers. *Lincoln County, Tennessee Tax List, 1829–1832*. Shelbyville, TN: Marsh Historical Publications, 1981.

Marshall, Doyle. *A Cry Unheard: The Story of Indian Attacks in and Around Parker County, Texas, 1858–1872*. Aledo, TX: Annetta Valley Farm Press, 1990.

Martínez, Oscar J. *Troublesome Border*. Revised Edition. Tucson: University of Arizona Press, 1998; rpt. 2006.

May, Robert E. *Manifest Destiny's Underworld: Filibustering in Antebellum America*. Chapel Hill: University of North Carolina Press, 2002.

Mayhall, Mildred. *Indian Wars of Texas*. Waco: Texian Press, 1965.

A Memorial and Biographical History of Johnson and Hill Counties. Chicago: Lewis Publishing Company, 1892.

Memorial and Genealogical Record of Southwest Texas. Chicago: Goodspeed Brothers, 1894; rpt. Easley, SC: Southern Historical Press, 1978.

Mercantile and General City Directory of Austin, Texas—1872–73. Austin: S. A. Gray, 1872.

Merritt, Dixon. *The History of Wilson County: Its Land and Its Life*. Nashville, TN: Benson Printing Company, 1961.

Michno, Gregory F. *Encyclopedia of Indian Wars: Western Battles and Skirmishes, 1850–1890*. Missoula, MT: Mountain Press Publishing Company, 2003.

———, and Susan J. Michno. *A Fate Worse Than Death: Indian Captivities in the West, 1830–1885*. Caldwell, ID: Caxton Press, 2009.

———. *Forgotten Fights: Little-Known Raids and Skirmishes on the Frontier, 1823 to 1890*. Missoula, MT: Mountain Press Publishing Company, 2008.

Millard, Bailey. *History of the San Francisco Bay Region*. Chicago: American Historical Society, 1924.

Miller, William Harris *History and Genealogies of the Families of Miller, Woods, Harris, Wallace, Maupin, Oldham, Kavanaugh, Brown*. Richmond, KY: privately published, 1907.

Missall, John, and Mary Lou Missall, compilers and editors. *This Miserable Pride of a Soldier: The Letters and Journals of Col. William S. Foster in the Second Seminole War*. Tampa: University of Florida Press, 2005.

Moller, George D. *American Military Shoulder Arms*. Volume Three. Albuquerque: University of New Mexico Press, 2011.

Monaghan, Jay. *Civil War on the Western Border, 1854–1865*. Boston: Little, Brown and Company, 1955; rpt. Lincoln: University of Nebraska Press, 1984.

Moneyhon, Carl H. *Republicanism in Reconstruction Texas*. College Station: Texas A&M University Press, 1980.

———. *Texas After the Civil War: The Struggle of Reconstruction*. College Station: Texas A&M University Press, 2004.

Moody, Ralph. *Stagecoach West*. New York: Thomas Y. Crowell Company, 1967; rpt. Lincoln: University of Nebraska Press, 1998.

Mooney & Morrison's General Directory of the City of Austin, Texas, for 1877–78. Austin: Eugene von Boeckmann, 1877.

Moore & DePue's Illustrated History of San Mateo County, California—1878. San Francisco: G. T. Brown & Company, 1878; rpt. Woodside, CA: Gilbert Richards Publications, 1974.

Moore, Albert Burton. *Conscription and Conflict in the Confederacy*. New York: Macmillan Company, 1924; rpt. Columbia: University of South Carolina Press, 1996.

Moore, John Basset, editor. *The Works of James Buchanan*. Volume Ten. Philadelphia: J. B. Lippincott Company, 1910.

Moore, Stephen L. *Eighteen Minutes: The Battle of San Jacinto and the Texas Independence Campaign*. Dallas: Republic of Texas Press, 2004.

———. *Savage Frontier: Rangers, Riflemen, and Indian Wars in Texas*. Four volumes. Denton: University of North Texas Press, 2002–2010.

Moorman, Donald R., with Gene A. Sessions. *Camp Floyd and the Mormons: The Utah War*. Salt Lake City: University of Utah Press, 2005.

Morrell, Z. N. *Flowers and Fruits from the Wilderness*. Boston: Gould & Lincoln, 1872.

Morrison & Fourmy's General Directory of the City of Austin, 1889–90. Galveston: Morrison & Fourmy, 1889.

Morrison & Fourmy's General Directory of the City of Austin, 1897–98. Galveston: Morrison & Fourmy, 1897.

Morrison & Fourmy's General Directory of the City of Austin, for 1881 and 1882. Austin: E. W. Swindells, 1881.

Morton, Oren F. *A History of Rockbridge County, Virginia*. Staunton, VA: The McClure Company, 1920.

Mullen, Kevin J. *Let Justice Be Done: Crime and Politics in Early San Francisco*. Reno: University of Nevada Press, 1989.

Murphy, Douglas A. *Two Armies on the Rio Grande: The First Campaign of the US-Mexican War*. College Station: Texas A&M University Press, 2015.

Muster Rolls of the Texas Revolution. Austin: Daughters of the Republic of Texas, 1986.

Nance, Joseph Milton. *After San Jacinto: The Texas-Mexican Frontier, 1836–1841*. Austin: University of Texas Press, 1963.

———. *Attack and Counterattack: The Texas-Mexican Frontier, 1842*. Austin: University of Texas Press, 1964.

———. *Dare-Devils All: The Texan Mier Expedition, 1842–1844*. Edited by Archie P. McDonald. Austin: Eakin Press, 1998.

The National Cyclopaedia of American Biography. Sixty-three volumes. New York: James T. White and Company, 1895–1984. Noyes, Stanley. *Los Comanches: The Horse People, 1751–1845*. Albuquerque: University of New Mexico Press, 1993.

Nye, Wilbur Sturtevant. *Carbine and Lance: The Story of Old Fort Sill*. Norman: University of Oklahoma Press, 1937; rpt. 1969.

Oates, Stephen B. *Confederate Cavalry West of the River*. Austin: University of Texas Press, 1961; rpt. 1992.

———, editor. *Visions of Glory: Texans on the Southwestern Frontier*. Norman: University of Oklahoma Press, 1970.

O'Gorman, Ella Foy. *Descendants of Virginia Calverts*. Los Angeles: s. n., 1947.

The Olio. Columbus, OH: A. C. Berlin & Co., 1895.

Olmsted, Frederick Law. *A Journey Through Texas, or A Saddle-Trip on the Southwestern Frontier*. New York: Dix, Edwards & Co., 1857.

O'Neal, Bill. *Fighting Men of the Indian Wars: A Biographical Encyclopedia of the Mountain Men, Soldiers, Cowboys, and Pioneers Who Took Up*

Arms During America's Westward Expansion. Stillwater, OK: Barbed Wire Press, 1991.

Oswandel, J. Jacob. *Notes of the Mexican War, 1846–47–48*. Philadelphia: n.p., 1885.

Paddock, Buckley B. *A History of Central and Western Texas*. Volume One. Chicago: The Lewis Publishing Company, 1911.

Parsons, John E., editor. *Samuel Colt's Own Record of Transactions with Captain Walker and Eli Whitney, Jr. in 1847*. Hartford: Connecticut Historical Society, 1949.

Peden, Henry C., Jr. *Revolutionary Patriots of Prince George's County, 1775–1783*. Westminster, MD: Family Line Publications, 1997

Petracek, Ruth. *The Wallace Collection*. Volume One. Santa Anna, CA: Petracek, 1979.

Philips, George Harwood. *"Bringing Them Under Subjection": California's Tejón Indian Reservation and Beyond, 1852–1864*. Lincoln: University of Nebraska Press, 2004.

Pierce, Gerald S. *Texas Under Arms: The Camps, Forts, and Military Towns of the Republic of Texas, 1836–1846*. Austin: Encino Press, 1969.

Piston, William Garrett, and Richard W. Hatcher III. *Wilson's Creek: The Second Battle of the Civil War and the Men Who Fought It*. Chapel Hill: University of North Carolina Press, 2000.

Polk, James K. *The Diary of James K. Polk*. Edited by Milton M. Quaife. Four volumes. Chicago: A. C. McClurg & Company, 1910.

Poyo, Gerald E., editor. *Tejano Journey, 1770–1850*. Austin: University of Texas Press, 1996.

Price, George F. *Across the Continent with the Fifth Cavalry*. New York: D. Van Nostrand, 1883; rpt. New York: Antiquarian Press, 1959.

Prucha, Francis Paul. *The Great Father: The United States and the American Indians*. Lincoln: University of Nebraska Press, 1984; rpt. 1995.

Ragland, Hobert D. *The History of Rush Springs*. Rush Springs, OK: Gazette Publishing Company, 1952.

Ramos, Raúl A. *Beyond the Alamo: Forging Mexican Ethnicity in San Antonio, 1821–1861*. Chapel Hill: University of North Carolina Press, 2008.

Reid, Samuel C., Jr. *The Scouting Expeditions of McCulloch's Texas Rangers; or, the Summer and Fall Campaigns of the Army of the United States in Mexico—1846*. Philadelphia: G. B. Zieber and Company, 1847.

Remington, Frederic. "How the Law Got into the Chaparral." *Crooked Trails*. New York: Harper and Brothers, 1898.

Richards, Gilbert. *Crossroads: People and Events of the Redwoods of San Mateo County*. Woodside, CA: Gilbert Richards Publications, 1973.

Richardson, Heather Cox. *West from Appomattox: The Reconstruction of America After the Civil War*. New Haven, CT: Yale University Press, 2007.

Richardson, Rupert Norval. *The Comanche Barrier to South Plains Settlement*. Glendale, CA: The Arthur H. Clark Company, 1933.

Ridley, Bromfield L. *Battles and Sketches of the Army of Tennessee*. Mexico, MO: Missouri Printing & Publishing Company, 1906.

Ripley, R. S. *The War with Mexico*. Two volumes. New York: Harper & Brothers, 1849.

Rister, Carl Coke. *Robert E. Lee in Texas*. Norman: University of Oklahoma Press, 1946; rpt. 2004.

Robinson, Charles M., III. *The Men Who Wear the Star: The Story of the Texas Rangers*. New York: Random House, 2000; rpt. New York: The Modern Library, 2001.

———. *Texas and the Mexican War: A History and a Guide*. Austin: Texas State Historical Association, 2004

Robinson, Duncan W. *Judge Robert McAlpin Williamson: Texas' Three-Legged Willie*. Austin: Texas State Historical Association, 1948.

Robinson, Sherry. *I Fought a Good Fight: A History of the Lipan Apaches*. Denton: University of North Texas Press, 2013.

Robinson, W. W. *Land in California: The Story of Mission Lands, Ranchos, Squatters, Mining Claims, Railroad Grants, Land Scrip, Homesteads*. Berkeley: University of California Press, 1979.

Rodenbough, Theophilus F., compiler. *From Everglade to Canyon with the Second United States Cavalry*. New York: D. Van Nostrand, 1875; rpt. Norman: University of Oklahoma Press, 2000. Originally published as *From Everglade to Cañon with the Second Dragoons*.

Rohrbough, Malcolm J. *Trans-Appalachian Frontier: People, Societies, and Institutions, 1775–1850*. Bloomington: Indiana University Press, 2008.

Roland, Charles P. *Albert Sidney Johnston: Soldier of Three Republics*. Austin: University of Texas Press, 1964; rpt. Lexington: University Press of Kentucky, 2001.

Rose, Victor M. *The Life and Services of Gen. Ben McCulloch*. Philadelphia: Pictorial Bureau of the Press, 1888; rpt. Austin: The Steck Company, 1958.

———. *Ross' Texas Brigade: Being a Narrative of Events Connected with Its Service in the Late War Between the States*. Louisville, KY: Courier-Journal Book and Job Rooms, 1881.

Rosebush, Waldo Emerson. *Frontier Steel: The Men and Their Weapons*. Appleton, WI: C. C. Nelson Publishing Company, 1958.

Rothbard, Murray N. *The Panic of 1819: Reactions and Policies*. New York: Columbia University Press, 1962.

Rowland, Dunbar, editor. *Jefferson Davis, Constitutionalist: His Letters, Papers and Speeches*. Volume One. Jackson: Mississippi Department of Archives and History, 1923.

Santleben, August. *A Texas Pioneer: Early Staging and Overland Freighting Days on the Frontiers of Texas and Mexico*. Edited by Isaac D. Affleck. New York: The Neale Publishing Company, 1910.

Scott, Mel. *The San Francisco Bay Area: A Metropolis in Perspective*. Second Edition. Berkeley: University of California Press, 1959; rpt. 1985.

Shea, William L., and Earl J. Hess. *Pea Ridge: Civil War Campaign in the West*. Chapel Hill: University of North Carolina Press, 1992.

Shelton, Perry Wayne, compiler, and Shelly Morrison, editor. *Personal Civil War Letters of General Lawrence Sullivan Ross, with Other Letters*. Austin: Shelly and Richard Morrison, 1994.

Sibley, Marilyn McAdams, editor. *Samuel H. Walker's Account of the Mier Expedition*. Austin: Texas State Historical Association, 1978.

Siegel, Stanley. *A Political History of the Texas Republic, 1836–1845*. Austin: University of Texas Press, 1956.

Silverstone, Scott A. *Divided Union: The Politics of War in the Early American Republic*. Ithaca, NY: Cornell University Press, 2004.

Simpson, Harold B. *Cry Comanche*: *The 2nd U.S. Cavalry in Texas, 1855–1861*. Hillsboro, TX: Hill Junior College Press, 1979.

Slap, Andrew L. *The Doom of Reconstruction: The Liberal Republicans in the Civil War Era*. New York: Fordham University Press, 2006.

Sleeper, John, and J. C. Hutchins, compilers. *Waco and McLennan County, Texas*. Waco: Examiner Steam Job Establishment, 1876.

Smith, E. Kirby. *To Mexico with Scott: Letters of Captain E. Kirby Smith to His Wife*. Cambridge, MA: Harvard University Press, 1917.

Smith, F. Todd. *From Dominance to Disappearance: The Indians of Texas and the Near Southwest, 1786–1859*. Lincoln: University of Nebraska Press, 2005.

Smith, Franklin. *The Mexican War Journal of Captain Franklin Smith*. Edited by Joseph E. Chance. Jackson: University Press of Mississippi, 1991.

Smith, Justin H. *The War with Mexico*. Two volumes. New York: The Macmillan Company, 1919.

Smith, S. Compton. *Chile Con Carne; or, The Camp and the Field*. New York: Miller & Curtis, 1857.

Smith, Thomas T. *The Old Army in Texas: A Research Guide to the U.S. Army in Nineteenth-Century Texas*. Austin: Texas State Historical Association, 2000.

———. *The U.S. Army and the Texas Frontier Economy, 1845–1900*. College Station: Texas A&M University Press, 1999.

Smithwick, Noah. *The Evolution of a State, or Recollections of Old Texas Days*. Compiled by Nanna Smithwick Donaldson. Austin: Gammel Book Company, 1900; rpt. Austin: University of Texas Press, 1983. Pagination refers to the 1983 edition.

Sowell, Andrew Jackson. *Texas Indian Fighters: Early Settlers and Indian Fighters of Southwest Texas*. Austin: Ben C. Jones & Co., 1900; rpt. Austin: State House Press, 1986.

———. *History of Fort Bend County*. Houston: W. H. Coyle & Co., 1904; rpt. Waco: W. M. Morrison, 1964.

———. *Life of "Big Foot" Wallace: The Great Ranger Captain*. Devine: Devine News, 1899; rpt. Austin: State House Press, 1989.

———. *Rangers and Pioneers of Texas*. San Antonio: Shepard Brothers & Co., 1884; rpt. Austin: State House Press, 1991.

Sparks, A. W. *The War Between the States as I Saw It: Reminiscent, Historical, and Personal*. Tyler, TX: Lee & Burnet, 1901.

Spaw, Patsy McDonald. *The Texas Senate*. Two volumes. College Station: Texas A&M University Press, 1990–1999.

Speer, William S., and John Henry Brown, editors. *The Encyclopedia of the New West*. Marshall, TX: United States Biographical Publishing Company, 1881.

Spurlin, Charles D. *Texas Volunteers in the Mexican War*. Austin: Eakin Press, 1998.

———, compiler. *Texas Veterans in the Mexican War*. Victoria, TX: privately printed, 1984.

Stanger, Frank Merriman. *History of San Mateo County*. San Mateo, CA: Arthur H. Cawston, 1938.

———. *Sawmills in the Redwoods: Logging on the San Francisco Peninsula, 1849–1967*. San Mateo, CA: San Mateo County Historical Association, 1967.

Stapp, William Preston. *The Prisoners of Perote*. Philadelphia: G. B. Zieber and Company, 1845; rpt. Austin: University of Texas Press, 1977.

Starr, Stephen Z. *The Union Cavalry in the Civil War*. Volume Three. Baton Rouge: Louisiana State University Press, 1985.

Stevens, Isaac Ingalls. *Campaigns of the Rio Grande and of Mexico*. New York: D. Appleton and Company, 1851.

Stout, Joseph A., Jr. *Schemers and Dreamers: Filibustering in Mexico, 1848–1921*. Fort Worth: Texas Christian University Press, 2002.

Swisher, Colonel John M. *The Swisher Memoirs*. Edited by Rena Maverick Green. San Antonio: The Sigmund Press, 1932.

Sword, Wiley. *The Confederacy's Last Hurrah: Spring Hill, Franklin, and Nashville*. Lawrence: University Press of Kansas, 1993.

———. *Mountains Touched with Fire: Chattanooga Besieged, 1863*. New York: St. Martin's Press, 1995.

Taylor, Zachary. *Letters of Zachary Taylor from the Battle-Fields of the Mexican War*. Rochester, NY: William K. Bixby, 1908.

The Texas Almanac. Galveston: Richardson and Company, 1856–1859, 1871.

Texas Almanac and State Industrial Guide, 1978–1979. Dallas: A. H. Belo Corporation, 1977.

Thomas, Emory M. *Robert E. Lee: A Biography*. New York: W. W. Norton & Company, 1997.

Thompson, Jerry D. *Cortina: Defending the Mexican Name in Texas*. College Station: Texas A&M University Press, 2007.

———. *Fifty Miles and a Fight: Major Samuel Peter Heintzelman's Journal of Texas and the Cortina War*. Austin: Texas State Historical Association, 1998.

———. *Juan Cortina and the Texas-Mexico Frontier, 1859–1877*. El Paso: Texas Western Press, 1994.

———. *Sabers on the Rio Grande*. Austin: Presidial Press, 1974.

———, and Lawrence T. Jones III. *Civil War and Revolution on the Rio Grande Frontier: A Narrative and Photographic History*. Austin: Texas State Historical Association, 2004.

Thorpe, Thomas Bangs. *Our Army at Monterey*. Philadelphia: Carey and Hart, 1848.

———. *Our Army on the Rio Grande*. Philadelphia: Carey and Hart, 1846

Thrapp, Dan L. *Encyclopedia of Frontier Biography*. Volume Two. Glendale, CA: The Arthur H. Clark Company, 1988; rpt. Lincoln: University of Nebraska Press, 1991.

Timmons, W. H. *El Paso: A Borderlands History*. El Paso: Texas Western Press, 1990.

Tise, Sammy. *Texas County Sheriffs*. Albuquerque: Oakwood Printing, 1989.

Townsend, Stephen A. *The Yankee Invasion of Texas*. College Station: Texas A&M University Press, 2006.

Tucker, Phillip Thomas. *The Final Fury: Palmito Ranch, The Last Battle of the Civil War*. Mechanicsburg, PA: Stackpole Books, 2001.

Tucker, Spencer C., editor. *The Encyclopedia of the Mexican-American War: A Political, Social, and Military History*. Volume One. Santa Barbara, CA: ABC-CLIO, 2013.

Tunnard, William H. *A Southern Record: The History of the Third Regiment Louisiana Infantry*. Baton Rouge, LA: printed for the author, 1866; rpt. Dayton, OH: Morningside Bookshop, 1970.

Urwin, Gregory J. W. *The United States Cavalry: An Illustrated History, 1776–1944*. Poole, Dorset: Blandford Press, 1983; rpt. Norman: University of Oklahoma Press, 2003.

Utley, Robert M. *Frontiersmen in Blue: The United States Army and the Indian, 1848–1865*. New York: Macmillan, 1967; rpt. Lincoln: University of Nebraska Press, 1981.

———. *Lone Star Justice: The First Century of the Texas Rangers*. New York: Berkley Books, 2002.

Vestal, Stanley. *Big Foot Wallace: Texas Indian Fighter*. Cambridge, MA: Riverside Press, 1942.

Wade, Houston, compiler. *Notes and Fragments of the Mier Expedition*. Two volumes. La Grange: La Grange Journal, 1936–1937.

Wallace, Ernest. *Texas in Turmoil: The Saga of Texas, 1849–1875*. Austin: Steck-Vaughn Company, 1965.

———, and David M. Vigness, editors. *Documents of Texas History*. Austin: The Steck Company, 1963.

Wallace, George Selden. *Wallace: Genealogical Data Pertaining to the Descendants of Peter Wallace and Elizabeth Woods, His Wife*. Charlottesville, VA: Michie Company, 1927.

Wallace, Lew. *Lew Wallace: An Autobiography*. New York: Harper and Brothers, 1906.

Wallace, Patricia Ward. *Waco: A Sesquicentennial History*. Virginia Beach, VA: The Donning Company, 1999.

Warde, Mary Jane. *When the Wolf Came: The Civil War and the Indian Territory*. Fayetteville: University of Arkansas Press, 2013.

Warner, Ezra J. *Generals in Gray: Lives of the Confederate Commanders*. Baton Rouge: Louisiana State University Press, 1959; rpt. 2008.

Watson, William. *Life in the Confederate Army: Being the Observations and Experiences of an Alien in the South during the Civil War*. London:

Chapman & Hall, 1887; rpt. Baton Rouge: Louisiana State University Press, 1995.

Webb, Walter Prescott. *The Texas Rangers: A Century of Frontier Defense*. Second Edition. Austin: University of Texas Press, 1965.

———. *The Texas Rangers in the Mexican War*. Austin: Jenkins Garrett Press, 1975. This slim volume is a reprint of Webb's M.A. thesis written for the University of Texas at Austin in 1920.

Webber, Charles Wilkins. *Tales of the Southern Border*. Philadelphia: Lippincott, Grambo & Co., 1853. The chapter dealing with Jack Hays was originally published under the penname Charles Winterfield as "My First Day with the Rangers. By a Kentuckian," *The American Review* 1, no. 3 (March 1845).

Weber, David J. *The Mexican Frontier, 1821–1846: The American Southwest Under Mexico*. Albuquerque: University of New Mexico Press, 1982.

Welsh, Jack D. *Medical Histories of Confederate Generals*. Kent, OH: Kent State University Press, 1995.

White, Gifford E. *1830 Citizens of Texas*. Austin: Eakin Press, 1999.

White, Virgil D. *Index of U.S. Marshals, 1789–1960*. Waynesboro, TN: National Historical Publishing Company, 1988.

Wilbarger, John Wesley. *Indian Depredations in Texas*. Austin: Hutchings Printing House, 1890; rpt. Austin: State House Press, 1985.

Wilcox, Shirley Langdon, editor. *1828 Tax List, Prince George's County, Maryland*. Bowie, MD: Prince George's County Genealogical Society, 1985.

Williams, Jack Kenny. *Dueling in the Old South: Vignettes of Social History*. College Station: Texas A&M University Press, 1980.

Williams, Mary Floyd. *History of the San Francisco Committee of Vigilance of 1851: A Study of Social Control on the California Frontier in the Days of the Gold Rush*. Berkeley: University of California Press, 1921.

———, ed. *Papers of the San Francisco Committee of Vigilance of 1851*. Berkeley: University of California Press: 1919.

Wills, Brian Steel. *The Confederacy's Greatest Cavalryman: Nathan Bedford Forrest*. Lawrence: University Press of Kansas, 1992; rpt. 1998.

Wilkes, William O., M.D. *History of the Waco Medical Association with Reminiscences and Irrelevant Comments*. Waco, TX; privately printed, 1931.

Wilkins, Frederick. *Defending the Borders: The Texas Rangers, 1848–1861*. Austin: State House Press, 2001.

———. *The Highly Irregular Irregulars: Texas Rangers in the Mexican War*. Austin: Eakin Press, 1990.

———. *The Legend Begins: The Texas Rangers, 1823–1845*. Austin: State House Press, 1996.

Wilkinson, Joseph B. *Laredo and the Rio Grande Frontier: A Narrative*. Austin: Jenkins Publishing Co., 1975.

Williams, Amelia W., and Eugene C. Barker, editors. *Writings of Sam Houston, 1813–1863*. Eight volumes. Austin: University of Texas Press, 1938–1943.

Williams, R. H. *With the Border Ruffians: Memories of the Far West, 1852–1868*. New York: E. P. Dutton and Company, 1907.

Wilson, James C. *Address on the Occasion of Removing the Remains of Captains Walker and Gillespie*. San Antonio: published by a committee of citizens, 1856.

Wilson, Robert Lawrence. *Colt: An American Legend*. New York: Abbeville Press, 1985.

Winders, Richard Bruce. *Crisis in the Southwest: The United States, Mexico, and the Struggle Over Texas*. Lanham, MD: SR Books, 2004.

———. *Mr. Polk's Army: The American Military Experience in the Mexican War*. College Station: Texas A&M University Press, 1997.

Winfrey, Dorman H., and James M. Day. *The Indian Papers of Texas and the Southwest, 1825–1916*. Five volumes. Austin: Texas State Historical Association, 1995.

Winkler, Ernest William, editor. *Journal of the Secession Convention of Texas in 1861*. Austin: Austin Printing Company, 1912.

———. *Manuscript Letters and Documents of Early Texians, 1821–1845*. Austin: The Steck Company, 1937

———. *Platforms of Political Parties in Texas*. Bulletin of the University of Texas, No. 53: September 20, 1916.

Wollenberg, Charles. *Golden Gate Metropolis: Perspectives on Bay Area History*. Berkeley: Institute of Governmental Studies, University of California, 1985.

Wood, M. W. *History of Alameda County, California*. Oakland, CA: Pacific Press, 1883.

Woodruff, W. E., Jr. *With the Light Guns in '61–'65: Reminiscences of Eleven Arkansas, Missouri, and Texas Light Batteries, in the Civil War*. Little Rock: Central Printing Company, 1903; rpt. Little Rock: Eagle Press, [1987].

Wood, J. C. *Report to Hon. A. V. Brown, Postmaster-General, on the Opening and Present Condition of the United States Overland Mail Route between San Antonio, Texas, and San Diego, California*. Washington, D.C.: privately printed, 1858.

Woodworth, Steven E. *Jefferson Davis and His Generals: The Failure of Confederate Command in the West*. Lawrence: University Press of Kansas, 1990.

———. *Manifest Destinies: America's Westward Expansion and the Road to the Civil War*. New York: Vintage Books, 2010.

———. *Nothing but Victory: The Army of the Tennessee, 1861–1865*. New York: Alfred A. Knopf, 2005.

Wooster, Ralph A. *Civil War Texas: A History and A Guide*. Austin: Texas State Historical Association, 1999.

———. *Lone Star Generals in Gray*. Austin: Eakin Press, 2000.

———. *Lone Star Regiments in Gray*. Austin: Eakin Press, 2002.

———. *Texas and Texans in the Civil War*. Austin: Eakin Press, 1995.

Wooster, Robert. *The American Military Frontiers: The United States Army in the West, 1783–1900*. Albuquerque: University of New Mexico Press, 2009.

———. *History of Fort Davis, Texas*. Santa Fe: Southwest Region, National Park Service, 1990.

Wooten, Dudley C., editor. *A Comprehensive History of Texas, 1685–1897*. Two volumes. Dallas: William G. Scarff, 1898.

Wright, General Marcus J., compiler. *Texas in the War, 1861–1865*. Edited by Harold B. Simpson. Hillsboro, TX: Hill Junior College Press, 1965.

Wyatt, Roscoe D. *Days of the Dons: On the Spanish and Mexican Ranchos of the San Francisco Peninsula and in the Santa Clara Valley*. Redwood City, CA: San Mateo County Title Company, 1949.

Wyatt-Brown, Bertram. *Southern Honor: Ethics and Behavior in the Old South*. 25th Anniversary Edition. New York: Oxford University Press, 2007.

Wyeth, John Allan. *That Devil Forrest: Life of General Nathan Bedford Forrest*. New York: Harper & Brothers, 1959; rpt. Baton Rouge: Louisiana State University Press, 1989. Originally published as *Life of General Nathan Bedford Forrest* in 1899 and 1908.

Wynkoop, J. M., editor. *Anecdotes and Incidents: Comprising Daring Exploits, Personal and Amusing Adventures of the Officers and Privates of the Army, and Thrilling Incidents of the Mexican War*. Pittsburgh, PA: n.p., 1848.

Yoakum, Henderson K. *History of Texas from its First Settlement in 1685 to its Annexation to the United States in 1846*. Two volumes. New York: Redfield, 1856.

Zanjani, Sally. *Devils Will Reign: How Nevada Began*. Reno: University of Nevada Press, 2006.

Internet Sources

Burkett, Nathan Boone. "Early Days in Texas." Unfinished manuscript dictated in April 1895 to son-in-law John T. Hogwood. Transcribed and edited by Wallace L. McKeehan from the original archived at Briscoe Center for American History, the University of Texas at Austin. 2008. *Sons of DeWitt Colony Texas*. Online at http://www.tamu.edu/faculty/ccbn/ dewitt/nathanmemframe.htm.

Davenport, Harbert. *Notes from an Unfinished Study of Fannin and His Men, 1936*. Edited by H. David Maxey. 2008. Texas State Historical Association. Online at http://www.tshaonline.org/ supsites/fannin/hd_home.html.

Find A Grave. Online at http://www.findagrave.com.

Handbook of Texas Online. Texas State Historical Association. Online at https://www.tshaonline.org/handbook.

Moore, Stephen L. "Texas Ranger William A. A. "Bigfoot" Wallace (1817–1899)." *The Texas Ranger Dispatch* 12 (Winter 2003). Online at www.texasranger.org.

Newspapers

Alameda Sun

Alexandria Gazette and Virginia Advertiser

American Flag (Matamoros)

Arkansas City Traveler

Arkansas Gazette (Little Rock)

Army and Navy Chronicle (Washington, D.C.)

Austin Daily Democratic Statesman

Austin Daily Statesman

Austin Weekly Statesman

Baltimore Gazette and Daily Advertiser

Brownsville Daily Herald

Brownsville Herald

Civilian and Galveston Gazette

Civilian and Gazette (Galveston)
Corpus Christi Caller
Corpus Christi Caller-Times
Corpus Christi Star
Corpus Christi Times
Daily Alta California (San Francisco)
Daily Constitutionalist (Augusta, GA)
Daily Delta (New Orleans)
Daily Globe (Washington, D.C.)
Daily Ledger and Texan (San Antonio)
Daily National Intelligencer (Washington, D.C.)
Daily Picayune (New Orleans)
Daily State Journal (Richmond, VA)
Daily Union (Washington, D.C.)
Dallas Daily Herald
Dallas Morning News
Dallas Weekly Herald
Democratic Telegraph and Texas Register (Houston)
Evening Star (Washington, D.C.)
Flake's Daily Bulletin (Galveston)
Flake's Weekly Bulletin (Galveston)
Florida Herald and Southern Democrat (St. Augustine)
Galveston Daily News
Galveston Weekly News
Houston Post
Houston Telegraph
Los Angeles Herald
Missouri Gazette and Public Advertiser (St. Louis)
Morning Star (Houston)
New York Commercial Advertiser (New York City)
New York Evening Post (New York City)
New York Evening Star (New York City)
New York Herald (New York City)
New York Times
Niles' Register (Baltimore)
Northern Standard (Clarksville, TX)
Nueces Valley (Corpus Christi)
Oakland Tribune
Placer Times (Sacramento)

Red-Lander (San Augustine)
Sacramento Daily Union
St. Louis Enquirer
San Antonio Daily Express
San Antonio Daily Light
San Antonio Express
San Antonio Herald
San Antonio Ledger
San Antonio Ledger and Texan
Semi-Weekly News (San Antonio)
Southern Intelligencer (Austin)
South-Western American (Austin)
Telegraph and Texas Register (Columbia and Houston)
Texas Democrat (Austin)
Texas National Register (Washington and Austin)
Texas Republican (Brazoria)
Texas Sentinel (Austin)
Texas State Gazette (Austin)
Texas State Times (Austin)
Texian Advocate (Victoria)
The Argonaut (San Francisco)
The Planter (Columbia, TX)
Tri-Weekly Telegraph (Houston)
Valley Star-Monitor-Herald (Brownsville)
Victoria Advocate
Waco Daily Examiner
Waco Tribune-Herald
Weekly Democratic Statesman (Austin)
Weekly Ledger and Texan (San Antonio)
Weekly State Gazette (Austin)
Western Texan (San Antonio)
Western Texian (San Antonio)

Public and Official Documents

Adjutant-General's Office. *Official Army Register, Corrected to August 31, 1847*. Washington, D.C.: Adjutant-General's Office, 1847.

Bandera County. Deed Records. Office of the County Clerk, Bandera, Texas. Copies in possession of author.

California Legislature. *Journals of Senate and Assembly of the Twentieth Session of the Legislature of the State of California*. Four volumes. Sacramento: G. H. Springer, 1874.

Kerr County. Deed Records. Office of the County Clerk, Kerrville, Texas. Copies in possession of author.

Los Angeles County. Record of Marriages. Volume Four: 1875–1877. Office of the Registrar-Recorder/County Clerk, Los Angeles, California. Copy in possession of author.

McLennan County. Marriage Records. Book B: March 28, 1878 to November 15, 1881. Office of the County Clerk, Waco, Texas. Copy in possession of author.

México. Comisión Pesquisidora de la Frontera del Norte. *Reports of the Committee of Investigation Sent in 1873 by the Mexican Government to the Frontier of Texas*. New York: Baker & Godwin, 1875.

Midland County. Marriage Records. Volume Two: June 1909-April 1911. Office of the County Clerk, Midland, Texas. Copy in possession of author.

Texas Bureau of Vital Statistics. Death Certificates. Department of Health, Austin, Texas. Copies in possession of author.

Texas Congress. *Journal of the House of Representatives of the Republic of Texas, Regular Session of the Third Congress, November 5, 1838*. Houston: Intelligencer Office, 1839.

———. *Journals of the Fourth Congress of the Republic of Texas, 1839–1840*. Edited by Harriet Smither. Three volumes. Austin: Von Boeckmann-Jones Co., 1930.

———. *Journals of the House of Representatives of the Ninth Congress of the Republic of Texas*. Washington, TX: Miller & Cushney, 1845.

———. *Journals of the House of Representatives of the Republic of Texas: Fifth Congress, First Session*. Austin: Cruger and Wing, 1841.

———. *Journals of the House of Representatives of the Seventh Congress of the Republic of Texas*. Austin: Thomas Johnson, 1843.

———. *Journals of the Sixth Congress of the Republic of Texas, 1841–1842*. Edited by Harriet Smither. Three volumes. Austin: Capital Printing Co., 1940–1945.

Texas Constitutional Convention. *Journal of the Constitutional Convention of the State of Texas, Begun and Held at the City of Austin, September 6, 1875*. Galveston: News Office, 1875.

Texas Legislature. House. *Journal of the House of Representatives, Being the Regular Session, Twenty-first Legislature*. Austin: Smith, Hicks & Jones, 1889.

———. *Journal of House of Representatives of the Sixteenth Legislature of the State of Texas, Extra Session*. Galveston: A. H. Belo & Co., 1879.

———. *Journal of the House of Representatives of the State of Texas, Twenty-second Legislature, Regular Session*. Austin: Standard Office, 1891.

———. *Journal of the House of Representatives of the Twentieth Legislature, State of Texas*. Austin: Triplett & Hutchings, 1887.

———. *Journals of the House of Representatives, Eighth Legislature*. Austin: John Marshall & Co., 1860.

———. *Journals of the House of Representatives of the First Legislature of the State of Texas*. Clarksville, TX: Standard Office, 1848.

———. *Journals of the House of Representatives of the State of Texas, Third Legislature*. Austin: William H. Cushney, 1849.

Texas Legislature. Senate. *Journal of the Senate of Texas: Being the Called Session of the Eighteenth Legislature of the State of Texas*. Austin: E. W. Swindells, 1884.

———. *Journal of the Senate of Texas: Being the Regular Session of the Eighteenth Legislature of the State of Texas*. Austin: E. W. Swindells, 1883.

———. *Journal of the Senate of Texas: Being a Special Session of the Seventeenth Legislature*. Galveston: A. H. Belo & Co., 1882.

———. *Journal of the Senate of the State of Texas: Being the First Session of the Seventeenth Legislature*. Galveston: A. H. Belo & Co., 1881.

———. *Journals of the Senate of the First Legislature of the State of Texas*. Clarksville: Standard Office, 1848.

Texas Provisional Government. *Journal of the Proceedings of the General Council of the Republic of Texas*. Houston: National Intelligencer Office, 1839.

———. *Journals of the Consultation Held at San Felipe de Austin, October 16, 1835*. Houston: Telegraph Power Press, 1838.

———. *Ordinances and Decrees of the Consultation, Provisional Government of Texas, and the Convention, Which Assembled at Washington, March 1, 1836*. Houston: National Banner Office, 1838.

Texas, State of. *Constitution of the State of Texas: Adopted by the Constitutional Convention Begun and Held at the City of Austin on the Sixth Day of September, 1875*. Austin: Institution for the Deaf and Dumb, 1877.

United States Congress. *American State Papers: Military Affairs*. Seven volumes. Washington, D.C.: Gales & Seaton, 1832–1861.

United States Congress. *Congressional Globe*. 29th-36th Congress. Washington, D.C.: Blair & Rives, 1846–1860.

———. *The United States Statutes at Large*. 126 volumes. Boston: Little, Brown and Company, 1848–1874; Washington: Government Printing Office, 1875–2012.

United States Congress. House of Representatives. *Additional Estimate*. House Executive Document No. 31. 32nd Congress, 1st Session. Serial No. 640.

———. *Annual Report of the Secretary of State*. House Executive Document No. 2. 28th Congress, 1st Session. Serial No. 463.

———. *Annual Report of the Secretary of War*. House Executive Document No. 1. 30th Congress, 2nd Session. Serial No. 537.

———. *Annual Report of the Secretary of War*. House Executive Document No. 1, 34th Congress, 3rd Session. Serial No. 894.

———. *Annual Report of the Secretary of War*. House Executive Document No. 2. 35th Congress, 1st Session. Serial No. 943.

———. *Annual Report of the Secretary of War*. House Executive Document No. 2. 35th Congress, 2nd Session. Serial No. 998

———. *Annual Report of the Secretary of War*. House Executive Document No. 4. 29th Congress, 2nd Session. Serial No. 497.

———. *Annual Report of the Secretary of War*. House Executive Document No. 5. 31st Congress, 1st Session. Serial No. 569.

———. *Annual Report of the Secretary of War*. House Executive Document No. 8. 30th Congress, 1st Session. Serial No. 515.

———. *Correspondence Between the Secretary of War and Generals Scott and Taylor, and Between General Scott and Mr. Trist*. House Executive Document No. 56. 30th Congress, 1st Session. Serial No. 518.

———. *Correspondence with General Taylor*. House Executive Document No. 119. 29th Congress, 2nd Session. Serial No. 500.

———. *Difficulties on Southwestern Frontier*. House Executive Document No. 52. 36th Congress, 1st Session. Serial No. 1050.

———. *Letter from the Postmaster General Transmitting a Report on Mail Contracts, &c.* House Executive Document No. 56. 32nd Congress, 1st Session. Serial No. 643.

———. *Letter from the Secretary of War*. House Document No. 115. 24th Congress, 1st Session. Serial No. 289.

———. *Message from the President of the United States*. House Executive Document No. 2. 35th Congress, 1st Session. Serial No. 942.

———. *Message from the President of the United States*. House Executive Document No. 2. 35th Congress, 2nd Session. Serial No. 997.

———. *Message of the President of the United States and Accompanying Documents*. House Executive Document No. 1. 40th Congress, 2nd Session. Serial No. 1323.

———. *Mexican War Correspondence*. House Executive Document No. 60. 30th Congress, 1st Session. Serial No. 520.

———. *Offers and Contracts for Carrying the Mails*. House Executive Document No. 86. 36th Congress, 1st Session. Serial No. 1057.

———. *Presidential Message Transmitting Information on California and New Mexico*. House Executive Document No. 17. 30th Congress, 1st Session. Serial No. 573.

———. *Protection of the Frontier of Texas*. House Executive Document No. 27. 35th Congress, 2nd Session. Serial No. 1004.

———. *Relations of the United States with Mexico*. Two Parts. House Report No. 701. 45th Congress, 2nd Session. Serial No. 1824.

———. *Texas Frontier Troubles*. House Report No. 343. 44th Congress, 1st Session. Serial No. 1709.

———. *Troubles on Texas Frontier*. House Executive Document No. 81. 36th Congress, 1st Session. Serial No. 1056.

United States Congress. Senate. *Annual Report of the Commissioner of Indian Affairs*. Senate Executive Document No. 2. 36th Congress, 1st Session. Serial No. 1023.

———. *Annual Report of the Commissioner of the General Land Office*. Senate Executive Document No. 1. 35th Congress, 2nd Session. Serial No. 974.

———. *Annual Report of the Secretary of War*. Senate Executive Document No. 1. 31st Congress, 1st Session. Serial No. 549.

———. *Annual Report of the Secretary of War*. Senate Executive Document No. 1. 31st Congress, 2nd Session. Serial No. 587.

———. *Annual Report of the Secretary of War*. Senate Executive Document No. 1. 36th Congress, 2nd Session. Serial No. 1079.

———. *Annual Report of the Secretary of War*. Senate Executive Document No. 2. 36th Congress, 1st Session. Serial No. 1024.

———. *Hostilities on the Rio Grande*. Senate Executive Document No. 21. 36th Congress, 1st Session. Serial No. 1031.

———. *Journal of the Confederate Congress*, Ten volumes. Senate Document No. 234. 58th Congress, 2nd Session. Serial Nos. 4610–4616.

———. *Journal of the Executive Proceedings of the Senate of the United States of America from December 6, 1852 to March 3, 1855, inclusive.* Volume Nine. Washington: Government Printing Office, 1887.

———. *Letter from the Secretary of War.* Senate Executive Document No. 19. 45th Congress, 2nd Session. Serial No. 1780.

———. *Memorial of Samuel Colt.* Senate Report No. 296. 30th Congress, 2nd Session. Serial No. 535.

———. *Petition of John C. Hays.* Senate Report No. 221. 32nd Congress, 1st Session. Serial No. 631.

———. *Reconnaissance of Routes from San Antonio to El Paso.* Senate Executive Document No. 64. 31st Congress, 1st Session. Serial No. 562.

———. *Report from the Secretary of the Navy.* Senate Document No. 503. 26th Congress, 1st Session. Serial No. 360.

United States Department of the Interior. *Official Register of the United States.* Washington, D.C.: Government Printing Office, 1885–1889.

United States Department of the Navy. *Official Records of the Union and Confederate Navies in the War of the Rebellion.* Thirty volumes. Washington, D.C.: Government Printing Office, 1894–1914.

United States Department of War. *Army and Navy Official Gazette: Containing Reports of Battles; also, Important Orders of the War Department, Record of Courts-martial, etc.* Washington City: John C. Rives, 1864–1865.

———. *The War of the Rebellion: A Compilation of the Official Records of the Union and Confederate Armies.* 128 volumes. Washington, D.C.: Government Printing Office, 1880–1901.

Theses and Dissertations

Bullock, Neal Terry. "The Confederate Services of General Ben McCulloch." M.A. thesis, University of Arkansas, 1957.

Crews, James Robert. "Reconstruction in Brownsville, Texas." M.A. thesis, Texas Tech University, 1969.

Dillard, Raymond L. "A History of the Ross Family and Its Most Distinguished Member, Lawrence Sullivan Ross." M.A. thesis, Baylor University, 1931.

Jones, Andrew McKee. "Comanches and Texans in the Making of the Comanche Nation: The Historical Anthropology of Comanche-Texan

Relations, 1803–1997." Ph.D. dissertation, University of Wisconsin-Madison, 1997.

Jones, Frank Leon, III. "With Zachary Taylor in Texas." M.S. thesis, Texas A&M University-Kingsville, 1995.

Knapp, Eric W. "'War Without Pity': Guerrilla Conflict in the Mexican War." M.A. thesis, University of Nebraska, 1995.

Lyles, Major Ian B. "Mixed Blessing: The Role of the Texas Rangers in the Mexican War, 1846–1848." MMAS thesis, Fort Leavenworth, 2003.

Marcum, Richard T. "Fort Brown, Texas: The History of a Border Post." Ph.D. dissertation, Texas Technological College, 1964.

Pierce, Gerald Swetnam. "The Army of the Texas Republic, 1836–1845." Ph.D. dissertation, University of Mississippi, 1963.

Whiteside, Myrtle. "The Life of Lawrence Sullivan Ross." M.A. thesis, University of Texas, 1938.

Yancey, William C. "In Justice to Our Indian Allies: The Government of Texas and Her Indian Allies, 1836–1867." M.A. thesis, University of North Texas, 2008.

Unpublished Manuscripts

"The Battle of Walker Creek, June 8, 1844: Tall Tales and Myths Removed, This is the Documented Drama of the Day the Texas Frontier Changed Forever." MS, n.d. Walker Vertical File, Texas Ranger Hall of Fame & Museum.

Stuart, Ben C. "Texas Indian Fighters and Frontier Rangers." Typescript, 1916. Archives and Information Services Division, Texas State Library and Archives Commission, Austin, Texas.

Walker, Samuel H. "The Walkers of Toaping Castle, Md." MS, 1883. Copy provided to the author by the Allen County Public Library, Fort Wayne, IN.

Index

A

B

C

F

G

H

I

J

K

L

M

N

O

P

Q

R

S

T

U

V

Y

Z